The
Ageless
Chinese A HISTORY

Third Edition

DUN J. LI

The
Ageless
Chinese

A HISTORY

THIRD EDITION

Charles Scribner's Sons, New York

Copyright © 1978, 1971, 1965 Charles Scribner's Sons

Library of Congress Cataloging in Publication Data

Li, Dun Jen, 1920-
   The ageless Chinese.

   Bibliography: p.
   Includes index.
   1. China—History.   I. Title.
DS735.L43   1978   951   78-7787
ISBN 0-02-370550-7

Maps by Jeanyee Wong

1 3 5 7 9 11 13 15 17 19 V/C 20 18 16 14 12 10 8 6 4 2
      9 11 13 15 17 19   20 18 16 14 12 10

Printed in the United States of America

Preface

On my first visit to Chinatown in San Francisco, in about 1959, I was looking in the shopwindows for a mandarin dress to buy for Jean. I went into one of the stores, but I just began to feel very uncomfortable and I left. I went into three different stores in Chinatown and walked out of each one before anybody could even wait on me. Back at the hotel, I realized that I was so anxious and insecure in the presence of the Chinese that I couldn't conduct a simple business transaction. All of my knowledge of Orientals was from movies, those Charlie Chan films that portrayed them as inscrutable personalities who could not be trusted. I'd get in there and feel that somebody was going to put opium in my tea or snatch me through a curtain and put me on a boat to China. I'd been programed by this society to respond in a racist way to Orientals.

> Andrew Young, U.S. Ambassador to
> the United Nations. *Playboy*,
> July, 1977, p. 70.

It is refreshing to hear anyone admitting racial prejudice; it is doubly so when the admission comes from so eminent a person as Ambassador Young. If our society has been successful in programing an urbane, sophisticated, and well-educated man like Ambassador Young to respond in a racist way to Orientals, certainly it can do even better with people of lesser caliber. Ultimately the fault seems to lie somewhere in our educational system, as it fails to produce men and women more congenial to a modern society, a society where racial prejudice should be as anachronistic as it is inimical to everything this country is supposed to have stood for. One wonders whether Ambassador Young or anyone else would have been "anxious and insecure in the presence of the Chinese" and been afraid of being poisoned and kidnapped for no reason at all had he, in his educational process, been required to read one good book on China or the Chinese—a book written not for the purpose of fostering or enhancing his prejudice but to help him liberate himself from it. Admittedly, even the best written book of Chinese history cannot hope to compete with Charlie Chan movies in influencing the public, but it will help reduce Sinophobia, commonly found even among the best educated people.

The idea of writing *The Ageless Chinese* was formed more than twenty-five years ago when, as a new arrival in the United States, I strove to improve my English by reading books on subjects most familiar to me. The books of Chinese history then recommended to me were among the best known, but somehow I could not relate to their contents. The Chinese described in these books were as alien and inscrutable to me as they were, presumably, to most Westerners. They walked mysteriously from page to page like phantoms or beasts, and the overwhelming concern of most of the authors was to instruct their readers how to cope successfully with these strange people with minimum damage to themselves. "I shall write a Chinese history myself once my command of the English language becomes adequate," I promised myself. The result was *The Ageless Chinese: A History*, which came into existence in 1965.

As soon as the book appeared on the market, I quickly realized that it was as foreign to many Western scholars as their books on China and the Chinese had been to me. While most critics commented favorably or at least gave me the benefit of the doubt, others subjected the contents and emphases of my book to severe criticism, little realizing that these contents and emphases had been the consensus of Chinese historians through centuries of effort. For the first several years of its existence, the book appealed mainly to two groups: China-born scholars and former Western residents in China, such as missionaries. To them the terrain was familiar and the scene intimate, and they may have liked the book for none other than reasons of nostalgia. As scholars of both groups either retired from active teaching or died of old age, it seemed that the book would also come to an end. The demand for it continues, nevertheless, largely because of the interest of scholars of the younger generation who, brought up during the civil rights movement, are less racially biased than their elders and are consequently more willing to evaluate the book according to its own merits. Certainly it is no small gratification to me that the book has gone into a third edition.

In this edition chapters VI and VII on the Sung dynasty have been completely rewritten. Most importantly, the coverage of the People's Republic has been expanded to two long chapters, providing substantial detail on the latest developments. Since the publication of the second edition seven years ago, events of great importance have taken place in that ancient country. The Cultural Revolution that was launched in 1966 continued its momentum in the early 1970s, and all aspects of Chinese life underwent a drastic change as a result. The Communist radicals, in power between 1966 and 1976, attempted to create a new man and a new society, unlike any other in the chronicle of modern history, in China or elsewhere. The impact was enormous, especially on education and cultural activities. Though a process of de-Maoization has been continuing since Mao Tse-tung's death in September 1976, the attempt to change the basic nature of man provides a fascinating area of study. For twenty-nine years since its establishment in 1949, the development of events in the People's Republic has been most complex and intricate; it would require volumes to cover all the details. It is hoped, however, that the reader will acquire a good grip of the situation involved, both foreign and domestic, after having read the last two chapters of this book.

The Ageless Chinese contains no grand theories—no theory, however comprehensive, can explain adequately the complexity of events over a period of four thousand years. The author describes and interprets events according to his own insight and understanding, and he obeys no higher authority than truth as he sees it. This point is particularly important in the description and interpretation of the most recent events, where emotions still run high. While he does not pretend to know all that is to be known, he has no intention of becoming an apologist for either the Nationalists or the Communists, the two bitter mutual enemies. Needless to say, partisans of either side will find certain passages in this book highly objectionable.

History objectively written is important not only for its own sake but also for its contribution to human understanding. The world has become too small for people to be strongly prejudiced against one another. Mine is not a book entitled "The Glory That Is China"; nor is it a book with which the lovers of Charlie Chan movies would feel at home. It is not flattering to those who speak constantly about their "five-thousand-year-old civilization" while achieving little in the meantime; nor is it pleasing to those who think of China only in terms of "water torture" or "Chinaman's chance," and merely want another "documentation" to rationalize their prejudice. It describes the Chinese as they are, with the dual traits of strength and weakness that characterize all the other peoples in the world.

While I cannot speak expertly about other cultures, it is interesting to note that certain aspects of Chinese culture have won acceptance in the West. Generally speaking, the more concrete or tangible these aspects are, the more easily they have been assimilated. They range from the easily appreciable Chinese cuisine to Chinese objects of art, notably paintings, ceramics, and sculpture. But the acceptance has not been extended to what the Chinese regard as more important, namely literature, history, and philosophy. For this lack of interest we specialists in the field are perhaps more responsible than anyone else. In other words, we have not succeeded in making our specialties less forbidding and more meaningful to our readers.

With the general public in mind, I have tried to make *The Ageless Chinese* as interesting as it is informative, so that the reader, even without any background of Chinese history, will find it easy to follow. It is a story of the triumphs, failures, happiness, and sorrows of the largest nation on earth. It is told in a simple, unpretentious language that no one can fail to understand. I would hope that the reading of it will be just as enjoyable as the writing of it has been.

Dun J. Li

Contents

ix

List of Illustrations

List of Maps

The
Ageless
Chinese A HISTORY

Third Edition

Introduction:
The Geographical Setting

If history is a continuous and, let us hope, unending drama, geography is the stage on which such drama is performed. While on the one hand the kind of drama man plays modifies the environment in which he lives, the environment itself influences or sometimes dictates what kind of drama can be played. Man and nature modify each other in a reciprocal manner. Though man is the most intelligent of all creatures, he is by no means omnipotent. He can exploit nature to his advantage, but he cannot change nature's basic pattern. Often does he work in vain when nature is harsh and unrewarding, and especially did his ancestors who had less knowledge and who lacked the experience which has evolved and accumulated through thousands of years. Though geography does not determine history, history is very much influenced by it. To understand a nation's history, we have to familiarize ourselves with its geography. Thus we begin our story of the Chinese with a description of the place where they live.

The Chinese live in Chung-kuo ("Central Nation") or Chung-hua ("Central and Flowery Land"), better known in the English language as China. The Chinese call their country "Central Nation" or "Flowery Land" because until modern times they had believed that they lived in the center of the civilized world, rich and beautiful beyond comparison. A better knowledge of the world reveals something different, but the old names have persisted. Americans and Europeans often refer to China as a Far Eastern country, a term as misleading as the "central nation," because such a term can only be justified if somehow we believe that the world begins somewhere east of Japan. China is located in the southeastern end of the Eurasian land mass, and since the eastern portion of this land mass is called Asia, it is more correct to say that China is an East Asian country, or a country in East Asia.

In terms of size China is the third largest country (after the Soviet Union and Canada) in the world, with an area totalling 3,760,000 square miles. From Pamir to the Pacific it extends 2,300 miles, and it measures 2,500 miles from northern Manchuria to the Himalayas. It lies between 18° and 54°N, from the tropical to the subarctic, excluding four groups of coral islands in the South China Sea which extend as far as 4°N. If China were imposed on North America, it would cover an area from the Atlantic to the Pacific, and from the southern Hudson Bay to the island of Jamaica in the Caribbean Sea. This vast expanse gives China a variety of climates and regional characteristics.

In the north China shares its longest boundary with the Soviet Union. At the eastern end of the boundary the Tumen and Yalu Rivers separate it from Korea. The Himalayas form a natural boundary between China in the north, and Pakistan, India, Nepal, and Bhutan in the south. Across its southwestern border China faces Burma, Laos, and North Vietnam. China's coastline of 4,000 miles is washed by the extensions of the Western Pacific: the Yellow Sea in the north, East China Sea in the middle, and South China Sea in the south. At the end of World War II, it had thirty-five provinces and two territories. One territory, Outer Mongolia, has since then become independent.

LANDFORMS

The land of China may be compared to a gigantic watershed, with Pamir and the Tibetan Plateau as the water divide and the Western Pacific as the water's final resting place. The entire area slopes eastward,

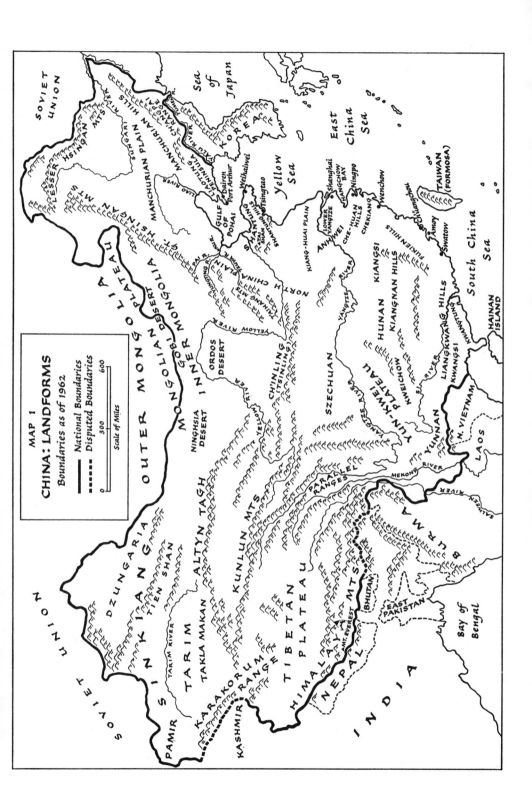

MAP 1
CHINA: LANDFORMS
Boundaries as of 1962

—— National Boundaries
----- Disputed Boundaries

0   300   600
Scale of Miles

and the altitudes of mountains and rivers diminish with it. Travelling westward, one ascends higher and higher, and when one reaches the Tibetan Plateau, the altitude is so high and the air so thin that breathing might be difficult. The Tibetan Plateau, nicknamed "the roof of the world," rises as high as 12,000 feet above sea level and is surrounded by even more formidable mountains. In the north are the Karakorum Range, the Altyn Tagh, and the Kunlun Mountains; all of them have peaks of over 20,000 feet. In the south are the Himalayas whose insurmountable height had guaranteed the "eternal" friendship between India and China until recent years. Their highest peak (also the world's highest), Mt. Everest, is located between Tibet and Nepal and rises 29,141 feet above sea level. Its towering height and treacherous slopes have been a challenge to the world's best mountain climbers.

Stretching northward and then eastward from Pamir is Tien Shan ("Heavenly Mountains") whose 1,000-mile length divides the Chinese Sinkiang province into two arid basins, Dzungaria in the north and Tarim in the south. Dzungaria has a greater annual rainfall than Tarim and is partially desert and partially pastoral. Tarim, on the other hand, is extremely dry and contains one of the world's most desolate deserts, the Takla Makan. However, fertile oases are found along the Tarim River which receives its water from the melting snow on surrounding mountains. Through these oases ran the ancient Silk Road to the Near East, and at one time camel-driving merchants risked their lives so that the Roman world could enjoy the luxuries from the East.

East of Sinkiang is the Mongolian Plateau which rises 3,000 to 6,000 feet above sea level and trends eastward. The southern and Chinese portion of the plateau is generally referred to as Inner Mongolia, as contrary to the larger, northern portion which is known as Outer Mongolia. Inner Mongolia is covered by deserts: the Gobi, the Ordos, and the Ninghsia. On the southern and eastern margin of the deserts are the steppe lands where rainfall is sufficient for a sparse growth of drought-resistant short grass and capable of supporting small herds of sheep and cattle. Oases are found wherever there is sufficient surface or underground water. Over the possession of these oases the Chinese and the non-Chinese nomadic groups fought many ancient battles.

South of the steppe lands are a loess plateau in the west and the North China Plain in the east. The plateau is formed by aeolian dust and silt blown from the northern deserts. Rainfall is light, and steppe conditions prevail over most parts of this region. Rivers dissect loess hills into deep valleys, and only the valleys can be cultivated fruitfully. The plateau is bordered in the east by the T'aihang Mountains which slope down eastward to merge with the North China Plain. The plain is drained by the Yellow River and the Ku River, together with their tributaries. The soil is the mineral-rich loess, and the plain, unlike the plateau, is one of the largest cultivated regions in China. At the eastern end of the plain and south of the Yellow River delta rise the Shantung Hills which stretch northeastward to form the Shantung Peninsula. The highest peak of this hilly complex is the historically famous Tai Shan which was visited often by Confucius.

East of the Mongolian Plateau are the Manchurian mountains and hills. The mountains—Greater and Lesser Hsingan Mountains—are located in northern and western Manchuria, slope down southeastward to merge with the Manchurian Plain, and rise again to form the Manchurian Hills. The Manchurian Plain consists of the drainage basins of the Liao and the Sungari and is a rich agricultural area. The Ch'angpai ("Everlasting White") Range stands majestically above the Manchurian Hills, and from here the Manchus once swooped down to conquer the Manchurian Plain and eventually all of China as well.

From the point of view of climate, the most important mountains in China are Ch'inling (also Tsinling) and its eastern extensions. They separate the dry north from the humid south, the Yellow River drainage from that of the Yangtze. The Yangtze and its tributaries create many fertile alluvial plains along their paths, from the Szechuan basin in the west to the Lower Yangtze in the east. In the east the Lower Yangtze plain merges imperceptibly with the North China Plain; together they form a vast, flat expanse from Shantung to Chekiang. The easternmost extension of Ch'inling, trending eastward, disappears in the Kiang-Huai Plain, the middle section of this vast expanse.

South of the Yangtze River the terrain follows the same pattern of diminishing its altitude eastward. Southeast of the Tibetan Plateau lies another plateau of lesser but equally staggering height. It is called Yun-Kwei Plateau because it covers Yunnan and Kweichow provinces. It averages 7,000 feet in its western, or Yunnan, portion and drops down to an average of 4,000 feet in its eastern, or Kweichow, portion. In its southeastern section are the Parallel Ranges where high mountains and deep valleys run southward and form a sharp, unique contrast. Water rushes its way along these valleys to join the Salween and Mekong Rivers. In some areas valleys are so deep and mountains so high that people who live on opposite sides of the same valley could say good morning to each other, but would have to journey all day before they could shake hands.

East of the Yun-Kwei Plateau the terrain lowers to become less rugged, more prosaic hills. South of the Yangtze drainage hilly regions dominate the terrain from Kwangsi to the East China Sea. These hilly regions are often named after the provinces in which they are located. They are, from west to east: (1) the Liangkwang (Kwangsi and Kwangtung) Hills, (2) the Kiangnan Hills (Hunan and Kiangsi excluding the central lakes region), (3) the Che-Huan (South Anhwei and East Chekiang) Hills, and (4) the Fukien Hills. In the hilly regions rivers are short and drainages are small. The only exception is the Si ("West") River which will be discussed later.

Wherever the hilly regions are washed by the sea, the coastline tends to be more serrated and contains many bays and harbors. Thus, in the Manchurian hilly region we find two superb harbors, Dairen and Port Arthur, located on the southern tip of the Liaotung Peninsula. Across the Gulf of Pohai is the Shantung Peninsula where the Shantung Hills make possible the fine ports of Weihaiwei and Tsingtao. South of Shantung and north of the Hangchow Bay the coastline is round and flat, as its hinterland is a vast expanse of alluvial plains. The prominent position of Shanghai does not depend on its importance as a harbor but on the fact that it stands at the mouth of the richest drainage basin in China. South of the Hangchow Bay the coastal areas are again hilly, and there are such fine harbors as Ningpo, Wenchow, Amoy, Swatow, and the historically famous Ch'üanchou. The potentiality of these harbors has not been fully developed, largely because transportation is extremely difficult over the hinterlands, and the rivers leading to them are short and swift.

DRAINAGE

As mountains in China trend eastward, so do all major rivers. The Yellow River and the Yangtze, the two largest rivers in China, are not exceptions. At their origin on the eastern fringe of the Tibetan Plateau, the two rivers are less than a hundred miles apart, but they become further apart as they wind their way eastward. Leaving the Tibetan Plateau, the Yellow River flows northwestward and then eastward to form the Ordos Bend. Moving southward, it serves as the boundary line between Shensi and Shansi. After receiving water from its two largest tributaries, Fen and Wei, it is blocked in its southward path by the Ch'inling Mountains; it turns eastward to enter the North China Plain. It passes across the Grand Canal in western Shantung before it pours into the Gulf of Pohai.

Economically, the Yellow River is less beneficial than the Yangtze and is in fact sometimes called the "Sorrow of China." Through its upper valley it is swift and, as it cuts through the loess plateau, it carries with it tons of sediment. From its muddy appearance the river acquired its present name. In Lungmen (between Shensi and Shansi) the river current is so swift that, according to an ancient myth, "fish which jump upstream across the rapids will automatically become dragons." East of Lungmen the river enters the North China Plain; as its current slackens, it begins to deposit its content. As a result, the river bed continues to rise and dykes have to be built higher and higher to confine the river within its course. In some areas the river bed is higher than the adjacent land, and once a dyke

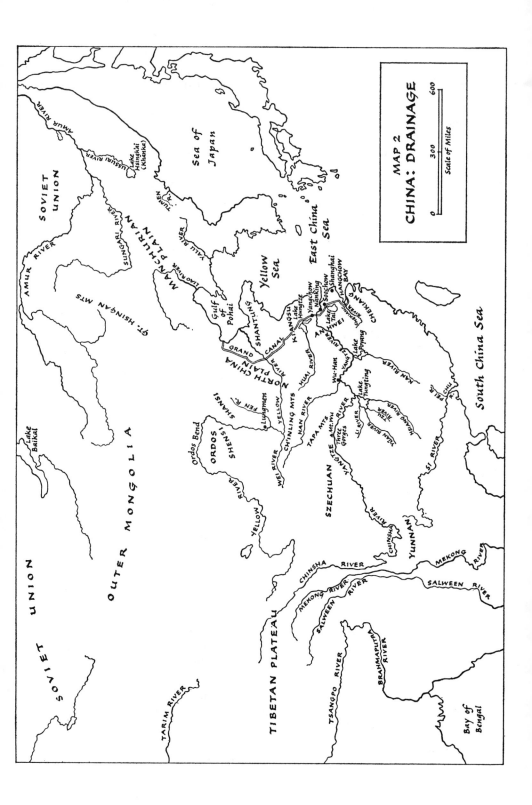

is broken during a heavy downpour, no little Dutch boy can save the area from a devastating flood. The eastern section of the North China Plain is only a few feet above sea level for the most part, and the river meanders through its own creation like a dying reptile. Consequently it often changes its course, and several major changes, with great loss of men and animals, have been recorded since history began. The last of such changes occurred in 1938 when Chinese field commanders, unable to check the advance of Japanese invaders, decided to break the dykes and cause a man-made flood. The Japanese were stopped for the time being, but countless Chinese lives were also lost in this catastrophe.

As the river is shallow, navigation on a large scale is all but impossible. Only the smallest boats of junk size can take advantage of the water surface. Irrigation, however, is practiced on a vast scale. Numerous canals, large and small, have been built to irrigate the adjacent fields. The irrigation works in the North China Plain were historically famous. Here the ancient Chinese civilization was born, and for more than 2,500 years it was the center of the civilized world known to the Chinese. Beginning in the Sung dynasty (960–1279), however, the situation changed. The once magnificent works of flood control and irrigation began to deteriorate, and this deterioration has never been successfully arrested. The economic and cultural center of China began to shift southward and, economically at least, the Yangtze basin has been more important than North China for the past one thousand years.

In its upper valley the Yangtze is the Chinsha River ("River of the Golden Sand") which collects the water of numerous streams on the eastern fringe of the Tibetan Plateau and flows southward. Cutting through the northernmost portion of Yunnan province, it goes northeastward to Szechuan. From then on it is called the Yangtze. Szechuan is a basin formed by the Yangtze and three of its major tributaries, and Szechuan, in fact, means "Four Rivers." Leaving Szechuan, the river cuts through the Tapa Mountains and passes through the famous Three Gorges. Overlooking one of the gorges is Mount Wu where, according to an ancient myth, a king of Ch'u had once met intimately the beautiful river nymph. The mountains rise almost vertically on both sides of the gorges, and the river rushes eastward over hundreds of treacherous rapids.

After the Three Gorges the river current slackens and travels more leisurely over the central lakes region. There are hundreds of lakes in this area, among which Lake Tungting and Lake Poyang are by far the largest. Here the Yangtze receives its longest and largest tributaries. From the south come the four rivers—Hsiang, Tzu, Yüan, and Li—which jointly drain the Hunan province and pour into Lake Tungting. From the north comes the Han River which joins the Yangtze at the Wu-Han metropolis. Further east, the Kan River drains the Kiangsi province, winds its way northward, and discharges its content into Lake Poyang.

Leaving the central lakes region, the Yangtze turns northeastward, cuts across the Grand Canal near Yangchow, and receives more tributaries before it pours into the East China Sea near Shanghai.

The third river in importance is the Si River and its drainage is the largest south of the Yangtze Valley. Its source is a dozen or more streams originating at the foot of the Yun-Kwei Plateau. As it travels eastward, it receives water from joining tributaries. West of Canton it merges with the Pei ("North") River and is then called the Chu ("Pearl") River. It pours into the South China Sea.

Three more rivers need to be mentioned. One is the Heilung ("Black Dragon") or Amur River which originates on the western slope of the Greater Hsingan Mountains, travels northeastward and then southeastward to serve as a common boundary between the Soviet Union and China, and pours into the Sea of Okhotsk through Russia's Maritime Province. Its most important tributary is the Sungari River which, together with the Liao River, drains the Manchurian Plain. The second river is the Huai River which winds its way eastward from one of the Ch'inling extensions to pour into Lake Hungtze, between Anhwei and Kiangsu provinces. Climatically, it is the dividing line between the North and the South in this part of China. Lastly, the Chekiang River drains its namesake province. It cuts the province into two parts, West and East Chekiang, as it goes northward to pour into the Hangchow Bay. The Hangchow Bay is geographically famous for its tidal waves. The tide enters as a racing wave of water up to 15 feet high and speeds up to 15 miles per hour on top of the normal water surface. Each year people travel far to see this unusual spectacle.

CLIMATE

There are many factors that affect the climate of China. First, continental China has a latitudinal difference of 36 degrees, which means large variations in temperature throughout the country. Hainan Island, below 20°N, is tropical, and the northernmost part of Manchuria, near 54°N, is subarctic. Between these two extremes are most parts of China which enjoy a middle latitude or temperate climate. Cyclonic activities are most active in middle latitudes, and in China's case, are an important factor in determining the amount of annual rainfall. The four seasons are sharply divided, though the lengths of summer and winter vary with latitude. Second, China faces the Pacific in the east and has as its hinterland one of the largest land masses in the world. The seasonal changes of temperature and air pressure on the continent vis-à-vis those on the ocean create what is known in this part of the world as the monsoon. The monsoon is a seasonal wind reversal and is responsible for the bitter cold winter in the

Northwest and heavy, summer rainfall in the Southeast. In summer, the continent is heated up faster than the ocean, and wind blows from the ocean towards the continent. The moisture-laden air discharges its load on the continent and causes heavy rain, especially along the coastal areas. In winter, as the continent cools off faster than the ocean, wind direction is reversed. The northern and northwestern winds, originating in continental polar regions, are cold and dry. They become even drier as they blow southward, for relative humidity becomes less as the air is heated up. Winter, therefore, is the dry season in China. Third, as major mountain ranges in China run along a west-east direction, they are effective barriers to the moisture-bearing winds from the ocean. Reaching a mountain, the air rises along the southern slope, discharges its water content as it ascends, and becomes comparatively dry on the lee side of the mountain. It becomes drier and drier as it passes over succeeding mountain ranges. Annual rainfall, consequently, diminishes northwestward.

There are three factors that determine the temperature of various parts of China: latitude, distance from the sea, and altitude. Temperatures—annual averages—range from 68° to 77°F in the Si River valley, 59° to 68°F in the Yangtze basin, 50° to 59°F along the Yellow River, 41° to 50°F in South Manchuria, and below 41°F in the northernmost section of Manchuria. Average temperatures, however, do not tell the whole story. Compared with many other parts of the world located on the same latitudes (North America, for instance), China has a much wider range of temperature between the coldest and warmest months. In other words, summer tends to be hotter, and winter much colder. Most parts of China have recorded maximum temperature exceeding 95°F; in some areas it exceeds 104°F. Kirin, located at 44°N in "cold" Manchuria, has recorded a maximum temperature at 104°F. In winter the high pressure system originating from Siberia dominates all of China. Its cold wind blows southeastward and penetrates as deep as areas south of the Tropic of Cancer. Canton, at 23.1°N, has recorded temperature at 27°F. The temperature of northernmost Manchuria sometimes falls to 40°F below zero.

The further an area is away from the ocean, the more continental its climate will be. Shanghai, on the coast, has a January average of 38°F and a July average of 80°F, with an annual range of 42 degrees. On the other hand, Urumchi, located deep in the hinterland in Sinkiang, has a January average of —3°F and a July average of 75°F, with an annual range of 78 degrees!

As in other parts of the world, altitude is also an important factor in determining temperature. In the southwestern section of the country are located high plateaus and many of the world's highest mountains. Northwestern Tibet, for instance, is located in comparatively low latitude (32–35°N); yet its annual temperature averages only 23°F in many

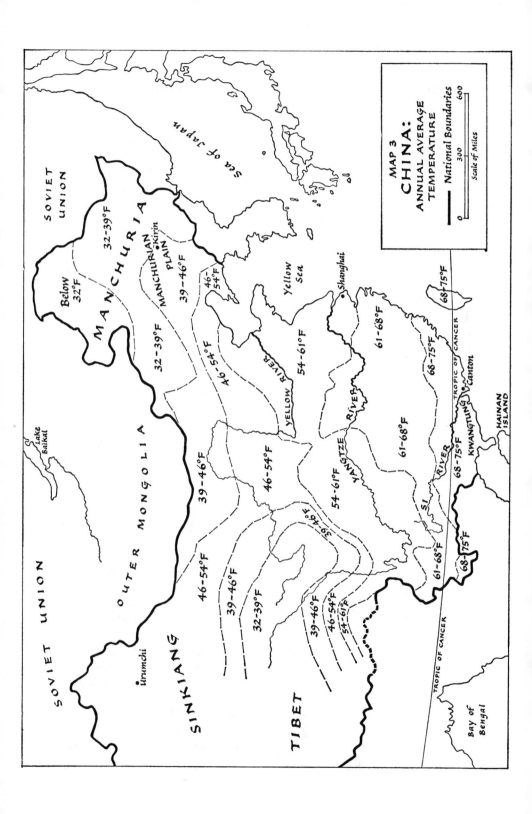

MAP 3
CHINA:
ANNUAL AVERAGE
TEMPERATURE

━━━ National Boundaries

Scale of Miles
0   300   600

SOVIET UNION

Lake
Baikal

OUTER MONGOLIA

Ürumchi

SINKIANG

TIBET

Bay of
Bengal

TROPIC OF CANCER

SOVIET
UNION

MANCHURIA

Below
32°F

32-39°F

32-39°F

39-46°F

MANCHURIAN
PLAIN

Kirin

Sea of Japan

46-
54°F

46-54°F

46-54°F

39-46°F

32-39°F

39-46°F

46-54°F

39-46°F

46-54°F

54-61°F

YELLOW RIVER

Yellow
Sea

54-61°F

Shanghai

61-68°F

YANGTZE RIVER

54-61°F

61-68°F

61-68°F

SI RIVER

68-75°F

68-75°F

Canton

KWANGTUNG

TROPIC OF CANCER

HAINAN
ISLAND

68-75°F

68-75°F

61-68°F

68-75°F

places. Because of its high altitude, a large portion of this region is permanently frozen.

The reasons described above cause the length of the growing season to decrease northward, and to a lesser extent, westward. Kwangtung, on the southeastern coast, has a growing season all year round, because rarely would temperature drop below 32°F. The middle and lower Yangtze valley, further north but close to the coast, has a growing season of eight to ten months. On the other hand, the Manchurian Plain has a growing season of only five to six months, and some of the mountainous regions in Tibet have practically no growing season at all.

Rainfall in China is mostly frontal or cyclonic in origin; only a small portion comes from convectional and orographic sources. The southern and southeastern monsoon brings precipitation to China from May to September and is responsible for much of the rainfall during the summer months. If in certain years the southern and southeastern winds are weak, they can only go as far as the Yangtze Valley, discharge all their water content, and leave little for North China. In such case, there are floods in the Yangtze and drought in the Yellow River region. If, on the other hand, the winds are unusually strong, they cause heavy rainfall in North China and little precipitation in the Yangtze Valley. Thus a flood or drought in North China is often accompanied by a drought or flood in the Yangtze region. Only when the winds are of the right strength will the rainfall be properly distributed and will all parts of China be benefited by its presence. In other words, when crops fail in the Yangtze, it is likely that they will also fail in North China, though for different reasons. If it is a good year, it would be a good year in both regions. Not surprisingly, the erratic behavior of the monsoon is a major concern to the Chinese people.

Superimposed on this monsoon pattern are the migrating cyclonic and anticyclonic disturbances which move along a west-east direction towards the coast and then northeastward towards Japan. Approximately eighty cyclonic depressions move across China each year. These storm centers are responsible for much of China's rainfall, expecially in the interior regions. Generally speaking, they are most widespread in the Yangtze and appear less often north of the Huai River. They occur every month of the year and are most numerous in the winter and spring. In late spring when they are blocked by the polar front in the north, they become stationary in the Lower Yangtze and cause continuous rain which the Chinese call mai-yü, or plum rain. It is most welcome to farmers because this is the time when rice seedlings, newly planted, need a great deal of moisture.

More intense and violent than the normal, mid-latitude cyclonic depressions are the typhoons. The typhoons originate in the ocean east of the Philippine Islands and cause strong winds and heavy storms on their destructive paths. In late summer and early autumn they repeatedly in-

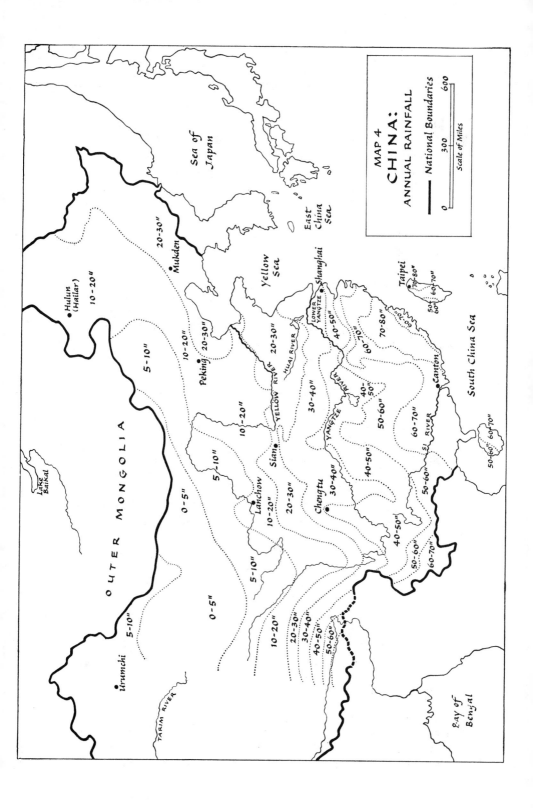

MAP 4
CHINA:
ANNUAL RAINFALL

— National Boundaries

Scale of Miles

0   300   600

vade China's southeast coast and cause heavy damages. Fortunately they curve northeastward once they hit the coast areas, and rarely do they penetrate far into the interior.

Three conclusions can be reached with regard to China's rainfall. First, it is heavily concentrated in summer; second, it is most plentiful on the southeast coast and diminishes northwestward towards the continent; and third, it is unreliable and unpredictable. Since rainfall is essential to the growth of vegetation and since it diminishes towards the hinterland at an accelerated speed, a large portion of China is unfit for cultivation. If we say that an annual rainfall of twenty inches is the minimum for profitable agricultural engagement, then about half of China's land surface would be unfruitful as farm land, no matter how good other conditions are. Actually, total arable land is much smaller, because other conditions, such as those of terrain and soil, are not so good as they should be.

Though China is fortunate in the sense that rainfall is concentrated during the growing season—in Lower Yangtze, for instance, almost seventy percent of annual rainfall falls between March and August inclusive —the unreliability of precipitation in a given year works havoc among farmers. Annual averages are often misleading, because what looks good in average may be disastrous in reality. In China's case, a wet year may have three or four times as much rain as a dry year. The disparity is more pronounced in North China than in the Yangtze Valley and the Si River basin. Flood follows drought and vice versa, even though the average appears to be the right amount. In view of these facts, it is not surprising that crops fail often and that they fail more often in North China. Since history began, the unreliability of rainfall has caused the greatest distress to Chinese farmers. During summer when rain is needed most, often none comes. The cumulus clouds drift slowly across the sky, and nothing happens. An ancient Chinese poet was so angry with them that he asked them pointedly:

> While myriads of seedlings
> Are dying of thirst,
> How can you leisurely
> Make peaks of mountains
> As if nothing had happened?

Today nature is as unmerciful to the Chinese as it has always been.

GEOGRAPHICAL REGIONS

Customarily, the Chinese speak of their country as composed of the Northeast, the Northwest, North China, South China, the Southeast, the Southwest, and finally, Mongolia and Tibet. There are two disadvantages in this division. First, each region is loosely termed, and individuals might

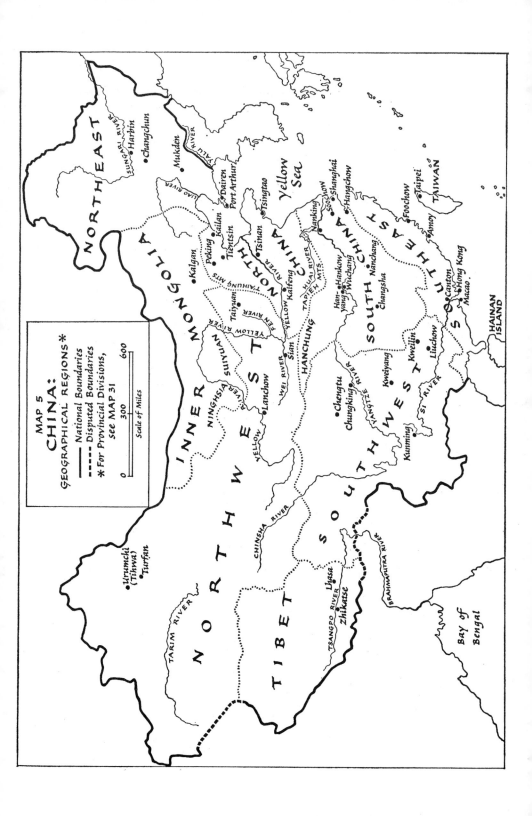

MAP 5

CHINA:
GEOGRAPHICAL REGIONS*

National Boundaries
Disputed Boundaries
* For Provincial Divisions,
see MAP 31

0   300   600
Scale of Miles

differ as to exactly what areas or provinces it contains. Second, this is not a division based entirely on geographical factors. These disadvantages, however, are more than offset by the advantage of a customary usage commonly understood. Furthermore, based on geographical factors alone, no two geographers could agree as to how China should be divided, because each geographer emphasizes a different factor or factors.

The Northeast   The Northeast is often referred to as Manchuria, because this was the ancient home of the Manchus. Chinese migration to Manchuria began more than two thousand years ago and most of the immigrants settled in the rich farm land in South Manchuria. When the Manchus ruled China beginning in the seventeenth century, Chinese were barred from moving to Manchuria for permanent settlement; this bar, however, was revoked during the last century. Subsequently Chinese from nearby Shantung and Hopeh provinces moved in in large numbers, and today there are approximately seventy million Chinese in Manchuria, of whom only a very small fraction still identify themselves as Manchus. The assimilation has been virtually complete.

Of all the geographical regions Manchuria is by far the richest in China. It offers great opportunities for agriculture and industry. Though rainfall and temperature diminish northwestward, South Manchuria is humid and warm enough to sustain an intensive farming as practiced by the Chinese. Only in the northwestern parts of Manchuria does rainfall become too light and growing season too short to practice agriculture profitably. The Manchurian Plain—sometimes referred to as the Sung-Liao Plain—is one of the major agricultural areas in China, and produces a variety of food and industrial crops. Since its population density is small compared with other agricultural areas in China, it has a food surplus. Soy beans are its most important food export.

Manchuria also has China's largest forest reserves. Lumbering is an important industry in eastern Manchuria, timber being shipped out downstream to the market via the Yalu and the Sungari Rivers. Fur trapping is a major source of income in forest regions, and sable is the most famous among a variety of furs produced. Harbin, located in the center of Manchuria, is its largest fur market.

Manchuria is the only region in China that is highly industrialized. It contains more than half of China's iron ore reserves, and its oil and coal reserves are also very large. It produces a variable amount of copper, manganese, lead, and sodium. China's largest gold reserve is located along the Amur River in northern Manchuria, though production has not been large. Modern hydroelectric plants along the Yalu River provide much of the electric power for industrial uses. All major cities and industrial centers are linked by railroads; in fact, Manchuria has more miles of railroad track than any other region in China. Mukden, with a population of more than 2,500,000, is the largest city in this region.

The Northwest   The Northwest extends westward from the T'aihang Mountains to the eastern border of Russian Turkestan. It includes Sinkiang, Kansu, Chinghai, the Shensi province north of the Ch'inling Mountains, and Shansi. Rainfall diminishes westward and climate becomes more continental along the same direction. The annual rainfall of Shansi, the easternmost province in this region, is about twenty inches. It steadily diminishes westward until it is less than four inches in southern Sinkiang (Tarim).[1]

Agricultural activities are greatly hampered by climatic limitations. In the eastern portion of the region where rainfall is comparatively heavy, agriculture is practiced only on riverine plains where irrigation water is available. Thus the Fen River basin, the Wei River plain, and the Lanchow area (Kansu) are the three major agricultural areas. The Wei River plain has one of the best soils and produces high-quality cotton besides the regular food crops. Sian (Ch'angan), an ancient capital, is still the largest city in the area.

Outside the riverine plains, the landscape is dominated by steppes and deserts. Here and there oases are found, and they please a man's eyes with their trees, shrubs, and cultivated fields. In addition to food crops, farmers in oases grow a variety of fruits, such as grapes, peaches, cherries, apples, apricots, and watermelons. Oases are by definition isolated areas, and most parts of the Northwest are agriculturally unproductive. As the land is unable to support a large population, the Northwest remains one of China's least populated regions.

Unfit for agriculture, a large portion of the Northwest is devoted to the livestock industry. Cattle and sheep are raised simultaneously, though sheep are more important in most areas. The best kind of pastures is often found in areas adjacent to high mountains where the melting snow provides the much needed moisture. The raising of livestock is the major occupation of non-Chinese groups, such as the Uighurs in Sinkiang. The Chinese, on the other hand, are mostly farmers and are concentrated in riverine plains and oases.

Containing China's largest coal reserves, the Northwest possesses great potentials for industrial development. There are also unknown quantities of gold, nitrate, lead, bauxite, and manganese reserves. However, these reserves will remain in the ground until better means of transportation can be built to reach them. Recently the Communist regime has begun to carry out an ambitious railroad-building program in this region.

North China   North China is bordered by the Great Wall in the north, and its southern boundary is the Tapieh Mountains in the west and the Huai River in the east. From the T'aihang Mountains it extends eastward to the Yellow Sea. Except for Shantung which is mostly hilly, North China is a vast plain. It includes Hopeh, Honan, Shantung, and the

[1] To locate provinces and cities, see Map 31, page 472.

northern sections of Anhwei and Kiangsu. It is sometimes called Chung-yüan, or Central Plain.

Among the factors that hamper North China agriculturally the most important is the lack of adequate rainfall. On the average, the amount of annual rainfall is only half as much as that of South China and is only one-third as much as that in the Southeast. The shortage of rainfall and its unreliability make farming extremely hazardous. Whenever it does rain, the rain floods the denuded earth. Since farmers have no other source of income except what can be gained by cultivating the field, a crop failure means famine for them. Thousands of years of settlement have made North China one of the most densely populated areas in China, and the supply of food can barely meet the demand even in good years. Time and again famine raises its ugly head, and faminie is too often followed by rebellion and war.

North China has two major coal fields, one along the T'aihang Mountains and the other in northern Hopeh. The Kailan coal mine is the largest of its kind in North China. The region is served by four major railroads: Ching-Han (from Peking to Hankow), Chin-P'u (from Tientsin to Nanking), Pei-Ning (from Peking to Mukden), and Lung-Hai which passes across North China along an east-west direction. (Map 6, page 27) All major cities are located along the railroads. Peking, the old imperial city, is now the capital of the Communist regime. It is famous for its libraries, museums, and scenic spots. Tientsin is the largest industrial and commercial center in this region. Industries include flour-milling, manufacturing of wool and cotton textiles, oil-pressing, leather-tanning, and paper-making. Its handwoven rugs, together with those from Peking, are internationally famous.

South China Since China's main wealth comes from agriculture, South China, by producing large quantities of agricultural products, is economically better off than its northern counterpart. For one thing, enjoying a warmer and more humid climate, the southerners are able to raise paddy rice which yields more calories per acre than wheat or any other northern crop. Besides, the Yangtze and its tributaries are far less troublous than the Yellow River.

South China consists of Hupeh, Hunan, Kiangsi, the Shensi province south of the Ch'inling Mountains (the Hanchung area), the sections of Anhwei and Kiangsu south of the Huai River, and the northern section of Chekiang (West Chekiang). Much of this region is hilly; only areas adjacent to lakes and rivers are intensively cultivated. Thus the central lakes region, Lower Yangtze, and the Hanchung area are three of the most productive areas in China, and their population density is also among the highest. The four major products are rice, cotton, tea, and silk, though considerable amounts of soy beans, sweet potatoes, and tobacco are also produced. Kiangsi and Hunan produce the finest hemp in China which, after being bleached, is woven into an airy cloth for summer wear. Besides timber, the most important forest products are tung oil and lacquer. The region is well supplied with fish, since it contains numerous lakes, rivers, and ponds and is close to the sea. Coal reserves have been found in every province, though production has not been large. In eastern Hupeh where coal and iron ore happen to be located together, there is an iron-steel center, the largest south of the Great Wall. South China also produces most of the nation's tungsten, antimony, lead, zinc, and silver.

Around the lakes and beside the rivers stand many of China's prosperous cities. Shanghai, with a population of eleven million, is by far the largest. It is the financial center of China as well as its largest port. Industries include the manufacturing of textiles, cement, tiles, glass, cigarettes and tobacco products, the milling of rice and flour, shipbuilding, printing and publishing, and a variety of others. West of Shanghai and on the southern bank of the Yangtze is Nanking, the former capital of Nationalist China. Nearby are Soochow and Hangchow which, rich and prosperous, are popularly referred to as the two "paradises on earth." Further up on the Yangtze is the Wu-Han metropolis. It consists of three cities: Hankow, Wuchang, and Hanyang. Hankow is the largest of the three and is the commercial center of the central lakes region.

The Southeast   The Southeast is mostly hilly, and level land can only be found in localized riverine plains and deltas. It includes the southern section of Chekiang (East Chekiang), Fukien, Kwangtung, Taiwan, and Hainan Island. It stretches from the subtropical to the tropical; south of Chekiang, there is little or no winter snow at all. Rainfall is plentiful and is concentrated in summer when the southeastern monsoon dominates the entire region.

As the growing season is long and rainfall is heavy, most areas in this region can grow two or even three crops a year. Whenever level land can be found or slopes are not too steep, rice is intensively cultivated. Thus, despite the limited areas available for cultivation, the Southeast is a major rice producing region in China. Taiwan serves as a good example to show the advantage of intensive farming. It is smaller than Denmark and less than twenty-five percent of the island is arable. Yet it produces enough rice to feed a population of seventeen million and exports large quantities besides. In addition to rice, there are also other crops, notably sugar cane. Taiwan is a major producer of cane sugar in the world and exports most of its refined sugar overseas. Located in the low latitudes, the Southeast produces a variety of tropical and subtropical fruits, including bananas, pineapples, oranges, and litchis.

As this region is mostly hilly, forests can be found in every province, and lumbering is an important industry. Its irregular coastline contains many fine bays and harbors, and fishing is an important means of earning a livelihood. The catches are dried, salted, or peppered to be shipped to

ARCHITECTURE IN PEKING

Marble Screen with Nine Dragons

Marble Arch Bridge

Walking Corridor

Temple Lion

The Cornice of a Palace

Marble Boat in the Summer Palace

Marble Pagoda of the Yellow Temple

A NARROW, CROWDED STREET IN HONG KONG   Notice the Chinese signs with, in some cases, their English equivalents. While most Chinese in this British colony are attired in the Western style, the woman in the foreground wears the traditional *ch'i-p'ao* which dates from the time of the Manchus.

many parts of the country. Mawei, ten miles east of Foochow (capital of Fukien province), has one of China's best shipyards.

Historically the Southeast is the seafaring section of the nation. Millions of its children have emigrated to other parts of the world, especially Southeast Asia. Macao and Hong Kong along the Kwangtung coast remind many Chinese of a colonial past. Hong Kong, once a rocky island with scattered fishing villages, has been prosperous ever since the British took it over in 1842 and is now one of the greatest commercial centers in East Asia. Canton is the capital of Kwangtung province and the largest city of this region within Chinese jurisdiction. Taipei, the major city of Nationalist China on Taiwan, is a commercial center as well as a political capital.

Because of its rugged terrain, the Southeast is poor in transportation. Poor transportation creates a unique situation: the diversity of dialects. There are so many dialects and subdialects in this region that sometimes people living less than a hundred miles apart cannot understand each other. In a less generous mood, ancient Chinese in the north often referred to these dialects as *niao-yü,* or birds' chatterings. Fortunately, all China uses the same written language, one of the oldest in the world. When a northern Chinese goes to a chop suey restaurant in the United States, he has to write his order because most Chinese-Americans came from China's Southeast.

The Southwest   The Southwest has two distinct regions: the Yun-Kwei Plateau and its eastern slopes, and the Szechuan basin. It includes four provinces: Yunnan, Kweichow, Kwangsi, and Szechuan.

Because of its high altitude, the Yun-Kwei Plateau is generally cool in summer and mild in winter. Kunming, for instance, has an average January temperature of 46°F and an average July temperature of 62°F. However, as the plateau slopes down eastward, annual range of temperature increases. The average July temperature of Kwangsi rises as high as 82°F. Szechuan, surrounded by high mountains, is also hot in summer. Winter, on the other hand, is comparatively mild; the eastward trending mountains protect this region from the bitter cold winds which plague most parts of China during this time. These same mountains also block the northern movement of summer monsoon and cause a large amount of precipitation throughout the entire region.

Climatic conditions being generally favorable, agriculture is intensively engaged in, wherever level land can be found. Szechuan, which has extensive alluvial plains, becomes one of the most important agricultural areas in China. Its most important crop is rice, followed by soy beans, cotton, wheat, corn, and sweet potatoes. Cane sugar is produced in the southwestern section of the province, and total annual production is only second to that of Taiwan. Nearby are China's famous salt wells, some of which, dug centuries ago, reach a depth of more than four thousand feet. In addition, Szechuan is first in the production of tung oil, and third (after Chekiang and Kiangsu) in the production of raw silk. The richness of Szechuan earns it the enviable title "Heavenly State" (*t'ien-fu chih kuo*) and, during World War II, enabled China to hold out against the Japanese demand for surrender for more than eight years.

Compared with Szechuan, the other three provinces in the Southwest are less fortunate. For the most part the terrain is too rugged to be useful. In the Yun-Kwei Plateau where level land is hard to find, terracing is widely used to wrest arable land from mountains. In Kweichow some of the terraced farms climb for several hundred feet and are a remarkable sight to see.

Chengtu, located in western Szechuan, is the industrial and commercial center of the surrounding area. The Chengtu-Chungking Railroad, completed in the early 1950's, has greatly enhanced its position as a commercial market. Chungking serves as an entrepot for a large drainage basin in central Szechuan and was the wartime capital of Nationalist China. Kunming is the capital of Yunnan and is noted for its "spring

RICE TERRACES IN CHINA   Notice the neat rows of rice plants in the field. The lower parts of the plants are covered by water during their growth. On the left side of the picture is a farmer's thatched hut. The clearing in front of the hut is used, among other things, for threshing harvested crops.

weather all year round." Kweilin is the largest city in Kwangsi   lo-cated beside a lake, is famous for its scenery.

    Mongolia and Tibet   Though geographically apart, Mongoli   Ti-bet are often grouped together because first, under the Nationali   me they were both territories contrary to the rest of the nation w   vas divided into administrative provinces; second, each is inhabit   an ethnic minority; and third, there are geographical characteristics   ion to both of them. Since 1945 when Outer Mongolia became officially independent, the word Mongolia has come to mean Inner Mongolia only. Inner Mongolia is sandwiched between Outer Mongolia in the north and the Great Wall in the south. Under the Nationalist regime it was divided into four administrative provinces: Ninghsia, Suiyuan, Chahar, and Jehol. Since then the Communists have made a realignment of administrative units. While Ninghsia remains separate, an Inner Mongolian Autonomous Region has been created to cover most of the other provinces.

The climate of Inner Mongolia is decidedly continental; summer is unusually hot and winter is extremely cold. Rainfall is small, and its annual amount diminishes westward. It averages between eight and twenty inches a year in the eastern section (Jehol) to less than two inches in the extreme western section. The region is a land of deserts and steppes.

Whenever rainfall is adequate to make grass grow, livestock is raised to take advantage of the natural environment. Sheep skin and wool are the two major items for export. Farming is conducted only in oases. That part of the Yellow River which separates Suiyuan from Ninghsia has a string of almost continuous oases which are cultivated by the Chinese. This is the only densely populated area in the entire region. The major mineral resources of Inner Mongolia are coal, iron ore, sodium, and sulphur.

Historically Tibet consisted of the Tibetan territory and the Sikang province. In 1954 Sikang was divided into two parts. The western part joined the Tibetan territory to form a newly created Tibetan Autonomous Region, and the eastern part was made a part of Szechuan province. That is the situation as it stands today.

The climate of Tibet varies a great deal, from a tundra type of climate in the northwestern section to a more humid, warmer climate in the southern section. Lhasa, located in the southern section, is cool in summer (average July temperature, 61°F) but cold in winter (average January temperature, 19°F). Rainfall for most parts of Tibet is very small, though the extreme southern section has a wide range of annual rainfall, from 10 to as much as 160 inches. The amount received each year varies with the strength of the Indian monsoon.

Agriculture is practiced along the river valleys of the southern section. The most important native crop is the hardy *ch'ing-k'o* (literally, green grain), though wheat, barley, and a variety of vegetables are also produced. Agricultural areas being extremely limited, the occupation of most Tibetans is the raising of livestock. The most important animal is the yak, an animal unique to the Tibetan region. The Tibetans drink its milk, eat its meat, and wear its fur and skin. Its fur is also woven into tents and rugs; its dung is burned as fuel; and its bones are made into utensils. The yak is also used as a means of transportation. The Tibetans drink a large amount of tea, which they do not grow, often mixed with butter. To obtain tea from outside sources, they ship out wool, animal hides, rugs, and such specialities as musk, deer antlers, and rhinoceros' and antelope's horns. These specialities, which are supposed to possess the power of rejuvenation, are highly priced, and they find their best customers among the well-to-do Chinese.

Tibet has a population variously estimated as between one and two millions. Although regarded as part of China since the early eighteenth century, it was not brought under China's effective control until 1951. Lhasa, with a .population of sixty thousand, is by far the largest city. The thirteen-story Potala Palace, from which the Dalai Lama once ruled all of Tibet, towers above the entire city. Zhikatse, the second largest city, is an important center of communication noted for its strategic value. Until recently there had been neither motor roads nor motorized vehicles in Tibet. When the Communists took it over in 1951, they began an intensive highway building program. Now there are more than three thousand miles of motor roads linking all major cities in Tibet with those in China proper. Following the highways came the Chinese whose number was insignificant before and is now estimated to be more than half a million.

ECONOMIC RESOURCES AND INDUSTRIAL PROSPECTS

Despite its emphasis on industrialization, China remains an agricultural country, and more than 75 percent of its people, directly or indirectly, depend upon farming for their livelihood. Yet, due to a number of unfavorable conditions—the lack of adequate rainfall, rugged terrain, poor soil, etc.—the amount of land that can be profitably used for agriculture is less than 20 percent of China's land surface. This percentage is further reduced by the amount of land allocated for other purposes, such as commercial and industrial establishments, houses, schools, roads, and cemeteries. Land under cultivation is roughly 10 percent of total land surface, approximately 260 million acres. This would mean only 0.31 acres per capita in a land of 850 million people. Land shortage and population pressure have always been among China's most serious problems.

Agriculturally unpromising, China has to depend upon mining and industry to cure its economic woes. Until the discovery of substantial oil reserves in the 1960's, coal was the only mineral of which China had plenty. Total coal reserve is estimated anywhere between 444 and 1,200 billion metric tons, a large portion of which seems to be of excellent quality. Even if the smaller figure is used, China still ranks fourth (after the United States, the Soviet Union, and Canada) in the world. The newly discovered oil reserves, located in Manchuria and North China,

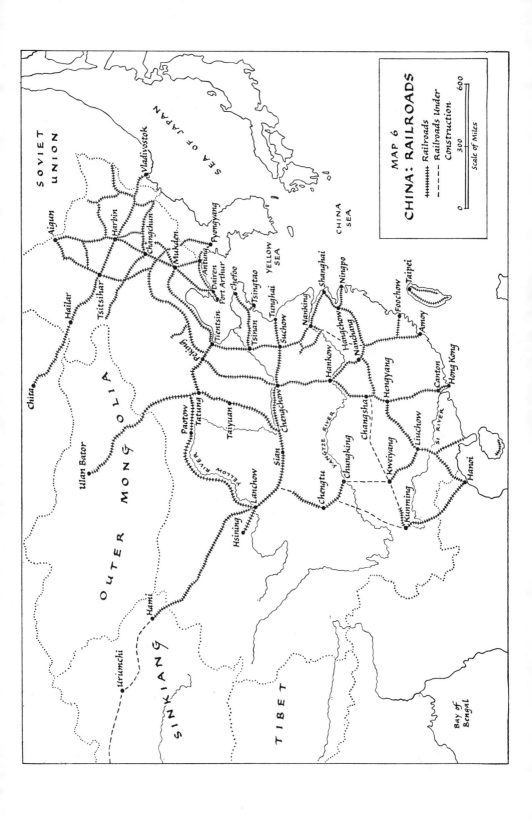

MAP 6

CHINA: RAILROADS

++++++ Railroads
------ Railroads Under
      Construction

Scale of Miles

0   300   600

SOVIET UNION

SEA OF JAPAN

OUTER MONGOLIA

SINKIANG

TIBET

CHINA SEA

YELLOW SEA

Bay of Bengal

Chita
Ulan Bator
Aigun
Hailar
Tsitsihar
Harbin
Vladivostok
Changchun
Mukden
Antung
Pyongyang
Dairen
Port Arthur
Chefoo
Tsingtao
Tunghai
Tsinan
Tientsin
Peking
Paotow
Tatung
Taiyuan
Suchow
Nanking
Shanghai
Ningpo
Hangchow
Nanchang
Foochow
Taipei
Amoy
Hankow
Hengyang
Canton
Hong Kong
Changchow
Sian
Chengchow
Lanchow
Hsining
Chengtu
Chungking
Changsha
Kweiyang
Liuchow
Kunming
Hanoi
Hami
Urumchi

YELLOW RIVER
YANGTZE RIVER
SI RIVER

have enabled oil production to increase steadily during the past decade, though total production is still very small when compared to the production of the world's major producers. In 1975, for instance, China's oil production was estimated to be 527 million barrels, as compared to 3,052 million barrels for the United States and 3,609 million barrels for the Soviet Union. Nevertheless, because consumer consumption of oil in the domestic market is severely limited (e.g., China has no privately owned automobiles), China has been able to export oil overseas, beginning in 1973.

While endowed with substantial coal and oil reserves, China is insufficiently supplied with iron-ore deposits. Known iron-ore deposits are estimated to be between four and eleven billion tons, and most of them are located in South Manchuria. Before World War II annual production of steel (including the production in Manchuria) never exceeded 1.5 million metric tons. It has been anywhere between 20 and 30 million metric tons in recent years. Either figure is still very small when compared to the 102, 106, and 141 million metric tons produced by Japan, the United States, and the Soviet Union, respectively (1975 figures). As for minor minerals, China has a large reserve of tunsten and antimony, but it is inadequately supplied with copper, zinc, lead, gold, and silver deposits. Though bauxite, from which aluminum is extracted, is widely distributed in China, not until recently has it been exploited on a large scale.

In addition to coal and oil, China is also favorably endowed with water power potential. There are excellent sites along the upper and middle valleys of the Yangtze and the Yellow Rivers where dams can be built to generate hydroelectric power. It is estimated that enough electricity can be produced to supply the needs of all major cities from Hankow to Shanghai if the turbulent water along the Three Gorges can be somehow harnessed. In 1957 the People's Republic announced an ambitious program of building forty-six dams along the Yellow River, scheduled to be completed in 1967. One year after the announcement, China entered a period of severe depression that did not end until 1962. The ambitious program was shelved, and the construction of most of these dams has not yet begun. Since then the Chinese have adopted a new approach to hydroelectric development. Instead of proceeding with large-scale projects that strain China's financial and technical resources and take too long a period to complete, the government encourages the construction of waterworks that do not require advanced technology and large expenditures. These waterworks, constructed with local resources, are designed to serve three purposes simultaneously: irrigation and flood control, as well as the generation of electricity. The new approach has proven to be remarkably successful.

To industrialize, a country has to satisfy a number of primary conditions. Among them are: (1) favorable social and cultural environment,

(2) the availability of trained personnel, managerial as well as technical, (3) easy access to fuel and raw materials, and (4) capital. In China's case, the problems posed by the first two conditions are transitional and have already been resolved. Traditional Chinese society did not provide a favorable environment for industrial development, since it downgraded industry and commerce and dissuaded young men of promise from pursuing an industrial or commercial career. Because this society has been slowly undermined since the impact of the West and is virtually destroyed under the Communist rule, there is no longer any question about favorable social and cultural environment. In fact, the People's Republic regards industrialization as the first step to the modernization of China. As for the availability of trained personnel, it is ultimately determined by the educational level of the country as a whole. Until recently education has been the privilege of a few. As mass education is being emphasized today, inevitably there will be more managerial and technical personnel. Nevertheless, new problems are created in the process of solving the old ones. The People's Republic, in promoting egalitarianism, has adopted an educational policy that emphasizes ideological indoctrination at the expense of academic excellence. Since modern science and technology require advanced training and sophisticated knowledge, the negative impact of this policy upon industrial development is obvious.

As for easy access to fuel and raw materials, China is not so well situated as the United States or the Soviet Union, but it is better off than most other countries. The unique problem China has to face is its huge population which must be fed and clothed. Natural forests have long disappeared from most parts of China as more and more forest regions are converted to farm land in order to grow food, and the output of industrial raw materials, in many cases, can be increased only at the expense of food production. Even with so much acreage devoted to the production of food, China produces barely enough to feed itself in good years and has to import grain in bad years. In short, China's prospect of industrial development lies as much in its ability to control population growth as in the availability of adequate natural resources. This does not mean, however, that the situation is hopeless. The discovery of new resources, such as the recent discovery of oil reserves, can make a world of difference. China has a territorial size smaller than that of the Soviet Union but larger than that of the United States. As one Chinese leader put it, "I simply do not believe that God likes the Russians and the Americans so much better than He likes us."

The inability to generate savings adversely affects capital formation, the lack of which in turn impedes industrial development. The extraction of savings from the agricultural section of the economy would mean undernourishment for millions, which no sensible leaders would contemplate. Yet China's industrialization has not been advanced far enough to enable it to sell industrial products in the world market on a large scale. A substantial increase of oil exports may make a difference, but it is still too early to tell how sizable it can be. Conceivably China can concentrate on the manufacturing of labor-intensive products that do not require advanced technology and large capital outlays, as Japan used to do and as Taiwan and South Korea are doing at this moment. This is perhaps where the future lies.

The Chinese, of course, can generate instant capital by borrowing from foreign sources or contracting long-term loans for the importation of capital goods. China's credit rating is excellent, and there should be no difficulty on this score. But the Chinese want no part in this kind of arrangement. The reasons are twofold: historical and ideological. The historical reason will be discussed in detail in the later part of this book; suffice it to say that the Chinese experience with foreign loans has not been pleasant. Ideologically, the Chinese believe that self-reliance is the best course for an underdeveloped country to follow, and to borrow is to mortgage one's own future, including one's own freedom and independence. Whatever the reasons are for turning down foreign assistance, China, lacking a solid base for capital formation from indigenous sources, is further handicapped in its industrialization effort without foreign borrowing.

While it is difficult to predict human events in general and the future of a nation in particular, it can be safely assumed that, all factors considered, China will not be an industrial and military power in the category of the United States and the Soviet Union. When the Chinese say that China will never become a superpower, they are not motivated by false modesty—they merely state the obvious. However, China's very size, in terms of both population and territory, commands attention, and its long history, uninterrupted for four thousand years, is an exciting, interesting field of study. Certain aspects of its culture provoke thought, if not providing alternatives. In any event, China is not a dull subject.

1

The Formative Period

The Chinese are a Mongoloid people who have lived in China for many thousand years. Despite theories to the contrary, there has been no proved evidence that they migrated to China from somewhere else. In 1927 skeletal remains were found in a small village near Peking of what is called the Peking Man, who is believed to have lived in this part of the world some 400,000 years ago. The Peking Man was a predecessor of *Homo sapiens* or modern man, and the fact that he possessed certain Mongoloid features has led many people to wonder whether he might have been the forerunner of the early inhabitants of North China. The question cannot be definitely answered because we know little about the transitional period during which subhuman beings were replaced by *Homo sapiens*. When the transitional period was over and when the first modern man appeared in this part of the world, he was a Mongoloid. Presumably, he was the ancestor of the modern Chinese. However, a long span of time had to elapse before his descendants could develop a semblance of culture. Throughout these long years progress was painful and extremely slow.

The question often arises as to why the Chinese civilization developed in the Yellow River basin instead of the Yangtze which, as we have said in the Introduction, is more beneficial economically. There have been many theories to explain this phenomenon, including the theory that a harsh environment stimulated better efforts on the part of the inhabitants and that they had to be inventive in order to survive. For instance, the frequency of floods necessitated creative work in irrigation and flood control. Furthermore, as both types of work required communal efforts, political organization was necessary to achieve the desired result. As floods in the Yellow River usually covered a large area, the political organization had to be strong and extensive enough to force cooperation among people of the area involved. There is even reason to believe that North China of ancient times was an easier place to live in than it is today. Centuries of deforestation have made flood-control more difficult and thousands of years of intensive farming have reduced the natural fertility of the soil. At one time North China was both challenging and rewarding enough to stimulate man to creative efforts but not rich enough to reduce him to lethargy and inactivity.

Unfortunately, we know little about his early activities. Archaeological findings, extensive as they are, are still inadequate in reconstructing a clear, reliable picture. Three major sites of Paleolithic culture have been located in North China, two near Peking and one in the Ordos Desert. Most common among the findings were stone choppers which, presumably, were all-purpose instruments used for cutting, boring, scraping, etc. Next numerous was a stone spade which might have been used for digging earth. The excavations at the Ordos Desert revealed a stone culture of a more advanced stage, as the findings included ground stone knives and bone needles. As the Paleolithic culture merged imperceptibly with that of the Neolithic period, the stone instruments became more refined and varied. What made the Neolithic culture remarkably distinct from its predecessor was the invention and the increasing use of potteries. Neolithic potteries have been found all over China, from Manchuria to Kwangtung, indicating wide diffusion of an advanced culture. However, most of the findings were made in North China, which might have been the source of the diffusion. Towards the end of the Neolithic period two pottery cultures stood as the most outstanding, the Yang-shao (Honan) and the Lung-shan (Shantung), named after the two sites where most of the typical potteries were unearthed. The artifacts of Yang-shao culture have been found in areas from Manchuria to Kansu, but none have yet been discovered in South China. Typical among these artifacts was a red pot painted with black, geometric designs and was perhaps used as a water container. The Lung-shan potteries were more advanced as they were more complex in pattern and design. They were found in the Yangtze Valley as well as North China. As they were typified by a shiny black hue, the culture they represented is sometimes called the black pottery culture.

We do not know whether the Chinese Neolithic culture was an independent development or had been influenced by the older cultures in West Asia. The similarity in geometric designs between the Yang-shao potteries and those unearthed in West Asia has led to the belief that borrowings did exist, but evidences have been too scanty to be conclusive.

How did the Neolithic people live? For one thing, we know that by the latter part of the Neolithic period they had entered the agricultural stage. Among the Yang-shao findings there were stone instruments which could only be interpreted as farm implements. Some kind of knitting and weaving must have also existed in view of the plaid patterns on the painted potteries and the discovery of spinning wheels in the Shansi and Honan excavations. For protection against wild animals as well as human enemies, many people lived together in villages. As villages existed, there must have been some kind of political organization among the villagers. Pig bones were numerous in these village ruins; the pig was perhaps the first domesticated animal. Towards the end of the Neolithic period potteries were not merely functional utensils; they were art pieces through which the potters gave vent to their sentiment and exercised their artistic skill. Sometimes animal images were engraved on these potteries such as those of cattle, horses, and sheep. These animals must have been domesticated by then. Since the potters were obviously experts devoted to their craft, it is safe to assume that a division of labor existed among the villagers and that the exchange of goods and services existed side by side with the division of labor. Among the Lung-shan findings not only were the tools, utensils, and ornaments skillfully fashioned from stone, shells, or bones but there were also animal bones that had been used for divination purposes. The belief in supernatural forces implied the existence of some kind of religion, albeit animistic.

While archaeological findings are too scanty to enable us to reconstruct the life of the Neolithic period, there are numerous written works which purport to describe it in detail. As these works were composed long after the alleged events they described had occurred, we cannot accept them as history in their entirety. Some of the described events are legendary, if not fictional; others are fairly reliable. The question as to where the line should be drawn has been a matter of debate ever since these works were written some twenty-two or twenty-three hundred years ago. Some of these works will be discussed in connection with Confucianism in the next chapter; the present concern will be the amount of information that can be derived from them with regard to the Neolithic culture. Generally speaking, the earlier the described events, the more legendary they tend to be, and the degree of reliability increases as the period during which the events had allegedly occurred comes closer to the time when these books were written. When reconstructing the history of this very ancient age, each writer has obviously to use his own judgment to differentiate facts from mere legends.

In a typically oversimplified way, the legends give a few culture heroes the major credit for bringing culture to the Chinese. Fu-hsi, one of these culture heroes, taught the domestication of animals, and thus the people were spared the daily necessity of hunting and fishing; he introduced the institution of marriage in order to remedy the rather awkward situation "when people knew only their mothers, with no knowledge of who their fathers were"; he invented the first musical instrument; and he was credited with the introduction of a calendar that numbered "360 days for each year." Another hero, Yu-ch'ao, persuaded people to come down from their "nests" in the trees or out from their dens in the caves to start building houses on the ground. Culture hero Shen-nung ("Divine Farmer") taught people the art of farming and the craft of trade; he even invented the art of prescribing herb cures, "after testing hundreds of herbs himself." Emperor Huang-ti ("Yellow Emperor") made the greatest contribution of all. He defeated the barbarian Miaos, thus clearing North China for Chinese settlement; introduced governmental institutions; and was even credited with the invention of coined money and the compass. His wife taught silk culture and domestic work. His minister Ts'ang Chieh invented the first written signs, thereupon "all spirits cried in agony, as the innermost secrets of nature were thus revealed."

When we come to the second half of the third millennium, the legend says that there was a golden age, when rulers were chosen from the best of men and ruled through their own examples and virtues. The best known of them were Yao and Shun whose virtues, it was said, were so great that by doing nothing in particular they brought peace and prosperity to all of their subjects. One thing, however, marred the history of the good emperors, namely, an unprecedented flood which occurred during their reigns. According to the legend, the Great Flood lasted for several decades, causing heavy damage to men and animals, for none was able to devise a means to stop it. First the incompetent Kun was appointed to supervise flood control. After nine years of building more dykes, the situation remained serious. Yü, the son of Kun, succeeded as superviser of flood control after his father's death. He dug canals following the natural routes of the Yellow River and planted trees along its banks and those of its tributaries. After thirteen years of diligent work during which he was said not to have visited his home even once, the turbulent current was tamed and was led calmly towards the sea. Yü became a popular hero, and the reigning monarch Shun decided to designate him as his successor.

Many historians wonder whether the good emperors had ever existed, let alone their good deeds. That these emperors sought "the most virtuous men," instead of their sons, to be designated as their successors seems to have been a legend too idealized to be true. If they did exist at all, these so-called emperors were perhaps the tribal chieftains best known among the numerous tribes then in existence in North China and might have governed better than other chieftains. Conceivably the various Chinese tribes had formed a confederation as a defense measure against non-Chinese tribes who lived around them and posed a constant threat. The "good emperors" could have been the heads of the confederation to whom all Chinese tribes owed some kind of allegiance. The designation of virtuous men as successors might have been an election process whereby the heads of the confederation were chosen. The incumbent chief of the confederation nominated "the most virtuous man" (which probably means "the ablest and the wisest") as his successor, and the nomination was subject to approval by all Chinese tribes other than his own. Once approval was secured, the nominee became officially the successor. When Yü was installed as the confederation chief, "ten thousand nations" (which means "numerous tribes"), we are told, came to him to pay their homage and tribute. It seems that once a tribal chief was proclaimed as the common suzerain of all Chinese tribes he was free to use whatever means at his command, including military force, to compel allegiance from the recalcitrant tribes. In any case, he could count on the support of those tribes which had already pledged allegiance to him.

If the above description is close to reality, the question arises as to why the "good emperors" are idealized beyond credibility in some of the earliest written records. To ancient historians, history was not merely an objective record of past events; it was also the means of providing moral lessons. The necessity of serving a moral purpose was such an overwhelming concern to these early historians that it often led them to a distortion of facts. The most unscrupulous among them even forged documents in order to drive home a point which to them was extremely important. In writing political history, most of these traditional historians subscribed to two basic principles, the principle of legitimacy and the principle of using the past to teach the present. These two principles were of course closely related. Legitimacy was not legitimacy in its biological sense; it was a legitimacy of "virtue" (tao-t'ung) which came to mean that only the most virtuous men were entitled to rule. This concept antedated Confucianism, though it was Confucianism which later strengthened it. It is not surprising that the most detailed description of Yao and Shun appears in the book of Mencius (372–289 B.C.), an architect of Confucian philosophy. As the theory of legitimacy was popularized, the tendency was to extend the line of legitimacy to the remotest years. One historian even composed an "imperial chronology" which extended the line beyond 4,000 B.C. Many of these "emperors" were said to have reigned more than one hundred years, which of course was a physical impossibility. Since traditional historians believed that history should serve as a moral guide to teach the present, they tended to glorify the past as the present became more unpleasant. Those who wrote about the "good emperors" lived between the eighth and the third century B.C., an age of chaos and war, and they were longing for a reappearance of the golden age which had allegedly existed in the past. To men like Mencius, history was always more important as a book of ethics than as history, and they read into it their own beliefs.

Unreliable as these early writings are as historical materials, it is totally unwarranted to dismiss everything in them as fictional or legendary. Each individual event has to be evaluated and judged according to its own merit. Skepticism, when carried to great extremes, could be as harmful as credulity. The Great Flood might serve as an example. While we cannot take as historical fact every detail about the Great Flood, it is nevertheless true that the flood could have occurred, because of the condition of the Yellow River and its tributaries, as we have described these in the Introduction, and because of the frequency of floods in North China during the historical period. It might have been a series of floods which occurred intermittently for a number of years. The fact that there was a legendary flood in West Asia does not necessarily mean that the Chinese had borrowed such a legend.

The accession of Yü as the common suzerain of all Chinese tribes was traditionally placed at 2205 B.C. Towards the end of Yü's reign, his tribe had become so strong and prosperous that the other tribes proclaimed his son Ch'i as his successor. The fact that Ch'i was an able and wise man might also have had something to do with this decision. A precedent was established and from then on the position of the common suzerain became hereditary. The dynasty which Yü established was called Hsia, the first dynasty in Chinese history. Though nominally suzerain, the Hsia was but one of the hundreds of tribes in the North China Plain. Inter-tribal warfare was frequent. Outside of forming a common front against the non-Chinese tribes ("barbarians") whenever it was necessary, they were free to conquer and annex one another. Even the Hsia tribe itself was eager to join the game. Originally located in western Honan, it expanded eastward until it covered parts of the modern Shantung and Hopeh provinces. As time went on, however, the Hsia rulers gradually lost the vitality which had characterized earlier leaders. Secluded in their palaces and sunk in sensual pleasures, they became puppets of their own ministers. In the twenty-second century B.C. one of the ministers actually ousted the king and usurped the throne. A dynastic revival ensued shortly afterwards, but it proved to be only temporary. In the eighteenth century B.C. one of the eastern tribes, called Shang, eventually replaced the Hsia as the common suzerain of all Chinese tribes.

SHANG

Shang originally was the name of a nomadic tribe, moving from place to place until it finally settled in Shangch'iu of modern Honan province. Through contacts with the more advanced Chinese tribes, it gradually adopted agriculture and acquired the sophisticated culture of a sedentary society. Meanwhile, it lost none of the vigor and vitality of a nomadic horde. In the eighteenth century B.C. a great leader emerged who, through diplomacy and warfare, annexed most of his neighboring states. This leader, T'ang, was not only noted for his military exploits, but even more so for his enlightened domestic policy. He ran an efficient government, worked hard for the welfare of his people, and was held in great esteem by them. In his struggle for supremacy, he promoted agricultural production to sustain his military campaigns, made alliances with those tribes that submitted to his will, and conquered those that resisted. As a showdown drew near with the Hsia, he successfully convinced most Chinese tribes as well as his own people how oppressive and corrupt the Hsia regime had become and why he had no choice except revolt. As a result, an increasing number of Chinese tribes switched their loyalty to him. Instead of rising up to meet the challenge, the last Hsia ruler, Chieh, became depraved and cruel. He reportedly killed his best ministers simply because they had offended him and he wasted manpower needlessly by building elaborate palaces for his concubines. As the military campaign progressed, more and more tribes joined T'ang's revolt. In the final battle Chieh was captured. After he had been exiled, the new dynasty, Shang, was formally established. The establishment of the dynasty was traditionally placed at 1766 B.C.

As the Shangs are closer to us than the Hsias in terms of time, we know a great deal more about them. Recent archaeological findings have further enriched our knowledge. For one thing, we know that they moved their capital often. This could have meant that they were not yet completely out of the pastoral stage or that they had repeatedly exhausted land fertility by constant cultivation. Both theories have perhaps an element of truth. Anyhow, agriculture was their main occupation. Crops included millet, wheat, and rice; millet seems to have been the main staple crop and was also used to make wine. Sericulture had been discovered before, and the silk produced was used to make clothes, kerchiefs, curtains, etc. For meat there were cattle, sheep, chicken, and hogs. Dogs had been domesticated. Other animals like oxen, horses, and elephants were used

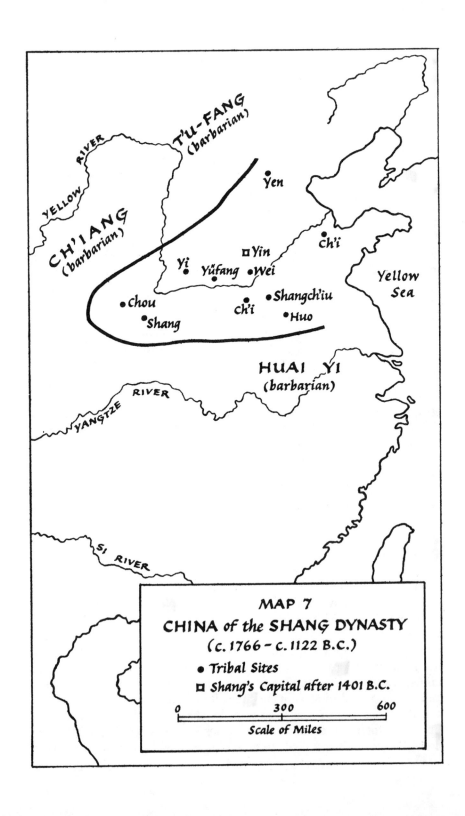

CH'IANG
(barbarian)

T'U-FANG
(barbarian)

YELLOW RIVER

Yen

Yin

Ch'i

Yi

Yüfang

Wei

Yellow
Sea

Chou

Shang

Ch'i

Shangch'iu

Huo

HUAI YI
(barbarian)

YANGTZE RIVER

SI RIVER

MAP 7
CHINA of the SHANG DYNASTY
(c. 1766 – c. 1122 B.C.)

• Tribal Sites
□ Shang's Capital after 1401 B.C.

0   300   600

Scale of Miles

for transportation; we know that the nobility and the wealthy had carriages drawn by animals. On the battlefield, while common soldiers fought on foot, the nobles attacked each other in horse chariots. Elephants were sometimes used for charging the enemy's defense lines. As forests could still be found in most parts of North China, game was abundant, and hunting was the most popular sport among the nobles. Even around the capital city Yin (after 1401 B.C.) there were large undeveloped areas to which agriculture had not been extended. We know that in one hunting trip a Shang ruler bagged 348 deer, and in another, 113 boars.

As for shelter, a peasant's house was no more than a thatched hut; the whole family lived in one large, rectangular room, divided by wooden boards or thatched curtains to make kitchen and living quarters. The houses of the wealthy were more elaborate. Stone and bronze foundations have been found on the Yin ruins; columns must have been extensively used for supporting the main beams. Since no tiles or bricks have been found on these sites, it is presumed that even among the wealthy, thatched roofing was common. Walls were generally made of hardened earth; doors usually faced south to admit more sunlight.

During the Shang dynasty two of the most epochal events occurred, namely, the discovery of bronze metallurgy and the development of a written language. Though we cannot place the date when bronze metallurgy was discovered in China, it must have undergone a long process of development before it reached the perfection evidenced by the bronzes unearthed in the Yin ruins. Experts have opined that the technique of casting bronze in the Shang dynasty was even superior to the famed craftsmanship of the European Renaissance. The unearthed bronzes were of many kinds, mostly household utensils and religious implements. There were wine pots, cups, plates and dishes, drinking vessels, and food containers of various shapes and designs. There were also religious vessels covered with elaborate designs in incised lines or in high relief. One bronze piece, perhaps serving the same purpose as our lazy Susan, had a beautifully designed central column around which four sculptured dragons rotated. Bronze was also cast into military weapons. The points of spears, javelins, and arrows, together with swords and knives, were made of bronze, as were warriors' helmets. However, bronze did not replace stone completely, as some weapons were still made of stone or animal bones.

Though overshadowed by bronzes, other handicraft products of the Shangs were scarcely less impressive. Some of the glazed potteries were made of clay of the finest quality, with paintings or relief drawings of animals and geometrical patterns. Jade was carved into many shapes representing men, wild animals, birds, fishes, and frogs; stone was sculptured into statues of men, tigers, rabbits, and birds. There was also a variety of ornaments made of jade and precious stones used for women's hairdressing. Since none of these materials were produced in the areas in which they were found, trade must have been very extensive. Cowrie shells were used as a medium of exchange; coined money was not yet invented.

The Shangs were said to be a religious people. They believed in spirits who, they thought, existed everywhere: in the forests, mountains, rivers, fields, and even in one's own house. However, most of the spirits were those of harmless, deceased ancestors. After a man died, his spirit presumably left the body and was wafted into the air, but it would extend protection to the family if properly humored and worshipped. By means of sacrifices and by magic incantations the spirits could be summoned before a priest and could be persuaded to reveal what the future held for the family. The Shangs would not do anything important without consulting the spirits, whether it be making a trip or fighting a war. For the kings who had to make important decisions affecting the entire nation, religious rituals became exceedingly elaborate affairs. Sheep or cattle used for each sacrifice sometimes numbered three or four hundred. The method of offering them, whether it was burning in open flames, drowning in rivers, or burying underneath the ground, varied according to occasions; even the color and sex of the animals were carefully prescribed. Sometimes prisoners-of-war were slaughtered as sacrifices. It was believed that the spirits, carefully attended to, would make their wishes known through the oracle bones. To conjure oracles, a priest drilled a turtle shell or a piece of animal bone with a hand piercer on one side and then placed the hollowed points on top of a flame. The other side of the shell or bone began to crack, and the cracks formed various patterns. The priest would then interpret the meaning of the patterns according to a magic formula; his interpretations were the alleged oracles. Thousands of these oracle bones have been unearthed from the Yin ruins.

When these oracle bones were unearthed, the archaeologists were amazed that there were written inscriptions on them. The inscriptions indicated the questions asked by the priest, the answers, and sometimes even the eventual outcome. Before 1899 when the first oracle bones were discovered, there had been two popular theories with regard to the origin of the Chinese written language. One theory traced the language's beginning to the knot-writing of the remote period; unfortunately, we know little about this type of writing. According to the other theory, the early beginning of the language was the Eight Diagrams, supposedly invented by the culture hero Fu-hsi. The Eight Diagrams will be discussed in connection with Chinese philosophy in a later chapter; suffice it to say that the Diagrams, having only simple, horizontal lines, were too simplified a form to generate a complicated language like Chinese. Since the discovery of the Shell-Bone script (*chia-ku wen*), as the inscriptions on the oracle bones are called, we have been greatly enlightened. More than two thousand written characters of this script have been deciphered, and most of them have been identified with their modern counterparts in the Chinese written system. It is beyond any doubt that the Shell-Bone script was the forerunner of modern Chinese. In fact, the modern script can be traced all the way back to this ancient script through several stages of development. The large number of written characters in the Shell-Bone script implied an advanced and sophisticated society which used it; the number of Chinese characters commonly used in China today does not exceed five thousand. The period during which this ancient script flourished is placed between 1700 and 1100 B.C.; since it had already reached an advanced stage by then, it is reasonable to assume that the rudiments of a written language first appeared in China around 2000 B.C., if not earlier. Perhaps we are not in great error when we say that China entered the historical period four thousand years ago.

The Chinese language, the oldest surviving language in the world, is unique in the sense that it is non-phonetic. Interestingly, it is still used by the largest number of people in the world. It began with pictographs and ideographs, and after 4,000 years they still constitute a sizable portion of modern characters, even though they have been stylized, simplified, or both. The words "sun" and "moon" were written ⊙ and 𝔇 respectively in the Shell-Bone script; today they are written 日 and 月 . The words for "one" and "two" have been written — and 二 throughout Chinese history because stylization and simplification are not necessary in these two cases. On the other hand, more complicated characters have passed through a long process of stylization and simplification. Here the words "turtle" and "horse" are used as examples.

Shell-Bone Script	Great Script	Small Script	Scribe Script	Modern Script
Shang Dynasty	Chou Dynasty	Ch'in and Former Han	Later Han	

One might notice that Small-Script characters are sometimes (such as in the case of "turtle") more complicated than the Great-Script characters that antedated them. The reason is that the Ch'in state which used the Small Script dictated its adoption by all Chinese after Ch'in had unified China in 221 B.C. The decision, politically motivated, might have deterred the simplification process for the time being. Both characters, even in their present forms, do not seem simplified enough to a Westerner. The present Communist regime apparently shares this sentiment, and since its establishment in 1949 has further simplified the more complicated characters. Today in all works published in Communist China, these two characters, "turtle" and "horse," are written respectively as follows:

龟　　　马

Most Chinese characters are not simple pictographs (such as in the case of "sun" and "moon") and ideographs (such as in the case of "one" and "two"); they are compound characters. A large number of compound characters are combinations of significs and phonetics. Both significs and phonetics are simple pictographs or ideographs and are characters themselves. However, when they become a part of compound characters, they lose their original meanings, except in an incidental sense. Take the word "village" which is written 村 . It is a compound character, composed of the signific 木 and the phonetic 寸 . The character 木 was originally written 木 which meant "tree" as it depicted a tree with branches on the top and roots at bottom. The character 寸 means a Chinese inch which obviously has nothing to do with a village. It is a phonetic and indicates that the compound character "village" should be pronounced the same way as the phonetic 寸 (*ts'un*). Why should the character "village" have the signific "tree"? Presumably, because there are trees around a typical village. There are other compound characters which cannot be so easily explained. Take the character 李 as an example. Besides being a surname, it means a plum tree and is pronounced *li*. It is a compound character, composed of the characters 木 and 子 . The character 子 ("son") is pronounced *tzu* and is therefore not a phonetic in this particular case. Most Chinese characters are of this type; they defy explanation or even rationalization because they have advanced too far from their beginnings. There could have been a logic in the composition of each of them, but that logic has been by and large lost.

When it is pointed out that each character can serve the purpose of an English letter or syllable besides being an independent word, it is easy to see what a versatile language Chinese is. On the other hand, since the language is not phonetic and since each character has to be memorized independently with regard to its pronunciation as well as its variety of meanings, Chinese is ackowledgedly one of the most difficult languages in the world. While a great deal could be said about the disadvantages of a non-phonetic language, the fact that in the Chinese language the written form (as contrary to pronunciation) counted most enabled it to spread to faraway places where it was adopted even though the pronunciation of the same item as indicated by a Chinese character was entirely different.

In other words, after foreigners had adopted the written characters, they pronounced the characters not as the Chinese pronounced them but as they had been pronouncing those words which they then began to write in Chinese. Today, a Japanese, a Korean, and a Chinese might not be able to communicate with each other orally, but they could do so with a piece of paper and a pen, because a written Chinese character conveys the same (or approximately the same) meanings to all of them. The same is true of a southern and a northern Chinese who write the same characters but pronounce them differently. Had the phonetic part of the language not been detached from its written part to a considerable extent, many written languages would have been developed in China in view of the difficulties in communication and transportation of the ancient years. The sharing of a common written language meant a common heritage and a common identity for all Chinese despite great distances between them. When it is pointed out that the word *Chinese* is more a cultural than a racial term, we can easily see what an important role the language has played in the development of China as a nation.

CHOU

In the twelfth century B.C. a western tribe called Chou replaced Shang as the common sovereign of all Chinese tribes in North China. The word "sovereign" is used deliberately, because during the early stage of the Chou dynasty there was a great deal of power concentrated in the hands of the central government. The ancestry of Chou's royal house was cloaked in mystery, and according to the legend, its founder, Hou-chi, was born of virgin birth after his mother had inadvertently stepped on a huge footprint in the field and thus become pregnant. During the Shang dynasty the Chou tribe pledged allegiance to the Shangs. Half nomadic and half agricultural, the tribe had moved from place to place until it settled down in the Wei River valley in modern Shensi. The Chou capital, Hao, was located near modern Sian. The fertility of the Wei valley strengthened the tribe economically; meanwhile, living among the "barbarians," the Chou tribe was able to maintain its martial spirit and fighting ability. During the twelfth century B.C. the royal house produced in succession several able leaders, notably King Wen (Wen Wang) and his two sons, King Wu (Wu Wang) and Duke Chou (Chou Kung). Before King Wen died in 1120 B.C. it was reported that more than two-thirds of the Chinese tribes had switched their loyalty from Shang to Chou. Two years later his son and successor, King Wu, formally declared war on Shang and led those tribes that had pledged allegiance to him for a final campaign against its king, Cheo. The declaration of war accused Cheo, among other things, of having been under the undue influence of wine

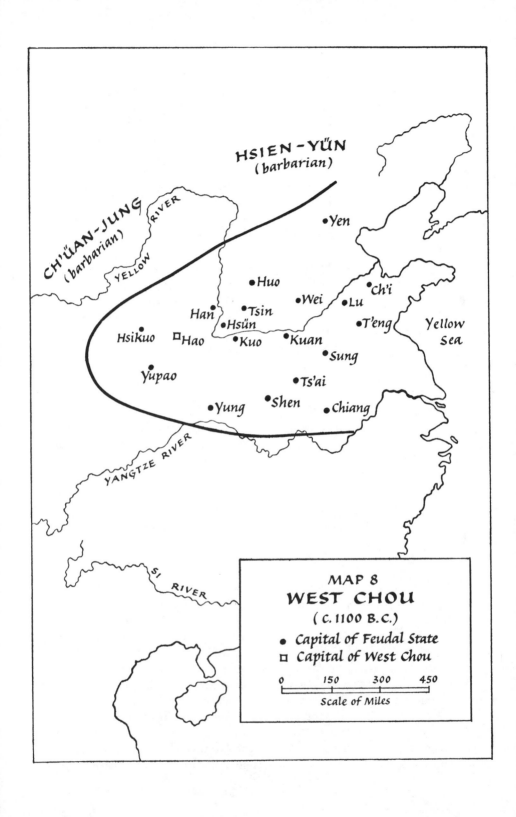

HSIEN-YÜN
(barbarian)

CH'ÜAN-JUNG
(barbarian)

YELLOW RIVER

•Yen

•Huo

•Wei   •Ch'i

Han•   •Lu
•Tsin
Hsĭkuo• •Hsŭn •T'eng   Yellow
    □Hao •Kuo •Kuan   Sea
•Sung
Yupao•

•Ts'ai
•Yung •Shen •Chiang

YANGTZE RIVER

SI RIVER

MAP 8
WEST CHOU
(C. 1100 B.C.)
• Capital of Feudal State
□ Capital of West Chou

0   150   300   450
Scale of Miles

and women in his political decisions, of having failed to perform religious services in honor of his ancestors, and of being cruel to his subjects. The debauched monarch committed suicide ("burned himself to death") after his army had been defeated. The Chou dynasty formally came into being in 1122 B.C.

The new dynasty was destined to be the longest in Chinese history, from the twelfth to the third century B.C. However, after the eighth century the Chou sovereignty was largely nominal; local states were essentially independent countries. Many historians call the period 722–481 B.C. the Spring and Autumn period, a period covered by the famous history, *Spring and Autumn Annals*. From 403 to 221 B.C. was the period of Warring States which ended in the latter year with the grand unification of China by the Ch'in state. Generally speaking, the first four centuries of the Chou dynasty was an era of peace and prosperity. The last five centuries witnessed a decline of central authority, the rise of local states, and the prevalence of anarchy and interstate warfare.

At the time when the dynasty was established, it was full of vigor and vitality. At the helm of the government were two of the greatest statesmen of ancient China, King Wu and Duke Chou. After the former's death in 1115 B.C. the Duke served as regent to King Ch'eng, his nephew, who was then a minor. Traditional historians credited the Duke with the suppression of a rebellion, the establishment of a central bureaucracy, and

BRONZE TIGERS These two tigers, weighing 47 pounds each, were cast during the Chou dynasty (c.1122–249 B.C.). Each has an open hollow chamber in the center, and its surface is decorated with low relief.

the introduction of a variety of institutions, including a nation-wide school system. Modern historians, however, tend to be more skeptical, since the book that records most of his achievements, namely *Chou Institutions* (*Chou kuan*), is a work of dubious origin. Nevertheless there is little doubt that Duke Chou, being an able organizer, contributed greatly to the stability of the early Chou regime.

Among the Chou institutions none was perhaps more important than *feng-chien* or feudalism. At the time when it was instituted, it was a centralizing rather than a decentralizing process. The Shang dynasty, Chou's predecessor, left the conquered tribes to manage their own affairs so long as they recognized the Shang suzerainty. The Chou, on the other hand, annexed or otherwise relocated many tribes and imposed a feudal order on all of them. A new theory was advanced that "all land belongs to the king and all men are the king's subjects," and the king could grant land to whomever he wished. Except areas around the capital which were under the king's direct management, all territories in China were distributed among the newly created lords. These feudal lords were either the descendants of the former royal houses (including Shang), the close relatives of the king, or the generals and statesmen who had helped the king in winning the war. Among the most notable of the feudal states thus created were Lu, Ch'i, and Tsin, which received the largest and the best arable land in North China. Five feudal ranks were instituted corresponding roughly to the English duke, marquis, earl, viscount, and baron. To avoid uncertainty and rivalry after the death of a lord, a new rule of succession was devised, covering the succession of all nobilities, including that of the king. The rule stated that legal wives were superior to concubines and that the elder sons were superior to the younger. After the king died, for instance, the eldest son of his legal wife (namely, the queen) would inherit the throne. This son might be younger than the oldest son of a concubine, but that did not make any difference in succession, because legitimacy had priority over seniority. This was contrary to the Shang practice wherein the dead king was usually succeeded by his next younger brother. With the Chou feudalism the other sons of the dead king were awarded the rank of duke. A duke's eldest son born to his legal wife would eventually succeed him as duke, while the rest of his male children would become marquises, and so on. As a baronate was the lowest feudal order, all the baron's sons, with the exception of one, had to step down as commoners. By this device the majority of noble descent would wind up as commoners eventually, and in numbers the nobility would not be overburdened. It was hoped that through the rigid enforcement of the succession rules internecine strife could be avoided.

Accompanying feudal ranks were feudal fiefs and feudal obligations. Feudal fiefs were land granted by the lord to his vassals in return for feudal obligations which consisted of tributes and services performed by the vassals for the lord. Fiefs varied in size. While a feudal state might be larger than New York state, some of the small fiefs were smaller than a large ranch in Texas. Relations between the lord and his vassals were carefully prescribed. Whenever he wished to, the king could inspect the administrative details of his vassalages; the vassals in return had to make periodic trips to the capital to pay tribute and to report personally to the king on the state of affairs within their domains. Failure to do so on the part of the vassals entitled the king to take retaliatory measures such as the suspension or deprivation of ranks and fiefs, and in more serious cases, sending troops against them. In many larger states key ministers were even appointed by the king. In time of war, the vassals were required to contribute troops to the king's defense, regardless of who the king's enemies were, barbarians or insubordinate vassals. They were obligated to defend the king, whenever and by whomever the king was attacked.

This, of course, represents an idealized stage of feudalism when practice more or less followed theory during the early period of the Chou dynasty. As time went on, some vassal states had become too strong to allow this theory to function effectively. After the eighth century B.C. the king's sovereignty became largely nominal, and each state pursued whatever courses it devised for itself.

Opposite the nobility and at the lower level of the social structure stood the commoners, such as the merchants, the artisans, and the peasants. The nobility constituted the governing class, the commoners the governed. Since the Chou society was agricultural, the overwhelming majority of the commoners were peasants. Landownership was vested in the nobility, however; the right the peasants had was that of utilization for which they paid the lord produce as rent plus labor. In a more or less typical situation a tract of land was divided into nine sections of about fifteen acres each. Each family tilled one of the eight surrounding sections, while all eight families tilled the central section in common. The harvest of the central section went to the lord as rent; the crops raised in each surrounding section belonged to the family which tilled it. Under feudal law the eight families should plow, seed, water, weed, and harvest the lord's common first before they could do the same with their own sections. Whenever this arrangement was found inconvenient, nine families, instead of eight, would till the nine sections as described above, and each family was responsible for its own assigned section. In this case each family gave one-tenth of its harvested crops to the lord as rent. Feudal obligations, however, did not end here. A portion of whatever the peasants produced, be it silk or wine, was customarily presented to the lord as gifts. Corvée could be imposed whenever necessity arose, such as repairing roads, building bridges, dredging rivers, or constructing dams. These obligations varied from place to place and from time to time, very much depending upon the kind of lord the peasants happened to have.

A poem in the *Book of Odes* describes vividly the life of a peasant who lived in Shensi in the early Chou period when feudalism was in its prime. According to this poem, the peasant started to repair his farm implements in the first month of the year for the seeding season ahead. In the second month he plowed the land; his wife prepared the food and carried the food basket to him at meal time. Meanwhile, his daughter went to the mulberry groves to pluck leaves for the hungry silkworms at home. Sometimes the lord's steward strolled by smiling and inquired how the work was going. In the eighth month harvesting began. His daughter was busy at home weaving silk cloth and dying it black, yellow, or flashing red to make clothes for the lord's children. In the tenth month when harvesting had been completed, the peasant began to brew wine so that he could present it to the lord as a birthday present sometime in the next spring. Then he went to work in the lord's house cutting reeds in the daytime and making ropes in the evening. Occasionally, there was a feast when all gathered in the lord's house, ate roasted lamb, and drank to the lord's health, shouting happily, "Long live the lord!" In the eleventh month the peasant hunted for foxes whose skins would be used to make the lord's winter coat. In the twelfth month, military training was conducted under the lord's supervision. The pigs which had been fattened were then presented to the lord. It was also the time to store ice underneath the ground to be used by the lord in the next summer or spring. All in all, the peasants seem to have existed only for the comfort of the lord. However, this poem also paints a picture of peace and prosperity, an orderly country life, and a warm relationship between the lord and his peasants. Though the peasant's life under feudalism was anything but enviable, the fact is that it was never bettered afterwards. After the eighth century B.C. when the country drifted into chaos and war, the peasants simply wished that they could have lived some centuries earlier.

Below the peasants and at the bottom of the social scale were the slaves. Slavery existed as early as men could recall, or at least as early as the Shang dynasty. After each battle the Shangs condemned most of their prisoners to slavery, no matter whether the prisoners were Chinese or barbarians. Slaves were employed in a variety of ways, as laborers in the farm, as household servants, or sometimes as expendable fodder on the battlefield. With the establishment of an orderly society in the twelfth century B.C. when warfare had become less frequent, the supply of slaves fell off. Fortunately for the slave owners, there were other sources. One source was provided by former freemen who, unable to pay their debts, were forced to sell their children or even themselves as slaves. There were also condemned criminals enslaved by the government. After the eighth century B.C. when wars became a normal state of affairs, prisoners-of war again formed a major source of supply, and slave-hunting was sometimes a major motive in waging warfare. After each war, all captives, including the nobles and high-ranking officials, were enslaved. If the warring parties so desired, captives could be exchanged and so saved from enslavement. On other occasions the state which held them asked for ransoms, the amount varying according to the worth of individual captives. In one case, the ransom was "five sheets of sheep skin." In other cases, ransom prices could be very high. In 611 B.C., for instance, the state of Sung was willing to pay a ransom of "one hundred chariots and four hundred horses" to the state of Ch'u to free a high-ranking official. If a person became a slave, his life was miserable indeed. His master not only monopolized his services but controlled his body as well. He could be bought and sold and was sometimes used as collateral for securing loans. In one instance, a lord commanded his slave to taste poisoned food even after it had been tested by a dog which died immediately. Cruelty like this might be an exception rather than a rule; it nevertheless shows the absolute control the master had over his slaves.

THE TURBULENT AGE OF WAR

King Yu, the ruler of Chou between 781 and 771 B.C., was not unlike the last monarchs of Hsia and Shang. He raised taxes, squandered them for his personal comfort, and was unconcerned with the welfare of his subjects. The immediate cause of his downfall, however, was his neurotic infatuation with a favorite concubine named Pao-ssu, according to traditional historians. When Pao-ssu gave birth to a son, he deposed his crown prince and named the infant as his heir apparent. The crown prince's mother, the queen, was the daughter of a powerful lord who, learning what had happened to his grandson, made a secret alliance with the barbarian tribe Ch'üan-jung for possible military action against the king in order to reinstate his grandson as the crown prince. Meanwhile, King Yu, not knowing of the conspiracy against him, sank even deeper in his infatuation with his favorite concubine. Despite her great beauty, Pao-ssu rarely smiled and the king tried in vain to induce her to smile often. Finally, he ordered the lighting of beacon fires which under normal circumstances signified a barbarian invasion and the urgent request for vassals' help to defend the king. The vassals arrived at the head of their armies, but there was no enemy. Amused by their bewilderment and awkwardness, Pao-ssu smiled. Having found a sure way to make her smile, the king lit the beacon fires repeatedly and often.

We do not know how much truth the above story contains, but it is recorded as history in one of the earliest writings. In 771 B.C. Ch'üan-jung, in alliance with the queen's father, invaded and quickly surrounded Chou's capital, Hao. The king ordered the lighting of beacon fires, but none of his vassals arrived as they obviously thought that the king was playing another practical joke upon them. The barbarians captured the capital and sacked it thoroughly, besides killing the captured king. Meanwhile, with the help of his maternal grandfather and the barbarians, the deposed crown prince ascended the throne as King P'ing. As the old capital was too close to the barbarians to be safe, the new monarch moved his capital eastward to Loyang. From then on the dynasty was never the same. Since Loyang was east of Hao, the Chou dynasty after 771 B.C. was often referred to as East Chou. The period of the East Chou (771–249 B.C.) overlaps with the Spring and Autumn period (722–481 B.C.) and the period of Warring States (403–221 B.C.). The Chou dynasty before 771 B.C. is sometimes called West Chou.

The five centuries after 771 B.C. were years of turmoil, war, and also social and economic changes. The central authority weakened, then became nominal, and finally ceased to exist. The weakening of central authority was accompanied by increasing frequency of foreign and domestic wars. The large states invaded and conquered the small states; the king had to confirm whatever had been accomplished, by naked aggression or otherwise. One king, trying to punish one of his subordinate vassals and thus to reassert his authority, found his army defeated and himself wounded on the shoulder (707 B.C.). As all states were free to conquer and annex one another, their total number decreased steadily. There were about two hundred states in the eighth century B.C.; towards the end of the fifth century B.C. and at the beginning of the Warring States period only seven major states remained.

During the Spring and Autumn period, efforts were made to bring some order out of chaos. Since the king was powerless and thus helpless, the leadership had to come from rulers of individual states. Among them Duke Huan of Ch'i (Ch'i Huan-kung, 686–643 B.C.) and Duke Wen of Tsin (Tsin Wen-kung, d. 629 B.C.) were the most prominent. Both pledged "respect for the central authority and repulsion of all barbarians" and claimed that their leadership would lead to the implementation of both principles. The real purpose, however, was to reach a *modus vivendi* among the major powers in North China and to prevent the barbarians and the less Sinicized powers such as Ch'u from threatening their dominant positions. From time to time force was used to compel small states to acknowledge such leadership. Duke Huan was said to have gone to war twenty-eight times during his reign of forty-three years; some of the wars were waged against the barbarians who had invaded the Chinese states, but the purpose of most of them was to make the other Chinese states his allies. Outside of North China he was greatly concerned with the rising power of Ch'u and in 656 B.C. he sent an army to invade that southern state on the ground that the latter had failed to pay tribute to the king of Chou, the nominal sovereign. This action earned him the reputation of protector of Chinese states against barbarians.

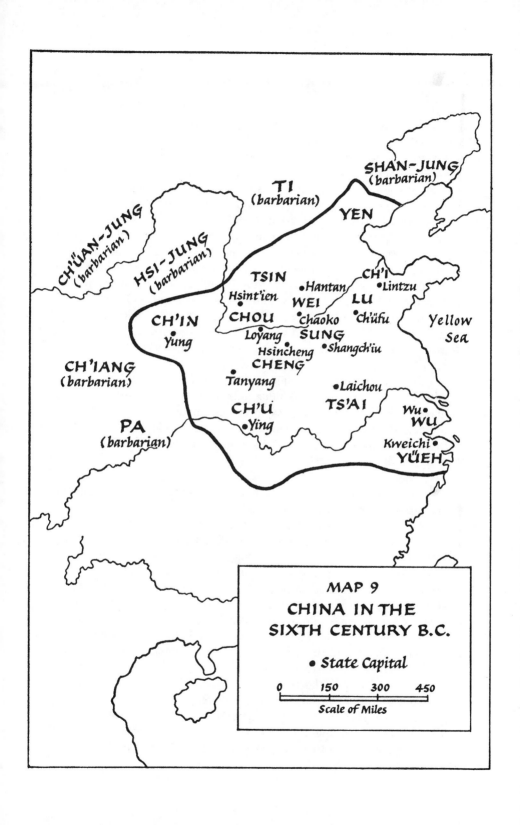

CH'ÜAN-JUNG
(barbarian)

CH'IANG
(barbarian)

PA
(barbarian)

HSI-JUNG
(barbarian)

TI
(barbarian)

SHAN-JUNG
(barbarian)

YEN

TSIN
Hsint'ien

CH'IN
Yung

CHOU
Loyang

Hsincheng
CHENG

Tanyang

Hantan

WEI
Chaoko

SUNG
Shangch'iu

CH'I
Lintzu

LU
Ch'üfu

Yellow
Sea

CH'U
Ying

Laichou

TS'AI

Wu
WU

Kweichi
YÜEH

MAP 9
CHINA IN THE
SIXTH CENTURY B.C.

• State Capital

0   150   300   450
Scale of Miles

To strengthen his leadership among the Chinese states, time and again (twenty-six times altogether) Duke Huan of Ch'i invited them to attend interstate conferences. Some of these conferences were called to deal with a particular emergency such as a barbarian invasion; others were convened to find some general principles to govern the relations among the Chinese states. In one of these conferences four major principles were adopted. First, the king's authority should be respected, though everybody knew that this was only a nominal gesture. Second, whenever there was a barbarian invasion against any state, all other states should hold consultations among themselves and should cooperate to repel the invader. This principle sounds like our modern concept of collective security. Third, if an internal revolt resulted in the assassination of the reigning prince and the establishment of a new regime, the regime would not be recognized, and all the states would send a joint force against the usurper until a legitimate ruler was installed. To prevent such an eventuality, each state promised, among other things, that it would not change its crown prince "casually" and would not "let women interfere with state affairs." Obviously, the conferees believed that these were the two major causes of internal revolt. Lastly, all states pledged non-aggression among themselves. In case of dispute among them, the leader state (Ch'i) would be called to arbitrate and to render judgment. Though these principles were often violated, the fact that efforts were made to bring a semblance of order among the northern states was a great achievement in itself. Without such efforts there would have been complete chaos. One hundred years after Duke Huan's death Confucius spoke highly of his achievement.

After Duke Huan's death in 643 B.C. Ch'i began to decline and the leadership of the northern states was later assumed by Duke Wen of Tsin. By then the potential enemies of the northern states were not the barbarians further north but the semi-Sinicized state Ch'u. In a ferocious battle fought in 632 B.C. (Battle of Ch'engpu) the advance of Ch'u was checked, and Duke Wen was proclaimed as the new leader of the northern states. The Duke died in 629 B.C., but Tsin, under a succession of capable leaders, continued to be the dominant power in North China. In 598 B.C. Ch'u defeated Tsin in the Battle of Pi (Honan), but it was unable to exploit its victory as it had overextended itself from its base in the Yangtze Valley. When Ch'i proceeded to challenge Tsin's leadership after the battle, Tsin quickly defeated it, and Ch'i was forced to acknowledge Tsin's leadership. The last of the three great battles between Tsin and Ch'u was fought in 567 B.C. (Battle of Yenling, modern Honan) when Tsin avenged its former defeat and was victorious. If the three battles indicated anything, they meant that neither side was able to challenge successfully the other's leadership in its own sphere of influence.

Tsin was the leader in North China, and Ch'u continued to be the dominant power in the south.

The stalemate produced one of the most interesting interstate conferences in ancient China. The small states had been victimized by the repeated warfare among the major powers, a warfare over which they had no control, and they were hoping for some kind of arrangement whereby the major powers would renounce war as an instrument of foreign policy. Sung, a small state between Tsin and Ch'u which had suffered greatly in the wars between the two giants, took the initiative in arranging a non-aggression conference. At its invitation the delegates of eleven states, including Tsin and Ch'u, gathered at its capital Shangch'iu in the summer of 546 B.C. There were numerous diplomatic maneuvers behind the scene, not unlike those which occur so often in our modern international conferences. A multilateral agreement was finally reached, and each signatory pledged non-aggression against its neighbor. The agreement paved the way for a peace of more than forty years, a remarkable achievement in view of the existing chaotic situation. When the peace was finally breached, it was breached by the southern state of Wu which had not been a signatory of the agreement in the first place.

So far we have been concerned mostly with North China, as this was the area where Chinese civilization was born and where the most important events took place. The rise of Ch'u indicated the increasing importance not only of an individual state but of the entire south as well. Ch'u's challenge of the dominant position of the northern states was more than political; it was also cultural and economic. It meant that the south which was customarily referred to as barbarian territories had become more and more Sinicized and that the southerners had been gradually absorbed by the Chinese culture as originated in the north. The southerners not only learned the northerners' written language but also adopted their institutions on a large scale. Though politically separated from the northern states, the south had become a part of the Chinese cultural system. Economically, it was intensely developed and was challenging North China in population and wealth. By the fourth century B.C. it had become so far advanced that it was able to produce such men as Ch'ü Yüan and Sung Yü whose poetry could be compared favorably with the very best written by the northerners.

The middle Yangtze, the home of Ch'u, was traditionally referred to as a barbarian territory. Early during the Chou dynasty when the king proposed to confer a feudal title on a Ch'u prince, the latter declined the honor on the ground that he was a barbarian and had no use for Chinese titles. In 706 B.C. the reigning Ch'u prince requested a feudal title, but this time Chou refused, because by then Ch'u had repeatedly invaded Chinese states in the north. Rebuffed, the prince of Ch'u proclaimed himself king two years later. Ch'u's power continued to grow throughout the seventh century B.C.; it conquered and annexed many Chou states and expanded northward to modern Honan province. Meanwhile, it held sway from the middle to the lower Yangtze valley. Time and again its troops penetrated deep into the North China Plain and at one time (598 B.C.) defeated Tsin in one of the most bloody battles in ancient history. It remained the strongest power in South China throughout the sixth century B.C. At the beginning of the fifth century B.C. Ch'u began to decline, as it had been weakened by repeated warfare with the northern states. Moreover, its rulers had slowly lost their martial vitality; and, exposed to the northern influence, they had succumbed to an easy, luxurious life as common among the northern rulers.

With the decline of Ch'u, others states emerged as contending powers in the Yangtze region. Among them Wu and Yüeh were the most prominent. Both states were located in the lower Yangtze; Wu in modern Kiangsu and Yüeh in Chekiang province. The lower Yangtze, being further away from the North China plain than the middle Yangtze, was exposed to Chinese culture at an even later date than Ch'u. While North China had advanced to a high stage of civilization early in the Chou dynasty, the people of the lower Yangtze were said to have such "barbarian" customs as "tattooing their bodies, cutting their hair short, and clearing the jungle to build cities." Progress, though slow, was nevertheless steady. Towards the end of the sixth century B.C. when Wu and Yüeh emerged as powerful states, the people of lower Yangtze had been greatly Sinicized, though the more advanced northerners still referred to them as barbarians. The emergence of the two southern states was followed by an interstate struggle which began in 506 B.C. and did not end until 473 B.C. At one time Wu not only defeated Yüeh; it almost wiped out Ch'u. Wu's supremacy, however, turned out to be short-lived. Flushed with victory, it sent its troops northward to attack Ch'i and Lu. This gave Yüeh a golden opportunity. In 473 B.C. it attacked Wu's home base and succeeded in conquering the entire state. From then on Yüeh dominated the lower Yangtze for seventy-three years. In 346 B.C. a revitalized Ch'u won a decisive victory against Yüeh. Soon Yüeh disintegrated into a number of small states and was no longer an important factor in interstate politics.

THE RISE OF CH'IN

In 403 B.C. Tsin disintegrated into three separate states, Han, Wei, and Chao. The disintegration marked the beginning of the Warring States period. After three centuries of conquests and annexations now only seven major states remained. These were Ch'in, Ch'i, Ch'u, and Yen, plus the three states that were the former Tsin. During this period military force

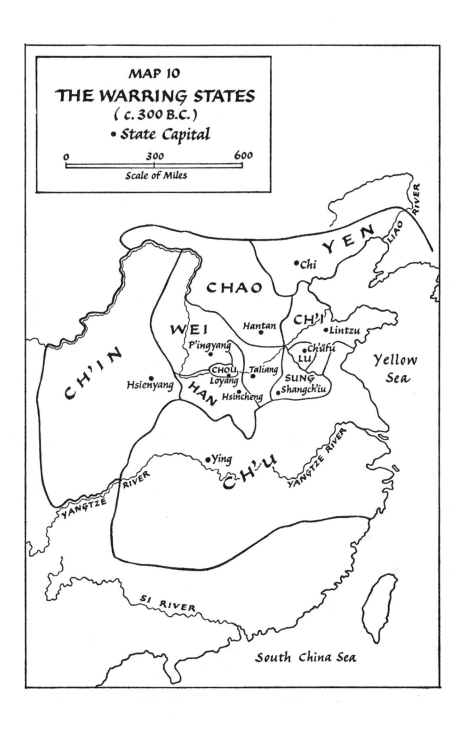

MAP 10
THE WARRING STATES
(c. 300 B.C.)
• State Capital

0   300   600
Scale of Miles

YEN

•Chi

CHAO

CH'IN

WEI

Hantan

CH'I

•Lintzu

P'ingyang

Ch'ufu
LU

Yellow
Sea

Hsienyang

CHOU
Loyang

Taliang

SUNG

HAN

Hsincheng

Shangch'iu

Ying

CH'U

YANGTZE RIVER

YANGTZE RIVER

SI RIVER

South China Sea

alone decided interstate issues—gone were the days of interstate conferences and sophisticated diplomacy. Agreements were made to be broken,
and diplomats were experts in treachery and deceit. Every prince was
bent on conquest, and might had become right. Prior to this period the
value of human lives was often taken into consideration even on the
battlefield. In one case the invading force of Ch'u, having heard that the
long besieged city of Sung was so starved that "people were forced to
exchange their children for food," voluntarily lifted the siege. The military
commanders during the period of Warring States would not give much
thought to moral scruples. Casualties ran to hundreds of thousands in each
of the many military campaigns, and no mercy was shown to prisoners-of-
war who were often slaughtered *en masse*. In this age of madness, generals were rated and rewarded according to the number of enemies they
killed. Bloodshed increased by the improvement in weapons and methods
of warfare. Cavalry and infantry replaced war chariots, and the wide use
of iron had made the new weapons more deadly. Besides, military strategy had become a specialized science. Top strategists like Wu Ch'i and
Sun Pin not only showed their talent on the battlefield but also wrote
books for the benefit of future generals. Each of the two large states,
Ch'in and Ch'u, boasted of an army of more than one million men; even a
smaller state like Han, Wei, or Yen was said to have several hundred
thousand men among its military rank and file.

Eventually the western state Ch'in was able to conquer the other six
states, and it unified China in 221 B.C. Located in the Wei River valley,
Ch'in was a comparative newcomer in the interstate community. For
centuries it was regarded as backward and semi-barbarian, and it exercised no great influence in the east where the more advanced states were
located. The attitude of the eastern states towards Ch'in was not unlike
the attitude of the Greek city-states towards Macedonia. As late as the
seventh century B.C. Ch'in's expansion towards the east was blocked by
Tsin and it had to be satisfied with being "the leader among the western
barbarians." In the long run, however, the unique advantages it enjoyed
enabled it to become the most powerful state and eventually to unify
China. First, it rose up among nomadic tribes and was surrounded by
them; it possessed a primitive vitality not shared by the more advanced
states in the east. Second, its home base, the Wei River valley, was perhaps the most productive area in the entire Yellow River basin. Besides,
the Ch'in people were known to be hardy, diligent farmers. Third, it was
bordered by high mountains in the east and in the south, and these
mountains were broken only by narrow passes. Behind its mountain
shield it could move to attack whenever opportunities presented themselves and shut itself behind its natural barriers when confronted with a
superior enemy. Moreover, being isolated in the west, it could exploit
whatever differences existed among the eastern states and even promote

such differences. Though these states knew about Ch'in's ambition, they were hopelessly divided among themselves.

Ch'in's supremacy was of course not achieved overnight. In addition to the natural advantages as described above, it benefited, time and again, from the presence of great leaders at the helm of its government. One of them was Shang Yang, who was Ch'in's chief minister before he died in 338 B.C. An interesting story tells us of his rise to power. Born in Wei, he became a protégé of Wei's chief minister at an early age. When the chief minister was about to die of old age, the reigning prince asked him whom he would recommend as his successor. The chief minister suggested Shang Yang, saying that he was the ablest man in the country for the position. Having noticed the prince's reluctance to accept his advice because of Shang Yang's youthfulness, he urged the prince to kill Shang, because, if the king could not use him, the young man would be employed by some other sovereign to Wei's great disadvantage. After the prince departed, the chief minister summoned Shang Yang to his death-bed, and advised the young man to flee for his life. Shang Yang was unruffled and replied calmly: "If the prince cannot accept your advice to appoint me as chief minister, how can you expect him to accept your advice to kill me? I am very safe indeed." Shortly afterwards, Shang Yang went to Ch'in and was granted a series of audiences with its prince, Duke Hsiao (Ch'in Hsiao-kung). The prince was so impressed that he soon appointed Shang Yang as his chief minister.

Historians classify Shang Yang as a follower of the Legalist school; the philosophy of this school will be discussed in the next chapter. For our immediate purpose, suffice it to say that the Legalists believed in the sanctity of law and the complete subservience of individuals to the state. Once a law was enacted, it should be obeyed by everyone in the state, including members of the royal household. Shortly after Shang Yang became the chief minister, the crown prince violated the law, whereupon Shang Yang announced his intention to punish him as if he were a com-moner. Others protested on the ground that the dignity of the heir appar-ent should be maintained, and finally the chief minister agreed to accept the prince's tutor as a substitute, and the latter was branded accordingly. Presumably, the tutor had not taught the prince how to behave and should therefore accept the blame. After this incident, "all Ch'in people learned to obey the law" and became "brave in public warfare and cow-ardly in civil strife." The observance of law was of course not an end itself; the real purpose was to channel each individual's energy to the service of the state. To mobilize manpower, Shang Yang ordered that all households in the state be organized into small groups and that each household be held responsible for the words and deeds of other house-holds within the same group. Civil strife was strictly forbidden, while bravery on the battlefield in the service of the state was abundantly rewarded. Economically, the goal was the maximization of production, especially the production of the two basic branches of the economy, farming and cloth-making. Every acre of land was to be tilled; the strength of every man was to be utilized. Those who were not engaged in useful occupation and those who suffered poverty because of their own laziness were condemned to slavery. As Ch'in was sparsely populated, Shang Yang offered favorable terms to attract immigrants from the east. These new immigrants were exempted from military service, so they could concentrate on opening up virgin land and forests. To provide more incentive, feudal land tenure was abolished; land transaction between individuals was legalized; and land enclosure was even encouraged to provide more efficient cultivation. Efforts like these did not fail to yield results. Ten years after Shang Yang began his tenure of office, it was said that every family was economically sufficient, banditry and thievery were completely eliminated, and Ch'in became one of the best governed states. Domestically strong, it was just a matter of time before Ch'in made its power and influence felt abroad.

By the second half of the fourth century B.C. Ch'in had become the most powerful state in China. Such being the case, it was clearly to the advantage of the other states to form a common alliance for defense. Such an alliance, sponsored by Chao's chief minister Su Ch'in, came into being in 330 B.C., and for a period of fifteen years it successfully stopped Ch'in's advance towards the east. The alliance, however, could not be maintained indefinitely. For one thing, while all the six states were afraid of Ch'in, they hated each other even more. There was the deep-seated hatred between Ch'i and Yen which resulted in two major wars in three years (314 and 312 B.C.). The hatred between Ch'i and Ch'u was equally bitter. While each state was debating about its foreign policy, Ch'in did not remain idle. It sent its own chief minister Chang Yi (who, incidentally, had been Su Ch'in's classmate and best friend at one time) to exploit the differences between the six states and to persuade them not to form a common front against the Ch'in state. Chang, an articulate man, combined persuasion with threat and coercion. Well equipped with gold, he distributed it generously to make the persuasion even more convincing. His strategy worked well. Su Ch'in's alliance collapsed, and the six states kept on quarrelling and fighting among themselves, much to Ch'in's gratification.

As the third century progressed, interstate warfare became more and more vicious. For each war, hundreds of thousands of fighting men were mobilized by each of the belligerents, and casualties reached many thousands at the end of each battle. Quarter was rarely given, and captured prisoners-of-war were often slaughtered in cold blood, as has been said before. In 274 B.C. a Ch'in general defeated Wei and reportedly killed 150,000 enemy soldiers. Fourteen years later, another Ch'in general, Pai

Ch'i, was said to have slaughtered 450,000 Chao soldiers in one single battle (Battle of Ch'angp'ing). These numbers were unquestionably exaggerated. It is nevertheless true that military commanders had become increasingly brutal and inhuman on the battlefield. After the Battle of Ch'angp'ing, it was clear that none of the eastern states could stop Ch'in's march towards final victory. Ironically, one of the last efforts to stop Ch'in was made by King Nan of Chou who led a hodgepodge force to attack a Ch'in stronghold in 256 B.C. As expected, he was defeated. After his defeat, he handed over his domain (30,000 people and 36 towns and villages) to his victorious enemy. Subsequently, another Chou prince claimed the throne. He was in turn defeated and forfeited his territory. In 249 B.C. the Chou dynasty formally came to an end.

Beginning in 230 B.C. Ch'in conquered one state after another, starting from its neighbors and working towards its neighbors' neighbors. Finally, there were no more neighbors left. The following table shows how quickly Ch'in moved.

	CONQUERED
230 B.C.	Han
228 B.C.	Chao
225 B.C.	Wei
223 B.C.	Ch'u
222 B.C.	Yen
221 B.C.	Ch'i

SOCIAL AND ECONOMIC CHANGES

As wars were frequent after the eighth century B.C., territories changed hands often. The common practice of a victorious state was to bring conquered territories under central or bureaucratic control instead of sorting them out as feudal fiefs. As this process continued, the territories under central administration increased while those under feudal control steadily declined. A state, large or small, might or might not have a feudal relationship with the reigning Chou king. Even if it had such a relationship, its allegiance to the king was nominal. In the territory within its control it was supreme and sovereign. It had officials who were familially related to the reigning prince and who bore feudal titles, but they were not different from other bureaucrats who served the state in an assigned capacity. A commoner, upon becoming a government official, might be given a feudal title, but this title indicated nothing except that he was a high-ranking official. For his service he might be assigned a certain number of households administered for his benefit. But the income he received from these households was in fact his salary, and the area in which they were located was not a fief in the true sense of that word. It could be taken away from him once he ceased to be a government official. Within each state the power of the prince was supreme and all people were his subjects. To be sure, feudal fiefs still existed as late as the third century B.C., but they constituted only a small part of the prince's territory. Moreover, the people within the feudal fiefs owed absolute loyalty to the prince as subjects rather than to the feudal lords as peasants. When there was a conflict between the two loyalties, the loyalty to the prince prevailed, as the feudal lord himself owed allegiance to the prince. The development of a centralized government took a long time to complete. In fact, before the fifth century there had been times when there was a decentralizing tendency within individual states, notably in Ch'i and Lu. The over-all tendency, however, was towards centralization. By the beginning of the fourth century B.C. such a development had been largely completed. In summary, while there was a power deconcentration after the eighth century B.C. as far as the king was concerned, there was an increasing concentration of power in the hands of individual states. Though moving in opposite directions, both processes contributed to the decline of feudalism.

Together with the political factors described above, there were social and economic causes that slowly undermined the feudal structure. One of these was the rise of the merchant class and the growth of cities. Feudalism thrived best in a self-sufficient economy within a small area, but geographical specialization in production was bound to destroy such self-sufficiency and eventually feudalism as well. While basic crops such as rice and wheat were raised practically all over China, different sections specialized in producing different products: "lumber, bamboo, and precious stones in Shansi; fish, salt, lacquer, silk and musical instruments in Shantung; fruits in the Yangtze River valley; and copper and iron in the mountainous regions in Szechuan." As society became more advanced, people desired more and better goods. This was especially true with the nobles who, being wealthy, could afford and consequently demanded luxuries produced in other areas. As such demands increased, each area, besides producing for its own needs, had to produce a surplus to exchange for what it needed and did not have. Hence there arose the merchant class which shipped goods from one place to another by performing a necessary economic service. Barter was no doubt the earliest form of trade, but as trade increased, money had to be used. Money in various forms was in use as early as the Shang dynasty, but it was not until the seventh or the sixth century B.C. that governments began to mint metallic coins. They came to different states at different times. The comparatively backward state of Ch'in, for instance, did not coin money until the fourth century B.C. After the fifth century B.C. gold began to circulate in large quantities. While the princes used it for rewarding their own ministers as well as bribing the ministers of other states, the merchants employed it as a medium of exchange. The use of precious metals as money unquestionably facilitated trade.

Trade also benefited from the increasing mobility of the people. Despite the fact that China was politically divided, there was no restriction of movement across state lines. A merchant could move freely from one state to another without encountering harassment from government on

PORCELAIN VASE   This vase was produced in the fourth or third century B.C. Notice the symmetrical designs and the balanced lines.

either side of the border line. No state would persecute a merchant simply because he came from another state; nor would it discriminate against him on behalf of its own merchants. It seemed that all governments had recognized the importance of his services. Under this benevolent atmosphere, many merchants became powerful and wealthy, so wealthy that in many cases they outshone the feudal lords in the display of luxuries. Often they doubled as moneylenders and even had kings and princes as their regular customers. One of the Chou kings, we are told, was so much in debt that he rarely chose to emerge from his palaces because he was afraid that he might bump into his creditors. As wealth increased, influence increased proportionally. The big merchants were granted audiences and were treated as equals by reigning princes in whichever states they happened to be. Often they exercised great influence over domestic and interstate affairs. It was said that Tzu Kung, a powerful merchant and also a former student of Confucius, in one trip, "saved Lu, deranged Ch'i, destroyed Wu, strengthened Tsin, and raised Yüeh to a position of supremacy." His feats were no doubt exaggerated. The fact nevertheless remains that the merchants were a powerful group to reckon with during this period.

The increase of commercial activities was reflected in the growth of cities. Cities became larger and more numerous, especially those located along the trade routes or chosen as state capitals. In North China four cities stood out prominently above others; they were, from west to east, Hsienyang, Hantan, Loyang, and Lintzu, each being a distribution center in its own area. In the fourth century B.C. Lintzu had a population of about 350,000; Loyang had a population of 500,000 toward the end of the third century B.C. In the south some cities were even larger. The outer wall of the capital of Wu, for instance, covered an area almost as large as present Peking (17 miles versus 18 miles in circumference), though statistics regarding its population are now unavailable. Cities with a population of 100,000 could be found in several regions. This booming scene was particularly noticeable in South China. Through the efforts of the southern states, Ch'u, Wu, and Yüeh, the Chinese frontier was extended steadily southward to the modern Fukien province and the southern portions of the modern Kiangsi and Hunan provinces. Here natural environment was more rewarding, land was more productive, and people were generally more spirited and carefree. All these, of course, were favorable conditions for the growth of commercial activities. There was the famous merchant Fan Li who, after retiring from an official career as Yüeh's chief minister early in the fifth century B.C., amassed a huge fortune in a period of nineteen years. He distributed much of his wealth among his friends and relatives, still leaving a large amount to his descendants. Today his supposed image is still hung in many Chinese stores whose owners are no doubt hoping to duplicate the achievement of this ancient financial wizard.

In the cities life was lively and interesting. Whenever a large number of people congregated, community activities existed; some of them were secular and others were religious. In the northern city of Lintzu, one of the most important events was the annual spring festival in honor of the Earth God. On that day all were dressed in their best, and the city provided a variety of entertainments including songs, dances, dramas, and acrobatics. Country people flowed into the city for the occasion, and many young maidens could enjoy overt flirtations without being criticized. After all was over and when evening drew near, there was plenty of wine for people to get intoxicated. The temple of the Earth God was perhaps the most important building in the city besides the palaces. Before a military campaign, meat and wine were offered to the Earth God to bring about good luck. After the campaign, victory was reported to him; sometimes the captured enemy commanders were killed in the temple as sacrifices. Natural disasters like flood and drought had also to be reported so he could give counsel with regard to the best of possible remedies. In a lawsuit when the judge was unable to render a judgment because of the lack of evidences, both sides were required to swear before the Earth God and wait for miracles to happen. Whenever there was an eclipse of the sun or the moon, people gathered in front of the temple, beating drums loudly to scare off the evil spirit who was about to swallow up the heavenly body.

As feudalism declined, land ownership was no longer confined to those who had inherited it as a hereditary right. It could be bought and sold like any other commercial product. Consequently, there was a growing tendency towards the concentration of land ownership in the hands of a few. The new landlords held no high sounding feudal titles; they were the powerful bureaucrats, the princes' favorites, and the wealthy merchants. This process of land concentration had gone on for a long time in North China. When the state of Ch'in formally abolished feudal land tenure and permitted the buying and selling of land ownership in the fourth century B.C., it only legally confirmed an existing practice. However, once legalized, this process of land concentration gathered additional momentum. For the farmers who had been until then under feudal protection, this was ominous enough. Either they were forced to sell their land because of incurred debt or they had to fight for subsistence against great odds. In either case, life was hard.

Chinese historians have preserved for us the budget of a typical farmer in Wei who lived in the fourth century B.C. He was the head of a family of five, and he cultivated 100 *mou* (15 acres) of land. His harvest averaged 1.5 piculs of grain per *mou* and his total harvest was 150 piculs

(1 picul = 133 lbs approximately). Each person consumed an average of 1.5 piculs per month; total yearly consumption for the whole family was 90 piculs. According to the market price, each picul was worth 30 standard coins; when he sold them, the remaining 45 piculs would bring him 1,350 standard coins in cash. After contributing 300 standard coins to religious causes like supporting of the temple of the Earth God, he had only 1,050 standard coins left. For a family of five, the minimum expenditure for clothes was 1,500 coins. So in a normal year he would wind up with a deficit of 450 standard coins. If additional taxes were collected, which occurred often, or if there were births, sickness, and deaths in the family, the annual debt would be even larger. When the accumulated debt became too large, he had to sell his land, and in sadder cases, sell his children or even himself as slaves. All in all, the decline of feudalism brought him only woes and misfortune. Under feudalism a peasant might not have plenty, but at least he had security. So long as he fulfilled his feudal obligations, he could keep his land and could count on a tolerable return for his labor. His more personal relationship with the lord forestalled oppressive extortions; it also entitled him to protection from his lord in time of need. With the decline of feudalism he was on his own. He was exposed to direct pressure from the big landlords, the money lenders, and worst of all, the impersonal government. There was no shield between him and forces bigger than his own. Sooner or later he might have to give up the struggle.

Disadvantageous though it might be to the peasantry, the decline of feudalism was not without its compensating effects. One of these was the spread of learning and education which, in turn, resulted in the increase of social mobility. When feudalism was at its prime, education was a monopoly of the nobility because feudalism thrived best on the rigidity of social stratification and the absence of social mobility; the spread of education to the lower strata of the population would have destroyed both. After the eighth century when wars were carried on almost incessantly, each state was in a constant struggle between survival and oblivion. It was ability rather than birth which could benefit a state and brought a man to power and wealth. With a good education, a man could rise above his humble background through sheer intelligence, ability, and an ambition to succeed. This emphasis on education was duly reflected in contemporary writings. Education rather than birth was hailed by many writers as the dividing line between the governing and the governed. To use the language of Mencius, there were two classes of people in a society: the gentlemen and the mean men. The gentlemen were the educated who, specializing in mental work, formed the governing class. The mean men, being the uneducated engaged in physical labor, constituted the governed class. Although Mencius was describing an ideal society where this division of labor existed, he nevertheless pointed out a direction in which the society was then actually moving. As education was expanded, a new elite man arose who was more proud of what he had in his mind than what he had in his blood.

The importance of education did not mean that everybody could have an education. For the most part, the privilege of enjoying it was confined to a small group. Though he was not legally restricted from obtaining an education, an average peasant was simply too busy in tilling his field and trying to make both ends meet to be seriously concerned with it. As has been noted earlier in this chapter, under Chou feudalism the great majority of the noble descent would eventually wind up as commoners. As time went on, a new class gradually emerged. The people of this class were of noble descent, but they were not nobles. They were commoners; yet, they had nothing in common with other commoners such as the peasants. They were *shih*, sometimes translated as gentry scholars. Two factors made them different from other commoners. First, they owned enough land or other means of support which spared them from the necessity of doing physical labor. Second, they had an education which provided them with the ways and means of acquiring leadership. Having enough to live by and yet not enough to discourage ambition, they were the most dynamic group during this period. But they were neither revolutionaries nor idealists. The aim of most of them was a worldly and selfish one, namely, winning the confidence and favor from a reigning prince and thus gaining power and wealth. As long as China was divided, they tried to exploit the existing situation to their own advantage. Many of them roamed from state to state and would serve whoever chose to hire them. They felt no patriotism or loyalty towards any state; they pledged allegiance only to those who hired them. Generally speaking, they were an unprincipled group and would not hesitate to use any means to achieve their selfish ends. During the period of Warring States their influence had become so great that many powerful princes made a habit of extending patronage and competed with one another in winning the allegiance of the roaming scholars. Prince Meng-ch'ang of Ch'i, for instance, supported three thousand roaming scholars from various states at one time. In other cases, roaming scholars held high-ranking and responsible posts in state governments. In Ch'in where feudalism was not so deeply rooted as in the eastern states and where innovations could be adopted with comparative ease, many able ministers came from this group. Shang Yang and Chang Yi were the two leading examples. Both were natives of Wei but served capably the Ch'in state. It was people like them who built a strong Ch'in regime which eventually unified China.

ᛉ ii

The Philosophers

THE IDEOLOGICAL PATTERN

The five centuries after 771 B.C. were a period of paradoxes. On the one hand, it was marked with incessant warfare, political anarchy, and moral degeneration. On the other hand, it was an era of dynamic social and economic changes and of great masters of new ideas. In fact, from the point of view of ideology, there has never been a period so constructive. The positive and negative aspects of this paradoxical age were not entirely unrelated. As the existing society degenerated further, there was more incentive to think in terms of an ideal society that could have existed but did not. After peace and justice had slowly disappeared, the longing for them became more intense. The great philosophers of this period were metaphysicians only in the most incidental sense; rather, they were overwhelmingly concerned with the imperfect world and the imperfect man. They were not interested in the supernatural forces either, because they believed that man's problems could only be solved by man himself. They were in this world, and they wished to make it a better place to live. They dealt extensively in politics, economics, and most importantly, ethics. Their interest in metaphysics and religion was confined to applying them if possible to the more mundane, worldly affairs. Theirs was a "man-centered" ideology to which all branches of knowledge must submit themselves.

The overwhelming concern about man marked distinctly the difference between Chinese philosophers and philosophers of other countries. The Greek and Indian philosophers of ancient times were also interested in man, but man's affairs formed only a part of their philosophical system. To the Chinese, man was the measure of all things, and without human values philosophies lost their basic meanings and could not even justify their own existence. There was no such thing as speculation for the sake of speculation; all learning was related, directly or indirectly, to human affairs. As theologians in medieval Europe believed that no knowledge was meaningful and worthy unless it contributed to the salvation of the soul, the Chinese philosophers of the classical age were equally scornful of pursuits that did not in any way help the physical man and his relationship with other people. The medieval theologians emphasized the importance of afterlife, while the Chinese were most concerned with this world. Both groups, seeing the universe from man's point of view, tended to neglect the universe as the universe was. In other words, they neglected to study our physical environment as an objective science. The European trend was reversed early in the modern period, and such a reversal paved the way for the advancement of modern science and technology. The Chinese, on the other hand, did not change their sense of values until the twentieth century.

This "man-centered" Chinese tradition is sometimes referred to as humanism. This term, however, should not be interpreted in the sense as Renaissance humanism in Europe. For one thing, the man in the tradition of Chinese humanism was an ethical being, and in that sense he had more in common with the man of medieval theologians than with the man in the spirit of the Renaissance. Secondly, the Chinese humanism emphasized man's relationship with other men rather than man as an independent, free individual. While Renaissance humanism freed man from his bondage to other men, especially his superiors in a manor, guild, or monastery, Chinese humanism, stressing human relations, strengthened that bondage. Chinese philosophers like Confucius were not interested in establishing a society composed of equal, independent individuals, but a society where man's position was clearly and carefully prescribed. Whereas Renaissance humanism led man out from medieval feudalism, Confucian philosophers wished to reestablish Chou feudalism which was then in the process of disintegration. The European humanists looked forward towards the future; the Chinese leaned back towards the past. Instead of freeing man from social control, Chinese humanism made such control even more formidable. Politically, it strengthened authoritarianism, in contrast to Renaissance humanism which, emphasizing individualism, might be said to have paved the way for modern democracy.

Such being the case, how could the Chinese system be still called humanism? It was humanism in the sense that it emphasized human welfare as man's most important concern and that man was the worthiest topic of all learning. By man was meant man as a social being rather than an independent individual. His relationship to other men was more important than he in himself. To the Chinese mind, the collective welfare of a group had priority over the well-being of individuals who composed it, and the enhancement of group welfare would presumably enhance individual well-being as well. Theoretically at least, human relations were more important than human beings. Such emphasis tended to degrade individuals rather than elevate them, because it made them mere points of conjunction in the intricate pattern of human relations.

Some of these relations were biological such as those between father and son and among brothers and sisters; others were nonbiological such as those between king and his ministers and among friends and neighbors. There were rules governing each of these relations, and altogether they constituted the moral code. Throughout centuries Chinese philosophers strove to find the rule that underlay all individual rules in the same spirit as our modern scientists strive to find the universal law that governs all natural laws. Their conclusions were of course different, and they debated among themselves throughout history. However, they did agree on one thing. Were human relations to be harmonious, individuals had to be virtuous, because it was impossible to establish a harmonious society if its members were woefully lacking in the basic attributes of worthy constituents. The improvement of individual character was therefore the first step towards the betterment of society. All ancient philosophers advocated the cultivation of personal virtues, though the definition of virtue might be entirely different. Those who failed to live up to the expectation of society were to be severely punished, by social or legal methods and often both. Thus, despite their humanistic beliefs, the ancient philosophers, with rare exceptions, showed little concern over the inhumanity of the penal code enforced in their times, which provided such diabolical punishments as branding, foot-amputation, and castration. The rules that governed relationship among men had to be maintained at all costs, including occasional but harsh punishment of individuals. These philosophers saw no contradiction in the advocacy of morality and ethics on the one hand and the inhuman punishment of individuals on the other. In fact, the latter was regarded by many of them as a necessary means to achieve the former.

According to Confucian philosophers, there were five cardinal relationships among men: those between king and his subjects, father and son, husband and wife, elder and younger brothers, and among friends. All these relationships were between superiors and inferiors, and even among friends the older were supposedly superior to the younger. The relationships did not cease with the death of the party involved; theoretically at least, they lasted indefinitely. The ancestors of a reigning emperor were revered by the nation as a whole, and the greatest men of the past such as Confucius were worshipped throughout history. This may account for the unique historical mindedness of the Chinese and their strong sense of identity with an ageless past. Within a family or a clan such sense of identity was even stronger. Ancestors were worshipped long after their death; the older the generation to which they belonged, the more they were honored. A man's mischiefs on earth were conveniently forgotten after his death, while his achievements, often exaggerated, were glorified. As a common practice, his eulogy was inscribed on his tombstone for the eyes of posterity, and a long time ago the Chinese had invented a literary style for the sole purpose of writing eulogies. When such style was followed, it was almost impossible to write anything derogatory of the dead man. The tablet that bore his name would appear in the family temple in due course, to be worshipped by his descendants for generations to come. The family register was one of the holiest books carefully preserved, and today many Chinese claim that they can trace their family beginnings to the time before the Christian era. The extension of human relationship to the deceased gave rise to the custom of ancestor worship which had been practiced by the Chinese from time immemorial. By the time that Confucius was born (551 B.C.) it was already a common practice.

The emphasis on human relationship personalized even the impersonal institutions such as government. The rulers were to rule by example, and they were "fathers and mothers" of the people. The moral calibre of those who enforced the law was more important than the law itself. Good government meant virtuous rulers, not necessarily good laws and sound institutions. In the Chinese thinking, the words in a legal contract were useless unless the parties who had concluded such a contract were morally strong enough to abide by it regardless of eventualities. A business agreement of bygone times was often an oral promise; to suggest otherwise would be regarded as an insult to the integrity of the contracting parties. Whenever difficulties arose, they believed that they could count on each other's sense of fairness to resolve their differences. In other words, they placed trust on the adherence by both parties to an unwritten moral code that governed human relations rather than an impersonal legal document. When a man pledged the hand of his baby daughter to his friend's baby son, he was not supposed to violate his pledge no matter how unworthy his prospective son-in-law turned out to be. When the children grew up, he and his friend relied on their filial obedience to carry out the arranged marriage. The parties directly involved might suffer from this alliance, but the rules that governed human relationship—the inviolability of promises among friends and the obedience of children to parents—had to be observed at all costs.

The observance of the ethical code came from no other consideration except that man, being a social being, had to live by certain rules. Rewards or punishments, either in this world or in the next, were immaterial. Man was unique among animals because he alone did not need inducement to be good. Otherwise, said Mencius, he could not have been different from other animals. Thus, most of the philosophers in ancient China based their hope of mankind on the essential goodness of man, and the ethics they taught was a "man-centered" ethics, totally devoid of the otherworldly connotations. A good man had no Heaven to look forward to; nor should a bad man be afraid of punishment after death. Religion and ethics were two separate fields, and they should be kept separate. An ethical man was not necessarily religious; nor was a religious man necessarily moral. Confucius said: "Worship the spirits, but keep them at a distance," because the spirits were not human and therefore had nothing to do with the rules that governed human relations. If a man was good simply because he expected reward or was afraid of punishment after his death, he would have lived a life of hypocritic pretensions. Was he really a good man in the first place? What would have happened to morality and ethics if he became an agnostic or atheist? What would have happened to society if all its members became agnostics and atheists? A man was expected to be good because he was a man, not a wild animal. He was born with goodness, said Mencius. He only needed to be taught to transform his innate goodness into righteous conduct.

How could immortality be achieved if a man's behavior in this world bore no relation to his life in the next? The ancient philosophers were not greatly concerned with this problem and did not regard it as particularly important. People like Confucius frankly admitted that they did not know the answer. "Not yet understanding life, how can you understand death?" said Confucius. When the question had to be answered, it was answered in the context of human relations. A Confucian classic, written perhaps in the fourth century B.C., said that there were three ways of achieving immortality. They were, in the order of importance: the establishment of virtues, the accomplishment of good deeds, and the writing of books. In other words, a man's immortality lay in the memory of his fellow men.. The more his life on earth benefited his fellow men and the longer his influence was felt, the more immortal he would become. It was not an immortality in the spiritual sense. As to spiritual immortality, the ancient philosophers provided no answer.

The separation of ethics from religion, a unique feature of the Chinese cultural system, was not without its blessing. In the Chinese mind, ethical standards were more important than religious standards, and in case of conflict between them, the former should always prevail. As the Chinese looked at it, these two standards were not necessarily the same and were sometimes contradictory. A religious sect that did not believe in wine-drinking had no right to condemn those who were convinced of the harmlessness of such habit, unless intoxication disrupted peace and order and affected adversely the relationship among men. In such case, the issue was a moral, ethical issue instead of a religious one. While religious standards were peculiar to a certain religion or religions, ethical standards were universal and should be applied to all men. One should not impose his own religious standards upon others who did not belong to his religion. To do so might be regarded as religious from his point of view; certainly it was not ethical. A religious fanatic bent on the condemnation and destruction of all other religions by whatever means he possessed was a social degenerate, deserving no mercy from his fellow men. Above religious beliefs was an ethical standard which all religions must abide by if society were to survive. Such a standard governed the relations between groups of individuals (such as religious sects) as well as individuals themselves. As ethics was separated from religion and was regarded as superior to religion, the Chinese were remarkably free from religious bigotry, and persecution on religious grounds, while not absent altogether, was noticeably mild compared with that of many other countries.

CONFUCIANISM

When we mention the Chinese cultural system, we inevitably associate it with Confucianism, and for more than two thousand years the word "Confucian" was virtually synonymous with the word "Chinese." Who was this man Confucius who exercised such a strong influence over so many people for such a long period? Throughout the centuries there have been so many words and deeds attributed to him that it is often difficult to differentiate the man from the myth. He was born in 551 B.C. or thereabouts and died in 479 B.C. Yet, a biography was not written about him until the second century B.C. Meanwhile, a legend had been built up, and his alleged words and deeds were scattered in many ancient writings. Fortunately, there is the book *Lun-yü* or *Analects* which was compiled by his disciples shortly after his death. The more cautious historians rely heavily on this book for a better understanding of this man, perhaps the greatest China has ever produced.

Confucius was a native of Lu which was located in modern Shantung province. By the time that Confucius was born, Lu had passed its prime as a political power and, located between three giants, Tsin, Ch'i, and

IMAGE OF CONFUCIUS This image of Confucius was painted by Prince Ho-shuo-kuo in the year 1735 A.D. On the top are Chinese characters of an ancient script which, roughly translated, read: "Confucius, the Sage and the Teacher." The small characters on the right read: "Respectfully painted by Prince Ho-shuo-kuo on the day of the full moon, in the ninth lunar month of the year of Chia-yin, during the reign of Emperor Yung-cheng." Below these characters are the prince's official seal which shows his name in Manchu on the left and Chinese on the right.

Ch'u, it had great difficulty in maintaining its precarious independence. Culturally, however, Lu had no peers. Originally the fief of Duke Chou, the state had been known for its cultural refinements for centuries. Both Confucius and Mencius, the two architects of Confucianism, were born in this state. As a child, Confucius was described as unusually inquisitive and showed great interest in rituals. Like other educated men of his time, he aspired to a governmental career and was reported to have served in various capacities in the Lu government. However, it was his teaching career that made him famous; what he taught became the basic tenets of what was later known as Confucianism. Accompanied by his students, he travelled a great deal, forever seeking the right prince who would give him a position of authority so that he could carry out his own teachings. In this matter he was bound to be disappointed because every prince he approached regarded his teachings as impractical at best. At one time during his travels he and his students lost their means of support and almost starved to death. At another time he was mistaken for a hated local politician because of physical resemblance and was almost mobbed. The Master, as he was generally called, took these ordeals in stride. Away from Lu for many years, eventually he returned home at an advanced age. It was then that he gave up any hope of a political career and concentrated on teaching. According to tradition, he wrote the *Spring and Autumn Annals,* besides commenting and editing many other works. Modern historians are more skeptical and even question whether he wrote anything at all.

Outwardly, it seems that he was a complete failure. Yet, in his unspectacular, prosaic way, he exercised the greatest influence over a large section of mankind for more than two thousand years. What was his secret? He succeeded by simply being himself. To millions of Chinese for centuries he represented perfection, a perfection which was expressed in human terms and was therefore easily comprehensible. He was unpretentious and honest, and he could be easily identified as one of the best among men, a good friend and a kind neighbor. He did not advise people to do the extraordinary and the impossible; he set up a standard which could be attained if they really tried. He had no use for pretension, whatever purpose it was meant to achieve. "When you know, say that you know; when you do not know, say that you do not know. This is the secret of knowledge." This advice came from Confucius; it could have come from any good school teacher.

This story is told of Confucius. A man was short of ginger and went to Wei-sheng Kao to borrow some. Instead of telling him that he did not have any himself, Wei-sheng Kao went out his back door without his friend's knowledge and borrowed some from his neighbor in order to lend it to his friend who had come to borrow. After Confucius heard this story, he criticized Wei-sheng Kao for being dishonest on the ground that he should have told his friend the truth. When his student Yen Yüan died, Confucius was overwhelmed with grief. Yet, when the dead man's father suggested that Confucius should sell his chariot to raise money to buy his son an outer coffin, the Master refused, saying that he had not sold his chariot on behalf of his own dead son and that he needed his chariot for travelling. We use these two examples to illustrate the humaneness of Confucius' moral standards, a touch of common sense which was ignored by later Confucians. They were never meant to be rigid and ritualistic as later they did become.

As a person, Confucius was gay, pleasant, and vivacious. He loved to sing, and according to the *Analects,* he stopped singing only when he heard that some one he knew had died. He liked outdoor life and one of his best recreations was to swim in a river with his friends. Besides, he loved the art of archery and chariot riding. Though he complained that he had not met a man who loved virtue more than sex, he did not regard sex as evil. In fact, a Confucian classic said explicitly that food and sex were the two basic, natural desires of man. When one of his students complained after Confucius had consented to meet a female admirer and famed beauty, Confucius was clearly irritated: "If I have done anything improper, let Heaven punish me, let Heaven punish me!" A sound and workable code of ethics had to be based upon the humanness of man. Deprived of its humanistic elements, it became inflexible, harsh, and penalizing and would do more harm than good. Virtue was to be enjoyed, not to be feared. Unattainable virtues ceased to be virtues because they became a source of fear rather than love. They contributed nothing to the well-being of man.

What were the Confucian virtues? Time and again the word *jen* appeared in the *Analects,* and each time Confucius gave it a different interpretation. The word has been variably translated as benevolence, love, and the like; it was the basic principle that governed the relationship among men. It was derived from man's innate goodness, though outwardly it was manifested in a variety of forms.

"When Fan Ch'ih asked about *jen,* the Master said: 'Love people.'

"When Yen Yüan asked about *jen,* the Master said: 'If you can control your selfish desires and subject them to the rules of propriety and if you can do this for a single day, it is the beginning of *jen* for the entire world. *Jen* is self-sufficient and comes from your inner self; it requires no outside help.' Yen Yüan asked for more details. The Master said: 'Don't see the improper; don't hear the improper; don't talk about the improper; and don't act improperly.'

"When Chung Kung asked about *jen,* the Master said: 'When you meet a person outside of your house, greet him as if he were a great noble. If, as a government official, you have to impose corvée duties on the people, you should approach your task with the same seriousness that you would use in performing a religious ritual. Don't do to others what you yourself do not desire.' " [1]

When a person was not sure whether he had done the right thing, he simply asked himself whether he would wish the same thing be done to him. He should be strict with himself as he had been strict with others. Goodness was implied in manhood; it needed no outside inducement. If a man performed good deeds for ulterior purposes, whether they be fame or wealth, his motives were not pure and there was little goodness in his deeds. In fact, motives were more important than results. Through vigorous self-discipline, a man would eventually reach a status in which he could do whatever he pleased without ever doing anything wrong. When such status was reached, he became a *chün-tzu,* or a morally superior man.

A superior man was not satisfied with his own perfection, because virtue, in order to survive, had to be contagious. There was an element of

---

[1] Fan Ch'ih, Yen Yüan, and Chung Kung were Confucius' students. All these passages appear in Chapter VI of the *Analects.* The translation is the author's own.

goodness in every man, and in such goodness lay the hope of mankind. "Among any three men walking in the street, there is one who could be my teacher," declared Confucius; "I shall follow their good traits, while correcting my own weaknesses which I have also found in them." A superior man, seeking perfection in himself, also tried to induce the best from others. For maximum results he could choose the career of a government official or that of a teacher because in either of the two capacities the people whom he could influence were large in number. As a government official, he influenced people by his own example; he could not achieve his purpose by instituting harsh laws and severe punishments. "The virtue of a superior man is like wind and the virtue of the people is like grass," said Confucius; "the grass bends towards the direction where the wind blows." He had no use for law, as law involved compulsion, and its observation arose from fear. A good government relied on morality to prevent wrong-doing instead of law to punish the wrongdoers. A student asked Confucius about the nature of good government. The Master said that there were three essentials that constituted a good government: sufficient food, adequate defense, and faith. If one of these three had to go, which one should go first? asked the student. The Master said defense. If one of the remaining two had to be abandoned, which one should be abandoned? The Master said food. "All men have to die," concluded Confucius; "without faith no nation can survive." By faith was meant the moral values of a nation that differentiated civilized men from wild savages.

Generally speaking, Confucius was a conservative in government and politics. He attributed the existing social ills and political anarchy to the disruption of authority and advocated return to the early form of Chou feudalism. He believed that only when authority was properly instituted and carefully observed could peace and order prevail. Society was composed of a variety of individuals and each individual had a special function to perform. However, authority did not and should not imply despotism. With each name, according to Confucius, there was a reality; without reality a name would be deprived of its meanings. Thus a prince (name) could not be rightly called a prince if he did not perform the functions (reality) assigned to him. If, for instance, he used his authority for selfish purposes instead of the welfare of his subjects, he was a prince in name only, but not a real prince. There was a heavenly imposed duty on the ruler as well as on the ruled. A ruler should set an example to his subjects. Only when the ruler was wise and virtuous could the people be expected to be loyal and obedient. The same principle was also applied to the household. Though the husband was superior to his wife, parents superior to children, and elder brothers superior to the younger ones, there were mutual obligations governing each other: love and protection on the part of the superiors and loyalty and obedience on the part of the inferiors. The respect and obedience a superior received was not automatic by any means. Only when a king treated his ministers with *li* (propriety), said Confucius, could the ministers reciprocate it with *chung* (loyalty). By the same token, a cruel, unloving father forfeited all rights of demanding filial piety from his son. A correct relationship imposed obligations on both sides; those who were not willing to give should not receive either.

Confucius was never given the opportunity to carry out his teachings as a government official; as a teacher, however, he was superb. He believed in the educability of man, whatever his natural endowment. The achievement might not be the same, but each man became better off after the educational process. The purpose of education was not merely the acquirement of knowledge or skill, however important that might be. The real purpose was the cultivation of virtues and the purification of personal character. According to the *Analects,* Confucius emphasized four main items in teaching his own students: literature, conduct, sincerity, and faith. Of the four items only the first one can be classified as academic learning. In another instance, the Master grouped his students into four categories in accordance with their attainments. They were: personal virtue, speech, politics, and literature. There is no question as to which category he emphasized most. As far as academic learning was concerned, it seems that he used the *Book of Odes,* the *Book of Rites,* and the *Book of Changes* as the standard texts, especially the first two whose importance was repeatedly emphasized in the *Analects.* As to teaching technique, the Master used the informal, conversational method. A question was raised, and the students tossed it around and expressed their own opinions. From time to time the Master came in and offered his ideas. There was no set answer or answers to each question. Like Aristotle, Confucius believed in the influence of music in refining a man's character. Archery and chariot-riding also formed a part of the curriculum. In short, the purpose of education was the cultivation of an all-round, versatile gentleman, setting a moral example to other people in private life and serving them ably and conscientiously whenever he was given an official post to hold.

Besides *jen,* the other virtue mentioned most often in the *Analects* was *li. Li* has been variably translated as propriety, ceremony, ritual, rite, mannerism, etiquette, etc.; it could have been any one of these, depending upon the context in which it was used. If *jen* was the manifestation of a man's innate goodness in acts that materially benefited his fellow men, *li* was the rule of conduct that reflected a person's goodwill which might not benefit the other party materialistically. To present a bag of rice to a hungry neighbor was an act of *jen;* to express sympathy and concern without providing material help was *li.* On the other hand, if one could help in a material way and yet chose to do nothing except express perfunctory sympathy, the outward *li* became meaningless because in that case it was devoid of content which should have been goodwill. If *li* were addressed to living beings, it could be translated as propriety, etiquette and so on; if it were addressed to deceased ancestors, spirits, and gods, it became religious rites and rituals. In short, it was a code of conduct that governed relations among men and also men's relations with gods and deceased ancestors.

One hundred and fifty years after the death of Confucius, Confucianism found its great champion in the person of Mencius. According to tradition, Mencius owed much of his fine character to his mother who, among other things, changed residence three times in search of a proper neighborhood for the boy to grow up. If the style of his book (*Book of Mencius*) indicates anything, he was forcible, aggressive, and uncompromising and was an expert in the art of speech and debate. Like Confucius, he aspired to a position of authority to carry out his own teachings and travelled from state to state for that purpose. He failed in his mission as Confucius had done so before him. For one thing, his program of "love and righteousness" was considered impractical in an age of political anarchy when the fate of a state depended upon the outcome of each conflict on the battlefield rather than the moral virtue of its rulers. However, wherever he went, he was received with consideration and respect, because by then the honoring of roaming scholars had become the fashion of the time as we have said in the preceding chapter. Unlike Confucius who travelled under conditions of extreme hardship, Mencius was at the head of "scores of chariots and hundreds of followers" wherever he went, and he chastised reigning monarchs like school children for their "evil" ways of governing their people. They listened attentively but discarded his suggestions once he had left.

What did Mencius teach? He elaborated and strengthened Confucius' basic beliefs and advanced some new ideas of his own. While Confucius only implied the natural goodness of man, Mencius said emphatically that human nature was good.

"Human nature is like water current," said Kao-tzu (a contemporary of Mencius). "If it is led to the east, it flows eastward; if it is led to the west, it flows westward. Like water which can be led to either of the two directions, human nature is neither good nor bad. It depends upon the direction towards which it is led."

"While it is true that water can be led eastward or westward, is it also true that it knows no difference between 'upward' and 'downward' "? asked Mencius. "The goodness of human nature is like water's natural inclination to move downward. As water is inevitably moving downward, there is no man in the world who is not good. If you beat water hard, it jumps up and can rise higher than your forehead. If you channel it and push it upward, it might even reach the top of a mountain. But, is this the nature of water? It acts contrary to its nature because it is given no other choice. If a man does bad things, he, like water, has been forced to do them and has not been given a better choice. His wrongdoing has nothing to do with his inherent nature which is good." [1]

Had Mencius never written or said anything else, the above passage alone would have made him one of the greatest thinkers in history. It elevated the dignity of man and raised the hope of mankind. More than two thousand years ago he anticipated our modern environmental theory. Enunciating his political theory, time and again he emphasized the importance of the people. While he did not challenge the hereditary right of monarchs to rule, he said that they should rule for the benefit of their subjects. Should a monarch fail to do so, his subjects had the right of rebellion because in that case he forfeited his own right as a monarch. During a time when casualties ran to many thousands in a single battle, Mencius maintained that no prince who mercilessly took away human lives could win the war and unify the country. Who could unify the country? It was the prince who practiced the "policy of love" (*jen cheng*). The prince who "humanizes his penal code, reduces taxation, promotes agriculture, and teaches people the virtue of filial piety, humility, loyalty, and faith" would eventually succeed. In any case, he should not exact more than ten percent tax of his subjects' produce. Unlike Confucius who had no use for material wealth ("Wealth is like floating clouds to me," said the Master), Mencius maintained that only when people were economically sufficient could they be expected to conduct a virtuous life.

An enlightened monarch should see to it that people should produce enough to support their parents and their wives and children. In good years they should have enough to eat, and in bad years they should not have to be starved to death. In such a case, it would be easy to lead them to as virtuous a life as they would be happy to follow. Nowadays people do not have the means to support either their parents or their wives and children. They suffer even in good years and cannot escape death in bad years. When they are confronted with possible death everyday, how can you expect them to have time to engage in rites and righteousness? [2]

While Confucius talked a great deal about *jen*, Mencius spoke often about *yi*. What was the difference between these two virtues? According to Kao-tzu (as quoted by Mencius), *jen* was the goodness within a person and *yi* was the righteous action that was derived from the innate goodness. Every action that benefited other people had to be motivated by goodwill, otherwise such action was meaningless and ceased to be righteous. The opposite of righteousness was profit, because profit was meant to benefit oneself instead of others. A virtuous man measured every step he took against a simple standard: was it profitable or was it righteous? Needless to say, he should reject the profitable and follow what was right.

[1] Translated from the *Book of Mencius,* Chapter VI.
[2] Translated from the *Book of Mencius,* Chapter I.

What kind of ideal society did Mencius visualize for mankind? It was a society where "men will not only honor their own parents and love their own children but will do the same with others' parents and children as well." It was a society where "all men are brothers." The first step towards that direction was of course the cultivation of personal virtues. When every person did the same, idealism would be eventually translated into reality. When that day arrived, peace and goodwill would prevail and war and injustice would be gone forever.

So far we have defined Confucianism as it was originally expounded by Confucius and Mencius. It was an ethical system, dynamic and humanistic. It deviated from its original meanings in later centuries as it became more rigid and formalistic. The Confucianism vigorously attacked by the twentieth-century liberals as a handicap to progress was not the Confucianism taught by Confucius. As Confucianism was a philosophy and a way of life, it did not have a priesthood or hierarchy; various schools interpreted it differently in their own ways. After the twelfth century the Sung School emerged as the most influential and dominated the intellectual scene for the next seven hundred years. It was then that Confucianism became more doctrinaire and dogmatic and consequently less humane. We shall have more to say about this in the coming chapters.

THE BASIC WORKS OF CONFUCIANISM

The basic works of Confucianism were those that were written before the second century B.C. when Confucianism was proclaimed as the state philosophy, as against those that were written afterwards. Some of them were so highly regarded that they were called *ching* or classics. By classics was meant more than masterpieces; they were also sacred. To an orthodox Confucian they contained the cream of all knowledge and wisdom, their words were to be memorized by heart, and their teachings were to be followed literally. What were the classics? Usually we say *Five Classics*, though occasionally the terms *Nine Classics* and *Thirteen Classics* were also used. In either of the latter case lesser works were added to the *Five Classics* to make the required number. The *Five Classics* were: *Book of Odes, Book of History, Book of Changes, Book of Rites*, and finally, *Spring and Autumn Annals*. The *Book of Music*, one of the original *Classics*, was lost in the third century B.C. during Ch'in Shih Huang-ti's book-burning campaign (see Chapter III). The *Five Classics*, however, have survived the long years.

The *Book of Odes* (*Shih ching*) was one of the oldest written works in history, dating from the tenth to the seventh century B.C. At one time it contained more than 3,000 poems; after Confucius' editing, said tradition, only 305 of them were allowed to remain. Of the 305 poems that constitute the present version, some are folksongs (*feng*), and others are political poems (*ya*), and ritual hymns (*sung*). The most charming and best known are the folksongs that have universal appeal regardless of time and space. The following is the conversation between a newly married couple who, according to Chinese tradition, lived under the same roof with the groom's parents.

> The cock is crowing;
> Oh, dear, it is already morning.
>
> It is not the cock crowing;
> It is only flies' droning.
>
> The east is brightening;
> The morning is here, my darling.
>
> It is the moonlight, not the sun;
> You must be mistaken.
>
> My head is dizzy;
> The flies are droning.
> I love to lie beside you longer
>   Sharing our unfinished dream.
> But what would others say,
>   When they come home from their gathering?
> Get up, sweet;
> Their scorn is frightening.[1]

What kind of moral could traditional Confucians derive from this piece of literature which was a love poem? To squeeze out a moral, they had to twist the meaning of the poem. This poem showed a virtuous wife, said the moralists, who urged her husband to get up early to attend the morning audience with the king. The "others" in the poem meant the "other ministers," and the "gathering" meant the "daily audience with the king early in the morning." The moral was: "Thou shalt not let passion blind your sacred duty to the king." Many other poems were given moral meanings in the same manner.

The *Book of History* (*Shu ching*) consists of historical and semi-historical documents dating from the early period of the Chou dynasty. During Ch'in's book-burning campaign, this book, like many other Confucian works, was ordered to be burned. After the establishment of the Han dynasty a search was made for the lost text, but in vain. As a last resort, the government invited a Confucian scholar named Fu Sheng (c. 180 B.C.) to reconstruct the lost text. Fu had memorized the entire work; now, more than ninety years old, he dictated what he had memorized

---

[1] Translated by the author from "The Folksongs of Ch'i" in the *Book of Odes*.

to his daughter who then transmitted the reconstructed text to the government. Since this text was written in the Han script, the same script as the Chinese are using today, it was called the *Book of History* in the "modern text." Later, when the old residence of Confucius was destroyed, a copy of the *Book of History* written in an ancient script was found inside a broken wall, and it contained sixteen more essays than the "modern text." Many scholars claimed that this was the original text, the text that had existed before Ch'in's book-burning campaign. Since the circumstances under which it was found were not exactly known, there were others who doubted the authenticity of the "old text." The debate regarding the comparative merits of the two texts has been going on for the past two thousand years. Generally speaking, the "modern text" is more reliable than the "old text" which contains a sizable portion of later forgeries.

The *Book of Changes* (*Yi ching*) is the only Classic that deals with the supernatural. As such, it was claimed by both Confucians and later Taoists as a part of their heritage. We know that Confucius read this book with great diligence and once remarked that he would be less subject to error if Heaven gave him more years to study this book more thoroughly. Why should it take him so many years to read a book which was small in volume? Obviously, readers like Confucius saw more meanings between the lines than the terse text contained. It is in fact a diviner's book, dealing with the meanings of the various combinations of the Eight Diagrams. A Diagram is composed of either two unbroken lines and one broken line or one unbroken line and two broken lines with two exceptions that are composed of either three unbroken lines or three broken lines. The unbroken line — symbolizes *yang*, the positive force in the universe, and the broken line - - symbolizes *yin*, the negative force in the universe. Their interactions, said the ancient diviners, created the universe and the things in it. Some scholars claim that the unbroken and broken lines represented the male and female sexual organs respectively and were therefore adopted as symbols for the two opposite but complementary forces in the universe. By arranging any three of the broken and unbroken lines in different positions, the ancient diviner obtained eight possible combinations which were called the Eight Diagrams.

The diviner, by doubling any two of the Eight Diagrams, could make a total of sixty-four possible combinations. As an illustration, we shall draw some of them as follows:

This may look like child's play to us, but to the ancient Chinese each of these combinations represented a particular form in which the cosmic forces expressed themselves. Each form foretold the future and the eventual outcome of prospective events. This was of course a different kind of divination from that practiced by the Shangs and perhaps did not come into wide use until the early period of the Chou dynasty. The terse, ambiguous text in the *Book of Changes* was traditionally attributed to King Wen and Duke Chou, the founders of Chou dynasty. It is more likely that they had nothing to do with it. The text was intentionally ambiguous to provide room for the individual diviner's own interpretations. Appendixes and comments were added to the text by later scholars and diviners; some of them were attributed to Confucius who, in this case, might have earned a reputation which he did not deserve.

The origin of the *Book of Rites* was even more ambiguous. We know that Confucius listed rites as one of the most important subjects in his curriculum. Was the present version of the namesake used at the time of Confucius? A portion of it might have been, but most of it was the creation of later scholars. The compilation, in its present form, did not come into being until the second century B.C. In the twelfth century A.D. two chapters of this book, *Great Learning* (*Ta hsüeh*) and *Doctrine of the Mean* (*Chung yung*) were taken out to form two of the *Four Books*. The other two books were the *Analects* and the *Book of Mencius*. After the twelfth century the *Four Books* and the *Five Classics* have been regarded as the basic texts of Confucianism.

The last of the *Five Classics* is a history of the state Lu entitled *Spring and Autumn Annals*. Tradition credited Confucius with its authorship. Thanks to its association with the great sage, its text has been carefully preserved. Its brief, terse remarks enabled Confucian scholars of succeeding centuries to read into them moralistic meanings.

In addition to the books described above, there were lesser works that were also a part of Confucian tradition. Closely related to the *Book of Rites* were *Ceremonies and Rituals* (*Yi li*) and *Chou Institutions*. The former appeared in the second century B.C.; the latter, also titled *Rites of Chou* (*Chou li*), was an idealized picture of Chou institutions. Though Duke Chou has been credited by tradition with its authorship, it was in fact a much later creation (second century B.C.?). Traditionally associated with the *Spring and Autumn Annals* were three other independent works: *Commentaries of Tso* (*Tso chuan*), *Commentaries of Kung-yang* (*Kung-yang chuan*), and *Commentaries of Ku-liang* (*Ku-liang chuan*). They were called commentaries (*chuan*) because they were supposedly to complement the *ching* which, in this case, was the *Spring and Autumn Annals*. They were variably dated from the fifth to the second century B.C. Among the three the *Commentaries of Tso*, attributed to a man named Tso Ch'iu-ming, was the most widely read during the later centuries as it contained many historical episodes lyrically written. Tso Ch'iu-ming was said to have also written *Conversations of the States* (*Kuo yü*) which was a description of events in the various states. *Documents of the Warring States* (*Chan-kuo ts'e*), by an anonymous author, was a book of similar nature dealing with a later period. The *Bamboo Annals* (*Chu-shu chi-nien*), a history of Tsin, was discovered in an ancient grave in the third century A.D. It bore that title because the text of the discovered copy was recorded on bamboo slips, an ancient material for writing. The original copy was subsequently lost, and the existing work, bearing the same title, is a reconstructed copy and contains mere fragments of the original. Finally, there was the *Book of Filial Piety* (*Hsiao ching*) which, since its composition in the third or second century B.C., had been a standard text used to indoctrinate school children on that virtue until the twentieth century.

The discussion of ancient Chinese literature is incomplete without mentioning the works of two southern poets, Ch'ü Yüan and Sung Yü, though their works did not form a part of the Confucian tradition. Ch'ü Yüan (343?–277 B.C.), according to a biography written in the second century B.C., was "broad in knowledge and clever with words." He had been a high-ranking official in Ch'u until the king listened to other people's slanderings and dismissed him. In despair, he eventually committed suicide. He left us several works among which are *Sorrows* (*Li sao*) and *Nine Songs* (*Chiu ko*). His poems were imaginative and lively, and his style was so unique that it was widely copied during succeeding centuries. The copied form, fully developed during the Han dynasty, was known as *fu*. Sung Yü was said to have been a disciple of Ch'ü Yüan, but we have no way to ascertain this tradition. We know little about his personal life except what he said about himself. If we can believe literally what he said, he was extremely handsome and was very popular with young damsels (a good indication that Confucian morality, the term as we understand today, was not yet known to the southerners in his life time). A dozen of his *fu* have survived, and they generally followed the same style as that of his alleged teacher.[1] The works of both writers are collectively referred to as *Elegies of Ch'u* or *Ch'u Tz'u*. They differed from the works of northern writers in content as well as in form.

TAOISM

In terms of influence over the life and thought of the Chinese people for the next two thousand years, Taoism was second only to Confucianism. As the Chinese did not regard philosophies (or religions) as mutually

---

[1] *Fu* is a literary form or style, but it is also the poem or poems written in such a form or style.

exclusive, the same person could be influenced by both philosophies without consciously identifying them. Both philosophies constituted a part of the Chinese cultural heritage, and a Chinese was a follower of the entire Chinese heritage rather than a particular school of philosophy. Since Confucianism was the dominant school of thought since the second century B.C., a Chinese before the twentieth century inevitably identified himself as Confucian, even though he also believed in other philosophies or religions such as Buddhism. This is very confusing to a Westerner who is brought up to believe that if a person follows one religion he cannot follow the other and that he has to leave his own church in order to join another church. As an average Chinese did not belong to a church organization in the Western sense of that term, there was no higher authority than himself with regard to religious matters. Such being the case, he wound up in believing a little of every major philosophy or religion as existed in China; he himself selected whatever he wished to believe. A Chinese intellectual might be said to be a synthesis of the entire Chinese heritage rather than a follower of a particular school of thought or religion. Since he was a recognized leader in his community, his approach and attitude towards different philosophies and religions were also shared, by and large, by his fellow countrymen who might not be able to read or write.

According to tradition, the founder of Taoism was a mystic figure named Li Erh, better known as Lao-tzu which means, literally, the Old Master. As a matter of principle, Lao-tzu was opposed to all activities, including the activity of founding a school of philosophy. However, Taoism came into being despite Taoist philosophy and has influenced Chinese life and thinking ever since. According to Ssu-ma Ch'ien, the great Han historian who lived in the second century B.C., Lao-tzu was born in Ch'u early in the sixth century B.C. He served as a librarian in the Chou Archives and was reported to have received and conversed with Confucius when the latter was a young man. After the interview, said Ssu-ma Ch'ien, Confucius was greatly impressed and compared Lao-tzu to a flying dragon who "rode the wind and cloud up in the sky." Seeing that Chou had begun to decline, Lao-tzu decided to leave his post for good. On his way to the west he was recognized by a warden on a mountain pass who begged him to write a book. The book was written in short order, amounting to some five thousand words. The biography ends by saying: "He (Lao-tzu) then went away, and nobody knew what had become of him." The book Lao-tzu had allegedly written was later known as *Tao-te Ching*, or *Book of Taoist Virtue*.

Modern historians wonder whether Lao-tzu in fact ever existed, let alone the correctness of these details of his life. The present version of the *Book of Taoist Virtue* was definitely a later creation, written in the fourth or third century B.C. Its authorship has not been determined and perhaps never will be. If it was written in the Warring-States period, as is generally assumed, it may be regarded as another form of reaction (as distinct from that of Confucianism) to the incessant warfare and political chaos of contemporary China. When a man becomes intensely dissatisfied with the existing situation, he either attempts to take positive steps to correct it as in the case of the Confucians, or resigns himself to his fate, takes a negative attitude towards the entire world, and resorts to drawing whatever comfort he can from an extremely disagreeable situation. The author who wrote the *Taoist Virtue* belonged to the second category. Like the Confucians, he condemned war, but in much stronger terms. What was the sense of this endless slaughtering? he asked. Every general was a murderer in disguise, because his glory was built on the dead bodies of thousands of innocent men. Every hero was an evil man by definition because his heroism indicated nothing except that he knew how to kill more people with better efficiency. Therefore, " a man of Tao avoids and loathes weapons as tools of bad omen" and "views every victory celebration as a funeral rite." A hero was to be pitied because he did not know his own guilt and ignorance.

The same kind of argument permeated the entire work. It condemned all values which contemporary society held dear. It subjected to scrutiny all conventions and traditions that men had long taken for granted. Its attack was as sweeping as it was intensive. What was the value of power, fame, and wealth? it asked. Had they done any good to the men who possessed them, not to mention the harm they did to others? If a government had to exist, let it govern the least. The best rulers were those who did not rule, and the less effective a government was, the better it would be. "The more there are laws, the more there will be thieves"; and mankind was much better off without any of them. Wisdom and knowledge contributed nothing to human welfare except discontent and unhappiness, and "the most ignorant is always the wisest." "By abandoning wisdom and discarding knowledge, the people will benefit a hundredfold." Education was worse than useless; as long as people were not taught to be good, they would not know what was bad and consequently would not become bad. A simple, primitive society was much more preferable than a complicated, advanced one where "luxury breeds envy and envy brings strife," and no one was happy in the end. An ideal society was economically self-sufficient and should produce nothing except necessities to satisfy the basic needs. No one envied another, as no one had more than the other had. As envy ended, so would rivalries and strifes. Wars would cease, since no state could gain anything by invading others. In such an ideal society, "there is no use for boats and vehicles, nor arms and soldiers. . . . While neighboring states are so close that people can hear the crowing of a cock or the bark of a dog in other states, they will not visit one another for the entire duration of their lives."

If all existing values were discarded, what would be the values a man of Tao should adhere to? His values were those of an infant, unspoiled by the existing society. He did not know gains or losses; honor or shame; ambitions or disappointments. He should be weak and meek; he should be withdrawing and submissive. Nothing was weaker than water; yet, it could destroy the hardest mountains. Nothing was lower than the ocean; yet, it received the mightiest rivers. The more we tried, the less we would succeed. A man of Tao, therefore, preferred a constant state of inactivity. What was Tao? Tao was formless and shapeless; it could not even have a name because a name presupposed a form. It could not be discussed because what could be discussed was beyond the sphere of Tao. Tao, in fact, was nothing, and "nothingness" was the essence of Tao. Why was "nothingness" so important? Because without "nothingness" nothing in the world could have existed. "Nothingness" was the "mother of all things," including the universe. From "nothingness" the universe had arrived and to "nothingness" it would eventually have to go. In the physical universe which "nothingness" had created, "nothingness" pervaded in everything and was the most useful thing of all existences. How could stars move without "nothingness" in between? Could they exist in the first place? What was the usefulness of a bowl? It was useful because it was hollow and contained "emptiness" within itself. A window or door was useful because "nothingness" dominated its existence. We could not exist one day had there been no "nothingness" around us. For one thing, we could not even breathe.

Thus, Taoist "mysticism," when reduced to common sense terms as the author of *Taoist Virtue* attempted to do, was nothing mysterious at all. The book did not attempt to explain the inexplainable; nor did it deal with the supernatural. It was in line with the secular, humanistic pattern as we have discussed earlier in this chapter. Besides *Taoist Virtue* the other important work in Taoism is the *Book of Chuang-tzu* whose author, Chuang Chou, was believed to have lived in the fourth century B.C. *Chuang-tzu* was a more substantial book, and its present version, edited and commented on by Kuo Hsiang (d. 312 A.D.), contains thirty-three separate essays. Generally speaking, it followed the same basic beliefs as those of *Taoist Virtue;* its style, however, was more biting and incisive. Its author was witty and humorous; invented conversations between ancient sages to strengthen his own argument; and was good with a tale or fable to bring home a particular point. Like *Taoist Virtue,* its major purpose was to smash conventional values, including those in morality and ethics. As expected, it singled out Confucianism as its main target of attack.

Confucian morality, argued Chuang Chou, benefited only those who were satisfied with what they had and discriminated against those who sought change. It glorified the mighty and the powerful, and it kept the lowly in their proper place. Take thievery as an example. Those who stole nations became kings and dukes, and those who stole such small things as "fishing hooks" were condemned as thiefs and were punished accordingly. Who were worse thieves, the kings and dukes who killed thousands of innocent people to steal a nation or the small man who was forced by hunger to steal a fishing hook? The bigger the crime, the more people glorified it. A crime ceased to be a crime and became heroic instead if it was big enough and involved the lives of thousands of people. The Confucians, by glorifying the bigger crimes and condemning the smaller ones, committed a hypocritic act. Moreover, the kings and dukes whom they glorified might not have the virtues as possessed by a common thief. Chih, one of the most notorious thieves of ancient times, was asked whether a thief had any virtues. "Certainly he has," Chih replied. "To know where the valuables are hidden indicates high intelligence. To enter into a house first shows bravery. To leave it last is an act of righteousness. To know whether to enter a house or not is wisdom. And to divide spoils according to merits is justice. It is impossible to become a great thief without possessing all of these five virtues."

If a thief could conceivably possess more virtues than the more respectable members of a society, the society might do well to reexamine its own sense of values. The continuous existence of fixed ideas and accepted conventions did not necessarily mean that they possessed irreparable, intrinsic values; it might have resulted simply from long usage. Did usage itself constitute a value? Should mankind subject itself to the bondage of convention simply because it had been hallowed by time? Man would have done a great service to himself if from time to time he stopped to reappraise his own beliefs. To illustrate, Chuang Chou invented a story about himself. Chuang Chou was about to die, he said, and his students were thinking of purchasing the best coffin in town when the inevitable arrived. "Why should you buy any coffin for me at all, not to mention a good coffin? I prefer to use the whole universe as my coffin," he protested. "We are afraid that your body would be eaten up by hungry vultures," replied his students. "It is true that without a coffin my body will be eaten up by vultures. But do you realize that with a coffin my body will be eaten up by ants? Now you are proposing to take my body away from the vultures and give it to the ants. Is that fair to the vultures? Why should you favor the ants and discriminate against the vultures?"

Being skeptical about Confucian rites, Chuang Chou was equally merciless in his attack on other Confucian virtues such as *jen* and *yi*. Moral standards were invented by man; they were superficial and superfluous. There was an inherent futility in man's endeavors, including his search for moral values. A wise man, knowing such futility, adhered to the principle of inactivity. What could be done would be done spontaneously by nature. The more man interfered with the function of natural order, the worse the situation would become. The futility of human endeavors did not stem from the incapacity of the human mind to acquire knowledge and ability; rather, it resulted from the very nature of reality itself. Reality was by definition contradictory, ironical, and uncertain. Its natural uncertainty was totally beyond man's control. A reality might be an illusion, and *vice versa*. What was the difference between these two anyway? They might be the same thing. To illustrate, Chuang Chou again invented a story about himself. He said that once in his dream he had become a butterfly, fluttering hither and thither, to all intents and purposes a butterfly. After waking up, he was confused. "Did I dream of becoming a butterfly or is the butterfly now dreaming of becoming me? Was the butterfly in my dream or am I now in the dream of the butterfly?" Such was the irony of life, the irony of all existences. "What it is" might be "what it is not," and *vice versa*. A crooked tree, said Chuang Chou, might live a long life because it was not good enough for making anything and was consequently spared by woodsmen. On the other hand, a goose that could not cackle ("has no virtues") would have to go to the kitchen table first. As far as he was concerned, Chuang Chou concluded, he preferred to live like an old tortoise "dragging my tail in the mud," rather than going around, trying to save mankind.

Why was Taoism so appealing to the Chinese? Its political and social theories were impractical, and its advocacy of returning man to his natural primitiveness was clearly an exercise in impossibility. To understand the appeal of Taoism, we have to understand the nature of man. Man was the most sentimental of all creatures, and the satisfaction of some of his emotional needs required the adoption of a Taoist mentality. Was a man really happy when he had acquired all elements that constituted wordly happiness: power, wealth, fame, etc.? Even during his "happiest" moment, there was a sense of sadness and he missed something which he could neither name nor describe. Man alone possessed such sensitivity which no other animals possessed. While a Westerner might renounce the worldly cares and seek comfort in religion, a Chinese might retreat to a mode of negativity in which all values, worldly or spiritual, became blurred and insignificant. Spiritual values were still values and were therefore not Taoist, because Taoism was the negation of all values, religious or otherwise. It was against any efforts, including efforts to attain a better life in the next world. If we have to use an analogy to drive home our point, Taoism was a state of drunkenness without being intoxicated. To be sure, not all men wished to adhere to the principle of Taoism at all times, because, whatever intrinsic merits it might possess, it was simply impossible to do so in the physical world. Yet, when it arrived, it provided great strength and comfort.

The appeal of Taoism might also have been related to China's social and economic environment. Life was extremely uncertain in China where one's fate was often beyond his own control. A prospective harvest might be suddenly ruined by a heavy storm, and a high ranking official might unexpectedly lose favor and be summarily dismissed. By recognizing the Taoist contention that one extreme was bound to be followed by another extreme in the opposite direction, one was more inclined to be moderate in success and acquiescent in failure. The recognition of the inevitability produced a Stoic indifference during the time of distress, engendered great courage to face what had to be faced, and provided cheer during even the most unhappy moment. It compelled modesty from the most proud and injected dignity into the most humble. Taoism was likely to be most popular during trying times: natural disasters, wars, and governmental oppressions, about which an ordinary mortal could do nothing except submit. Knowing the inevitability and facing it with resignation were in themselves a source of strength.

So far we have confined our discussion to Taoism as a philosophy (*Tao chia*). There was also Taoism as a religion (*Tao chiao*). The standardized English translation makes no distinction between these two, and consequently there is a great deal of confusion. As to the Taoist religion, it developed along independent lines and will be discussed in a later chapter.

"A HUNDRED SCHOOLS CONTEND"

The ancient philosophers made no distinction between philosophy as a speculative science and philosophy as a way of life. As their major concern was human relations, a philosophy was meant to be lived by rather than to be discussed in abstract terms. How a philosopher conducted his personal life spoke more eloquently of his philosophy than anything he might have said or written. In other words, he was a living manifestation of his philosophy. Aside from Confucianism and Taoism there were numerous other schools during the period under discussion, and each of them came into being as it sought the best remedy against the background of a turbulent, disorganized society. Confucianism and Taoism have survived, but most of the other schools did not. It is a matter of debate whether survival was a reflection of merit. Perhaps not. Since the other schools exercised less influence on later Chinese than the two main streams of thought, we shall discuss them more briefly.

Among the various schools one of the most outstanding was unquestionably the philosophy of Mo Ti, or Mo-tzu, which means Master Mo. He was born to a humble family in North China about the time that Confucius died. One hundred years later, his philosophy had become so widely accepted that it challenged Confucianism as the leading system of thought in the fourth century B.C. The main themes of his philosophy were two, universal love and non-militarism, the latter being a supplement to the former. While Confucians defined love as emanating from man's inner self and extending towards the outward world in different degrees according to the closeness of the receiving persons, Mo Ti believed in universal love, the same in intensity for all men under Heaven. Confucius emphasized the importance of filial piety, but Mo Ti ridiculed it on the ground that to place priority on family was clannish and selfish and that family welfare was often advanced by Confucian believers at the expense of the welfare of the whole society. It was the welfare of the whole society, said Mo Ti, that should be a gentleman's first concern. The welfare in Mo Ti's mind was a material welfare, as contrary to the moral welfare expounded by Confucius. As universal love implied equal well-being, not until the humblest man in the nation acquired a satisfactory standard of living could any one else have the right of enjoying the same. Customs and conventions that presupposed wasteful spendings with no real increment of material well-being should not be condoned, and they should be in fact abolished. In this respect, Mo Ti singled out Confucian rites as the target of his strongest criticism because he regarded them as purely wasteful. There was no sense of spending so much for a funeral, argued he, when one had not enough to eat; nor was it a sound logic to favor the dead at the expense of the living. To oppose waste, he urged the practice of thrift and the finding of ways and means to increase production. This utilitarian approach led him to elevate Yü above all China's past heroes, as Yü was the hard-working, legendary engineer who many centuries before had dug canals and built dams to protect North China from future floods. Emphasizing the importance of basic, material needs, Mo Ti spoke for the poor and the humble. An ideal society in his mind was a welfare state of material sufficiency rather than a moral commonwealth with emphasis on intangible values.

No mere theorists, Mo Ti and his followers substantiated what they believed with concrete actions. Coming largely from the lower strata of society, most of them artisans and engineers, they were deft in technical and manual work. Mo Ti led them to tasks which he believed would bring about a better human relationship. In order to love, one had to learn first not to hate. Of all the forms of showing hatred, warfare was unquestionably the worst. Hence non-militarism was the first step towards universal love. Non-militarism, however, was not synonymous with non-violence; nor did it mean "turning the other cheek." While violence was deplorable, sometimes one had to use it to prevent further violence because persuasion, however convincing, yielded only slow and often ineffective results. As wars were frequent then, Mo Ti mobilized his followers to help the defense of a city or state which had been unjustifiably attacked. Being engineers and artisans, they were expert in defense and in making defensive weapons, and they often gave a good account of themselves. More than once were the invaders stopped when Mo Ti sided with the defenders. This organized group of soldiers and engineers pledged no loyalty to any sovereign or state but only to a principle as interpreted by Mo Ti himself. To this principle his followers were willing to commit anything, even their own lives.

Despite many differences, Mo Ti and Confucius had much in common. Both were motivated by a sincere interest in human welfare and in taking positive steps to advance it, and both accepted the existing form of government, monarchy, as the best kind of government. Like Confucius, Mo Ti insisted that the ruler should be virtuous and should set examples to his subjects, so that "his rule would be in harmony with the wishes of Heaven." The difference was on the emphasis regarding the attributes of a good sovereign. While Confucius talked in moral terms, Mo Ti was more practical and utilitarian. In the treatise *Universal Love* he said:

> I have heard that a man of gentle character loves his friend as if his friend were he himself, and treats his friend's relatives as though they were his own relatives. . . . I have also heard that a good prince places the welfare of his subjects above that of his own. He feeds them when they are hungry, clothes them when they are cold, nurses them when they are sick, and buries them when they die.

Another school of importance was Legalism. There were no conscientious efforts on the part of the Legalists to form an independent school; it came into being as a result of grouping together the writings of those who emphasized the importance of law as the sole means of attaining efficiency in government and orderliness in society. One of these works was *Kuan-tzu*, attributed to Kuan Chung, the chief minister of Ch'i under Duke Huan. It was, however, the creation of a later age. Another work was the *Book of Lord Shang* (*Shang-chün shu*) which, traditionally attributed to Shang Yang, was actually written by an anonymous author in the third century B.C. The leading thinker of the Legalist school was Han Fei (d. 233 B.C.) who wrote *Han-fei-tzu*, the most comprehensive presentation of the Legalist philosophy. Han Fei was a disciple of Hsün Ch'ing, a Confucian philosopher who, unlike Mencius, believed that human nature was basically bad. Hsün Ch'ing's other disciple, equally famous, was Li Ssu who served as Ch'in's chief minister before he died in 208 B.C. If Han Fei was the theoretician, Li Ssu was the practitioner who, as the chief minister, put the Legalist theory into practice. However, there was a strong personal rivalry between these two. Eventually, Li Ssu threw his former schoolmate into jail and forced him to commit suicide. The Legalists, like the modern Fascists, did not believe in such things as love and compassion; power was to be maintained and secured at any cost, including murder.

While Hsün Ch'ing believed in education as a sure means to improve the evil nature of man, his disciple Han Fei proposed the enactment and enforcement of law to prevent his evil nature from running its wild course. To expect goodness from people of their own accord was unrealistic and wishful, said Han Fei. The so-called virtues proposed by Confucians were at best hypocritic pretensions, readily utilized by the pretenders for their own selfish purposes. In fact, no virtue existed without some selfish motive behind it. To build society on virtues, false, fleeting, and unreliable, was like building a house on sand which, being unstable, would collapse eventually. The Confucian *li*, the outward manifestation of virtues, was as superficial as it was wasteful. Confucius' admonition of returning to the golden past was an outmoded thought because the times were different and the need was also different. No institution had a permanent value; the best was such as most fitted each historical period. Therefore, let no one admire any longer "the virtues of Yao, Shun, Yü, T'ang, Wen, and Wu"; new sages should come forward to devise new means for a new age.

What was the current need? The Legalists said that it was law. To use Han Fei's analogy, law was like measures to a carpenter. As a carpenter could not build without the help of measures, a prince could not rule without laws. Law should be just and fair; but whatever the law was, once instituted, it should be equally enforced upon all, for the nobility as well as the peasants. Law should be made exact and clear so that people would know what to do and what to avoid. The offenders should be severely punished, and abiders richly rewarded. In fact, reward and punishment were the two basic weapons in the hand of a prince. Emphasis on law spared the necessity of searching for motives which simply could not be known. Motives unknown, it was the external conduct of which the prince should take account. Virtue could only be measured by external conduct, and laws should be the standard of measurement. What was inside a person was not the prince's business.

The enforcement of law necessitated a strong government and government should be strengthened at all costs. In order to create a centralized and all-powerful state any means was justifiable regardless of moral or ethical considerations. Machiavelian methods were definitely advisable, as long as they could bring results. Every prince had to face the fact that the conflict between the rulers and the ruled was an inevitable and uncompromising one. To safeguard his own superiority, he should employ the inducement of fame and wealth to win him supporters, and coercion and punishment to compel obedience from others. Genuine gratitude never existed, and it was all to the good that it did not exist, since no man would do anything without expecting something in return. A man became moral or law-abiding only when he had no other choice. This kind of cynical argument permeates all of Han Fei's writings.

In an ideal society of the Legalist image, material welfare was definitely more important than the cultivation of virtues. "Only when people are well fed and clothed can they be expected to know the difference between honesty and shamefulness," as Kuan Chung was reported to have remarked. When Shang Yang was the chief minister of Ch'in, he organized the whole state to the last man for the purpose of increasing agricultural production. In Han Fei's thinking, man's virtues should be expressed and judged in two fields only: diligence in work and bravery in warfare. An ideal society was a society composed of well-organized farmer-soldiers governed and controlled by an all-powerful state headed by an omnipotent prince. All men should be good farmers in peace and brave soldiers in war. In peacetime military training went side by side with the tilling of the soil. In such a society there was no need for philosophy or literature, said Li Ssu. Law was the sole subject of learning; government officials were alone the teachers. Conventions and traditions were untrustworthy, however good once they might have been. The most important was the present, and the urgent need of the present, argued Han Fei, was a centralized state wealthy and powerful enough to unify China so to bring back order from chaos. After a copy of Han Fei's work reached Ch'in's reigning prince, later known as Ch'in Shih Huang-ti, he sighed with regret that he was not fortunate enough to have lived in the same age as the author, thinking that Han Fei must have been an ancient sage. He did not know that the author's schoolmate was his own chief minister Li Ssu who was then doing his very best to carry out Han Fei's philosophy.

Confucianism, Taoism, Moism, and Legalism constituted four major schools of thought prior to Ch'in's unification of China in 221 B.C. There were, of course, the lesser schools. The Agriculturalists believed that all material values were derived from land and that farmers alone were producers. They regarded people of other occupations as exploiters and proposed that even kings and princes, to justify the material support they received to maintain their livelihood, should till the field side by side with other farmers. There were also the Dualists (*Yin-yang chia*) who believed that the essence of the universe was the two opposite but complementary forces, *yin* and *yang*, and that all things in the universe were made of varying combinations of the five primary elements: metal, wood, water, fire, and earth. The basic theory of the Dualists was later incorporated into Taoism and was also accepted by many Confucians.[1] Finally, there was the School of Names (*Ming chia*, often translated as School of Dialecticians) whose philosophers, like the Greek Sophists, loved a good argument for the sake of argument. They debated on such matters as whether a white horse was a horse or a hard rock was really a rock. To people of other schools this kind of debate was an exercise in futility. Since it bore no relation to man and his relationship with other men, it was regarded as trivial and insignificant. This school of thought which might have devel-

---

[1] For a detailed description of Dualism, see Chapter VII.

oped as a basis for our modern logic died shortly without an heir. The overemphasis on human relations in China's intellectual heritage killed off the potential growth of a pure, impersonal science.

SCIENCE

Though science was not emphasized in ancient China, there were individuals whose natural inquisitiveness carried them beyond the ordinary confines of human relations. They never received the attention accorded to humanistic philosophers, and most of their contributions remained anonymous. Like many other ancient peoples, the Chinese believed that the revolutions of heavenly bodies had a direct bearing on human affairs. It was not surprising that their major interest should be in astronomy and its related field mathematics. The *Book of History* mentioned one of the earliest solar eclipses on record which was placed at 2137 B.C. Modern archaeologists examined the Shell-Bone inscriptions and found that the total eclipse of the sun in 1137 B.C. as well as the total lunar eclipse in 1311 B.C. were duly observed and recorded. The *Spring and Autumn Annals* recorded thirty-seven solar eclipses of which thirty-three have been positively identified as actual occurrences. In 28 B.C. sun spots were first observed, more than sixteen centuries before Johannes Kepler made his discovery in 1607.

The greatest Chinese work on mathematics before the Christian era was the *Chou-pi Mathematics* (*Chou-pi Suan-ching*), written perhaps in the third century B.C. It contained the Pythagorem theorem ($a^2 + b^2 = c^2$), computations of the distance between the sun and the earth as well as the sun's orbit, quadratic equations, and formulae for prisms, cones, and cylinders. It was stated in this book that a mathematician named Shang Kao was told by Duke Chou (twelfth century B.C.) to measure the "height of the sun." Shang Kao placed three rods of equal length at three different cities with a distance of 1,000 *li* (c. 333 miles) between any two of the three cities. All the three cities were located on a straight line running from the north to the south. On the day of summer solstice (c. June 21) when the sun reached its northernmost point and began its southward journey, the sun shadow of each of the three rods was measured. Knowing the differences between the lengths of the three shadows, continued the story, Shang Kao had no difficulty computing the "height of the sun." The concept of π seems to have antedated the writing of *Chou-pi Mathematics;* however, it was not until the third century A.D. that the Han mathematician Liu Hui came out with a nearly perfect answer, 3.1416.

The ancient Chinese of the pre-Ch'in period used the frequency of a musical tone as the standard of determining correct measures and weights, just as modern scientists use the velocity of light for the same purpose. The standard tone was that of Yellow Bell (named after the legendary ruler Huang-ti or Yellow Emperor), a pitch pipe which, according to modern scientists, yielded a sound frequency of 348. One-ninth of the Yellow Bell was a standard Chinese inch (*ts'un*); the internal space of the Yellow Bell which contained 1,200 standard grain was the smallest unit of volume, *sha*; and the total weight of 2,400 standard grain (which filled up two Yellow Bell pipes) constituted the basic weight, *liang*. *Liang*, literally, means "double" or "two." Applying the principle of sound frequency, the ancient scientists were able to make different kinds of pitch pipes as music instruments. Lengthening or shortening the Yellow Bell pipe by one-third of its existing length repeatedly, they were able to produce a variety of harmonious, melodious notes. It was reported that as early as the sixth century B.C. they had discovered the seven pitch notes which we are using today. Of course, they called these notes by different names (*kung, shang, chüeh*, etc.) instead of do, re, mi, etc.

In the field of applied science the Chinese paid great attention to irrigation work and flood control as dictated by circumstances. We know little about the engineering details that accompanied the construction of numerous dams and dykes in North China before the Warring-States period. However, by the third century B.C. hydraulic engineering had become an advanced science. The Ch'in engineer Li Ping built one of the most intricate irrigation systems in western Szechuan which, after more than two thousand years, is still in working order. The soundness of his engineering seems to indicate that the basic principles of hydraulics must have been known to his predecessors. Another example was the Great Wall. As early as 500 B.C. individual states began to build long walls as a defense measure against northern nomads. However, it was not until the third century B.C. that the Ch'in regime connected them to form what was later known as the Great Wall. Crawling a distance of 1,700 miles, it was an engineering feat of first magnitude.

Though overwhelmingly concerned with humanities, the ancient Chinese did not seem to have done badly in the field of science. Unfortunately, the Chinese achievements were individual, isolated events. There was no such thing as a scientific community in which different scientists could exchange each other's findings and inspire and stimulate their common interests. This contrasted sharply with the lively activities of philosophers. Nor was there a conscientiously accumulated knowledge in a particular discipline which enabled a scientist to follow up what his predecessors had achieved and eventually reach a new height in his own field of specialization. Practically every discovery or invention was the work of an individual genius. There was no precedent to follow; nor was a man sure that his efforts would be appreciated by his contemporaries, let alone posterity. Any scientific or technical invention was regarded as a "small skill" (*hsiao chi*), unworthy of the attention of great statesmen and scholars. Brought up in the Chinese sense of values, a discoverer or inventer tended to look down upon his own achievement. If historians bothered to record his contribution at all, they did so more out of curiosity than out of appreciation. Moreover, being scholars rather than scientists, they could only describe the outward phenomena instead of the underlying principles. Their recordings would not help people of succeeding generations who might have a similar interest. Many new discoveries and inventions must have come into being during each generation, but most of them disappeared with the death of the scientists involved because there were no follow-ups. The few inventions that possessed commercial value (such as drugs) were carefully guarded as family secrets and passed through one designated male member of each succeeding generation. If he died suddenly or prematurely before he had the opportunity to transfer the family secrets to a member of the next generation (usually his oldest son), the invention was lost to the society as a whole. Daughters were not allowed to share such secrets, because they would be married and would carry the secrets to other families. Behind all these impediments to a continuous growth of scientific and technological knowledge was of course the traditional contempt the Chinese held for such knowledge. Confucian scholars had successfully convinced their countrymen of the trivial nature of "small skills" as compared with the overwhelming importance of morality and ethics that governed human relations. If China lacked a tradition in science and technology, these scholars were at least partially responsible.

iii

The Grand Unifications

THE CH'IN REGIME

Early in 221 B.C. the Ch'in state conquered Ch'i, the last of the six rival kingdoms, and all of China, for the first time in history, was brought under control within one jurisdiction. The new administration, known to historians as the Ch'in dynasty, had a territory that extended from South Manchuria to North Vietnam and from the East China Sea to the eastern slope of the Tibetan Plateau, a territory that was one of the largest political units ever appearing on the face of the earth. "Your Majesty has achieved a Great Deed," wrote one of the ministers in his memorial to the king, "a deed that can be achieved only once in thousands of years." Doubtless flattered by remarks like this, the king issued a decree, saying that from then on he should be addressed as the First Emperor, or Shih Huang-ti, and that his successors should be known as Second Emperor,

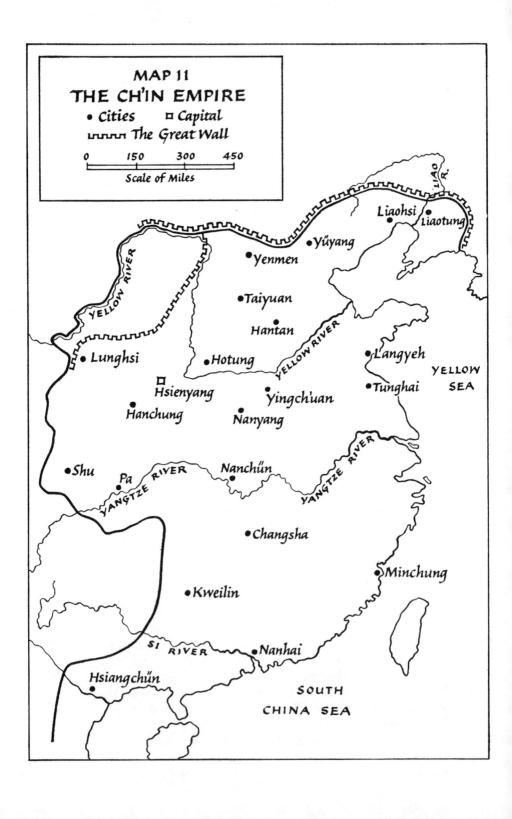

MAP 11
THE CH'IN EMPIRE
• Cities   □ Capital
⌐⌐⌐⌐ The Great Wall

0   150   300   450
Scale of Miles

LIAO R.

Liaohsi
• Liaotung

• Yüyang
• Yenmen

• Taiyuan

Hantan

YELLOW RIVER

• Lunghsi

• Hotung
□
Hsienyang   • Langyeh

YELLOW
SEA

• Yingch'uan   • Tunghai

• Hanchung   • Nanyang

• Shu
Pa   Nanchün
YANGTZE RIVER   YANGTZE RIVER

• Changsha

• Minchung

• Kweilin

SI RIVER   • Nanhai

• Hsiangchün

SOUTH
CHINA SEA

Third Emperor, and so on, "until thousands of generations to come." Two years after the unification, Shih Huang-ti went to Tai Shan, the sacred mountain of Shantung, where he officially received the mandate of Heaven "to rule all that is on earth." A stone monument was erected on the sacred mountain to mark the event; on the monument were inscribed the details of his achievement. "Let posterity abide by the Imperial Will without fail," stated the last sentence of the inscription.

Egoistic as the emperor may sound, there is no indication that his rule was not welcomed. Several centuries of intermittent warfare entailed enormous loss of lives and properties; the weariness was such that people were willing to accept any kind of regime as long as it could bring peace. One may even argue that this political unity, when it finally materialized, was not really unexpected, since all Chinese shared essentially the same cultural background despite the fact that prior to the unification they had lived in different states. Group loyalty, including that to one's own home state, was never very strong during this particular period of Chinese history; there was, however, a shared attachment to a common culture, explicitly expressed in a generally understood written language and a body of literature couched in that language. People could move freely across state lines, and within each state no legal or social discrimination was enacted against residents from other states. The Ch'in state, for instance, regularly searched for the best brains in the country to serve as its chief ministers, regardless of which state they came from. Cosmopolitan in outlook, the Chinese believed that even the difference between Chinese and barbarians was culturally tentative. The people of Ch'u and Yüeh who had been looked down upon as barbarians were readily accepted as equals by their more advanced brethren in the north, once they modeled their institutions after the northern states. This cultural assimilation continued in spite of the frequency of warfare or, perhaps more correctly, was really accelerated by it. All factors being considered, it seemed that political unification was merely a matter of time.

Now that all of China had been brought under his control, how would Shih Huang-ti propose to govern it? He invited suggestions, and soon he found opinions evenly divided between those who favored a revival of the Chou feudalism and those who advocated a highly centralized administration. On the grounds that he had never encountered a trustworthy vassal within the feudal framework, the emperor intervened decisively for centralized administration. All of China was to be divided into thirty-six provinces (forty-one provinces after 213 B.C. when more territories were brought under control) each of which was in turn to be divided into districts. All governors were appointed by and responsible to the emperor, and all officials, high or low, served solely at the imperial pleasure. Though the establishment of centrally controlled administrative units began a long time before (page 59–60), their adoption on a nation-wide scale by the

Ch'in dynasty proved to be a measure of great significance in the long run. In whatever forms feudalism did reappear during the later dynasties, its existence was generally brief, and the establishment of a centralized national government headed by a theoretically omnipotent prince (called Son of Heaven in Chinese) was regarded as a normal course to follow. This marked the beginning in China of what historians often refer to as autocracy or despotism which lasted for more than two thousand years until 1912 when it was replaced by a republic. Though actual power wielded by individual monarchs may have varied from time to time, no Chinese, prior to the modern period, had ever thought of the feasibility of entertaining an alternative, since any alternative to autocracy, in their minds, could only mean anarchy and chaos.

To enable his regime to last "thousands of generations," Shih Huang-ti took concrete measures to eliminate local influence so as to discourage any decentralizing tendencies. Natural fortresses and local fortifications were ordered to be destroyed; military weapons hitherto scattered over the country were collected, melted, and cast into huge bells and statues; and no one was allowed to possess any kind of weapons without specific authorization from the government. To deprive local communities of leadership that might develop and become strong enough to challenge the central authority, the very wealthy were ordered to take residence at the capital, Hsienyang, where their actions could be easily observed. It was said that no fewer than 120,000 families actually moved. Trunk roads with trees planted along both sides at regular intervals were built to link major cities with the capital, so that imperial troops could quickly appear on the scene, wherever trouble occurred. Hsienyang itself was rebuilt to inspire awe and to serve as a symbol of imperial strength. Two hundred and seventy palaces were lined up for a distance of many miles, and towering over all of them stood the magnificent Afang Palace which, we are told, measured "1.5 miles in length, 3,000 feet in depth, and more than 400 feet at its highest point." The emperor himself made regular inspection trips to the four corners of his empire; one trip, for instance, took him all the way to modern Chekiang province.

Following the Legalist adage that it was more important to control people's thought than to control their actions, Shih Huang-ti and his chief minister Li Ssu, a Legalist, introduced a series of programs aimed at cultural regimentation and thought control. The four centuries prior to the establishment of the Ch'in dynasty had been one of the most creative periods in China's cultural history when "thousands of flowers blossomed and a hundred schools of thought contended." Many of these schools continued to advocate their own ideas and criticized what they did not believe even after China had been unified. The new regime concluded that if this trend were unchecked and criticisms of governmental policies unsuppressed, they would soon generate dissension and discontent which in turn might weaken its control over the people, induce revolts, and eventually break up the empire. Accordingly, in 213 B.C. the chief minister Li Ssu petitioned the emperor as follows:

All histories, except the official history of the Ch'in state, should be burned. With the exception of the imperial professors who are authorized to keep books in their respective fields, all others who have in their possession the *Book of Odes,* the *Book of History,* and other works of the various philosophies should report to local authorities and hand to them their holdings, all of which would be subsequently burned. Those who dare to discuss among themselves the contents of the *Book of Odes* and the *Book of History* should be executed in public. Those who dare to criticize the present regime by invoking the ancient writings should be likewise put to death, together with all the members of their families. Government officials who know that violations have occurred but choose not to prosecute would be regarded as having committed the same crime as that committed by the offenders. If books are not burned thirty days after the order has been issued, the offenders should have their faces branded and should be exiled to the northern frontier to build the Great Wall.

Books not to be burned are books of medicine, divination, and forestation. Those who wish to study law could do so under the guidance of government officials.

Shih Huang-ti's approval of the above proposal was followed by a book-burning campaign so thoroughly and viciously conducted that when learning once again became respectable one generation later, many books had to be rewritten from memory, while others were permanently lost to posterity. To cap the book-burning campaign, dissent was vigorously suppressed and dissenters severely punished. In 212 B.C., for instance, more than 460 scholars at the capital were found to have "slandered the emperor" and "spread heretical ideas to confuse the public," and were all sentenced to be buried alive, while those in the provinces, who had been accused of committing similar crimes, were exiled to the frontiers as soldiers. Given this anti-intellectual bent, it is not surprising that when rebellion mushroomed a few years later, few intellectuals rallied to the support of the regime, and ever since few historians have had much good to say about China's first totalitarian regime.

To be sure, not all of the Ch'in regime's policies were as destructive as thought control. Such measures as the codification of legal statues and the standardization of written script and weights and measures were definitely beneficial in the long run. Prior to the unification, legal codes and economic systems were altogether different in different parts of China. Since differences in weights and measures hampered the movement of trade and variances in statutes caused confusion in law enforcement, the Ch'in regime ordered the adoption on a nation-wide scale of a new system of weights and measures as promulgated by the imperial government and the replacement of the legal codes of individual states by the universal Ch'in code which was to be enforced throughout the empire. The Ch'in code followed the Legalist emphasis on "generous reward and severe punishment," and it covered everyday life so thoroughly that it was said to have served the purpose of "a fishing net through which even the smallest fish cannot slip out." From hindsight the most beneficial of the Ch'in regime's reforms was without question the standardization of written script. Before 221 B.C. different scripts of the Chinese language had existed side by side, a situation not dissimilar to the writing of modern German language in either the Roman or the Gothic script except that in the Chinese scripts the variety was much more numerous. In that year the government proclaimed that the Small Script, which had been the official script in the Ch'in state prior to the unification, was to be the standard for all writing and that the use of other scripts would be punishable by law. While this measure no doubt facilitated communication within the empire, the government also was able thereby to erase the last excuse for misunderstanding or misinterpreting the law, since all statutes were to be written in the same script. In its eagerness for standardization the government even decreed that all vehicles were to be equipped with axles of standard lengths. We have no idea, however, how successfully this decree was carried out, since no extant materials have shed any light on this matter.

Ironically, what triggered a rebellion against the Ch'in regime had nothing to do with any of those things described above; it came as a result of the abusive use of manpower. The construction of the Great Wall, irrigation projects, and other public works, the maintenance of a huge standing army for the possible use against the northern nomads and internal rebels, and the conscription of peasants to open up new frontiers of agriculture all required the extensive use of manpower. To be specific, it was said that a regular force of 300,000 worker-soldiers was maintained along the northern frontier; 500,000 persons were sent to the deep south to open up virgin fields; and the construction of the Afang Palace alone engaged some 700,000 coolies. To be sure, corvée had been an old practice in ancient China, but the conscripted workers, prior to the Ch'in period, had been mostly used locally to repair bridges, build roads, or dig irrigation canals, usually in winter after harvest when farmers had more time to spare. Under the Ch'in regime, however, farmers were conscripted whenever the government thought it needed them regardless of winter or summer and were sometimes sent hundreds or even thousands of miles away to be employed in the construction of public projects. The working period was indefinite; many of the conscripted did not expect to return and never did. Outside the government the question that many had only whispered but now began to utter aloud was: how long could the people endure this kind of tyranny?

In 209 B.C. two obscure farmers, Ch'en Sheng and Wu Kuang, were ordered to report for work at Yüyang (modern Hopeh province), many miles away from their home. There was a heavy storm; the roads were destroyed by the flood; and they knew that they could not possibly arrive in time. According to the Ch'in law, the penalty for late arrival in corvée assignment was death. Choosing between certain death and rebellion to stay alive, they did not hesitate. They persuaded their fellow conscripts to do the same and started a revolt which spread like wildfire. Shih Huang-ti had died in the year before (210 B.C.), and his son Erh-shih, or Second Emperor, was theoretically in charge. But the real power was in the hands of the chief minister Chao Kao who, in 207 B.C., put the Second Emperor to death and proposed to install on the throne a nephew of the slain emperor named Ying. Before the new emperor could even be installed, wave after wave of rebels stormed into the capital amid widespread confusion. All members of the royal family, including Ying, were subsequently put to the sword, and all the palaces, including the Afang Palace which, to the rebels, was an example of sheer idiocy at the expense of taxpayers, were set on fire and burned to the ground. The Ch'in empire, one of the most eventful in the history of China despite its short span of life, finally came to an end.

THE HAN REGIME

The capture of Hsienyang by the rebels in 207 B.C. was followed by intensified warfare between two contenders for the vacated Ch'in throne, namely, Hsiang Yü (d. 202 B.C.) and Liu Pang (d. 195 B.C.). On the surface Hsiang Yü seemed to have a better chance to succeed because of not only his noble birth but also his forceful personality which invariably compelled attention or even diffidence, though not necessarily compliance. By comparison, Liu Pang, a commoner, was colorless. He himself readily admitted his lack of proficiency as either a general or a strategist; yet somehow in his own prosaic way he managed to hold the loyalty and service of some of the best brains of contemporary China, notably Hsiao Ho, Chang Liang, and Han Hsin, the triumvirate of wisdom who, according to many historians, were more responsible for the establishment of the Han dynasty than Liu Pang himself. The difference was that while Hsiang Yü relied on his commanding personality and sometimes ruthlessness to compel obedience, Liu Pang was more likely to do the right thing at the right time, thus creating the impression of being more statesmanlike. Nothing can demonstrate this point better than the way each treated the surrendered Ch'in soldiers. Hsiang Yü simply slaughtered them; in one instance, we are told, he buried alive 200,000 of them over the period of one evening. Liu Pang, on the other hand, made conscientious efforts to win them over and convert them into his own following. When

Hsienyang was captured, the first thing Liu Pang searched for and later obtained was the tax register of the Ch'in empire; Hsiang Yü, on the other hand, seized every piece of treasure and every beautiful woman he could find, while setting on fire all those things which he could not carry. Given a contrast like this, there was no question as to who, ultimately, would win.

The Han dynasty, which Liu Pang (also known by his imperial title Han Kao-tsu) founded, proved to be one of the longest and greatest in Chinese history. Except for a brief interruption early in the first century A.D. it lasted more than four hundred years. Before the interruption it was called the Former Han or West Han (202 B.C.–8 A.D.) with its capital at Ch'angan; after the interruption, it was called the Later Han (25–220 A.D.), or sometimes East Han since its capital, Loyang, was located east of Ch'angan. The interruption was caused by Wang Mang (d. 23 A.D.) whose Hsin dynasty lasted only fourteen years (9–23 A.D.).

Having been convinced that the Ch'in regime's quick collapse was largely due to the absence of support from members of the royal family, Liu Pang decided to revive feudalism on a regional basis, combining it with a basically centralized administration to form what we today may call a dyarchy. In other words, two political systems, for administrative purposes, existed side by side throughout the empire: the feudal, hereditary domains that were awarded to members of the royal family, and the centrally controlled administrative units run by bureaucrats who served solely at the imperial pleasure. Total areas for each were approximately the same. Though theoretically sound, this dyarchy did not work very well even during Liu Pang's own lifetime. The purpose of creating feudal domains was to safeguard the royal house; yet in 200 B.C. when he himself was besieged and almost captured by a nomadic tribe in the northern frontier, the forces that came to his rescue were led by provincial governors rather than feudal lords whom he had titled dukes and counts. The lesson was unmistakable, and from then on succeeding monarchs made repeated efforts to reduce the power and influence exercised by their vassals. As one may expect, these efforts were rigorously resisted by the lords, some of whom, powerful and wealthy, sometimes openly defied imperial wishes. It was merely a matter of time before a showdown would arrive.

During the reign of Han Wen-ti (r.179–157 B.C.) Chia Yi (201–168 B.C.), then a young and precocious scholar, suggested to the emperor the breaking up of large duchies to create small ones, but the suggestion was ignored. When Emperor Han Ching-ti (r. 156–141 B.C.) took this suggestion seriously, it immediately provoked a revolt as had been generally expected. Thanks to its able generals, the imperial government quickly crushed the revolt, thus ending the so-called Seven States' Rebellion (154

B.C.). After this, powerful lords were ordered to divide their domains among their offspring; as for those who died without an heir, their territory went to the imperial government. As time went on, areas of central administration continued to expand at the expense of feudal domains. By the time of Han Wu-ti's reign (r.140–87 B.C.) whatever feudalism remained was abolished in toto, *de facto* if not *de jure*.

The disappearance of the Han dyarchy meant that all of China became centrally controlled and that the imperial will, theoretically at least, was to be enforced at every corner of the empire. This necessitated the establishment of an elaborate bureaucracy which, at the time of Han Wu-ti, was by and large completed. At the pinnacle of this bureaucracy and immediately below the emperor stood the Three Chancellors (*San kung*) the senior member of whom, titled Prime Minister (*Tsai hsiang* or *Ch'eng hsiang*), was in charge of the civil administration of the empire. Of the other two, the Grand Chancellor (*T'ai wei*) was responsible for military affairs, while the Grand Censor (*Yü-shih ta-fu*) served as the head of the censorate and concurrently as the Deputy Prime Minister. Below the Three Chancellors were the Nine Secretaries of State (*Chiu ch'ing*) who had jurisdiction over all such matters as that ranging from the supervision of religious worship to the collection of revenues. Their functions were largely administrative as contrary to those of the Three Chancellors who advised and consulted with the emperor on policy matters. On the local level the Han government followed the Ch'in precedent by dividing China into provinces and districts. Altogether there were approximately one hundred provinces, each of which had within its jurisdiction ten to twenty districts. Provincial governors and district magistrates were all appointed by the central government; often provincial governors were transferred to the central government to serve as Secretaries of State, and *vice versa*. Overlapping provincial delimitations was the division of the empire into thirteen inspectional circuits, each of which was headed by a censor (*tz'u-shih*), appointed by and responsible to the Grand Censor at the capital. The duty of the censor was to investigate and report on all matters of public concern, such as famine, banditry, and governmental corruption and to impeach any official within his circuit, including a governor, for delinquency in the performance of his duties. His rank was comparatively low; yet he was given the duty of keeping a watchful eye on the highest-ranking governor.

Bureaucracy needed bureaucrats. How did the Han government find so many of them to staff its own bureaucracy at various levels? This indeed was a problem. Prior to the Ch'in period (221–207 B.C.) this problem did not exist since each prince, within his own feudal domain, simply chose his officials the same way as he would choose his personal servants. The Ch'in dynasty unified China, but it lasted too short a period for an institution of recruiting bureaucratic personnel to develop. At the beginning of the Han dynasty the shortage of qualified civil servants was keenly felt by all concerned, including Liu Pang who, in a decree issued in 196 B.C., promised to confer honor and fame to any "able or virtuous man" who would share with him "the burden of the state." But the shortage continued despite his effort.

It was not until the reign of Han Wu-ti that the recruitment of governmental personnel became for the first time institutionalized. At the capital city of Ch'angan the emperor founded a Central University which each year graduated two kinds of students: the sons and nephews of the highest-ranking officials (annual salary: 2,000 piculs of grain) and the sons and nephews of those who were not so high-ranking, including commoners. The first group, though officially titled "members of the imperial guards," actually served as a manpower reservoir from which all the ministries and commissions in the central government recruited their officials, usually at the lowest rank. The second group, on the other hand, returned to their native provinces or districts where they served as local officials. In addition to this recruitment via the Central University there was also the nation-wide selection system (hsüan-chü). The system itself consisted of two parts, regular selection and imperial invitation. Regular selection was a process whereby local governments recommended "able and virtuous men" to the central government to be appointed as government officials and was conducted regularly, usually once a year. Imperial invitation, on the other hand, was held sporadically when unusual circumstances called for the recruitment of unusual talents, such as the recruitment of flood-control experts after the Yellow River had broken its dikes or the recruitment of "unconventional scholars" (who must know foreign languages besides other qualifications) to serve as the emperor's envoys to distant kingdoms. Moreover, whenever a national disaster occurred, whether it be widespread famine, foreign invasion, or even the eclipse of the sun, the emperor would normally issue an invitation to all who were "wise and knowledgeable" to deliberate and make recommendations on the affairs of the state. Needless to say, those who were recruited via the emperor's special invitation always enjoyed great prestige and commanded high respect. Tung Chung-shu (second century B.C.), generally regarded as the greatest Confucian scholar of the Han dynasty, was recruited in this manner in 134 B.C.

Most of the institutions described above were introduced during the reign of Han Wu-ti, with an impact not to be erased for the next two thousand years. Thus, as early as the second century B.C., the Chinese had built a bureaucratic system with such a refinement that it was unequalled anywhere in the contemporary world and was not to be surpassed until the modern period. This bureaucracy doubtless strengthened the autocratic form of government; but, without it, argued many Chinese scholars, the empire simply could not be efficiently governed.

MILITARY EXPANSION

Throughout the Ch'in-Han period (221 B.C.–220 A.D.) China's most formidable foreign opponent was the Hsiung-nu, a Turkish-speaking nomadic tribe which, at its apex of power early in the second century B.C., held sway over a territory that extended all the way from Eastern Mongolia to the Aral Sea (Map 12). From time to time its cavalrymen rode southward and raided, much to the distress of the people in the border regions. Shih Huang-ti pushed them back in the Ordos area (modern Suiyuan province), but even he could not do more than erect the Great Wall to discourage future incursions. Early in the Han dynasty when Liu Pang felt strong enough to meet its challenge head-on, his army was routed and he himself almost captured, as noted earlier. Two years later (198 B.C.) he had to appease the Hsiung-nu chief by marrying one of his princesses to him, sending him silk, wine, and rice as "gifts," and calling him "brother." But the kind of peace he established through appeasement did not last long. Throughout the first seventy years of the Han dynasty invasions and counter-invasions went on intermittently, with the Chinese usually winding up at the losing end.

Why were the Han Chinese not able to cope with the Hsiung-nu whose population was merely a fraction of that of China and whose material wealth was equally inferior? To answer this question is to examine the advantages of the Hsiung-nu warrior, advantages which a peasant soldier cf China did not have. First, he was better trained for warfare, having been taught to "shoot foxes and rabbits during childhood" and human beings when he grew older. "He can stand the elements better, tires less easily, and can fight for a much longer time without water or food," commented the Han statesman Ch'ao Ts'o (d. 154 B.C.). Second, he was more efficient as a cavalryman, "shooting accurately while galloping at full speed" and possessing a mobility which the Chinese peasant soldier could not match. Third, being a nomad, he had no cities or population centers to protect and could therefore "move about like birds." The Chinese, of course, had certain advantages too. Their military equipment, either defensive or offensive, was far superior; more importantly, they were much more disciplined as a group, as contrary to their nomadic counterparts who "fight for their own material ends like hungry vultures, but disintegrate quickly upon a setback and disperse readily like flying clouds." It is difficult to compare these two sets of advantages between the Chinese and the Hsiung-nu; the key factor that could tip the balance

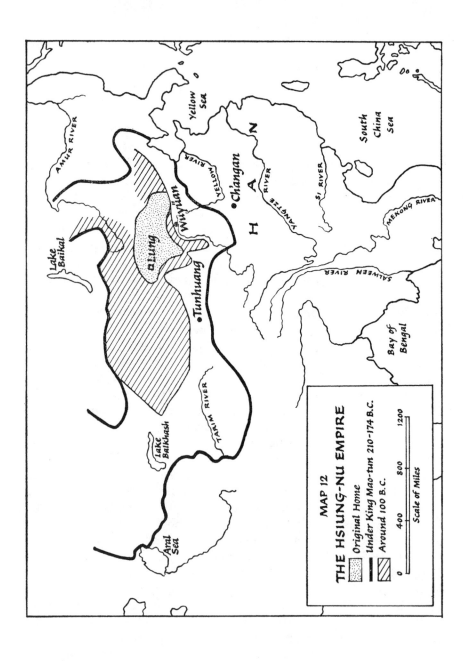

MAP 12

THE HSIUNG-NU EMPIRE

Original Home

Under King Mao-tun 210-174 B.C.

Around 100 B.C.

Scale of Miles

0   400   800   1200

in favor of one side or the other seems to be the quality of leadership. At the peak of their ascendancy (210–174 B.C.) the Hsiung-nu had Mao-tun as their khan, easily the greatest leader they had ever produced. In 140 B.C. when Han Wu-ti ascended the throne, the situation materially changed because this emperor was not only a Chinese Mao-tun but also much more.

Dynamic and full of vitality throughout his life, Han Wu-ti devoted himself to military conquests and territorial expansion besides introducing many domestic reforms, some of which have been previously described. The conquests and the expansion may be briefly summarized as follows:

1. In 127 B.C. a major expedition against Hsiung-nu was sent north-ward under the command of General Wei Ch'ing (d. 106 B.C.); as a result, most of the modern Inner Mongolia was annexed as part of the Han empire. Again in 119 B.C. an even larger force was organized under General Huo Ch'ü-ping (d. 115 B.C.) who cleared Outer Mongolia of Hsiung-nu forces and reached as far as Lake Baikal. Between 104 and 102 B.C. General Li Kuang-li (d. 90 B.C.) went westward, passed across the Pamir mountains, and brought under the Chinese control what is known today as Russian Turkestan.

2. In 109 B.C. two expeditions, one on land and the other by sea, were simultaneously launched against Korea. In the following year four administrative provinces were established in what is now North Korea.

3. In 112 B.C. all the areas known today as Kwangsi, Kwangtung (including Hainan Island) and North Vietnam were conquered, and nine administrative provinces were established in their stead.

4. In 111 B.C. the territories that covered modern Kweichow and Yunnan were brought under the Han control.

In due course the conquered areas where agriculture could be profit-ably practiced became either Chinese provinces (such as Yunnan and Kweichow) or culturally Sinicized states, such as Korea. The territories north of the Great Wall and west of the Hohsi Corridor (modern Kansu province), however, could not be so easily converted, since they were either arid or semi-arid and the Chinese type of agriculture, with the exception of isolated oases, could not be successfully carried out. Thus the impressive victories which Han Wu-ti had scored against the Hsiung-nu could only provide a temporary relief and could not, in the long run, solve the basic problem of conflict. Whenever the Chinese became weak, it was almost certain that the nomads would march southward again. During the first two decades of the Christian era when China was in the midst of dynastic changes, the Hsiung-nu were again on a rampage, looting and burning in the border provinces. Fortunately for the Chinese, they soon split into two groups hostile toward each other. The northern group was more aggressive and warlike, and the southern group, pressed by its northern neighbors, had to seek protection from the Chinese. The Chinese

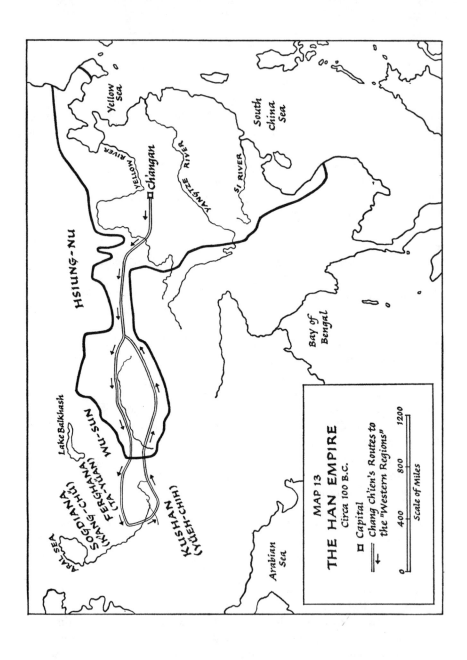

Yellow Sea

South China Sea

Yellow Sea

YELLOW RIVER

□ Ch'angan

YANGTZE RIVER

SI RIVER

HSIUNG-NU

Bay of Bengal

Lake Balkhash

WU-SUN

SOGDIANA (K'ANG-CHÜ)

FERGHANA (TA-YÜAN)

ARAL SEA

KUSHAN (YÜEH-CHIH)

Arabian Sea

MAP 13

THE HAN EMPIRE

Circa 100 B.C.

□ Capital

⟶ Chang Chien's Routes to the "Western Regions"

0   400   800   1200

Scale of Miles

settled them in Inner Mongolia, hoping to erect a bulwark against the more aggressive northerners. One generation after China had been once again unified under the Later Han regime, the Chinese began to go on offensive and, allied with the southern Hsiung-nu, twice (once in 73 A.D. and again in 88 A.D.) pushed the enemy all the way to the Altai Mountains. The Hsiung-nu, after this defeat, never recovered their former strength.

An important by-product of the Hsiung-nu campaigns was the opening up of the eastern section of a trade route which appears in many maps of the ancient world as the Silk Road. The Road began at Loyang and Ch'angan, passed across Central Asia, and eventually reached the Mediterranean, with a total distance of almost four thousand miles. The first episode that led to the opening up of this route was the exploration by Ch'ang Ch'ien (d. 114 B.C.) who, in 139 B.C., was sent by Han Wu-ti to Central Asia to seek allies against the Hsiung-nu. In his first trip the Chinese emissary failed in his primary objective of obtaining allies; but, having been detained by hostile tribes along the road for a total of thirteen years, he learned a great deal about their customs and traditions, goods they produced as well as goods they wanted but could not produce, in addition to geographical information which was of obvious military value. His second trip, conducted in 119–115 B.C., was more successful, culminating in an alliance with the Wu-sun, a nomadic tribe living in the Ili valley (modern Sinkiang). The second episode that had a direct bearing on the establishment of the Silk Road occurred two hundred years later and was centered on the exploits of Pan Ch'ao (d. 102 A.D.) of the Later Han dynasty who, by sheer daring and ingenuity, brought most areas of Central Asia under the Chinese control (73–97 A.D.). Then he sent his lieutenant Kan Ying westward, with the ostensible purpose of getting in touch with the Roman Empire (called Ta Ch'in by the Chinese). Kan Ying went as far as the head of the Persian Gulf where he was advised not to advance further by native sailors who warned him of the great danger of sailing on the uncharted Arabian Sea. His mission failed, and the two great civilizations of the ancient world, Roman and Chinese, never did officially meet.

Once the trade route was opened up, it benefited people and governments of all sides. The Chinse imported horses, cattle, and furs and hides from Central Asia, while the Central Asians placed an even greater value on Chinese manufactured products, especially silk, some of which eventually found its way to the imperial city of Rome. Imports other than horses and cattle proved to be more significant in the long run, such as cucumber, walnut, sesame, and caraway seeds, all of which enriched the Chinese diet; grapes that served as a new material to make wine; and clover that could be planted as forage or plowed under as fertilizers. From the Central Asians the Chinese also learned to play such musical instruments as *heng-ch'ui* (a variation of flute), *p'i-p'a* (a string instrument similar to the guitar), and *hu-ch'in* (often translated as Chinese violin). All in all, it would seem that the Chinese were more indebted to the Central Asians in this interchange than the other way around.

ECONOMIC POLICIES AND WANG MANG'S REFORM

Before the 120's B.C. when Han Wu-ti began his numerous campaigns of conquest, the country had been at peace for many decades, and the laissez-faire policy of some of his predecessors, such as Han Wen-ti and Han Ching-ti, had brought about an economic prosperity seldom seen before. "Imperial granaries were filled to capacity with grain, so much so that it overflowed its containers, rotted, and became inedible," recorded historian Ssu-ma Ch'ien (d. about 85 B.C.), a contemporary of Han Wu-ti. "The imperial treasury had an abundant supply of cash in reserve, so abundant that a large number of coins had not been in circulation for a long time, the strings used to hold them together were often found to have been broken, and it became extremely difficult to count them." This picture of affluence was equally observable among the people. While the wealthy drank the finest vintage wine and rode in the most expensive carriages, the lesser well-to-do also earned enough to make both ends meet. The reason for this affluence, partially at least, was the steady decrease in taxation. For instance, the poll tax of 120 standard coins for each adult male per year that had been introduced in 203 B.C. was reduced to 40 standard coins, to be paid triennially, by the 170's B.C. Even this small amount, that approximated 13 standard coins per year, was sometimes waived altogether. After Han Wu-ti ascended the throne, however, the situation quickly changed. His conquests may have brought greatness to the nation, but, from a taxpayer's point of view, it was definitely much easier to live before rather than during or after his reign.

To raise revenue to finance his military campaigns, Han Wu-ti introduced a variety of measures, such a governmental monopoly of the salt and iron industries as well as that of coinage, an increase in the poll tax, a tax on liquor, the debasement of currency, and the sale of ranks and titles. Though none of these measures was welcome to taxpayers, the most damaging turned out to be a property tax. Beginning in 129 B.C. a series of imperial decrees called for the periodical reports by taxpayers on the value of their properties and the imposition of taxes on the reported items. Since the rate (5 percent) seemed to be no better or worse than that for most of the taxes then in existence, the property owners showed no great alarm about it. Yet in the law there was this crucial provision that "those who fail to report on the properties they own or make false reports will be exiled to the frontier for one year and their property confiscated, with half of the confiscated property awarded to the informer." In 114 B.C. when the government was hard pressed for more financial resources, it took full advantage of this provision to raise additional revenues and shamelessly encouraged people to inform on one another. A nation-wide hysteria ensued, and the result was predictable. Many merchants with more than an average income became bankrupt, while the government confiscated and acquired large quantities of movable and immovable assets, including land and slaves. "For the first time in a long period," commented a Han historian, "the government had more than enough to meet all its expenses."

Prior to this disaster, the merchants had enjoyed a good life under the Han regime. It is true that Liu Pang had once prohibited them to wear silk and ride in carriages, but this social discrimination was rarely, if ever, carried out. In fact, their strength continued to grow despite discriminatory legislations. "Our law degrades the merchants," said Ch'ao Ts'o in 156 B.C., "but the merchants have become increasingly wealthy nevertheless." Early during Han Wu-ti's reign a number of families had amassed enormous fortunes, especially those in the iron-mining and iron-smelting business. The influence of businessmen can be demonstrated by citing the career of Sang Hung-yang who, as a merchant's son in Loyang, rose steadily higher in the bureaucracy until he eventually became the finance minister of the empire. The first blow to the businessmen came in 118 B.C. when the iron-mining and iron-smelting industry was nationalized. Four years later, a more serious blow was delivered when practically all wealthy or well-to-do merchants lost all they had in a nation-wide, hysterical campaign against alleged tax evasions, as has been previously described. To substitute the merchants for some of the roles they traditionally played, the government introduced in 110 B.C. the so-called market stabilization program, buying goods that glutted market and selling them when they were in strong demand. Though the ostensible purpose of this program was the stabilization of prices, the government had also in mind the realization of a handsome profit that had normally belonged to the merchants. After a series of anti-mercantile measures like this, business confidence was never the same and businessmen never recovered their former financial health. The equilibrium between commerce and agriculture was destroyed for good, and the Han economy almost exclusively oriented toward agriculture.

In agriculture the most serious problem confronting the Han government was the inequality of landownership. After the Ch'in state abolished feudal land tenure and permitted the buying and selling of landownership (p. 63), the ancient ideal of equal landownership was invariably destroyed. The situation was not helped by its policy of encouraging the enclosure of small farms to promote efficiency and the opening up of new fields by great landlords. The process of land concentration continued, only to be accelerated further when the Han dynasty was established. By the end of the second century B.C. the situation had become so serious that Tung Chung-shu, in a memorial to the emperor, strongly recommended remedial measures. "While the wealthy have land that extends from one tract to another," said he, "the very poor do not have a spot of earth where they can plant their two feet." For those who tilled others' land, the rent was as large as 50 percent of harvested crops. Taxes were high; requisitions were numerous. Often in debt, sometimes they had to sell their crops immediately after the harvest when prices were low. Then in the spring they had to borrow money at high interest to start the sowing season and thus incurred an even larger debt. As debts accumulated, they sometimes had to sell their women and children as slaves. The moment would eventually arrive when they either quit farming of their own accord or faced forcible eviction. Without a means of livelihood, many of them resorted to banditry in order to keep themselves alive. "Thousands of bandits were convicted and sentenced to death each year," said Tung Chung-shu.

Among the remedial measures Tung Chung-shu suggested were the reduction of taxes and corvée assignment, the abolition of government monopoly of salt and iron, and most importantly, the limitation of land-ownership to forestall land aggrandizement. Han Wu-ti, however, was not in a receptive mood, since he needed the cooperation of great landlords to finance his military campaigns. Consequently nothing constructive came out of Tung's suggestion. As the first century progressed, population continued to grow until it reached the official figure of something like 60 million (59,594,978) by 2 A.D. The actual figure was perhaps twice as much, since most people, to avoid the increasingly heavy taxation, never reported their presence on the face of the earth. Increasing population reduced the amount of land per capita and worsened the already deteriorating situation. Finally in 6 B.C. a program was formulated whereby the amount of land and the number of slaves owned by each individual were made proportional to his rank and position in the government. The maximum amount of land and the total number of slaves that the highest-ranking prince was entitled to own were limited to thirty *ch'ing* (454 acres) and two hundred persons, respectively. But this program was never implemented, as powerful interests connected with the royal family successfully sabotaged it before it could be carried out. It was not until Wang Mang usurped the throne and established himself as the emperor that drastic measures were taken to reverse a trend that had gone on for more than three centuries.

Economic factors aside, Wang Mang's ascension to power was closely related to and partly resulted from some of the basic weaknesses that then existed in the power structure. In an autocracy such as that practiced in China where all power, theoretically at least, was vested in the monarch, no factor in government was more important than the kind of leadership he could provide. Good leadership was difficult to find in any case, especially in a Chinese palace environment where the emperor, as a normal practice, was isolated from outside contact by concubines and eunuchs. After Han Wu-ti, mediocre monarchs succeeded one another. With nothing better to occupy themselves, they indulged themselves in debauchery. One emperor (Han Yüan-ti, r. 48–33 B.C.), having too many concubines to know all of them personally, kept a complete file of their portraits in order to decide with whom he should spend a particular evening. Not to be outdone, his successor (Han Ch'en-ti, r. 32–7 B.C.) died of a heart attack while making love to one of his favorites. As these monarchs shielded themselves from the unpleasant affairs of the state behind a feminine screen, their maternal and conjugal relatives fought for the control of the state. The fate of one emperor was so pathetic that after his death he was officially titled Ai-ti, or Emperor Sadness (6 B.C.–2 A.D.). Since this situation obviously could not last any longer, Wang Mang lost no time in taking advantage of it.

The Wang family, by supplying the reigning monarchs with empresses, was the dominating power toward the end of the Former Han dynasty. While the female members of the Wang family controlled the royal weaklings, its male members occupied the highest positions in the imperial government. Not all of them were bad ministers, however; they served the government as well as their family interest to the best of their knowledge. Wang Mang, the last member of the Wang family to achieve great power, was particularly reputed for his proficiency in Confucian learning, modesty, and hard work. He had built his reputation so well that once when he was forced into temporary retirement by his political enemies, hundreds of Confucian scholars petitioned for his reinstatement. On another occasion after he had refused to accept a high honor out of professed modesty, a petition of half a million signatures urged his acceptance. As he became more popular, his power and influence increased proportionally. In 6 A.D. Baby Emperor Ying, aged two, ascended the throne, and Wang Mang was appointed the regent, with the title of Acting Emperor. Many Confucian scholars stated openly that the Han dynasty had lost the mandate of Heaven and that Wang Mang was the new sage destined to found a new dynasty. In 8 A.D. Wang Mang took the advice and called his new dynasty Hsin which, in Chinese character, means "New."

Today historians refer to Wang Mang as a reformer; what he had in mind was really a revival, a revival of the golden past that had allegedly existed early during the Chou dynasty. Whenever criticized, he defended himself by quoting Duke Chou and Confucius, saying that these two sages would have done the same thing had they lived in the time as he did. Of criticisms there were plenty, since his programs were the most revolutionary in memory. In 9 A.D., the very year his dynasty was formally established, the following decree was issued:

From now on all land belongs to the nation, all slaves are private possessions, and neither land nor slaves are subject to trade. A household which has a male membership of less than eight but a landholding of more than one *ch'ing* [about 15 acres] should distribute the excessive amount among its relatives, neighbors, or fellow villagers. The landless will receive land from the government in accordance with the law. Those who dare to criticize this well-field system, a system devised by our ancient sages, will be exiled to the frontier where they will serve as defenders against the monstrous barbarians.

Wang Mang's other reform measures included the market stabilization program, patterned closely after a similar program introduced earlier by Sang Hung-yang (p. 113), and also the money lending program which entitled people, whenever in need, to borrow money from government operated banks. The interest was 10 percent per year, as contrary to the free market interest that went as high as 30 percent. Important enterprises such as the manufacturing of liquor, iron, salt, and coins were declared government's monopolies upon which the government relied for raising revenue to meet its administrative expenses.

However good the motives were behind these reforms, they never achieved the results that Wang Mang had hoped. For one thing, they were thrust upon an ill-prepared nation without adequate planning. No sound organization was ever established for their implementation; in many localities wealthy merchants were employed as regulation agents, though they were more interested in enriching themselves than serving justice. Whenever a law encounterd opposition in its enforcement, the government quickly changed it, instead of giving it adequate time to yield results. As the law changed often, people had no idea what the law was, especially in remote areas where communication and transportation were more difficult. The outcome was confusion and anarchy. The small farmers whom the reforms were supposed to benefit suffered with the rest of the population. When Wang Mang finally realized the futility and called an end to the whole reform program, enough damage had been done and revolt had already begun. Moreover, the powerful landlords had never reconciled themselves to the new regime which proposed to confiscate their properties. Once started, the revolt against Wang Mang soon spread over the entire country. The landlords provided the leadership; the peasants filled up the rank and file. It was this combination which overthrew the short-lived Hsin dynasty.

THE LATER HAN

An ironical aspect of the revolt against Wang Mang was its peasant background, indicating that either the peasants had never heard of the new emperor's reform programs aimed at the improvement of their welfare or circumstances had become so desperate that promises, however well-phrased, simply came too late to do them any good. The immediate cause of the rebellion was classical: widespread famine and the government's inability to cope with it. Toward the end of Wang Mang's reign harvests failed in large areas, and the most adversely affected were Shantung and Hupeh. In Shantung the rebels called themselves Red Eyebrows, as they painted their eyebrows red to distinguish themselves from government troops whenever they went to battle. The Hupeh rebels, on the other hand, were often referred to as the Green Foresters, since they started their rebellion at a place named Green Forest (Lulin), near Tangyang of modern Hupeh province. In no time the rebellion snowballed to hundreds of thousands of angry peasants for each group, looted wherever they went, and defeated every contingent which the government sent against them. To make its rebellion more "legitimate" or "respectable," each group installed a descendant or alleged descendant of the Liu family as its "king," so as to take full advantage of the popular belief that Wang Mang had unjustifiably usurped the throne and that the royal house of Liu would in due course be restored to its former position. In the fall of 23 A.D. the rebels entered Ch'angan, put Wang Mang to the sword, and solemnly declared the imperial city their war booty where they pillaged with a joy that amounted to ecstasy.

Obviously rebels of this nature could not accomplish anything constructive, and the restoration of peace and the establishment of a new regime would have to come from some other source. Liu Hsiu (d. 57 A.D.), with a better grasp of the situation, quickly took the task upon himself. Orphaned at the age of nine, he was reared by his uncle, a powerful landlord who had at one time sent him to Ch'angan to study Confucian classics. In 22 A.D. famine spread to his native district Nanyang (modern Honan province) where the landlords, unable to mollify the anger of hungry peasants, decided to lead them in revolt. When Liu Hsiu, generally known as a cautious, conservative person, showed up in their strategic conference, they were really amazed. They were even more surprised when they learned that whenever a city was captured, his army was the only one that did not engage in looting. "What did you join the rebellion for?" asked his mystified colleagues. Liu Hsiu did not answer this question to the best of our knowledge, but we know what the answer was. One year later Wang Mang died; the competition for the vacated throne became thus a free-for-all struggle. It took five more years, however, before Liu Hsiu defeated all his competitors, including the Red Eyebrows and the Green Foresters, and brought all of China under his control. Even before this came to pass, he had, in the summer of 24 A.D., assumed the imperial title. He chose the ancient city of Loyang as his capital since Ch'angan, having been sacked repeatedly by the rebels, was no longer presentable enough to serve as a center of power.

The Later Han dynasty, founded by Liu Hsiu (known also by his posthumous title of Han Kuang-wu), lasted 13 emperors and 195 years (25–220 A.D.). The first eighty-one years (25–106 A.D.) were a period of conquests and consolidation, landmarked by successful military campaigns against the Hsiung-nu and Pan Ch'ao's conquests of Central Asia (p. 111). The next thirty-one years (106–147 A.D.) were a period of drift, generally downward, and witnessed nothing particularly important, with the possible exception of China's repeated defeats at the hand of the Tibetans. Beginning in 147 A.D. when Han Huan-ti (r. 147–167 A.D.) ascended the throne, the downward drift began to pick up momentum, accelerated with the passage of time, and eventually raced the dynasty to its inevitable plunge into history. For those interested in the study of dynastic cycle, the Later Han provides a good model to follow.

After 88 A.D. when the Hsiung-nu were finally and completely defeated, the most powerful group the Later Han regime had to contend with was the Ch'iang, located in modern Tibet. They raided China's border areas repeatedly in the 100's A.D. and at one time (108 A.D.) penetrated deep into Northern Szechuan, thus threatening to cut off the transportation lines that linked Northwestern and Southwestern China. Chinese border officials, unable to cope with the invaders, forcibly moved Chinese residents eastward by destroying their crops and houses and resettled them further away in safer regions. It was not until 117 A.D. that a counteroffensive proved successful and pushed the Ch'iang back to their home in Tibet. But the matter was far from being settled. In the 140's and again in the 160's the Ch'iang once more launched their attacks, only to be defeated by a massive Chinese force in 167 A.D. Seventeen years later these invasions and counterinvasions started all over again and, in fact, went off and on long after the Later Han dynasty itself had gone into oblivion. Meanwhile all the border areas that extended from modern Ninghsia to Sikang had been so ravaged that their recovery was not to come about until 150 years later.

In the administration of its bureaucracy the Later Han regime followed the pattern of its more illustrious predecessor with some modifications. In addition to the Three Chancellors who supervised the work of the Nine Secretaries of State, a new post, that of the Grand Tutor (*T'ai fu*), was created. As the imperial counsellor, he outranked the Three Chancellors; but actually his duty was that of Chancellor-at-large without portfolio, advising the emperor when the latter wished to listen to him. Another important new post was that of the Grand General or Marshal (*Ta chiang-chün*), usually created on an *ad hoc* basis to meet a military emergency. In theory he was a subordinate of the Military or Grand Chancellor (see p. 105); once he was outside the boundary of China (such as in a military campaign), however, only the emperor could give him direct orders. Tou Hsien (d. 92 A.D.), the conqueror of the Hsiung-nu during the first century A.D., was the most famous general to hold that post. As time went on, the power of the administration slowly moved away from the Three Chancellors and the Nine Secretaries of State to the Imperial Secretariat (*Shang-shu t'ai*) which, charged with the handling of all incoming petitions and outgoing decrees, was in a better position to influence policy decision than the regular administrative organs. The Imperial Secretariat was headed by a Secretary-General (*Shang-shu*) who, assisted by a Deputy Secretary-General, had under his jurisdiction six bureaus. The bureaus were divided on a functional basis such as "local administration" and "barbarian affairs."

In the matter of local administration the Later Han regime followed the Former Han example by adopting a two-tiered system consisting of provinces and districts. For the purpose of imperial inspection (as contrary to civil administration) several provinces were grouped into a circuit headed by a censor, in the same manner as they were done during the Former Han dynasty (pp. 105–106). In 188 A.D., however, an important change was made, a change that was of great significance in the long run. The censor, whose power was confined to that of inspection and impeachment, was replaced by a governor-general (*mu*) with civil and military authority; and the governor of a province, who outranked the censor, now became an administrative subordinate of the higher-ranking governor-general. In short, the inspectional circuit had became an administrative viceroyalty (*chou*); and the three-tiered system that consisted of viceroyalties, provinces, and districts had replaced the two-tiered system. The imperial government thought that by enlarging the highest administrative unit on the local level, it would increase the power and efficiency of local administration, at a time when there were increasing disturbances in the countryside such as banditry, riots, and, most seriously, an open rebellion staged by a group of people who called themselves Yellow Turbans (see p. 130). In other words, the creation of the three-tiered system resulted from the chaotic state of affairs then existing in the empire and was in itself indicative of the downward trend of the dynasty's fortune. Once created, viceroyalties quickly became semiautonomous, when the central government was continually weakened by internal strife and corruption. By the beginning of the third century A.D. the so-called governors-general were to all intents and purposes independent warlords who fought among themselves and helped bring about the dynasty's eventual demise.

The inability of the central government to control warlordism resulted partly from the structural weakness of the power center. Of the thirteen emperors of the Later Han dynasty only the first two (Han Kuang-wu and Han Ming-ti) ascended the throne as adults. The age of the rest ranged from two to nineteen when they were solemnly proclaimed as Sons of Heaven. Since as children they could not very well govern the empire themselves, their mothers, as a general rule, served as regents. While in rare cases a capable empress dowager might actually rule in behalf of her son, most of them, living in isolation as dictated by custom, relied on the men they trusted, usually their relatives, for advice and counsel before making policy decisions. These relatives, consequently, were placed in the position of power and actually ran the government. As the emperor grew up, he found himself surrounded and forcibly advised by his mother's relatives who, to keep themselves in power, isolated him from outside contact. This, naturally, caused great resentment.

To whom could the young man turn for help? Other than his mother's relatives the only males with whom he had daily contact were his personal servants, namely, the eunuchs. Though the eunuchs were never known for their principle or wisdom, the young emperor, in his eagerness to assert himself, would have to take them as his allies. The leaders of the eunuchs were consequently appointed to high and responsible posts in order to counterbalance the power of the dowager's relatives. Two factions were thus formed, and they soon clashed against each other. With the emperor's blessing the eunuchs often won out and the dowager's relatives were either executed, exiled, or sent to prison. This was especially true if the dowager no longer lived. Having purged their opponents and gained the reins of government, the eunuchs eventually became too powerful even for the emperor who by then had found himself a mere puppet of his nominal servants. They with their followers built their own political machines from the imperial to the local level with no other objective in mind except maintaining themselves in power. This situation continued until a new child emperor came to the throne. The new empress dowager would serve as regent, purge the eunuchs, and elevate her relatives to high positions. And then the whole process would be repeated. Though greatly simplified in its description here, this tragic succession of events occurred repeatedly during the Later Han dynasty.

Both the eunuchs and the dowager's relatives had a third party to contend with, namely, the scholar-gentry. After the time of Han Wu-ti Confucian teachings had become a universal subject of learning among the country's elite and the only avenue whereby an obscure scholar in the countryside could make himself known. Since only the leisurely rich could devote full time to the many subtle interpretations of the Confucian classics, the landowners inevitably furnished most members of the scholar-gentry class. The selection system, first introduced in the second century B.C. but greatly institutionalized during the Later Han dynasty, provided this class with a means of acquiring power since the criteria of selection invariably centered on such Confucian virtues as filial piety and such Confucian learning as the *Five Classics*. To defend their interests as well as a lofty Confucian principle, the scholar-gentry insisted that only those who had been objectively chosen through the selection system or had passed successfully a competitive examination could receive appointments from the imperial government as officials. They called themselves the "pure group" (*ch'ing liu*), implying clearly that those who had obtained their positions through avenues other than Confucian learning were less than pure, including, presumably, both the dowager's relatives and the eunuchs. However, whenever they were forced to make a choice between the two groups, they invariably chose what they regarded as the lesser evil, namely, the dowager's relatives who, though not Confucian scholars themselves, had been raised up to respect Confucian learning, and would not mind letting the scholar-gentry occupy lesser positions as long as they could have absolute power themselves. With the eunuchs, on the other hand, the matter was entirely different. Once their power was established, they made the selection system either a dead letter or an outright farce and employed only those who pledged absolute loyalty to them rather than the government. This most Confucian scholars were reluctant to do. The scholar-gentry may have been as much self-motivated as the other two groups; but, in a society like China where most people were illiterate, they represented whatever public opinion there was and could, if they so chose, serve as an effective bulwark between the masses and an increasingly oppressive government. There is no question as to which group was the least evil among the three.

The first major clash between the eunuchs and the scholar-gentry occurred in 166 A.D. and was triggered by a murder case involving a Taoist magician. The magician, confidently predicting that a general clemency was forthcoming, instigated his son to commit murder, in order to prove beyond any doubt his ability as a diviner and the confidence he had in it. The murder was committed within the jurisdiction of Governor Li Ying, a recognized leader of the scholar-gentry, who lost no time in arraigning the murderer and sentenced him to death. Before the sentence could be carried out, however, an imperial decree of general clemency arrived, invalidating the death sentence. Furious over the accuracy of the magician's prediction which he denounced as superstitious nonsense and knowing only too well that the magician was a political henchman of the eunuchs, he ordered the immediate execution of the murderer, despite the imperial order to do otherwise. The eunuchs induced a disciple of the magician to sue the governor, accusing him of having not only wilfully violated an imperial decree but also conspired with scholars and students to form an illegal alliance against the government. The emperor ordered the arrest of all leaders of the alleged illegal group known as the prohibited party, and more than two hundred persons were subsequently thrown into jail. Three years later several hundred leaders of the scholar-gentry, including a former Grand Censor, were convicted of conspiracy and were later either executed or exiled. The conflict reached a climax in 172 A.D. when more than one thousand students at the Central University in Loyang were summarily arrested for harboring conspiratorial and antigovernment thought. By then the victory of the eunuchs was complete.

The abuse of power by the eunuchs finally forced an alliance between the dowager's relatives and the leaders of the scholar-gentry. However, with the imperial seal in their hands and occupying important positions in the government, the eunuchs were hard to dislodge. In desperation, Ho Chin (d. 189 A.D.), the brother of Empress Dowager Ho, decided to take drastic action. In 189 A.D. he invited Tung Cho (d. 191 A.D.), a military governor then stationed at Hotung (modern Shansi province), to send troops to help his cause. But the plot was discovered, and Ho Chin was murdered in his residence. Upon hearing about his death, two sympathizers of the prohibited party decided to go ahead with their original plan without waiting for the arrival of Tung Cho's troops, for they feared that they themselves might be next in line to be murdered. They and their followers quickly surrounded the palace and threatened to set it to fire if the eunuchs did not come out of their own accord. When the threat failed, they stormed in. The order of the day was to kill all the beardless, and more than two thousand persons were slaughtered on the spot, including many who were not eunuchs but unfortunately happened to be beardless. Soon Tung Cho arrived at the head of a large force and proved to be as ruthless as any of the eunuchs. He deposed and then put to death the reigning emperor as well as his mother Empress Dowager Ho and installed on the throne a nine-year-old prince of his own choice later known as Han Hsien-ti (r. 189–220 A.D.), while reserving absolute power for himself.

The assumption of power by Tung Cho as a dictator ended the Later Han dynasty all but in name. Since no one except the puppet emperor had in the meantime assumed the imperial title, traditional historians chose not to pronounce the dynasty's end until 220 A.D. when the leader of another house officially replaced Han Hsien-ti as the emperor and founded a new dynasty. As for this, more will be said in the next chapter.

CULTURAL ACTIVITIES

Liu Pang, who at one time used a scholar's hat as a urinal to show his absolute contempt for all intellectuals, soon learned that intellectuals, when properly humored and regularly paid, were an asset rather than a liability, especially to an emperor who had a large bureaucracy to staff. But his interest in intellectuals never went beyond civil bureaucrats and trial judges, and it was not until the reign of his son Han Hui-ti (r. 194–188 B.C.) that the out-dated Ch'in law of prohibiting the ownership and traffic of forbidden books was annulled (191 B.C.). From then on learning and education continued to gain in general esteem and popular support. Learned men were often invited to serve the government as "imperial professors" (po-shih) who allegedly "know all about the past and the present" but who actually functioned as catalysts in the discussion of contemporary issues. Chia Yi, a precocious scholar previously mentioned, served in that capacity in the 170's B.C. With the ascension of Han Wu-ti to the throne in 140 B.C. things began to move more quickly, in education as well as in practically everything else. In 136 B.C. government-endowed professorships on the *Five Classics* were created in the capital, and eleven years later (125 B.C.) fifty young men of eighteen years old or older, who "look respectable, love learning, and have always been dutiful toward their elders," were recruited as the professors' students. These professors and students formed the nucleus of what was then known as the Central University (*T'ai hsüeh*) which continued to grow with the passage of time until it had a student enrollment of more than three thousand shortly before the beginning of the Christian era and of more than thirty thousand toward the end of the second century A.D. Besides doing research and teaching students, the professors were often called upon by the government to deliberate and advise on foreign and domestic issues, to give expert opinion on rituals and ceremonies for important occasions, and sometimes even to serve as roving envoys in the provinces, reporting local conditions and suggesting improvements. As for the students, they sometimes got themselves deeply involved in politics, as noted earlier, though their main concern was supposed to be their studies.

Even on the local level the promotion of learning relied heavily on official patronage. Early during the Han dynasty one of the most famous patrons of learning was Liu An (d. 122 B.C., also known by his feudal title of King Huai-nan) who had on his payroll several thousand Taoist scholars and hangers-on at one time. Under his guidance these Taoist scholars wrote and compiled the *Huai-nan-tzu* ("The Work of Huai-nan"), later acclaimed as an important contribution to the Taoist tradition. Another example of local initiative was provided by Wen Ong who, as governor of Szechuan in the 140's B.C., established his own schools in Chengtu and sometimes sent some of his brightest products to Ch'angan to study law with the imperial professors. He was so successful with his educational work that it was decreed as a model to follow by the imperial government; shortly afterwards, we are told, schools were established in all the provinces.

It is interesting to note that while Liu An was promoting Taoism in Huai-nan (modern Kiangsu province; south of the Huai River), Wen Ong, a specialist in the *Spring and Autumn Annals*, personally taught his students the various aspects of Confucianism in Szechuan. This indicates that as late as the 140's B.C. "a hundred schools of thought" still contended; if anything, Taoism seemed to be more in vogue than others since both Han Wen-ti and Han Ching-ti, the two succeeding emperors before 140 B.C., patronized Taoism more than any other ideology. Soon, however, there was a reversal of royal patronage. The man primarily responsible for this reversal was Tung Chung-shu who, through his own erudition and courage, successfully won approval from the imperial government of a number of pro-Confucian measures, such as the creation of government-endowed Confucian professorships, the establishment of the Confucian-oriented Central University, and most importantly, the proclamation of Confucianism as the state ideology. "Those teachings that lie outside of the Six Arts [Six Confucian Classics; see p. 79] or Confucian learning should not be allowed to advance and in fact should be abolished," he said in a memorial to Han Wu-ti. The acceptance of this proposal by the emperor proved to be a step of monumental importance. For the next two thousand years Confucianism was the officially patronized ideology for practically all the Chinese regimes; prior to the Communist triumph in 1949 rarely could a Chinese advance far in governmental circles without professing some belief in the teachings of Confucius. Since then Tung Chung-shu has often been hailed as the greatest contributor to the Confucian cause since Mencius.

Differences in ideology, even in those ancient days, were never so clear-cut as their partisans hoped to make them, and the synthesis of seemingly opposite ideas could be observed even in the writings of such professed doctrinaire as Tung Chung-shu. The Taoists spoke eloquently of nature, while the Confucians' interest was mostly about man. Yet Tung Chung-shu's most important contribution as an ideologist was the elaborations he made on the theory of harmony between nature (literally Heaven) and man. As nature was always perfect, it was man's duty to accommodate and adjust himself to it, for the purpose of not only maintaining his internal peace but also creating a humane and orderly society. Tung Chung-shu, of course, did not originate this theory; he merely refined it. As early as 178 B.C. we find this interesting decree issued by Han Wen-ti:

I have heard that Heaven installs rulers to govern the people it creates and that it will warn a ruler with natural disasters if he has lost virtue or if his rule has become unjust. On the eleventh month of this year there was an eclipse of the sun. No natural disaster can be more serious than this: Heaven has reproached me!

An important aspect of the theory of harmony between nature and man was man's ability to influence nature by doing what was *naturally* expected from him rather than what his human weakness had compelled him to do. Thus, whenever a natural disaster occurred, whether it be flood, drought, or the eclipse of the sun, a conscientious monarch was mandated to think seriously about his shortcomings, reduce taxes and corvée impositions, or stop an expensive foreign war, had he already been engaged in it. By doing any or all of these things it was hoped that nature would not cause more disasters and would in fact be restored to order, and the harmony between nature and man would be once more established. If he continued his evil ways by doing what was not *naturally* expected from him as either the Son of Heaven or the Father of Man, he became an obstruction in the smooth functioning of natural order and should therefore be either destroyed or replaced. In that case his subjects had both a right and an obligation to overthrow him and his government by staging a rebellion. Thus the theory of harmony between nature and man formed an integral part of the theory of the mandate of Heaven which charged the ruler to rule only for the benefit of the ruled and entitled the people to revolt whenever he ceased to do so.

Aside from government-sponsored scholarship there were works of great importance initiated and completed entirely by individuals. The most famous among them were the *Historical Records* (*Shih chi*) by Ssu-ma Ch'ien and the *History of the Han* (*Han shu*) by Pan Ku (d. 92 A.D.). The former was intended as a universal history of the Chinese world, dating from the dawn of civilization to the time of Han Wu-ti and consisting of a total of 130 rolls. The purpose of this book, said the author, was "to find the laws that govern Heaven and Earth and the reasons that underlie the changes of ancient and modern times." Pan Ku's work, on the other hand, was later known as a dynastic history, covering only one dynasty which, in this case, was the Former Han. It was started by his father Pan Piao (d. 54 A.D.) and completed by his sister Pan Chao (d. about 105 A.D.) who was credited with the eight chronological charts and the treatise on astronomy in the completed work. Since most of it was Pan Ku's own writing, the book has always borne his name alone. His work, together with that of Ssu-ma Ch'ien, set a precedent for the writing of later dynastic histories that followed its format almost without fail, such as their division into royal biographies (*pen-chi*), treatises (*shu* or *chih*), ordinary biographies (*lieh-chuan*), etc.

In passing, one may add a personal note to these two historians.

Ssu-ma Ch'ien, like his father Ssu-ma T'an, was an imperial astronomer and historian. In 99 B.C. he, "forgetting his inferior position," voluntarily offered testimony to the defense of a Chinese general named Li Ling (d. 74 B.C.) who, having been defeated and captured by the Hsiung-nu, should have committed suicide according to the Chinese custom but did not. For this "unforgivable" crime of defending a "traitor," Ssu-ma Ch'ien was punished by castration, a punishment next only to the death sentence in severity according to popular estimation. "The misfortune fell upon me before my book [*Historical Records*] was completed," said he. "Knowing what I had to accomplish, I went through the worst punishments without anger or fear." One hundred years later Pan Ku, a brother of the conqueror of Central Asia named Pan Ch'ao (p. 111), was convicted on a trumped-up charge and died in jail. Prior to his death he had served with distinction under General Tou Hsien in a military campaign against the Hsiung-nu, and his description of that nomadic tribe, based on first-hand knowledge, is still the most authentic among the Chinese sources. The tragic story of these two historians gives ample evidence of the autocratic nature of the Han regime.

For most people who read these two monumental works the appeal is more literary than historical. Both indeed are great masterpieces of literature, and a person can immediately stir up a debate among his learned colleagues if he prefers one author to the other. The style of writing they used is popularly known as the Han style, characterized by its clarity, conciseness, and vigor. When well-executed, it conveys a beauty so aesthetically powerful and moving that it gives a knowledgeable reader an almost indescribable sensation. In addition to the works of Ssu-ma Ch'ien and Pan Ku, such quality can be also observed in some of the best writings of such men as Chia Yi, Ch'ao Ts'o, and Tung Chung-shu, all of whom have been mentioned before. The Han style was repeatedly imitated during the later periods, but this imitation, like all other imitations, was never close to the original. Unfortunately, it is virtually impossible to transplant this literary quality untarnished to a Western language, however able the translator is, because of the great dissimilarity between Chinese and Western languages. The reverse is equally true; one has to read a Chinese translation of Shakespeare to be fully convinced of the validity of this point.

In poetry two forms prevailed over others during the Han dynasty, namely, *shih* and *fu*. We can trace the former to the *Book of Odes* (pp. 79-80) of North China and the latter to the *Sorrows* and *Nine Songs* (p. 83) of South China. In *shih* the Han poets used extensively the five-character style which, according to the T'ang essayist Han Yü (768–824), made its first appearance early in the first century B.C. In this style each line consists of five characters and the last character of every first, second, and fourth lines rhymes. A typical example and also one of the best written is

PAINTED SHELL   The hunting scene on this shell was painted in red and black during the period of either East Chou (770–249 B.C.) or Former Han (202 B.C.–9 A.D.). There are no words on it; the painter is unknown.

the *Nineteen Old Poems* (*Ku-shih shih-chiu shou*), written by an anonymous author or authors. *Fu*, a generally lengthy and more adorned form of poetry, has topics that range from the *Song of a Tailor Bird* (*Chiao-liao fu*, by Chang Heng 78–139 A.D.) to the *Glory of Imperial Hunts* (*Yü-lieh fu*, by Yang Hsiung 53–18 B.C.). The writing of verses in this form was such a mentally exhausting and challenging experience that Chang Heng, we are told, spent ten years polishing and repolishing his *Serenade to the Two Capitals* (*Liang-ching fu*; Loyang and Ch'angan) before he showed the final copy to his friends. Of all the *fu* poets during the Han dynasty the ultimate fame belonged to Ssu-ma Hsiang-ju (179–117 B.C.) who, patronized by Han Wu-ti, produced such masterpieces as *Laments of Ch'ang-men* (*Ch'ang-men fu*) and *Refutation to the Szechuan Elders* (*Nan Shu fu-lao*). The former expresses the sorrows of a scorned mistress, while the latter attempts to allay the anger of weary taxpayers.

Chang Heng, the *fu* poet previously mentioned, is generally regarded as one of the most versatile of the Han scholars. His interest and expertise extended from poetry all the way to astronomy and mathematics. At one time he constructed an armillary sphere to locate planets and stars and traced their movements with remarkable accuracy. More impressive, however, was a seismograph he invented. It was described as composed of a bronze cylinder of eight feet in diameter with the central opening "bulging up like a wine cup." Surrounding a central column in the middle of the cylinder were eight sculptured dragons which represented eight different directions. Whenever an earthquake occurred, one of the dragons would eject a small ball which was then received by a carved toad attached at the base. It was said that by using this device an earthquake taking place several hundred miles away could be easily detected and located. Unfortunately, we know nothing about the underlying principles upon which he built this remarkable instrument. Another scientist worth mentioning was Chang Chi (lived in the 170's A.D.) who wrote *Typhoid Fever and Other Diseases* (*Shang-han tsa ping lun*). Hailed by contemporary physicians as a great saver of lives, the original book, consisting of sixteen rolls, was lost to posterity sometime after 220 A.D. when China was once again plunged into chaos and war. The present version, reconstructed from fragments of the original early in the fourth century A.D., has in it only ten rolls. It is still a standard reference book for Chinese physicians practicing traditional medicine.

Finally, there was Wang Ch'ung (d. *c.* 100 A.D.) who showed great originality in a different field. Skeptical of his fellow scholars' efforts in tracing the many subtle meanings of Confucian classics and critical of their so-called virtuous conduct, he doubted whether Confucianism was the universal truth. Having dismissed the theory of harmony between nature and man, he maintained that nature was no more than a blind but orderly mechanical force and that there was no observable relationship between the movement of heavenly bodies and human events. Nor was the existence of a spiritual world possible, said he, because its existence was contrary to sound logic and good reasoning. As a healthy society could not be created on false assumption, a man could not be true to himself if he simply followed the popular, established conventions without using his own reasoning and knowledge to guide himself. Throughout his book, *Critique of Opinions* (*Lun heng*), he tore into pieces what he regarded as false values. Like many Taoist philosophers before him, he called upon man to return to nature, though his "naturalism" (*tzu-jan*) was not clearly defined anywhere in his book. Being vastly different from the orthodox Confucian philosophy, his ideas may be viewed as a belated reaction against the seemingly endless pursuit of Confucian dogmas which had been the prevailing trend after the second century B.C. On the other hand, they may also be regarded as an indictment against many of his fellow scholar-gentry whose great concern with Confucian virtues often carried them to ridiculous pretensions. Although Wang Ch'ung did not know it, a growing tendency toward Taoist skepticism started with him which was to dominate China's intellectual scene for centuries to come.

ぷ iv

Disintegration
and Amalgamation

DISINTEGRATION

The massacre of eunuchs in 189 A.D. ushered in a long period of turmoil and wars. Except for the West Tsin regime (265–317) which unified China for a short period, China remained politically disunited until late in the sixth century when unification was again achieved under the Sui dynasty. The four hundred years from the second to the sixth century were not only noted for China's military and political weaknesses, which in turn invited barbarian invasions, but they were also noted as a period of political and social disintegration, mass migrations, and culturally, as the time of the reappraisal of traditional values. On the more constructive side, this period witnessed a continuous process of Sinicization among the non-Chinese and the rise of South China as a political and cultural equal of the North. Ideologically, Taoism gained new adherents among the scholar-gentry class as the strength of Confucianism declined. Buddhism had been introduced earlier and now spread far and wide. It became a strong spiritual force and even challenged the supremacy of Confucianism in the field of morals and ideals. Taoism, Buddhism, and Confucianism remained the main spiritual and ethical forces in China until modern times.

Towards the end of the Later Han dynasty, nominal sovereignty was still vested in the emperors, but actually they were puppets of whichever ministers or governors were in a position to control them. As rumor gained ground that the Han dynasty had lost the mandate of Heaven, rebellions sprang up like bamboo shoots after an early spring shower. Some had noble, well-defined purpose; others were simply organized banditry. Among the rebels the most destructive was a group called Yellow Turbans, a religious sect which claimed the ability to cure bodily ills through the use of charms and incantations. It was sometimes called "the Sect of Five Bushels," because initiation into membership cost five bushels of rice. As Han prestige continued to decline, the Sect began to exploit popular discontent and transformed its religious functions into those of a political conspiracy; it even had some powerful eunuchs as its allies. In 184 A.D. it raised the standard of revolt; its members wore yellow turbans to distinguish themselves from others. Organized first in the modern Hopeh province, the revolt soon spread to other areas, from Manchuria in the north to as far as Fukien province in the south. City after city fell before the looting and marauding rebels. Governors and magistrates fled as fast as they could. If they were captured, they might be conveniently used as sacrifices for the rebels' "Heavenly God." Powerful as they were, the Yellow Turbans had no appealing ideology nor any constructive programs. Their followers soon became disillusioned and the rebellion collapsed as speedily as it had arisen. By 190 A.D. it had already run its course, after devastating eight provinces for six years. Its leaders were either killed or captured, and most of its followers simply disappeared.

To defend themselves against rebels like the Yellow Turbans and to combat wide-spread banditry in the country, provincial governors were authorized by the imperial government to organize their own fighting forces. Sometimes great landlords took the initiative in mustering large followings for similar purposes, with or without authorization from the imperial government. In such cases, the imperial government usually confirmed the *fait accompli*, granting ranks and titles to local leaders in accordance with their military and political strength. As localism increased, the whole country was divided among military governors and local leaders who owed a nominal allegiance to the crown but who were actually independent warlords fighting one another to expand their own territories. One of them, Tung Cho, marched into the capital and assumed absolute power, as has been described in the preceding chapter. With his army stationed near the capital and his opponents eliminated, Tung Cho could do whatever he pleased. He deposed the reigning sovereign and placed on the throne a young prince, Han Hsien-ti, who turned out to be the last emperor of the Han dynasty. After the imperial authority had all but disappeared, military governors lost their last scruples and one after another declared their independence from central control. In 192 A.D. Tung Cho was murdered by one of his own men. Amid the confusion that ensued, the capital Loyang became a looting ground for soldiers and bandits alike, who enjoyed "burning palaces and starving government officials." This situation continued until the arrival of Ts'ao Ts'ao who managed to restore some kind of order in North China.

Of all the warlords of this period, Ts'ao Ts'ao (d. 220 A.D.) was perhaps the ablest and certainly the most colorful. As his father was an adopted son of a eunuch, he had no family prestige to be proud of and had to depend upon his own ingenuity for his drive towards power. He first became nationally known when, as a military governor, he successfully defended his province against the Yellow Turbans who had run wild in other areas. Through a series of conquests and successful manipulations, he became the new strong man and took over the reins of the imperial government as prime minister. With the imperial authority behind him, he defeated and eliminated one warlord after another until he brought North China under his control. However, he was stopped short in his attempt to annex the south and the southwest. In the south the house of Sun Ch'üan had long established itself as the rallying point of the southerners against the more aggressive north. In 208 A.D. Ts'ao Ts'ao marched his victorious army southward with the explicit purpose of eliminating the last block to the unification of China. The ensuing battle was one of the best known in Chinese history, immortalized in the famous novel *The Romance of the Three Kingdoms*. Though the northerners seemed invincible in land warfare, they were not so skillful in handling warships. Sun Ch'üan and his generals out-maneuvered Ts'ao Ts'ao and forced him to fight a river battle at Ch'ihpi along the Yangtze River in the modern Anhwei province. The northerners were decisively defeated and were forced to withdraw, and Ts'ao Ts'ao had to forget about the unification of China for the time being. After the battle, Liu Pei, an ally of Sun Ch'üan, went westward to conquer the modern Szechuan province. In 220 Ts'ao Ts'ao died, and his son Ts'ao P'i succeeded him as prime minister. Ts'ao P'i lost no time in deposing the last Han emperor (Han Hsien-ti), assumed the imperial title, and named his new dynasty Wei. In the following year, Liu Pei also proclaimed himself emperor and named his regime Shu. Soon Sun

Ch'üan did the same and called his state Wu. Thus China entered the period of Three Kingdoms, Wei in the north, Shu in the southwest, and Wu in the southeast. Of the three kingdoms, Wei was by far the strongest. Yet she was unable to conquer the other two as long as the latter cooperated in their defense. A stalemate ensued and lasted about half a century. After the death of Liu Pei and Sun Ch'üan in their respective countries, Shu and Wu underwent a process of deterioration and were no longer able to resist the more powerful north. Meanwhile the house of Ssu-ma, endowed with able and vigorous leaders, replaced the house of Ts'ao as the real ruler of North China. In 263 Wei conquered Shu. Two years later Tsin Wu-ti (d. 290 A.D.), a member of the Ssu-ma family, deposed the last Wei monarch and proclaimed himself emperor. He changed the dynastic title from Wei to Tsin, sometimes referred to as West Tsin. In 280 Tsin conquered Wu, and China was again unified for a brief period.

BARBARIAN INVASIONS

While the Three Kingdoms were fighting for supremacy in China proper, events of great importance developed in the grassland belt below the Gobi Desert. Towards the end of the Former Han, a precedent was established whereby Mongolian tribesmen who had either voluntarily surrendered themselves or sought protection from Han authorities against their enemies, were granted right of residence within the Chinese border provinces and lived side by side with native Chinese. As the number of these tribesmen grew over the years, Han began to fear that in case of an internal upheaval within China proper they might be incited to revolt by ambitious leaders and become military vanguards to invade China proper. Early in the third century Ts'ao Ts'ao divided them into five tribes, resettled them in the northern parts of the modern Shensi and Shansi provinces, and appointed a Chinese official who resided with each tribe to supervise its activities. After the establishment of the West Tsin regime, this policy of settling nomadic tribesmen within Chinese provinces was continued, despite repeated warnings that in case they revolted, the capital Loyang would be within their easy march. While this policy was originally motivated by the desire of winning goodwill from the otherwise hostile tribes and of bringing them under closer supervision by Chinese authorities, it backfired badly when it became evident that succeeding Chinese governments had neither the tact to win their friendship nor the strength to command their respect. To make the situation worse, both Wei and Tsin habitually looked southward in their struggle for the conquest of China proper; they were negligent in their defense against the northern nomads. Moreover, in their dealings with the barbarians, they

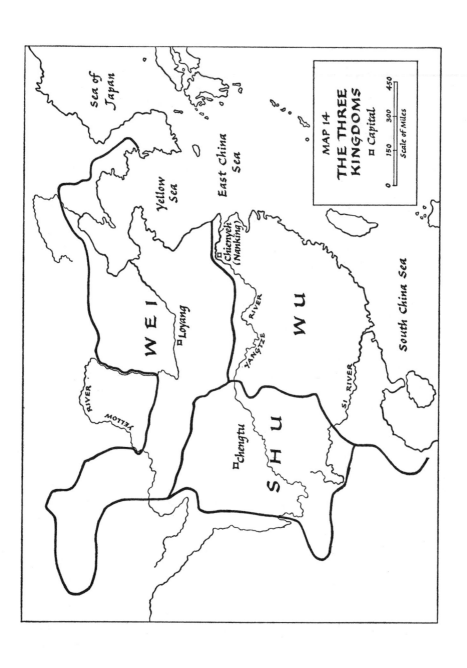

MAP 14

THE THREE KINGDOMS

□ Capital

Scale of Miles

0   150   300   450

Sea of Japan

Yellow Sea

East China Sea

South China Sea

WEI

□ Loyang

YELLOW RIVER

Chienyeh (Nanking)

YANGTZE RIVER

WU

SHU

□ Chengtu

SI RIVER

had no historical lessons to guide them and to enable them to see the forthcoming danger, for until then no barbarian tribes had ever been able to maintain a permanent occupation of China proper. By the time the danger was recognized, it was already too late.

Of course, the invasions could at least have been postponed if there had been no internecine strife within Tsin itself. Even before he unified China, Tsin Wu-ti had unwisely revived a semi-feudal system by dividing large areas of his kingdom among his close relatives. Most of these newly created dukes and counts lived in the capital, even though their fiefs were outside in the country. No sooner had Tsin Wu-ti died than intrigues and conflicts began to develop. To make the situation worse, his son and successor, Tsin Hui-ti, was one of those royal weaklings who had an intelligence no better than that of a child. Once when he was told that people had no rice to eat because of a bad famine, he allegedly retorted, "Why do they not eat meat instead?" His wife Queen Chia, a strong-willed but stupid woman, took over the reins of government and started to arrest and execute those whom she regarded as her enemies. This precipitated a series of murders, assassinations, and even open wars, with the high ranking dukes and counts fighting on one side or another at different times. By 306 A.D. when the strife finally ended, Queen Chia, Tsin Hui-ti, and several dukes had all been murdered in cold blood, not to mention thousands of their followers who had been slaughtered in open warfare. As a result, Tsin was greatly weakened and so there was an excellent opportunity for the barbarians to march southward.

The designation "barbarians" was given by the Chinese to cover all nomadic tribesmen living in a grand semicircle extending from Tibet in the southwest to Manchuria in the northeast, for a distance of more than 2,500 miles. They were barbarian in the sense that first, contrary to the agricultural Chinese, they were pastoral and nomadic; and second, they lacked many refinements generally characterizing a more advanced, sedentary society. During the fourth century many barbarian tribes participated in the invasion of China proper at one time or another. In the north it was the Mongolian and other related tribes that played the leading role; in the west it was the Tibetans who made frequent incursions along the border provinces. In 311 A.D. one of the Hsiung-nu groups, later known as Ch'ien Chao, captured Loyang, sacked the city thoroughly, murdered more than 30,000 government officials, and carried away the rest, including the reigning monarch and an empress dowager. No sooner was a new sovereign proclaimed on the throne than another Mongolian tribe marched southward and captured him too. Meanwhile all North China fell into the hands of the barbarian invaders. With the capture of the last emperor in 316 A.D. the West Tsin dynasty came to an end. Those who managed to escape migrated southward to establish the East Tsin regime south of the Yangtze River.

In the north political power was in a continuous state of flux. One tribal chief made his claim to an imperial title only to be overthrown and replaced shortly afterwards by another chief of a more powerful tribe. Altogether five major tribes established sixteen kingdoms in a period of less than one hundred years; some of them lasted only a few years. Many of the so-called kings were among the worst of their kind: even the worst Chinese tyrants looked like angels compared to these barbarian chiefs. Together they created a Dark Age of one century for future historians to remember. Caring little for moral scruples, they killed and burned whereever they went; sometimes they did this merely for the fun of doing it. By the middle of the fifth century the modern Shensi, Shansi, and Honan provinces were completely devastated. According to one eyewitness, one could walk miles without seeing one house standing or hearing one dog barking. According to another, for every one hundred households less than one had survived the disaster. These were the same provinces that had been the cradle of Chinese civilization for more than two thousand years. Ch'-angan, once the capital of mighty Han, had about one hundred households left. The whole city of Loyang was described as looking like a gigantic garbage dump. The worst among the barbarian chiefs was unquestionably Shih Hu (literally Shih the Tiger) who ruled North China for a brief period during the first half of the fourth century. Among the many outrageous things he did was the conscription of 260,000 farmers to build his palaces in which he kept an official harem of 30,000 concubines and a nonofficial harem of 20,000 more, temporarily recruited from his subjects' wives and daughters. He found great enjoyment in tortures, such as pulling out people's hair, cutting tongues, and gouging out eyes. Fortunately, his reign lasted barely a decade. Shortly after his death, one of his generals ordered all city gates closed, and murdered all people who were directly or indirectly related to the Shih clan. Few survived this massacre.

SINICIZATION

In time even this primitive savagery could be mollified. First, to maintain a permanent occupation, there was the necessity of restoring order and establishing governmental institutions. Since no institutions of their own were capable of coping with the many problems of an agricultural society, the alien rulers had to rely on their Chinese subjects for advice and counsel. It gradually became clear to them that it was much more profitable to tax than to rob and that killing would certainly reduce the number of taxpayers. Eventually they adopted Chinese institutions, ways of life, and even ideologies, and operated their governments within the Chinese framework which had been refined for many centuries. This process of Sinicization was also carried on on the lower level. Though mass Chinese migrations to the south occurred under the immediate impact of barbarian invasions early in the fourth century, the majority of native inhabitants remained and they lived side by side with the invaders. In such broad contacts the backward were invariably inclined to learn from the more advanced in a variety of fields, from language, philosophy, and literature to custom, habits, and even mores. One manifestation of this voluntary assimilation was the mass adoption of Chinese names which made the Chinese and the aliens eventually undistinguishable after two or three generations. Furthermore, there was no bar to interracial marriages, which became a common occurrence, especially among the upper class. The alien rulers took great pride in collecting Chinese beauties. The offspring of these interracial marriages, raised under the Chinese cultural atmosphere, were more inclined to identify themselves as Chinese. All these, of course, helped in speeding up the process of Sinicization. Many of the alien rulers were so Sinicized that they patronized Chinese learning and even read Confucian classics themselves. By the fifth century, barely one century after the armed invasions, the so-called barbarians were in every respect Chinese, and barbarian only when one took pains to trace their genealogy.

The first Sinicized monarch of any importance was Fu Chien who came from a tribe racially related to the modern Tibetans. He unified North China in the 370's and built an empire with territories extending from South Manchuria to modern Sinkiang province in the northwest and southward to the Yangtze River basin. Chinese leaders in the north gave him substantial support and many of them served his government as high ranking officials. In time the regime was Sinicized enough to consider itself a direct descendant of the many Chinese kingdoms of the past, such as those of Yao and Shun, the ideal rulers in Confucian ideology, and regarded as barbarian other nomadic tribes in the north and the northwest which had not been brought under its rule. With broad support from both the Chinese and the non-Chinese after it had unified North China, it seemed logical that it should attempt to conquer South China, then under the East Tsin regime. In 383 Fu Chien mobilized one million men for his southward march, 270,000 in cavalry and the rest in infantry. The East Tsin, his opponent, could only muster 100,000 men to face him along the Fei River in modern Anhwei province. The Tsin army, though small in number, was a well-disciplined group and was under the command of an able general, Hsieh Hsüan. Fu Chien's one million men, on the other hand, was a motley army of green troops most of whom had only recently been conscripted. The battle was one of the most dramatic in military history. After an initial setback the northerners became panicky; everyone took to his heels, including the generals. Men and horses ran into each other; thousands were trampled to death, as the Tsin troops followed them in hot pursuit. Fu Chien himself was wounded in the shoulder by a flying arrow. After his return, he found his empire rapidly disintegrating. The various tribes which had been subject to his rule took the opportunity of his defeat to reassert their independence. The North was again divided and was plunged into intertribal wars for many more decades. The Battle of the River Fei was one of the turning points in Chinese history. Had the North won, South China would have been conquered, and the whole of China would have been unified under a non-Chinese regime for the first time in history.

About half a century after the Battle of River Fei another powerful Mongolian tribe emerged from the grasslands in the North. Endowed by a long succession of capable rulers, it conquered one kingdom after another until in 439 it unified the entire north. The dynastic title of this regime was Wei, but more often it was referred to as North Wei, Later Wei, or Topa Wei, to distinguish it from the Wei dynasty established by the Ts'ao family some two centuries before. It was an energetic and enlightened regime; during its prime it was unquestionably one of the best regimes ever established by a non-Chinese group in the north. The man most responsible for raising it to such high standard was Wei Hsiao-wen-ti who ascended the throne in 471.

Hsiao-wen-ti's contribution as a statesman lay more in his success in domestic reforms than in any achievements he made in military conquests. Realizing the impossibility of conquering the south without running the risk of political disintegration and economic bankruptcy, he concentrated his energy upon consolidating his empire and creating economic prosperity for his subjects. In this respect he continued the policy of his predecessors by promoting agricultural production, reforming the tax structure so as to reduce taxes and other requisitions, and simplifying and making more efficient his administrative apparatus. He periodically sent roving envoys to the provinces to report on local conditions, to reward the honest and punish the guilty.

Hsiao-wen-ti's most significant achievement, however, was his success in carrying out land reforms. After the collapse of the West Tsin regime, North China had been in a state of intermittent warfare for two centuries. The farmers who bore the direct brunt of war suffered the most. In each village many perished and others left their homes and never returned. Farms were abandoned and deteriorated into patches of wilderness. For those who had returned, there were the unending lawsuits involving land titles, for deeds had been lost and official records had been destroyed during the wars. Many claimed ownership to land which might not rightly belong to them. While good farms continued to lie idle, many bona fide farmers found no available land to till. In 485 the government made a drastic move and enacted a law to arrest waste and to rationalize land ownership. According to the law, every male subject was entitled to receive seven acres of land from the state after he reached the age of fifteen; he could receive more if he possessed additional capacity of production as measured by the number of people in his household. This land would be returned to the state for redistribution after he died or when he became too old to carry on agricultural activities. Besides, an adult male was granted an additional 3.5 acres of land which did not have to be returned to the state even after he reached old age, and which could be inherited by his children. This additional land provided the necessary means of support for the aged. In addition, there were lands granted for specific purposes, such as the construction of domiciles, the growing of mulberry trees and flax, and vegetable gardening. The land of convicted criminals, together with the land of those who voluntarily left their homes without expressing a desire to return or who died without heirs, would be returned to the state for redistribution among the needy farmers. In return for land granted, the grantees paid tax in produce, which was generally light. A married couple, for instance, had to pay a yearly rate of only one bolt of silk and two piculs of grain; for a boy of premarital age, it was only one-fourth as much. However, tax rates would be proportionally increased if the taxpayer owned male or female slaves. Of the total amount of tax collected, two-thirds went to the imperial treasury; the other third was left with local authorities to meet administrative expenses, including the salary of governmental employees.

On the village level, village chiefs were chosen from local leaders who collected taxes and carried on many other administrative functions. While they were not paid salaries, they did receive exemption from taxation and military services. Besides mediating local disputes and punishing offenders for small crimes like thievery, they saw to it that the needs of the aged, the sick, the orphaned, and the destitute were taken care of by the entire village.

The Later Wei thus achieved what many reformers had failed to achieve during the previous centuries. In this respect, Hsiao-wen-ti was particularly fortunate; he did not encounter the same strong opposition as Wang Mang had encountered previously. His reforms were less drastic and consequently more enforceable. Though there was a minimum amount of land granted to each individual male, the amount increased in direct proportion to the number of people in the grantee's household (including females). Two-thirds of the land was to be returned to the government for redistribution upon the death of the grantee; his heirs were nevertheless allowed to inherit the other one-third. By this device the wealthy could keep the land they owned and the poor, in the meantime, could be assured of a minimum means of support. Moreover; since the disintegration of the Later Han regime, there had never been a time better for land reform than the time of the Later Wei. After two centuries of intermittent warfare, large tracts of land were unclaimed,

either because the original owners had perished during the wars or because they had left their homes as war refugees and never returned.
The mass migration towards the south under the initial impact of barbarian invasions alone left millions of acres of unclaimed land, for those who
could afford to migrate southward were generally the wealthy. Throughout the years much of the abandoned land was uncultivated; in other
cases, deserted land was cultivated even though the tillers could not show
certificates indicating their ownership. As ownerless land was available
for distribution among the landless, the government did not have to take
land away from the rich in order to give it to the poor. While Wang
Mang's land reforms provoked strong opposition from the landlords and
precipitated a revolt which resulted in the downfall of his regime, a
similar measure adopted by the Later Wei was carried out peacefully
without causing a social upheaval.

A more difficult task, however, was the implementation of a Sinicization program. Though assimilation of nomadic tribes into the Chinese
cultural system had begun when the first contact of the two groups was
made, it was Wei Hsiao-wen-ti who first made it an official policy enforced by legal measures. To show firm determination to Sinicize his regime, he moved the capital southward from P'ingch'eng (modern Shansi)
to Loyang which was not only a trade center but also an ancient Chinese
capital for many centuries. He could move the capital only after he had
successfully crushed a rebellion among his own followers who feared that
movement of the capital would mean the destruction of the hardy, nomadic tradition and the acquirement of Chinese "softness" which might
eventually weaken the regime. The tribesmen became more alarmed
when it was clear that in the formulation and implementation of governmental policy the emperor relied on the advice of Confucian scholars,
while showing an undisguised contempt for the nomadic fighters. As opposition was strong and widespread, he even found it necessary to order
the execution of his own son, the crown prince, who had refused to go
along with his Sinicization program. By royal decrees, not only was
nomadic costume to be discarded and replaced by Chinese dress, but the
Chinese language was proclaimed as the official language and had to be
learned by all persons under the age of thirty. All family names were to
be Sinicized, including the name of the royal family which from then on
was to be known as Yüan instead of its original form Topa. Interracial
marriages were encouraged. The emperor himself took Chinese wives and
asked his ministers and subjects to do the same. Confucian learning was
made a requirement for the educated. Scholars with special contributions
were rewarded with fame and position.

The policy initiated by Wei Hsiao-wen-ti was generally followed by
other alien dynasties which succeeded Later Wei in the north. Thus by

conquering North China wave after wave of nomadic invaders were absorbed into the Chinese cultural system. Eventually, they all became Chinese.

THE SOUTHERN AND NORTHERN DYNASTIES

When the first wave of barbarians swept down on the North China plain and captured Loyang in 311 and again in 316, it was the signal for a mass migration to the south. The emigrants came mostly from the upper classes because first, they alone had the means of moving for such a long distance and second, they had more to lose if they ever fell into the hands of the invaders. According to one record, six or seven out of every ten gentry families joined the southward march. In many cases, entire clans including neighbors and servants left their homes and travelled hundreds of miles to establish new homes south of the Yangtze River. Millions of people moved southward, probably the largest migration ever recorded in history. By the time they reached their destination, they found that a new Chinese regime had already been established. In 317 the military commander in the south, a member of the royal family, formally proclaimed the creation of a new regime, after news came from the north that the last emperor of West Tsin had been killed by the invaders. The new regime was known as East Tsin (317–420) and the new emperor was Tsin Yüan-ti (r. 317–322). To accommodate the newly arrived refugees, the government set up administrative provinces south of the Yangtze River for their settlement. As members of the upper class, the refugees brought to the south their wealth, experience, and technical skills which benefited their adopted homeland greatly in cultural and economic matters.

The sudden arrival of a large number of northerners caused great resentment among the native inhabitants. At the beginning the southerners refused to cooperate with the new government. But Tsin Yüan-ti was tactful and patient. Eventually, he was able to persuade the southern leaders to cooperate with his regime. After the leaders had given in, others soon fell in line. Frictions between northerners and southerners flared up from time to time, but they never reached major proportions. From the southerners' point of view, there were genuine reasons for complaint. For one thing, the northerners were preferred as office-holders; rarely were the southerners given high and responsible posts in the imperial government. To minimize their complaint, the government was careful enough not to interfere with the privileged position and the vested interests of the leading southern families. They were the original leaders of the south; as long as they did not choose to lead a revolt, the government was safe. Generally speaking, these families kept aloof from the northern orientated government, neither actively supporting it nor openly hostile to it. When the government decided not to interfere with their vested interests, they did not see the necessity of openly defying it at the risk of losing whatever they had. Throughout the long period of northern domination there was never a revolt organized on regional issues.

When the northerners first came to the south, they thought that their stay would be only temporary and that soon they should be able to reconquer the north and return to their ancient homes. Throughout the East Tsin dynasty this hope was kept alive by the division among the alien kingdoms in the north and by the prospect of revolt organized by the northern Chinese who were then living under alien rule. No sooner was the East Tsin regime established than an expedition was sent northward to recover the lost territories. But this attempt, like several others that followed, ended in failure. On the surface it seemed strange that these expeditions should fail, as the alien kingdoms fought among themselves and none had any popular support. But the Chinese regimes in the south were even weaker. The southern Chinese showed no enthusiasm in supporting the reconquest of the north for the northerners; moreover, there was not a single leader in the south who could inspire confidence and trust from both the northerners and southerners and mobilize all the resources for a sustained campaign in the north. In fact, practically all expeditions were organized by individuals on a personal or clan basis. They were supported by the government only reluctantly, for it feared that a successful and popular general would become unmanageable and would pose a threat to the government itself. The nearly successful campaign was made by an East Tsin general named Liu Yü who conquered the modern Honan province and captured Loyang and Ch'angan in 417. His success, however, proved to be short-lived. After he returned to the south, his subordinates began to quarrel among themselves. The reconquered territories again fell into the hands of the alien invaders.

After 417 Liu Yü became the strong man in the south. Three years later, he forced the last emperor of East Tsin to abdicate on his behalf. He called his regime Sung, sometimes referred to as Liu Sung to distinguish it from the Sung dynasty of a later period. Meanwhile in the north, the alien regime Later Wei was conquering and consolidating its gains in the Yellow River basin; it eventually unified North China in 439. The year 420, when the Liu Sung regime was established, marked the beginning of the period of Southern and Northern Dynasties. As far as the north was concerned, this period was ended in 581 when Sui replaced North Chou. In the south this period ended eight years later when Sui conquered the last of the southern dynasties, Ch'en, in 589.

The northern and southern regimes are listed as follows:

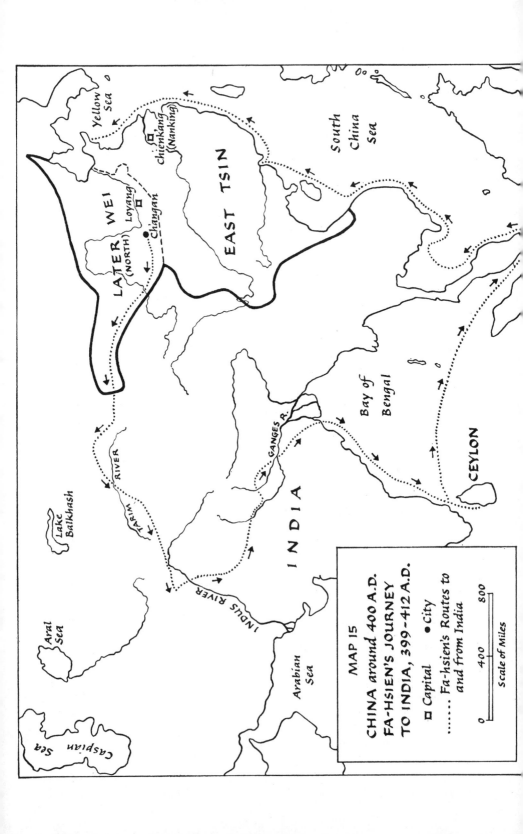

MAP 15
CHINA around 400 A.D.
FA-HSIEN'S JOURNEY
TO INDIA, 399–412 A.D.
□ Capital • City
.... Fa-hsien's Routes to
and from India

0   400   800
Scale of Miles

NORTH CHINA	SOUTH CHINA
Wei (220–265)	Wu (222–280)
West Tsin (265–317)	East Tsin (317–420)
Later Wei (386–535)	Sung (420–479)
West Wei (535–556)	Ch'i (479–502)
East Wei (534–550)	Liang (502–557)
North Ch'i (550–577)	Ch'en (557–589)
North Chou (557–581)	

The six southern regimes with their capital at Chienk'ang (modern Nanking) were sometimes referred to as the Six Dynasties.

After Liu Yü's northern expedition, there were no more serious attempts to reconquer the north throughout the period of the Southern Dynasties. Meanwhile the north, under the regime of Later Wei, was more interested in consolidating its gains than in making new conquests. When the north was again divided into rival kingdoms after 535, it was too disunited to attempt to conquer the south. Thus a period of peaceful co-existence endured for about one hundred and seventy years. Ambassadors were often exchanged between the northern and the southern regimes, as the northern kingdoms after the Later Wei were no longer viewed as barbarian by their southern counterparts. Though their boundary line fluctuated, it divided the land into roughly the same areas which are today termed North and South China. Loyang in the Yellow River basin was the administrative center for the northern dynasties; Chienk'ang on the southern bank of the Yangtze River was the capital of the southern regimes.

PERSONAL LOYALTY AND THE FAMILY ELITE

Since the unification of China by Ch'in, the disintegration of the Later Han marked the beginning of the longest period during which China was politically divided. The divisive tendency began long before the barbarian invasions, though the barbarians, by occupying North China, prolonged it. The grand unification of the Former Han had as its theoretical basis one of the cardinal principles of Confucianism, namely, loyalty to the monarch as the symbol of the entire state. As the Later Han progressed, such loyalty slowly weakened and eventually became only nominal. After the Yellow Turbans' rebellion, it all but disappeared. The loyalty which had hitherto been expressed to the emperor as the symbol of the state was now transferred to local strong men who received such titles as governors and governors-general after they had acquired a large following through their own initiative. As national loyalty to the emperor was replaced by local loyalty to individual strong men, localism replaced nationalism as the focus of political ideals among the educated elite. National loyalty to the emperor could be justified on the ground that the emperor embodied the will of the state; such loyalty, consequently, strengthened power concentration and political unity. Personal loyalty to local strong men, on the other hand, served exactly the opposite purpose.

Since personal loyalty was hailed as one of the greatest virtues, it in due time degenerated into a blind faith, bearing no relation to the principles of the man to whom such loyalty was addressed. In other words, if a man was hired as a government official, he was socially and morally bound to obey and support his superior, even though the actions of his ·superior could not be morally or legally justified. It was expected that such loyalty would continue even after the official superior-inferior relationship had long been terminated. Once a personal loyalty was established, it was supposed to last forever. Sometimes such loyalty was expressed in the most abject terms. We know that one official resigned from his post in order to enter a period of mourning after the death of a former superior, when such an extreme form of mourning was customarily reserved only for one's parents. Towards the end of the Later Han, the warring governors fought constantly among themselves, and each of them, pursuing his own selfish purposes, could always count on the support of his subordinates. After a process of elimination among the warring governors, this personal loyalty eventually became centered on the three most successful regional leaders, Ts'ao Ts'ao in the north, Liu Pei in the southwest, and Sun Ch'üan in the southeast. Even after West Tsin had unified China, localism was as strong as it had been before. It weakened the regime so much that West Tsin became an easy prey to the invading barbarians. After the barbarians had twice captured and sacked Loyang, the Confucian concept of a unitary government was damaged beyond repair, and for the following centuries the Chinese had to learn to live under a new system of divided rule. This passive acceptance of political division was particularly remarkable in view of the fact that most of the northern kingdoms were non-Chinese regimes. In the south, personal loyalty to local leaders was continually emphasized and was partially responsible for the quick succession of dynasties.

This overemphasis on personal loyalty came into being partly because the normal avenues to a governmental career no longer existed. A person, to enter governmental service, had to rely on the goodwill of an official in power who could extend to him the benefit of patronage. In a society where the only way of winning power and prestige lay in employment with the government, the avenues to a governmental career were extremely important. During the golden years of the two Han dynasties, there were normal ways of entering governmental service, and theoretically, it was possible for men of humble origin to attain the highest positions in the nation. In due course this remarkable system deteriorated.

Towards the end of the Later Han, great emphasis was laid on Confucian virtues, especially filial piety, in the selection of prospective officials. Hoping to be elected, a sizable number of the intelligentsia went to great extremes to show that they were "virtuous." After the establishment of the Wei dynasty it was thought that a better defined system was needed for the recruitment of governmental personnel. Consequently in 220 the nine-rank system was adopted at the suggestion of the Minister of Personnel, Ch'en Ch'ün. Under this system all gentry scholars in the country were rated and grouped into nine grades in accordance with their "virtues and abilities," from the highest first to the lowest ninth. In each province or district, officials appointed by and responsible to the imperial government were stationed for the specific purpose of rating and evaluating personnel within their jurisdiction, elevating them to higher ranks if they followed a Confucian pattern of virtuous life and degrading them if their behavior was regarded as unbecoming to the status of the scholar-gentry.

While the original motive for the establishment of the nine-rank system was doubtless sound, this system too deteriorated after it had been consistently abused. First, only the outward and often superficial "virtues" were appreciated, and no attempt was made to appraise a person in a more profound manner. Filial piety was the virtue most revered, and many prominent men (such as the famous historian Ch'en Shou) suffered degradation either because they did not resign from their official posts after the death of their parents or because they did not perform the ritual of mourning in an approved manner. With such emphasis on outward and often superficial conduct, this system promoted conformity at best and encouraged hypocritical acts at worst. Second, not all evaluators were impartial and objective. Impartiality and objectivity were even harder to obtain when members of influential families became subjects of evaluation. Even when evaluators were conscientious and unbiased, the great number of people to be judged within their respective jurisdictions made the task too huge to yield trustworthy results. So they would not antagonize the powerful and the wealthy, but ingratiate themselves with them, most of the evaluators, ignoring the so-called virtues, simply rated persons in accordance with the power, position, and wealth of the evaluated. By the early West Tsin dynasty, it was found that "there are no poor families among the higher ranks; nor can the old elite be found among the lower rated."

Despite its original purpose, the nine-rank system had thus become a device of providing additional luster and prestige to a small group of elite families called *shih chia* or old families. It should be noted, however, that these families did not come into being because of the system; they had existed long before it. We can trace their origin to many sources, and one of these sources was the emphasis given to Confucian learning after the second century B.C. when Confucianism was proclaimed as the state philosophy. As time went on, traditions developed in certain families as the recognized authorities on the interpretation of a Confucian classic after its interpretation had become a specialized affair which required the undivided attention of a lifetime. As Confucian learning was closely related to office holding, the families that produced prominent Confucian scholars were the same families that had power and influence with the government. Even out of office, they were the recognized leaders in their own communities. Once a family had reached such an elevated status, it enjoyed great prestige regardless of whether at a given time it had among its members any scholars or government officials. Its social standing did not change with the change of dynasties. In fact, monarchs of each succeeding regime had to ingratiate themselves with the old families in order to win their support. Generally speaking, the old families cooperated with any successful political leader so long as he did not initiate measures to change the status quo which they had long enjoyed.

The power and influence of the old families further advanced as a result of the political and social disintegration after the second century A.D. For self-protection against marauding soldiers and bandits, powerful landlords took the initiative in organizing local militias, recruiting supporters from the lesser landlords and independent farmers since the imperial authority could no longer be counted on to maintain peace and order. Sometimes the lesser landlords and independent farmers had to send their children or relatives to live with the great landlords as hostages to guarantee their unswerving loyalty. A psuedo feudal relationship was thus established in which the lesser landlords became *pu-ch'ü* or subordinates to the most powerful of the local landlords. During the barbarian invasions, most of the old families moved southward with the East Tsin, taking their subordinates with them. In the south their lofty position was recognized as it had been in the north; they enjoyed more social prestige than even the leading families in the south. Those which chose to stay in the north cooperated with the non-Chinese regimes which were anxious for their cooperation and support. In fact, the non-Chinese monarchs considered it a social honor to be able to marry their children into some of these old families. Even a liberal-minded emperor like Wei Hsiao-wen-ti made a habit of choosing his officials from this group.

In the south the old families enjoyed even greater prestige and influence throughout the Southern Dynasties. In selecting officials the government invariably checked with genealogies; members of the old families practically monopolized high positions regardless of individual merit. As genealogy was a key to office holding, the government made special efforts in correcting and editing the genealogies of the old elite, for falsifications of family origins, as would be expected, had become a common practice. The oligarchic control of governmental positions accounted partially for the complacency with which the government regarded China's political division into the Southern and Northern Dynasties, for the old families had more to lose than to gain in a renewal of warfare with the north. There was no reason to change the status quo, when its maintenance was to their own advantage.

Social differentiation existed even among the old families themselves. They were grouped into different classes, according to the various degrees of prestige they commanded; Hsieh, Ts'ui, and Lu were acknowledged as highest. Under such circumstances, snobbishness and prejudice were bound to occur. Families of the upper classes did not even try to conceal their contempt for those socially below them, and the families of the lower classes were just as anxious to be accepted by those socially above. This was shown poignantly in the matter of marriage. The upper class families customarily intermarried with families of their own standing, while the lower class families considered it a great honor to be able to marry their children into the upper classes. Social status was achieved through tradition; power and wealth were only contributory factors. During the Ch'i dynasty, upon the decision of a Wang family to marry one of its daughters to an extremely wealthy man of lower standing, a court censor thought it was a good case for judicial indictment. When Hou Ching, a high ranking official, asked for Emperor Liang Wu-ti's good office to secure a wife from the Wang or Hsieh family, the emperor replied that the prospective groom should not aim so high and that he should seek his bride among families below those of Chu and Chang. Later, when Hou Ching started a rebellion and captured Chienk'ang, he murdered in cold blood many of the old elite, probably in revenge for a past social slight. The old families and their prestige, however, survived his massacre. A man of humble origin might occasionally rise high in governmental service, but he would be still looked down upon as an upstart, with whom the old elite would have nothing to do socially. Sometimes social snobbishness was carried to such an extreme that two persons of different social standing were not supposed to ride in the same carriage or sit on the same bench. Family classification according to prestige existed throughout the Southern Dynasties and persisted as late as the seventh century. When the T'ang Emperor T'ai-tsung ordered a codification of family registers throughout the empire, the royal family Li was rated third in prestige, two ranks below the leading family Ts'ui.

It should be noted, however, that the social differentiation described above was applicable to the gentry families only. It did not affect the majority of the population, namely, the peasants. As far as the peasants were concerned, they had always been on one of the lowest levels of the social strata, and they still were.

REACTIONS AGAINST CONFUCIANISM

During the golden years of the two Han dynasties Confucianism was not only a system of government but also a code of personal behavior. As long as the basic teachings of Confucianism were observed, they provided an aim and a purpose for society as well as for individuals. Towards the end of the Later Han dynasty, the perversion of Confucianism in the name of "virtuous" conduct gave rise to skepticism and cynicism which led to the renunciation of Confucian values. A reaction had thus set in and lasted more than four centuries. The new cynical attitude was best shown in the famous *Three Decrees* issued by Ts'ao Ts'ao in which he asked anyone with extraordinary ability to join his staff, even if "he had once stolen his sister-in-law, accepted bribes, murdered his wife, or failed to return home for his mother's funeral." This kind of statement would have been unthinkable one century before. As Confucian virtues were discredited, Confucian learning was given even less emphasis. It is interesting to note that during the period of Southern and Northern Dynasties whatever Confucian learning was left was promoted more in the north under the alien dynasties than in the south under the Chinese regimes.

As Confucianism declined, Taoism won new adherents among the country's intellectual elite. In an age when life was most uncertain and rewards, either of social recognition, power, or wealth, did not necessarily follow talents and hard work, the best brains sought refuge in a philosophy of resignation and escape. Unwilling to submit to a world they could not change, they built a world of their own and shut themselves off from unpleasant realities. In this small world of their own they met friends of similar inclinations, conducted philosophical conversations, and found self-satisfaction in their own speculations. Confucianism had lost its appeal partly because it had failed to meet the challenge of a disorganized world. This new elite of intellectuals repudiated completely the traditional Confucian virtues such as loyalty, self-discipline, and filial piety, and advocated instead a code of behavior based upon natural inclinations rather than established conventions. They believed in self-expression unfettered by old dogmas and popular beliefs. They themselves did not favor any set of principles either as a philosophy or code of behavior except the cardinal principle of being honest and true to oneself. It was natural that they should seek refuge in the teachings of Lao-tzu and Chuang-tzu, as these teachings repudiated established values and emphasized naturalism and non-activity as the most important virtues. The *Book of Changes,* though generally considered a Confucian classic, was singled out as the most praiseworthy, largely because of its mystic and metaphysical attractions. Despite their principle of non-activity, the new intellectual elite did a remarkable work in editing and commenting on the writings of Lao-tzu and Chuang-tzu and the *Book of Changes.*

In the pursuance of truth and wisdom, the Taoist philosophers of the Wei-Tsin period attached great importance to verbal exchange. During the course of verbal exchange, truth and wisdom came into being not through logical reasoning but as a result of sudden flashes of insight. The answer to a question was likely to be concise in words and broad in implication, leaving much room for individual speculation and interpretation. Even the tone and placement of voice contributed to the most propitious atmosphere; the best voices were often described as "golden" or "cool," or as "sounds from a harp." Argumentative statements during the conversation had to be avoided, as they would destroy the very purpose of Taoist passivism. In fact, the manner of expressing an idea was just as important as the idea itself. Even clothes worn by the conversationalists should be appropriate for the occasion, generally described as wide, loose, and comfortable. Besides, there was the indispensable horsewhisk in the hand of the conversationalist as a symbol of detachment and non-involvement. The purpose was not so much to convince as to express, leaving individual listeners complete freedom to digest and infer for themselves.

This new vogue of *ch'ing t'an,* or "purified conversation," was begun in the 240's during the Wei dynasty and reached its apex of popularity during the West Tsin dynasty. Its architects were Ho Yen (d. *ca.* 250), Wang Pi (226–249), and Kuo Hsiang (d. 312), all of whom were not only expert conversationalists but also writers of considerable originality. However, their basic ideas did not exceed the confines set up by Lao-tzu and Chuang-tzu several centuries before. Like those two masters, they emphasized such key teachings as "nothingness" (the beginning of the universe), "non-activity" ("everything will be done when nothing is being done"), and "naturalism" (the right path to genuine behavior). They ridiculed all efforts aimed at the improvement of personal conduct and the betterment of political and social institutions. The Taoist attitude was an attitude of perfect detachment from worldly endeavors, and they conducted their personal life according to what they called natural inclinations, with little or no regard for conventional restraints. While most of their personal behavior might be simply amoral, there were others who interpreted the new teachings as a form of sensual escapism. A treatise of anonymous authorship entitled *Yang Chu,* probably written during the Former Han dynasty, enjoyed a sudden popularity, as it neatly filled the gap left in the writings of Lao-tzu and Chuang-tzu. In this treatise the author advocated the avoidance of pain and the pursuit of pleasure, as he assured his reader that life was short and most uncertain and that the other world was unknown. Once this path was followed, Taoism, originally interpreted as a means of achieving personal purification, was now perverted into a teaching advocating sensual self-satisfaction.

In practice, the patterns of behavior on the part of its adherents varied a great deal, from conduct which was highly moral and purely ascetic to that which was downright absurd. On a higher level, we may cite T'ao Ch'ien and Wang Hui-chih as examples. T'ao Ch'ien (376–427) was a noted poet and prose writer whose works have been universally praised for their aesthetic beauty in describing natural environment. During the time he was a magistrate, he decided to "hang up his official seal" (indicating his resignation) on the ground that he could not humiliate himself by bowing to an unworthy superior for the "five bushels of rice" which he had received as his salary. Wang Hui-chih was the son of the famous calligrapher Wang Hsi-chih (321–379). One beautiful moonlit evening, he thought of a good friend who lived many miles away and decided to pay him an unannounced visit. He arrived at his friend's residence early in the morning after a long drunken voyage by boat during the previous night, only to return immediately without making the intended call. Asked by his boatman the reason for his peculiar behavior, he replied that he was enthusiastic to see his friend when he started his journey but that such enthusiasm was gone after he had reached his destination, so there was no sense in then seeing his friend.

While conduct like this might be genuinely "naturalistic," other men, such as the famous Seven Sages of the Bamboo Grove, went to great extremes to prove their point. As a rule, they sought satisfaction in the wine cup, and one of them had a record of being drunk consecutively for sixty days. One of the Sages, Liu Ling, was regularly accompanied by a servant with a shovel wherever he went. He instructed his servant to bury him wherever he should be when he dropped dead. Often remaining completely naked at home, he would protest when surprised by visitors: "The universe is my dwelling place and my house is only my clothes. Why, then, do you enter into my pants?" Behavior such as this could have been dismissed as individual eccentricity and would hardly be worthy of notice by historians were it not for the fact that these people were the elite of the scholar-gentry, and it was this class that traditionally provided leadership and guidance for the entire nation. The point has been raised that in an age of injustice under a corrupt, despotic regime, to shield oneself behind the Taoist philosophy was the best means of achieving survival. It was nevertheless true that the traditional sense of public responsibility generally expected from this class was completely lost in a selfish indulgence which China then could least afford. In this new age, life had no meaning except the pleasure one could derive from it:

> When there is wine,
> There should be a song.
> Life is like morning dew
> That disappears
> Soon after the sun rises.[1]

---

[1] These are the first lines of a poem written by Ts'ao Ts'ao.

After the fall of the West Tsin regime to the barbarians early in the fourth century when most of the northern gentry families moved to the south, they found that the south, having suffered no major war devastations and being economically more productive, enjoyed such prosperity as had seldom been seen before. The term Six Dynasties often reminds one of a life of ease and plenty. The easy life produced a typical gentleman of this age, weak in limbs, short-sighted in outlook, ignorant of practical matters, but expert in witticism and repartee. Let us look at a description of these gentlemen by a northern contemporary:

The gentlemen of the Liang dynasty all wore ponderous dresses with wide belts, tall hats, and high-soled shoes. When they went out, they rode in carriages; at home they were waited on [by their servants]. . . . During the Hou Ching rebellion many of them were physically so weak that they could hardly walk. Being bony in body and becoming breathless in the mildest physical efforts, they could stand neither summer nor winter. Many of them simply waited for death, when the rebellion occurred suddenly . . . The ancestors of these gentlemen passed across the Yangtze River when the Tsin dynasty was established in the south. For eight or nine generations they did not participate in tilling the fields, and all depended upon government salaries for their support. Those who owned land relied on their servants for its cultivation; they themselves had never seen the plowing of one spot of earth or the planting of one single tree. Nor did they know the time to sow and the time to reap. Being so impractical as they were, how can you expect them to know the rest of the worldly affairs? They were incompetent as government officials and ineffective as heads of households. This is all due to the fault of having too much leisure.[1]

However, these gentlemen had little difficulty in finding ways to spend their leisure. For the more sophisticated, there were literature, calligraphy, painting, music, and other recreations. The writers of the Six Dynasties developed a new style of writing, called *p'ien t'i* or parallel form. Sentences were constructed in such a way that each phrase or sentence was neatly balanced by a phrase or sentence of equal length (namely, the same number of characters), and the last characters of both phrases or sentences usually rhymed with each other. The result was a literary form lying somewhere between prose and verse, and when recited, it conveyed a flow of sound extremely pleasant to the ears. Since sentence construction had to conform strictly to the parallel form, obscure characters which would not have been used ordinarily had to be employed. The use of obscure characters and the concise sentence structure accounted partially for the difficulty of understanding the composition itself. The parallel form was sometimes called the ornamented form as phrases and sentences were lavishly embellished with flowery, elegant words which were sometimes empty in meaning. Too often content had to be sacrificed to form. As its writing required great knowledge in charac-

[1] Translated from *Family Instructions for the Yen Clan* (*Yen-shih chia-hsün*) by Yen Chih-t'ui. This passage appears in the chapter on "Worldly Affairs" (*shih-wu*).

ters and rhythm, it was no mean achievement to be able to write a presentable essay in parallel form. It remained a mental exercise for the country's gentry scholars for many centuries to come. As for calligraphy, it had long been a cherished art form. Being composed of pictographs and ideographs, the Chinese written language was uniquely fit for calligraphic development. The Tsin dynasty produced Wang Hsi-chih whose style was noted for character and strength and has been emulated ever since. During the Six Dynasties the extremely cursive grass style acquired increasing popularity;[1] expertly executed, its graceful and sweeping lines conveyed a sense of beauty, power, and even mental exaltation. Writing with the grass style, a calligrapher sometimes had to make omissions (and occasionally additions) in each character in order to achieve the desired result. Many contemporaries complained about this corruption of Chinese characters, but to the admirers of the grass style, this was a small price to pay for a superb form of artistic expression. As for music the lute remained the major instrument. Like the ancient Greeks, the Chinese believed that music had a beneficial effect on a person's morale and character. To be able to play the lute was regarded as a necessary refinement for a gentleman. As the Chinese then did not have a system of musical notation but depended on memory for their performances, we have no idea how music was played during this particular period.

Besides literature and art, there were chess and games of chance for the southern gentry to indulge in. From what we can gather, the chess game played was the traditional *wei-ch'i*, or game of encirclement (called *go* in Japan). If they played with the same rules as modern Chinese do, a good game would have taken hours or even days to finish and might be regarded as a mental exercise par excellence. However, it was such a waste of time that Confucius once remarked: "Is there any one who does not like chess? If there is, will he not be rightly said to be wise?" Many contemporaries condemned chess on the same ground, but it remained as popular as ever. Another ancient game which enjoyed a new vogue was the pitch-pot game in which arrows were thrown into a vase placed at some distance. This, of course, required skill as well as luck. One man, we are told, never missed his target, even though his view of the vase was cut off by a screen. Sports of a more strenuous type, however, were not indulged in, for vigorous physical exercise was regarded as vulgar, not becoming the dignity of a gentleman. The same pleasurable life was also enjoyed by the ladies. Since they were not allowed to mingle socially with men or share their activities, they had a world of their own and spent a considerable part of their time in making themselves pretty. Cream, powder, and rouge were widely used, as they had been used before. One

---

[1] It is called "grass style" because the strokes that compose a character are supposedly shaped like grass.

of the fads then was the wearing of high, popped-up wigs, called false heads. The wigs had different forms; some of them, we are told, were shaped like "flying birds."

From the Confucian point of view, the personal life of China's rulers during the Southern Dynasties was anything but exemplary. With the possible exception of Liang Wu-Ti, none of the rulers in the Southern Dynasties could be described as able and conscientious. Many of them were mischievous, malicious, and outright wrongdoers. One crown prince, for instance, murdered his father. Another king tried to poison his mother. Still another used the navel of a fat minister as target to practice archery and stole dogs from a neighboring Buddhist temple to be cooked as food. Nor did the fair sex behave any better. Complaining that her brother the king had thousands of concubines while she had only one husband, a princess asked the king to obtain for her some handsome men as consorts and received thirty of them. One empress dowager received a gift of thirty handsome men from her son (the king) to serve in whatever capacity she chose. In short, these rulers were anything but virtuous and lived a life directly opposed to what would be expected from a Confucian ruler. They could not look beyond their immediate concerns; sensual enjoyments and private feuds occupied most of their time. Even the best of them, Liang Wu-ti, was more concerned with his spiritual salvation than the national welfare for which he was supposedly responsible. Though unimpeachable in private life, he was so enchanted with the other-worldliness of Buddhism that twice he had to be implored not to relinquish his throne to enter a Buddhist monastery as a monk. So the best rulers during this period were so other-worldly as to ignore the welfare of this world, and the worst of them simply made the best of this world by living a life of corruption and immorality. In either case the people did not benefit.

TAOIST RELIGION AND BUDDHISM

So far Taoism has been discussed as a philosophy and a way of life. Quite different from this was Taoism as a religion. Partly due to the paradoxical messages contained in the *Book of Taoist Virtue* and partly due to the traditional belief that Lao-tzu never really died after he had disappeared in the mountainous west, his name had long been associated with alchemy, the magic art of achieving earthly immortality. The fear of death prompted the desire to prolong life indefinitely; this fear was found especially among emperors who had acquired great power and wealth and would like to enjoy them forever. The court of Ch'in Shih Huang-ti, for instance, was frequented by alchemists and magicians. One of them, Hsü Fu, was sent by the emperor to the eastern seas to search for immortal drugs. He left with several thousand boys and girls and never returned. The legend had it that they became the first settlers in Japan from the mainland. The great expanse of the Western Pacific stimulated imagination; many people believed that beyond that great expanse lived immortals whose blessings must be sought before they could attain immortality for themselves. Early in the Han dynasty, the name of the legendary emperor Huang-ti, for reasons never satisfactorily explained, was often combined with the name of Lao-tzu; thence the Learning of Huang-Lao became known as the magic formula of extracting elixir. Even an emperor like Han Wu-ti could not resist the popular fad, and one of the court magicians was said to have been successful in arranging a meeting between the emperor and his long deceased concubine.

In addition, religious Taoism also contained strong elements of animism. The Taoists believed that there was a spirit in charge of every mountain or river whose good grace must be sought to prevent natural disasters and to bring prosperity to the community. To communicate with the spirits, the help of Taoist priests who alone knew the appropriate rites had to be invoked. Their help became absolutely necessary when the emperors made their periodical sacrifices to the greatest spirits of them all, Heaven and Earth.

Taoist mysticism was further enriched by the injection of divination and prognostication which had become very popular towards the end of the Former Han dynasty. The theory that the universe together with its constituent parts was created through the interaction of the two opposite but complementary forces, *yin* and *yang*, was given a new meaning: namely, by watching closely the changing patterns of these two forces at work one might be able to foretell the future. Thus the Taoist priests acquired a role similar to that of an astrologist. Meanwhile, new elements of Taoism were also introduced. While the rulers were interested in the search for immortal drugs, the common people had a more practical concern; after all, alchemy was too expensive a practice for men of ordinary means. Towards the end of the Later Han dynasty a man named Chang Ling (also known as Chang Tao-ling) attracted large followings due to his reputation as a successful magician, curing diseases through the use of charms and spells. He was later proclaimed by his followers as the founder of Taoism as a religion (as distinguished from Taoism as a philosophy), and he is still regarded as such. A pantheon of Taoist gods and goddesses soon developed; some were imaginery divinities and others were historical figures. Throughout later ages Taoist priests continued to practice medicine through charms and spells; they also performed funeral services to assure the deceased a place in the heavenly kingdom of spiritual bliss.

Though Taoism as a philosophy had speculative merit, Taoism as a religion was a medley of mystic practicums. It had no elaborate theology; nor did it provide a system of ethics aimed at the improvement of human relations. Though many books written throughout the ages were generally classified as Taoist, they were most concerned with personal salvation and immortality through meditative retirement, alchemy, and many other such means. The road to salvation was a technical one and bore little relation to personal conduct in this world. Consequently, their impact on social and moral institutions was rather limited. However, Taoism filled a vacuum left in Confucian ideology which provided no spiritual domain for one to look forward to, and it made available a spiritual comfort to satisfy a basic human need. While Confucian scholars might dismiss Taoist religion as a form of superstition and preferred the practical wisdom of Confucianism, the less intellectual masses found this wisdom useless if they had nothing to hope for after death. Throughout the long centuries Taoist religion was a cherished faith in the hearts and minds of the common people in China and was a convenient vehicle through which the masses expressed their emotions and feelings. Perhaps it was no mere coincidence that whenever a rebellion occurred, more often than not Taoism was hailed as a rallying standard, for the government was practically always Confucian in outlook. In this sense Taoism might be said to be a people's religion.

However, a more serious challenge to the supremacy of Confucianism was an alien religion called Buddhism. Buddhism means the teachings of Buddha, or the Enlightened One. The real name of the Enlightened One was Siddhartha, born to the Gautama family in a small country south of Nepal. His birth date was traditionally placed at 563 B.C. or thereabouts. Since the details of his life were not put in writing until several hundred years later, what we know about this man is at best semihistorical. He was said to have been born to a rich, aristocratic family with a loving but perhaps overprotective father. As the boy grew up, his father gave him everything a man's heart could possibly desire, including a harem of beautiful girls. But the old man would not let him go out of the palace ground, because outside of the palace ground there were the unpleasant realities which he did not wish his son to see. Overcome by curiosity, the young man finally sneaked out with his charioteer to the outside world without his father's knowledge. He saw an old man, a sick man, and then a dead man. "Why is it that people have to suffer so much?" he asked. He wanted the answer, but he could not find it. He returned to the palace, but he was no longer the same happy prince. One night he took a last look at his sleeping wife and his infant son and silently left the palace. Outside of the city and at the edge of a forest, he cut off his long hair with a sword, discarded his princely robes and put on those of a beggar, and set out to seek the answer for himself.

He wandered from place to place and sought answers from India's holy men. Their answers, however, were not satisfactory. For six long years, he meditated and he fasted, but the answer was as remote as ever.

Meanwhile, he had been so weakened by self-imposed mortifications that he had all but wasted away. All these efforts, however, were not exercised in vain. One day as he sat underneath a tree in a grove a flash of insight struck him, and all of a sudden the absolute truth about life and death was revealed to him. He knew The Answer and he had become the Enlightened One or Buddha. The stage he had reached was *nirvana,* the "unconditioned world where there is neither time nor space." He could have left the physical world then, but out of infinite compassion for his fellow men he decided to stay longer so that he could transmit his own experience to others. Why was it that human beings had to suffer so much? It was because life was a painful process by definition. One life was merely the reincarnation of a preceding life; while the wheel of births and rebirths rolled on unceasingly, there would be no end to man's sufferings. To liberate oneself from the endless cycle of deaths and rebirths, one needed to recognize that the physical world was illusory and that one should not seek for the fulfillment of worldly desires, whether they be fame, wealth, power, or the opposite sex. Desires were the basic cause of pain, and to stop pain, a person had to eliminate desires. Meanwhile, he should conduct his life in accordance with the Eightfold Path: right views, thought, speech, conduct, livelihood, effort, mind control, and meditation. The Eightfold Path was the Middle Way that led to "pure compassion," the "selfless love for all that lives." Those who followed the Middle Way would of course abstain from killing, stealing, falsehood, unchastity, etc.

Though Buddhism was born in India, it was in countries east of India that it achieved its greatest triumph. Spreading to Southeast Asia was the Hinayana ("Lesser Vehicle") School which was closer to the original Buddhism as taught by Buddha. The school that spread to China and eventually to Korea and Japan was the Mahayana ("Greater Vehicle") School which, recognizing the distinction between absolute and relative truth, was more tolerant of non-Buddhist ideas and was consequently more welcome to the Confucian Chinese. In due course Mahayana Buddhism developed a pantheon of deities: the Bodhisattvas who dedicated themselves to the saving of weaker souls. The Buddha Amitabha was known to the Chinese as O-mi-t'o-fo, and Avalokitesvara, changing his sex, became the Chinese Kuan-yin, or the Goddess of Mercy. They were two of the most popular deities in China. Once in China, Buddhism adjusted itself to its new environment by emphasizing charity and good works: to contribute to one's own salvation by helping others. Meanwhile, those who followed Buddha's original teaching of celibacy and asceticism could always join the monastic ranks. Mahayana Buddhism appealed to both the clergy and the laity as it provided a path of salvation for both groups.

Until modern times there was never a foreign impact so great and so

BODHISATTVA, LATER WEI DYNASTY (386–535) This figure was found in the Lungmen cave (modern Shansi province), a fragment of a large statue. The Chinese copying of Indian works in depicting the Bodhisattvas was perhaps responsible for the clearly discernible Greco-Roman influence in this figure.

influential as Buddhism. There were many reasons for the tremendous success of this imported faith. First, Taoism aside, there was not a native ideology in China which satisfied a universal spiritual need. The Buddhist emphasis on compassion and love contrasted sharply with the selfish motives behind many Taoist practices; it struck a tender response from the best part of human nature. By providing a spiritual substance it substantiated such Confucian virtues as *jen* and *yi* which even at their best were only worldly and human. For the less intellectual the meaning was even greater. It raised hope for the next and better world which Confucianism did not elaborate and which Taoism defined only in the vaguest terms. Furthermore, it was the only religion known to the Chinese which linked ethics in this world and heavenly bliss in the next. Its moral teachings attracted the Confucian intellect and its other-worldliness appealed greatly to the masses. Secondly, it was introduced to China during a period which was most opportune for its growth. Eccentric conduct on the part of many Confucian scholars in the name of filial piety and righteous action had been so extreme that it was often denounced as hypocritical, and Confucianism as a moral force consequently declined. On the other hand, Taoism as a philosophy had come to mean a doctrine of self-protection from cruel, worldly realities, and Taoism as a religion was unfortunately mingled with many superstitious elements. A spiritual and moral vacuum had to be filled, and it was filled by Buddhism. Thirdly, this was an age of political disunity, turmoil, and wars, with their implications of human sufferings. The need for spiritual comfort was never so great. Being able to look forward to a promising unknown helped one forget the unpleasant realities, and the Buddhist theory of reincarnation provided an additional relief. Finally the Chinese under Confucianism were essentially a tolerant people, relatively free from religious prejudice and bigotry. Believing in Confucianism by no means limited them from accepting another faith. In fact, when Buddhism was introduced, many Confucian scholars welcomed it as a supplement to Confucian beliefs. Though persecutions of Buddhists did occasionally occur, they were confined to the clergy for short durations; most of them were instigated by Taoists rather than Confucians. For the average Chinese, religions did not need to be mutually exclusive, and he saw no contradiction in holding two or three faiths at the same time.

Through trading with Central Asia the Chinese heard of Buddhism as early as the second century B.C. In 2 B.C. a Chinese scholar travelled to one of the Central Asian kingdoms to learn about this new faith, but nothing consequential came out from this trip. Many decades later Emperor Han Ming-ti (r. 58–76 A.D.) was said to have dreamed of a golden image of Buddha. Curiosity aroused, he sent a Confucian scholar named Ch'in Ching to India with the intended purpose of bringing back Buddhist scriptures. Ch'in Ching returned with two Indian monks, and many

Buddhist scriptures loaded on white horses were transported to China. After his return, the emperor ordered the erection of a Buddhist temple at his capital Loyang, called the Temple of White Horses, the first Buddhist temple in China. Buddhist monks came to visit China and Chinese students and monks went to study in India. From then on a cultural exchange of unprecedented scale followed. One of the most famous monks during this period was Fa-hsien who set out for India in 399 and did not return until fifteen years later. He wrote a book on India, and his observations provide historians with valuable information about the India of this period. Through the joint efforts of Indian and Chinese monks, most of the Buddhist literature was translated into Chinese. The translation was a difficult task, as many Buddhist terms did not have their counterparts in Chinese. In translating, colloquial rather than literary Chinese was preferred, so that the new gospel could reach larger masses.

Although China had never been conquered militarily by a foreign country, she was completely captivated by the Buddhist faith. Because of Buddhism, China learned to respect India; India was perhaps the only country in the world which the Chinese have never called barbarian. Encouraged and patronized by Chinese monarchs, Buddhism spread fast and wide. Buddhist believers multiplied; so did Buddhist temples. Of course, not all the faithful were truly sincere. There were exceptions even among the Buddhist monks. Some joined the monastic ranks because they wished to avoid military service. The tumult and turmoil of a warring age, ironically, helped Buddhism to spread. During the period of the Southern and Northern Dynasties, Buddhism made more converts in the north than it did in the south. In the north, Buddhism claimed more than 40,000 temples and more than three million monastic monks at its peak of popularity, not to mention millions of Buddhist laymen. In the south, Buddhism was most popular during the Liang regime which had within its jurisdiction 2,846 temples and 82,700 monks at one time. Monarchs competed with wealthy laymen in donating funds for the building of temples and the erection of Buddhist statues. One of the Liang monarchs even wished to abdicate his throne for a more meditative, monastic life as has been mentioned before.

The impact of Buddhism was not confined to religious and philosophical fields; its influence was felt in other areas as well. In literature it introduced logic and organization in essay writing; the lack of sound logic and good organization had been notoriously obvious in ancient Chinese writings. It gave prestige to the writing of stories and novels which had been traditionally held in contempt by Confucian scholars, though this effect was not fully felt until several centuries later. Buddhist influence was also felt in sculpture and architecture. When Buddhist statues were in great demand, sculpture, previously neglected as an art form, attracted many new talents. Sculptors and painters commissioned by kings and

BUDDHIST PAGODA   Located outside the city of Hangchow, this modern pagoda has inscribed on it excerpts of a Buddhist scripture.

wealthy patrons produced numerous Buddhist statues and images of artistic taste. They were made of various materials: iron, stone, wood, or clay. One such statue, we are told, rose as high as 70 feet. Many of them were gilded with gold; historians since then have blamed this expensive devotion for the comparative scarcity of gold in later periods as compared with its apparent abundance prior to the introduction of Buddhism. Many stone statues were carved out of mountain cliffs. Today the impressive Yünkang statues at Tatung, Shansi province, bear witness to the skill of the sculptors as well as to the devotion of their patrons. So far as architecture was concerned, most important was the introduction of an architectural form known today as pagoda. A pagoda during the Later Wei period had either a round or many-sided base and rose several stories high, with a total height of as much as nine hundred feet (a later source, four hundred feet), as in the case of the famous Yungning temple built in Loyang in 516 A.D. While Confucian scholars had traditionally condemned extensive buildings, religious or otherwise, as unnecessary luxuries, the new Buddhist converts spared no expense to build great temples in honor of Buddha and the Bodhisattvas. Many even went bankrupt in doing so.

From China, Buddhism spread to Korea and eventually to Japan. It succeeded wherever it went. Meanwhile in China it had become mature or popular enough to split into many sects. As for this, more will be said in the forthcoming chapter.

v

Sui and T'ang

THE SUI REGIME

Like Wang Mang and Tsin Wu-ti before him, Yang Chien (d. 604), founder of the Sui dynasty, "stole the crown from orphans and widows" and came to power through the back door. His family, though Chinese, had served succeeding non-Chinese dynasties in North China for several generations, and he himself rose to become Duke Sui under the proto-Mongolian (known as Hsien-pi) regime named North Chou in 568. In 580 the reigning emperor (Chou Hsüan-ti, r. 578–579) died; his son, aged seven, was installed by Yang Chien as Emperor Chou Ching-ti. One year later, a decree of abdication was issued in the boy emperor's name, stating, among other things, that heavenly and earthly phenomena had been such that they

162

unmistakably indicated the loss of the mandate of Heaven by the North Chou regime, and that Duke Sui, being virtuous and wise, had been designated by Heaven as the rightful successor. Amid pomp and ceremony the imperial seal was then presented to Duke Sui who, having gone through the motion of refusal out of expected modesty, accepted it when "clearly no alternative is really available." Thus Yang Chien, a ruthless and unprincipled Chinese, finally put to an end the last of a long series of non-Chinese regimes whose ancestors had ravaged and then occupied North China for more than three centuries, and established a new dynasty named Sui. Four months later the ex-emperor, aged eight, died under suspicious circumstances.

If the position of a political leader in history depends more on how he used his power than on the means of acquiring it, Yang Chien (also known by his imperial title Sui Wen-ti) certainly should not be considered such a bad monarch as the above paragraph seems to imply. Perhaps because of this reason, traditional historians in China have spoken generously of him. Not only did he end the last alien regime in North China, but he also, in 589, conquered Ch'en, the last of the Southern Dynasties and thus, for the first time in almost three hundred years, brought all of China under one jurisdiction. The pacification of China was followed by vigorous campaigns abroad, notably against the T'u-chüeh (Turks) who, after 552, were the most powerful tribe in the north. In 582 the T'u-chüeh split into two rival groups; and the Sui regime, by allying itself with the more amenable western group, decisively defeated the eastern group the following year. From then on, through manipulation of their rivalries plus an optimum use of military force, the Sui regime was continually able to weaken the T'u-chüeh strength until, by 603, it reduced them to virtual impotence. In that year it helped install on the T'u-chüeh throne a tribal prince named Chi-min who subsequently "showed his gratitude" by acknowledging the Sui emperor as his overlord. Four years later Chi-min came to Ch'angan to pay his tribute and, formally, pledged his allegiance. This much-celebrated event marked a dramatic reversal in the balance of power in this part of the world. The non-Chinese domination of North China as well as the grasslands to the north that had lasted for more than three centuries finally came to an end, and the Chinese domination, that officially began in 607, was to continue for approximately one hundred fifty years (607–755).

In domestic construction the Sui regime is most noted for two accomplishments, namely, the establishment of a nation-wide, ever-ready granary system and the construction of the Grand Canal. The concept of an ever-ready granary did not originate with the Sui, of course; its beginning was attributed to a man named Li Hui (sometimes romanized as Li K'uei) who, as the chief minister of the feudal state of Wei early in the fourth century B.C., introduced a graduated tax system whereby each farmer would pay as his taxes an amount of produce determined by the size of the crops he actually harvested each year. In a good year when bumper crops prevailed, his tax rate could be as high as 75 percent of the harvested crops; in a bad year he would pay little or nothing. In the latter case the government would sell in the open market the stored grain that had been collected as taxes during the bumper years; the amount to be released for sale would depend upon market demand as well as actual need. The purpose of this device, said Li Hui the innovator, was to prevent the fluctuation of grain prices and to safeguard a satisfactory livelihood for all, regardless of how good or bad the harvest was. Implemented in various degrees by later regimes, this device became known as the ever-normal granary system (ch'ang-p'ing ts'ang). Meanwhile another system, known as the communal (she ts'ang), or relief, granary (yi ts'ang), was also introduced. The primary function of a communal, or relief, granary, as its name implies, was to provide relief during the time of famine on a local or communal basis, whereas the ever-normal granary, controlled and operated by the central government, was aimed at the stabilization of grain prices. Each system complemented the other and worked more effectively because of the existence of the other.

In 583 Yang Chien ordered the establishment of ever-normal granaries in the key cities along the Yellow River and its major tributaries. Seventeen years later (606) his son Sui Yang-ti (r. 605–616) began to construct two of the largest grain storages ever known, namely, the Lok'ou Granary southeast of Kunghsien (Honan province) and the Lo Granary north of Loyang. The former measured seven miles in circumference and contained 3,000 individual bins, each of which had a capacity of holding 8,000 piculs (532 tons) of grain. The latter was much smaller and had a capacity only one-tenth as much. Together these two granaries had a storage space for 26,000,000 piculs (1,729,000 tons) of grain. In 616 when Sui Yang-ti died, the stored grain in these and other ever-normal granaries was said to be of such a large amount as to be equivalent to the total payroll of the imperial government for a period of fifty or more years. This indeed was a new record of governmental affluence.

As for the communal or relief granaries, they were first established during the Sui dynasty in 585. Each year at harvest time when taxes were paid in produce, a surcharge of various amounts but not exceeding one picul per household were imposed on the taxpayers. The grain thus collected would go to a communal or relief granary, headed by a local manager who served simultaneously as the accountant. During the lean years when the harvests were bad, the stored grain would be distributed among the poor without charge. Meanwhile the imperial government was supposed to sell its grain hitherto stored in the ever-normal granaries at the

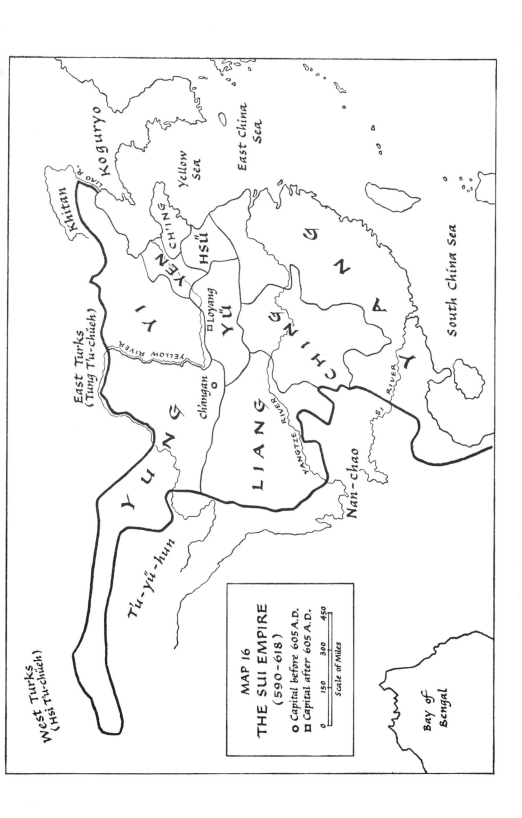

West Turks
(Hsi T'u-chüeh)

East Turks
(Tung T'u-chüeh)

Tu-yü-hun

YUNG

Ch'ang-an o

YELLOW RIVER

Khitan

LIAO R.

Koguryo

YEN

CH'ING

HSÜ

□Loyang

YÜ

CHING

YANGTZE RIVER

LIANG

Nan-chao

SI. RIVER

YANG

Yellow
sea

East China
sea

South China Sea

Bay of
Bengal

MAP 16

THE SUI EMPIRE
(590–618)

o Capital before 605 A.D.
□ Capital after 605 A.D.

0	150	300	450

Scale of Miles

market or below-the-market prices, thus preventing prices from continually moving upward. When the relief granary was in operation in a community, it mollified the impact of famine and saved lives, at least for a short period of two or more years. However, if bad harvests persisted for a much longer period and famine spread to a large section of the population, the stored grain in the relief granary would be inevitably exhausted and, in that case, serious difficulties could really begin.

From the point of view of lasting impact, the Sui regime's second accomplishment, namely the construction of canals, proved to be much more significant. Topographically China slopes eastward, and great mountains and rivers, with rare exceptions, move along the same direction. Thus transportation was made comparatively easy by following the natural courses of rivers that run from the west to the east, but was extremely difficult over the land routes from the north to the south and vice versa. Prior to the Sui dynasty the situation was not too serious, since North China was more or less economically self-sufficient. What caused the subsequent decline is still very much in debate among the historians; the neglect in water conservation during the alien occupation, the deterioration of soil quality as a result of thousands of years of continuous cultivation, the process of deforestation for the purpose of creating more farm land, or even the change of climate—all these have been cited as possible causes. Meanwhile South China was intensively developed as an agricultural region and, by the sixth century, could normally produce a yearly surplus readily available to meet the needs of other less fortunate areas such as North China. Since there were no natural water routes between the north and the south whereby this surplus could be transported, Sui Yang-ti set out to construct an artificial one, later known as the Grand Canal. The Grand Canal ranks as one of the greatest public works in history; in terms of cost in manpower and materials, its construction was often compared to the building of the Great Wall.

The first Sui canal was built by Yang Chien in 584; its completion provided a water route between T'ungkuan on the present Honan-Shensi border and Ch'angan, a distance of approximately one hundred miles. This, of course, was only the beginning of a much larger project to come. The Grand Canal, constructed under Sui Yang-ti, had three sections, all connected in a general north-south direction. The central section was the T'ungchi Canal which, built in 605, linked the southern tributaries of the Yellow River with the northern tributaries of the Yangtze River. Thus, for the first time in history a water route was provided between the valleys of the two most important rivers in China. The canal was said to be forty paces in width, with state highways along its banks, and these highways were planted with willows on both sides. In 608 building of the northern section of the Grand Canal, called the Yungchi Canal (from Panchu on the

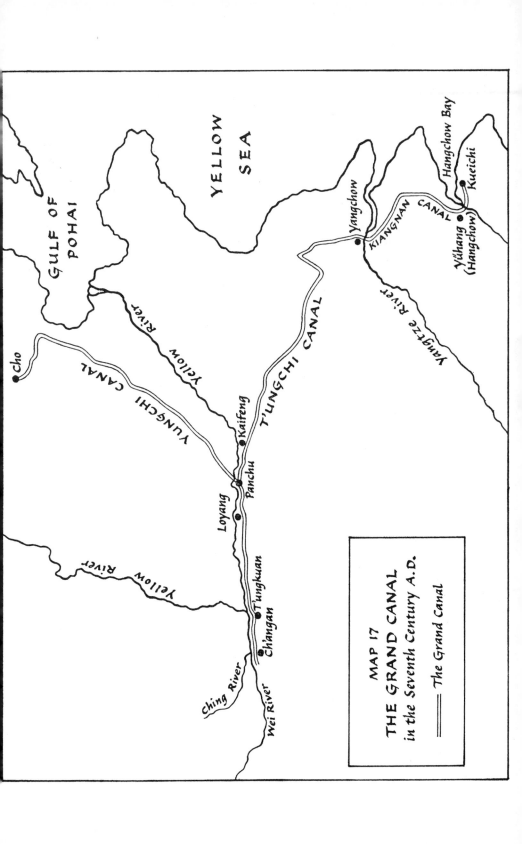

GULF OF POHAI

YELLOW SEA

Hangchow Bay

Yellow River

● Cho

YUNGCHI CANAL

● Kaifeng

T'UNGCHI CANAL

Yangchow

KIANGNAN CANAL

● Kueichi

Yühang (Hangchow)

Yangtze River

● Loyang

● Panchu

Yellow River

● Tungkuan

Ch'angan ●

Ching River

Wei River

MAP 17
THE GRAND CANAL
in the Seventh Century A.D.

——— The Grand Canal

Yellow River to the city of Cho near modern Peking), was started. More than one million people were conscripted to work on this project. This project was followed two years later by the construction of the southern section, called the Kiangnan Canal, which began at Chinkiang on the Yangtze River and extended southward to Hangchow on the Ch'ient'ang River (the lower valley of the Chekiang River). Upon the completion of the Grand Canal produce from South China could be shipped by boat to North China for a distance of approximately 900 miles. Its importance cannot be overemphasized. More than anything else it fused North and South China as an economic and cultural whole and strengthened their interdependence. It was only after the introduction of railroads in modern times that the canal began to outlive its usefulness and deterioration set in. Prior to this time each dynasty had always considered the good maintenance and efficient operation of the Grand Canal one of its primary concerns.

Sui Yang-ti's other public works, such as the construction of his elegant palaces, were less praiseworthy since they brought benefit to no one except himself. Toward the end of his reign he became more and more unscrupulous in the use of manpower and lived a life so extravagant that on one occasion, we are told, he employed 18,000 musicians for thirty days to entertain his guests from abroad. Taxes had to be continually increased, and soon they reached a point too burdensome even for the well-to-do. His pleasure trips to the Yangtze areas were not only an annoyance to his subjects, but often meant financial ruin to the local gentry who had to wait on him. The popular saying was: "People are angry, but dare not speak." They had to wait for a disaster to fall on him before they would speak with a mighty clash of arms. The disaster they awaited did happen when his military campaigns against Korea met with reverses.

Since Han Wu-ti's conquest of Korea in the second century B.C., the Hermit Kingdom had been an off-and-on tributary state to the Celestial Empire for more than seven centuries. During the period of Southern and Northern Dynasties there was no interference of Korean affairs on the part of China, since China herself was divided. After Yang Chien had unified China, Korea, being afraid that China would intervene again, took defensive measures on the Sino-Korean border. The fear was soon realized. In 597 Yang Chien sent an ultimatum to the Korean king, enunciating a number of reasons why he had to declare war: the tribal allies of China on the northeastern border had been repeatedly attacked by Korea; Koreans had often passed across the border to murder Chinese; Korea had shown openly her displeasure when the Sui regime unified China, and so on. The following year an expeditionary force was sent to subdue Korea but failed to achieve its purpose. During Sui Yang-ti's reign, three times the emperor personally led military expeditions against the Hermit Kingdom, but each time the brave Koreans fought the invading forces to a standstill. Because of the enormous difficulty of shipping supplies over the rugged mountains in eastern Manchuria, a large portion of Chinese troops died of starvation and disease before they could even reach the front. It did not help that the defenders adopted a Fabian strategy by fortifying themselves behind well-built strongholds and refusing to give battle. The invaders, frustrated and eventually exhausted, had to give up the siege, once their supplies such as food diminished at a fast rate. It was not until 668 that Korea was finally conquered, when the T'ang dynasty under T'ang Kao-tsung (r. 650–683) threw in all its resources and captured Korea's capital of Pyonyang.

As the 610's progressed, all signs indicative of a dynasty's downfall were clear for all to see: foreign adventures had failed; taxes and labor conscription had been increased beyond endurance; and to trigger the rebellion, famine again appeared after a devastating flood had raged over Shantung, Hopeh, and Honan provinces, where "people ate tree bark and sold themselves as slaves in countless numbers." As one would expect, the revolt began in Shantung and Hopeh, the two provinces that had served as supply bases during the Korean campaigns and were most adversely affected by the war. What followed is too familiar. Warlords and bandits sprang up all over the country, fighting against the government and also among themselves. In 618 Sui Yang-ti was murdered in the gay city of Yangchow whereto he had repaired to enjoy himself. Two months later Li Yüan (566–635), another rebel leader, assumed the imperial title at Ch'angan and called his dynasty T'ang.

THE T'ANG REGIME

What would the moral judgment be if one were placed in a position to kill or be killed and succeeded in doing the killing? Whatever the answer to this question is, there is little doubt as to what a person would strive to do if unfortunately he found himself in such a terrible dilemma. This was precisely the dilemma Li Shih-min faced in 627. Though the successful revolt against the Sui regime was, in a formal sense, led by his father Li Yüan, Li Shih-min was in fact its primary initiator, promotor, and executor, more responsible for the founding of the T'ang dynasty than anyone else, including his own father. Yet, legally and customarily he could not succeed as the next emperor, since he was not his father's first-born son, but the second. Would he stage a revolt against her elder brother Chien-ch'eng once the latter, as the crown prince, inherited the throne? How would his elder brother treat him if, on the other hand, he simply submitted himself to his brother's authority? While the first question was very much in the mind of his elder brother, he himself had the second question to ponder. He could not help recalling the tragic ending of all of Sui Yang-ti's brothers who were either killed or thrown into jail, even though the new emperor, before ascending the throne, had been known as a kind, generous, and brotherly prince. Besides, his own elder brother, as far as he knew, had never been brotherly toward him. Ever since 624 when all of China was brought under the T'ang control, Yüan-chi, the youngest and most belligerent of the three brothers, had repeatedly urged Chien-ch'eng to kill him "before it is too late." What could or would Shih-min do under the circumstances other than strike first so as to save his own life? On the morning of July 20, 627, he and his veteran warriors hid themselves on both sides of the Hsüan-men Gate that led to the imperial palace, knowing in advance that his two brothers would arrive soon to attend an imperial conference. The moment they arrived, heavy fighting ensued. Both Chien-ch'eng and Yüan-chi were shot to death by piercing arrows; Shih-min was thrown from his mount in a wild chase but somehow escaped injury. Shocked and saddened by the tragic event, Li Yüan abdicated on behalf of his only surviving son.

While one may question the dubious way whereby Li Shih-min (hereafter referred to by his imperial title T'ang T'ai-tsung) acquired absolute power, there is no question whatsoever about his subsequent achievement. The empire he founded flourished gloriously for 137 years (618–755); not until 755 did it begin to move downward, and not until 907 did it finally end. This period of 137 years is known as one of the golden eras in Chinese history when China stood alone in radiance and splendor among the contemporary civilizations of the world. Once again the Chinese extended their jurisdiction northwestward to Central Asia, westward to the eastern border of Persia, southward to Vietnam, and northeastward to Korea. Even the "unconquerable" Tibet was brought in as a Chinese vassal state. Domestically old institutions were renovated and strengthened, while new ones were added as the necessity arose. This was also the period of intellectual and cultural refinement, equal to any in history. The over-all achievements were so numerous and exceptional that many Chinese in the United States, even after generations of Americanization, still proudly refer to themselves as T'ang jen, or men of T'ang.

Among the rulers of this period the most outstanding were T'ang T'ai-tsung (r. 627–649), Empress Wu (624–705), and T'ang Hsüan-tsung (r. 713–755). T'ang T'ai-tsung ranks high among China's historical leaders not so much for his military conquests or domestic construction as for his attempt to live up to a Confucian ideal, namely, that the purpose of governing was to bring maximum benefit to the governed. "The first principle in kingship is to preserve the people," he stated. "A king who exploits the people for his personal gains is like a man who cuts his own thighs to feed himself. As there is no such thing as a crooked shadow following a straight

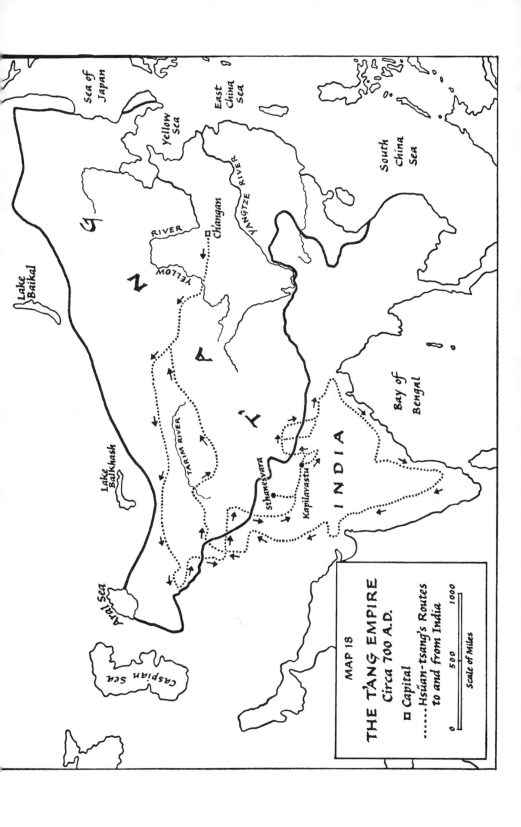

Sea of Japan

East China Sea

Yellow Sea

South China Sea

Lake Baikal

RIVER

YELLOW

Ch'angan

YANGTZE RIVER

Bay of Bengal

Lake Balkhash

TARIM RIVER

INDIA

Sthaneśvara

Kapilavastu

Aral Sea

Caspian Sea

MAP 18

THE T'ANG EMPIRE

Circa 700 A.D.

□ Capital

..... Hsüan-tsang's Routes to and from India

Scale of Miles

0   500   1000

object, it is inconceivable that the people can be disloyal when their rulers are virtuous." These remarks have been dear to the hearts of all Confucians ever since they were made some thirteen hundred years ago. During the best years of his reign, we are told, "no banditry occurred anywhere in the empire, and consequently the jails were often empty." Polished rice cost less than forty standard coins per picul, and taxes were only one-fortieth of the annual harvest, the lowest rate ever recorded in Chinese history. For those who believe that a virtuous ruler can indeed induce the people to do the almost impossible for the common good, there is this episode that allegedly occurred during T'ang T'ai-tsung's reign. Approximately three hundred convicted criminals had been sentenced to death in the various parts of the empire and were scheduled to be executed. The emperor ordered them to be set free so they could live the last few months of their lives with their families, on the condition that they would voluntarily surrender themselves to the executioners no later than the day before the scheduled execution. To the surprise of the watchful citizens, every one of the three hundred returned of his own accord and reported to the executioner on the scheduled date.

Empress Wu, at one time the consort of T'ang Kao-tsung (r. 650–683), has been praised and condemned with equal vigor by historians. She has been condemned because of her ruthlessness in the pursuance of power as well as the "rottenness" of her personal life. To seek power, she murdered three of her own children, including one daughter, and installed and dismissed two emperors in one year (684), both again of her own blood. After acquiring absolute power in 685, she openly invited the recommendation of supersexual young men for her royal pleasure, in a society where all "decent" women were supposed to be modest and sexually innocent. Despite all this, she has been praised highly as an able, conscientious, and enlightened ruler. She entrusted governmental affairs to the very best men she could find, and they proved to be unswervingly loyal to her. Her reign of twenty years (685–705) was among the most memorable during the T'ang dynasty.

The elegance of T'ang court life reached its most refined stage during the reign of T'ang Hsüan-tsung, also known as T'ang Ming-huang. Though acclaimed as the most generous patron of fine arts and literature among the T'ang emperors, to most Chinese he has been known primarily for his central role in a story of love, a story which reflects most convincingly the kind of easy, pleasurable life during a period of abundance. Many poems were written in praise of the unsurpassed beauty of this commoner's daughter named Yang Kuei-fei with whom the emperor had fallen in love at first sight. Enchanted by her charm, the emperor did all he could to keep her happy and amused. A music and dance troupe of several hundred persons was kept in the court to entertain her, and horses and riders, we

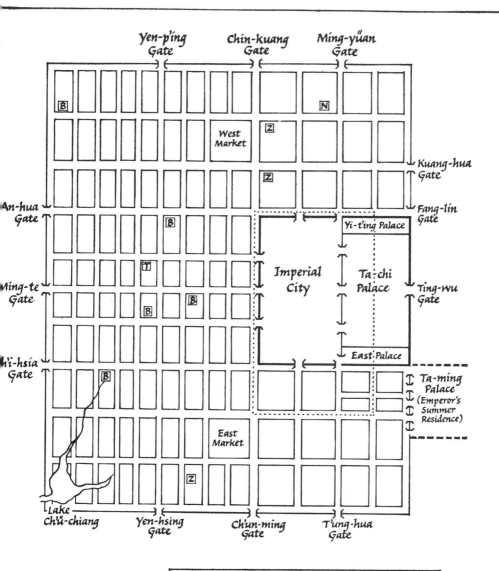

Yen-p'ing Gate

Chin-kuang Gate

Ming-yüan Gate

An-hua Gate

Ming-te Gate

Ch'i-hsia Gate

West Market

East Market

Imperial City

Ta-chi Palace

Yi-t'ing Palace

East Palace

Kuang-hua Gate

Fang-lin Gate

Ting-wu Gate

Ta-ming Palace (Emperor's Summer Residence)

Lake Chü-chiang

Yen-hsing Gate

Ch'un-ming Gate

T'ung-hua Gate

W
S — N
E

MAP 19

T'ANG'S CAPITAL: CH'ANGAN

Total Area: 972 ch'ing or 14,752 acres

)(City Gate

Famous Churches and Temples: B Buddhist;
N Nestorian; T Taoist; Z Zoroastrian

---- Walls of modern city of Sian

are told, ran around the clock from Canton to Ch'angan to carry fresh litchi—her favorite fruit—to the royal court, a distance of more than 1,500 miles. Each year on the seventh evening of the seventh month when every happily married Chinese couple was supposed to pledge eternal fidelity toward each other, the emperor vowed repeatedly that he and his beloved would indeed live and die together. Her male relatives were made dukes and counts, and there was a saying in Ch'angan: "Don't grieve when the new born is that of the female sex."

"No feast can last forever," however; and this feast, that had gone on for 137 years, came to an abrupt end in 755. Toward the end of that year news arrived at Ch'angan that An Lu-shan (d. 757), the governor-general of Fanyang (modern Hopeh), had revolted. The government was so ill-prepared for this unexpected event that in less than a month the rebels reached the Yellow River, crossed it, and soon captured the city of Loyang. Subsequently An Lu-shan sent his veteran warriors westward to attack Ch'angan which he captured six months later. Previously the emperor and his favorite Yang Kuei-fei could not even believe their own ears when they heard of this revolt, since An Lu-shan, though an illiterate barbarian, had been their most trusted general and protégé and had been for this reason given the important command of defending China's northeastern frontier. Now that the enemy was knocking at the front door of Ch'angan, the emperor and his favorite decided to flee in the darkness of the night, hoping eventually to reach the safe province of Szechuan. In a postal station twenty-eight miles west of the capital, the dispirited and half-starved soldiers refused to march forward unless, they said, the culprits responsible for this miserable state of affairs were punished. Yang Kuei-fei's brother who was then the prime minister was cut into pieces by the mob of soldiers, and still they demanded more blood. With tears in his eyes, the emperor ordered his favorite to be led away, and she hanged herself on a nearby tree. Throughout the rest of his life, the emperor was a sad, depressed man, "washing his face everyday with a fountain of tears."

To suppress An Lu-shan's revolt, the T'ang regime made the short-sighted move of inviting military help from barbarian tribes beyond the northwestern frontier. The most powerful group among them was a nomadic, Turkish-speaking horde called Hui-heh (Uighurs) which had its base of operation in modern Kansu province. It readily accepted the T'ang government's invitation, on the condition that all the wealth of recaptured cities should be regarded as its war booty and that it had free disposal of all captured persons, including women and children. Given a condition like this, one can easily visualize the madness that followed the recapture of Loyang in the fall of 757. Long after An Lu-shan's rebellion had been suppressed (757), the same Hui-heh roamed freely in Shensi and Honan provinces, "torturing people and insulting local officials," besides carrying on the customary looting. Even the capital city of Ch'angan was not spared. One day early in 766 a Hui-heh envoy was busy directing the kidnapping of Chinese civilians right in front of the Bureau of Barbarian Affairs, while Chinese officials helplessly looked on. Fourteen more years had to elapse before the Hui-heh, torn by internal dissension, began to decline; and the T'ang emperors, following an ancient custom, supplied its rulers with Chinese princesses as consorts.

The T'ang government's appeasement of the Hui-heh was partly due to its fear of another powerful tribe of Tibetan origin, namely, the T'u-fan. Beginning in 756 year after year these Tibetans raided areas deep within China proper until in 763 they captured their biggest prize, Ch'angan, which they sacked for fifteen days before leaving it in ruins. This miserable state of affairs continued off and on until the middle of the ninth century when the T'ang government was finally able to recover from the T'u-fan all of its lost territories. By then the once powerful tribe had disintegrated into many small groups that could no longer pose any threat.

An important factor that contributed to the T'ang regime's inability to cope with these foreign invaders was the existence of a deep-rooted malaise in the power center. With one possible exception, all the T'ang emperors after T'ang Hsüan-tsung were mediocre or worse; real power, consequently, fell into the hands of the self-seeking eunuchs. This power was more absolute than that enjoyed by the eunuchs of the Later Han since in the T'ang case there were no empresses' relatives or scholar-gentry strong enough to provide a counterbalance (see pp. 120-122). They installed and dismissed emperors at will; twice (once in 820 and again in 827) they found it necessary to murder a reigning emperor in order to crown a younger and more pliable puppet. One emperor (T'ang Wentsung, r. 827–840), having attempted but failed to assert himself, was forced to witness the slaughtering of hundreds of his loyal supporters in cold blood (December 14, 835). Though his own life was spared, he lived in virtual confinement for the rest of his life. "Why should Your Majesty not be content with the enjoyment of life when your humble servant can easily handle such mundane affairs as the running of the government?" inquired the eunuch leader who pretended to be genuinely surprised. With people like this eunuch running the government, the T'ang court, once the center of elegance and culture, had by then become a hotbed of corruption, intrigues, and open assassinations.

As the court lost its dignity, the people lost their respect for it. Discontented elements in the provinces took full advantage of local grievances engendered by corruption and injustice to organize revolt. The most damaging among these revolts was the one led by Huang Ch'ao (d. 884) which, beginning at Shantung in 875, ravaged the eastern half of China proper for a period of nine years. In 878 the rebels captured Canton where, we are told, they slaughtered 120,000 foreigners (Christians, Muslims, Jews, and Persians) in cold blood, presumably because they were "too wealthy." While robbing the rich, Huang Ch'ao gave some of his loot to the poor, with whom he was quite popular. His success culminated in the capture of Loyang and Ch'angan in 880; he sacked both cities thoroughly, as the barbarians had done several times before. However, without the support of the scholar-gentry whom he despised, he was never able to organize an efficient government, even though at one time most of China proper was under his control. In 884 after his hordes had been repeatedly defeated by a T'ang general, he asked one of his devoted friends to kill him and to take his head to the T'ang headquarters for a reward. When his friend refused to do so, he committed suicide.

To cope with rebellions like this, governors-general were given extraordinary powers; often several viceroyalties were put under the jurisdiction of one man to achieve more efficient military campaigns. As one may expect, eventually these governors-general became too powerful for the imperial government to control after the rebellions had been suppressed. They collected their own taxes, appointed their own officials, and maintained their own armies. Theirs were independent kingdoms in all except name. To perpetuate their independent status, they often appointed their successors (usually their own children) before they died, and the imperial government could do nothing except confirm the *fait accompli*. Thus the most powerful governors-general were not only independent but also hereditary rulers. They fought among themselves and annexed each other's territories. It often happened that when a T'ang emperor decided to punish the most recalcitrant of them, being militarily weak he had to seek help from other governors-general. By becoming a partner in the wars between the governors-general, he degraded himself in the game of annexing territories which nominally belonged to him anyway. Almost without exception he wound up on the loser's end, as the governors-general whose assistance he had requested gained most of the territories conquered from the defeated and consequently became even more unmanageable. Were he on the losing side, he found himself in the most embarrassing position of having to issue a decree publicly denouncing himself and apologizing to his nominally inferior subordinates. In either case, he could not win.

With invasions from abroad and disunity and rebellions at home, it was only a matter of time before the T'ang dynasty would come to an end. In 907 the last T'ang emperor abdicated in favor of one of his generals named Chu Ch'üan-chung (852–912). The latter called his dynasty Liang, known as Later Liang to historians. Following this change of dynasties, five dynasties rose and fell in quick succession; it was a matter of one strong man replacing another. The five dynasties were known as the Later Liang (907–923), the Later T'ang (923–936), the Later Tsin (936–947), the Later Han (947–950), and the Later Chou (951–960). Under none of these dynasties was China unified. The many warlords in the provinces continued their independent or semi-independent status. This shifting situation finally ended in 960 when Chao K'uang-yin, a scholarly general, conquered most of the warlords and founded a new dynasty called Sung.

T'ANG INSTITUTIONS

The slow movement of administrative jurisdiction from the Three Chancellors and Nine Secretaries of State to the Imperial Secretariat that began during the Later Han period had been completed by the time when the T'ang dynasty was established. In name not only did the Three Chancellors still exist; they were also the Three Tutors (*San shih*), derived originally from a single post, namely, the Grand Tutor of the Later Han dynasty. But these Chancellors and Tutors were appointments advisory or honorific in nature, carrying with them little power or responsibility. Actual power of administration was vested in the Three Secretariats (*San sheng*), Six Ministries (*Liu pu*), and one Board of Censors (*Yü-shih t'ai*). The first two were jurisdictionally related, while the last-mentioned was independent of both.

The Three Secretariats derived their origin from the Imperial Secretariat of the Later Han dynasty and consisted of the First Secretariat (*Chung-shu sheng*), the Second Secretariat (*Men-hsia sheng*), and the Executive Secretariat (*Shang-shu sheng*). The First Secretariat participated with the emperor in the formulation of laws and drafting of decrees, but these prospective laws or decrees, to be legally valid, had to be endorsed by the president or other responsible officials of the Second Secretariat which, in this case, held a power amounting to veto. Originally operating in separate buildings and checking and balancing each other, the two Secretariats merged during the reign of T'ang T'ai-tsung to form what was then known as Council of Political Affairs (*Cheng-shih t'ang*). The chairman of this council, who could be the president of either the First or the Second Secretariat, was often referred to as the *real* prime minister, as contrary to the presidents of individual Secretariats who were called prime ministers without being characterized as "real" (*chen*). In 720 the Council of Political Affairs was renamed First-Second Secretariat (*Chung-shu men-hsia sheng*), though its basic functions remained the same.

If the First-Second Secretariat can be compared to the legislative branch of a Western government, the Executive Secretariat, as its name implies, was the executive branch of the government. Since T'ang T'ai-tsung, before ascending the throne, had served as the president of the Executive Secretariat, no one, from then, was "audacious" or "impudent" enough to occupy that post, which remained vacant throughout the remainder of the T'ang dynasty. Instead there were two vice-presidents, the first and the second, and the first vice-president served simultaneously as the acting president. Under the first vice-president were the Ministries of Rites, Personnel, and Finance, and under the second vice-president were the Ministries of War, Justice, and Public Works. Together they were called the Six Ministries that formed the backbone of the central administration. While the functions of most of these ministries are self-evident, those of the Ministry of Rites may need some explanation. The Ministry of Rites was in charge of not only "rites," such as religious worship, but also matters relating to education, civil service examinations, and "barbarian affairs." Interestingly enough, all officials in the Three Secretariats, including the "real" prime minister, enjoyed a rank no higher than that of the third degree, thus conforming to the fiction that they were merely the emperor's personal secretaries. Meanwhile, the Chancellors and the Tutors, who enjoyed higher ranks, had little or no responsibility at all, as noted earlier.

Independent of the Three Secretariats was the Board of Censors headed by a Grand Censor (Yü-shih ta-fu) who, during the Han dynasty, had been a member of the Three Chancellors (p. 105). The Board was responsible for the examination and scrutiny of the personal as well as official life of all officials under active tenure, and could start impeachment proceedings against any of them, including the "real" prime minister, if its investigation so warranted. For inspectional purposes the empire was divided into ten circuits each of which was headed by a censor, popularly known as the inspector general (chien-ch'a shih or kuan-ch'a shih). An inspector general travelled regularly within his circuit and listened to complaints; he could initiate indictment against any official within his circuit, including a governor, if in his judgment there was a genuine case calling for action. Thus armed, his power continued to increase with the passage of time until eventually he was as much administrative as he was inspectional. In short, he had to all intents and purposes become a governor-general heading an administrative viceroyalty instead of an inspectional circuit. The same change occurred during the Later Han dynasty, as described in an earlier chapter (p. 119).

Prior to this change the T'ang dynasty had practiced a two-tiered system in local government: the empire was divided into 358 provinces that in turn were divided into 1,573 districts. Now that viceroyalties had been inserted between the central government and the provinces, a three-tiered system of viceroyalties, provinces, and districts prevailed as a result. The increase of local power did not end here, however. In 722 the government created ten military viceroyalties with heavy concentration of troops in the northern and northwestern provinces as a defense measure. The heads of these viceroyalties, called military governors-general (chieh-tu shih), enjoyed military commandership as well as administrative and inspectional powers. One of them was named An Lu-shan who, by 755, had become powerful enough to stage a rebellion. To combat An Lu-shan's rebellion, governors-general in the interior regions were also given military command until the whole empire was divided into military viceroyalties, headed by autonomous or semi-independent warlords. The wars they waged against one another eventually brought the T'ang dynasty to an end, as noted earlier.

Traditional historians in China tend to dismiss the increase of local power after 755 as an abnormal development resulting from unusual circumstances; they find much greater pleasure in discussing the golden age when the T'ang bureaucracy functioned with remarkable efficiency. One reason for this efficiency, as they point out, was the adoption of the civil service examination system introduced earlier during the Sui dynasty. This system differed from the selection system of the Han dynasty in the sense that it emphasized written examinations as a means to measure the qualifications of a candidate to governmental posts, as contrary to the selection system that placed great weight on the recommendations by local governments. The difference was a difference in emphasis nevertheless, since the examination system, as a normal procedure, also called for the recommendation of candidates by local governments, and the selection system, especially that practiced during the Later Han dynasty, sometimes required the taking of a written examination before a recommended candidate was given a governmntal post to hold. Early during the T'ang dynasty six categories of examination existed side by side; they ranged from the all-embracing "flowering talent" (*hsiu-ts'ai*) to the more technical fields such as "expertise in law" (*ming lü*) and "expertise in mathematics" (*ming suan*). In 651 the category of "flowering talent," which had been the most prestigious, was abolished altogether, on the ground that "it was so difficult that rarely could any one succeed in it." Of the remaining, the categories of "advanced scholarship" (*chin-shih*) and "expertise in classics" (*ming ching*) were the most popular and attracted the largest number of candidates. Since "expertise in classics" emphasized memory, the most talented candidates gravitated naturally toward "advanced scholarship" which required, among other things, the writing of five essays on contemporary affairs. Beginning in 754 the candidates for "advanced scholarship" were also required to write two poems, one in the *shih* and the other in the *fu* style. From then on poetry continued to overshadow essays in importance until in 834 the writing of essays was abolished altogether, and the candidates were tested in the writing of poetry alone. Eager candidates circulated their poems among the powerful and the influential long before the examination date; if their products were judged to be of the finest quality, they were designated to pass, even before they actually took the examination. This was especially true for a candidate who was to pass the examination as "number one."

This does not mean that the examination was easy, however. Before the category of "flowering talent" was abolished in 651, the candidates who had passed the examination under that category totaled no more than fifteen or thereabouts. The number of candidates for "advanced scholarship" varied from 1,000 to 2,000 each year; those who succeeded numbered anywhere from 10 to 20, at a ratio of approximately 100 to 1. "Half of the candidates will have white hair before they reach this level," commented the T'ang essayist Han Yü, "and most of the others can never make it no matter how many times they are going to try." The examinations that led to an "advanced scholarship" degree were administered by the Ministry of Rites; before a degree-holder was actually appointed to a governmental post, usually at the lowest rank, he had to take another examination administered by the Ministry of Personnel. Han Yü himself failed three times in the latter examination and was without a governmental post for ten years after he had acquired his "advanced scholarship" degree.

The civil service examination system marked a sharp departure from the general practice of the preceding period when family background was emphasized in the recruitment of bureaucratic personnel (pp. 145–147). By stressing talent and ability in a prospective official's qualifications, the T'ang government attempted to cultivate a national purpose of solidarity so as to destroy localism that had been blamed for the division of China after 220 A.D. As the examination system took no consideration of family or local background, the glamor hitherto attached to the old families would disappear, and the government would be the sole dispenser of fame, power, and wealth. By dangling rewards constantly in front of the country's educated, the government obtained the undivided loyalty of a most powerful group, and those who had been rewarded abundantly after passing the examinations could be counted on to support the status quo. It is no wonder that with modifications and occasional interruptions the civil service examination system continued in force for the next twelve centuries; it was not abolished until the twentieth century.

The examination system may have contributed to the strengthening of Chinese autocracy; its advantages, on the other hand, cannot be denied either. First, it definitely broadened the government's base by drawing officials from all levels of society and thus introduced a democratic element into an otherwise oligarchic society. Theoretically at least, a man of the humblest origin could, by passing the examinations, rise in power, wealth, and prestige. More than anything else, the examination system accounted for the large degree of social mobility in China that had been denied to many other societies. Second, to find the right man for the right task, nothing could be more objective than a test impartially administered, and the civil service examination system was adopted with that purpose in mind. Many great statesmen in China were a product of this system. Third, the examination system reminded the people of the importance of education and learning and thus indirectly raised the cultural level of the country as a whole. While in other countries landlords, merchants or industrialists might be men of the greatest prestige, in China the most respected had always been the scholars.

In economic matters the early T'ang dynasty practiced a land distribution system introduced earlier by the Later Wei regime (386–535). The land law of 624 that governed this system read in part as follows:

Each adult male is to be given one *ch'ing* of land. A person who is incurably ill or disabled will receive forty *mou* of land. A widowed wife or concubine will receive thirty *mou*. The head of a household will receive twenty *mou* in addition to his regular allotment. Of the amount of land each person receives, 20 percent is hereditary and the rest is redistributable. Upon the death of the grantee, the herditary portion can be inherited by the head of the household next in line, while the redistributable portion is to be returned to the government for redistribution among other people. [1 *ch'ing* = 100 *mou* or 15.13 acres.]

For land received, a farmer paid grain as rent (*tsu*), contributed silk or cloth as requisitions (*t'iao*), and performed corvée as labor services (*yung*). Each year rent amounted to two piculs of grain; requisitions measured seven yards of silk or eight and half yards of cloth; and twenty working days constituted the total labor service. He could, if he chose to, translate his corvée duties into payment in kind, or work extra days as a substitute for his "rent" and "requisitions" obligations. This was known as the tripartite tax system that imposed taxes on "persons" rather than "income." Since a person who paid taxes received approximately the same income from the land he tilled as his neighbors, the so-called "personal tax" was indeed the same as "income tax." It was fair and equitable as long as the land distribution system was in force. It could not and would not work once this system was destroyed.

Beginning in the 660's the land distribution system began to deteriorate; a considerable time had to elapse, however, before it completely disappeared. Among the reasons that could be cited for this deterioration and eventual disappearance, the primary one seemed to be the continuous increase of population which, in the end, made land distribution physically impossible to be carried out. In short, there was simply not enough land to be distributed. Once again land was bought and sold like commodities, with the inevitable result that a few had large tracts of land, while most of the others had little or no land at all. Yet the landless and the poor, legally speaking, had to pay the same amount of taxes as the well-to-do since the tripartite tax system, as noted earlier, only recognized "persons" rather than "income" in the assessment of tax payment. Beginning in 755 when China was plunged into chaos and war, people moved constantly from one place to another to escape the ravages of war; births and deaths were no longer recorded; even population registers were in most cases permanently lost. Tax collectors roamed the countryside using whatever ingenuity they had to collect as much as possible, with little or no regard for the principle of equity. Under the circumstances the tripartite tax system simply ceased to function.

This confused state of affairs continued until 799 when Yang Yen (727–781), then the vice-president of the Second Secretariat, introduced a new tax system to restore some stability. According to this system, the government at the beginning of each year estimated its expenditures and then, using this estimation as a basis, decided how much tax would be levied for that year. Taxes were assessed according to "income" rather than "persons," and all taxes hitherto paid in produce and labor services were now combined into one single tax to be paid in cash. However, if a taxpayer chose to pay in produce, he could do so by paying an amount equivalent to his cash assessment, the conversion rate varying according to market prices. Payment was to be made twice a year, once before the end of the sixth month and once before the end of the eleventh. Because of its simplicity and fairness, this new system—called *liang-shui fa*, or semiannual tax system—was a great improvement over the previous one. It or its derivatives continued in force until the twentieth century.

RELIGION AND CULTURE

As far as ideology was concerned, the T'ang regime, like other Chinese regimes before or after it, made a clear distinction between those ideas that governed secular matters and those that concerned themselves primarily with the spiritual or the otherworldly. Confucianism emphasized correctness in the relationship among men and was therefore the state ideology that governed all mundane affairs, ranging from governmental organization to personal ethics. To promote Confucianism, the T'ang government not only made Confucian learning the primary requisite for all those who wished to enter governmental service, but also encouraged the establishment of Confucian-oriented schools and the writing and publication of Confucian subjects. In areas other than mundane, however, there was definitely more competition; in fact, the early T'ang emperors often prided themselves as patrons of all religions, including Buddhism, Taoism, Zoroastrianism, Nestorianism, and Islam. Individual monarchs may have had their preference for one religion or another, but none, before 845, persecuted those that were not his personal choice. In the capital city of Ch'angan as well as in many other Chinese cities, the followers of different religions quietly built their temples or churches, with little or no interference from the government whatsoever (Map 19). Nor is there any indication that this peaceful coexistence among different religions was interrupted by the desecration, let alone destruction, of one holy place by the followers of another, though rivalry among themselves and competition for new adherents continued to persist. Each temple or church was like a store that offered different wares, and a customer was free to shop around to find what he needed. As far as the government was concerned, the more diverse the temples were, the better the people's spiritual need would be satisfied.

Of all the religions prevalent during the T'ang dynasty, the most influential and popular was still Buddhism which embraced within its fold people of all walks of life. Monasteries and temples continued to translate Buddhdist scriptures into Chinese; some of the translations were done under government sponsorship. Indian and Central Asian monks were invited to China to teach, and Chinese pilgrims travelled to India, over almost impassable mountains and deserts, to obtain more authentic copies of Buddhist scriptures. The most famous of these pilgrims was Hsüan-tsang (c. 596–664) who left Ch'angan in 629 and did not return

EWER IN THE
FORM OF A
COURT LADY,
T'ANG DYNASTY

until sixteen years later (Map 18). Upon his return he was interviewed repeatedly by Emperor T'ang T'ai-tsung who, as a result, became a Buddhist devotee later in his life. Empress Wu was even more generous in her patronage, having been assured by some Buddhist monks that female rule of a great empire was more than merely sanctioned according to Buddhist scriptures, though it was condemned by Confucians as a matter of principle. T'ang Hsüan-tsung, the last emperor of the golden era, personally preferred Taoism; but even he did not initiate any harsh measures against Buddhism which, in fact, reached its apogee of glory during his reign. By then Buddhism had become so deep-rooted in Chinese society that it would continue to grow, with or without royal patronage.

In the wake of Buddhist growth and prosperity came Buddhist schism. The multiplication of Buddhist sects was facilitated by the absence of a religious council or papacy that could have mediated or settled theological differences—each Buddhist master could indeed interpret the scriptures the way he wished and elaborate his own emphasis. Among the Buddhist sects that emerged and finally established themselves during the T'ang dynasty, the Pure Land and the Ch'an (known as Zen in Japan) were the most influential and popular. According to the Pure Land sect, a man's salvation depends upon not only his personal effort in the accumulation of Buddhist deeds but also, most importantly, the assistance he can invoke from Amitabha, the Buddha of Infinite Light who presides over the Pure Land. The Pure Land is the Western Paradise where the immortals live in an atmosphere of eternal bliss and where "the rivers are running with scented water and the land is dotted with jewel trees." To invoke the assistance of Amitabha, one needs to practice the *nien-fo*, or "remembering Buddha by calling his name." Thus the name of O-mi-t'o-fo, which is the Chinese transliteration of Amitabha, becomes a most familiar word in Chinese Buddhism, that has been uttered an infinite number of times in prayers ever since the Pure Land established itself as one of the most popular Buddhist sects in China. The more often one repeats that name, the better the chance one will have to achieve nirvana. One monk of the seventh century advised the use of beans in keeping track the number of times the name of O-mi-t'o-fo was repeated, and a disciple of his, following his advice, accumulated eighty feet of beans in height, though we are not told the length or the width.

It is easy to see why the Pure Land was so popular in T'ang China. According to this sect, a man's salvation did not depend upon bookish learning at a time when most Chinese people were illiterate. Nor was it contingent upon the accumulation of good deeds (*e.g.*, bridge building and road repairing) that involved financial expenses, at a time when most Chinese people were poor. It merely required the performance of a simple act, namely the repetition of Buddha's name which all people—rich or poor, high or lowly—could easily do, including a mute who was specifically allowed to do it in a mental fashion. Moreover, it appealed directly to the center of all religions, namely faith, the simplicity of which not only enhanced its popular appeal but also created an emotional beauty all of its own.

Parallel to the development of the Pure Land was that of the Ch'an which, literally, means meditation or concentration of mind. The Ch'an Buddhists taught the attainment of enlightenment through the examination of one's inner consciousness, bypassing all the external paraphernalia such as rituals, images, scriptures, and even the Lord Buddha himself. To know all realities and thus attain enlightenment was to know one's own mind, said the Ch'an Buddhists, because "the thing is where the mind is." The examination of one's own mind through meditation was therefore the key to knowledge, since all the physical objects or phenomena were merely reflections, like those in a mirror, of the inner mind. The inner mind was indeed The Reality, the total mastery of which would enable one to attain enlightenment. When a Ch'an Buddhist was asked whether the wind moved the pennant or the other way around, he replied that neither the wind nor the pennant had moved: it was the beholder's mind that had moved!

While this explanation of the movement of the pennant may not be rational or scientific, it is still comprehensible. The teachings of Ch'an Buddhism after the eighth century became more abstruse and consequently less comprehensible. One of these teachings was the doctrine of instant enlightenment, according to which enlightenment could be attained through the use of such methods as beatings of the faithful by a stick or the utterance of a single magic word. These methods were to open the door to Buddha in the same manner as the shouting of *Sesame* was to open up some hidden treasure in the *Arabian Nights*. Verbal exchange was greatly emphasized, and the following may serve as an example of the kind of conversation the Ch'an Buddhists conducted:

Monk: Who knows the meaning of the apricots?
Master: The Buddhists know.
Monk: Can a monk know?
Master: I don't know Buddhism.

The last statement was supposed to be the most important. Both the monk and the reader could make their own interpretations.

This anti-logical, anti-literary, and highly speculative sect called Ch'an began with the Indian missionary Bodhidharma who came to China in 526 (variant 520) and is reported to have sat facing a wall in meditation for nine years until his legs atrophied. Six generations later the Ch'an mandate was passed to Hui-neng (638-713) who proved to be the greatest Ch'an propagator since Bodhidharma. After his death in 713, many legends have developed around this illiterate worker of peasant background who, in a period of eight months, was elevated to the Sixth Patriarchy of Ch'an Buddhism. According to one legend, the Fifth Patriarch Hung-jen (602–675), in the process of choosing a successor, asked each of his disciples to write a poem which, when completed, would indicate whether the writer possessed any Buddhist spirit. Shen-hsiu (600–706), the primary contender who later lived to the advanced age of one hundred six, wrote his poem as follows:

My body is the *bodhi* tree;
My mind a shining mirror.
The mirror I dust constantly,
Lest dust would accumulate.

Hui-neng, then serving as a rice pounder in the monastery, refuted the above poem as follows:

Bodhi is not a tree;
Nor is a mirror a mirror.
Since none of these exists,
How can dust accumulate?

It does not require much knowledge of Ch'an Buddhism to see which poem is superior.

The honeymoon between Buddhism and the T'ang government suffered a sudden setback in 845 when the half-insane emperor named T'ang Wu-tsung (r. 841–847), primarily motivated by greed, ordered the confiscation of Buddhist properties and the forcible return of the clergy to lay life. "When this measure [of confiscation] takes effect," said the royal decree, "good land amounting to hundreds of thousands of *ch'ing* will be appropriated by the government, together with 150,000 male and female slaves, all of whom will be reclassified as taxpaying citizens." All the former clergy, "who have lived on other people's toil," would have to seek gainful employment and start to pay taxes, and "statues made of gold, silver, and precious metals are to be melted and then handed over to the Board of Revenue." The full impact of this draconic decree lasted less than seven months (from the eighth month of 845 when the decree was issued to the third month of 846 when T'ang Wu-tsung died), though sporadic persecution may have begun as early as 842. Needless to say, no physical violence had ever been committed against any Buddhist monk or nun; nor was there any measure of suppression directed against Buddhist lay believers.

Whatever the impact of this persecution was on the later development of Buddhism as a whole, the two most popular sects, namely the Pure

Land and the Ch'an, seemed to be the least affected. The popularity of the Pure Land did not depend upon the prosperity of Buddhist establishments or hierarchies that T'ang Wu-tsung had destroyed. On the contrary, "A Buddhist temple is wherever the name of Amitabha is invoked," which could be one's own living room. As for Ch'an Buddhism, it had always been iconclastic, anti-establishment, and individualistic. A true Ch'an Buddhist could not care less if his temple were burned down. To destroy Ch'an Buddhism, one would have to destroy the Buddhist state of mind, which no government could do. Moreover, the Ch'an Buddhists emphasized the importance of manual work, such as tilling the fields, which enabled them to refute the charge that all Buddhist monastics were parasites. As for other sects that relied on literary tradition and religious establishments for their continual well-being, the persecution of 845, regarded by many as the worst persecution against Buddhism in Chinese history, doubtless had an adverse and depressing effect.

Outside the sphere of religion, Confucian or Confucian-oriented scholars predominated. These scholars were so prolific in their literary output that when the imperial library at Ch'angan catalogued its holdings in the 710's, it had 28,469 entries by contemporary authors as compared to 53,915 entries by all the writers prior to the T'ang dynasty. In history the two outstanding authors were Liu Chih-chi (661–721) who wrote *The Understanding of History (Shih t'ung)* and Tu Yu (d. 812) who wrote *The Study of Institutions (T'ung tien)*. The former book is a critical review of Chinese historiography, and the latter book traces in detail the development of Chinese institutions. In prose writing Han Yü and Liu Tsung-yüan (773–819) were credited with the revival of the "ancient style" (Han style, see p. 126) that had been eclipsed in importance by the "parallel form" during the preceding period (see pp. 151–152). From a historian's point of view, a most interesting development in T'ang literature was the emergence of the *ch'uan-ch'i* which, literally, means "unusual events according to tradition;" they are actually what we today might call short stories. The best known among the extant *ch'uan-ch'i* is a political moralizer by Tu Kuang-t'ing (850–933), entitled *The Story of the Curly Beard (Ch'iu-jan ke chuan)*. The moral is that great leaders like T'ang T'ai-tsung are born, not made, and that to know the limit of one's own ambition is indeed the font of wisdom. The story contains surprises, suspenses, and finally relief, all neatly arranged in less than 2,100 Chinese characters.

In poetry the T'ang dynasty produced three of the truly great of all times. They were Li Po (701–762), Tu Fu (712–770), and Po Chü-yi (772–846). Often hailed as a true genius, Li Po wrote beautiful poems "as easily as water flows out from a fountain." His products, consequently, possess a liveliness and spontaneity none of the other poets could match.

They deal with sentiments and emotions, generally without social content. Tu Fu, on the other hand, was more socially conscious, since most of his poems were written after 755, the year that marked the end of peace and the beginning of wars. A typical poem of his is *The Army*

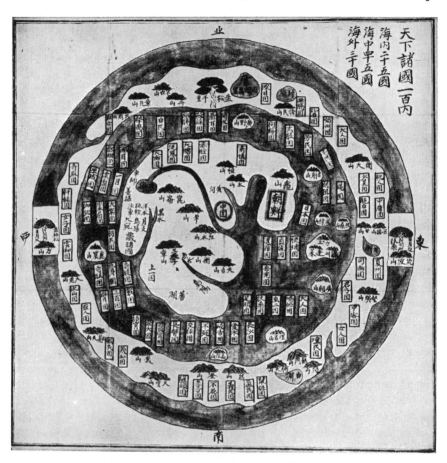

AN ANCIENT MAP SHOWING THE CHINESE CONCEPT OF THE WORLD   China is located at the center of the map (white area) surrounded by water (black area) dotted with island kingdoms including Japan. Further beyond is an enveloping ring of land (white area) on which are located countries with such odd names as "Country of Giants" and "Country of Gentlemen." Beyond this land is the universal ocean (black area) which extends outward indefinitely. On the upper right is the explanation which reads: "There are one hundred nations in the world: twenty-five surrounded by the Seas, forty-five on the Seas, and thirty beyond the Seas." The four Chinese characters around the map indicate directions: "East" in the right, "North" on the top, etc. The calligraphy on this map is embarrassingly poor, indicating perhaps that the map was an amateurish production.

Recruiter of Shihhao (*Shih-hao li*) that describes the misfortune of an old peasant whose one son has been recently killed in action while the other two are still serving in the army. Yet in the middle of one night when Tu Fu happens to stay in his house as an overnight lodger, the local army recruiter comes to seize the old man as another draftee. Having heard the knocking of the front door, the old man runs to the rear wall over which he jumps and then disappears in the darkness of the night. Meanwhile his wife, with an infant grandson in her arms, tearfully pleads with the recruiter to take her as an army cook instead of drafting her husband as a soldier. The next morning when Tu Fu leaves the village, only the old peasant is around to bid him good-bye and farewell. Po Chü-yi, the last of the trio, expresses in his poems the sadness of departure, the tragedy of wars, and the loneliness of the deserted. Two of his best known poems are *Eternal Sorrows* (*Ch'ang-hen ko*) and *Song of P'i-p'a* (*P'i-p'a hsing*). While the former traces T'ang Hsüan-tsung's romance with Yang Kuei-fei, the latter relates the ill fate of a once famous courtesan. Both works, depicting the transiency of happiness and the vicissitude of life, contain a strong element of Taoist fatalism—the sense of complete helplessness against overwhelming or even supernatural odds. Since this feeling of impotence is doubtless shared by most people in a similar situation, Po Chü-yi has been often referred to as a people's poet.

In the field of fine arts the T'ang dynasty was most noted for its painters. The greatest painter of the early T'ang period was Yen Li-pen (d. 673) who, as a specialist in the painting of people and architecture, once served in the court of T'ang T'ai-tsung. Yet he was not happy with his own talent. "I am deeply ashamed," he once said to his son, "that I cannot make a name for myself except through my paintings." He resented particularly the fact that he was often treated like a household servant or errand boy by members of the royal household. This attitude toward the fine arts was to change quickly, however. By the second decade of the eighth century, painting had definitely become a most respectable profession. The man most responsible for this change was T'ang Hsüan-tsung who, as the T'ang regime's greatest patron of arts and literature, invited to his court not only such famous men of letters as Li Po but also such renowned artists as Wu Tao-tzu, Li Ssu-hsün (651–720), and Wang Wei (699–759). Needless to say, all of the invited were treated like "friends and guests" instead of "household servants" or "errand boys." Wu Tao-tzu is regarded as the first great landscapist in Chinese history, though none of his paintings, except a few in facsimile (see illustration, p. 236), has survived. Li Ssu-hsün and Wang Wei were also famous for their landscapes which by then had become the most popular subject matter among the painters. Wang Wei, also known as a great poet, is said to have been able to "inject poetry into his painting and painting into his poems." Ironically, the extant T'ang paintings are mostly those of the lesser known, such as the horse paintings of Han Kan (c. 720–780) that were exibited in a tour of American museums in 1960.

Had T'ang Hsüan-tsung known a little about European history, he could have correctly stated that Ch'angan was the school of Asia just as Athens had been once the school of Hellas. During the golden era of the T'ang dynasty China was like a magnet of culture to all the peoples around her, especially the Koreans and the Japanese who came to her to learn all that a great civilization could offer: religion, philosophy, the arts, technology, and political and economic institutions. Korea had been subject to Chinese cultural influence since time immemorial; Japan, however, was a comparative newcomer. The first systematic account of Japan did not appear in China until the third century A.D., describing the Japanese in a generally favorable vein and stating specifically that they were a moral people with good customs. The mention of paddy rice and sericulture in this account, plus the recent discovery of Han coins on Japanese soil, seems to indicate that long before any formal contact was made, a cultural exchange of informal nature had gone on for centuries. However, it was not until the second half of the sixth century that the Japanese became fully aware of the advantages of the Chinese civilization and decided to go all-out to learn about it. By then the Japanese had already adopted the Chinese written language as their own, and the familiarity of the language doubtless facilitated the learning process.

From the latter part of the sixth to the last decade of the ninth century Japanese envoys, monks, scholars, and students arrived in China in increasingly larger numbers. After their return, their influence was immeasurable in shaping Japan's cultural development along the Chinese pattern. Chinese philosophy and religion were transplanted to Japan without much change, though the adoption of Chinese political and economic institutions proved to be less successful. In technology Japan learned from China the more advanced methods in making textiles, paper, woodworks, and, later, the printing press. The Chinese influence was ever greater in architecture; in fact, the two Japanese capitals, Nara and Kyoto, were built as small replicas of Ch'angan, then the capital of T'ang China (Map 19). More sophisticated Japanese learned to write poetry and prose in the Chinese style, sculptured and painted in the Chinese fashion, and even played Chinese games of intellect such as the popular wei-ch'i, known in Japan as go.

By the early tenth century the Japanese had apparently learned all they wished to learn from China; consequently, they ceased to come. Culturally the Japanese had matured and increasingly asserted their own independence.

☫ vi

The Two Sungs (1)

A CENTRALIZED ADMINISTRATION

On Chinese New Year's Day (January 31), 960, Kaifeng was alerted by urgent dispatches from two governors in the northern frontier that the Khitans, a nomadic tribe originating in Inner Mongolia, were about to march southward to invade Chinese territories. An emergency meeting was called, and it was decided that Chao K'uang-yin (927–976) should head an expeditionary force to meet the invading enemy. Two days after the alarm was sounded, the commander and his troops were speeding northward.

The rise of Chao K'uang-yin as the most powerful man in Kaifeng was no less than phenomenal. Only a year before he was one of those young generals who had plenty of ambition but was quite uncertain of what the future would hold. It was a surprise to him and to everybody else that suddenly the reigning emperor, Chou Shih-tsung (922–959), decided to promote him to the position of Commander of the Imperial Army, by-passing the older and better-known generals, including the emperor's closest relatives. Chou, however, had his own reason for the appointment. He was suffering from an incurable disease and his days were numbered; he wanted a conscientious, dependable man to take care of his six-year-old crown prince (later known as Chou Kung-ti, 953–973) when he could no longer do so himself. From among the candidates he had in mind, he finally decided on Chao K'uang-yin. First, Chao was incorruptible at a time when practically everyone used his position to enrich himself. Second, he loved learning. To the emperor a man genuinely interested in books could not possibly be bad. Chao had once been accused of having accepted bribes and of having shipped large trunks of gold and precious stones to his home after a successful military campaign in the south. The emperor ordered an investigation, and the investigators found nothing in those trunks except books which Chao had carefully collected and preserved from the devastation of war. Then and there the emperor decided that this was the man for whom he had been looking for a long time.

On the third of the first lunar month (February 2), the expeditionary force reached Ch'ench'iao where the soldiers stayed overnight after a long day's march from the capital. Early in the morning of the next day, Chao K'uang-yin was wakened from his sleep by loud, repeated shoutings in the inn where he stayed. Opening his bedroom door, he saw hundreds of soldiers swarming into the inn, and some of the generals, their swords unsheathed, stood on both sides of the inner court. The noise reached a crescendo when the soldiers spotted their commander. When the commotion finally subsided, the generals cried in unison: "Be our commander, the emperor of China!" Before Chao had time to respond, one of the generals put a yellow robe—symbol of imperial authority—on his back, and all the soldiers knelt down immediately, shouting at the top of their lungs: "Long live the emperor!" Subsequently the soldiers carried him to his horse, and the entire expeditionary force moved southward toward Kaifeng. In Kaifeng Chou Kung-ti, the child emperor, abdicated, and Chao K'uang-yin formally assumed the imperial title as the founder of a new dynasty named Sung. Meanwhile the Khitans, after looting some of China's border provinces and thus achieving their purpose of invasion, had withdrawn.

Though there had been instances of emperors installed by soldiers during the Five Dynasties, the mutiny at Ch'ench'iao proved to be most consequential, since the Sung dynasty, founded by Chao K'uang-yin (hereafter referred to by his imperial title Sung T'ai-tsu), lasted more then three hundred years (960–1279). Before Kaifeng, its capital, was captured in 1127 by a non-Chinese tribe called the Nuchens, it was referred to as the North Sung (960–1126). South Sung, with its capital at Hangchow in South China, lasted 152 years (1127–1279) before it was conquered by the Mongols.

Even today historians have not agreed on the true nature of the Ch'ench'iao mutiny that led to the establishment of the Sung dynasty. Was it an impulsive, spontaneous outburst or a carefully planned, cleverly manipulated event? Whatever the answer is, the way the dynasty was founded affected fundamentally the nature of the regime itself. After most of China had been brought under his control, Sung T'ai-tsu did not forget for a moment that he had become emperor only through a mutiny engineered by his subordinates, and he was fearful that he himself might be deposed in a similar manner. What followed was one of the most curious episodes in Chinese history, known to historians as "disarmament over a wine cup (*pei chiu shih ping ch'üan*). As the story goes, the emperor one evening invited his top lieutenants to a banquet in his palace. In the midst of joyful drinking he dismissed all attendants and then remarked that he was worried and often sleepless at night after he had ascended to the dragon throne, even though he was extremely grateful for the support that the generals had given to him.

"Why?" asked the generals.

"This is not difficult to see. Who does not wish to occupy my place?"

Upon hearing this all the generals present knelt. "The mandate of Heaven has already been bestowed upon Your Majesty. Who can and dares to challenge it?"

"You might not," the emperor replied. "But how can you control your subordinates who wish to acquire power and wealth as once you did when you proclaimed me your sovereign? If and when they put the yellow robe on your back, how can you refuse?"

Then the emperor gave them a lecture on the meaning of life, saying that the purpose of life was pleasure for oneself and one's descendants. This purpose would be better served, he added, if the generals would relinquish their military authority and retire to their private estates, so that no suspicion could possibly exist between the sovereign and his generals, and everyone present, with God's help, would live a long span of life. Having received the message, the generals resigned from their respective posts the very next day, all on account of "illness."

The "disarmament over a wine cup" formally ended a long period of warlordism that dated to the An Lu-shan's revolt in 755 (pp. 174–175). To prevent the reappearance of regionalism and to concentrate all the power in the hands of the emperor, Sung T'ai-tsu proceeded to reorganize the entire government, from the central to the local level. In central government the Sung regime followed the T'ang practice by maintaining the Three Secretariats (p. 177), but only the First-Second

Secretariat, known also as Council of Political Affairs and located inside the palace, had direct access to the emperor. The First and Second Secretariats no longer functioned as independent organs, and the Executive Secretariat, together with the Six Ministries under its jurisdiction, also lost much of its influence. The power in military affairs, for instance, was transferred from the Ministry of War to the Privy Council (*Ch'u-mi yüan*) that, like the First-Second Secretariat, was also located inside the palace. The First-Second Secretariat and the Privy Council, known as the Two Offices (*Liang fu*), were the nation's highest civil and military organs, respectively, and both were under the emperor's direct command. The Ministry of Finance, traditionally vested with the authority of managing the nation's fiscal matters, became almost an empty shell, as its power was taken over by the Finance Commission (*San ssu-shih*), again under the emperor's direct command. During the T'ang dynasty the duty of the imperial counsellors (*chien-kuan*) was to admonish or remonstrate with the emperor (p. 350); now they served as the emperor's mouthpieces, as they criticized or censored governmental officials upon the emperor's command. In short, all the checks upon the exercise of

The Sung Administration

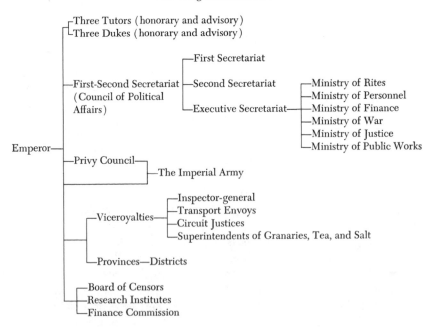

imperial power, that had been built into the Chinese government, were now totally lost. The enhancement of imperial authority was visually demonstrated by the fact that a prime minister of the Sung dynasty (President of the First-Second Secretariat) had to stand still when discussing state affairs with the emperor, no matter how long the discussion lasted, while his counterpart during the T'ang dynasty was customarily granted a chair. The new practice, while elevating the dignity of the emperor, was quite a strain for the prime minister, especially if he was advanced in age.

As for local administration, the Sung regime had, theoretically, a three-tiered system, but actually it had only provinces and districts. The highest local administration was supposed to be *lu*, here translated as viceroyalty, but *lu* was more a functional than a territorial administration, since there was no governor-general heading a viceroyalty. In each *lu* were four chief officials in charge of different duties, independent of one another and responsible directly to the emperor. They were (1) the inspector-general (*an-fu shih*), the emperor's eyes and ears over provincial and district administrations, (2) the transport envoy (*chuan-yün shih*), who supervised the shipment of local revenue (money and grain) to the central government, (3) the circuit justice (*t'i-tien hsing-yü kung-shih*), who conducted hearings on cases of appeal, and (4) the superintendent of granaries, tea, and salt (*t'i-chü ch'ang-p'ing ch'a yen kung-shih*), who oversaw not only the ever-normal granaries (pp. 163–166) and the tea and salt monopolies but also irrigation and water control projects.

With most of its normal functions taken away from it, the provincial administration (*fu, chou, chün,* or *chien*) became mostly a bureaucratic medium between the central government and the districts (*hsien*) over which it had direct jurisdiction. The magistrate of a district served not only as the administrative chief but also as the chief judge, the commander of local militia, and the superintendent of waterworks. He was, as the Chinese would say, the "father and mother" of the people.

The number of local administrations varied during the Sung dynasty and was considerably smaller after 1127 when the Nuchens conquered most of North China. In 1122, five years before this conquest, the Sung regime had 26 viceroyalties, 351 provinces, and 1,243 districts. The total number of households in 1110 was reported to be 20,882,258, the highest on record during the Sung dynasty. Historians disagree on the average membership of a Chinese household, ranging anywhere from 5 to 10. If we take the number 7 as the average membership, the population of China in the 1110's must be around 150 million. This population declined sharply after 1127, of course, when China, once again, was plunged into warfare. (Source of statistics in the paragraph: *Sung shih,* roll 85.)

To concentrate local power in the central government, the Sung regime regarded all local officials as officials of the central government who, for the time being, had been assigned to local duties. Legally there were no local officials; there were only local duties to be performed on the spot by central government officials. Theoretically at least, the lowest-ranking magistrate of a district was as much controlled by the emperor as the highest-ranking prime minister in the capital. Needless to say, officials were regularly rotated between the capital and the provincial posts. A magistrate might be dismissed from his district post (*ch'ai-ch'ien*) by provincial authorities on account of incompetence, but he would not lose his rank (*kuan*) and position (*chih*) in the central government unless he had been convicted of such heinous crimes as murder and treason. While the purpose of this practice was to enhance the power of the central government, it also protected individual officials in terms of financial security. Not surprisingly, practically every educated Chinese aspired to become a government official.

The normal way of entering officialdom was, of course, to pass the civil service examinations. Though the Sung regime inherited the examination system from the T'ang, it nevertheless made some important changes. While during the T'ang dynasty the number of candidates participating in the metropolitan examination was comparatively small, and those who succeeded were even fewer (p. 180), the numbers for both increased enormously during the Sung dynasty. In "advanced scholarship," which remained the most prestigious of all the categories, the number of candidates varied from ten to twenty thousand during each of the metropolitan examinations, and the number of successful candidates varied from six to seven hundred. Unlike his T'ang counterpart who had to pass another examination administered by the Ministry of Personnel before he was granted a governmental post to hold, a successful candidate of the Sung dynasty was immediately ranked and salaried, even though no official opening was available.

The most important innovation, however, was the determination of a candidate's merit solely upon the test results, regardless of other considerations. During the T'ang dynasty the candidates of a metropolitan examination circulated their written works, especially poetry, among the capital's intellectual elite and political notables, and the successful candidates were often pre-determined before the examination actually took place, especially the candidate who was to be ranked "number one." If the test results were such that the examiners could not make a clear-cut decision as to who should pass or fail, the candidates themselves might be asked to vote for their own choices, and their choices would then be officially designated as the successful candidates. The Sung dynasty changed all that. In 992, the practice of "name covering" was introduced, so that an examiner would not know whose tests he was reading or grading. Beginning in 1011 all the answers in a test had to be copied, and only the copies, instead of the originals, were presented to the examiners for evaluation. In this way an examiner would not be able to show either favoritism for or prejudice against certain candidates whose handwriting he had recognized. Hopefully total impartiality could thus be maintained.

A successful candidate was one most proficient in the writing of sophisticated poetry or eloquent prose, plus erudition in Chinese history and Confucian ideology. Yet the same person, who had no military background whatsoever, might someday be called upon to head an army of several hundred thousand men to stop the invasion of China by some ferocious barbarian tribe. To forestall the reappearance of warlordism that had plagued China for two centuries, Sung T'ai-tsu made it a dynastic rule that only intellectuals, and certainly not professional soldiers, could command an army. This rule was not violated until 1127 when most of China was overrun by the Nuchens, with whom the poetry-writing generals did not know how to cope. Though the intellectualized generals were regarded as more amenable to the wishes of the central authorities than the professional variety, they were nevertheless regularly transferred from one post to another, so that no permanent loyalty could be forged between the generals and the troops they commanded. The loyalty of troops to a local strong man, as critics pointed out, was primarily responsible for the division of China and the chaos it created after 755.

The Sung armed forces could be divided into two categories: the regular army and the militias. The militias, operating in the countryside and commanded by local magistrates, confined their duties to the catching of thieves and bandits; they were not important as fighting units. The real strength in the armed forces lay with the regular army that was in turn divided into the Forbidden Army (*Chin chün*) and the Garrison Army (*Hsiang chün*). The Forbidden Army, named after the Forbidden Palace where the emperor lived, was to be the emperor's personal guards; it actually constituted the bulwark of the nation's defense. At the beginning of the Sung dynasty it had approximately 200,000 men, but the number continued to increase until it reached 826,000 by the 1030's. Half of the Forbidden Army was stationed in the capital and its environs, while the other half was deployed along the northern frontier, face to face with the nomadic enemy. Army units were rotated between the capital and the frontier as a matter of routine, so each unit could be exposed to battle conditions on a regular basis. As for the Garrison Army, it was inferior in both quantity and quality. In fact, once a Garrison Army unit distinguished itself, either in training or in combat, it would be automatically absorbed by the Forbidden Army. If, on the other hand, a Forbidden Army unit did less well than was expected, either in training or in combat, it would be downgraded to the Garrison rank. The Garrison Army units, stationed in less strategic areas, were regularly rotated among cities and towns, so that no army unit could generate a local attachment detrimental to the imperial interest. All the soldiers in the regular army, contrary to the militias, were volunteers, recruited from the rural unemployed or semiemployed. The strong ones would go to the Forbidden Army, and the Garrison Army had to be satisfied with the leftovers. Once joining the army, a volunteer would normally stay with it for his entire life.

The concentration of power in the central government served the imperial interest only in the sense that it effectively forestalled the reappearance of warlordism and kept the country united. With one major exception which will be discussed later, few revolts occurred throughout the Sung dynasty. But what was good for the royal household and its intellectual allies, in terms of the preservation of internal peace, may not be good for the nation as a whole. It is this contradiction that eventually doomed the Sung regime, as we shall presently see.

PEACE AND WAR

If, as the Chinese say, a picture is worth one thousand words, a good map is worth at least ten times as many. The map of China's annual precipitation that appears on page 13 perhaps speaks more eloquently about China's foreign relations than a long essay of great erudition. The agriculturalists tell us that intensive farming, the kind that has been practiced by the Chinese since history began, becomes virtually impossible if annual rainfall falls below fifteen inches. Since China has always been an agrarian society, not surprisingly the line of fifteen-inch annual precipitation, which runs from Manchuria to an area near the Burmese border, has by and large marked the boundary between China proper and the outer territories. The Great Wall, built by the Chinese to protect the agrarian south against the nomadic north some twenty-two hundred years ago, also zigzags along this line.

Between the lines of ten-inch and fifteen-inch annual precipitation are the grasslands, the traditional zone of contest between the nomadic tribe to the north and the agrarian Chinese to the south. Often the Chinese pushed agriculture as far as the line of ten-inch annual precipitation, only to fall back, either because of below-normal precipitation over an extended period or, most likely, because of the physical pressure the nomads were able to exercise. There were, of course, occasions when the Chinese, under such strong regimes as the Han and the T'ang, conquered not only the grasslands but also the deserts beyond. But these occasions were rare and infrequent. Normally it was the nomads, rather than the Chinese, who controlled this strategic zone of grasslands.

When the nomads and the Chinese were equal in strength, peace prevailed and normal intercourse, including trade, was regularly conducted between them. Economically the agrarian society of China and the pastoral society of the tribes were complementary and mutually dependent, as each imported from the other what it could not, or could only poorly, produce. China imported from the nomads furs, skins, hides, and above all, horses, which were in great demand by both the military

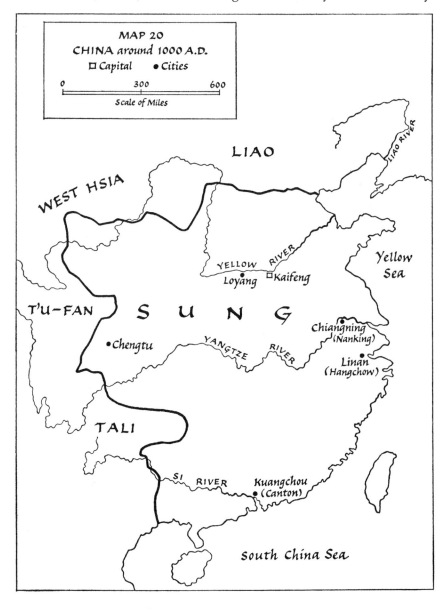

MAP 20
CHINA around 1000 A.D.
□ Capital   • Cities

0   300   600
Scale of Miles

and the civilians. The nomads, on the other hand, imported from China agricultural and industrial products, notably grain, silk, cloth, and tea. As pastoral products were not essential to the maintenance of daily life in the sense that grain and cloth were and since they (*i.e.*, horses) could be domestically raised or imported from other sources if the need became too great, the Chinese had an advantage not enjoyed by the nomads. Whenever there was a population pressure in the pastoral areas, a situation almost unavoidable if peace persisted for a relatively long period, the need for agricultural and industrial products from China would become more pressing. Since physically it was impossible for the nomads to produce these products in their own land, they had to trade to obtain them. If trade was denied to them or if it became unfeasible because they could not offer goods of equal value in exchange, they might conclude that war was the only means whereby they could obtain what they needed from the Chinese. This need for Chinese products accounted for the frequent raids on China's border provinces even in time of peace. When a strong leader emerged and was able to organize a large fighting force, the nomads would invariably march southward in order to seize what they could not obtain by peaceful means.

The political division and chaos during the Five Dynasties, when the Chinese were fighting among themselves, provided the nomads one of those reccurrent opportunities to assert themselves and surge forward. Then the most powerful of the nomads were the Khitans, a Mongolian tribe originating in the Liao River basin of Manchuria. Early in the tenth century the Khitans produced an outstanding leader named A-pao-chi (872–926), who conquered one tribe after another until he brought Inner Mongolia, as well as South Manchuria, under his control. To develop his country economically, he encouraged the immigration of Chinese farmers who would plow up the grasslands and convert them to farming. He built towns and cities, opened salt and iron mines, coined money to facilitate trade, and established exchange centers along the border to barter with the Chinese. A new written language was invented by simplifying Chinese characters, and Chinese scholars were invited to serve his government, notably a man named Han Yen-hui (d. 968) who served as chief adviser. With his encouragement, Chinese immigrants continued to arrive until eventually they outnumbered the Khitans. A dyarchy was then set up, whereby the Chinese would be governed by a bureaucratic administration, while the Khitans continued to live under a tribal system. The Khitans served as administrators and warriors, and the Chinese, by and large, were the producers. Having successfully combined nomadic vitality with Chinese industry, A-pao-chi was ready for a career of conquest. Repeatedly he sent his troops to raid China's border provinces and wreak havoc. Later, meeting stiff Chinese resistance, he switched his energy eastward to annex the kingdom of P'o-hai (713–926) which, at its height, had a territory comprising the eastern section of Manchuria, part of North Korea, and the Maritime Province of modern Russia. When he died in 926, he had an empire large enough to extend from the Ordos Desert all the way to the Sea of Japan. This was a formidable foe for whatever Chinese regime located further in the south.

In 936 a Chinese general named Shih Ching-t'ang (892–942) usurped the throne and proclaimed himself founder of the Tsin dynasty, known to historians as the Later Tsin (936–947). Facing challenges all around him, he pledged himself as a vassal to the Khitans whose support he eagerly sought in order to face his Chinese enemies. Though flattered by this gesture, the Khitans were not at all impressed; they wanted something more concrete and useful, namely Chinese territories, the denial of which, they said to the Chinese usurper, would mean the absence of their support. This left the self-styled Chinese emperor two choices: either presenting Chinese territories to the Khitans as demanded or foregoing his own pretensions as an emperor. He made the first choice, most naturally, since there had rarely been a Chinese ruler who placed national above personal interest. In 937 Shih Ching-t'ang presented to the Khitans as a tribute the Sixteen Yen-Yün Provinces, which covered the northern sections of modern Hopeh and Shansi, including Peking. Now that the Khitans had by-passed the Great Wall and were deep inside China proper, all of North China was within their easy march. In 947, strong and confident, they changed their national title from the tribal "Khitan" to a more Sinicized name "Liao."

Sung T'ai-tsu, founder of the Sung dynasty, was too busy unifying and consolidating his regime to pay much attention to the northern threat. When his younger brother Sung T'ai-tsung (r. 976–977) ascended to the throne, an effort was made to recover the Yen-Yün Provinces. In his attempt to recapture Peking, Sung T'ai-tsung's troops were routed, and two flying arrows struck his shoulders while he was fleeing southward. Two more attempts were made during his reign, one in 980 and again in 986, but in each case the result was humiliating defeat. In the winter of 1004 Liao took the offensive. The Sung troops were easily routed, and the invaders were pushing hard toward the Sung capital. Kaifeng was in a panic, and some Sung ministers openly advocated the abandonment of the city and the transfer of the capital either southward to Nanking or westward to Chengtu. When the panic finally subsided, Sung Chen-tsung (r. 998–1022), the reigning emperor, was persuaded to take personal command of the army and meet the invaders in the north. Near the city of Tanyüan, less than forty miles north of Kaifeng, a battle was fought, with no decisive victory for either side. A stalemate ensued and both sides were ready for a negotiated peace. The peace agreement consisted of notes exchanged between the Sung and the Liao emperors. The Sung note reads in part:

To help disburse military expenses, the Sung Government agrees to deliver to Liao an annual gift of 200,000 bolts of silk and 100,000 taels of silver. . . . Garrisons on each side defend their respective territories along the frontier, and trespassing by either civilian or military personnel is strictly forbidden. Thieves and bandits who escape from one side should not be given quarters by the other and should in fact be extradited. Farmers on both sides should be left alone to live in peace; they and their farms should not be interfered with. The cities and their fortifications are to remain the way they are; no additional walls or canals are to be built by either side to strengthen defense. May the above agreement be witnessed by Heaven, Earth, the gods, and the spirits, and be reported to our ancestral temples. Be it observed by our descendants until eternity to come. He who violates it—may he not live long to enjoy his country. Heaven be the witness, he shall die a violent death.

The purpose of Liao's invasion, as later events revealed, was to exact tribute; it had no intention to conquer the Sung regime, certainly not at this time. The peace agreement, known to historians as the Agreement of Tanyüan, paved the way for a peace of 118 years (1004–1122), the most glorious of the Sung dynasty. It was a period of such emperors as Sung Jen-tsung (r. 1022–1063) and Sung Shen-tsung (r. 1067–1085), of such statesmen as Fan Chung-yen (990–1053) and Wang An-shih (1021–1086), of such philosophers as Ch'eng Hao (1031–1085) and Ch'eng Yi (1032–1107), of such historians as Ssu-ma Kuang (1018–1086) and Ou-yang Hsiu (1007–1072), of such poets as Yen Chu (991–1055) and Chou Pang-yen (1057–1121), and of such artists as Mi Fei (1051–1107) and Li Kung-lin (1049–1106). Above all, it was the age of the gay genius Su Shih (also known as Su Tung-po, 1036–1101), the incomparable poet, essayist, painter, and the superb connoisseur of beautiful women and vintage wine. The silk at Hangchow and the porcelain at Chingtehchen (located at the northeastern corner of modern Kiangsi province) reached their finest stage during this period, and the ownership of a Chingtehchen vase, manufactured during this period, can easily retire this author to a life of comfort.

One thing, however, marred this beautiful scene. In 1038 news arrived from the western frontier that Yüan-hao (d. 1048), hereditary ruler of the Tanguts, had declared independence and called his regime Great Hsia (known to the Chinese as West Hsia). Most alarmingly, he had sent his troops to invade China's border provinces. The nation of the Tanguts, a Tibetan tribe located in modern Kansu province, had been an off-and-on Chinese vassalage beginning in the seventh century, and its hereditary rulers, known for their "high degree of Sinicization," had been granted the surname "Li," the surname of China's royal house, during the T'ang dynasty. After the Chao family had founded the Sung dynasty, Sung T'ai-tsung conferred upon the Tangut ruler the surname "Chao" as a special honor, desperately hoping that the Tanguts would show the same consideration for China's new regime as they once did for the mighty T'ang. Nevertheless, the Tanguts raided China's border provinces time and again, primarily for looting purposes. When the Chinese protested, the Tanguts assured them that these raids would stop immediately if they were able to acquire the things they needed without having to conduct these raids. Taking the hint, the Chinese periodically presented them with gifts of silver, silk, and tea.

The Sung-Tangut relations took a sudden turn for the worse when Yüan-hao succeeded his father as the Tangut ruler in 1032. To him treasures freely given were not the same as treasures stolen, and the latter were definitely more valuable. Deploring the fact that for thirty years his father had been "softened" by Chinese bribes, he emphatically stressed the importance of maintaining the tribe's nomadic vitality— wearing animal skins instead of silk and living in tents instead of houses. Otherwise, he added, the Tanguts would be assimilated by the Chinese and lose their identity as a nation. To combat Chinese influence, he invented a written language for his tribe, into which many useful books in Chinese were translated. "He was not only a vigorous and persevering leader," said his Chinese admirers, "but also an artist and scholar, especially versed in Buddhist ideology." When he declared independence by changing his surname from "Chao" back to "Li" and raised the standard of revolt, he boasted of a fighting force of half a million men.

In the Sung capital of Kaifeng, opinions were divided on the best way to cope with the crisis. One school called for the organization of a strong expeditionary force to seek the enemy and destroy him, thus solving the problem once and for all. For a time this strategy was followed. The result proved to be disastrous, as the Chinese infantrymen were easily routed by the hard-riding, fast-moving nomadic warriors. The Sung government, by necessity, had to find a new approach. Under the leadership of Fan Chung-yen, whose name has been mentioned earlier, the Sung government cut off all trade with the Tanguts and encouraged and rewarded all the friendly tribes who did the same. In other words, the Chinese and their allies were staging an economic blockade. When the Tanguts attacked, the Sung forces would scorch the earth before they retreated and then shut themselves behind well-built fortifications. They refused to engage in open battle, where the Tangut cavalrymen enjoyed a clear advantage.

This Fabian strategy, criticized by many Chinese as being too cowardly, paid off eventually. Having all their male population mobilized for war and being confronted with an economic blockade as tight as an iron ring, the Tanguts quickly found out that their war materials, including food, were diminishing fast, while the heavy toll on the limited manpower continued. There was widespread discontent; Yüan-hao, in the end, had to concede defeat. In 1044 he proposed peace, saying that the revolt against the Sung regime, instigated by "evil elements," had been a mistake, that he was willing to return all the territories he had seized from China, and that he himself would be more than delighted to resume his former status as a Sung vassal. The Sung government accepted his proposal readily and promised to reopen markets for trade. The annual grant of silver, silk, and tea was renewed, and once again peace prevailed on the northwestern frontier.

The Tangut war, lasting six years (1038–1044) and confined to the northwestern corner of China, had only a limited impact on the general well-being felt by most Chinese during this period (1004–1122). When war was resumed with Liao in 1122, a glorious era suddenly came to an end, with consequences so disastrous that few could possibly have foreseen them. As for this, more will be said later in this chapter.

PROBLEMS AND REFORM

The seeds of war are sown in peace, and the inadequacy of the Sung regime was clearly recognizable during even its best years. The Sung China of the eleventh century was the largest nation on earth; yet she had to fight for six years in order to reach a stalemate with a small tribe called the Tanguts, and then only by waging protracted warfare. All the Sung statesmen, including Sung T'ai-tsu, realized that Kaifeng was indefensible in case of war. Located in the middle of a vast plain and having no natural barriers to speak of, the city was within easy march of nomadic cavalrymen, who had always given the Chinese infantry difficulty, especially in battles fought on a flat terrain. Once an enemy reached the northern bank of the Yellow River, Kaifeng was as good as lost, since the river, instead of serving as a natural barrier, became a solidly frozen highway in winter. Why did the Sung regime not move its capital to Loyang or, better still, to Ch'angan where the mighty Han and T'ang seated themselves? The answer is that the regime relied on South China, especially the Lower Yangtze, for tax revenue to support its huge bureaucracy and army. The tax revenue, in the form of grain and silk, could be shipped only as far as Kaifeng via the Grand Canal, since the westernmost section of the canal, the section that ran from Kaifeng to Ch'angan via Loyang, had been so neglected and silted during the turbulent centuries after 755 that it was now unnavigable (see Map 17, p. 167). Why did the Sung regime not work on the canal and restore it to completely operational form? In the answer to this question lay the fundamental cause of the Sung ills. As long as grain and silk could flow easily to Kaifeng where they could enjoy them, the bureaucrats did not wish to bother. In other words, it was the sense of complacency and the lack of foresight that proved to be the Sung's eventual downfall.

Unfortunately, the problems were not confined to the choice of the capital. Public policies in many other areas were equally faulty, if not worse. The Sung regime prided itself as having a government by intellectuals, but it quickly turned out to be a government for intellectuals as well. As previously noted, to reach the status of a bona fide intellectual, with all the prestige and financial rewards associated with that term, one had to pass a competitive examination held in the capital. During the first twenty-seven years of the dynasty the metropolitan examination was held once every year, as it was during the T'ang dynasty, and the number of successful candidates for each examination was still small. Beginning in 978 the examination was held once every two or three years, and the number of successful candidates skyrocketed to six or seven hundred on each occasion. Not until 1064 was the triennial system of examination introduced, a system that was to be followed by succeeding dynasties. With the passing of years the number of successful candidates kept on accumulating, and each and every one of them had to be supported by the government for his entire life, even though there might not be any meaningful duties for him to perform. In the 1060's the number of scholar-officials was about twenty-four thousand, not including officials of nonexamination or minor ranks (clerks, secretaries, advisers, retainers, etc.) whose membership must have been several times larger. In all of China's history there had never been so many paid so much for doing so little.

The financial drain on the nation would not have been too great had the pay been moderate or reasonable. But the pay was extravagant. Take the prime minister as an example. His monthly salary was 300,000 standard coins, plus 20 bolts of damask silk, 30 bolts of gauzy silk, and 100 ounces of floss, to be distributed on a yearly basis. In addition, he received 100 piculs of grain per month as food stipend, even though he and his family could not possibly consume one-tenth as much. He was entitled to have 70 servants, all paid by the government. If he were transferred to the provinces to serve temporarily in a local capacity, he received an additional "hardship pay" that could be as high as 20 million standard coins per year. (The Sung Chinese used paper currency, and the 20 million standard coins would be just so much paper printed with large denominations.) Every three years when the emperor conducted the grand ceremony of Heaven worship, the prime minister expected to receive 4,000 taels of silver and 4,000 bolts of silk as an extra bonus. Before he died, he could sponsor twenty or more persons to be designated as officials, and those designated could be either his relatives, friends, or protégés. To be sure, not all officials received the kind of compensation described above, since the lower-ranking officeholders had to be satisfied with less. Added together, however, the total expenses involved could only be described as stupendous.

Besides the bureaucracy there was also the army to support. In 1065, for instance, members of the regular army were estimated to be 1.2 million, divided in a 7 to 5 ratio between the Forbidden Army and the Garrison Army. A soldier in the Forbidden Army received an amount of grain and cash equivalent to 50,000 standard coins per year, while his counterpart in the Garrison Army was paid an equivalent of 30,000 standard coins. Though either amount was adequate to support one person, a soldier had to moonlight if he wished to marry and support a family. Meager though his salary was, total expenditure for soldiers' salaries amounted to 5 billion standard coins in 1065, while the government's total revenue for that year was only 6 billion. The Sung army was a professional army of volunteers, and all the soldiers had to be supported by the government throughout their lives. They could function well as warriors from the age of twenty to forty, but lost their valor afterwards, even though they still filled up the ranks. Thus the Sung army, even in its top form, was only half combat-effective.

The third major outlay from the Sung government's finances was the annual tribute or gift paid to its northern enemies. Too weak to fight and too comfortable to risk the consequences, it regarded bribery as a normal way to peace. It successively and successfully bribed the Khitans, the Tanguts, and the Nuchens, and managed to preserve China's political identity as a nation. Later, when the Mongols refused to be bribed and wanted to convert China into their private domain, the Sung regime collapsed and all of China, for the first time in history, was conquered.

It was against this background of military weakness and financial insolvency that the Sung reforms must be viewed. The first reformer was Fan Chung-yen who, in 1043, proposed the rectification of "ten areas of vital concern." In summary, the proposal called upon the government to eliminate bureaucratic waste by laying off superfluous personnel, by carefully selecting those who were able to serve, and by raising the standard for the civil service examinations. It also called upon the government to build a strong army through professional management and to abolish all the miscellaneous taxes, especially the unauthorized corvée which had been the greatest burden to the peasantry. Moderate though the proposal was, it precipitated strong, immediate opposition. "By one stroke of a pen," said one opponent, "you will make thousands of families cry." "It is better for a few families than for the whole nation to cry," Fan Chung-yen replied. Nevertheless, the proposal for reform was rejected.

Wang An-shih was a young man of twenty-two when Fan Chung-yen issued his reform program. No extant record shows how he reacted when he read about the reform, but it is not difficult to visualize. The problems China then faced were common knowledge, and the question had always been how to cope with them or, more precisely, how to cope with them without stepping upon vested interests and thus precipitating insurmountable opposition. In 1058, after he had already established his reputation as a literary genius and a rising star on the political horizon, Wang An-shih presented Sung Jen-tsung, the reigning emperor, with the famous "ten-thousand-character memorial," which has remained one of the finest pieces of Chinese literature ever written. It struck the capital like a flaming meteor from the sky. "There is no such thing as an economic crisis," said the petitioner boldly, "but there is such a thing as the lack of talent." He did not advocate retrenchment, which would have generated too much opposition; he advocated instead the opening up of new resources.

If Sung Jen-tsung could not accept Fan Chung-yen's mild reform during his younger years, obviously he could not accept a more radical one at an advanced age. But time was on Wang An-shih's side. As a crown prince, Sung Shen-tsung had been one of his greatest admirers and it was not surprising that shortly after his ascension to the throne in 1068 the new emperor summoned Wang for an audience. The interview went well, so well in fact that early in 1069, when the first opportunity arrived, Wang An-shih was appointed the prime minister. "What is the first priority in launching a successful administration?" asked the emperor. "The most urgent is a change of atmosphere and the introduction of new programs," Wang replied.

Today many historians consider Wang An-shih a socialist, but a socialist he was not. The purpose of his reform was to enrich and strengthen the nation, so that the Sung regime could negotiate with its enemies from strength and fight more effectively if war came. The idea was not new, of course; what made him so distinctly different from his contemporaries was his recognition that the nation could not be enriched or strengthened without in the meantime enriching or strengthening individual households that constituted the nation. However, national or governmental interest, instead of individual welfare, had always been his primary concern.

Wang An-shih's reforms conveniently fall into three main categories: economic, military, and educational. Of the economic programs the most significant and also the most controversial was the green sprouts program (*ch'ing miao fa*), which called upon the government to provide ready credit for needy farmers at a standard, low interest. When serving as magistrate of Yinhsien (also known as Ningpo, located in modern Chekiang province), Wang An-shih had carried out this program among people within his jurisdiction, and it was viewed by all as a great success. Now he wanted it adopted nationwide. Before its adoption the prevailing annual interest on money borrowed from private sources ranged anywhere from 60 to 70 percent, and such a high interest had bankrupted many small, independent farmers. Under the new program the government lent money twice a year to needy farmers at a semiannual interest of 20 percent, with capital drawn from the government-operated, ever-normal granaries. The borrowers were required to pay both principal and interest twice a year when they paid their regular land tax, usually in spring and autumn. In case of a bad harvest they might be granted a moratorium from payment for a one-year period. It was called the green sprouts program because each year the first loan was made in spring when rice sprouts were green and when farmers most needed money.

To protect both producers and consumers and also to stabilize prices, the marketing and exchange program (*shih yi fa*) was introduced in 1072. Under this program the government established more than twenty marketing agencies in the capital and other large cities for the purpose of buying and selling commercial products. These agencies would buy products when their prices had been depressed during the time of over-supply and would sell them in the open market when their prices had been bid up too high during the time of strong demand. In selling a product to the marketing agency, a producer or merchant was paid at cost when the market price of the same product was too low to cover the cost. If he so chose, he could waive cash payment and request instead the exchange of his overstocked merchandise for goods that had been in short supply in the market and therefore commanded better prices. When certain merchandise was in short supply, trustworthy merchants might be allowed to borrow such merchandise from the marketing agency and sell it in the open market; they would in that case pay the agency a semiannual interest of 10 percent. Through these devices it was hoped that supply and demand would be well balanced, that prices would be stabilized, and that consumers, as well as producers, would be protected. The government, of course, would also make a handsome profit in the process.

Under the semiannual tax system introduced by Yang Yen in 799, labor services traditionally required from the peasantry were incorporated into the tax system, and a peasant who had paid his regular taxes was supposed to be free from any corvée obligations (pp. 181–182). But these obligations reemerged during the Five Dynasties as local authorities, in a time of chaos and war, did whatever they pleased. When the Sung dynasty was founded and peace finally prevailed, this illegal imposition had become a common practice. Still, theoretically speaking, corvée could only be imposed according to need, *e.g.*, when a dam had to be built or a bridge repaired. But this principle, more often than not, was violated in practice, as farmers were called upon to perform labor services when they should have been working on their own farms. By the eleventh century, *yao yü,* or compulsory labor, had become the most burdensome among all of the government's exactions as far as the peasants were concerned. In 1070 Wang An-shih introduced the corvée exemption program (*mien yü fa*), which proved to be the most popular of all his reforms. Conscripted labor was thereafter abolished, and a new tax, called the corvée exemption tax, was imposed. The amount to be paid by each household varied in accordance with its income, and the revenue thus collected would be used to hire volunteers, thus freeing all others from the burden of compulsory labor. Peasants were elated and thankful when news about this program reached their village.

The least controversial of Wang An-shih's reforms were those dealing with irrigation, flood control, and the reclamation of wasteland. While large projects were undertaken by the government, farmers were encouraged to proceed with projects of their own, and in such cases the government would grant loans on easy terms with capital procured from the ever-normal granaries. In 1077, seven years after this measure had been adopted, 361,178 *ch'ing* (*c.* 5.5 million acres) of wasteland were reported to have been reclaimed. All tracts of land, regardless of their ownership, were classified into five grades, and taxes were determined by grades instead of crops actually harvested. It was hoped that by taxing land in this manner, all land would be utilized most efficiently, and total farm production would be greatly increased for the nation as a whole.

To strengthen the nation's defense, Wang An-shih introduced the *pao-chia* system in 1071 and the horse conservation program (*pao ma fa*) in 1072. The *pao-chia* ("protection and shield") concept dated from as early as the fourth century B.C. when Shang Yang, as chief minister of the Ch'in state, put into practice a similar idea (pp. 57–58). Under Wang An-shih's system, every ten households were organized into a *pao* ("protection") and all able-bodied men in each household, with the exception of one, were required to join the militia. Each *pao* was headed by a *pao* captain, selected from independent farmers or landlords. Five *pao* formed a *ta pao* ("great protection"), and ten *ta pao* were organized as a *tu pao* ("capital protection"). On each organizational level part-time officials were chosen from among the constituent members to carry on the daily administration. Whenever a crime or any other irregularity occurred within a *pao*, the person aware of its presence was duty-bound to report it to the *pao* captain; he who failed to make such a report would be regarded as an accomplice and punished accordingly. The militiamen were taught the fundamentals of war and were drilled at times when farming activities were at a minimum, usually in winter after harvests had been collected. Their duty was to maintain order in the countryside during peacetime, and they served as reserves at the time of war.

The purpose of the horse conservation program was to provide an abundant supply of horses for civilian use in peacetime and for military combat in case of war. Fully aware of China's inferiority to the nomads in battles fought on flat terrain, Wang An-shih proposed to build a strong cavalry to supplement the infantry which had always been the backbone of her armed forces. Traditionally the best of China's horses came from Manchuria, Inner Mongolia, Kansu, and Ninghsia, but all these territories, by the eleventh century, had been lost to the nomads. The horse conservation program, successfully implemented, would hopefully rectify this situation. Under this program farmers might either borrow horses from the government or take cash payment to buy horses from private sources. In either case the ownership of horses resided with the government, while the farmers had the right to use them in farming or transportation. To encourage participation in this program, the government provided special tax relief for the participants. Once each year government-appointed veterinarians would inspect and examine these horses to make sure that they had not been abused. If a horse died, all the households within a *pao* were held jointly responsible for making adequate compensation. All the horses under private care would be automatically surrendered to the government for military uses when and if a war came. To standardize military weapons and to improve their quality, a new office was created in the capital to supervise the manufacturing of all weapons within the empire.

In education Wang An-shih's proposal called for a reappraisal of the civil service examination system and the reorganization of the Central University at Kaifeng. The examination system had not produced men of ability, he said, because of its overemphasis on memory and because of the impracticality of the subjects tested. Upon his recommendation all categories in the metropolitan examination, with the exception of "advanced scholarship," were abolished; in "advanced scholarship" the candidates were tested on their knowledge of Confucian classics and of such practical subjects as geography and economics. The test on poetry, so much emphasized in the past, was abolished altogether. While not advocating the abolition of the civil service examination, Wang An-shih nevertheless believed that men of true talent could be better cultivated in schools. Accordingly, he reorganized the Central University with the hope that supervised studies leading to degrees would eventually replace the civil service examination system. All students in the university were grouped into three grades in accordance with their academic achievements: low, middle, and high. They were tested on their assigned work every month; each year there was a final examination covering the entire year's assignments. Those who successfully passed the examination were promoted to a higher grade and were given rights and privileges corresponding to those on the similar levels of the civil service examination system. For instance, the high-grade students who had completed their work at the top of their class would be recommended to the Ministry of Personnel for assignment as government officials, as if they had passed the metropolitan examination with high honors.

Early in 1074 a severe drought spread across many provinces, and there was serious doubt as to whether spring planting could ever begin. Countless peasants left their homes in search for food, as the future looked gloomier with each passing day. "It is Wang An-shih's fault that it has not rained," reported one official to the emperor. "It will rain as soon as he is dismissed from office." As pressure increased, Wang An-shih eventually resigned, though continuing to insist that he was not responsible for the lack of rain. Later he was called upon to assume office again, but his second premiership lasted only one year. As soon as he was out of office, all his programs were terminated, including the corvée exemption program which had been most popular.

The controversy over Wang An-shih's reform is known to historians as a conflict between the Old and the New Parties, a conflict that persisted throughout the remainder of the North Sung period. It was a conflict in ideology as well as approach to programs. To Ssu-ma Kuang, an orthodox Confucian and leader of the Old Party, a good government was a government of good men and not necessarily of good laws, since only a good man would enforce good laws and refrain from enforcing the bad ones, while a bad man would do exactly the opposite. He pointed out that many unprincipled officials, to earn credit for promotion purposes, forced people to borrow money from the government under the green sprouts program and then applied torture to exact payment from borrowers who were short of funds when payment was due. A wealthy nation, said he, was one where wealth was scattered among the people, rather than concentrated in the government, and it was morally intolerable for the government to compete with the people for profit. To Wang An-shih and members of the New Party, however, the argument raised by Ssu-ma Kuang was academic, if not exactly unsound. They called attention to the fact that this was no ordinary time and that the Sung regime must rise above its own inertia and complacency if it were to meet successfully the challenges from abroad and at home. The reforms, they contended, were the answer to China's problems.

Upon Wang An-shih's death in 1086, the conflict between the Old and the New Parties quickly degenerated into a conflict in personalities, rather than programs or ideology. Early in the twelfth century the standard-bearer of the New Party was a comic figure named Ts'ai Ching (1047–1126) who seemed to believe that the only way to become wealthy was to spend money; he spent so wastefully that by the end of his pre-

miership of almost twenty years the treasury was empty and the government was bankrupt. The Kaifeng regime became so weakened that it
took only a single push by its enemy to bring about its collapse.

DECLINE AND FALL

In the famous novel *Shui-hu chuan* (p. 330) Sung Chiang, the bandit
chieftain, stated repeatedly, often with tears in his eyes, that he and
his "108 marsh heroes" revolted only because the government had never
given them a chance to do otherwise. While greatly romanticized in the
novel, Sung Chiang was in fact a historical figure. He and his men staged
a rebellion early in 1120 but surrendered one year later—a fact that has
prompted the Communists in China today to conduct a nationwide campaign to denounce him as a capitulationist. Shortly after their surrender,
they were sent southward to help crush a much more serious revolt led
by a man named Fang La (d. 1122) who happened to be a Manichaean
(p. 372).

As described earlier in this chapter, the Sung government incurred
enormous expenses each year. To meet the expenses, it depended heavily
on tax revenue from the Lower Yangtze; East Chekiang, where the Fang
La rebellion began, had been one of the areas that bore the heaviest
burden. As if this were not enough, two financial imbeciles came to power
in 1100: Sung Hui-tsung (r. 1100–1125) as the emperor and Ts'ai Ching
as his prime minister. Jointly they sent the North Sung regime into a tailspin, not to end until the regime came to an end itself. In the name of
grandeur, they spent lavishly and foolishly. Statutory limits on the number of personnel in each bureau or office were abolished, and a favored
official could occupy ten posts and receive ten salaries simultaneously,
while doing nothing except amuse himself. Fancying himself as a living
Taoist deity, Sung Hui-tsung ordered the construction of Taoist temples
across the nation and spent millions in honor of the gods in the Deep
Void on each religious day. A cultured man of fine taste, he loved an-
tiques, curios and artifacts, referred to by his contemporaries as "rare
flowers and stones." Beginning in 1102 and continuing for almost twenty
years, the people in the Lower Yangtze were required to send "rare
flowers and stones" to Kaifeng as a special tribute three times a year.
Unprincipled bureaucrats used each occasion to practice barbarity and
blackmail, as they ordered troops to storm into houses suspected of having artistic objects. Once an artistic object was found, it would be
covered with a piece of yellow silk, which instantly transferred its ownership to the royal household. If the object was too big to go through the
door, the door would be demolished; if a bridge was too low for it to
go underneath in a boat, the bridge would be destroyed. In either case,

the owner of the house or the community that owned the bridge would have to do the repair at his or its own expense. If an owner threw his valuable possessions into a river before their presence could be discovered, he might soon learn that he had to fish them out himself. For every piece of "rare flowers and stones" that eventually reached Kaifeng via the Grand Canal, the cost to the taxpayers was large enough to support several people comfortably for their entire lives.

It is not known to what extent Sung Hui-tsung, surrounded in his Forbidden Palace by master paintings and beautiful women, knew about the sufferings that his search for "rare flowers and stones" had caused among his subjects. He had to be held responsible, however, since he could have easily stopped it by waving his hand. "The emperor is supposed to be a father to his subjects," said Fang La; "what kind of father is he if he causes his children to suffer so much?" In the fall of 1120 he raised the standard of revolt, and in less than ten days thousands joined him. Two months later he captured his biggest prize, Hangchow. Stunned at the beginning, the emperor quickly asserted himself and sent his best troops southward. By the spring of 1122 when the rebellion was finally crushed, two million of the so-called riotous mob (*luan min*) had perished.

If Sung Hui-tsung congratulated himself, his joy proved to be short-lived. Far in the northeast a new enemy called the Nuchens emerged, an enemy with whom even his best troops could not cope. Prior to their career of conquest, the Nuchens had lived in northeastern Manchuria and the modern Maritime Province of Russia. A nomadic people, they moved with their cattle and horses from place to place during summer months, but they always returned home in winter. Home was a hole dug deep in the ground, so the occupants could protect themselves from the bitter wind of Siberia. Family formed the basic social unit, tribe constituted the highest political organization, and from time to time tribes gathered to forge a confederation to conduct war or make peace. Without a written language, the Nuchens governed themselves by custom and tradition. When a man committed a murder, his family was required to surrender one of its members, normally but not necessarily the murderer, to be at the disposal of the injured family, plus ten horses, ten heads of cattle, and six taels of gold. Less serious offenses were compounded into a fine, paid in horses or cattle. There was no such thing as a jail sentence.

For centuries the Nuchens subjected themselves to the overlordship of whichever happened to be the strongest nation in that part of the world. They were a vassal to Korea early in the seventh century, but quickly switched their loyalty to the Chinese after T'ang China had conquered Korea in 668. Early during the Sung dynasty two groups developed among the Nuchens: those who lived closer to the Chinese and had been more or less Sinicized were called the assimilated Nuchens; those who lived beyond and further to the north and continued to maintain their rugged existence were referred to as the unassimilated Nuchens. Early in the twelfth century the latter group produced a great leader named Wan-yen A-ku-ta who, in a short lifetime, materially changed the power structure in North China.

To explain A-ku-ta's rise, it is not enough to say that he combined nomadic vitality with a superb talent for organization—a combination that all the great leaders in the grasslands had, whether they were A-pao-chi, Yüan-hao, Genghiz Khan, or others. It is just as important to describe the kind of circumstances he was born into and the kind of opponents he had to face. In the 1110's when A-ku-ta was the head of the Nuchens, the Liao regime, to which he had pledged himself as a vassal, had lasted for about two hundred years. As a Sinicized state, it had reached the lower end of a dynastic cycle and was suffering the same kind of decline as many Chinese regimes. As if to verify the Confucian stereotype of a degenerate monarch in a dying regime, T'ien-tso, the last Liao emperor, abused his power by increasing taxes among his subjects and by demanding more tributes from his vassals. His demand for a special tribute of falcons and pearls from the Nuchens and the disturbances it caused precipitated A-ku-ta's revolt in 1115, just as Sung Hui-tsung's demand for "rare flowers and stones" generated Fang La's rebellion in 1120. A-ku-ta called his rebellious regime Chin, on the hopeful assumption that *chin* or gold was stronger than *liao* or iron.

After declaring his independence, A-ku-ta won one battle after another and was pressing hard upon the disintegrating Liao forces. As Liao was greatly weakened, Sung, against its better judgment, thought this was a golden opportunity to recover the Sixteen Yen-Yün Provinces, including Peking. In 1122 Sung and Chin concluded a military alliance. Sung was to attack Liao from the south and Chin from the north, with the Great Wall as the dividing line between the two zones of operation. After hostilities had resumed, Chin forces pushed relentlessly southward, encountering little or ineffective resistance, while Sung, on the other hand, failed miserably in its repeated efforts to capture the prized city of Peking. As the last resort, Sung sought Chin's help. Thus invited, Chin forces quickly defeated the remaining Liao army, passed across the Great Wall, and captured Peking. Throughout its existence, Sung was never able to dislodge them.

Now that the state of Liao had disappeared, the Sung and Chin forces were facing each other across a new but undefined border. Sung wanted Chin to hand over the Sixteen Yen-Yün Provinces as agreed upon by both sides in the military alliance, but Chin refused, saying that Sung had not done anything constructive during the war to deserve them. As the diplomats could not agree on the spoils of victory, it took only a few border incidents to transform the former allies into new enemies. In the fall of 1126 the Chin forces launched an all-out offensive and quickly overran the ineffective opposition. In the bitter winter of 1126–1127 they passed across the Yellow River and laid siege to Kaifeng. Facing an untenable situation, Sung Hui-tsung abdicated in favor of his son, known as Sung Ch'in-tsung (r. 1126–1127). When the new emperor sued for peace, he was told by the invaders that the thought of peace could not be entertained unless he paid them an indemnity of 10 million taels of gold, 20 million taels of silver, and 20 million bolts of silk. A city-wide search was conducted to find the gold, the silver, and the silk, but the Sung government could not come up with the amount demanded. The enemy resumed the attack, and Kaifeng quickly fell. The emperor and the ex-emperor, together with the entire royal household, were carried northward. In his new capital of Peking, the Chin ruler (Chin T'ai-tsung, r. 1123–1134) celebrated his victory by ordering the two prisoners to appear in blue robes (commonly worn by servants) and serve him drinks. To make sure that everyone knew his feelings about them, he titled Sung Hui–tsung "Duke of Confused Virtues" and Sung Ch'in-tsung "Marquis of Recurrent Confusions."

Among members of the royal household who managed to sneak through the enemy's dragnet was Prince K'ang, a younger brother to the captured emperor. On June 12, 1127, he was proclaimed by the Sung forces that had survived the Chin attack to be a new emperor, known by his imperial title as Sung Kao-tsung (r. 1127–1162). But these forces did not do any better than those that had been defeated, and quickly the new emperor had to flee southward. For three years the enemy went up and down the eastern half of China and at one time penetrated as far as Hangchow (January 27, 1130) and Ningpo (February 11, 1130). By then he had obviously overextended himself. Meanwhile the regrouped Sung forces had cut off his logistical supply along the Yangtze River. The invaders called a hasty retreat and soon abandoned most of the areas that they had only recently conquered. Sung Kao-tsung returned from his exile in Wenchow, and a new regime, known to historians as South Sung, slowly took roots in Hangchow.

What should the new government do about North China, still under enemy occupation? One group, called the Idealists (*Yi-li p'ai*), contended that the struggle against the enemy must continue as a matter of principle until all the lost territories were recovered. Most military commanders, intellectuals, and university students belonged to this group. Their opponents were the Realists (*Shih-shih p'ai*), composed largely of politicians in power, including the emperor. The Realists condemned the Idealists as illusionists who could not and would not face reality. They firmly believed that to resume the war was a sure way to disaster, since the enemy was so much stronger. Besides, no regime based in South

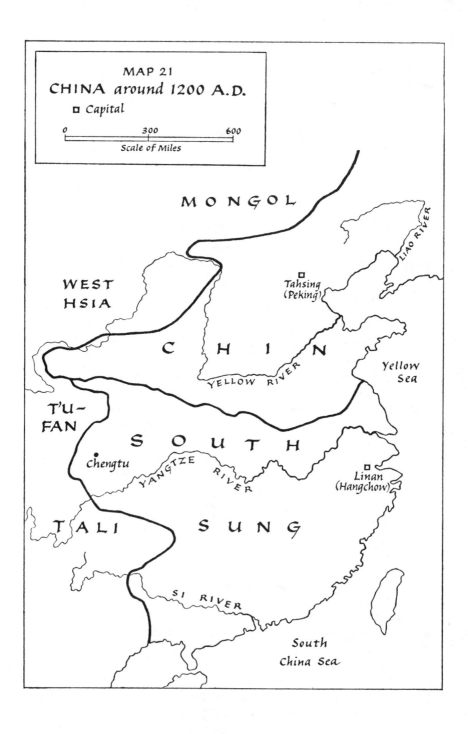

MAP 21
CHINA around 1200 A.D.
□ Capital

0   300   600
Scale of Miles

MONGOL

WEST
HSIA

CHIN

Tahsing
(Peking)

LIAO RIVER

YELLOW RIVER

Yellow
Sea

T'U-
FAN

SOUTH

Chengtu

YANGTZE RIVER

Linan
(Hangchow)

TALI

SUNG

SI RIVER

South
China Sea

China had ever conquered the north and unified China; it had always been the other way around. The conflict between these two groups culminated in the trial and eventual execution of General Yüeh Fei (1104–1142), the hero of the Idealists. The general rose from the rank and file and had a good rapport with the men under his command. Having won many surprising victories against the enemy, he was one of the most vociferous in demanding the continuation of the war. To prime minister Ch'in Kuai (1086–1151), however, these victories were more illusory than real because the enemy, when aroused, might decide to launch an all-out invasion again, a situation that he did not wish to face. In the latter part of 1141, while he and his men were operating in North China, Yüeh Fei was called back to face a charge of disobedience and conspiracy. Upon his return, he was tried, found guilty, and executed. Since then he has been the best known among Chinese martyrs. Today his body lies in a scenic spot outside Hangchow, and the temple built in his honor has become a national shrine.

The death of Yüeh Fei paved the way for a peace treaty that was concluded in April, 1142. Besides the customary annual tribute (250,000 taels of silver and 250,000 bolts of silk), Sung acknowledged Chin as its suzerain and called itself a vassal state. The boundary between the two states generally followed the Ch'inling Mountains in the west and the Huai River in the east. The agreement continued in force until 1164 when Sung, taking advantage of internal strife within the Chin government, pressed for betterment of the terms. As a result, the amount of annual tribute was somewhat reduced, both states regarded each other as equals, and the Sung emperor would address the Chin ruler as "younger uncle" instead of "lord" in all state communications. The boundary between the two states nevertheless remained the same.

Historians refer to the South Sung period as *p'ien an*, which means partial or precarious peace. As long as peace lasted, however, the Sung Chinese proceeded to conduct life as usual, work hard, and enjoy themselves. South Sung might be militarily inferior to Chin, but economically it was much more affluent. For instance, products such as rice, porcelain, silk, and tea, which had been traditionally associated with China or the Chinese, were products of South China rather than North China. As trade flourished under the South Sung regime, cities became bigger and more prosperous; the very mention of such names as Yangchow, Nanking, Soochow, and Hangchow was a reminder of not only economic affluence but also cultural sophistication. In fact, Soochow and Hangchow have since been referred to as the "two paradises on earth." Further down in the south there were such ports as Ch'üanchou and Canton that attracted traders from far and wide, including Arabs, Persians, and Jews. In these and many other cities, there were fine libraries, reputed academies, and learned scholars. Scholars drank wine, contemplated the moon, and often wrote poems to commemorate the occasion. Meanwhile the world leisurely and pleasantly slipped by.

Marco Polo (c. 1254–1324), the Venetian who visited Hangchow toward the end of the thirteenth century, when the Sung spirit still survived under alien rule, described the people of that city in the following words:

> The inhabitants take such delight in ornaments, paintings, and elaborations that the amount spent on them is something staggering. The natives of Kinsai [Hangchow] are men of peace, through being so cosseted and pampered by their kings [the emperors of South Sung], who were of the same temper. They have no skill in handling arms and do not keep any in their houses. There is prevalent among them a dislike and distaste for strife or any sort of disagreement. They pursue their trades and handicrafts with great diligence and honesty. They love one another so devotedly that a whole district might seem, from the friendly and neighborly spirit that rules among men and women, to be a single household. This affection is not accompanied by any jealousy or suspicion of their wives, for whom they have the utmost respect. A man who ventured to address an unseemly remark to any married woman would be looked upon as a thorough blackguard. They are no less kind to foreigners who come to their city for trade.[1]

The Venetian may have exaggerated a little about the virtues of the South Sung Chinese, but his characterization of their shortcomings was relevant and real. The "distaste for strife" and the lack of skill in handling arms proved to be their undoing, as we shall see in another chapter.

[1] *The Travels of Marco Polo,* tr. by R. E. Latham, The Penguin Classics, 1958, p. 191.

᚛ vii

The Two Sungs (2)

THE SUNG SPIRIT

Traditional historians in China do not divide their country's history into ancient, medieval, and modern periods as Western historians do for theirs; to them history has always been a continuous but cyclic process. Though the concepts of "ancient (*ku*) and "modern" (*chin*) do exist, their definitions are ambiguous and entirely subjective. In Ssu-ma Ch'ien's *Historical Records* (pp. 125–126), for instance, the word "modern" means the second century B.C., the time when the author lived; it is clearly implied that no event could be characterized as "ancient" unless it occurred prior to 1,000 B.C. Later historians likewise defined "ancient" and "modern" in their own individual fashions. Though no common ground for agreement existed, the issue involved was not regarded as really important, since all of these historians believed in the cyclic, instead of the progressive, development of history. Their time reference was the cyclic "dynasty" rather than the progressive "period."

This does not mean, however, that no important changes have occurred during the four thousand years of China's recorded history. These changes may have been imperceptible on a year-to-year or decade-to-decade basis; they are noticeable in a broad perspective of centuries or, better still, millenniums. In other words, the development of Chinese history has been more in the form of a whirl than in the shape of a circle. As a whirl, it can go either upward or downward; in most cases, however, it gyrates with great speed while standing still. If democracy is the ultimate in political development, we have to say that the whirl has been moving steadily downward, since monarchal power has steadily increased throughout the ages until, at this time, every statement made by Mao Tse-tung is regarded as infallible. No Chinese monarch in the past, however brilliant, has ever been regarded as beyond the realm of error. Technologically, the whirl has moved upward, though the upward movement was barely noticeable until modern times when the Western impact brought about a qualitative change. There is disagreement, however, about the field of arts and literature. Are the Ming paintings superior to the Sung paintings? Perhaps not. Are the Ch'ing vases more artistic than the Yüan vases? Perhaps yes. Is the best prose of Chang Ping-lin (also known as Chang T'ai-yen, 1868–1936) comparable to the masterpieces of Ssu-ma Ch'ien and Pan Ku? The answer depends upon the person who ventures an opinion.

In determining the nature of a society, more important than the activities—military, political, economic, social, and cultural—is the priority given to them, since every society, however advanced or primitive, conducts all of these activities. In this regard the Sung dynasty clearly marked a turning point, since it overemphasized certain activities at the expense of the others. Prior to the Sung dynasty a model man was supposed to combine physical valor (*wu*) with cultural refinement (*wen*) or, as the ancient Greeks would put it, to have a good mind in a sound body. If this combination was not possible within one individual, the pre-Sung society promoted an equitable distribution of both groups of people by providing equal recognition and similar material reward for all of them. Thus the Han dynasty benefited from the presence of such men of valor as Li Kuang-li (p. 109) and Pan Ch'ao (p. 111) as well as such men of cultural refinement as Ssu-ma Hsiang-ju and Yang Hsiung (p. 127), though the former group was generally more favorably regarded than the latter. The T'ang dynasty corrected the imbalance by introducing the civil service examinations whereby "men of thought" could receive the same kind of recognition as "men of action." Nevertheless, the avenue to prominence, by the way of examinations, was carefully controlled, so that imbalance in the opposite direction would not occur either. The T'ang dynasty, during its best years, had indeed the happiest combination, as it produced great men in both categories.

This equilibrium was destroyed in the beginning of the Sung dynasty, purposely and for political reasons. The early Sung emperors were determined to prevent a reappearance of the kind of warlordism that characterized a divided China after 755, hopefully to keep China unified under a strong, centralized government for a long time to come. To achieve this purpose, they elevated civil above martial virtues, mental above physical activities, and civic above military personnel. The only avenue to power, wealth, and prestige was through book learning, as measured by an impartially administered, competitive examination. Passing the examination, preferably with high honors, became a profound dream for all ambitious men, including those who, intellectually and psychologically, were not oriented to book learning. "He who uses pen commands," a popular saying then went; "he who uses hands obeys." Scholars let their fingernails grow long as a symbol of prestige, indicating that they never had to do any physical labor.

Thus, at a time when the nation's survival depended upon the valor and self-sacrifice of the military, those in that profession were among the most abused and downtrodden groups. No self-respecting family would allow its sons to volunteer in the army, and the recruits had to come from what the government called *wu lai* or worthless men—the rural unemployed who joined the army as the last resort. They were forced by economic necessity to enlist, just as their sisters, in time of famine, had to be sold as concubines or prostitutes. As soon as a man enlisted, his face would be branded (and sometimes his arms too), so he could in no way escape the humiliation associated with his profession. Prior to the Sung dynasty branding had been a form of punishment for an offense such as thievery; now it was required for every soldier. Would he be interested in sacrificing his life to defend the privileged position of those who had condemned him for no reason other than his lowly profession? He fled from the battlefield when confronted with a strong enemy, but fought like a tiger once he switched his loyalty to the enemy side. Numerically small, the Khitans, the Nuchens, and later the Mongols could not have succeeded so well in China without Chinese help, as most of their soldiers were indeed Chinese. When the Fang La rebellion began, the government had to send foreign troops to help suppress it, since it could not completely trust its own men. After a government had sunk so low, it deserved to die. It did die, of course, a few years later.

All the Sung virtues and vices were nowhere better exemplified than in the person of Emperor Sung Hui-tsung. A man of impeccable taste for the finer things in life, he was the Sung regime's greatest patron of arts and literature. He was a painter of considerable talent (some of his paintings have survived), a poet of note, and an accomplished musician. He surrounded himself with artists, men of letters, and, of course, beautiful women. His women had not only pretty faces and willowy bodies but also special talent as singers or dancers. His liaison with the famous courtesan Li Ssu-ssu was a legend of his own time. In order to visit her anytime he wished, he built an underground tunnel that linked his residence with her house outside the palace. One evening, while she was entertaining a renowned poet by the name of Chou Pang-yen (1057– 1121), the emperor suddenly arrived without advance warning. Hurriedly she pushed the poet underneath her bed, and the poet, hearing but not seeing the tender moment between the emperor and his favorite, wrote a most beautiful poem to commemorate the occasion. When the emperor learned about the poem, he immediately recognized that the "hero" in it was none other than he himself. He summoned the poet for an audience, but the poet had already fled. The poem has survived and is widely read even today.

Unfortunately for the nation and eventually himself as well, Sung Hui-tsung's generosity and sentiments were reserved exclusively for his intellectual equals, certainly not for the soldiers who had to risk their lives to safeguard his throne or the peasants who had to labor doubly hard to support the kind of luxuries he and his intellectual equals enjoyed. Perhaps this was not his fault, since he, surrounded by sycophants and isolated from outside contact, had no idea of how miserable life was outside the palace wall. He cried when he heard about Fang La's rebellion; for the first time he had to face the reality that had escaped him in his idiotic and obsessive search for "rare flowers and stones." Perhaps he regretted, but the regret had come too late. The title given him by his Nuchen captors a few years later, "Duke of Confused Virtues," was most appropriate for a man who, had he not been an emperor, would have been a true Renaissance man of his time.

Despite its shortcomings, the Sung regime perhaps conformed better to the Confucian ideal than any other regime in history. It had a government by intellectuals as Confucius would have wished. Socially, all the Sung people were divided into two classes—those who labored with their brains were the rulers and those who worked with their hands were the ruled—a division of labor that Mencius regarded as natural and ideal. The two philosophers also stated, repeatedly, that a good ruler ruled by example. Though not all the Sung emperors could be described as exemplary rulers, there were no outright brutes among them; the worst among them were merely incompetent and stupid. If the quality of life in a society is determined by the level of its cultural activities, certainly no Chinese society, before or since, rates more highly than the Sung dynasty. For centuries Confucian philosophers had stressed the importance of *wang tao*, or the way of peace, and condemned unequivocally *pa tao*, or the way of war, elaborating in great detail that a barbarian invasion occurred only because Chinese rulers had not been virtuous enough. Not sure of their own virtues, the Sung rulers most naturally thought of bribery ("annual tribute") to buy the enemy off when he invaded. When Wang An-shih spoke of the necessity of "enriching the nation and strengthening its armed forces," his opponents characterized him as a Legalist in disguise—a most damaging characterization in a Confucian society. Nevertheless, the Sung rulers did violate a cardinal Confucian principle, namely, that they must keep taxes to a minimum. Sung taxes were among the highest on record, and the Sung government, not surprisingly, did not enjoy popular support.

The Sung values, good or bad, were not confined to the Sung dynasty alone; they became the norm for Chinese of succeeding centuries. Chinese pacifism is an example. From the Sung times to the twentieth century when Western values began to prevail, the Chinese condemned soldiery as a most contemptuous occupation. A popular saying observed, "Good men should never become soldiers as good iron should not be used to make nails." Parents taught their children not to play "wild games" that required physical exertion, as children must be always polite, gentle, and unaggressive. To be healthy was all right, but to have muscles was disgraceful. Physical education had no part in the school curriculum, and archery, which was occasionally practiced, was more an art than a sport. There were many outstanding colleges throughout these long centuries, but not a single military academy of any consequence before the twentieth century. The martial arts, known to the Western world as *Kung-fu,* were practiced mostly by people outside the mainstream, such as Buddhist monks and members of the secret societies. In the hundreds of traditional novels, short stories, and dramas, a hero was usually a delicately built, pretty-faced, and sophisticated scholar, the kind of person too effeminate to be taken seriously in a Western society. Even in *Shui-hu chuan,* a novel about cutthroat bandits, the supreme commander was an ex-clerk who could not handle either a knife or a bow. Prior to the Sung dynasty and for more than twenty-five hundred years of her recorded history, China had never been conquered by a foreign power; since then she has been conquered twice, first by the Mongols and then by the Manchus. During the past 718 years (1260–1978) the Chinese have lived under alien rule for 376 years (1260–1368 and 1644–1912). They were very much an easy prey to the Western powers and Japan in modern times. All this may have been a coincidence, but most likely it is not.

THE INTELLECTUALS

Admittedly the Sung society was not ideal. But if one happened to be intelligent and love book learning, one could not have been born to a better time than the Sung period, however humble one's background might be. With the exception of a small minority known as the "mean people" (p. 354), all Chinese were entitled to take part in the civil service examinations, and the examinations, being impartially administered, served as the greatest mechanism in keeping the political and intellectual elite in a continuous flux. Some may say that the increase of social mobility as generated by the examination system was more apparent than real since allegedly only the wealthy could afford to send their children to school. This assertion is valid only to a certain extent. To a family that had designated one of its sons (usually the brightest) to pursue an academic career, the major sacrifice was to lose him as a full-time worker on the farm. Since the farm was most likely small, his service on it might not have been needed in the first place. Tuition paid to a village teacher was nominal and could always be compounded into a few pints of rice. The length of formal schooling was also short because, once a student learned to read independently, he was practically on his own. If by then he had shown some promise as a scholar, there would be no dearth of eager, more affluent families that would try to help him out—to produce a distinguished scholar, as measured by the civil service examinations, was not only a matter of local pride, but it also had social and political implications that no farsighted person could ignore.

Countless examples of the Chinese version of from-rags-to-riches can be cited, but one of the best concerns Fan Chung-yen, whose name has been mentioned repeatedly earlier. Born to a poor family in Soochow, he was still an infant when his father died. Out of economic necessity his mother remarried, and he spent an unhappy childhood in his foster father's house. In 1011, at the age of twenty-one, he decided to make a name for himself. He left home for Honan where he studied with a private academy, later known as Ying-t'ien. For the next four years, we are told, he studied day and night, washing his face with cold water whenever he was too tired to continue and eating nothing more substantial than a daily fare of thin gruel. The endurance paid off in 1015 when he passed the metropolitan examination in his first attempt. He received appointment as magistrate of Kwangteh (located in modern Anhwei province), and among his first actions was to send for his mother, so she too could enjoy the glory and the material reward due to a holder of the *chin-shih* ("advanced scholarship") degree. From then on he rose steadily in the bureaucracy until he eventually became the prime minister.

While in Kaifeng, he proposed reform for the enormous waste and in-efficiency in the central government, but his proposal, as mentioned earlier, was rejected. During the Tangut war, he was called to head an army to defend the northwestern frontier after several Sung generals had failed. He stopped the Tanguts' advance and was in due course able to impose on them a peaceful settlement. During his long, distinguished career, he set aside part of his salaries to establish a relief fund to help the deserving poor. When in retirement, he was a good friend and fine neighbor, always kind and helpful to anyone who needed his counsel and advice.

People like Fan Chung-yen were the conscience of their time, and his maxim that "an educated man should suffer before anyone else suf-fers and should enjoy only after everyone else has enjoyed" may have been too lofty an ideal for all of his fellow intellectuals to reach. Never-theless, there were enough intellectuals with a good conscience to make the Sung period a truly memorable one. They served as a buffer between an unbending bureaucracy bent on collecting as much tax as possible and the voiceless masses from whom most of them came. Often at the risk of their own careers, many of them spoke eloquently about social in-justice and economic exploitation, sometimes with good results. When in retirement, they, as recognized leaders in their respective communities, supervised the maintenance of Confucian temples and the worship therein, the operation of communal granaries and relief work in time of famine, the establishment of schools and the proper education of the young, the continued operation of such welfare establishments as or-phanages and houses for the aged, the administration of justice for crimes less serious than murder or armed robbery, and many other matters. Above all, they were the transmitters of Chinese heritage from one gen-eration to another. They were supposed to set a moral example for others to follow and many of them did.

Wherever they lived or worked, these intellectuals formed part of a nationwide community. The community was not a society or association in its modern sense, with membership cards and paid dues; it was an informal comradeship of common interest, devotion, and pride. A success-ful candidate of the metropolitan examination would be an automatic member since his name would be immediately known to everyone in the community, and those who passed the examination in the same year had a special feeling for one another and called each other *t'ung-nien* ("same-year"), an affectionate term for "brother." For a person who had failed or, for personal reasons, had not tried to obtain a *chin-shih* degree, entry to this exclusive community was more difficult, since he had to do something special to attract nationwide attention. Maybe his essay on current affairs or on a specific point about Confucian philosophy was judged to have special merit; maybe some of his poems were so well phrased that they resembled the work of a genius. Even a *chin-shih* degree holder recognized that not everyone who had passed the examination was brighter than everyone who had failed it. Members of the community took their superiority for granted—so did practically everyone else. They protected one another's interests and formed a solid front as far as outsiders were concerned. If they failed as government officials, they could always return home as recognized leaders of their own communities. Even in total defeat, they were still regarded as better than anyone else.

Below the national community of intellectual elite were the second-echelon aspirants known only locally in their own communities. They were a mixed group, ranging from those who barely knew how to write a presentable letter to those who had passed the lower level of the civil service examination and had received the *hsiu-ts'ai* ("flowering talent") degree. The kind of influence they were able to exercise depended less upon their scholarship, which was difficult to measure, than upon their family background which was more tangible and familiar. A *hsiu-ts'ai* degree holder from a wealthy, established family might be a power in his own right, but his colleague from a poor background might have great difficulties in surviving since the government did not subsidize holders of lower degrees. To make a living, an impoverished *hsiu-ts'ai* might, for a fee, compose eulogies of the dead, write petitions for the illiterate or less well educated, or peddle calligraphy among the peasants who, following tradition, pasted calligraphic works on doors and walls when a special occasion such as the New Year had arrived. He might be able to secure a position in the magistrate's office as a secretary or clerk if he had good connections; more often than not, he became a schoolteacher. Despite his reputation as a scholar, his life was anything but enviable.

All the local scholars, rich or poor, held the *chin-shih* degree holders in awe as the kind of persons they themselves wanted, but failed, to become. A *chin-shih* living in his own community was an acknowledged leader whose opinion must be sought on all important matters. Even the local magistrate would not make an important decision without consulting him in advance. If, when a local issue developed, he was serving in the capital or some other part of China, and if, in the meantime, the issue had become too complicated to be settled to everyone's satisfaction, he might be requested to serve as an arbitrator; his decision, under normal circumstances, would be followed without fail. The general principle governing local disputes was to avoid litigation that would impose financial burden on all parties concerned. If two *chin-shih* degree holders stood on the opposite sides of a local issue, a *cause célèbre* ensued, no matter how insignificant the issue really was. Normally this would not happen since the intellectual elite preferred a united front vis-à-vis outsiders and would not wish to damage their own reputations and prestige in endless lawsuits.

While most intellectuals who became teachers did so out of economic necessity, there were others who purposely chose teaching as a lifelong profession. To them life as a bureaucrat, with its implied necessity of having to please one's superiors regardless of the issue involved, was simply too demeaning to entertain. Great masters emerged because, of all the things they could do in life, they preferred teaching. Ch'i T'ung-wen, a master teacher in the latter part of the tenth century, attracted students from all parts of China, and fifty-six of them later succeeded in passing the metropolitan examination. It was at the academy he founded, later known as Ying-t'ien, that Fan Chung-yen studied. Ying-t'ien, Pai-lu-tung (located in modern Kiangsi province), Shih-ku (located in modern Hunan province), and Yüeh-lu (also located in modern Hunan province) were then hailed as the Four Great Colleges of China. In Lower Yangtze there was a master teacher named Hu Yüan who, besides being a classicist, also specialized in acoustics. In the 1040's, after more than forty years of teaching in Huchow, he came to Kaifeng as a visiting professor in the Central University. So many students wished to enroll in his classes, or just be close enough to have a glimpse of him, that the regular dormitories were found to be inadequate and the university authorities, we are told, had to erect temporary buildings to accommodate the surplus. Sometimes a renowned scholar would travel hundreds of miles to engage in open debate with colleagues who held a different point of view, as the audience listened in awe of their erudition and eloquence. A scholar of this kind attracted followers from far and wide, and quickly he and his followers would found a new school of learning with a different philosophical emphasis.

Scholars like Ch'i T'ung-wen and Hu Yüan were universally admired and respected because, among other things, they never allowed themselves to get deeply involved with political feuds and bickering. Being nonpolitical, however, was more an exception than a rule. While as individuals most Sung scholars could be characterized as good men, the Confucian obsession with "learning for the purpose of application" (hsüeh yi chih yung) could not but transform academic differences into practical politics, and scholars of different philosophical emphases soon found themselves political enemies as well. Various philosophical and political cliques emerged, and each of them made alliances and created enemies as the occasion arose. Before 1100 the political feuds, such as those between the Old and the New Parties, were still conducted on a high level because, among other things, the participants (Wang An-shih, Ssu-ma Kuang, Ou-yang Hsiu, Su Shih, and others) were not only scholars but also gentlemen. Their differences were those of a policy or ideological orientation, and there was no personal vendetta of any kind. The situation deteriorated when Ts'ai Ching became the prime minister. In 1102 he drafted a list of 120 persons whose "evil" example no officials were supposed to follow. Two years later the list was enlarged to 309 persons who, said a royal decree, had no right to speak on any issue concerning public policy. The same kind of vindictive feuds continued even after the Sung regime had lost North China and moved its capital to Hangchow. Today historians regard Chu Hsi (1130–1200) as one of the greatest philosophers of all times; but, in his own time, he was denounced by his political opponents as a "bogus head," and his philosophy was condemned as "false learning."

Despite the vindictiveness, no intellectual was ever jailed or executed when his faction or clique lost power. The worst that could happen to him was the loss of his bureaucratic post and consequently his power base; he might even have to leave the capital and return home where he would remain a celebrity and an authoritative voice. In short, the political feuds of the Sung dynasty were the most gentlemanly ever recorded in Chinese history, never equalled before or since. Sung T'ai-tsu, a scholarly emperor, had made it a dynastic rule that no corporal punishment should ever be inflicted upon intellectuals, and his successors, for more than three hundred years, followed this rule without fail.

As the intellectuals formed the most powerful group in politics, traditional power blocks, such as the eunuchs and the emperor's maternal or spousal relatives, were completely overshadowed in terms of influence. One may argue, perhaps convincingly, that the Sung intellectuals, in power for more than three centuries, did not do any better for the Sung people than the groups they condemned did for their respective regimes. One may also argue, perhaps less convincingly, that their failings resulted less from personal faults than from the inherent imperfection of a chaotic world they had to face. Nevertheless, the very idea that the avenue to power was education, instead of birth, wealth, or any other consideration, was unique and refreshing. The examination system may not be the best way to measure a person's worth; still, no one in traditional China had been able to devise a better system. In any case, it kept alive the hope of a peasant's son who, with good intelligence, hard work, and much luck, might someday become one of the most powerful men in the nation. In view of the competition, the odds against his success were of course overwhelming; but few societies other than traditional China had ever even given him a chance.

NEO-CONFUCIANISM

The pattern of behavior that we sometimes associate with the Chinese, from overpoliteness to poker face, does not originate in Confucius who, when insulted, would probably not have thanked the insulter for "enlightening" him and then have gone home calmly to contemplate his own "unworthiness." To be sure, not every Chinese could live up to this model behavior by "turning the other cheek"; he who could would be regarded as a gentleman of the first order. Sometimes this model behavior is carried to such an extent as to make the practitioner look cowardly, hypocritical, or simply silly, and the Chinese are, of course, viewed as inscrutable. Whatever this behavior may imply to a non-Chinese, Confucius certainly should neither be given the credit nor assigned the blame, since it began no earlier than the Sung dynasty. It originates in Neo-Confucianism, rather than classical Confucianism of the pre-Ch'in period.

The beginning of Neo-Confucianism can be traced to two major sources: the reaction to the kind of Confucianism practiced from the Han times and the response to the challenge of Taoism and Buddhism, especially the latter. Prior to the T'ang-Sung period the study of Confucianism meant primarily the philological and etymological study of Confucian texts, notably the *Five Classics*. Great masters in this field of study emerged from time to time, such as Ma Yung (79–166) and Cheng Hsüan (127–200). What had this study to do with Confucianism, asked the Sung scholars, other than mountains of words that it had produced? Would this study not distract people from understanding the true nature of Confucianism which, after all, was a code of behavior? Even as a code of behavior, Confucianism had declined as a moral force after the Han times. Filial piety, for instance, was hailed as the first virtue of the nation, but it had been carried to such an extent that it often seemed a farce rather than a genuine expression of filial devotion. The mourning period for a deceased parent was supposed to be three years during which the mourner abstained from doing anything pleasurable, including sex, but many sons extended it to six or, in some cases, twenty years, only to be confronted with the fact that their wives, during the mourning period, had given birth to not only one but sometimes several children. Confucianism had been adulterated, said the Sung scholars, and they vowed to return it to its original form. In the process of purifying Confucianism of its alien elements, they, of course, added a few alien elements of their own.

The emergence of Neo-Confucianism could be also viewed as a reaction to the increasing popularity of Buddhism and Taoism. During the

T'ang dynasty scholars like Han Yü called upon China's intellectual elite to rebuke Buddhism as a form of superstition, but to combat it they did not develop a new ideology. They merely reiterated some ideal society that had allegedly existed in China's remote past. To the Sung scholars, however, one must have one's own system to fight an alien system, and they searched diligently in the Confucian classics for those ideas that were regarded as most appropriate for the occasion. When these ideas were found inadequate, they did not hesitate to borrow from their opponents, while denying adamantly that they had adopted any alien ideology. The result was a Confucianism strongly imbued with Buddhist and Taoist influences. The Chinese call it the Rational School (*Li hsüeh*), known to the West as Neo-Confucianism.

As noted in an earlier chapter of this book, classical Confucianism concerns itself with human relations and social welfare, and neither Confucius nor Mencius had ventured far cosmologically or metaphysically. To build a cosmological system, the Sung scholars had to borrow heavily from the Taoists. Pioneered by Chou Tun-yi (1012–1073) and later elaborated by others, Sung cosmology presupposes a rational universe that functions according to well-defined rules. The universe begins with The Infinite (*Wu chi*), the eternal but invisible force that is the very essence of its being. Once acquiring form, The Infinite becomes The Absolute (*T'ai chi*), the beginning of the physical universe that could be known through the five senses of man. The Infinite and The Absolute provide, respectively, the universe's content (*chih*) and form (*hsing*); they are inseparable since form could not exist without content and content would remain unknown without form. The monolithic Infinite-Absolute multiplies itself and creates things through the interaction between two opposite but complementary forces within itself, namely, *yin* and *yang*, or the negative and the positive. Things thus created can be either *yin*-dominated, such as the moon, or *yang*-dominated, such as the sun. Likewise, men are *yang*, and women are *yin*. "Things" refers to not only concrete objects but also abstract concepts. South and brightness are *yang*, and north and darkness are *yin*. Though the two forces maintain their separate identity, each existed in the existence of the other. There could not have been men without women, and the concept of darkness is impossible unless there has been brightness.

Yin and *yang* are forces, not things. Most things in the universe, whether they be trees or clouds, are the final, rather than the immediate, products of their creations. The immediate products of the *yin-yang* interactions are the five primary elements, namely, metal, wood, water, fire, and earth. The five primary elements are the simplest forms of physical existence; they, through their various combinations, create the more complicated things such as trees and clouds. In each of the things they have created, one of the five elements had a more dominating position than the others. The trees, for instance, had a "wood virtue" (*mu teh*), and the clouds, water. While maintaining their separate identities in each given instance, the five primary elements successively produce and destroy one another, and no element can maintain its present status indefinitely. Their mutual relations are indicated in the following graphs:

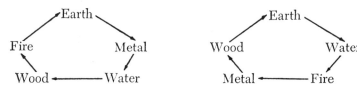

THE GENERATION CYCLE   THE DESTRUCTION CYCLE

In the left graph, earth generates metal, metal generates water, etc. In the right graph, earth destroys water, water destroys fire, and when wood destroys earth, the cycle is completed. During each generation or destruction process, none of the five elements is lost; it only changes its form. In both cycles nothing can be gained or lost.

Thus the universe maintains its dynamic existence through the continuous interaction between *yin* and *yang* and the incessant permutations of the five primary elements as they successively produce and destroy one another. The law of the universe is the law of change; it is change that keeps the universe living and dynamic. Change, however, does not go on in a random or blind fashion. It follows a definite pattern, the pattern of the Eight Diagrams. The two opposite forces, *yin* and *yang*, interact in accordance with the form as provided by one of the Eight Diagrams. In the first two diagrams one force so completely dominates the other that the latter does not appear. They are the purest *yang* and *yin* diagrams (*ch'ien* and *k'un*), representing Heaven and Earth, respectively. The other six diagrams have either two *yin* and one *yang*, or two *yang* and one *yin*. In the former case the diagram is a *yin* diagram, and things created through this kind of combination are *yin* things, such as the moon. In the latter case it is a *yang* diagram, and things thus created are *yang* things, such as the sun. As has been said earlier (p. 81), in each diagram a broken line represents the *yin* force, and an unbroken line the *yang* force. As a reminder, two typical *yin* and *yang* diagrams are drawn as follows:

Yin Diagram   *Yang* Diagram

Through a continuous process of combination, dissolution, and re-combination *yin* and *yang* destroy and create the constituent parts of the universe. In summary, the whole cosmology may be pictured as follows:

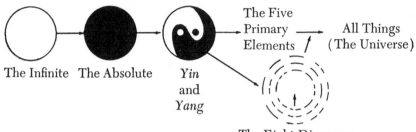

The Infinite   The Absolute   *Yin* and *Yang*   The Five Primary Elements   All Things (The Universe)

The Eight Diagrams

It should be pointed out, however, that the basic ideas of Sung cosmology did not originate with the Sung scholars. The concept of The Absolute first appeared in the *Book of Changes,* and the idea of The Infinite was introduced in the *Book of Taoist Virtue.* The concepts of Eight Diagrams and five primary elements were equally old. The Sung scholars' contribution was, in essence, the coordination and systematization of the existing ideas into a rational, logical system. Han scholars like Tung Chung-shu had in fact written a great deal about the *yin-yang* interactions.

The Sung scholars did not, of course, study cosmology for its own sake. Following a Confucian tradition that every field of learning must serve a human purpose, they were more than anxious to apply the dualist principle to the well-being of man. A man has in him a combination of heavenly reason (*yang*) and earthly desires (*yin*), and he must carefully maintain an equilibrium between them and should never allow the latter to usurp the position of the former. The possession of a human form does not necessarily make a man a man; more important is the principle or reason (*li*) that underlies the essence of being a man. This principle that governs man is his humanity or, as Mencius puts it, his sense of compassion and his ability to distinguish right from wrong. As a chair is not a chair if it cannot sustain the weight of a human body, a man is no longer a man and is in fact indistinguishable from the lowest animals if he has lost his sense of humanity or his essence of being a man.

While human nature is good and everyone is born with human qualities, the amount of humanity varies with individuals, and the amount a person actually has depends upon how well he has developed his *ch'i*. *Ch'i* enlarges the humanity within a person just as heat pushes up the mercury in a thermometer. To develop *ch'i* to its fullest extent is to attain moral perfection (*chih sheng*)—the highest goal, which every man should strive to achieve.

How does a person develop his *ch'i*? The Sung scholars could not agree on the answer and a major dispute soon developed between two schools, led respectively by Chu Hsi and Lu Chiu-yüan (1139–1192). Chu Hsi, quoting the *Great Learning*, asserts that the development of personal ethics requires the acquisition of knowledge, and the acquisition of knowledge "lies in the investigation of objects and things." There is a hidden truth in every object, and the understanding of one truth will help unravel truths in all other objects. As a person continues his studies conscientiously and diligently, says Chu Hsi, eventually all truths will appear in their proper places and the universal truth, of which individual truths are only constituent parts, will be "suddenly" revealed to him. He will then know the innermost secrets of nature and man, and for the first time he will be truly "enlightened." He will be not only wise but also free. His will be moral perfection without the slightest effort and despite himself.

To Lu Chiu-yüan, however, the investigation of outward things in the physical world means the pursuance of an unlimited goal by the limited means, and it cannot but be a fruitless and wasteful process. Besides, the attainment of moral perfection has nothing to do with the physical world; it comes about only when the mind has been truly rectified. There is nothing to investigate outside the mind, says he, since "the truth of the universe is within oneself." To acquire truth and therefore virtue, all a person needs to do is to examine himself. To discipline oneself is more important than to right outside wrongs, and the whole world will be peaceful and orderly if one's own mind has been rectified first. To do otherwise, says Lu Chiu-yüan, is to "confuse end and means" (*pen mo tao chih*) and cannot yield good results.

The investigation of objects and things did not mean, of course, scientific research—a product of the modern era for which the China of the twelfth century was not yet ready. It meant, to all intents and purposes, book learning. Even confined to book learning, the amount of work involved had to be enormous. "I have been deeply buried in a mountain of words from which I do not seem to be able to free myself," said Chu Hsi on one occasion. If Chu Hsi could not read all the books, obviously nobody else could either. While all knowledge was desirable, he later concluded, there were certain works that contained the basic truth and should be studied with great diligence. He singled out the *Four Books* (p. 82) for emphasis and started to write extensive comments on them. Though these comments, from a modern historian's point of view, contain as much distortion as clarification, they, together with the main texts, were among the first to be taught in schools, and no candidate in the civil service examination could expect to succeed if he deviated from them. Chu Hsi's influence persisted for the next seven or eight centuries and remained viable long after the establishment of the Chinese Republic in 1912. When this author went to school at the age of five, his first assignment was to chant the opening sentence of the *Analects* as commented by Chu Hsi. What kind of gentleman would a person be if he followed scrupulously Chu Hsi's instructions? Most likely he was an expressionless and unemotional individual who, internally, was supposed to know the right from the wrong at all times. It was this kind of individual that the Westerners encountered in China during the nineteenth century; not surprisingly, the "notoriety" of Chinese inscrutability began to spread.

HISTORY, LITERATURE, AND THE FINE ARTS

People of traditional China were among the most historically minded in the world, and the wealth of their written record was also unique. To them history was not only a rendering of the past, but it also taught personal ethics and good government. It was said that when Confucius wrote the *Spring and Autumn Annals,* "rebellious ministers and unfilial sons trembled"; they trembled because Confucius's book was meant to condemn them. Beginning with Pan Ku who wrote the first dynastic history, scholars maintained that the lessons of the immediate past should not be lost and that once a new regime was established, it must authorize or sponsor the writing of an authoritative history of the old regime it had replaced. Because of the enormous prestige attached to the authorship of a dynastic history, there was no dearth of volunteers, and sometimes individuals would proceed with their work with or without governmental authorization. In that case two or more versions covering the same regime might emerge, and only time could ultimately judge as to which of them would be accepted as a dynastic history.

When the Sung regime was established, a dynastic history covering the T'ang had already been in existence. It was *T'ang shu* (*History of the T'ang*) written by Liu Hsü (*c.* 885–944), a onetime premier under the Later Tsin regime, and his colleagues. Emperor Sung Jen-tsung detested Liu Hsü, whom he described as "a despicable character," and ordered Ou-yang Hsiu (1007–1072), then the acknowledged dean of scholars, to write a new version. It took Ou-yang Hsiu and another scholar named Sung Ch'i (998–1061) seventeen years to complete the new version, known as *Hsin T'ang shu* or *New History of the T'ang.* Since historians of later ages could not agree on the comparative merit of the two versions, both were subsequently classified as authoritative histories covering the T'ang period. On his own initiative, Ou-yang Hsiu also wrote the *Hsin wu-tai shih* (*New History of the Five Dynasties*), with the intended purpose of replacing an earlier work (*Wu-tai shih* or *History of the Five Dynasties*) by Hsüeh Chü-cheng (912–981). The new version was only half the size of the old version (75 versus 150 rolls), but doubt remained as to which of the two was really better.

A much more influential work than any described above was *History as a Mirror* (*Tzu-chih t'ung-chien*) by Ssu-ma Kuang, Ou-yang Hsiu's friend and colleague. As its title implies, it was meant to be a guide for future emperors and statesmen, so that they would not repeat the mistakes of the past. To make sure that the reader would not miss the significance of the events he described, the author added comments whenever appropriate. Designed as a successor to the *Spring and Autumn Annals,* the book covers a period of 1,362 years, from the beginning of the Warring States in 403 B.C. to the last year of the Five Dynasties in 959 A.D. Though recognized as one of the greatest works ever written, it has the obvious disadvantages of all chronicles. For one thing, it is difficult for a reader to follow an event from the beginning to the end, as its description may spread over several rolls, interrupted by the description of other events that occurred in the same year or years. To provide a remedy for this inconvenience, a man named Yüan Shu (1131–1205) later grouped all the major entries in Ssu-ma Kuang's book in accordance with "events" instead of "years" and titled his book *Events in the History as a Mirror* (*Tzu-chih t'ung-chien chi-shih pen-mo*). Though originally compiled for the convenience of his own reading, the book became immediately popular since it was much easier to read than the original.

Equally as important as those mentioned above are two other works written according to "topics" instead of "events" or "years." They are *General Records* (*T'ung chih*) by Cheng Ch'iao (c. 1104–1162) and *A Study of Cultural Heritage* (*Wen-hsien t'ung k'ao*) by Ma Tuan-lin (d. c. 1317). The contents of the former book are divided into twenty major topics, with more emphasis on the humanities, such as music, literature, and phonetics. Ma Tuan-lin's book, on the other hand, is much stronger on institutions, as its twenty-four main topics include such subject matters as land taxation, money and exchange, population, commerce, finance, education, civil service examinations, religious worship, and the administration of criminal justice. The author records the pros and cons of the major issues involving institutional changes and often concludes with his own assessments.

It took Ssu-ma Kuang seventeen years and Ma Tuan-lin twenty years to write their respective masterpieces, and historians, at least those in traditional China, had to be a patient breed. When a historian finally became well known, more often than not he was no longer around to enjoy his own fame. Understandably, most authors preferred writing shorter pieces, the impact of which could be immediately felt. Early in the 1060's when Wang An-shih was hailed as "a new sage" by the capital's political and intellectual elite, Su Hsün (1009–1066), father of the better known Su Shih (1036–1101), wrote an essay entitled "How Can You Tell a Hypocrite" (*Pien chien lun*). In it he stated that a man who never combed his hair or washed his face must be a hypocrite, even though he spoke eloquently about the ways of ancient sages. Wang An-shih's name was never mentioned in the essay, but everyone knew whom the author had in mind. The essay became an immediate sensation because it expressed an opinion contrary to the consensus. Later it became a rallying point for those who vigorously opposed Wang An-shih's reforms.

Su Hsün wrote in what was then known as the ancient style, pioneered by such T'ang essayists as Han Yü and Liu Tsung-yüan (p. 187). After the eighth century and throughout the Five Dynasties the ancient style was once again eclipsed by the "parallel form" (pp. 151–152), the popularity of which persisted until the eleventh century. According to Ou-yang Hsiu, the ancient style had been a lost art when he was a young man; he was determined to revive it, he said, after reading Han Yü's writing and being enormously impressed with the beauty of its style. Later, as the most prestigious scholar in the capital, he took under his wings such talents as Su Hsün and his two sons, in addition to Tseng Kung (1019–1083) and Wang An-shih, all of whom pledged that they would write prose only in the ancient style. This decision, plus their enormous output, soon reestablished the ancient style as the standard form of prose writing. The most outstanding among them proved to be the versatile Su Shih (also known as Su Tung-p'o) who, in a letter to his younger brother Su Ch'e (1039–1112), described his style as follows:

My essays are like thousands of fountains shooting with a violent burst from an uncharted wilderness. When the water reaches the plain, it becomes a roaring torrent, sweeping thousands of miles with complete ease. When it encounters rocks and mountains, it changes its course and adjusts itself to its surroundings. It it completely unpredictable. It goes wherever it should go and only stops whenever it should stop.

Great though its achievement in prose was, the Sung period was even better known as a golden era in poetry. By then poetry had developed into two distinct forms, *shih* and *tz'u*. In *shih* each line has the same number of characters as the other lines, and since each character has always one syllable, all lines provide even rhythm throughout the entire poem. It is the general practice for each poem to have either five-character or seven-character lines, though many of the very ancient poems, such as those in the *Book of Odes*, have four-character lines. Though poetry in the form of *shih* reached its most glorious age during the time of Li Po and Tu Fu, Sung poets like Su Shih and Wang An-shih could not be said to be much inferior without causing a heated debate. Usually it is personal taste, rather than the inherent merit of the poems themselves, that makes ratings differ. Whatever the opinion might be in the case of *shih*, there is a consensus that in the other form of poetry, *tz'u*, the Sung dynasty surpasses all other periods, before or after, in the number of great masters and in the quality of poems they produced.

Nobody knows for sure when *tz'u* first began. It began perhaps no earlier than the seventh century because no *tz'u* has survived from before that period, if it ever existed. As with all forms of literary expression, it passed through a long evolutionary process before it reached its final form. It was first found in the houses of entertainment where the songs sung by female entertainers were arranged in such a way that each line in a song contained a definite number of characters (syllables), usually from two to nine. The line and metric arrangement in each song was called *p'ai*, and the words were *tz'u*. It was and still is customary to entitle each poem by the name of an original *p'ai* that it followed, rather than the content of the poem itself. Since the number of *p'ai* was limited, theoretically there could have been thousands or even millions of *tz'u* with the same title. But, as only the very best have survived the test of time, the actual number of extant *tz'u* with the same title is comparatively few. At the beginning the *tz'u* as sung by the girls in the entertainment houses were perhaps no better than those found in similar places in today's Hong Kong or Macao, but quality improved once the great poets took an interest in composing them.

It is not difficult to understand how these houses of entertainment flourished. In a society where every aspect of outward conduct was strictly regulated and where all marriages were arranged, the houses of entertainment provided an emotional outlet not to be found anywhere else. Here alone could a man discard his socially required respectability and do whatever his true self dictated. He left his Confucian propriety behind when he entered a house of "wild flowers." Sometimes genuine friendship or even romance developed between the "wild flowers" and their patrons, and such romance appeared in numerous novels and short stories. If the patrons happened to be talented poets, there was no reason why they should not write lyrics for the songs sung by their favorites. Some of the "wild flowers," such as the ninth-century Hsüeh T'ao, were talented poets in their own right and composed their own songs.

Though originating in the house of ill repute, *tz'u* became a respectable form of literary expression as soon as members of the intellectual elite took a hand in composing it. As time went by, it was divorced from its original purpose of singing; people wrote it merely to express their sentiments and emotions. *Tz'u* of the late T'ang period, as represented by the works of Wen T'ing-yün (*c.* 812–872) and Li Shang-yin (813–858), lack depth and conviction, as they are too artificially ornate. Not until the tenth century did *tz'u* find its great champion in the person of

Li Yü (936–978), the last ruler of a small kingdom called South T'ang in the Lower Yangtze that was eventually conquered by the newly established Sung regime. As a king, Li Yü was a miserable failure, as he spent more time with dancing girls and musicians than he did with his cabinet ministers. His earlier works are good, but not exceptional. Only when he was living in captivity, after having lost his kingdom, did his literary talent fully bloom. While he wrote only to quench his emotional thirst, many of his immortal lines have been on the lips of his countrymen for the last one thousand years.

As a form of poetic expression, *tz'u* remained popular throughout the Sung dynasty. There was a Liu Yung (*c.* 998–1063) who had written so many *tz'u* that it was said "whenever there is drinking water there are girls who know how to sing his songs." His popularity was partly due to the fact that he preferred commonly used words and thus made his poems more comprehensible to the less educated singers. After passing the metropolitan examination in 1034, his experience with a bureaucratic life was not a happy one, partly because, to use his own words, he "prefers to exchange illusory fame for some light drinking and low singing." Finally, at the end of a long, libertine life, he was so poor that his admiring brothel girls had to contribute funds for burial expenses. One century later there was another *tz'u* poet named Hsin Ch'i-chi (1140–1207) who differed from Liu Yung both in temperament and in the nature of *tz'u* produced. By then the golden age of peace and prosperity had passed, and the Chin horsemen had swept down as far as the Yangtze River. As a war veteran, Hsin Ch'i-chi wrote to express his own patriotic sentiments. As one critic put it, his poems were not meant to be sung by brothel girls; they were to be shouted aloud by marching soldiers.

Between Liu Yung and Hsin Ch'i-chi there were many poets whose *tz'u* have survived. The most memorable among them was a woman named Li Ch'ing-chao (b. 1081) who wrote with a subtlety and delicacy unmatched by any of the others. Born to an intellectual family in Tsinan, modern Shantung province, she had been reared in the best of China's cultural tradition before she was married to a university student named Chao Ming-ch'eng (1081–1129). The marriage was a happy one, she said many years later. She and her husband spent many happy evenings in matching wits and in outdoing each other in guessing the sources of famous literary quotations, recalling not only the titles of books but also the volumes and page numbers. After her husband had left for the south as a government official, she sent him one poem after another, expressing the sadness of separation and the hope and joy of a reunion. So impressed was he with the beauty of these poems that he tried to surpass her by writing many himself. He showed both of their poems to a friend without identifying the authors, and the friend did not hesitate for a moment to point out the best lines, all of which happened to be hers.

Unfortunately this happy life did not last long. The Chin forces marched southward, and Li Ch'ing-chao's home, together with the rest of North China, fell into the enemy's hands. The refugee's life was further saddened by the early death of her husband, and without any children of her own, she stood alone in a man-dominated world. Still she had her talent, and she used it to attack those whom she accused of having treated her unfairly. Shunned by the intellectual elite, she died in poverty and misery, in a year that historians have not been able to determine. Little did she realize that after her death she would be hailed as one of China's greatest literary geniuses.

Poetry, in the form of either *shih* or *tz'u,* was written in the classical language, which the less educated could not comprehend. Their needs had to be satisfied in some other manner. Long before the Sung dynasty professional storytellers had traveled from town to town, from village to village, and, for a small fee, made their audience laugh or cry. Usually they stopped at the moment of suspense so that their listeners would come back the next day. The stories were told in spoken Chinese, which was easy to understand, and they were called *p'ing hua,* or vernacular tales. At the beginning these tales were handed down orally from generation to generation, and considerable time must have elapsed before the popular ones were put down in written words. Many of them, written during the Sung period, have survived. The basic theme of these tales is simple and straightforward: to punish the guilty and to reward the deserving. They are not well written as a rule. Looked down upon by traditional China's intellectual elite, they are, nevertheless, extremely valuable from a historian's point of view, since they provide firsthand information on the life of the common people during the Sung dynasty. This information is not available in the more orthodox sources, such as the dynastic histories, where only the mighty and the great receive adequate attention. They are now serving a purpose never intended by their authors.

Speaking of Chinese arts, one invariably thinks of paintings and porcelains, and the Sung dynasty produced the best of both. By then the art of painting had been so specialized that a painter was often referred to by the subject matter in which he was particularly proficient, whether it be landscape, people, animals, or plants. Nevertheless the painters best known to posterity were the landscapists, such as Li Ch'eng, Fan K'uan, Tung Yüan, and Mi Fei and his son Mi Yu-jen. Li Kung-lin specialized in the painting of "people," Huang Ch'uan in "flowers," and Sung Hui-tsung in "birds" as well as "flowers." Some painters even specialized in "gods, devils, and ghosts." Su Shih, the incomparable genius, was

A CHINESE PAINTING   This painting is attributed to Ma Yüan of the Sung dynasty. The Chinese characters on the upper right read: "Ma Yüan plays with the moon in the shade of a pine tree."

an expert painter of "bamboo." Regarding his technique, he said the following:

> To paint bamboo, the painter holds the brush steadily, looks intently at the paper, and visualizes the broadest outlines of the proposed painting. When the vision flashes, he follows it quickly, and with his brush sweeping across the paper, he pursues it as a falcon chases an elusive rabbit. If he slackens his pace, vision escapes and may never return.

Early in the twelfth century the painters found their greatest patron in Sung Hui-tsung, the reigning emperor, and it was under his direction that the *Hsüan-ho Catalogue of Painting* was compiled. The book contained 6,396 paintings by 231 artists, divided among ten different categories according to subject matter ("landscape," "people," etc.). Unfortunately most paintings in this catalogue have been permanently lost.

With ink brushed on silk, all the extant Sung paintings appear faded and yellowish, and the coloring is not so bright as it ought to be: a lapse

LANDSCAPE BY AN ANONYMOUS PAINTER OF THE TWELFTH CENTURY Taoist influence plays an important part in practically all landscapes of the traditional style. Notice the dominance by mountains and water in this picture and the comparative insignificance of man. Man accommodates himself to nature; he does not change it.

of one thousand years has taken its toll. It is a different matter with the Sung porcelains, however. Time cannot change their shapes or coloring: today they stand in the great museums of the world as beautiful and proud as on the day when they were first created. Though porcelains were produced all over China, none were better known than those manufactured in Ch'angnan, located in the northeastern corner of modern Kiangsi province. In the first decade of the eleventh century the reigning emperor (Sung Chen-tsung) conferred on the city an unusual honor by renaming it Chingtehchen, or City of Chingteh, after his own royal title. Ever since then Chingtehchen has been the porcelain capital of the world. Today fragments of Sung porcelains can be found in such faraway places as East Africa, the Middle East, and the Indian subcontinent, indicating that even then their appeal was worldwide.

PRINTING

Nobody knows when the first printed books appeared; but, as far as the record goes, the first mention of printing did not occur until 593 when Emperor Sui Wen-ti ordered the printing of Buddhist images and scriptures. Before this event occurred, however, printing had obviously undergone a long, evolutionary process. The use of personal seals, carved from wood or stone or cast from bronze, dated from the fifth or sixth century B.C., and the erection of stone monuments, with inscription on them, was also an ancient tradition. Late in the third century B.C., for instance, the Ch'in emperor Shih Huang-ti ordered stone monuments to be erected in the "four corners of the earth," and on them were inscribed eulogies of the emperor and his regime. When the Christian era began, Tai Shan, the sacred mountain that Confucius used to climb, was said to have contained more than 1,800 stone monuments with carved words, including, presumably, one erected by the Ch'in emperor. In the second century B.C. Confucianism was declared a state cult; not surprisingly, the government would sponsor the inscription of Confucian classics on stone slabs so as to standardize the texts and to popularize Confucian teachings. In 1 A.D. Wang Mang ordered the inscription of Confucian classics on stone slabs as a way to standardize the texts; in 175 A.D. Emperor Han Ling-ti issued a similar order, with specific instruction that the slabs be erected on the campus of the Central University, so that students, even without their own books, could still read the ancient sages whenever it was not raining.

One can easily imagine that some enterprising student, with or without the university authorities' approval but with a plentiful supply of paper and ink, would try to make a book or books from the stone inscriptions. All he needed to do was to place a piece of damp paper on the stone, press it into the inscriptions, apply ink on the plain surface of the paper, and then rub it gently with a brush. As his brush swept across the paper, the words and pictures soon appeared on the paper exactly as they were on the stone. By binding together successive rubbings, he would, of course, have a book, even though it was enormous in size and difficult to carry. In due course rubbing itself became a highly developed art; it has been practiced throughout Chinese history and is still practiced today.

It took only a little imagination to transform the concept of rubbing into block printing. Instead of a huge slab with words carved into the stone, one needed a small-sized wooden block with words appearing in relief and, of course, in the mirror's image. Each wooden block corresponded to one Chinese page which, with ink on only one side and being folded in the middle, meant two pages in the Western style. The printed words would be in black, as words from rubbing had appeared in white. Pages were bound together by thread to make a volume (*ts'e*) that might contain several rolls (*chuan*), and two or more volumes might be packed in a box made of paperboard reinforced with silk. One volume or one box might be more than adequate for a small-sized book; but, for a giant work like *History as a Mirror,* two or three boxes might be required. The Chinese have manufactured books in this manner since the invention of printing, and an observing person may have noticed on television that Mao Tse-tung's study, where he received foreign dignitaries, was piled high with this kind of book.

While we do not know when and where the first printed books appeared, we do know that by the ninth century books had been produced in huge quantities in the province of Shu (modern Szechuan province) and had been distributed on a nationwide scale. They were books of Buddhist scriptures, Confucian classics, dictionaries, and books of medicine, poetry, or any other subject matter that had an appeal great enough to justify publication. Many of the Buddhist books contained the names of those who subsidized the publication, as well as the names of authors and publishers, but one rarely found this kind of individual sponsorship for any other kind of book. Since Confucius never promised a blissful afterlife, the printing of Confucian classics, whenever it needed subsidy, had to be sponsored by the government. In 932 the government of Later T'ang, acting on the recommendation of prime minister Feng Tao (882–954), ordered the printing of the *Nine Confucian Classics* for wide circulation. The Department of Cultural Affairs (*Kuo-tzu chien*) was made responsible for the selection and editing of texts, for the employment of hand carvers and other personnel, and for the printing operation itself. Consisting of 130 volumes, the entire work took some twenty years to complete. While the government was sponsoring the publication of more serious works, there were individuals who were so proud of their own writings that they published them at their own expense. We know that in 953 a man named Ho Ling printed several hundred copies of his own poetry and distributed them among his friends and relatives.

The Sung dynasty was founded by a scholarly general who loved to collect books, and by 966 his personal collection was said to have exceeded 80,000 volumes. Inspired by his example, the dynasty promoted culture throughout its existence, and the publishing industry flourished as a result. Early during the dynasty the publishing center was still Szechuan, but it soon moved southward. By the eleventh century two publishing centers had emerged, namely Hangchow of Chekiang province and Chienan of Fukien province. In Hangchow the two major publishers were House of Ch'en and House of Yin; in Chienan the House of Yü dominated the field and continued in operation as late as the Ming dynasty. These private publishing houses operated on a business basis, and they put out books with the market in mind, such as dictionaries, medicine books, vernacular tales, and, of course, the *Four Books* which every school child was required to read. Whenever a masterpiece emerged, they would publish it too, even though it might be heavy in content. For instance, *History as a Mirror* was published in Hangchow almost as soon as the manuscript was completed—a sharp contrast to another masterpiece of the first century B.C. (*Historical Records*) that had to wait for twenty years before it was even discovered (pp. 125–126). For books that were regarded as culturally important but might not yield any profit if pub-

RUBBING This rubbing was made from a stone monument on which one of the earliest known images of Confucius was inscribed. The image was painted by the great T'ang painter Wu Tao-tzu who lived in the eighth century, but was not cast into stone, however, until 1107 A.D. The Chinese text on the top, also inscribed in stone, was written by a Professor Shang in the same year. The purpose of casting this image into stone, said Professor Shang, was to preserve for posterity the best image of Confucius then known. The man on the right was believed to be Tseng-tzu, one of Confucius' disciples. In ancient times a student habitually walked a few paces behind his teacher, to show his respect.

lished, such as the *Five Classics* and the dynastic histories, the Department of Cultural Affairs, an organ of the Sung government, would subsidize their printing, so that they would continue to be available to the public. Partly because of the enormous popularity of the civil service examinations, the market for serious books remained large and continuous.

Meanwhile important improvements were made in the manufacturing of ink and paper, and the fact that some of the Sung books have survived seems to underscore this point adequately. Even today the term *Sung pan*, or Sung edition, still represents the highest ideal in publishing to many Chinese. None of the innovations, however, was more important than the invention of movable type. The invention, which occurred in the 1040's, was attributed to a man named Pi Sheng about whose life, unfortunately, we know very little. Shen Kua (1021–1085), Pi Sheng's contemporary, described the printing of first books by movable type as follows:

Pieces of movable type are made of moistened clay, and on each of them is carved one Chinese character. The type is ready for use after it has been hardened by fire and thus made permanent. To proceed with the process of printing, a printer smears an iron plate with a mixture of turpentine, resin, wax, and burned paper ash. Pieces of movable type are then arranged on the plate in such a way as to reflect the text of a book to be printed. They are confined within the plate by an iron fence fastened tightly to the plate . . . The plate is then placed on a gentle fire in order to melt the mixture previously described. A wooden board with smooth surface is pressed upon the type so that the heads of all pieces would appear on the same level. The plate is then ready for printing.

Usually two plates are used when a book is printed. While one plate is in the process of printing, pieces of movable type are arranged and set on the other plate. When the required number of copies has been printed by the first plate, the second plate is ready. Thus the two plates change their role alternately.

For books that commanded a steady market, each page was cast into a copper plate that could be used again and again for reprinting purposes. The first mention of printing from copper plates occurred in the 930's, and by the time of the Sung dynasty the use of copper plates for printing popular books had become a common practice. The government, meanwhile, was using copper plates to print its paper currencies. Early in 1127 when Kaifeng was under siege, the invading Nuchens demanded not only gold, silver, and silk but also book-printing plates, then housed in the Department of Cultural Affairs. Culturally the invaders had paid the Sung regime a great tribute, even though they were much superior militarily.

ᛒ viii

Yüan

THE MONGOLS

The Mongol Empire of the thirteenth century was the largest the world had yet seen, covering most of the Eurasian continent and extending from the Pacific to the Mediterranean Sea. Within its jurisdiction were peoples of many nationalities, religions, and cultural backgrounds. They were the subjects of the Great Khan, the world conqueror to whom they owed allegiance and paid tribute. The rise of the Mongols was spectacular indeed. Throughout history no other people had built such a large empire in such a short time. It had taken the Romans almost four centuries to bring within their control the territories around the Mediterranean; it took the Mongols less than one century to build an empire much larger than that of the Romans. The total Mongol population was estimated to be somewhere between 1,000,000 and 2,500,000, and the number of their fighting men, at the top of their strength, probably did not exceed 250,000. Yet, besides slaughtering millions on their warpath, they brought under their control, directly and indirectly, several hundred millions. In all history rarely had so many been conquered by so few.

What made the Mongols so powerful? To begin with, the very nature of nomadic life bred a warlike spirit, and until the invention of firearms the nomads had always been among the world's best fighters. Life was extremely hard in the arid and semiarid regions, and to live the nomads had to struggle successfully against fellow men as well as their natural environment. The amount of usable land was limited in nomadic regions, and the population increase of one tribe could only be accommodated by depriving other tribes of their holdings. Besides, a slow change of climatic conditions might render marginal land unusable, and a sudden burst of animal epidemics could strike terror among the nomads. In either case, the nomads had to move or die, and when they moved, war began. Thus the precarious conditions of steppe life made war a common occurrence, and the nomads had to prepare for war while living in peace. In fact, the difference between life in peace and life in war was never a clear-cut one. A nomad made his livelihood on horseback and fought on it too. He killed wild animals with arrows from his strong bow and shot his enemies in the same way. Hardiness, endurance, and bravery were as much required in peace as in war. Since war frequently occurred, the nomad was used to it. He changed his life from peace to war with complete ease, and there was no such problem as adjustment.

North of the Great Wall and south of the Arctic Circle the basic pattern of nomadic life had changed little from time immemorial. From pasture to pasture the nomads moved on their camels and horses, thrived on meat and milk, and slept at night in portable tents. Outwardly peaceful, they turned into ferocious warriors whenever their leaders asked them to do so. From time to time battles were fought, and emerging from each battle was a great hero, only to be eclipsed in time by even greater ones. Savagery accompanied each battle, and no mercy was shown towards the vanquished. As a normal practice, men captives were put to the sword, and women and children were condemned to slavery. While such battles could not achieve any purpose in the long run, temporarily they did have the benefit of easing population pressure. The sad fact was that the steppe land, unfit for cultivation, could not support a dense population, and survival of the militarily fittest had always been the steppe law. Chinese historians have recorded time and again barbarian brutality towards the Chinese. It should be remembered that the barbarians were no less barbaric towards their fellow barbarians.

Whenever a tribe had successfully defeated its neighbors and unified a considerable portion of the grassland, it was inevitable that it would cast an envious eye on the rich agricultural land to the south. Its objective could be either temporary raiding and looting, or the looting might be part of a grandiose plan for the conquest of China proper. Only when China was strong could she stop the nomad hordes short of the Great Wall.

In fact, the history of China's external relations, until modern times, was largely a history of peace and war with her nomadic neighbors. Such relations began as early as history. During the second millennium and the first half of the first millennium B.C., the Chou people called all the northern nomads Ti, and those who lived west and northwest of their border were differentiated as Jung. One of the Jung tribes captured the Chou capital Hao in the eighth century B.C., sacked the city, and killed the reigning king. The Chou government, forced to move its capital eastward to Loyang, never really recovered from this defeat. During the Ch'in, Han, Wei, and Tsin dynasties, the most formidable nomads were the Hsiung-nu, a Turkish-speaking group who dominated the northern grassland for almost a millennium. From the fourth century A.D. on, other tribes began to play a more important role. The Mongol Topa tribe established the first Sinicized regime in North China in the fifth century. With its decline in the sixth century, other groups reasserted themselves. During the Sui and T'ang dynasties, the most powerful tribes were the T'u-chüeh (Turkish) in the north, the Uighurs (Turkish) in the northwest, and the Tanguts (Tibetan) in the west and the southwest. They were held in check as long as T'ang remained strong. After T'ang's decline in the eighth century, the nomads were again on a rampage. Throughout the Five Dynasties they fought among themselves as well as against the Chinese. When the dust finally settled, the Khitan Tartars (Mongolian) emerged triumphant and established a Sinicized regime called Liao. Liao was eventually replaced by a more vigorous tribe from the northeast, a Tungusic group called Nuchens who, on the Liao ruins, established another Sinicized regime called Chin.

Thus the balance of power shifted time and again in the northern grassland; the change of overlordship was as frequent as dynastic change in the south. Whatever Chinese regime happened to rule the rich, agricultural south, one of its greatest concerns was its relations with the more warlike nomads in the north. The past showed that while Chinese domination of the grassland, whenever it infrequently occurred, was indirect and temporary, the nomads, with the help of their Chinese collaborators, had been able to maintain a more direct and more permanent rule in the south. The balance of power seemed to have been in favor of the nomads. However, until the thirteenth century the nomads, at their very best, had been able only to bring part of China proper under their control, and no alien regime had ever extended its jurisdiction beyond the Yangtze River. The situation changed with the arrival of the Mongols. The Mongols not only subjugated China; they went beyond, conquered much of Burma and Vietnam, and brought many South and Southeast Asian kingdoms under their tributary system.

The accomplishment of the Mongols was no less than sensational. Less than a century before their conquest of China they had been among the least promising of all nomadic tribes. They lived in the arid wastes of what is known as Mongolia, and life was as hard then as it is today. Good pastures were few and far between, and the Mongols had to move from one pasture to another so that there would be enough grass for their multitude of flocks. Like seasonal birds they migrated southward during the winter months, and with each approaching summer they began their northward journey, grazing their beasts as they went. Each man's house was a portable, circular tent, supported by wooden rods and covered with felt. To set it up was as easy as tearing it down, and whenever its owner moved, it was transported on an ox-pulled or camel-drawn wagon. The Mongols lived on meat, milk, and game, and they had "no objection to eating the flesh of horses and dogs and drinking mares' milk." Wealth was measured by the number of beasts that one owned and was expressed by the better clothing (silk and rich furs) he wore or the number of wives he had. Polygamy was an accepted custom, though women were held in high respect by men. While men's major interests were hunting and warfare, less strenuous tasks, such as buying and selling, the care of children, and the maintenance of households, were within women's jurisdiction. Men and women both believed in a supreme High God who resided in Heaven. The most popular deity, however, was an earthly god who watched over their beasts, crops, and children.

What made the individual Mongol a formidable opponent on the battlefield was his ability as a horseman and archer. He was taught to ride a horse as soon as he learned to walk. As a scout and hunter, he rode his horse as a matter of daily routine. When war turned him into a fighter, he could ride his horse during the day and sleep on it at night, while his mount fed itself with whatever grass it could find on the ground. If need be, he could go or stay for a whole month without provisions, drinking mare's milk and eating wild game. If no water was available, he cut a vein of his horse and drank its blood. There was no supply problem, as far as a Mongol warrior was concerned. He was able to endure exertion and hardship as few men could. As an archer, he was equally unsurpassed. Constantly using his bow and arrows against wild animals, he had no difficulty in switching his target to one of the human species, and to the dismay of his enemies, he was deadly accurate. Riding hard and aiming constantly he and his colleagues dropped their enemies before the latter could come close to them. They could often win even though they were far outnumbered. Fighting alone or jointly with others, a Mongol warrior possessed a mobility unsurpassed before the invention of motorized vehicles. He struck quickly when he was sure to win and disappeared equally fast if, in his judgment, the odds were heavily against him. To begin a career of conquest, all he needed was a great organizer to lead him. Early in the thirteenth century he found such a leader in the person of Temujin, later known as Genghis Khan.

Temujin was born to a Mongol tribal chieftain, and historians have not yet agreed on the year that he was born. A Chinese source says that he was born with his right hand holding a lump of blood which looked like a red stone and that the name of Temujin was given to him because his father was then celebrating his victory over a rival chieftain of the same name. Temujin's father died when Temujin was young, and the boy attached himself and his tribe to On-Khan, the chief of the Kereit tribe. He was so successful in defeating the many enemies of the Kereit tribe that On-Khan eventually felt uneasy himself because he was not sure that an ambitious man like Temujin would be satisfied to be his vassal permanently. Having sensed On-Khan's suspicion and distrust, Temujin decided to strike first, and without warning he marched toward his former lord and decisively defeated him. He annexed the Kereit tribe and thus enlarged his base of operation. From then on it was one victory after another, and by 1206 all Mongol tribes had been brought under his control. In that year he called upon all his vassals to gather in the upper valley of the Onon River, and in a solemn ceremony he was proclaimed the Almighty Emperor, or Genghis Khan.

Though there was nothing unusual about tribal warfare, Genghis Khan's victory was different in the sense that for the first time in history the Mongols had produced a true conqueror of rare proportions. While information about him as a person is meagre, he seems to have been a conqueror in the truest sense of that word. He conquered for the glory of conquest, and the benefit of material gain, if it was in his mind, was secondary and unimportant. He made a life of conquest, lived it, and would not leave it until his breath failed him. "Man's highest joy," he is believed to have said, "is in victory: to conquer one's enemies, to pursue them, to deprive them of their possessions, to make their beloved weep, to ride on their horses, and to embrace their wives and daughters." While this advice had nothing to recommend it to a more civilized society, it expressed the highest ideals of a nomadic warrior. The purpose of conquest was victory itself, pure, simple, and therefore noble. Such purpose allegedly justified the most wanton brutality that human beings ever committed: the slaughtering of the entire populations of cities, the enslavement of women and children, and the senseless destruction of many ancient centers of civilization. As the Mongols galloped, the world trembled.

Having unified all Mongol tribes, Genghis Khan began his conquest of non-Mongol tribes and kingdoms. From Manchuria to the Black Sea one victim fell after another. Southward he sent his hordes across the

Great Wall and captured modern Hopeh, Shantung, and Shensi provinces, including Chin's capital, Peking. The Chin ruler was forced to retreat southward to Kaifeng. In the fall of 1227 Genghis died of a battle wound suffered in the siege of Hsingchungfu, the capital of West Hsia. Several days later West Hsia surrendered, and in accordance with the dead Khan's wish, the entire city was put to the sword. Ogodei, the third son of Genghis, succeeded his father as the Great Khan. Under him continuous conquests were made:

1. Kaifeng, the new capital of Chin, fell in 1233, and the former Chin territory, most of North China, was annexed.

2. Korea was conquered in 1231–1232.

3. Ukraine and South Russia had been previously conquered by Genghis Khan. In 1235 the famous Mongol general Batu pushed northward and eventually occupied what is known today as Great Russia, including Moscow. One column captured the ancient city Novgorod, not far from the Gulf of Finland.

4. In 1240 Batu invaded Poland, Bohemia, Hungary, and the Danube Valley. One column advanced as far as Venetia. All of Western Europe might have fallen to the Mongol hordes had it not been saved by an unexpected incident. In the spring of 1242 news arrived that the Great Khan Ogodei had passed away, and Batu, eager to participate in the election of a new supreme ruler, called off further invasions. Thus Western Europe was saved by Mongol domestic politics.

After several years of internal struggle during which foreign expansion was temporarily suspended, Mangu, a grandson of Genghis, was proclaimed as the supreme ruler in 1251. During his reign of eight years the Mongol Empire expanded southwestward to Persia, Mesopotamia, and Syria. His brother, the famed Kublai Khan who ascened the throne in 1260, finally conquered South Sung. Thus the Mongol Empire, begun with Genghis' military exploits two generations before, was completed during the reign of Kublai. The empire, because of its huge size, was divided into four khanates:

1. The Khanate of the Great Khan, extending from Eastern Siberia southwestward to Tibet. It included Mongolia, Korea, Manchuria, China, and the northern sections of Burma and Vietnam.

2. The Khanate of Chaghadai (Ili) which covered Afghanistan and Russian and Chinese Turkestan.

3. The Khanate of Persia (Il-Khans) in the Near East, including modern Iraq, Iran, and Southern Caucasus.

4. The Khanate of Kipchak (Golden Horde), extending from Chinese Turkestan to Eastern Europe. It included Western Asia, Russia, and Ukraine.

Theoretically, the Great Khan who sat on the dragon throne in Pe-

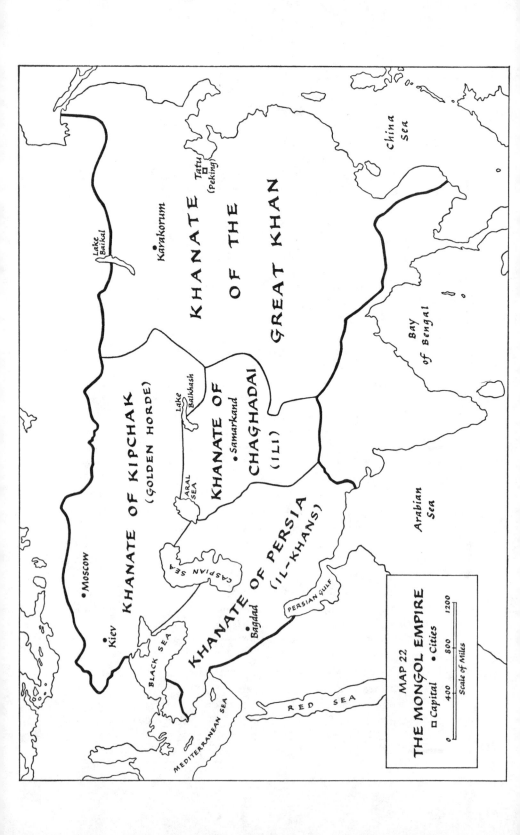

China Sea

Lake Baikal

Kavakorum

Tatu (Peking)

KHANATE OF THE GREAT KHAN

Bay of Bengal

Lake Balkhash

KHANATE OF KIPCHAK (GOLDEN HORDE)

KHANATE OF CHAGHADAI (ILI)

Samarkand

ARAL SEA

Arabian Sea

Moscow

CASPIAN SEA

KHANATE OF PERSIA (IL-KHANS)

Kiev

BLACK SEA

Bagdad

PERSIAN GULF

MEDITERRANEAN SEA

RED SEA

MAP 22

THE MONGOL EMPIRE

□ Capital   • Cities

Scale of Miles

0   400   800   1200

king had jurisdiction over all three other khans. However, due to the great distances between them, such jurisdiction was more nominal than real, and each khanate was virtually independent.

THE CONQUEST OF SOUTH SUNG

The Mongol conquest of South Sung turned out to be more difficult than the relative strength of the two countries would have warranted. While the Mongols swept across Central and Western Asia with comparative ease, it took them more than a generation to subjugate their southern opponent. The reasons were not difficult to find. To begin with, the Mongols were better fighters on the desert and the steppe than in the agricultural areas where the performance of the cavalry, wherein their strength lay, could be considerably hampered by the paddy fields and the undulating forest hills. Secondly, the existence of numerous cities and the high density of population in China proper slowed down conquest and made it more difficult, for a city could not be taken unless the city leading to it had been taken previously. This was contrary to the situation in Central and Western Asia where population centers were few and far between. Thirdly, and perhaps most important of all, the Mongol invaders aroused a strong sense of nationalism among the South Sung Chinese. Under good leadership such nationalism could be harnessed into an iron will of resistance which in turn slowed down the victorious march of even the seemingly invincible Mongols. A case in point was the heroic defense of the twin cities Hsiangyang and Fanch'eng (modern Hupeh province) which, although completely surrounded, managed to hold their own for five years (1268–1273). In the long run, however, the military superiority of the Mongols foretold the final outcome. They might be slowed down, but they could not be stopped.

Previously, when the Mongols attacked Chin, South Sung made the mistake of allying itself with the rising Mongols against a much weakened neighbor. It did so because it hoped to recover its lost territories south of the Yellow River. For a while it did occupy Kaifeng and Loyang after Chin's defeat. In 1234, when Chin was finally conquered, South Sung found itself face to face with a ferocious horde. In the following year the Mongols attacked South Sung along several fronts. The western column, under the able general Kublai, soon captured Szechuan province. Meanwhile Kublai's fellow generals on the eastern front ravaged the area between the Yellow River and the Huai. In 1252 Kublai invaded Yunnan and extinguished a small kingdom called Tali (former Nanchao). One of his generals continued southward and invaded northern Vietnam. By 1259 the entire Southwest fell into Mongol hands, and the Mongol control of the upper Yangtze Valley extended eastward to include Wuchang

TEMPLE OF HEAVEN   The temple, dating from the thirteenth century, is located in Peking. The emperors used to worship here.

(Hupeh province). Then Kublai received the news that the Great Khan Mangu had died. He quickly arranged a truce with Sung commanders in the field and hurried back to Karakorum, the capital of all Mongols. In the following year Kublai, dispensing with the formality of being elected, assumed the title of Great Khan. It was not until 1271, however, that on the recommendation of a Chinese scholar the national title was changed from Mongol to a Sinicized name Yüan. By adopting a Sinicized national title the Mongols considered themselves legitimate heirs to the fast disappearing Chinese Sung dynasty. Thus Kublai and his successors assumed a dual role, one as a Chinese emperor and the other as the Great Khan for all Mongols.

After Kublai became the supreme ruler, the invasion of South Sung was renewed with eagerness. The heroic defense of Hsiangyang and Fanch'eng upset the conqueror's schedule, but after the fall of the two cities in 1273 other cities were captured with comparative ease. In 1276 Hangchow surrendered without a fight, and the Mongol invaders, spearheaded by their Chinese collaborators, pushed hard against the remnants of the disheartened Sung forces. Since then many historians have contended that the Sung forces could have held much longer on the rugged terrain of the Southeast had it not been for the "treacherous betrayal" of an Arab merchant. The Arab merchant, known by his Sinicized name P'u Shou-keng, came to China in his boyhood and rose to become a Sung official in charge of the Superintendency of Merchant Shipping at the flourishing port of Ch'üanchou in modern Fukien province. For thirty years he monopolized the lucrative trade between Fukien and Southeast Asia and grew in wealth, power, and influence. Under his control were not only the merchant marine but also powerful battleships. Many people contended that if he had supported Sung's cause, the Southeast would not have fallen so fast, because the Mongols, despite their invincibility on land, were quite inadequate in sea warfare. But P'u Shou-keng chose to surrender his ships to the Mongols on the ground that "continuous warfare is bad for business." Under his supervision, hundreds of warships were constructed at Ch'üanchou for the invaders. As an admiral under his new overlord, he cleared up the remnants of Sung's naval force along the southeastern coast and was partially responsible for the breakdown of Sung's last resistance. In 1279 the last claimant to the Sung throne, caught between the pursuing enemy and the blue sea, chose the latter and drowned himself.

Though triumphant on the Chinese mainland, Kublai was not successful in his attempt to subjugate Japan. He had repeatedly sent envoys to demand Japan's acknowledgement of his overlordship but each time he was haughtily refused. In 1275 he dispatched from Korean ports 25,000 troops for the invasion of the island kingdom. The invading force, after winning an initial victory, was forced to re-embark by foul weather and return to Korea with heavy losses. The second and much larger invasion occurred six years later, after Kublai had conquered South Sung and had brought the captured Sung navy to strengthen his invading armada. The invaders managed to establish a beachhead in North Kyushu but were unable to penetrate much beyond. For the second time the weather came to Japan's rescue. A typhoon struck and destroyed or disabled most of the invading ships. Having been deprived of their ships, those invaders who had been stranded ashore were easily liquidated by the Japanese. Of 140,000 men who began the invasion less than half returned home.

From their bases in southwestern China the Mongols repeatedly invaded Vietnam and Burma, ravaged as they went, and caused great damage. In the 1280's Mongol envoys were successful in persuading many small kingdoms in South and Southeast Asia to acknowledge Yüan's overlordship and send tribute to China. However, Mongol influence was never substantial in the tropical regions.

CHINA UNDER MONGOL RULE

From the year 936 when a Chinese garrison surrendered the Sixteen Yen-Yün Districts to the Khitan Tartars, China proper was not unified under one regime until 1279. What the Sung emperors had vowed to accomplish but had failed to do was attained by the alien ruler Kublai

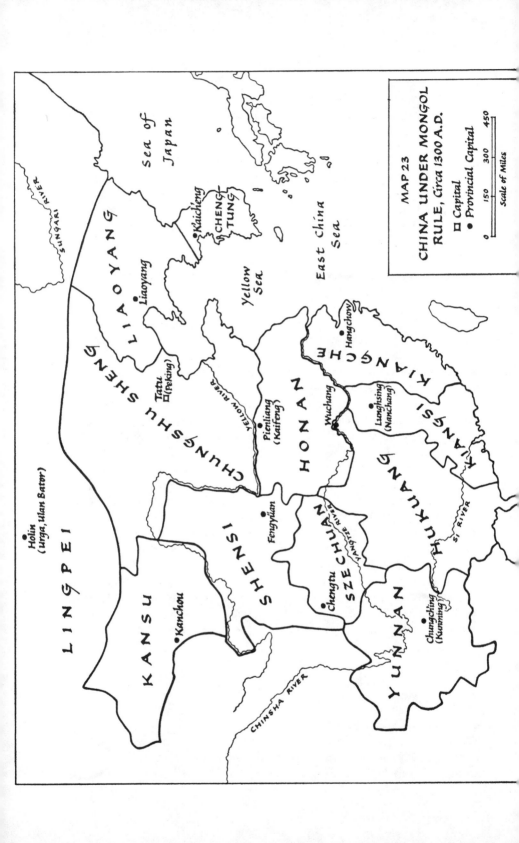

MAP 23

CHINA UNDER MONGOL RULE, Circa 1300 A.D.

□ Capital
● Provincial Capital

Scale of Miles
0   150   300   450

LINGPEI

Holin
(Urga, Ulan Bator)

SUNGARI RIVER

Sea of Japan

LIAOYANG SHENG

Liaoyang

Kaicheng

CHENG-TUNG

Yellow Sea

East China Sea

CHUNGSHU SHENG

Tatu
(Peking)

YELLOW RIVER

Pienliang
(Kaifeng)

HONAN

Wuchang

Hangchow

Lunghsing
(Nanchang)

KIANGSI

KANSU

Kanchou

SHENSI

Fengyüan

Chengtu

SZECHUAN

YANGTZE RIVER

HUKUANG

SI RIVER

YUNNAN

Chungching
(Kunming)

CHINSHA RIVER

Khan, known to the Chinese as Yüan Shih-tsu. Shih-tsu was perhaps the ablest and the most enlightened among Yüan rulers, but most Chinese did not take kindly to him and regarded him as no better than half-barbarian. There were reasons for this. Other alien rulers, such as Hsiao-wen-ti of North Wei or later the Liao and Chin rulers, had been thoroughly trained in Chinese ways before they ruled Chinese subjects. Yüan Shih-tsu, on the other hand, was basically a nomadic warrior, and he never "dismounted to rule" as his Chinese subjects thought he should. His major interest was conquest, and when he needed recreation, he found it in hunting and falconry. From the Chinese point of view, he should have devoted more time to the patronage of art and literature and to the cultivation of Confucian virtues. In this respect his successors were regarded as worse than he, for none of them was ever Sinicized in the real sense. In the Chinese mind, to be civilized meant to be Sinicized, and the Yüan rulers, in their efforts to maintain a separate identity, remained outsiders forever to the Chinese. The Yüan dynasty was one of the most unpopular in Chinese history, and the eighty-nine years of Mongol rule were regarded by many Chinese as among the worst China had ever encountered. Despite its military grandeur, the Yüan dynasty was nevertheless a period of cultural recession.

Overwhelmed by a superior military force and betrayed by many of their own leaders, the Chinese were slow in acquiescing to the Mongol rule. Marco Polo, travelling in China in the 1280's, commented repeatedly on Chinese resentment against their new rulers. Mongol garrisons were stationed in all sizable cities to prevent revolt and to crush it if and when it occurred. The authority of the garrison was supreme, and if it were challenged, the whole city would have to pay dearly for its defiance. The Venetian said that the entire population of Chinkiang (east of Nanking on the south bank of the Yangtze River) was slaughtered, after a party of madly drunken Mongol soldiers were slain by some irresponsible local citizens. Not surprisingly, the Chinese resented the garrison soldiers. "They cannot bear the sight of a soldier or of the Great Khan's guards," remarked Marco Polo. Thanks to the Mongols' iron hand, few revolts occurred, and whatever resistance there might have been was soon driven underground. It was not until the 1340's when the Mongol rule had been considerably weakened that Chinese revolts met with some degree of success.

Culturally backward and numerically outnumbered, the Mongol rulers realized that they could not rule China indefinitely unless they could devise and adopt a system whereby their Chinese subjects would never be in a position to challenge their supremacy. Out of this consideration came a caste system in which people of lower groupings were discriminated against in favor of those of higher groupings. Discrimination was practiced in all fields of human activities, political, legal, and socioeconomic. There were four castes altogether, and a person's enjoyment of rights and privileges, or the lack of it, varied in accordance with the caste to which he belonged. However, the emperor, sitting at the pinnacle of the hierarchy and being the sole dispenser of all favors, could at any time, if he chose to, grant exceptions; theoretically he could raise even the humblest to the noblest regardless of the caste system. For instance, he could appoint a Chinese as his prime minister if he wished to, though under normal circumstances he was not expected to take such an unusual step. The highest caste was the ruling oligarchy to which all Mongols belonged. It was followed by se-mu jen (literally, "color-eye" people), or people whose skin colors and eye shapes were different from those of the Chinese and the Mongols. They were what the Chinese called hsi-yü jen, or "people from the western regions," whether they be Persians, Uighurs, or any of the Central Asian groups. Religiously they were predominantly Muslim; many of them, however, were Buddhist or Nestorian. Northern Chinese belonged to the third caste, and Southern Chinese were at the bottom of the caste system. Northern Chinese were the former subjects of Chin who, having lived under alien control before, were not so resentful of the Mongol rule as their southern brethren who, before the Mongol conquest, had been the citizens of the Chinese dynasty, Sung.

Discrimination was most pronounced in the selection of government officials. Practically all high posts were occupied by Mongols, assisted by their Muslim collaborators. Rarely could a Chinese rise to cabinet rank, and few Chinese were appointed as governors. Throughout the Yüan dynasty all but three prime ministers were Mongols. Of the three, one was a Uighur and two were Northern Chinese. At local levels Chinese could serve as staff assistants, but they could not become the head of a department or an office. This differentiation in official appointment created much confusion in local administrations. At one time it was reported that in the Yangtze area none of the provincial officials knew how to read or write. Towards the end of the Yüan dynasty, the government, hard pressed by financial needs, began to sell offices of lower ranks to whoever wished to buy them regardless of caste origin. Few Chinese, however, took advantage of this offer. Those who did buy them were characterized by local population as "scoundrels" (wu-lai).

The enforcement of law also took into consideration caste differences. One of Genghis Khan's famous orders was that if a Mongol murdered a Muslim, he should pay 40 palishi of gold, but if the victim happened to be a Chinese, he should hand over to the injured family a donkey or its equivalent. Judicial discrimination was extended to all of China after the Mongol conquest of South Sung. Under no circumstances were Chinese allowed to do physical harm to Mongols, but the law did not say that Mongols could not harm Chinese. For the same crime Chinese were punished more severely than Mongols. Chinese were not allowed to possess arms or to learn military skills, and in 1289 an imperial decree ordered them to hand over to the government all their horses. In cities they were forbidden to walk in the streets at night, and they could not gather in any large numbers, whether for religious worship or for commercial purposes. While discrimination was applied to all Chinese, the Mongol rulers were somewhat lenient with craftsmen and artisans, such as blacksmiths, goldsmiths, carpenters, and the makers of bows and arrows. Whenever a city was captured, they made a point of sparing the lives of artisans. According to one story, the entire city of Kaifeng would have been put to the sword after its fall if the Mongols had not been afraid that they might kill by mistake many artisans whom they needed.

Culturally the Yüan dynasty was one of the most sterile periods in Chinese history. By all counts it was an anticlimax after the brilliant era of the two Sungs. The Mongol rulers singled out intellectuals for the worst repression, partly because they neither appreciated nor understood cultural activities and partly because they distrusted intellectuals as loyal subjects. Intellectual activities were looked down upon as a profession. In the Mongol concept of the relative importance of different professions, intellectuals were placed a little above beggars and were much below prostitutes (another source says "common people"). Teachers and beggars were considered the most useless and they were often mentioned in the same breath. Though they learned quickly to appreciate the services of artisans and physicians, the Mongols, at the beginning, had no use for farmers. When Ogodei Khan entered China proper for the first time, he had hoped to turn North China into empty pastures. Later when the Mongol conquerors learned that farmers could pay more taxes than nomads, they went to great lengths to promote agriculture. However, they never thought highly of intellectuals. During their conquest of China, they condemned all captured intellectuals to slavery, if they chose to spare their lives. Later, when it was apparent that government could not function without literate clerks, they allowed many of them to buy their freedom. By then intellectuals had become a necessary evil to be tolerated. Most of the Yüan emperors did not know how to read or write and did not care to learn.

This mixed feeling of contempt and distrust was reciprocated by Chinese intellectuals who regarded the Mongols as the worst kind of barbarians China had ever encountered. The best among them boycotted the new government. Those who had illusions learned fast. The famous Sung historian Ma Tuan-lin, for instance, served under the new regime for a while and quit as quickly and as graciously as he could manage it. The civil service examination system which had been the traditional way of selecting government personnel was not revived until 1315. The government did not attach much importance to it and it never produced men of any prominence. Among the Yüan bureaucrats less than one percent was the product of the examination system. The best among Chinese intellectuals did not participate in it, even though the examination was held as frequently as once in every three years. In each examination two tests were given, one for Chinese and one for Mongols and "people of western regions." The test for the Chinese was much stiffer, and the test for others was often a formality. Many Mongols and "westerners" who had passed the examination were later found to be illiterate. Power, fame, and wealth, which under the Sung could be obtained through academic excellence and ability to serve, were now based upon race and nationality. Many intellectuals, denied their traditional outlet for advancement, busied themselves with their own petty projects, such as the verification of an ancient text or the editing of an old classic. Without government sponsorship, schools were established and maintained through local initiative. There were students but few scholars, and among scholars few were original thinkers.

By virtue of conquest the Mongol rulers regarded China as their private domain and thus revived a feudal concept which had been abandoned by the Chinese many centuries before. The purpose of ruling China was to enjoy what China could offer: land, population, and natural resources, and governmental policy was formulated with that purpose in mind. The Mongol conquerors, knowing nothing about financial matters and distrusting their Chinese subjects, often turned over the execution of such policy to their Muslim collaborators. When Ogodei first entered China, he sold the right of collecting taxes to a Uighur merchant. Even a monarch like Kublai had no better appreciation of fiscal policy than the collection of the largest tax revenue. Those who knew how to collect the largest amount with the least expense were regarded as able and were promoted fast. Tax revenue continued to increase so that by the 1330's the total yearly amount was said to be one hundred times as much as that collected during the 1280's. After South China was pacified, large tracts of farmland together with Chinese households were awarded to Mongol princes, princesses, and others who had unusual military deeds to their credit. The number of households awarded to each person varied, from scores to more than 100,000. Other Mongols took over Chinese land on their own initiative, and some of them, wishing to be surrounded by a more familiar scene, turned rich agricultural land into empty pastures. The existence of pastures side by side with paddy fields caused frequent frictions between Mongol cattlemen and Chinese farmers.

Ironically, the group singled out by the world conquerors for preferential treatment was the professionally religious. In the Mongol concept of the relative importance of different professions, the priests were ranked second highest, next to government officials. Within their empire the Mongols followed a policy of religious toleration. Different faiths existed side by side, and within one city could be found the religious establishments of Buddhism, Taoism, Islam, and Nestorianism. The Mongols themselves, however, preferred Lamaism, a mixture of orthodox Buddhism and a Tibetan faith called Bon. Lamaism was given extensive royal patronage, and millions of acres of land were granted to leading Lamaist monasteries. A leading monastery in Shantung, for instance, was granted land amounting to 323,000 *ch'ing* (about 4,887,000 acres), and another monastery was given 37,059 farm households for support besides 100,000 *ch'ing* (about 1,513,000 acres) of land. Each year government expenses for Buddhist and various religious services accounted for more than one-half of its total expenditure! In 1292 it was said that altogether there were 42,318 Buddhist temples and monasteries and 213,148 monks and nuns.

To speculate as to what might have made the warlike Mongols so religious is beyond the field of a historian, but any historian knows that not all religious men practiced what they taught. While most of these Buddhist monks were doubtlessly pious and sincere, many joined the monastic rank simply because it was the easiest way of making a living. The behavior of some others was anything but exemplary. One government censor reported in 1310 that many monks were married and had children, and another censor reported in 1324 that often monks invaded private homes, chased out the male residents, and raped the wives and daughters. According to a widely circulated story, one Mongol prince did not wish to have anything to do with Lamaism until he was advised by his father, the emperor, to experience it personally. Accordingly, a lama was assigned to teach him "the secret way of attaining great joy in Buddhism." After one instruction, the prince remarked happily: "Mr. Li has taught me Confucian classics for years and I don't understand a thing about them. The great lama from the West taught me the Buddhist way to great joy and I understand everything about it in one evening." This incident allegedly occurred towards the end of the Yüan dynasty, almost one century after the Mongol conquest of China. Even then the Mongol rulers seemed to be no less barbarian than their forefathers who had founded the Yüan dynasty.

MONGOL ACHIEVEMENT

It would be an oversimplification to say that all was darkness under the Mongol rule. When they first entered China proper and knew nothing about governing a sedentary people, the Mongols had to rely on Chinese and Sinicized non-Chinese for advice and counsel. One of the greatest men serving in this capacity was a Sinicized Khitan named Yeh-lü Ch'u-ts'ai who served both Genghis and Ogodei with distinction. It was he who advised Ogodei not to turn North China into empty pastures, and he was also credited with having saved millions of lives from the Mongol sword.

During the early reign of Kublai Khan efforts were made to secure Chinese cooperation, and many Chinese did join his government. Unfortunately, this policy was not followed by his successors. What Chinese influence there was moderated somewhat the naked barbarity of the nomadic warriors. Though Chinese were never allowed to play any substantial role in the Yüan regime, as time went on there were Mongols Sinicized enough to promote peaceful pursuits. Under their direction there were many outstanding achievements.

Foremost among Yüan's achievements was its transportation system. The Mongols, maintaining the world's largest empire, depended upon efficient transportation to hold the empire together. Roads were built through the length and breath of the empire, and all of them, directly or indirectly, were linked with the nerve center, Peking. In peace time traders and travelers used them, and in time of war, troops could be sent with dispatch to trouble spots. An efficient postal system was maintained, mostly for the transmission of messages from Peking to the provinces and vice versa. Marco Polo gives us a vivid description of Kublai Khan's postal service. According to him, courier stations were built along the roads, and there were both mounted and unmounted couriers. The unmounted couriers could "travel a ten days' journey in a day and a night," and "in the fruit season it often happens that this means fruit gathered in the morning in the city of Khanbalik (Peking) is delivered on the evening of the next day to the Great Khan in the city of Shang-tu, ten days' journey away." The Great Khan's mounted messengers, of course, travelled even faster. "They ride 200 miles in a day, sometimes even 250; indeed, in extreme urgency, they can achieve 300 miles," says the Venetian. During the reign of Kublai, more than 200,000 horses were regularly maintained for courier service.

The Yüan regime also improved river and sea transportation substantially. All major rivers in China ran from west to east; how to ship food from the rice producing areas in the Lower Yangtze to North China had been a problem faced by many dynasties in the past. To solve this problem, Sui constructed the Grand Canal which was later improved by Sung. Since both regimes located their capitals along the southern bank of the Yellow River, the Grand Canal as then completed was adequate to meet their needs. But it was a different matter with Yüan which chose Peking as its capital. To feed the swelling population in the new capital, Yüan ordered the construction of two canals: Chichou and Huit'ung, both running northward through western Shantung. Boats carrying farm products could thus sail from the Lower Yangtze all the way to the Peking area. Two and a half million coolie laborers were employed in this project, which was not completed until 1289.

Side by side with shipping through the Grand Canal was a sea transport service whereby ships loaded at Shanghai sailed northward along the

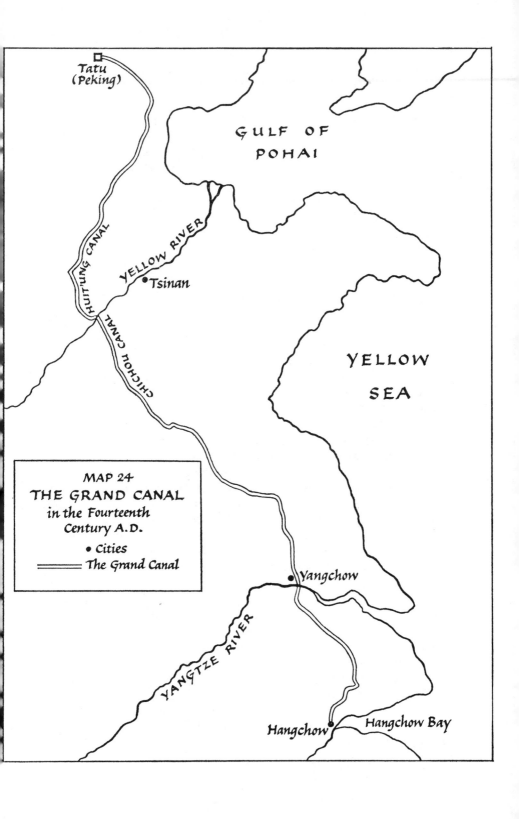

Tatu
(Peking)

GULF OF
POHAI

HUI'T'UNG CANAL

YELLOW RIVER

• Tsinan

CHICHOU CANAL

YELLOW

SEA

MAP 24
THE GRAND CANAL
in the Fourteenth
Century A.D.
• Cities
═════ The Grand Canal

• Yangchow

YANGTZE RIVER

Hangchow •   Hangchow Bay

sea coast until they reached Takuk'ou at the mouth of the Ku River. This
sea route, however, was much more hazardous and therefore less practical.

Equally as important as the improvement of transportation facilities
was Yüan's promotion of agricultural activities. Though Genghis never
thought much of agriculture, his grandson Kublai, upon assuming the role
as a Chinese emperor, soon recognized its importance. Among the many
new measures he adopted, the most far-reaching was perhaps the commune system. In a decree issued in 1286 he ordered the organization of
every fifty to one hundred farm households into a commune. The purpose
of the commune, said the decree, was mutual help and better farming
among constituting households so as to increase farm production. Each
commune would be captained by an elderly, experienced farmer whose
duty was to reward the diligent and punish the laggard, besides teaching
and advising on better farming methods. Within each commune was an
elementary school where children were taught the fundamentals of reading and writing during times when they were not needed in the field.
There was also an ever-ready granary to which each household contributed a small amount of its harvest during good years and from which
the poor could draw relief during the years of famine. While land was
individually owned, each commune member had the obligation to help
others, especially when they could not till their land themselves on account of sickness, death of family members, or other legitimate reasons.
In case of a major disaster such as an epidemic when the resources of one
commune could not cope with the situation, other communes were obligated to help on a basis of reciprocity. Judging from available evidence,
the commune system seems to have functioned fairly well.

More controversial than the commune system, however, was Yüan's
wide use of paper currency. The use of paper currency had not originated
with Yüan. Its origin could be traced back to the ninth century when the
T'ang government, considering the inconvenience of shipping cash to
distant areas where government purchases were made, paid local merchants with money certificates called "flying cash." These certificates bearing different amounts of money could be converted into hard cash on
demand at the capital. Since they were transferable, they were exchanged
among merchants almost like currency. However, "flying cash" was not
meant to be currency and its circulation was rather limited. Real paper
currency was not introduced until early in the Sung dynasty, when it was
utilized by a group of rich merchants and financiers in Szechuan, the
same province where the art of printing had been invented. Each banknote
they issued had printed on it pictures of houses, trees, and people. Red
and black inks were intermittently applied; the seals of the issuing banks
were affixed; and confidential marks were made on each bill. All these
devices made counterfeiting extremely difficult, if not impossible. These

banknotes could be converted into hard cash at any time in any of the issuing banks. Widely circulated, they were readily accepted for the payment of debt and other financial obligations. Later, however, some of the banks apparently printed too many notes without adequate backing. When the bearers went to them for cash, they were unable to honor their obligations. Lawsuits resulted and there was considerable confusion. Eventually the government decided to prohibit the issuing of banknotes by private banks and made it a government monopoly. Government issues made their first appearance in Szechuan and, because of their success, were later introduced in other areas as well. After Chin entered China proper, it followed Sung's practice. In 1154 it established a Bureau of Paper Currency in Kaifeng as the central agency in charge of all issues. Two kinds of paper currency were issued, one of large denominations, consisting of one to ten strings (each string was worth 1,000 standard coins) and another of small denominations, bearing the amounts of one to seven hundred standard coins. The validity of each issue was limited to seven years.

There was nothing wrong with paper currency as long as it had sufficient backing and, on demand, could be readily converted into hard money. When the government printed too much paper money and these two principles could no longer be practiced, inflation resulted and the whole paper structure eventually collapsed. That was exactly what happened during the Yüan dynasty. In 1260 Yüan's first paper currency was issued. Various denominations were printed, ranging from a face value of two standard coins to the highest denomination of two strings. Excessive printing year after year soon flooded the market with depreciated paper money until the face value of each certificate bore no relation whatsoever to its counterpart in silver. In 1272 a series of new issues was put in circulation, and the old issues were converted into the new ones at the ratio of five to one. The new issues were printed with copper plates instead of wood blocks, as had been the case before. As the printing press was overworked, a new round of depreciation began, and by 1309 another conversion became necessary. The 1272 issues were converted into the new issues again at the ratio of five to one. Thus in fifty years (from 1260 to 1309) Yüan's paper money was depreciated by 1,000 percent. As the value of paper money came down, prices of commodities moved up. Counterfeiting was widespread despite severe penalties. To make the situation worse, the government often refused to exchange for new issues old certificates that had been worn out through a long period of circulation. This legalized robbery, naturally, did not endear the government to its people.

From hindsight, the greatest achievement during the Yüan dynasty was neither its transportation system nor its paper currency, but its music drama. Musicales began at least as early as the fifth century, but it was not until the eighth century that they reached their most glorious age under the patronage of T'ang Hsüan-tsung. Musicales, however, were not music dramas. They could be sung and danced to, but each piece of music stood independently and there was no story linking all of them together. Music drama, in fact, did not begin until the Sung dynasty. Even then, men of literary fame did not bother to write them, and no outstanding works appeared. The situation changed early in the Yüan dynasty. Music drama became a popular form of literary expression and attracted many men of talent. Some historians attribute this phenomenon to the fact that Chinese intellectuals, denied their traditional outlet of advancement in government, applied their talents to the less consequential fields, such as music drama. Whatever the real cause, Yüan's achievement in this field was superb and has never been surpassed.

There were dozens of drama writers during the Yüan dynasty. However, only 116 of their works have survived. The greatest of the writers were Kuan Han-ch'ing, Ma Chih-yüan, and Wang Shih-fu, all living during the middle decades of the thirteenth century. We know little about their personal life, and all seem to have been unsuccessful as government officials. Kuan Han-ch'ing left us ten of his dramas, the best known of which is the *Butterfly Dream* (*Hu-tieh meng*), a story about the philosopher Chuang-tzu and his unfaithful wife. Among Ma Chih-yüan's six extant dramas, it is commonly recognized that the best is *Autumn in the Han Palace* (*Han-kung ch'iu*), a story describing the sorrow of the Han emperor Yüan-ti after his beloved concubine had left for a Hsiung-nu prince in the northern desert.

None of the extant Yüan dramas, however, is more popular than *The Romance of the West Chamber* (*Hsi-hsiang chi*), written by Wang Shih-fu. Some critics regard it as the best music drama ever written. According to an unsubstantiated story, Wang often lay flat on the ground whenever he was thinking hard to find the right words for his songs. One day in writing a departure scene between the hero and the heroine in *The West Chamber*, he searched so hard for the words most appropriate to the scene that finally when he found them, he rose up, wrote them down, fainted away and died. The unfinished portion was later completed by Kuan Han-ch'ing. The drama tells the story of a student who, while studying in a Buddhist temple in preparation for the imperial examination, was attracted to a young lady who was living next door with her family. Through the aid of the young lady's maid, they met and their love was consummated. One month later, when the secret affair was discovered, the girl's mother refused to give her consent for marriage until the young man could establish himself by passing the imperial examination. With his departure for the capital to take the examination, the story ended.

While stories varied, all Yüan dramas followed a commonly accepted pattern. All persons who appeared in them fell into three categories, *mo* who were the male leaders, *tan* who played the leading females, and *tsa* who played supporting roles, including the ubiquitous jesters. When an actor appeared on the stage, the audience could immediately identify the role he played because the make-up and the dress he wore were highly conventionalized. Each drama began with an introduction which was followed by the standard four acts. The story of each act was told by singing, acting, and dialogue. Besides the songs, the words of the dialogue and each of the actors' movements were all recorded as part of the drama. The songs were written in semiliterary form, and when sung, were perhaps difficult to understand. But there was no question about understanding the dialogues which were written in colloquial and even slangy Chinese. Thus the drama appealed to the illiterate as well as the intellectuals.

THE FALL OF THE YÜAN REGIME

Sung, a militarily weak regime, lasted more than three hundred years; Yüan, the most powerful dynasty in Chinese history, collapsed in less than a century. How can this be explained? First, as we have noted, the Yüan regime never had popular support. Second, the regime began to deteriorate soon after the death of Kublai Khan, and such deterioration resulted largely from the degeneration of the Mongol ruling class.

When Kublai died in 1294, all the territories which the Mongols had intended to conquer had been conquered. The only exception was of course Japan. As conditions of peacetime replaced the state of war, the Mongols had no more use for their greatest asset, their fighting ability. Peace, ironically, turned out to be their unconquerable enemy. Living in peace, the Mongols slowly lost what had made them fearsome and great on the battlefield. Meanwhile, they had not yet acquired qualities that would have made them successful rulers in peace. Having dispensed with bow and arrows and not yet learned to use the pen, the Mongol emperors after Kublai Khan were ludicrous misfits on that dragon throne in Peking. They did not possess the same valor and vitality as their nomadic ancestors; yet, they were unwilling or unable to master the arts of peace. Corrupted by power and wealth, they acquired many Chinese vices (such as love of luxuries) without at the same time acquiring some of the Chinese virtues (such as love of literature and learning). This was true not only of the Mongol emperors but of the entire Mongol hierarchy as well. From lofty princes and princesses to lowly garrison soldiers in a remote city—they were all softened by the wealth of the nation which they conquered. The once simple, hardy Mongol princes, no longer needed on the battlefield, had now become parasitic, and they had no other desire except to enjoy the material best which China could provide. The garrison soldiers, once the backbone of Mongol strength, were corrupted by an easy life from which they seemingly had no way to escape. With no check or restraint, nepotism and corruption were rampant from top to bottom. To make the situation worse, the Mongols, as the ruling class, were neither required nor allowed to learn any useful profession. As there was no more fighting to do, they were completely lost in the labyrinth of civilization. As they were corrupted, they were no longer the same invincible Mongols.

Undisputed power tended to corrupt itself. Since their authority was no longer challenged from the outside, dissensions soon developed among the Mongols themselves. Intrigues, conspiracies, and strifes which had been common in Chinese politics reappeared in the Mongol court as well. Power struggles intensified themselves during the time of succession when each powerful faction within the Mongol hierarchy attempted to place its own candidate on the throne. This, however, was not the situation before Kublai Khan when the Mongols had a remarkable system of choosing imperial successors. After a Great Khan died, an election was held among the Mongol princes, and theoretically everyone related to the dead khan was eligible to be elected to succeed him. This system worked very well during the period of Mongol expansion because the man elected was usually among the ablest of the electors. These were the years when the Mongols were engaged in their conquests, and the Great Khan had to be a man of character and valor to command the respect of his fellow princes and inspire the entire nation to a continuous war effort. Kublai was the first man to violate the tradition of election, as he assumed the imperial title without bothering to be elected. However, he was so highly regarded by his fellow princes that there was only ineffective opposition to his assumption of the title.

Once it was violated, the election system was never revived. Immediately after the death of an emperor, the struggle began among the Mongol princes to seize the throne. According to a Mongol custom, every prince related to the dead emperor could succeed him, whether he were an uncle, a brother, a nephew, or a son. Though normally the strongest candidate succeeded, it often occurred that the leaders of powerful factions blocked each other's chances, and often they had to compromise on a less prominent and less forcible person. In such a case, the new emperor became a mere figurehead, and the real power was in the hands of his supporters. If a reigning emperor chose to designate a crown prince (as some did), such designation would be challenged by his other relatives. Often they backed up their verbal challenge with the threat or the actual use of military force. In the latter case, civil war began. The problem of succession first appeared after the death of Kublai Khan and continued to plague the Yüan regime throughout its existence. More than anything else, it sapped the strength of the Mongol ruling class.

Contrary to the Mongol custom, the Chinese system called for the oldest son of the first legal wife (the empress) as the logical successor, unless the reigning emperor had expressly designated some one else as the crown prince. Due to the emphasis the Chinese placed on filial piety and ancestor worship, rarely was the dead emperor's wish defied, once he had made it known. Whatever disadvantages the Chinese system might have, it provided an orderly transmission of power from one generation to the next, and it lessened, though it did not prevent, the intensity of the power struggle generally following the death of an old emperor.

Despite internal differences, the Mongol ruling class presented a united front insofar as their Chinese subjects were concerned. Living in a hostile land and numerically outnumbered, perhaps they could not do otherwise. They enforced strictly the separate identities between themselves and their Chinese subjects because they knew that any relaxation on this score would eventually lead to their Sinicization and assimilation, a situation which they did not wish to see arise. This emphasis on separate identities, arising from political necessity, antagonized further the Chinese who concluded that their rulers could not be Sinicized, and in their opinion, civilized. Though there had been alien regimes in China before, with the Mongols the gap between the ruling and the ruled seemed to be unbridgeable. While they could do nothing about unuttered resentment, the Mongols took extreme measures to prevent potential revolts; some of these measures have been described earlier. By degrading intellectuals they hoped to deprive the Chinese of their traditional leadership, and by concentrating all military power in their own hands they tried to prevent the development of warlordism which had toppled many Chinese dynasties before. When the Yüan regime was finally overthrown, it was overthrown by popular revolts, led by neither intellectuals nor warlords.

While the Mongol rulers kept an watchful eye on the intellectuals, Chinese nationalism was driven to reside within the lower strata of the population where it remained dormant. Toward the end of the Yüan dynasty when the Mongol power began to show weakness, this nationalism revived and emerged. When it emerged, it took the form of religious propaganda, organized banditry, and popular uprisings. The uprisings which eventually crystallized into mass revolts were led by people of the humblest origin, with little or no education. What triggered the uprisings, however, was the classical case of famine. When famine occurred, people were no longer their rational selves. Driven by hunger, the usually submissive peasants became overnight a massive wave of defiance. Ambitious leaders were quick to exploit the situation. When they called for a revolt against all injustices, real or imaginary, the peasants followed them in a blind fashion.

The first revolt against the Yüan regime was organized by the White Lotus Society, a secret religious sect. It took its beliefs liberally from Taoism and Buddhism, and its leaders claimed the power of communicating with the spiritually unseen. Through the use of magic formulae, they said they could cure the sick, predict the future, and do numerous other miracles. The White Lotus Society first appeared in the area north of the Huai River (modern Anhwei province), and with the passage of time it attracted a large following among the ignorant, superstitious peasants. From time to time it was prosecuted by the Yüan government, and many of its leaders were exiled from their homes as a form of punishment. However, the more the government prosecuted it, the more influential it became. Governmental prosecution, in fact, turned it into a symbol of resistance against an unpopular, alien regime and converted it into an underground nationalist movement. Early in the 1350's repeated famines hit the Huai River area, and the White Lotus Society confidently predicted a major social upheaval and a dynastic change. Because of its pseudo-religious nature, Confucian intellectuals wished to have nothing to do with it, and it was led by poorly educated, mass agitaters. Acting according to its prediction, the Society secretly prepared a revolt. To exploit the nationalist sentiment and to rally popular support, Han Shan-t'ung, its leader, claimed that he was a direct descendant of the Sung emperors. However, the plot of revolt was discovered before it could be carried out, and Han was arrested and subsequently executed. Liu Fu-t'ung, one of Han's top lieutenants, installed Han's son as the figurehead "Sung emperor," and vowed to drive the Mongols out of China. The once invincible Mongols retreated before the hastily organized peasants, and the rebels captured city after city until they had practically the entire Yellow River basin under their control.

For a while it seemed that the Mongol regime would fall at any moment. This, however, was not to be the case. While Liu Fu-t'ung and his generals were ravaging North China, other rebel leaders emerged in the Yangtze River basin. All of them, with the possible exception of one, came from a humble background; among their ranks were a cloth peddler, a fisherman, a pirate, and two salt merchants. Perhaps because of their background, they were as much anti-establishment as they were anti-Mongol. Underneath the nationalistic veneer with which they camouflaged their rebellion was the traditional socioeconomic grievances that had kindled so many revolts in the past. One rebel leader (Chang Shih-ch'eng, d. 1366) killed all the rich men he could find, regardless of whether they were Mongols or Chinese, and at one time even allied himself with the Mongol regime against other Chinese rebel leaders. Whatever nationalism there was, it is fair to say that as far as most peasants were concerned, the primary objective of joining a rebellion was to search for food. In any case, the basic issue that precipitated this widespread anti-Mongol rebellion was never clearly defined, for the simple reason that the rebels, being uneducated or poorly educated, were not articulate enough to express their thought in a logical manner. Even today historians are still debating whether this rebellion was primarily nationalistic or socioeconomic.

However, the very fact that South China played a major role in this rebellion seems to indicate that for the first time in Chinese history nationalism was indeed an important factor in the anti-establishment struggle. Traditionally the Southern Chinese were less rebelliously minded than their northern brethren, and great rebellions, with a few exceptions (such as the Fang La rebellion of the twelfth century), generally originated from the north. The reason is that South China, being economically more productive, experienced famine less frequently than North China and consequently had less reason for staging a rebellion. The Mongol regime, by adopting a policy of discrimination against South China, changed the picture completely. The political and social discrimination against South China has been discussed earlier; more harmful, from a southerner's point of view, was the economic exploitation that took the form of not only higher tax rates but also the appropriation of large tracts of land for the support of Mongol princes and princesses. The nationalistic and socioeconomic factors were in this case mutually productive and strengthened each other, and a Southern Chinese hated the Mongols because they were not only alien rulers but also economic exploiters. It was one thing to be looked down upon; it was quite another matter to be deprived of the means of a livelihood.

At a time when rebellion was ravaging all of China, the Mongol rulers in Peking, instead of rising to the occasion and facing the challenge, were hopelessly divided among themselves. The kind of court strifes described earlier in this chapter had in fact reached a new climax. A new twist was added, however, in the sense that for the first time an empress was actively conspiring against her own husband the emperor. The emperor in question was Yüan Shun-ti (r. 1333–1369), a fun-seeking, spineless ruler whose preoccupation with Lamaist rather than state affairs provided his ambitious Korean wife with the opportunity to exercise real power in the making of policy decisions. As the emperor showed lesser and lesser interest in running the government, the empress intensified her effort to depose him in order to install as the new emperor her own son, namely the crown prince. The crown prince, as one might expect, was more than cooperative in this matter. Thus two political factions emerged in the Mongol court, supporting respectively the emperor and the empress. Meanwhile, their counterparts in the countryside were waging open war against each other. On two or three occasions the conspiracy to oust the emperor almost succeeded; it failed at the last minute when powerful Mongol princes rallied behind the emperor and thwarted the scheme. In 1369 when the emperor finally rose from lethargy to decide to eliminate his crown prince and thus end the conspiracy once and for all, the anti-Mongol rebels were marching fast towards the capital, Peking. There was no sense to kill one's own son, the emperor concluded, when the regime could not even preserve itself.

While the Mongols were feuding among themselves and became greatly weakened as a result, they ceased to be an important factor in the struggle for supremacy in China. As the 1360's began, it had become clear that whoever emerged as the most successful rebel leader would overthrow the Yüan regime and become the new ruler of China. Not surprisingly, the rebel leaders were more concerned with eliminating one another than with fighting against the Mongols. All over China the game with the highest stake was being played among the rebel leaders, as it had been played at the end of each previous dynasty: the winner would become the founder of a new dynasty, to be adulated by historians for generations to come, while the losers would inevitably be branded as bandits, to be disposed of in the manner the winner chose.

The eventual winner, surprisingly, came from an unexpected corner. His name was Chu Yüan-chang, a protégé of Kuo Tzu-hsing. Early in the 1350's when revolts sprang up like wildfire all over China, Kuo, a wealthy landlord in northern Anhwei, distributed his wealth among the able-bodied, discontented peasants in his district and organized a rebellion of his own. It was then that Chu Yüan-chang, an unemployed ex-Buddhist monk about whom more will be said in the next chapter, decided to join him. This band of rebels captured some cities from the Mongols in northern Anhwei; it was soon weakened, however, by internal dissension. For a while it seemed that these rebels would follow the footsteps of so many others into oblivion. In 1355 Kuo died and Chu inherited the leadership. It was then that the situation changed materially for the better as far as this group of rebels was concerned.

In Chu Yüan-chang China again encountered a true leader of rare proportions. With Anhwei as his base of operation, he successfully defeated his rebel opponents, one after another. By 1367 when practically all areas south of the Yellow River had been brought under his control, he dispatched 250,000 of his battle-proven veterans northward to capture Peking. The Mongol military machine, once the best in the world, collapsed overnight. Yüan Shun-ti left Peking for Mongolia in the summer of 1368, and with his departure the Yüan dynasty formally came to an end. Earlier in the same year Chu Yüan-chang assumed the imperial title at Nanking and called his regime Ming.

℞ ix

Ming

CHU YÜAN-CHANG

Chu Yüan-chang (1328–1398), the founder of the Ming dynasty, came from a very humble background. Even by the low Chinese standard, the family was exceedingly poor, and rarely could it maintain itself above the starvation level. Born the youngest of four sons in Fengyang (Anhwei province), he had a harsh life during his childhood. In 1344, when he was sixteen, a severe drought hit his native province, and whatever crops had remained in the fields were soon destroyed by swarms of locusts. A famine ensued, and his parents and brothers perished in the widespread disaster. He was so poor that he did not even have the money to buy a small lot to bury them. Having lost his home, he was taken in by a Buddhist monastery as a novice. He left the monastery shortly afterwards and wandered aimlessly for three years. During this period he was beset with sickness and hunger and had to beg for food to keep himself alive. Finally he returned to the monastery for more regular meals.

Early in 1352 the revolts against the Mongol regime spread to his native province. The commander of the local Mongol garrison, not daring to attack the rebels, chose instead to capture thousands of innocent farmers as prisoners of war and reported this to Peking as great victories in order to win rewards. Not knowing what to do under the circumstances, Chu asked a diviner for advice, and the diviner, invoking the power of the spirits, replied "no" to his inquiry about whether he should continue to stay in his native city or leave to avoid being captured by the Mongols. Asked again whether he should join the ranks of the rebels, the spirits answered with an emphatic "yes." After this alleged incident, Chu went to see Kuo Tzu-hsing, and the latter, taking a look at him, was greatly impressed with his unusual appearance; reportedly he was one of the ugliest men ever to appear on earth. The young man was awarded an orphaned girl as his wife, who was later to be the first empress of the Ming dynasty. He soon proved his worth by defeating repeatedly the Mongols and their collaborators. By 1355 when his old patron died, he was the logical successor, and with an increased following he was ready to contend for the highest prize in the kingdom. How he succeeded has been briefly described in the preceding chapter. Thus in sixteen years (1352–1368) a former beggar rose to become the emperor of China.

Though there was more than a millennium between them, Chu Yüan-chang and Liu Pang are often compared as the two commoners in Chinese history who founded new dynasties. Both came from the most humble backgrounds and rose to supreme power through native ability, personal magnetism, and the uncanny gift for doing the right thing at the right moment. With little or no formal education, both were contemptuous of the intellectuals who, they believed, could only be used but should never be trusted. Both were shrewd, calculating, and ruthless; when power was at stake, they forgot even the most common decency. Both were outrageous for ingratitude to their lieutenants who had helped most to put them on the throne. Once the regime was established and stabilized, the new emperors liquidated them one by one, fearful that these lieutenants, with their increased power and prestige, might threaten the security of the imperial line. However, in the eyes of most Chinese they were heroes because they successfully overthrew two of the most tyrannical regimes in Chinese history. Chu Yüan-chang was perhaps the more heroic, for the Yüan regime was not only tyrannical but also alien.

As with every success story, sheer luck was as important a factor as personal ability. Certainly Chu was not dreaming of becoming the future emperor of China at a time when he had to beg for food from door to door. Many years after he had ascended the dragon throne, he was still sensitive to any mention of his humble background, especially of his brief experience as a Buddhist monk. At least two Confucian scholars were found guilty and were sentenced to death when inadvertently they used the word "birth" (*sheng*), which seemed like a possible pun for "monk" (*seng*), in their congratulatory memorials. According to a widely circulated story, one day the emperor visited one of his palaces under construction, and, pleased with himself and thinking that nobody was nearby to hear him, he said to himself: "Who would believe that a humble monk could have a day like this!" Raising his head, he saw a workman on one of the beams, who had obviously heard what he had just said. The workman was ordered to come down, and after finding that he was both mute and deaf, the emperor decided to spare his life. Later, when it was learned that he was neither, nowhere could the workman be found. He never reported again for work; in fact, he completely disappeared. This incident may or may not have occurred, but it does say a great deal about Chu Yüan-chang, the commoner who had become an emperor.

Moreover, this story speaks eloquently of the absolute power Chinese monarchs enjoyed. Though Chinese monarchy had always been absolute, monarchic absolutism reached new heights under the Ming regime. With reference to autocratic rule, a history student cannot fail to notice the continuous growth of monarchic power throughout Chinese history. In other words, Chinese monarchy became more absolute with the arrival of each succeeding dynasty. This trend began as early as recorded history began and did not end until the monarchical system itself ended in 1912. While this was the general trend, it should be quickly added that the actual power exercised by each individual monarch varied a great deal, and it varied in accordance with his personality (strong or weak), ability, and the circumstances under which he ruled. Generally speaking, the first emperors of each dynasty were more powerful than the last ones, for the power of monarchs declined as each dynasty declined. However, it was still true that over the long run, monarchic power increased and that the monarchy of each succeeding dynasty was generally more absolute than that of the preceding dynasty. For instance, Ming monarchy was more absolute than Yüan; Yüan was more absolute than Sung; and so on.

The continuous increase of monarchic power did not result from any change in political theory; rather, it came as a result of innovations and accumulated usage. In theory the emperor was the Son of Heaven, and being responsible to nobody on earth, he enjoyed absolute power by definition. The checks on the exercise of that power could only be imposed by the emperor himself, *e.g.*, his own willingness to observe custom and tradition, his fear of potential revolts, and the conviction, if he chose to have it, that he should always rule for the benefit of the ruled. There was no way of getting rid of a bad government except by successful revolt, and if a monarch abused his power, revolts were justified in theory as had been done often in practice. But revolts, even successful ones, were

extremely costly and time consuming, and as both monarch and his subjects agreed, they should not be indulged in lightly. Until modern times,
China had never practiced any other form of government except absolute
monarchy because to the Chinese the alternative was anarchy, which
should be avoided at all costs.

Since absolute monarchy was the accepted form of government, the
only way to avoid its abuse lay in the betterment of the monarch himself:
he should be intelligent, wise, and able, and he should rule not for his
own self-glorification, but for the welfare of his subjects. As taught by
Confucians, the education of monarchs was the most important education
in the realm, for they believed that a good government was impossible
unless the monarch was virtuous and that the prerequisite to an orderly
society was the "cultivation of virtues" among the rulers. Thus in Chinese
politics personnel was always more important than institutions since the
basic institution, that of absolute monarchy, remained the same throughout centuries.

When Chu Yüan-chang emerged as the emperor of China, one of his
major concerns was the security of the imperial line and the best way to
preserve it. A man of commanding personality and unusual ability, he had
no fear of any challenge to his own authority, but he was greatly concerned with what could happen when he was no longer in charge of state
affairs. His eldest son, the crown prince, was a weak figure. After the early
death of the crown prince, Chu Yüan-chang designated the crown prince's
eldest son, then a child, as his heir apparent. To secure the throne for his
successor, he thought that before he died he had to eliminate all potential
enemies of the future emperor. Two purges (in 1380 and again in 1393)
were conducted, and each was a bloodbath. The two purges were centered on two prominent figures, Hu Wei-yung, the prime minister, and Lan
Yü, a marshal and field commander. Both had been his top lieutenants in
overthrowing the Yüan dynasty and in establishing the new regime. The
two main characters might or might not have been guilty of treason as
charged (the prime minister, for instance, was accused of having com-
municated secretly with the Japanese and of having invited them to land
on the eastern coast of China for a common effort to topple the Ming
regime), but there was no question about the innocence of thousands of
others who had to perish because they were directly or indirectly, personally or otherwise, associated with the two accused. After the two purges,
all political figures who could be remotely considered a threat to the
throne were liquidated. With the comforting thought that the crown had
been secured for his grandson, Chu Yüan-chang died in peace in 1398.
Little did he realize then that the danger to his grandson's crown would
come from an unexpected corner.

Rejecting the revival of feudalism on a large scale and yet entertaining the hope that the royal house in Nanking would be defended by its

own members in case of need, Chu Yüan-chang placed three of his eldest sons in three strategic areas of North China in command of concentrations of troops, while his other sons were given rank, title, and wealth, but little real power. The role of the three was twofold: to come to the rescue of Nanking whenever help was needed and to defend North China against possible Mongol invasion, since the Mongols, though driven out of China proper, were still a potential threat. When Chu Yüan-chang's grandson, Ming Hui-ti, inherited the throne in 1399 at the age of sixteen, he was greatly concerned with the semi-independent status which his three uncles enjoyed, and he proposed to reduce their power which, he believed, threatened his own security as emperor at Nanking. His real target, however, was third uncle Chu Ti, who was by far the ablest and the most powerful of his numerous uncles. Declaring that his nephew was badly advised by evil elements and that there could be no peace until they were removed, Chu Ti personally took command of his troops and

MARBLE STATUES OF ANIMALS   These statues, erected in the fourteenth century, line the tomb of Chu Yüan-chang, founder of the Ming dynasty. The tomb is located outside of Nanking and is a major tourist attraction. The names of some of the tourists are scratched on the bodies of the two elephants in the foreground, a destructive way of achieving immortality practiced everywhere in the world.

marched southward from his base at Peking. The resultant war lasted three years, and while the fortunes of war changed from time to time, the uncle's greater ability decided the final outcome in the end. Nanking fell in 1402, and the boy emperor disappeared when his palace caught fire and was burned to the ground. It was not known whether he had been burned alive or had managed to escape. In the following year Chu Ti ascended the throne and was then known by his reign title Yung-lo. The capital was moved northward to Peking.

The reigns of Hung-wu (Chu Yüan-chang's reign title) and Yung-lo, which jointly covered more than a half century, were the most dynamic of the Ming regime. Hung-wu was regarded as one of the ablest monarchs China ever produced, and his innovations were followed without question by his successors. He disregarded all limitations on his power imposed by custom and tradition, and his reign was marked by a despotism unprecedented in Chinese history. Angered by Hu Wei-yung's alleged treason, he decided to abolish the institution of premiership once and for all, and "anyone who dares to petition for its reëstablishment will be ordered to perish immediately together with the rest of his family." The Six Ministries (Rites, Finance, Personnel, War, Justice, and Public Works), which formerly had been headed by a prime minister, were now made directly responsible to the emperor alone. Thus the institution of premiership, which was almost as old as Chinese politics itself, came to an end, and it was not reëstablished throughout the Ming dynasty.

The abolition of premiership strengthened further the power of Chinese monarchs. Though appointed by and responsible to the emperor, a prime minister enjoyed a certain degree of independence as the head of the government, as against the monarch who was the head of the court as well as the head of the state. He was usually promoted from the rank and file of a professional bureaucracy, and being raised up among the people, he presumably knew "the people's sickness and sorrows." The monarch, on the other hand, was usually a product of palace life and had no personal experience with the life of his subjects outside the palace. Generally speaking, the prime minister, being one of the people, had in mind the welfare of the nation as a whole, while the monarch was more concerned with the security of his crown and the welfare of the royal household. A monarch inherited his throne through no virtue of his own, while a prime minister earned his position by academic excellence and personal ability. Against an impulsive or capricious emperor, a conscientious and upright prime minister upheld the principles he stood for. Respecting his position and prestige, even the most despotic monarch would think twice before he inflicted upon his prime minister undeserved punishment. Thus a good prime minister always served as an effective check on the absolute power of the supposedly omnipotent prince.

The emperor Hung-wu, by abolishing the premiership, created a

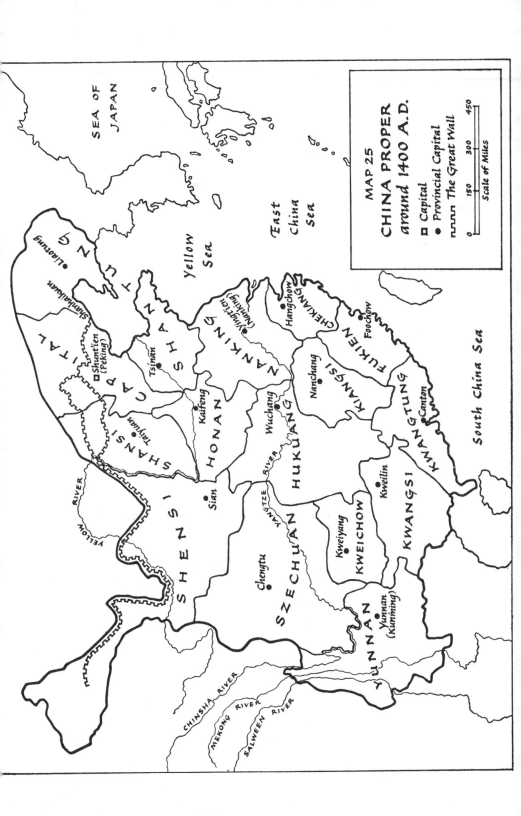

MAP 25

CHINA PROPER
around 1400 A.D.

□ Capital
● Provincial Capital
ⅢⅢⅢ The Great Wall

0   150   300   450
scale of Miles

SEA OF JAPAN

Yellow Sea

East China Sea

South China Sea

LIAOTUNG
●Liaoyang

Shanhaikuan

CAPITAL
□Shuntien (Peking)

SHANTUNG
●Tsinan

SHANSI
●Taiyuan

HONAN
●Kaifeng

SHENSI
●Sian

NANKING
●Yingtien (Nanking)

CHEKIANG
●Hangchow

FUKIEN
●Foochow

KIANGSI
●Nanchang

HUKUANG
●Wuchang

KWANGTUNG
●Canton

KWANGSI
●Kweilin

KWEICHOW
●Kweiyang

SZECHUAN
●Chengtu

YUNNAN
●Yunnan (Kunming)

YELLOW RIVER

YANGTZE RIVER

CHINSHA RIVER

MEKONG RIVER

SALWEEN RIVER

most unfortunate precedent for his successors to follow. Though able monarchs like Yung-lo had no difficulty in carrying out a prime minister's duties, the less fortunate ones, with tremendous power in their hands and yet not knowing how to use it, turned to their personal favorites for guidance and counsel. Surrounded in the Forbidden City by concubines and eunuchs, they increasingly turned to the latter for consultation on state affairs. To be sure, the Board of Censors was allowed to function even after the abolition of premiership. But the censors, being officials of lower ranks, could only remonstrate with their superiors at their own peril. They were neither supposed to nor did they actually serve as an effective check on the omnipotence of absolute monarchs.

Ming despotism was vividly demonstrated by a new custom, the corporal punishment of government officials. The ancient tradition that "a gentleman could be ordered to die, but he should never be humiliated" was no longer observed under the new regime. Though corporal punishment had been frequently used against common criminals, it was for the first time legally sanctioned by a Chinese regime against intellectuals. In Chinese thinking, the intellectuals, as the standard bearers of the Chinese heritage, should always be held in respect and should never be humiliated in public. If a member of the intelligentsia committed a crime of an unforgivable nature, tradition called upon him to commit suicide; and, if he were true to his Confucian principles, he should do so without complaint even though he might be fully convinced that he was innocent. The Ming regime dispensed with this honorable custom and introduced instead corporal punishment. Whether the new regime inherited this practice from the Mongols is a matter of conjecture, but Chu Yüan-chang would have started it even if there had been no precedent. For the founder of the Ming dynasty was an unusually cruel man, and coming from a humble background with no formal education to speak of, he might have subconsciously enjoyed the humiliation and tormenting of the seemingly self-centered intellectuals. Whatever the real motive was, he made the flogging of public officials a court routine, and those who died of injuries included a duke and a Minister of Public Works. The floggings became so indiscriminate and deadly that it was said that court officials bid farewell to their wives every morning when they left for the imperial conference and congratulated each other for having lived another day if they came home alive. One court official who dared to petition the emperor for some relief from this cruel practice was thrown into jail and never came out alive.

Once the precedent of corporal punishment was established, later Ming emperors followed it as a matter of common usage, and none of them ever questioned its advisability and wisdom. In fact, "court floggings" (t'ing chang) developed into ritualistic affairs and were done with well-defined, specified rules. Whenever a public flogging occurred, all court officials were required to wear ceremonial robes and to be present to observe in the emperor's audience hall. Once the victim was brought in, his guilt was publicly announced by an imperial guard. He would then lie flat on his stomach, with both arms and legs tied tightly so he could move neither left nor right. A wooden rod was used to flail his exposed buttocks after his underwear had been publicly stripped off. The number of blows he would receive depended upon the seriousness of his offense. Usually he died before the last blow could be delivered.

Barbaric though it might be, the severe punishment of government officials did yield one good result: the elimination of bribery and corruption. Early during the Ming dynasty the law stipulated that any official who accepted bribes exceeding sixty taels of silver was liable to capital punishment, and those who had accepted less would be flogged and then condemned to an indefinite period of hard labor. Meanwhile, able and conscientious officials were honored and abundantly rewarded. The imperial government periodically sent inspectors down to the provinces, punishing the guilty and rewarded the deserving. Rarely in Chinese history had government officials been so honest.

MARITIME EXPEDITIONS

If Chu Yüan-chang could be compared to Genghis Khan in foresight and personal ability, Yung-lo was certainly another Kublai Khan. In both cases their successors were far behind them in performance as vital, capable rulers. The reigns of Hung-wu and Yung-lo were not only marked by a new height in autocratic rule at home, but they were also characterized by the implementation of a vigorous foreign policy abroad. In this respect the first few decades of the Ming dynasty have been often compared with the expansion years of the Han and T'ang regimes. Chu Yüan-chang not only drove the Mongols out of China but repeatedly sent his troops deep into the enemy's territories. Twice the Ming forces captured Karakorum, and the Mongol chieftains were forced to sue for peace. The fact that Yung-lo located his capital only forty miles south of the Great Wall indicated an extremely confident regime which felt strong enough to be face to face with China's traditional enemies from the northern steppes. Like many Han and T'ang emperors, he took offensive actions to achieve an essentially defensive goal: time and again his men invaded and penetrated deep into the grasslands, seeking out the enemy's forces and destroying them. Throughout the Yung-lo reign the nomads were forcibly kept within their own boundaries. But for reasons we have discussed before, the very nature of the grasslands prohibited any permanent success of an agricultural ruler. When the Ming regime began to show signs of decline after the 1430's, China's traditional enemy once again threatened her northern frontier.

Believing that all peoples on earth should be brought under the benevolent influence of the Son of Heaven, the first Ming emperor sent envoys overseas demanding the acknowledgement of his overlordship shortly after his accession. For reasons of their own, many of China's peripheral states and some in faraway South and Southeast Asia allowed themselves to be persuaded to join Ming's tribute system. Korea, Japan,

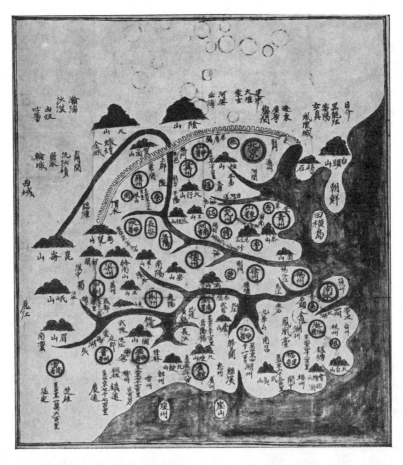

A MAP OF CHINA MADE DURING THE MING DYNASTY The Great Wall is shown on the upper part of this map. The two heavy tree-like lines indicate the Yellow River in the north and the Yangtze in the south. Within the large circle on the upper right is the Chinese word "Peking." The black area on the right and lower side is, of course, the ocean.

Liu-ch'iu, Annam (Vietnam), Cambodia, Siam (Thailand), Borneo, Java, Sumatra, several Malay states, and some small kingdoms on the southeast coast of India, directly or by implication, acknowledged Ming's overlordship at one time or another. Hung-wu's efforts along this line were continued by his son Yung-lo. It was during the latter's reign that Chinese influence was expanded overseas in a manner never before accomplished.

Under Yung-lo and his two immediate successors the Chinese launched a series of maritime expeditions on an unprecedented scale. From 1405 to 1431 Chinese armadas led by the court eunuch Cheng Ho made seven voyages to the "Western Ocean" (a term used during this period to cover the general area of South and Southeast Asia) for the ostensible purpose of "glorifying Chinese arms in the remote regions and showing off the wealth and power of the Central Kingdom." In 1405 when the first expedition began, a powerful fleet of 62 vessels carrying 27,800 men sailed from Fukien, visited many Southeast Asian countries, and went as far as India. In the places it visited, it "proclaimed publicly the decree of the Son of Heaven" (of demanding their submission), and "if they refused to submit, force was used to coerce them." On the other hand, if the local chieftains decided to cooperate, gold, silk, and other valuables were showered on them as rewards. The first expedition, successfully accomplished, was followed by six others, and most of them went as far as the Persian Gulf or Aden at the southeastern end of the Red Sea. In at least two of the voyages Chinese vessels personally commanded by Cheng Ho called on some of the small kingdoms on the east coast of Africa. As a result of these expeditions it was reported that altogether thirty-six countries in the "Western Ocean" sent tribute missions to China and acknowledged Ming's overlordship. These thirty-six countries included eight from the East Indies, eleven from India and Ceylon, five from Persia and Arabia, and five from the east coast of Africa.

Cheng Ho's voyages were the most spectacular maritime expeditions the world had yet seen. From a historian's point of view, they raise more questions than have ever been satisfactorily answered. First, what were the motives behind this adventure? What did it try to achieve? Second, what seamanship did the Chinese then possess which made these expeditions not only possible but also remarkably successful? Third, why did not the Chinese follow up their initial success, as later the Western Europeans did, with the establishment of a commercial and perhaps a political maritime empire? Lastly, what was the true meaning of the tribute system which, the Chinese insisted, was the only proper basis in their relations with non-Chinese countries?

Chinese sources give two reasons for this unprecedented maritime adventure: first, to trace the whereabouts of Ming Hui-ti who was believed by some to have escaped from Nanking and who might be some-

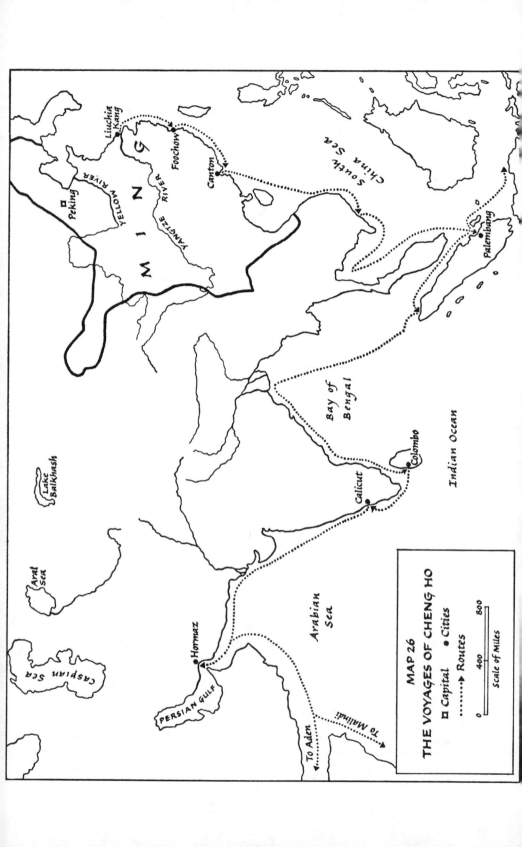

MAP 26
THE VOYAGES OF CHENG HO

□ Capital   ● Cities
······► Routes

Scale of Miles

0   400   800

Peking

MING

Liuchia Kang

YELLOW RIVER

YANGTZE RIVER

Foochow

Canton

South China Sea

Palembang

Bay of Bengal

Colombo

Calicut

Indian Ocean

Lake Balkhash

Aral Sea

Caspian Sea

Arabian Sea

Hormuz

PERSIAN GULF

To Aden

To Malindi

where in Southeast Asia, and second, to "impress people overseas with Ming's power and wealth" and to "bring ten thousand nations to bear tribute missions to the Central Kingdom." The first reason might have had something to do with the first voyage, but even then it was secondary at best, for there were no extensive efforts made during any of the seven voyages to find the ex-emperor. If this were a genuine reason, there would have been no need for these voyages to go as far as the Near East or Africa. The second reason was more plausible, since so far no other motives have been found. In other words, these expeditions were launched for ideological reasons and prestige. The material or commercial motive which prompted European expansion at a later date was notably absent.

Ideologically, the Ming emperors regarded themselves as the Sons of Heaven, thus representing all people on earth. Once such an assumption was made, it seemed logical that they should wish to bring as many foreign nations under their overlordship as they physically could. While the Han and T'ang emperors looked northward and overland for the extension of their pretensions, the Ming emperors looked southward and overseas for the same purpose. Perhaps by then history had shown them the futility of expansion across the grasslands and deserts on account of geographical and cultural factors. If a southern expansion was to be equally unprofitable, as later it did turn out to be, they had no historical lessons to guide them at that time. The word "profit," of course, should not be interpreted in its material sense, since the Chinese did not believe that material profit should be a primary factor in governing the relationships among nations. Traditionally against commercialism which seemed to be the only practical reason for such an adventure, they undertook one of the most costly operations in history for nonmaterial purposes.

Despite the basic attitude of anticommercialism on the part of the Chinese government and most of the Chinese people, the fact that China had a long coastline indented with many fine bays and harbors should explain why a certain portion of its people became orientated to the sea and depended on the sea to earn a livelihood. Regardless of what other people thought of them and their activities, the people on the southeast coast had long been engaged in commercial endeavors overseas. Since they lived far away from the Yellow River basin where more important history was made and since the Chinese had traditionally looked down upon trade and commerce, what they did in the faraway areas of Fukien and Kwangtung was only scantily recorded by the agriculturally minded historians. On the southeast coast where the rugged terrain dropped abruptly into the sea to form an irregular coastline with many bays and harbors, the land was poor and arable areas were few. As the pressure of population increased with the passage of time, people were forced by necessity to look beyond the blue horizon for a livelihood. With or without government approval, they sailed abroad with Chinese products and brought home goods of exotic origins. Many perished on the high seas or on remote islands; others brought back uncountable wealth. For every family that succeeded, many others mourned the loss of their beloved ones. Merchants who had found a more rewarding existence overseas settled down there permanently and never returned. Early in the 1560's it was reported that tens of thousands of Chinese resided in Luzon, and a Chinese community of several thousand families had been established in the city of Palembang (Sumatra).

As overseas trade expanded, numerous trade ports on the southeast coast flourished. The most important among them was Ch'üanchou (Map 1) which remained the leading shipping and trading center throughout the Sung, Yüan, and Ming dynasties. Government posts in charge of merchant marine and shipping were so lucrative that they were eagerly sought after, and officials who occupied them grew in power and wealth. One of them, P'u Shou-keng, became so powerful that his change of loyalty shortened the life of the South Sung regime, as has been mentioned before. Despite a basic anticommercial attitude, overseas trade was so profitable and prosperous that both government and people benefited from it. The large amount of wealth that could be acquired from overseas trade and the great risk involved in it gave birth to a new custom in Fukien province, the adoption of foster children. Abandoned children and orphans were adopted by families even when they had children of their own. They were sent abroad for commercial enterprise after they had grown up, while the true sons were generally kept at home. If they made good, the whole family benefited; if they were lost forever, their families would be somewhat comforted by the thought that they were not true sons in the first place.

Since seafaring had a long history on the southeast coast, seamanship improved with the passage of each generation. The merchants who roved the seven seas for profit could be easily converted into naval captains for manning warships, once their government demanded their service. When Kublai Khan decided to invade Japan again in 1281, enough seamen and ships to transport 140,000 troops were gathered in short order. When Yung-lo ordered his men to venture into the south seas, the people on the east coast were equally ready to provide what he needed. Generations of experiments and improvement enabled the Chinese to manufacture ships that were among the most seaworthy the world had yet seen. Some of the vessels used in Cheng Ho's first voyage, for instance, had a length of 44 *chang* (c. 517 feet), and a width of 18 *chang* (c. 212 feet), built with four decks and watertight compartments. With favorable winds they could make as fast as six knots an hour. The compass, which had been used for centuries to locate proper burial places for the dead, was now an indispensable instrument in navigation. Early during the fifteenth century when

Cheng Ho made his voyages, the Chinese had the men and the skill to undertake such feats of seamanship as had never before been seen in world history.

Despite their monumental success in seamanship, the maritime expeditions of the Ming dynasty were discontinued as suddenly as they had been launched. Cheng Ho goes down in history as an earlier Columbus who was not followed by a Cortes or a Pizarro, and his overseas voyages turned out to be the first and the only large-scale maritime adventure ever undertaken by a Chinese government. If the Chinese had continued his efforts, the economic and political structure of the world in the subsequent centuries, or at least that in Asia, would have changed considerably. The immediate causes of their discontinuance were rather obvious. First, these maritime expeditions were extremely costly, and yet they brought back nothing except dubious prestige. The Ming regime simply could not continue them indefinitely. Second, other areas began to demand more attention from the government after the 1430's, especially the northern frontier where the Mongols again threatened an invasion. The real causes, however, went much deeper. Had the maritime region on China's southeast coast constituted an independent state acting in observance of its own interests, it could have been another Portugal or Spain, one of the first maritime nations in the world. Its sailors, having touched the east coast of Africa early in the fifteenth century, could conceivably have reached the Cape of Good Hope later, and eventually might have been able to "discover" such strange places as England and France. This, however, was not to be the case. China remained land-centered and anticommercial. Instead of discovering more new territories, China and its tributary states were "discovered" by Western Europeans in a later age.

The reasons for the failure to follow up Cheng Ho's initial success with sustained interest and effort can be found in the nature of Chinese culture itself. In other words, the sense of values contained in the Chinese cultural system would not allow maritime success on a sustained basis. The Chinese lacked the motivations that prompted Western Europe to discover and explore new areas in a later period. First, as a people the Chinese were unusually self-centered. Separated from other centers of civilization by oceans and almost impassable mountains and deserts, the Chinese developed their culture independently. They had been little affected by foreign influence, except Buddhism from India, until modern times. The result was a self-centered "culturalism" which regarded the Chinese culture as the most unique and incomparably great. While foreigners were welcome to come to China to be Sinicized and, in the opinion of the Chinese, civilized, it was considered improper for the Chinese to go overseas for the sole purpose of propagating Chinese beliefs. Active proselyting was to be avoided because it could not serve any purpose except to place doubt on the advocated beliefs. In the Chinese mind, true values needed no persuasion, and if the Chinese culture were truly great (as they believed it was), foreigners would follow it of their own accord. Throughout Chinese history individual Confucians might go to foreign countries to teach if they were invited, but there were no organized efforts on the part of the Chinese or their government to send missionaries overseas. Thus the missionary zeal which played such an important role in Europe's discovery and exploration of new territories during the age of commercial revolution was singularly absent so far as the Chinese were concerned. Second, there was the traditional anticommercialism in China. Ever since the Han dynasty the merchants had been regarded as exploitative and parasitic, and despite the useful functions they performed, they were discriminated against socially and occasionally even persecuted. During the Ming dynasty the fact that the seafaring merchants generally came from the lower strata of the population and were the least cultured in Confucian learning strengthened further an ancient prejudice. In the minds of most Chinese, the merchants who voluntarily left their parents and their ancestors' graves to seek fortunes overseas were the most contemptible because by doing so they neglected to observe two cardinal virtues of Confucianism, i.e., filial piety and ancestor worship. Third, rightly or wrongly the Chinese believed that they were economically self-sufficient and that they needed nothing from foreign lands. That Cheng Ho's expeditions brought back nothing remarkable except such curiosities as ostriches, zebras, and giraffes further convinced them that while foreigners depended upon trade with China for the improvement of their livelihood, China had nothing to gain in trading with foreigners. This belief was strengthened in a later period by the insistence of Western Europeans on opening China to trade.

Spectacular as Cheng Ho's expeditions were, they did not represent a basic need from the Chinese point of view. Many Confucian scholars regarded this maritime adventure as being wasteful and unnecessary and merely "a eunuch's enterprise" with which they would have nothing to do. Though they had no objection to bringing many foreign lands into the tribute system, they believed that this should be done on a voluntary basis and that no coercion or "persuasion" should be applied for that purpose. The tribute system, as they saw it, was based upon a cultural relationship between superior and inferiors. China, being culturally superior, extended its benevolent influence to its neighbors, and its neighbors sent tribute missions to China out of gratitude and appreciation. Foreign countries that sent tribute missions should be given Chinese products in return that were worth more in monetary value than the tributes they sent in order to show "the generosity and abundance of the Central Kingdom." There should not be any motive for material gain in the operation of the tribute system. The tribute system, enshrined in tradition and history, was the only basis of international relations Confucian scholars would recognize. Clearly they did not believe in equality among sovereign nations because in their mind no nation except China was truly sovereign. This self-centered "culturalism," as one might call it, had worked fairly well throughout Chinese history until modern times when China was brought into contact with Western Europeans.

The actual performance of the tribute system fell far short of the ideal as conceived by Confucian scholars. The material motive, theoretically absent, played an important role as early as the tribute system began. The gifts given by Chinese emperors to foreign rulers and their emissaries were often subsidies and bribes in disguise; the Chinese hoped that foreigners, given the choice of obtaining what they needed by peaceful means, would not resort to the use of more violent methods. On the other hand, foreign countries perhaps had no objection to being considered as inferiors so long as the manifestation of inferiority did not extend beyond the nominal, ritualistic gestures such as the adoption of the Chinese calendar and the receiving of Chinese ranks and titles. Moreover, tribute embassies were often foreign trade missions in disguise and brought material benefits to the countries that sent them. Thus the tribute system rationalized foreign trade and gave it an aura of respectability which otherwise it would not have had. Traditionally anticommercial, the Chinese government would have been hard put to sanction foreign trade if it were not disguised as tribute missions. During the Ming dynasty the so-called tribute bearers were often the representatives of foreign trade interests. In many cases these representatives were Chinese exiles who had been chosen by foreign traders to represent them because of their expert knowledge of Chinese affairs. Oftentimes, the Chinese government threw these exiles into jail or even executed them, once their identity was established. From the government's point of view, the fact that these exiles left their ancestors' graves for foreign lands spoke eloquently of their rascality for which, it believed, they deserved no mercy. Needless to say, the government did not favor Chinese emigration overseas.

JAPANESE PIRATES

Like many dynasties before it, the Ming dynasty underwent a familiar dynastic cycle. The first stage of the cycle was the stage of exuberant energy characterized by expansion abroad and peace and prosperity at home during the reigns of Hung-wu and Yung-lo. Then followed the stage of stability during which a power equilibrium existed between China and its "barbarian" neighbors. While there were occasional clashes of arms between them, neither side was able to advance decisively against the other. Domestically, as population increased following a period of peace and prosperity, the balance between food supply and demand had become marginal and delicate, and a serious drought or flood would tip the balance and cause a famine and possibly an internal revolt. From 1424 when Yung-lo died to 1628 when the last Ming emperor, Ch'ung-chen, ascended the throne, there were several serious revolts, not to mention riots of a more local nature. The government, however, was able to suppress each revolt after considerable bloodshed. The rebels could challenge the imperial authority, but they could not threaten its existence. The last years of the stage of stability merged imperceptibly with the first years of the stage of decline. The decline was a gradual and continuous process, and it is difficult to say exactly when it began. During the period of decline, as the scope and the frequency of internal revolts became increasingly larger, the government was less and less able to cope with them. Meanwhile, the non-Chinese tribes beyond the Great Wall became stronger and bolder; they invaded, or threatened to invade, border provinces. At home, corruption, incompetence, and factional strife continued to sap the strength of the government. The Ming regime finally ended when it was too weakened to last any longer.

The first indication that all was not well with the state was its inability to suppress Japanese pirates on the east coast in the 1520's. Since 1401 when Japan had sent its first tribute mission to China, extensive trade had been conducted between the two countries under the guise of tribute missions. Ningpo (Chekiang province) was designated as the port of entry, and both sides seemed to benefit greatly from the exchange. However, problems soon developed, and there were constant bickerings and wranglings between traders of both sides. To simplify the matter, the Ming government decided in the 1430's that the Japanese could send only one tribute mission every ten years, that each mission should not consist of more than two ships and two hundred persons, and that only authorized representatives of the Japanese government would be recognized as members of the mission. This policy, however, did not work so well as the Ming government had hoped.

Trade being exceedingly profitable, the competition to send tribute missions was intense. Since Japan was not unified at that time, different feudal lords sent their own missions to China, each claiming to represent Japan. When the tribute missions arrived at Ningpo, the Chinese government had to decide whom to recognize. It often occurred that Chinese officials in charge recognized the mission that offered the largest bribe and turned back the rest. With so much at stake financially, the Japanese who had been turned back simply would not accept the Chinese decision. Since they could not trade legally, they resorted to smuggling. When engaged in smuggling, they had no difficulty in finding Chinese collaborators who were eager to help for a commission. Thus the rejected tribute bearers transformed themselves into smugglers overnight, and with the help of their Chinese collaborators they were remarkably successful. As their success story spread, other Japanese merchants followed suit. Together they made smuggling a widespread affair on the east coast of China. When the Chinese authorities set out to suppress them, they fought back and ravaged the coastal villages and towns in retaliation. The very same Japanese would be tribute bearers, legitimate traders, smugglers, or pirates, depending upon when and where they made their appearance.

In 1523 when again it was time to send tribute missions to China, many Japanese lords competed for the prized privilege. When two rival delegations arrived at Ningpo, the Chinese official in charge (a eunuch) violated the principle of priority—"first come, first served"—by inspecting first the goods of the delegation that arrived later but had offered a large bribe to the Chinese. The rival delegation led by a Buddhist monk attacked the delegation which the Chinese had favored. Chinese officials, instead of offering their good offices, secretly helped the side they favored with military weapons. Learning about this, the rival delegation and its auxiliary warriors retaliated by burning and looting Chinese towns and cities. When peace was finally restored, the Ming government ordered the suspension of trade with the Japanese "now and forever," and all Japanese were ordered to leave China immediately. Recognizing the weakness of its defenses along the coast, the government thought that this was the best policy to follow; but it was to backfire shortly afterwards.

As long as trade was legalized and officially supervised, it benefited both Chinese and Japanese merchants, despite friction and occasional outbursts of violence. Once it was suspended, the legitimate trade went underground and became a clandestine operation. By then trade had become so prosperous that merchants of neither side wished to abandon it. While the government had in mind coastal defense and consequently prohibited trade, the merchants on the east coast were so anxious for profits that they continued to trade with the Japanese despite the government's prohibition. Unwilling or unable to check the illicit trade, local officials adopted an attitude of "salutary neglect." Well-bribed, they could be counted on to close their eyes.

Without government supervision and regulation, trade became a private affair between Chinese and Japanese merchants, and they had to settle whatever difficulties that arose by themselves. One of the recurring difficulties was the inability or unwillingness on the part of many Chinese merchants to pay their debts to the Japanese exporters after they had received goods. Refusing to go home empty-handed, the Japanese took temporary residence on the nearby islands off the coast and waited and demanded to be paid. When their food and other provisions were exhausted, they found it necessary to raid coastal villages to obtain the means of livelihood. The Chinese debtors would then accuse them of piracy and demand the local garrisons to chase them out. Meanwhile, they secretly informed their Japanese creditors of the coming raid to make sure that they would leave safely for Japan before the arrival of Chinese troops. By these devious maneuvers these Chinese merchants hoped to achieve a double purpose: they did not have to pay the debts they owed, and the Japanese merchants, once safely home, could be expected to return with more goods next time. If they did return, the same scheme would be again used. Though most Chinese and Japanese merchants were honest in their dealings, there were among them enough such black sheep to cause constant friction between the two groups.

While honest Japanese traders could not find redress for their legitimate grievances, the dishonest ones resorted to illegitimate means to achieve their purpose. They would trade when they were allowed, smuggle when legitimate trade was denied to them. They resorted to piracy if they believed that the returns could be even larger. The long coastline and Ming's weak defense made piracy extremely difficult to suppress, and once one piracy went unpunished, others followed suit. Piracy being so profitable, the entire coast from the Liaotung Peninsula to Kwangtung was soon infested with pirates. From 1523 when trade with Japan was officially suspended to 1564 when piracy was finally suppressed, the merchant-pirates from Japan went up and down the coastline, looting, burning, and killing, encountering little or no opposition. Ming's defense was so weak that on many occasions pirates not only ravaged the coastal areas but penetrated deep into the interior. In one instance, a small band of Japanese pirates went as far as South Anhwei and then turned northward to attack Nanking.

While officially they were lumped together and were called "dwarf (Japanese) pirates," most of these pirates were actually Chinese. From the very beginning, Chinese took an active part in these lawless activities. At one time it was estimated that they constituted about 70 percent of the pirate force. These Chinese came from various walks of life, and all of them, for one reason or another, had become dissatisfied with their previous occupations. Among them were dismissed government officials, students who had failed in the civil service examinations, jail-breaking prisoners, runaway Buddhist monks, and professional ruffians. Many of the local gentry either connived at or were actually involved in this lawless but profitable occupation. Though these pirates ravaged the entire coast, it was Kiangsu and Chekiang provinces that suffered most, partly because there were many islands off the coast of these two provinces which conveniently served as jumping-off places for piratical raids. The Chushan Islands, for instance, were notorious as pirate strongholds. After 1558, however, the pirates moved southward and concentrated their efforts on Fukien and Kwangtung provinces. It was not until the 1560's that their energy was spent and they were finally suppressed.

INTERNAL DECLINE

The fact that bands of pirates could devastate such large areas for such a long time was a clear indication of Ming's decline as a military power. Military commanders were usually political appointees who knew little or nothing about warfare. They fled before the arrival of the enemy and left towns and cities wide open to the invaders. In 1555, for instance, a band of sixty-seven Japanese pirates swept across three provinces for several hundred miles, looted in a dozen cities, and killed more than four thousand persons in a period of three months. More than anything else, this incident reflected an almost unbelievable bureaucratic incompetence. More than a century of unchallenged, autocratic rule had created such complacency among government leaders that minor rebellions and piratical raids could not even create a stir of urgency and arouse them to a better effort. During this period the emperors were all products of an easy palace life, and most of them knew or cared little about state affairs. Two of the emperors shared a notorious record for not having received any of their ministers for twenty years. Instead of delegating power to legally constituted authorities, the emperors turned over the reins of government to their personal servants, the eunuchs. As eunuch power increased, the Ming regime slowly declined.

A combination of circumstances made eunuchs a unique factor in Chinese politics. They were: (1) the seclusion of emperors from the outside world, (2) the emperors' unlimited power and unchallenged position, (3) the great size of the imperial harem, (4) the daily contact between emperors and eunuchs, and (5) the general acceptance by the Chinese people of the above practices. The special privileges reserved for an emperor alone were also a handicap which he must overcome if he wished to become a successful ruler. He had to be unusually wise not to be corrupted by the power he enjoyed. But monarchs, like any other group of people, had their share of mediocrities. The soft, femininized palace was no place to breed hardy, strong leaders. During his daily routine, an emperor saw only women and eunuchs. He could not venture into the outside world without causing great alarm among court officials since his safety was their most important concern. He knew little about his subjects except whatever information his ministers and eunuchs chose to give him. Yet his power was so great that he could order the death of anyone who, in his opinion, had shown "disrespect" or had personally offended him. Under such circumstances it took an unusually courageous minister to be frank, and courageous ministers were only too few. The Ming record shows that time and again ministers trembled with fear in an emperor's presence, and when pressed to speak, spoke what they thought the emperor would like to hear. They were anxious to keep bad news from his knowledge, lest in a sudden burst of anger they might be punished more severely than they deserved. For instance, the last Ming emperor Ch'ung-chen had no idea where the rebels were until they began to climb the walls of the Forbidden City and attack his palace. Pampered by women and eunuchs and cut off completely from the outside world, an emperor had to be an exceptional man to govern successfully the largest nation on earth. But most emperors were not exceptional. Many of the Ming emperors, for instance, relied on their eunuchs for information and judgment, since the eunuchs alone saw them everyday and could perhaps talk with them on a personal basis. In some cases, an emperor simply turned over the whole government to a head eunuch, while he could enjoy "wine, women, and song" without being disturbed by state affairs.

With the possible exception of the Sung, practically all major Chinese dynasties were plagued with the usurpation of power by eunuchs in various degrees. After the establishment of the Ming regime, Chu Yüan-chang took extra precautions to prevent eunuchs from acquiring power and formulated strict rules to govern their lives. The number of eunuchs was limited to one hundred, and they were not allowed to read and write. They served in the palaces only, and under no circumstance would they be allowed to become government officials. To remind the eunuchs of their place, Chu Yüan-chang ordered that an iron plate be placed on one of the palace doors, on which was inscribed: "Eunuchs should not meddle in governmental affairs. Let those who violate this rule be punished by death." Though this rule was meant to be permanent, it was soon violated by Chu Yüan-chang's son, the emperor Yung-lo. To reward the eunuchs who had helped him win the war against his nephew Hui-ti, Yung-lo appointed them to high positions with great responsibilities. Some were sent to foreign countries as his personal envoys. The most prominent of them was Cheng Ho whose maritime expeditions have been discussed earlier. Yung-lo, a strong ruler, could use the eunuchs according to their talents and ability without prejudicing his own power as a sovereign. His successors, however, were not so fortunate. They often handed over the power of government to the eunuchs and shut themselves off from outside contact. While they enjoyed the various forms of dissipation within the Forbidden City, the eunuchs ran the government.

The apogee of eunuch power was reached during the reign of Ming Hsi-tsung (1621–1627) when the head eunuch was a man named Wei Chung-hsien. Wei was described as a listless loafer during his boyhood, and he reportedly castrated himself in a sudden burst of emotion after he had lost a great deal in gambling. Subsequently selected for service in the imperial palace, he ingratiated himself to the wet nurse of the crown prince. When the crown prince, a boy of fifteen, ascended the throne as Ming Hsi-tsung, he showed his gratitude to his former nurse by appointing her friend Wei to high offices in the government. Though an illiterate who could not even write his own name, Wei was a shrewd, crafty man with an extraordinary memory. When it became clear that he was the emperor's favorite who could dispense favors, all officials, high and low, sought his patronage and competed to join "the eunuch's clique." As his power increased, he rewarded and punished government officials in accordance with their loyalty to him. Meanwhile, he kept the young emperor happy and content with "prostitutes, entertainers, good horses, and fast hounds." At the height of his power, all high-ranking officials, from cabinet ministers to provincial governors, were his personal followers, and no man could hold office long if he were considered the eunuch's enemy. Many governors, only too eager to please the new strong man, launched a shameless movement of temple building to honor the "grand" eunuch. The building of temples to honor great men of the past such as Confucius and Chu Hsi was a common practice in China, but to build temples to honor a contemporary was a rare occurrence. The temples of Wei Chunghsien went up all over China; in Confucian temples sometimes the "grand" eunuch's name was placed side by side with that of Confucius. Of course, not all gentry scholars joined "the eunuch's clique." Those who opposed the "grand" eunuch formed their own clique called Tung-lin, named after an academy at Wusih (Kiangsu province) where many of the anti-eunuch Confucian scholars taught. But as long as the emperor placed confidence in eunuch Wei, there was nothing these Tung-lin members could do. It was not until 1627 when Ming Hsi-tsung died that the eunuch's political machine finally collapsed.

What made eunuch rule particularly objectionable was that whenever it occurred, it was inevitably accompanied by nepotism and corruption. Most of the eunuchs were either illiterate or poorly educated. Usually they came from families of dubious background, for obviously no decent family would allow its members to pursue the career of a eunuch. The lack of education may be responsible for the fact that, as a group, they were the most unprincipled in Chinese politics. To them power and wealth were an end, not a means. They had no interest in national welfare; nor could they stand political opposition. They rated government officials according to their loyalty rather than their performance and, as a result, the incompetent and morally degenerate occupied the key positions in the government. These people had no other desire except to stay in power and to enrich themselves further. Early in the sixteenth century when one of the eunuchs was sentenced to death on the ground that he had "peddled influence, dismissed upright scholars, and conspired to commit treason," he was found to have possessed, among other things, 2.5 million taels of gold and 50 million taels of silver. The confiscated valuables of Wei Chung-hsien were said to have been even larger. Whenever it appeared, eunuch rule was always one of the worst in Chinese history.

However strong it was, eunuch power was basically transitory and unstable because it had no theoretical or constitutional basis. Confucian theorists had always condemned it on principle and denounced eunuchs in power as usurpers. A eunuch might rise quickly, but his power could also collapse at any moment. During the Ming dynasty, for instance, a eunuch could enjoy power as long as he enjoyed the emperor's confidence. The withdrawal of favor meant not only political oblivion but very likely death as well. Most of the Ming eunuchs who had exercised great power died an unnatural death. After an emperor died, his successor invariably found it politically wise to punish the eunuchs severely for real or imaginary crimes they had committed. Wei Chung-hsien, for instance, was forced to hang himself soon after the new emperor Ch'ung-chen ascended the throne.

As the Ming regime declined, nepotism, corruption, and incompetence were found in local as well as the imperial government. The first century of honest and efficient rule was now past. In the provinces, local officials and big landlords often worked together to advance their respective interests. These officials were appointed by and responsible to their bureaucratic superiors, and they could, if they chose, completely ignore local opinion. As long as their superiors were satisfied, there was little the local populace could do, unless they wished to express their grievances in a violent manner such as riots and revolt. These officials could hardly be expected to be virtuous when their superiors in the capital were the even less virtuous eunuchs. The officials enriched themselves as fast as they could and by whatever means they could find before a shift of power in the capital sent them home jobless and powerless. As all government officials were appointed, they, in turn, rewarded their own henchmen with governmental positions within their jurisdiction. When there were no positions, they created new ones. In fact, many officials were paid salaries even though they had nothing in particular to do. In some areas the office of superintendency of rivers was maintained long after such rivers had changed courses and when there were no more rivers to supervise. This expanded, wasteful bureaucracy necessitated higher taxation which placed an additional burden on the taxpayers.

The big landlords, on the other hand, were interested in enlarging their estates. During the Ming dynasty private landholdings of large size were called *chuang-t'ien*, or plantations. Among them the royal plantations (*huang-chuang*) owned by the imperial household were by far the largest. Most plantations were created by royal decree. After the founding of the Ming regime, Chu Yüan-chang rewarded his relatives, generals, and ministers with large tracts of land. His successors followed this practice as a matter of usage. These plantations varied in size, from 100 *ch'ing* (c. 1,500 acres) to sometimes 7,000 *ch'ing* (c. 105,900 acres). Once they were created, they were often enlarged by illegal or pseudo-legal methods. Farmers who owned land adjacent to the plantations were often "persuaded" to sell their holdings at lower than market prices to the plantation owners. If they refused to be "persuaded," the plantation managers might decide to use force to evict them from their holdings. To bring complaints before the law was often worse than useless because local officials were in no position to challenge the authority of plantation owners and could only do so at their own peril. With odds heavily against them, small farmers sometimes found it wise to hand over their holdings "voluntarily" to the big landlords without asking for compensation, once they knew that their powerful neighbors had coveted their land for some time. In other cases their holdings were "offered" to plantation owners as "presents" without their knowledge; apparently someone had forged their names to make such a presentation. It was useless to protest when the plantation owners had already expressed their "gracious appreciation for such generous gifts."

The owners of these big plantations lived in the capital or in other large cities; it was their managers who supervised the operation of their estates in the countryside. These managers were so anxious to produce "good" results that often they employed the most dubious means in achieving them. The managers worked closely with local officials who were expected to support them in their various schemes. Whenever their overt actions aroused public anger, these officials were counted on to minimize legal consequences. In 1489 the Minister of Finance Li Min, in a memorial to the reigning emperor, described the situation as follows:

> Within the capital area there are five royal plantations with a total acreage of 12,800 *ch'ing* (c. 193,860 acres). Besides these, there are 332 plantations with a total acreage of 33,000 *ch'ing* (c. 499,290 acres) owned by royal relatives and eunuchs. Plantation managers and their subordinates hire hoodlums and ruffians to do their bidding. They forcibly take over people's land, extort their money and other valuables, and debauch their wives and daughters. If people dare to make the slightest protest, they find themselves being sued on fabricated charges. The sheriff comes to arrest them, and their whole families tremble with fear. This is why people hate the plantation managers to the marrow of their bones.[1]

While plantations represented the largest and perhaps the worst form of land concentration, there were lesser landlords who exercised power and influence in their communities in proportion to the size of their holdings. To be sure, not all landlords were ruthless exploiters; nor were all

---

[1] Translated from the official *History of the Ming* (*Ming shih*). This passage appears in the first section of *Economics* (*Shih-huo chih*) dealing with land tenure.

government officials corrupt. The truth seems to be that as members of the gentry class most of the landlords tried to live up to their reputation as respectable community leaders. They supposedly set moral examples for their peasant neighbors and perhaps most of them did. However, in a country where there was a large population in proportion to the amount of land suitable for cultivation, land concentration intensified the contrast between the rich and the poor, for whatever was gained by one person had to be the loss of somebody else. As bureaucratic corruption became more widespread, small and tenant farmers found an increasingly unsympathetic or even hostile government unresponsive to their complaints. The few government officials who chose to champion their cause could only do so at the risk of their own positions. The Lower Yangtze basin was one of the richest areas in China, but early in the seventeenth century taxes were so heavy that sometimes small, independent farmers "have to sell their children to meet tax payments. When they still cannot pay the amount due, they desert their farmsteads, and their farms are left behind in waste. Meanwhile, the amount of tax due on these farms is piled up year after year." The lot of tenant farmers was even worse. According to Ku Yen-wu, a famous scholar who lived towards the end of the Ming dynasty, nine out of every ten farmers in the Lower Yangtze region were tenant farmers. He described their life as follows:

> The fields they till are small in size. In assessing land for tax purposes, the government considers all ditches and roads that run through the farm as taxable areas. A tenant farmer reaps one harvest each year in the fall and collects anywhere from 1 to 3 piculs of unpolished grain for each mou of land. From this amount he pays his landlord anywhere from 8 pecks (0.8 piculs) to 1.3 piculs as rent. He works hard all year round, and a considerable time is devoted to the collection of human and animal waste to be used for fertilizers. His cash expenses for each mou of cultivated land are about one string of cash. Thus after the expenses are deducted, his harvest amounts to less than 1 picul per mou. It is not unusual that after his rent is paid today, he has to beg for food tomorrow.[1]

THE DOWNFALL

In 1628 when the last Ming emperor Ch'ung-chen ascended the throne, the regime had deteriorated to such an extent that nothing except a miracle could reverse the trend. Ch'ung-chen was one of the better emperors, conscientious and hard-working, but he could not stop the accelerating decline of the Ming regime. No sooner was he proclaimed emperor than he heard of a dreadful famine in Shensi province. One of the memorials he read described the situation as follows:

[1] Translated from *Jih-chih lu* or *The Daily Accumulated Knowledge*, roll 10.

Your humble servant was born in Anse subprefecture, Shensi province. I have read many memorials submitted by Your Majesty's officials in connection with the present state of affairs. They say that famine has caused fathers to desert their children and husbands to sell their wives. They also say that many people are so starved that they eat grass roots and white stones. But the real situation is worse than what they have described. Yenan, the prefecture from which your humble servant comes, has not had any rain for more than a year. Trees and grasses are all dried up. During the eighth and the ninth lunar months of last year people went to the mountains to collect raspberries which were called grain but actually were no better than chaff. They tasted bitter and they could only postpone death for the time being. By the tenth lunar month all raspberries were gone, and people peeled off tree bark for food. Among tree bark the best was that of the elm. This was so precious that to consume as little as possible people mixed it with the bark of other trees to feed themselves. Somehow they were able to prolong their lives. Towards the end of the year the supply of tree bark was exhausted, and they had to go to the mountains to dig up stones as food. Stones were cold and tasted musty. A little taken in would fill up the stomach. Those who took stones found their stomachs swollen and they dropped and died in a few days. Others who did not wish to eat stones gathered as bandits. They robbed the few who had some savings, and when they robbed, they took everything and left nothing behind. Their idea was that since they had to die either one way or another it was preferable to die as a bandit than to die from hunger and that to die as a bandit would enable them to enter the next world with a full stomach. . . .[1]

While starved peasants in northern Shensi ravaged the countryside in search of food, garrison soldiers in South Manchuria and Shensi mutinied because they had not been paid for a long time. To make the situation worse, the government decided in 1629 to cut down some of its administrative expenses by reducing the number of coolie couriers in Shansi and Shensi provinces. These coolie couriers, employed by government posts in carrying mails, were suddenly without jobs, and they too decided to join the rebels. In the same year the Manchus moved southward to attack Peking. Responding to the call from the imperial government for help, the governors from Shansi, Suiyuan, and Kansu led their soldiers eastward, only to see them mutiny on the road before they could reach the capital. These soldiers, like those of the Shensi and Manchuria garrisons, had not been paid for some time and they refused to obey any more orders. Thus the rebellion, first started by bands of starved peasants, was quickly joined by unemployed coolie couriers and soldier mutineers. The number of rebels continued to grow as other dissatisfied elements joined them en masse.

Early in the 1630's Chang Hsien-chung and Li Tzu-ch'eng emerged as the two leaders of the rebel forces. Both were born in Shensi, had a

---

[1] A copy of the Chinese original can be found in Chou Ku-ch'eng, *A History of China* (*Chung-kuo t'ung-shih*) (Shanghai, 1947), vol. 2, pp. 880–881.

common peasant background, and had received little or no education. Before the rebellion Chang was a mercenary soldier, and Li was first a coolie courier and then a Buddhist monk. Both had been once sentenced to death on account of crimes or alleged crimes and managed to escape through some devious methods. When the starving peasants began to revolt in 1628, Li was among the first to join them. Chang joined two years later after he had collected a small following. From 1628 to 1635 the rebels were most active in the Northwest, though occasionally they moved eastward to Honan and Hupeh and southward to Szechuan. In the latter year rebel forces had snowballed to more than 400,000, and at the suggestion of Li Tzu-ch'eng their leaders decided to move eastward to contend for all of China. Government troops that were sent against them retreated or otherwise dispersed before the marauding hordes. City after city surrendered without a fight, and others were captured after a brief engagement. To encourage surrender, the rebels announced that they would not take away a single life if a city surrendered the day they arrived. However, if it chose to defend itself for one day, 30 percent of the city's population would be put to death; 70 percent would be killed if it were defended for two days; and the entire city would be destroyed if it hesitated for more than three days before opening its gates. Among the things they looted they kept for themselves horses and arms; food, cloth, and money were generously distributed among starving peasants. They promised to abolish taxation forever if they won. And many peasants believed in them.

The rebel ranks soon split into two groups. One group led by Li Tzu-ch'eng ravaged the Yellow River basin; the other, led by Chang Hsien-chung, moved up and down the Yangtze River valley, killing and burning as it went. Chang Hsien-chung was one of the most bloodthirsty persons ever recorded in Chinese history and was said to have felt uncomfortable if he did not see somebody killed each day. His favorite targets were the Ming nobility, the bureaucrats, and the intellectuals. In one instance, he called students to take his civil service examinations, but when they arrived, he ordered all of them to be slaughtered in cold blood. His generals were rated according to the number of people they had killed; some of his generals were sentenced to death simply because they had not killed enough to meet the norm. In Chengtu, Szechuan province, there stands a monument believed to have been erected by Chang Hsien-chung. The monument bears the following inscriptions:

> Heaven produces myriads of things to nourish man;
> Man never does one good to recompense Heaven.
> Kill, kill, kill, kill, kill, kill, and kill!

It seems that he sought neither fame nor wealth, but the power to destroy. In one case, he dammed a river and placed millions of dollars' worth of gold, silver, and precious stones on the dried river bed, and then ordered the dam be broken so that all these valuables would be washed away towards the sea. Why did he do this? Because, said he, he wanted these valuables to be denied to posterity. From 1630 when he joined the rebels to 1646 when he was finally captured, millions of innocent people died victims of this psychopath. The most devastated area was Szechuan which at one time was said to have "few" people left. When the Manchus marched towards Szechuan, many people looked to them as their saviors. In 1646 one of Chang's generals deserted him and led the Manchus to his stronghold. Chang was wounded by a flying arrow and the pursuing Manchus found him hidden underneath a pile of firewood in a small village. He was captured and subsequently beheaded.

Equally ferocious but perhaps less brutal was Li Tzu-ch'eng, nick-named "The Dashing King." In the beginning he was no better than other rebels; his hordes plundered, burned, and slaughtered wherever they went. After most of North China was brought under his control, he began to think seriously of being a contender for the Ming throne. He promised to abolish taxation to win the support of peasants and imposed some discipline on his marauding soldiers. His soldiers were no longer allowed to plunder and rape, while money, grain, and cloth which he stole from the rich were handed over to the very poor as relief. In 1643 he declared the establishment of a new regime at Sian (formerly Ch'angan) and organized his government according to the Ming pattern. In the same year his troops entered Peking without encountering much opposition. The last Ming emperor Ch'ung-chen hanged himself on the Coal Mountain behind the Forbidden City, after his wife the empress had committed suicide before him. Fearing that his beloved daughter, the First Princess, would be molested by the rebels if she fell into their hands, he proposed to kill her with a long sword. Sobbing audibly, he said to her: "Why did you have to be born a princess?"

Thus the Ming dynasty came to an end after an existence of 277 years.

INTELLECTUAL AND CULTURAL ACTIVITIES

Though he distrusted intellectuals and often subjected them to public humiliation, Chu Yüan-chang knew that he needed educated men to staff his bureaucracy and assist him in running his empire. In 1375 he ordered the establishment of a nation-wide school system. Schools were to be established in every prefecture and subprefecture, and their maintenance would be subsidized by the government. To enroll in one of these schools, a prospective student had to be a relative of a government official. If he were not, he had to possess additional qualifications: he must be over the age of fifteen, had to show promise as a scholar, and must already have mastered the *Four Books*. The same decree also called for the establishment of village schools, "one in every thirty-five households," though we have no idea how effectively this was carried out. These village schools taught the fundamentals: reading and writing, simple mathematics, and Confucian morality. Students who had shown promise as scholars would be encouraged to continue their education in nearby cities. Besides the government-sponsored schools, there were also private institutions supported by high officials, big landlords, or sometimes rich merchants. There were more than three hundred private academies (*shu-yüan*) in the country, and generally speaking, they were of a better quality than government-sponsored schools. To attend school was, of course, not compulsory. A child of wealthy parents was more likely to be tutored at home, and often his teacher was a disappointed, unsuccessful candidate in the civil service examinations. Tutoring provided the most intensive training and was preferred by parents if they had the financials means, because tutors, in most cases, roomed and boarded in the houses of their employers and had daily contact with their charges. Sometimes two or three families pooled their resources and jointly hired a tutor.

The decisive moment arrived when the student took the lowest level of the civil service examination. According to the Ming practice, a student had to pass the preliminary examination in his subprefecture (*hsien,* sometimes translated as "district" or "county") first before he could take the lowest level of the civil service examination which was held twice every three years in the capital city of a prefecture (*fu*). If he passed the prefectural examination, he received the degree *hsiu-ts'ai* ("flowering talent") which qualified him to take the preliminary test for the second level of the civil service examination. The second level of the civil service examination was held in the provincial capital once every three years, and the successful candidate was called a *chü-jen* ("recommended man"). Only a *chü-jen* was eligible to compete in the imperial or metropolitan examination which, like the provincial examination, was held triennially. Students all over the country gathered in Peking for this occasion, and the successful competitors were awarded the highest degree *chin-shih* ("advanced scholarship"). All *chin-shih* were personally interviewed by the emperor who, after the interview, would decide the order of the top candidates. The person whose name was placed at the head of the list was called *chuang-yüan* ("number one"), the highest goal of every scholar in the nation. He and his fellow *chin-shih* were entitled to appointment to governmental posts. Without much modification, the examination system described above was followed throughout the Ming-Ch'ing period.

Most of the successful candidates in the imperial examinations could look forward to governmental careers on the lower levels of the bureaucracy, and they were sent out to various parts of the empire to be "fathers and mothers" of the people. A selected few who had shown great talent and originality would be appointed as research fellows in the nation's highest academic institution, the Hanlin ("Forest of Culture") Academy. The origin of this institution can be traced back to the T'ang dynasty, but it was not until the Sung dynasty that it was perfected as a purely academic institution. Under the Sung the research fellows were not assigned any particular task to perform; rather, they were paid to read or write whatever they pleased. The institution was referred to by contemporaries as a "talent reservoir" from which, it was hoped, the greatest and ablest ministers would eventually emerge. Generally speaking, the Ming regime followed the Sung precedent with regard to the purpose and functions of the Hanlin Academy, though from time to time the Hanlin scholars would be called to perform such "practical" tasks as drafting decrees for the imperial government or giving counsel on historical precedents. They could also take the initiative to petition the emperor with regard to policy, and in that case they became actively involved in politics. Oftentimes, a government official was assigned to the academy as a research fellow when there was no appropriate opening suited for his talent. When he was given a post to hold, he could expect higher rank and a more responsible position compared to those ordinarily awarded to *chin-shih* scholars. After Yung-lo became the emperor, he enlarged the Hanlin Academy by creating the position of "research associates" (*shu-chi-shih*). As their title implied, the research associates did not command the same prestige as the research fellows. They were chosen from the *chin-shih* scholars who did not score high in the metropolitan examinations. The Hanlin Academy remained the nation's highest academic institution throughout the Ming-Ch'ing period.

As for intellectual achievements, the Ming dynasty lagged behind its more illustrious predecessors, Han, T'ang, and Sung. It did not produce great thinkers of originality with the possible exception of Wang Shou-jen (also known as Wang Yang-ming, 1472–1529). Wang, a holder of the *chin-shih* degree, had a distinguished career as a government official, but he was most famous for his philosophy of "innate knowledge" (*liang-chih*). He maintained that all knowledge existed within one's inner self and that it could not be obtained by investigating outward things. To seek knowledge outside oneself was to place the cart before the horse and was useless and futile, because there could not be any truth if one's mind did not exist. He only needed to look at his own inner mind to obtain the absolute truth, and if his inner mind were rectified, the truth of the outside world would reveal itself. He, in fact, was the center of all truths, and "all things are complete within me." To find truth and knowledge was therefore to find oneself. How to find oneself? He needed to investigate his inner mind and concentrate his thought, and the truth of the universe would ultimately come to him through a sudden flash of insight. He and the universe would then become one, a single entity inseparable.

This sounds like Ch'an Buddhism; in fact, Wang Shou-jen was perhaps influenced by it. However, the truth in Wang's philosophy was not a metaphysical truth as it was in Buddhism; it was a moral truth as it had been advocated for centuries by Confucian scholars. Using Buddhist tools, Wang attempted to achieve an essentially Confucian purpose. To him, knowledge and truth were not ends by themselves. They should lead to right conduct, conduct that would benefit one's fellow men. To use his own words, "Knowledge is merely the beginning of conduct; conduct is the completion of knowledge." Knowledge was meaningless and useless without conduct. In other words, the acquirement of absolute truth was not the attainment of *nirvana* as it was in Buddhism; it merely equipped the enlightened man with the necessary means to enlighten others. The ultimate purpose was not the salvation of individual souls; it was the betterment of society. Wang did not advocate escape from the physical world; on the contrary, he urged people to go deeper into it. In that sense, his philosophy was worldly and humanistic; it was basically Confucian. It was similar to the doctrine that had been expounded earlier by the Sung scholar Lu Chiu-yüan. In fact, this philosophy of emphasizing "innate knowledge" has been referred to as the Lu-Wang School by historians.

Unlike Wang Shou-jen, most Ming scholars were busy with less abstract work, commenting, editing, and compiling existing works. In terms of influence on later generations, few works of the Ming period were more important than *The Outline of Herb Medicine* (*Pen-ts'ao kang-mu*) edited and compiled by Li Shih-chen. Since its completion in 1578, it has been the basic text in the hands of every Chinese doctor who practices the traditional medicine. Remarkable as Li was, the authors of the official *History of the Ming* (*Ming shih*, compiled under the the Manchu government's sponsorship and completed in 1739) devoted only a few paragraphs to him, even though his book had perhaps saved more lives than any other Ming scholar or statesman ever did. His brief appearance in the dynastic history shows the traditional antiscience bent, and to traditional historians the moralists who taught people how to live were always more important than the scientists who taught people how to live longer. According to this brief biography, Li Shih-chen consulted more than 800 existing works, checked and rechecked their possible errors, and worked thirty years before his work was completed. The final work consisted of 16 volumes of 52 rolls. It listed 1,932 different animal, vegetable, and mineral drugs and more than 8,000 prescriptions. All drugs were classified and itemized; each of them was accompanied by an illustration, with detailed information on its origin, color, shape, and smell. It was the most complete medical work China had ever produced.

A POET WANDERING IN
THE MOONLIGHT This
picture was painted by
Tu Chin, who lived in
the fifteenth century.
The Chinese characters
in the picture are a
seven-character poem
written by the painter
to describe the scene.
A typical seven-charac-
ter poem has four lines,
each consisting of seven
characters. These lines
are rarely separated,
however; nor are punc-
tuation marks used.

Monumental though it was, *The Outline of Herb Medicine* was a small work compared with the gigantic *Yung-lo Encyclopedia* (*Yung-lo ta-tien*). The compilation of this encyclopedia began in 1403 under the sponsorship of the emperor Yung-lo and was completed four years later. It consisted of all major works in Confucian classics, history, philosophy, and miscellaneous subjects, totalling 22,877 rolls and involving the work of 2,316 scholars. Originally, the government planned to print it, but abandoned its project when the estimated cost proved to be too great. Consequently, only three hand-written copies were made; two were housed in Peking and one in Nanking. The compilation of the *Encyclopedia* was by far the largest literary project ever undertaken by the Ming government.

In the field of fine arts the Ming dynasty was most famous for its painters. Among the painters one of the best known was T'ang Yin who lived in Soochow (modern Kiangsu) early in the sixteenth century. Proclaimed a true genius by his contemporaries, he nevertheless decided to forego a governmental career after he had passed the provincial level of the civil service examination and chose a life of "wine, women, and song" instead. His numerous antics included the impersonation of a humble servant to seek employment in a gentleman's house so that he could be close to a maid whose beauty he greatly admired. He achieved what he had set out to achieve and cared not what other people thought of his personal life. Interestingly enough, his "improper conduct" was dismissed by many of his contemporaries as an unavoidable attribute of a true genius who happened to be a libertine by nature. Though he was described as a prolific painter to whose door "people of all walks of life come daily to beg for paintings," only a few of his paintings have survived. The other famous painter was Tung Ch'i-ch'ang (d. 1636) who, unlike T'ang Yin, lived a virtuous, Confucian life for 83 years and had a distinguished career as a government official. Besides, he was a historian, a calligrapher, and above all, a painter. According to the official *History of the Ming*, even a short note of his was a collector's item, eagerly sought after in the open market and commanding a high price. As a painter, he first followed the style of the Sung painter Mi Fei and eventually established an independent style of his own. He specialized in landscape, and his landscapes were said to have synthesized the best of all paintings since the Sung dynasty. To many of his contemporaries, he was the greatest painter of the Ming dynasty, surpassing all others, including T'ang Yin.

X

Ch'ing

The Great Wall, originally built in the third century B.C., served as a defense shield against northern nomads throughout most of Chinese history. The eastern end of the Wall was the city Shanhaikuan which occupied a narrow level land between the rising mountains in the west and the Gulf of Pohai in the east. Shanhaikuan, literally translated, means "the Pass between the Mountain and the Sea." The pass was so narrow that those who held it controlled the access to or from Manchuria and, once it was taken by an enemy, the road to Peking would be wide open. To defend Peking, the Chinese had to defend Shanhaikuan at all costs. Early in 1644 when Li Tzu-ch'eng and his rebels entered Peking, the Ming garrison commander at Shanhaikuan was a man named Wu San-kuei. After entering the capital, the rebels captured his father and used him as hostage to demand Wu's surrender. Fearing for his father's life, Wu led his troops westward with the intention of complying with the demand. However, he soon learned that his favorite concubine Ch'en Yüan had been kidnapped by one of the rebel generals, and hating the thought that she was now in the arms of another man, he vowed revenge. Instead of surrendering to the rebels, he returned to Shanhaikuan and decided to fight. Yet he knew that the odds were heavily against him if he fought alone. In desperation he sought help from the Manchus. He opened the Pass between the Mountain and the Sea, and the Manchus poured in. The invited "barbarians" not only defeated Li and his rebels but established a new dynasty in China as well. The new dynasty was Ch'ing which lasted more than two and one-half centuries until 1911.

The Manchus sprang from the same Tungusic stock as the Nuchens who at one time occupied North China and founded the Chin dynasty (1122-1234). Their home was the woodlands in southern and eastern Manchuria, east of the Liao River and west of the Manchuria-Korean border. Their economy was largely pastoral, though centuries of contact with the Chinese had converted a considerable portion of them into sedentary farmers. The conflict between the Chinese and the Tungus began as early as written history began, mostly because both sides coveted the rich, agricultural area in South Manchuria. During the period of Warring States (403–221 B.C.) the northernmost state Yen pushed the Tungus deep into the wooded north and forcibly took over the Liao River basin. After Ch'in's unification of China (221 B.C.) Manchuria was incorporated as part of China and governed as an administrative province. Enticed by the cheap, rich farmland, Chinese immigrants came in increasingly large numbers. However, located on the frontier and surrounded by hostile nomads, South Manchuria was difficult for China to hold. Whenever the central authority in China proper weakened, South Manchuria would be conquered by the Tungus or other non-Chinese tribes. The Tungus annexed it during T'ang's decline in the eighth century and created a new kingdom called P'o-hai (713–926). At its height, P'o-hai's territory covered southern and eastern Manchuria and the northeastern corner of Korea. Throughout the Sung dynasty South Manchuria was a part of the Khitan empire of Liao and then a part of the Tungusic empire of Chin. During the Yüan dynasty practically everyone in Asia was either directly or indirectly under the Mongol rule, including the Chinese in South Manchuria and the various Tungusic tribes such as the Manchus.

Thus, after the eighth century South Manchuria had been continuously under non-Chinese rule, and it was not brought under Chinese jurisdiction until the Ming dynasty when again the Chinese extended their military might north of the Great Wall. Chinese immigration to South Manchuria was revived, and the land-hungry Chinese peasants opened the virgin forests as eagerly as their countrymen had done before the eighth century. As the Chinese relentlessly pushed forward the frontier of agriculture, they ran into difficulty with the non-Chinese tribes who naturally wished to keep these wooded areas as their pastoral preserve. This difficulty was further compounded by other problems involving trade. The non-Chinese tribes in Manchuria were not economically self-sufficient, and they needed trade to obtain agricultural products from the Chinese. Realizing their need, the Chinese government often used trade as a political weapon; it suspended or threatened to suspend trade whenever it thought that "the barbarians had behaved in an outrageous manner." As trade was officially supervised, Chinese officials were in a position to regulate price, and prices of foreign products were often artificially depressed to the disadvantage of tribal traders. Moreover, tariff duties imposed on imported and exported merchandise were heavy and unspecified. This uncertainty of tariff levies provided a flourishing ground for the growth of corruption on the part of Chinese officials.

Whatever injustices the Ming government might have done to the Manchus and other non-Chinese tribes in Manchuria, it could always make its will prevail as long as it remained militarily strong. It could no longer do so when its military strength declined during the second half of the sixteenth century. The Ming government, like many of its predecessors, incorporated South Machuria as a part of China. As Ming's military strength declined, South Manchuria became more and more a military liability since it was surrounded on three sides by hostile non-Chinese tribes and was linked to China proper largely through the narrow pass of Shanhaikuan. Logistical support became extremely difficult if the enemy could somehow cut off the normal supply line along the northern shore of the Pohai Gulf. During the second half of the sixteenth century the Chinese settlements in the Liao River basin were subject to increasing pressure from the surrounding nomads who raided and ravaged whenever these settlements were inadequately defended. Often the Ming government retaliated by suspending trade with the offending tribes, only to see the raids become more frequent and more intensified because the enemy, denied trade to obtain what he needed, resorted to more violent means to achieve his purpose. Early in the seventeenth century the government found that it could no longer defend all Chinese settlements in South Manchuria, and those located on its fringe and close to the nomadic areas had to be abandoned. Whenever the settlers refused to leave, they were forcibly evicted and resettled in more defensible regions. The abandoned areas were soon taken over by the non-Chinese tribes.

While the Ming government was making a strategic retreat in South Manchuria, the Manchus rose steadily to take its place. Nominally they were Chinese vassals and as such they were allowed to trade at specifically designated places. Their main exports were horses, lumber, and genseng. The last-mentioned was a herb medicine believed to have the power of rejuvenation and had a large market in China proper. As Ming power declined, the Manchus, like other non-Chinese tribes, found it more profitable to raid than to trade. At the beginning the raids were largely economically motivated, but early in the seventeenth century these desultory raids were coordinated and became part of an over-all strategy aimed at military conquest. This shift took place under the great leader Nurhachi (1559–1626), who succeeded his father as a tribal chief and Chinese vassal in 1584. Secretly preparing his tribe and himself for "the great deed," he tried to avoid Ming's suspicion by performing faithfully all the rituals required of a Ming vassal and by repeatedly sending tribute missions to Peking. At one time (1590) he personally led a tribute mission to pay his homage to the reigning emperor. Little did the Ming government know then that underneath his humble appearance was the burning ambition of a powerful opponent.

While Ming's suspicion was in abeyance, Nurhachi annexed and unified all Manchu tribes under his personal control. He organized his own military machinery through the creation of the "banner" system. The banner system was a politico-military organization to incorporate all Manchu tribesmen into new administrative units (first four and later eight) called banners, and all Manchus, including their captives and slaves, were required to register under assigned banners. Each banner was headed by an appointed official personally loyal to Nurhachi rather than the hereditary tribal chieftains. It was called the banner system because each organizational unit was identified by a banner of a specified color. After the Manchus began to expand and brought non-Manchus under their jurisdiction, sixteen more banners were added, eight Chinese and eight Mongol, making a total of twenty-four. Each banner contributed a certain number of fighting men whenever a Manchu ruler was engaged in war, the number varying in accordance with the purpose and scope of the war efforts. By 1644 when the Manchus began the conquest of China proper, the total number of their fighting men was approximately 170,000.

In 1616 when his preparations were complete, Nurhachi raised the standard of revolt and called his newly created regime Later Chin. Two years later he announced his famous "Seven Grievances" against the Ming regime and declared war. The Ming government retaliated by sending 200,000 men to Manchuria, only to see them decisively defeated by the outnumbered but hard-fighting Manchus. Realizing their relative weakness in fighting pitched battles, later Ming generals adopted the Fabian strategy of building strong fortifications at strategic points and shutting themselves behind these strongholds, hoping to wear out the limited resources of the enemy and eventually to force him to sue for peace. However, the Manchus captured the countryside to isolate these strongholds and in due time were able to capture cities as well, such as Mukden. In

1626 Nurhachi died of battle wounds sustained during an attack on a Ming stronghold and was succeeded by his son Abahai, known also by his posthumous title, Ch'ing T'ai-tsung. Abahai attacked and defeated Korea in 1627 and concluded the war with a peace treaty whereby Korea promised to supply the Manchus with grain and open markets for trade. Korea, in fact, became a Manchu protectorate. With his rear safe and secure, he attacked the Ming fortification Ningyüan but was pushed back with heavy losses. With the resources of all China at its disposal, it seemed that the Ming regime could have held South Manchuria indefinitely had it not deteriorated so fast at home.

After 1628 and for almost two decades the regime was beset with nation-wide rebellions. It could no longer concentrate its efforts on the Manchurian campaign. The situation was not helped when it executed some of its ablest generals whenever they suffered a temporary setback. Summary punishments like this inadvertently helped the enemy's cause; several Ming generals surrendered to the enemy because they no longer felt safe. In 1634 the Manchus completed the conquest of Inner Mongolia, and thus the entire northern frontier was subject to the Manchus' direct attack. Two years later (1636) the Manchus changed their dynastic title from Later Chin to Ch'ing. With their rear safely secured, they repeatedly entered China proper and at one time (1638) went as far as Shantung province and captured its capital Tsinan. They withdrew only when they had obviously overextended themselves. Many Chinese generals, tempted by Manchus with offers of higher positions and more responsibilities, voluntarily surrendered; two such generals brought with them Portuguese cannons which greatly facilitated the capture of Ming's walled cities. From the point of morale, the most damaging surrender was that of Hung Ch'eng-ch'ou who had under his command some 130,000 troops at one time. An upright statesman and scholar, he was expected to commit suicide when his army was defeated and he himself was captured. When the news arrived at Peking that he had surrendered to the enemy, the shock was greater than any reverse the Ming regime had suffered. In the minds of many Chinese a man like him symbolized the "national spirit," and when he surrendered, the nation's morale and pride were damaged beyond repair.

In 1643 Abahai died and was succeeded by his six-year-old son Shunchih (1644–1661). Abahai's brother Dorgon (1612–1650) served as regent. One year later the Ming general Wu San-kuei surrendered Shanhaikuan to the Manchus. Rebel Li Tzu-ch'eng fled westward to Sian and the Imperial City fell into the hands of the Manchus. Once again China was ruled by an alien regime.

However, it took many more years before China was completely pacified. In South China the Ming loyalists continued to fight and installed various members of the royal house as claimants to the Ming throne.

There were Prince Fu at Nanking, Prince Lu at Chekiang, Prince T'ang at Fukien, and Prince Kuei at Kwangtung. But the resistance movement was neither coordinated nor effective. The Manchus pushed relentlessly southward, and their Chinese generals such as Hung Ch'eng-ch'ou and Wu San-kuei paved the way as vanguards. In the spring of 1645 the victorious Manchus passed across the Yangtze River and captured Nanking. In the next year the resistance movement centered at Fukien also collapsed. The last claimant to the Ming throne, Prince Yung-ming, moved from Kwangtung to Kwangsi and then to Yunnan, always with a pursuing enemy behind him. In 1659 he escaped to Burma where he established a government-in-exile for two years. The Burmese, fearing that the Manchus might use his presence in Burma as an excuse to invade their country, attacked and captured him and handed him over to the Manchu garrison commander across the border. He was subsequently hanged, and the Ming line was thus exterminated.

CONSOLIDATION AND EXPANSION

In less than three generations a small tribe succeeded in conquering and imposing its rule on the largest nation on earth. How was the success to be explained? First, the Manchus rose at the propitious moment of Ming's decline. Early in the seventeenth century all the classic features indicating the approaching of the dynasty's downfall were in evidence: feeble and effeminate rulers, a corrupt bureaucracy, incompetence and factional strife among government officials, natural disasters, and finally internal rebellions. If the Manchus had not replaced the Ming regime, it was likely that some other foreigners or internal rebels would. On the other hand, the fact that it was the Manchus and not any other group who succeeded in overthrowing the Ming regime spoke eloquently of their intrinsic strength. When Nurhachi succeeded his father as a tribal chief in 1584, he is believed to have had no more than five or six hundred fighting men under his control. With these men as a nucleus he built a strong military machine which enabled him to start his career of conquest. Among the many factors that contributed to the Manchus' spectacular success, none was more important than the fact that they had a long string of capable leaders. Nurhachi was succeeded by the equally able Abahai. After Abahai died, it was fortunate that Dorgon—the Conqueror of China—served as regent while the boy emperor Shun-chih was a minor. This string of capable leaders extended long after China had been conquered. The three emperors after Shun-chih, in the order of succession, were K'ang-hsi, Yung-cheng and Ch'ien-lung. It was during their reigns that the Ch'ing dynasty reached its most glorious age. Thus for six consecutive generations, one able emperor followed another. This had not happened to any other dynasty in the course of Chinese history.

All the early Ch'ing emperors realized that to conquer China and to rule it successfully, they had first, to adopt Chinese culture and Chinese institutions, and second, to win the support of the Chinese population, especially that of the scholar-gentry class. The banner system, first introduced by Nurhachi, was essentially an adaptation of a bureaucratic system to tribal conditions, and as such, there was no difficulty in utilizing it within agrarian China, once the Manchus had conquered Chinese territories. Nurhachi ordered the translation of Confucian works and Ming penal codes into his newly invented Manchu alphabet and adopted Chinese institutions to suit his own purpose. This voluntary Sinicization was continued by his successors. The dynastic title was the Sinicized word Ch'ing (pure), and all Manchu rulers assumed, and were given posthumously, Chinese titles. Chinese scholars were invited to staff the Ch'ing bureaucracy, and Chinese generals were encouraged to surrender. Once they surrendered, they were given higher or better positions in the new government. Sometimes the same generals who had suffered repeated defeats under the Ming regime performed remarkably well once they switched their loyalty and fought for the Manchus. Some of the most famous field commanders who conquered China for the Manchus were Chinese, such as Hung Ch'eng-ch'ou, Wu San-Kuei, Keng Chung-ming, and Shang K'o-hsi. All of them had served the Ming government at one time or another. The decaying Ming could not use fully their talents, but the young, vigorous Ch'ing regime could.

Fortunately for the new dynasty, it had a wise, intelligent statesman to give it direction during the most crucial years after it had entered China proper. He was Dorgon (1612–1650), fourteenth son of Nurhachi and uncle of the reigning emperor Shun-chih. He was learned in Confucian ideals and Chinese institutions, and one of the letters, addressed to a Ming general, that bore his name can still be found, as an example of literary excellence, in many Chinese textbooks. His whole regime was Chinese orientated. The administrative apparatus of the defunct Ming government was adopted without much modification, and Ch'ing regarded itself as the legitimate heir to Ming which, it believed, had lost the mandate of Heaven. After the Manchus' entry into China proper, Dorgon, on behalf of the boy emperor, adopted a series of measures aimed at winning Chinese support. All incumbents of the old regime were encouraged to stay on their jobs and could expect to be promoted by one rank if they voluntarily surrendered themselves to the victorious Manchu army. Local officials were requested to recommend men of wisdom and ability to serve the new regime, and no questions would be asked about their past loyalties. Taxes were to be reduced and all extra levies besides the regular tax load were to be thereafter abolished. The new government vowed to punish severely all incompetent and corrupt officials, and the inspector-generals and censors were instructed to personally visit the populace "to inquire about their sicknesses and sorrows." The Manchus were forbidden to behave like conquerors and to use their privileged position to violate the law and enrich themselves. This policy of winning Chinese support worked well and yielded good results. When the Chinese were ordered to shave part of their heads to indicate their loyalty to the new regime, all Chinese except the staunch Ming loyalists complied. By winning Chinese support, the Manchus, who constituted no more than 2 percent of the population in China, were able to maintain themselves in China for almost three hundred years.

The general cooperation on the part of the Chinese population enabled the Ch'ing government to crush two simultaneous, though not coordinated, rebellions. The leader of the first rebellion was Wu San-kuei who in 1644 had opened Shanhaikuan to lead the Manchus into China proper, and who, together with other Chinese collaborators, was responsible for the elimination of Chinese resistance. The Manchus rewarded him lavishly, awarding him the title of prince and marrying one of the Manchu princesses to his son. He was made a virtual dictator in China's Southwest. He recruited his own bureaucratic personnel, maintained his own army, and strengthened his domains economically by establishing mining and trade monopolies. Meanwhile, the central treasury at Peking subsidized him with a yearly amount of nine million taels of silver.

As his power and wealth increased, he became more arrogant and indiscreet. Obviously this situation could not last indefinitely. In 1673 the Ch'ing government decided to take away his command and ordered him to leave for Manchuria to live in retirement. Facing the prospect of political oblivion, he raised the standard of revolt. He persuaded two other governors-general (one at Kwangtung and another at Fukien) to join his revolt because these two governors-general had also enjoyed a semi-independent status and had been ordered to leave their command. At one time more than one-third of China proper fell into the rebels' hands and rebel influence extended from Kwangtung and Fukien in the Southeast to Kansu and Shensi in the Northwest. But slowly and steadily the Ch'ing government fought back. After Wu San-kuei died in 1678, the rebellion soon collapsed.

Why did this happen? First, the majority of the Chinese population, especially the scholar-gentry class, were on the side of the existing government and against the rebels. The regime was young and vigorous and there was a rising prosperity. The Chinese were in no mood for another change. Second, the cause of nationalism which Wu and his fellow rebels invoked to rationalize their revolt was no longer a valid issue because most Chinese had accepted the new dynasty as legitimately Chinese.

Furthermore, it was not convincing because all of the three rebel leaders had once served and then betrayed the Chinese Ming regime and had led the way to the conquest of China by their Manchu masters. As far as most Chinese were concerned, they should be the last ones to advocate Chinese nationalism.

The other rebellion was led by a man of higher principle named Cheng Ch'eng-kung or Koxinga (1624–1662). Cheng's father was an ex-pirate who surrendered to Ming in 1627 and, then being made a Ming official, came to control overseas and coastal trade in Fukien province. When the Manchus marched to the Southeast, he surrendered his men and ships to ingratiate himself with the new regime. His son, then a boy of twenty-two, regarded his father's actions as disgraceful and decided to go his own way and follow an independent course. He and his small following pledged themselves to the continuous support of the Ming cause when other Chinese generals with thousands of troops had switched to the winning side and surrendered without a fight. From 1651 to 1659 he ravaged the Chekiang and Fukien coast and turned down all Ch'ing's overtures requesting his surrender. In the latter year he felt strong enough to invade the Lower Yangtze valley. His troops landed on the Shanghai coast, captured Chinkiang and laid siege on Nanking. Many garrisons in South Anhwei responded to his call for revolt and joined the rebels. Peking was alarmed and reinforcements were quickly dispatched southward to stop his advance. With odds greatly against him, he left the Lower Yangtze and returned to Amoy in Fukien. As the Manchus increased their pressure, he and his followers sailed across the Taiwan Strait and reestablished themselves on the island of Taiwan.

Taiwan is an island shaped like a drifting leaf, 150 miles off the coast of Fukien province. It is 250 miles in length and 90 miles in width at its widest point, with a total area of some 13,800 square miles. It is also known as Formosa which means "beautiful" in Portuguese. Early in the Ch'ing dynasty, two major ethnic groups were to be found in this island. The first group was the aboriginal Taiwanese who seemed to be racially related to modern Indonesians. Today the Chinese call them Kao-shan Tsu, or High Mountains People, largely because they live in the mountainous regions on the eastern and central sections of the island. The majority of the inhabitants on Taiwan were in the second group, the Chinese. Financially hard-pressed at home where arable areas were few and small, the Chinese on the Fukien and Kwangtung coast found the Taiwan land irresistible and inviting. Since the first immigration began sometime during the Sui-T'ang period, it was continued throughout succeeding centuries. However, it was not until the sixteenth and the seventeenth centuries that Chinese came to Taiwan in increasingly large numbers. Most of the newcomers were farmers; others were fishermen and traders. The farmers opened up the virgin lands and found them so fertile

that they had no difficulty in raising three crops each year. Soil, temperature, and rainfall were all ideal for a rice economy. In the early 1660's it
was estimated that total acreage of paddy fields was approximately
30,000 acres. This acreage was considerably enlarged during the succeeding decades. For the poverty-stricken Chinese peasants, Taiwan was a
bright new haven indeed.

Loosely organized as a Chinese prefecture and separated from the
mainland by the Taiwan Strait, early in the seventeenth century Taiwan
was successively occupied by Chinese pirates, Japanese traders, and in
1623, Dutch adventurers. Though their interest was largely commercial,
the Dutch promoted agriculture by reducing land tax, constructing irrigation works, and even providing small loans to enable the poorest peasants
to acquire oxen, farm implements, and seeds. Their benevolent rule encouraged even more immigrants from Fukien province. In 1659 Cheng
Ch'eng-kung returned to Amoy, after his unsuccessful attempt to seize the
Lower Yangtze Valley. Two years later, hard pressed by the victorious
Manchus, he decided to take over Taiwan and to use it as the last stronghold to rally all Ming loyalists. After he defeated the Dutch and captured
the island, Cheng turned his energy to the establishment of a new government and invited Chinese scholars to staff it. He opened schools, promoted
the opening-up of virgin fields, and encouraged immigrants from the
mainland. Unfortunately, dissensions soon developed among his successors after his death in 1662. Though the island government continued to
maintain its independence for more than twenty years, it was no longer a
threat to Ch'ing's authority on the nearby mainland. In 1683 the Ch'ing
regime took the offensive, and the last Ming stronghold subsequently
collapsed. Taiwan was incorporated as a Ch'ing prefecture and remained
under Chinese jurisdiction until 1895.

The pacification of China proper was followed by a vigorous policy
of expansion towards the grasslands beyond China's traditional borders.
By now the Ch'ing emperors regarded themselves as Sons of Heaven à la
Chinese, and as such, they thought they should bring all "barbarians"
under their "benevolent" influence. A more important motive, however,
arose from a practical, strategic consideration. Throughout Chinese history the danger to China proper had always come from the grasslands in
the north, and to safeguard China proper, the Chinese believed that they
had to neutralize that danger either directly or indirectly by controlling
part or all of these grasslands. The success story of the Manchus provided
additional weight for this argument. The Manchus, upon becoming rulers
of China, thought along the same lines as the great Chinese emperors of
the past. Before their entry into China proper in 1644, they had succeeded
in subjugating Korea and Inner Mongolia as their protectorates. As their
northeastern frontier was thus comparatively secure, their subsequent ex-
pansions were directed northwestward. In 1697 the emperor K'ang-hsi

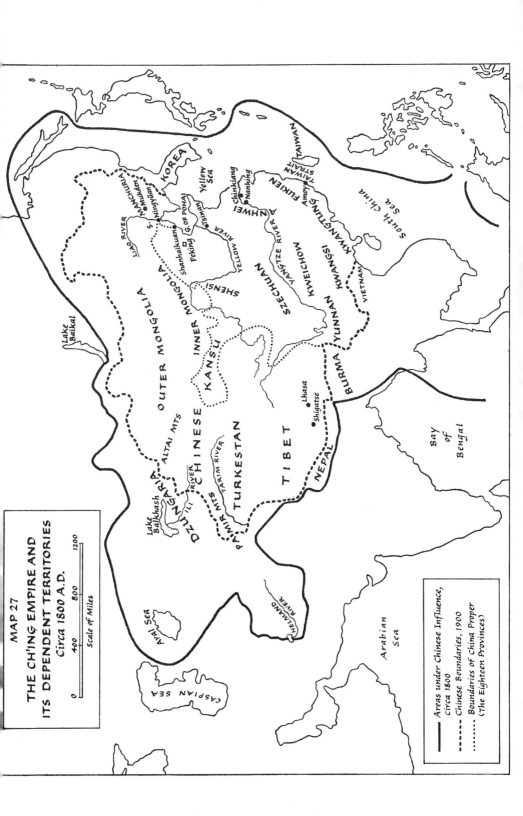

MAP 27
THE CH'ING EMPIRE AND
ITS DEPENDENT TERRITORIES
Circa 1800 A.D.

Scale of Miles

0   400   800   1200

Areas under Chinese Influence,
circa 1800

Chinese Boundaries, 1900

Boundaries of China Proper
(The Eighteen Provinces)

CASPIAN SEA

Aral Sea

Arabian
Sea

Bay
of
Bengal

HELMAND RIVER

NEPAL

Lhasa
Shigatse

TIBET

BURMA

VIETNAM

YUNNAN

KWEICHOW

KWANGSI

KWANGTUNG

South China
Sea

FUKIEN

Amoy

ANHWEI

Nanking

Chinkiang

SZECHUAN

YANGTZE RIVER

SHENSI

KANSU

INNER MONGOLIA

CHINESE
TURKESTAN

DZUNGARIA

PAMIR MTS

TARIM RIVER

ILI RIVER

ALTAI MTS

Lake
Balkhash

OUTER MONGOLIA

Lake
Baikal

MANCHURIA

LIAO RIVER

Mukden

Ningyüan

S.

Shanhaikwan

Peking

G. OF POHAI

Tsinan

YELLOW RIVER

Yellow
Sea

KOREA

TAIWAN

TAIWAN STRAIT

Vietnam

Arabian
Sea

personally led an expeditionary army to Outer Mongolia and in a crucial battle near Urga, the Mongol power was destroyed. Outer Mongolia became a Ch'ing vassalage and remained so throughout the Ch'ing dynasty.

The conquest of the area west of Outer Mongolia, however, turned out to be a long, protracted process. In this area was located the Mongol kingdom of Dzungaria which at its peak of power in the 1670's covered Chinese Turkestan, the Ili River Valley, and the Altai Mountains. In 1697 and again in 1732 the Ch'ing regime sent expeditionary forces to conquer it, but each time the invaders fell short of their desired goal. One generation later when Ch'ien-lung was the emperor, the Manchus made an all-out effort, and after a military campaign of three years (1755–1757), they finally succeeded in conquering this Mongol kingdom. The conquest was accompanied by a ruthless slaughter which practically wiped out the Dzungars. One year after the conquest of the Dzungars, the Muslims in Chinese Turkestan revolted, as if they had never heard what had happened to their neighbors in the north. The rebellion, however, was quickly suppressed. As a result of these operations the Ch'ing regime extended its jurisdiction north of the Ili River basin and west of the Pamir Mountains. The Greater Northwest was incorporated as a part of the Manchu empire.

The Manchu conquest of Tibet, on the other hand, was complicated by a religious factor, Lamaism. Lamaism, originally developed in Tibet, won its largest following during the Yüan dynasty when the Mongols gave it special privileges and extended patronage. The downfall of the Mongol Empire in the fourteenth century did not in any way reduce its influence among the Mongols. Early in the fifteenth century a reform movement took place within the Lamaist church, and the reformers emphasized a more secluded, meditative life as a way to enlightenment. A new sect emerged from the reform movement, known as the Yellow Hat Sect to distinguish it from the older Red Hat Sect. The founder of the new sect, Tsong-kha-pa, died in 1419, but his branch of Lamaism continued to grow. In time his divinity was supposedly divided among two lines of successors, the Dalai Lamas and the Panchen Lamas, the successors to his first and second disciples respectively. Lama succession was achieved through a process called reincarnation; the new Dalai or Panchen Lama was supposedly the reincarnation of the old ones. When a Dalai or Panchen Lama died, a search was made among the newly born, and the wise men of the Lama court would decide, with divine guidance, on the reincarnated Lama. Theoretically both Lamas shared the same degree of divinity, but historically the Dalai Lama had always enjoyed a greater temporal power.

As Lamaism was deeply rooted in Tibetan life, it seemed natural that the Ch'ing government should wish to use the two grand Lamas to achieve its political control. Even before entering into China proper, the

Manchus made useful connections with the fifth Dalai Lama (1617–1662) at Lhasa, and after moving the capital from Mukden to Peking, they invited the grand Lamas to send tribute missions. However, Ch'ing influence in Tibet was then nominal and it amounted to no more than Tibet's recognition of Ch'ing as suzerain. In an attempt to extend their influence in Tibet, the early Ch'ing emperors had to compete with the Dzungars who had a similar design of their own. In 1717 the Dzungars moved in with a strong force, captured Lhasa, and terrorized the country. Ch'ing responded in 1720 when it sent two armies into Tibet and drove out the Dzungars. It installed the seventh Dalai Lama in the Lhasa palace (Potala) and a Ch'ing garrison was left behind to maintain peace and order. The easternmost part of Tibet was incorporated as a part of Szechuan province. The successful intervention of 1720 was followed by similar interventions afterwards. A Tibetan civil war in 1727–1728 brought another Ch'ing expeditionary force whose purpose was to make sure that the pro-Ch'ing faction in the civil war would remain in power. In 1750 the Ch'ing regime intervened again when there was a general breakdown of order following a series of murders of political leaders and a continuous state of anarchy and confusion. After order was finally restored, the emperor Ch'ien-lung let it be known that the Dalai Lama would be the sole temporal ruler and that a council of ministers would be created to advise him on state affairs. His spiritual rival, the Panchen Lama, would remain at Shigatse, located to the west of Lhasa. A Ch'ing garrison would stay in Lhasa permanently to maintain order, and the Dalai Lama, in exercising his state functions, was to seek advice from Ch'ing ministers in residence. Through these devices China was able to maintain its indirect rule in Tibet, which remained a vassal and protectorate throughout the Ching dynasty.

To strengthen its southwestern frontier, the Ch'ing government decided in the 1720's to bring the various minority peoples in Kwangtung, Kwangsi, Kweichow, Szechuan, and Yunnan provinces under direct control. These minorities were often lumped together and called Miao, but there were numerous sub-groups under that term. They lived in the remote, mountainous regions and there was little or no cooperation among the various sub-groups. It was said that their ancestors were driven out from China proper in ancient times by the Chinese, but historians have not been able to prove or disprove this assertion. Throughout the centuries there had been constant clashes between the Chinese and the Miao minorities. Miao revolts occurred from time to time and each time they were suppressed with considerable bloodshed and vengeance. During the Ming dynasty the government succeeded in instituting a system of indirect rule whereby hereditary tribal chieftains were awarded Chinese ranks and titles and were brought under the overall supervision of Chinese governors. Though this system worked fairly well, it prevented Chinese officials from having direct jurisdiction over the Miao people. This lack of direct jurisdiction created considerable difficulties, especially in areas where Chinese and Miao lived side by side. If a Miao committed a crime, Chinese officials could not bring him to justice without his chieftain's approval. Moreover, Chinese governors could not evaluate, promote, or dismiss tribal chieftains according to their performances as they could with Chinese officials. They could only dismiss them at the risk of inviting a rebellion. In 1726 at the suggestion of the Yunnan governor Oh-erh-t'ai, the system of indirect rule was abolished and all minorities were brought under central administration. Officials in charge of Miao territories were appointed by and responsible to their respective governors and could be promoted and dismissed like any other Ch'ing officials. Oh-erh-t'ai was so successful with his work that he was soon promoted to the rank of governor-general in charge of Yunnan, Kweichow, and Kwangsi provinces. By 1731 he had succeeded in extending bureaucratic administration to all minorities in the Southwest.

Beyond the southeastern border, the Vietnamese pledged their allegiance to the Ch'ing regime soon after the Manchus entered China proper. Succeeding Vietnamese kings were awarded titles and honors. Ch'ing's subjection of Burma, on the other hand, encountered difficulties. Two Ch'ing expeditions (one in 1767 and another in 1770) suffered defeat when they ventured into the inhospitable jungle areas of northern Burma. It was not until 1789 that the reigning Burmese king, facing great difficulties at home, decided to surrender and become a Ch'ing vassal.

THE CH'ING EMPERORS

In contrast to the Mongols of the Yüan dynasty who conquered and ruled China through the use of naked military force, the Manchus attempted to base their rule on some form of popular support. It has been mentioned earlier that they made conscientious efforts to Sinicize their regime before they entered China proper. This policy of winning Chinese support was continued after the regime had established itself at Peking. In the imperial government the Chinese shared power and responsibility with their Manchu colleagues. Each of the Six Ministries had two ministers, one Manchu and one Chinese, and four deputy ministers, two Manchu and two Chinese. On the provincial level, while most governors-general were Manchus, the governors were mostly Chinese. The magistrates in charge of prefectures and subprefectures were of course overwhelmingly Chinese. Only in military commandership were the Manchus given priority and preference. The better-trained banner troops were mostly commanded by Manchus, while Chinese commanders had to be satisfied with the militia-like "green battalions." Except for the emperors, who had to be Manchus by virtue of heredity, theoretically there was no limit for the Chinese in ascending the bureaucratic ladder. Rumor even had it that the great emperor Ch'ien-lung was actually Chinese, though the validity of that statement is generally discounted by serious historians. By and large it is safe to say that the Manchus intended to rule China jointly with the Chinese.

To justify their rule in China, the Manchus had to overcome a tremendous ideological difficulty. Many Chinese scholars, invoking the Confucian teaching about the uncompromising "difference between Chinese and barbarians" (Hua yi chih pien), regarded alien rule as an affront to the dignity of the Central Kingdom. This nationalist sentiment was particularly strong in the Yangtze River basin. The three outstanding scholars in this area, Huang Tsung-hsi (1610–1695), Wang Fu-chih (1619–1692), and Ku Yen-wu (1613–1682) all had fought against the Manchus in the past and refused to serve the new regime after it had succeeded in conquering China. It was to the credit of the new regime that these men were left alone to pursue their scholastic interests despite their known antigovernment beliefs. While the government could do nothing to change the opinion of the staunch Ming loyalists, it was very successful with the less staunch ones who were by far in the majority. To be sure, there were occasional purges conducted by the government to eliminate the disloyal elements among the academic ranks, but they were no worse than those conducted by some Chinese emperors in the past such as Chu Yüan-chang.

To combat the sentiment of Ming loyalists about alien rule, the Manchus had to justify their regime in China. In 1727 a plot engineered by a group of Ming loyalists to overthrow the government was discovered and the conspirators were brought to trial. The reigning emperor Yung-cheng decided to use this occasion to refute once and for all the loyalists' contention that barbarians could not rule China and that all Chinese were morally bound to fight against the Manchus. The court proceedings together with the emperor's comments were compiled and published and distributed among Chinese scholars. The book, entitled A Record of Awakening to Great Righteousness (Ta-yi chüeh-mi lu), contained a key document written by Emperor Yung-cheng himself. The document began by saying that sages were not a monopoly of China and that foreign lands would in due time produce their own share of the truly great. In fact, said the document, many Chinese heroes in the past were born in barbarian lands, such as the legendary emperor Shun and the founder of the Chou dynasty King Wen. They were barbarians, but they were hailed in history as legitimate Chinese emperors. The important thing, continued the document, was not a person's birthplace but the possession of a unique "virtue" which entitled him to rule over China. The document implied that by the 17th century the Manchus had already possessed such a virtue.

The first Ch'ing emperors, as we have already said, were men of outstanding ability, especially K'ang-hsi, Yung-cheng, and Ch'ien-lung. K'ang-hsi inherited the throne at the age of seven and ruled China con-

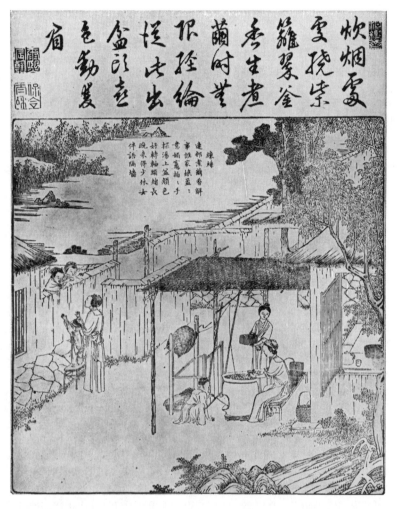

A WOODCUT SHOWING THE PEACEFUL COUNTRY SCENE The women on the right are unreeling silk fibers. On the left a woman and her child chat with their neighbors over a fence. The Chinese characters in the picture are a five-character poem describing the scene. On top of the picture is a seven-character poem believed to have been composed and written by Emperor K'ang-hsi.

secutively for sixty-one years (1661–1722). It was during his reign that the revolt of Wu San-kuei was crushed, Taiwan was incorporated as part of China, Outer Mongolia and Dzungaria were conquered, and Tibet became a Ch'ing vassal and protectorate. However, he was remembered by posterity not only as a great conqueror but also as a conscientious, enlightened monarch. He advanced agriculture by reducing land taxation and by promoting the construction of flood-control and irrigation projects. His policy of limiting the number of Buddhist monks and nuns especially pleased Confucian scholars. A generous patron of education and academic activities, he was an outstanding scholar in his own right. It was said that as a boy K'ang-hsi was so obsessed with book learning that he would not stop reading even when he was dangerously ill, and the habit remained with him throughout his life. He strove to become a Confucian model monarch and set a moral example to his subjects. In an imperial edict issued during his reign and hung on the walls of all schools in China, he commanded his subjects to do the following:

1. Observe filial piety and brotherly love to improve the basic human relations.

2. Respect your clansmen to promote the virtue of concord.

3. Live harmoniously with your fellow villagers to avoid quarrels and lawsuits.

4. Promote agriculture and sericulture to assure an adequate supply of food and clothing.

5. Practice thrift to save expenses.

6. Exalt schools to rectify the conduct of scholars.

7. Discard heretic ideas to strengthen orthodoxism.

8. Be familiar with the law to avoid ignorance and rascality.

9. Be humble and modest to cultivate good customs.

10. Be diligent in your profession to stabilize your will.

11. Warn your children and younger brothers aginst lawless activities.

12. Stop lawsuits to preserve good will.

13. Do not protect lawless elements in order to avoid involvement in conspiracies.

14. Pay your taxes to ward off tax duns.

15. Strengthen the *pao-chia* system to prevent robbery and thievery.

16. Patch up quarrels to protect your own life.

All teachers and students in each school were ordered to assemble twice a month to recite aloud the above edict, once on the first of the month and once on the fifteenth. The edict, called the *Sixteen Sacred Injunctions,* summarized the basic attributes that a Confucian monarch expected from his loyal subjects.

One thing, however, marred the happy tranquility of K'ang-hsi's old age. He had sired thirty-five sons, and as he grew more advanced in age, intrigues developed among his sons as many of them wanted to be designated as his successor. His personal favorite was Yün-jen, the first born son of the empress, who under normal circumstances should have been the crown prince anyway. However, the crown prince became mentally unbalanced, conducting himself in such an unprincely manner as to, among other things, bring in country girls to the Forbidden Palace. Much to his grief, K'ang-hsi found it necessary to depose him as the crown prince. After that, intrigues and feuds among his numerous sons became even more intensified. It was not until 1722 when he was on his death bed that he finally decided on his fourth son who, after accession, was known by his reign title Yung-cheng.

In contrast to his father who was known as being tolerant and lenient, Yung-cheng was strict and harsh. To prevent any challenge to his authority, he threw several of his brothers into prison, where they eventually died, and their supporters were liquidated *en masse.* He placed informers and spies in both the palace and the government to warn him in advance of any plot or conspiracy. Remembering well the fraternal strife involving the designation of a crown prince during his father's reign, he refused to let his choice of successor be known while he was living. In the very first year that he became the emperor, he secretly wrote down the name of his successor and placed it in two sealed envelopes, one kept in the Outer Court and the other in the Inner Court. Nobody else knew the designated successor, and he ordered that these envelopes should not be opened until immediately after his death. In 1735 when he died, the court officials opened the envelopes and found the name of his fourth son who, after accession, was known as Ch'ien-lung.

Despite his suspicious nature, Yung-cheng was an able, conscientious, and just ruler. He was shrewd in the management of the nation's finance, impartial in his selection of government officials, and rewarded and punished in accordance with his subordinates' performances. Under him were some of the ablest governors of the Ch'ing dynasty, such as Governor-general Oh-erh-t'ai of Yunnan-Kweichow-Kwangsi provinces. To concentrate imperial power in his hands, he created a new organ called the Privy Council (*Chün-chi ch'u*) which formulated governmental policy under his personal command, bypassing the regular government apparatus. He personally read all important documents and rendered decisions, and he made all governors directly responsible to him, rather than indirectly through the Six Ministries.

Yung-cheng was succeeded by Ch'ien-lung, the last of the great Ch'ing emperors. His long reign of fifty-nine years (1736–1795) marked the apex of Ch'ing power and saw further expansion of the Ch'ing empire. The kingdom of Dzungaria was annexed, the Muslim uprisings in Chinese Turkestan and the Miao uprisings in Kweichow were successfully suppressed, Vietnam and Burma were brought in as Ch'ing vassals, and

Nepal was made a tributary state. At home peace and prosperity continued to prevail. The imperial exchequer was so full of unused money that four times during his reign the emperor ordered cancellation of all tax payments. The unprecedented prosperity was nowhere better indicated than in the tremendous increase of population. From 1749 to 1793 population in China proper was more than doubled. Towards the end of Ch'ien-lung's reign, however, the regime began to show some internal weaknesses. The military campaigns against China's neighboring states, victorious and glorious in appearance, were extremely costly. It was estimated that altogether they cost more than 150 million taels of silver. His six pleasure tours of the Lower Yangtze cost even more, estimated to be 200 million taels. As he grew older and more complacent, he delegated authority to a favorite of his called Ho-shen. Ho-shen served as his Grand Chancellor for twenty years, and through various corrupt means amassed a great fortune. When he was finally brought to trial after the death of Ch'ien-lung, he was found to have possessed more than 800 million taels of silver, equivalent to ten years' revenue of the Ch'ing empire! Most of this money was found in his mansion, including 260 million taels hidden inside the walls.

CULTURAL ACTIVITIES

Both K'ang-hsi and Ch'ien-lung prided themselves on being grand patrons of learning and literature. Though the Manchu written language was still one of the two official languages in the government, it remained mostly a formality, and with the passage of time even many Manchus did not bother to learn it. On the other hand Manchu intellectuals—including the above-named emperors—found great challenge and enjoyment in the literary tradition of China. Militarily China was conquered by the Manchus, but culturally China's conquest of its conquerors had never been so complete. Both emperors were literary men of considerable talent and were versed in Chinese philosophy and literature. Ch'ien-lung reportedly wrote more than 100,000 poems and was a discriminating critic of painting and calligraphy. K'ang-hsi was even more versatile: he studied astronomy, geography, mathematics, and music, besides Confucian classics and traditional literature. He was even said to have had a smattering of the Latin language. During his reign he personally supervised the printing of twenty-six items on Confucian classics, sixty-five items on history, thirty-six items on philosophy, and twenty items on miscellaneous subjects. The famous K'ang-hsi Dictionary was also compiled under his patronage.

The most significant literary task during K'ang-hsi's reign, however, was the compilation of an encyclopedia entitled *A Collection of Books* and *Illustrations of Ancient and Modern Times* (*Ku-chin t'u-shu chi-ch'eng*). In this effort the emperor obviously attempted to vie with another great patron of learning in the past, *i.e.*, the emperor Yung-lo of the Ming Dynasty, who, as we have said in the preceding chapter, sponsored the compilation of the *Yung-lo Encyclopedia* (*Yung-lo ta-tien*). During the change of dynasties all but one copy of the *Encyclopedia* had been destroyed, and even the extant copy was incomplete. The compilation of *A Collection of Books* was undertaken in 1700 and was not completed until 1725. Its size was comparatively smaller than the *Yung-lo Encyclopedia*, but it was the largest work ever printed to that date anywhere in the world. Two generations later when Ch'ien-lung was the emperor, an imperial decree ordered the collection of all major works on all subjects, whether they be printed, out-of-print, or hand-copied. This gigantic task took nine years to complete (1773–1782) and the resulting collection was entitled *The Complete Library of the Four Treasuries* (*Ssu-k'u ch'üan-shu*), consisting of 3,457 entries in 93,556 fascicles. The *Four Treasuries* was even larger in size than either the *Yung-lo Encyclopedia* or *A Collection of Books*. Seven hand-written copies were made, housed in seven newly built libraries, four in North China and three in the Yangtze River basin. Those in the north were open only to selected scholars; the three in the south, however, were open to the general public. Though historians since then have universally praised Ch'ien-lung's foresight in undertaking this gigantic task, critics pointed out that many works of great value had been destroyed during the compiling process. Any work that described the Manchus in terms that were only slightly derogatory was ordered to be destroyed. Censorship was also extended to Sung works criticizing Liao and Chin, and to Yüan and Ming works criticizing the Mongols. In other cases, books were destroyed simply because they did not appear "literary" enough to the censors or because they allegedly dealt with "trifles" or "nonsense."

Among the different Confucian schools the early Ch'ing emperors singled out the Rational School of Chu Hsi for emphasis. The emperor K'ang-hsi, for instance, regarded Chu Hsi as the greatest philosopher since Confucius and Mencius. The elevation of Chu Hsi was not new; the Ming emperors had honored him before. Obviously his teachings were more appealing to Chinese monarchs than those of other Confucian scholars. First, he believed that the building of moral character among individuals was the first step to the betterment of society. To discipline oneself was therefore more important than to criticize others. Second, he taught the importance of using reason to combat human desires, whether they be for fame, wealth, or power. He maintained that within every man there was a perpetual conflict between "Heavenly reason" (*t'ien li*) and "human desires" (*jen yü*), a battle between the good and the evil, and that a person could eliminate the evil by conscientiously cultivating the good. Every man had to make his own choice because between the good and the evil there could not be any compromise. Third, the purpose of academic learning was its practical application, and a Confucian scholar should serve his government whenever the opportunity presented itself. In a Confucian sense, the nation (*kuo*), the government (*cheng*), and the monarch (*chün*) were almost synonymous, and to serve the nation was by implication to serve the monarch. Loyalty to the monarch was one of the greatest Confucian virtues. Fourth, Chu Hsi, like many other Sung scholars, advocated government by legitimate rulers. By legitimacy was not meant legitimacy in its hereditary sense; legitimacy came into being through the possession of a traditional virtue (*tao t'ung*). This traditional virtue supposedly began with the legendary emperors Yao and Shun and passed through many great dynasties of the past such as Chou, Han, T'ang, and Sung. Though such virtue was never adequately defined and was only vaguely understood, its possession was regarded as the prerequisite to legitimate government. By elevating Chu Hsi the Ch'ing emperors believed that they had followed the great emperors of the past in the possession of that virtue which entitled them to the ruling of China.

Finally, Chu Hsi proposed the dual existence of "form" (*hsing*) and "reason" (*li*), the two inseparable elements of everything in the universe. Form was what we know through the application of our senses, and reason was the law that governs the existence of the form. To use Chu Hsi's own example, a boat has a form which enables us to know its physical existence, but a boat is not really a boat if it cannot sail. The capacity to sail is the "reason" for its being a boat and this capacity existed before any particular boat existed. "Reason" was *a priori*, and "form" was *a posteriori*. Chu Hsi, like all other Confucian scholars, was interested in the application of his theory to human relations. The correct relations between fathers and sons and between monarchs and their subjects, said he, existed before the existence of the parties involved. The virtue of fathers and monarchs was "benevolence" (*jen*) towards their sons and subjects respectively, while "reverence" or "respect" (*ching*) should be the virtue of the inferior parties. The law ("reason") governing the relationship among men existed before particular men existed and was superior to the parties involved. It was eternal, while men themselves were ephemeral. An orderly society could be established only when each individual knew his assigned role and respective place in the society.

In view of what Chu Hsi advocated, it is not difficult to see why his philosophy appealed greatly to monarchs. Both the Ming and the Ch'ing emperors ordered that in Confucian temples his name should be placed beside that of Confucius, to be honored by all students and scholars. The *Four Books* originally selected by him as the basic works of Confucianism were the standard texts which students who wanted to pass the civil service examinations must master thoroughly.

Influential though it was, Chu Hsi's philosophy was not altogether unchallenged. Since it was sponsored by the government, such a challenge, as expected, came mostly from unofficial circles and independent thinkers. Early in the Ch'ing dynasty, Ku Yen-wu attacked the Rational School on the ground that the followers of this school, emphasizing the cultivation of personal virtues, tended to cut themselves off from the outside world and that they failed as leaders of society when they did not recognize and find a remedy for social and economic ills. The metaphysical speculation of the Rational School served no useful purpose, and its overemphasis tended to take a scholar away from a more important concern: the welfare of the society and its people. A true gentleman, said Ku Yen-wu, "should regard social well-being as his own private end to strive for," and knowledge failed to be true if it could not advance human welfare in a practical way. Following his own philosophy, Ku Yen-wu wrote two books, both on "practical" matters: *Problems and Challenges of Various Areas in China (T'ien-hsia chün-kuo li-ping shu)* and *The Daily Accumulated Knowledge (Jih-chih lu)*.

A more vigorous and systematic attack on the Rational School came from another Ch'ing scholar named Tai Chen (1724-1777). Tai Chen was born to a poor family in South Anhwei, the same region which had produced Chu Hsi more than seven centuries before. It is said that he was inquisitive and critical about everything he read when he was a child and that he often asked questions which even his teacher could not answer. When he was sixteen, he reportedly had committed to memory all the Confucian classics and their major commentaries. Talented though he was, he failed repeatedly in the civil service examinations. He earned a living by teaching, and through his writings he was regarded by his contemporaries as one of the greatest Confucian scholars. His most important work was *A Commentary on the Words and Meanings of Mencius (Meng-tzu tzu-yi shu-cheng)*. During his declining years he was invited by the emperor Ch'ien-lung to help in the compilation of the *Four Treasuries*. He died of overwork at the age of fifty-four.

Tai Chen, like many other critics of the Rational School, attempted to bypass the Sung period in his search for the meaning of Confucianism. These critics believed that one had to go to the writings of the Han dynasty and before in order to ascertain the true intention of the great Confucian masters. Because of their emphasis on the Han writings, their school of thought was called the Han School or Han Learning, as opposed to the Rational School represented by Chu Hsi. They maintained that post-Han writings, especially those of the Sung scholars, were influenced by Taoism and Buddhism and could not be relied on in understanding Confucianism. What was wrong with "human desires?" asked Tai Chen. Had not the *Book of Rites* said that food and sex were man's two basic, indispensable desires? Was it not true that the elimination of desires was originally a Taoist and a Buddhist teaching? The sages taught a person to channel his desires along the right direction, and there was no mention in the ancient texts that he should suppress them with "reason." Moreover, what was the definition of "reason"? What one person regarded as "reason" might not be "reason" for others. "Reason" being such a loose term, every one used it to advance his own interest. "The haughty use it against the humble, the elders use it again the young, and the aristocrats use it against the common people." But, if the inferiors used it in front of their superiors, "they are accused of being rebellious even when they are right." "How many injustices have been done under the disguise of 'reason'?" asked Tai Chen. "Harsh and cruel officials kill people by invoking the law, and later [Sung] scholars killed people by invoking 'reason.'" "The sad thing is," he continued, "that while people might feel sorry for those killed by law, none expresses sympathy for those killed by 'reason.'"

Wishing to have nothing to do with metaphysical speculation, Tai Chen and other "Han School" scholars applied themselves to "practical" research. They made great contributions in the fields of phonetics, philology, etymology, and textual criticism. Theoretically, these studies were not ends in themselves. They were meant to contribute to the understanding of Han and pre-Han writings.

POPULAR LITERATURE

The debate between the Han and the Sung Schools was confined to the highly sophisticated intellectuals. The majority of the Chinese people did not understand and cared little about it. When they read, they wished to be entertained and amused, and certainly they could not find entertainment in philosophical works that were written in a classical style. Fortunately there were many works with popular appeal, and among them novels stood as the most outstanding. Historians call them Ming-Ch'ing novels, though some of them (such as *The Romance of the Three Kingdoms*) were actually written during the Yüan dynasty. Chinese intellectuals looked down upon novels as a form of literary expression, and some of these novels did not even bear the name of the author. Presumably they were not proud of their own works, and they wrote them simply because they wished to "kill time." Unshackled by this ancient prejudice, today we are perhaps better equipped to judge their works than they themselves were. Modern scholars agree that the best Ming-Ch'ing novels are among the greatest literary creations of all countries.

There must have been a long evolutionary process between the plain vernacular tales of the Sung dynasty and the superbly written novels of the Ming-Ch'ing period. Whether written in classical or vernacular form, the Ming-Ch'ing novels, at least the best among them, possessed a refinement which the Sung tales had never attained. They appealed to learned intellectuals as well as to those who heard them retold by professional story-tellers in the tea houses. They were the popular literature, appealing to people of all walks of life and of all social standings.

Among the novels in question one of the best written and most popular was *The Marsh Heroes* (*Shui-hu chuan*), translated by Pearl S. Buck as *All Men Are Brothers*. It was originally written by Shih Nai-an and subsequently completed by Lo Kuan-chung, both authors living in the fourteenth century. It was a work of historical fiction, the story of Sung Chiang and his fellow bandits who early in the twelfth century had ravaged the countryside and captured many cities before they were finally suppressed. In *The Marsh Heroes*, however, they are portrayed as the victims of oppression and injustice and as Robin Hoods who robbed the rich and aided the poor. Altogether there were 108 "heroes" in this book, but the author concentrated on a dozen or so of the most colorful figures. There was the runaway monk whose hate for all evil was as strong as his love for good wine and tasty food. There was the ex-captain of the imperial guards who had to forego a promising career to become a bandit because a powerful official coveted his unusually attractive wife. There was also the tall, handsome Wu Sung who spurned the overtures of his brother's wife, only to find himself accused of having seduced her. After the woman had found a great lord as her lover and poisoned her husband, Wu Sung took the law into his own hands and slaughtered her in cold blood right in front of his brother's dead body. Thus he became a wanted man and joined the bandits. The leader of these bandits was the ex-clerk Sung Chiang. He became an outlaw because he was forced to murder his wife who had threatened to expose his underworld connections. Throughout the book the author's sympathy was with these bandit-heroes.

Scarcely less popular was another work of historical fiction, *The Romance of the Three Kingdoms* (*San kuo yen-yi*), reportedly written by Lo Kuan-chung. The book begins with the ominous remark that "an empire is founded to be broken, as a broken empire is bound to be reunited in the course of time." The broken empire described in this book was the Later Han which early in the third century was broken into Three Kingdoms (see Chapter IV). While the book covers a long period from the time of the Yellow Turbans rebellion to the reunification of China by Tsin Wu-ti, its central figure was a man named Chu-ko Liang who served as an adviser and then prime minister to the King of Shu, Liu Pei. His ingenuity and cleverness, according to *The Romance*, enabled South China to successfully resist Ts'ao Ts'ao, who was singled out as the villain in this work. Written in a semiclassical style, *The Romance* was easy to read, and reportedly many Chinese, by reading this book and imitating its style, learned to write their first presentable letters. Its numerous episodes were adapted in many plays and operas of succeeding centuries. There was hardly anyone in China who did not know some of these stories.

Less popular but perhaps of greater literary value was *The Dream of the Red Chamber* (*Hung-lou meng*), by Ts'ao Hsüeh-ch'in who lived in the eighteenth century. It is a story of love between two cousins, Chia Pao-yü (Precious Jade) and Lin Tai-yü (Black Jade). The story ends with the death of the heroine and the insanity of the hero who subsequently joined the monastic ranks. Pao-yü could not marry his true love because his grandmother had her eyes on a more wholesome and less clever girl named Hsüeh Pao-ch'ai. The day he married Pao-ch'ai was also the time when his true love departed from the earth. The romance of the two cousins was conducted on a platonic level; they exchanged notes and poems and made subtle, remote remarks whenever they saw each other. Physically delicate and emotionally oversensitive, Tai-yü would cry for days and vow never to see him again if he made some remarks that could be remotely construed as offensive. Meanwhile, she might write long, sad poems of self-pity and murmur them while "collecting and burying fallen flowers." The love story itself might be regarded as over-sentimental, but the book throws much light on the life of the leisurely rich and the operation of a scholar-gentry family of high standing. It is still one of the best books to read for anyone who wishes to study the Chinese family system. Most Chinese, however, read it for the story.

Another book, beautifully written in a classical style, was a collection of 431 short stories entitled *Strange Stories from a Lonely Studio* (*Liaochai chih-yi*), by P'u Sung-ling (1640–1715). The heroes in these stories were mostly men, but the heroines were usually either ghosts or fox-fairies. The love and romance between them make interesting, if weird, reading. Almost without exception, the ghosts and fox-fairies described in this book were more honest and trustworthy than human beings. Did the author mean to satirize the imperfections of human beings? According to Chinese hearsay, foxes, once transforming themselves into human beings, were sexually irresistible, and when approached, their victims were completely helpless to maintain their chastity. How did this superstition begin? One explanation is that even in a society where males and females were strictly segregated and their private meetings were socially taboo, cases of unwed mothers did occasionally occur; and that to save the family of an unwed mother from social disgrace, there had to be a face-saving formula to explain the supposedly unexplainable. "This is not her fault," her parents would like to hear people say when their unwed daughter became unexpectedly pregnant, "because you could not expect her to resist a male fox who came in through a window crack and made her unconscious by the waving of a hand." In such a case, her parents might be persuaded not to punish her too severely (as by putting her to death) in order to save the family's reputation. The Chinese being a practical people, even the most intelligent among them did not bother to attack this superstition as long as it served a useful purpose.

Among other interesting novels is *An Unofficial History of the Lite-roti* (*Ju-lin wai-shih*), by Wu Ching-tzu (1701–1754). It is a well-written satire attacking the hypocritical behavior of many shallow, worldly scholars. *Flowering Plum in a Golden Vase* (*Chin p'ing mei*), which first appeared in printed form in the 1570's, was an anonymous work describing the amorous adventure of a man named Hsi-men Ch'ing. Hsi-men the Lord, as he is called in this book, captured one beautiful woman after another until he debilitated his health and died of exhaustion at an early age. The moral of the book, which appears on the last page, is that overindulgence does not pay, but the book's chief attraction has been its pornographic details.

Another popular novel, written in a different vein, was *Journey to the West* (*Hsi-yu chi*), by Wu Ch'eng-en. It describes the successful journey of the Buddhist monk Hsüan-tsang to India in the seventh century and the colorful exploits of his escort, a monkey, who, among other things could "cover eighteen thousand *li* (about 6,000 miles) in one jump." Less well-written but equally popular was *The Romance of Deification* (*Feng-shen yen-yi*), by an anonymous author of the Ming dynasty. It describes the war between Chou and Shang in the twelfth century B.C., with all gods and goddesses fighting on one side or another. Some of the gods travelled in the sky and others did so underneath the ground. Chou won because all good deities happened to be on its side.

We cannot leave the topic of popular literature without mentioning the charming autobiography of Shen Fu who lived in the eighteenth century. The present version of the autobiography, *The Six Chapters of a Floating Life* (*Fou-sheng liu-chi*), has actually four chapters, the other two chapters having long been lost. It describes the life of an unsuccessful, impoverished gentry-scholar, enjoying what he had and accepting what he could not change. It is permeated with Taoist and Buddhist influences. The most charming chapter is perhaps the first which deals with the author's domestic life. Though Shen's marriage was arranged, rarely has there been a happier couple. To show what an understanding wife he had, the author mentioned the fact that his wife had been looking for a good concubine for him for a long time without his knowledge. Their happy life, however, was marred by the misunderstanding between his wife and his parents and by the recurrent poverty that beset them for their entire lives. But as long as money lasted, they enjoyed boat rides under the moonlight and the flowers they planted in their small garden. The story ends tragically when his wife died at an early age.

DYNASTIC CYCLE

The internal strength of the Ch'ing regime reached its apex during the middle decades of the eighteenth century, and the decline began to set in towards the end of Ch'ien-lung's reign. The revelation of Ho-shen's grand larceny in 1799 was a great shock to the nation. To many who believed in the dynastic cycle, it signified the end of a glorious era and the beginning of a downward trend. No sooner was the new emperor Chia-ch'ing installed on the throne than a mighty rebellion swept across the Upper Yangtze basin. The rebellion, led by the White Lotus Society, lasted nine years and was not suppressed until 1804. Thus weakened, the Ch'ing regime continued to decline throughout the first half of the nineteenth century. Once a regime began to decline, very likely it would deteriorate to the very end. Like a river seeking an outlet towards the sea, there might be some reverse currents, but the general direction was unmistakably downward. This has been noticed with regard to the Ming dynasty, and the Ch'ing dynasty provides another excellent example for studying the dynastic cycle. During the stage of decline there were domestic rebellions and foreign invasions. What made the Ch'ing situation different was first, that foreign invasions came overseas from the south instead of overland from the north as had been traditionally the case; and second, that the new "barbarians" were of a different kind and were by far the most sophisticated China had ever encountered. They were not only superb warriors, but they possessed a highly advanced, though quite different, culture. That the Chinese made no distinction between these new "barbarians" and those with whom they had had experience before worked only to their own disadvantage. More will be said about this in a later chapter.

Internal rebellions, foreign invasions, and the inability of the government to cope with them characterized the declining stage of a dynastic cycle. Chinese historians long realized the existence of the dynastic cycle, and they explained it in terms of Confucian and Taoist philosophy. Dynastic change, said they, was as inevitable as any other change in the universe, and the permutation of the five primary elements was equally applicable to dynastic successions. The Ch'in regime, for instance, believed that it possessed the "water virtue" (*shui te*) and was therefore entitled to succeed the Chou regime which was said to have possessed the "fire virtue" (*huo te*). After the Han regime was established, its historians maintained that the new regime possessed the "earth virtue" (*t'u te*) which enabled it to succeed the Ch'in regime. Towards the end of the Former Han dynasty, some historians contended that the Ch'in regime was too short to be considered a regular dynasty and that the entire "virtue" system should be rearranged. In the new arrangement, the Chou dynasty was said to have possessed the "wood virtue" (*mu te*), and Han, the "fire virtue." When the Wei regime succeeded Han, it believed that it possessed the "earth virtue," which destroyed and replaced the "fire virtue."

What interests us most is that this theory of dynastic permutation presupposed the organic development of a political regime. A political regime, like a living organism, grew, matured, decayed, and finally ceased to exist. Then it would be replaced by a new regime which would pass through the same process. When a new regime was born, it was said that it had received the mandate of Heaven to rule; when it declined, allegedly Heaven had withdrawn its mandate and was in the process of designating a successor. Natural disasters, famines, incompetence and corruption in the government, internal revolts, and foreign invasions—these were indications of Heaven's displeasure with the existing regime. What should a ruler do under such circumstances? He should repent and should cultivate his virtue more diligently, said Confucian moralists. Tradition dictated that whenever a national disaster occurred, whether it were natural or man-made, the emperor should take full responsibility for its occurrence and issue proclamations to condemn himself, with the hope that Heaven, taking into consideration his repentance, would not punish him further by sending more disasters. The past shows that Heaven rarely intervened in those matters and that once decay set in, it continued until the existing regime was extinguished. Under the most auspicious circumstances the decay might be arrested for a short span of time, but rarely could it be stopped. During the Ch'ing dynasty, a dynastic regeneration occurred in the 1860's, but the decline continued beginning with the 1870's. The "cultivation of virtue" on the part of emperors contributed little in reversing the downward trend, once a dynasty reached the stage of decline. Though most emperors during the declining stage of a dynastic cycle were weaker leaders compared with their predecessors, it cannot be said that all of them were not "virtuous." The last Ming emperor Ch'ung-chen, for instance, was a strong, conscientious monarch, and few of the Ch'ing rulers had tried so valiantly to rejuvenate a deteriorating regime as Kuang-hsü, one of the last Ch'ing emperors.

It seems that there were forces beyond human control that worked to effect the rise and fall of each succeeding dynasty. Chinese scholars traditionally explained the existence of the dynastic cycle in abstract and philosophical terms and moralized upon it for the benefit of posterity. Modern historians, on the other hand, view it from a more rational angle and explain it in social and economic terms. We have mentioned in an earlier chapter that in China the frontier of agriculture had virtually disappeared as early as the Han dynasty and that the amount of land available for the production of food did not increase by any substantial amount for more than two thousand years. As the Chinese remained predominantly agricultural, they could not establish permanent settlements on the grasslands beyond the northern and western frontiers, and as they were land-centered, they were either unwilling or unable to expand overseas. Thus the geographical size of China was naturally limited by the grasslands and deserts in the Northwest and the Pacific Ocean in the Southeast. The increase of population throughout Chinese history had to be accommodated within the natural confines of China, and such an accommodation became increasingly difficult with the passage of time.

Chinese historians recorded land shortage as early as the fourth century B.C., and by the time of the Former Han dynasty, population pressure had become an acute problem. Population increased at an accelerated rate during the rising stage of a dynastic cycle when peace and prosperity prevailed. Sooner or later a point would be reached when the fixed amount of land could no longer support even the barest existence. When natural disasters struck, widespread famines would ensue, and open rebellions against public authority often came in the wake of widespread famines. The country was then plunged into chaos and war, and the barbarians, taking advantage of the situation, raided the border provinces and sometimes occupied part of China proper. This situation would continue until a strong man or a succession of strong men emerged, defeated all opponents, and reunified the country. Normalcy returned when all China was brought under the new leader's jurisdiction, barbarians were repelled, and he himself was installed as the founding emperor of a new dynasty. In the case of Ch'ing, the new emperor was a barbarian himself, but once he had come to the throne of China as a Chinese monarch, he regarded it as his duty to repel other barbarians as strong Chinese rulers would. During the period of dynastic change, famine, war, diseases, and a high death rate helped to reduce the population. When a new dynasty was established, again there was enough land to support a much reduced population. Population pressure thus eased, the rising stage of a new dynastic cycle began, and once again there was peace and prosperity. As the amount of land was not enlarged and farming techniques remained the same, peace and prosperity again brought about population pressures which in turn prompted another dynastic decline.

These, of course, are much simplified statements about a complicated phenomenon. Nevertheless they are basically valid. The Chinese of old were not very statistically minded and they left us few figures to work on. However, whenever statistics are available, they tend to support this land-population theory. The following is a list of population figures:

1575 (Ming dynasty)	60,692,000
1661 (Ch'ing dynasty)	19,138,000
1749	177,495,000
1783	284,030,000

1793	307,460,000
1812	361,690,000
1842	413,021,000
1860	360,925,000
1885	377,636,000
1910	438,425,000

These were the population figures of China proper as they appeared in tax registers, and they are at best approximations. The comparatively small figure for 1575 reflects the declining stage of the Ming dynasty. By 1661 population had been reduced to the almost incredible nineteen millions, less than one-third as large as that in 1575. What a heavy toll the change of dynasties had taken! Once the Ch'ing regime was established, population increased at an accelerated speed. The increase was so fast that it can best be described as an explosion. From 1842 to 1885 population actually decreased, indicating that the dynasty was in a stage of decline.

Land shortage and population pressure were duly reflected in the increase of land prices. On the Lower Yangtze basin the best farm land was sold for about two taels per *mou* (0.15 acre) in the 1640's.[1] It rose to ten taels per *mou* in the 1730's and went further to sixty taels in the 1780's. Thus the price of farm land rose thirty times as much in 140 years and six times as much in fifty years. The rising price for land speeded up the process of land concentration, as only the very wealthy could then afford to acquire additional acreage. Small farmers, once forced to sell their land on account of accumulated debts, became tenant farmers or unemployed. Moreover, as population swelled and the unemployed increased, the competition to obtain tenancy became more intense, and the landlords were in a good position to drive a favorable bargain for themselves. This often left the tenants very little once they paid their rent and fulfilled their contractual obligations. Those who were rejected by the landlords as tenants joined the rank of the rural unemployed. Thus, the increase of population caused land shortages which in turn caused higher land prices. As prices rose, land became more concentrated in the hands of a few and the rural unemployed became even larger in number. All these resulted in one thing: increasing poverty among the rural population. The increasing poverty among the peasants and the existence of a large army of the unemployed combined to create a potentially explosive situation for all concerned.

As long as there was no immediate danger of mass starvation, the traditional Confucian values which emphasized correct relationship and mutual help among neighbors, friends, and relatives kept in check the

[1] Unless otherwise indicated, a tael is always a tael of silver. It is equal to one ounce approximately.

dissatisfied elements and prevented a precarious situation from deteriorating into mass violence. Once a natural disaster struck and famine ensued, such values could no longer hold people within their normal confines, and the once scattered bandit groups soon coalesced and rose up in open rebellion. Whatever cause the leaders might have used to rationalize their revolt, so far as most peasants were concerned, hunger was the only reason for joining a rebellion. As China entered the stage of civil war, war itself generated more famines which further swelled the rank and file of the rebels. Farms were deserted and production slackened as able-bodied men were either drafted into the army or joined the rebels. When a social upheaval of such magnitude occurred, life meant little or nothing, and millions died as a result of war, starvation, and disease. By then most people were convinced that the existing regime had lost the mandate of Heaven.

ﾉ xi

Traditional Chinese Society

THE COMING OF THE WEST

So far we have discussed Chinese history as an independent development, little affected by outside influences. This independent development was largely due to geographical isolation, as has been said before. During the past four centuries, however, the situation has completely changed. The Commercial Revolution which began with Columbus' historical voyage to the New World affected China as well as the rest of the world. The oceans which had been viewed as insurmountable barriers to men's contact and knowledge of one another now became international highways over which travelled traders, missionaries, and adventurers. The expansion of European influence during and following the Commercial Revolution was unprecedented in scope, and as such expansion continued, many of the hitherto unknown or inaccessible parts of the world were either occupied by Western powers outright or were subject to strong Western

338

influences. By the nineteenth century there was no inhabited part of the world which had not felt the Western impact.

For the first time in its history China faced a cultural rival and was presented with a cultural alternative with which it had never been confronted before. The impact of the West was so great that its full meaning and scope will perhaps not be understood for a considerable time to come. Before modern times the only major foreign influence on Chinese culture came with the introduction of Buddhism from India. But the impact of Buddhism could not be compared with the pervasiveness of modern Western influence. Even at its prime, Buddhist influence was largely religious and philosophical. Chinese institutions, ethical values, and traditional loyalties and beliefs were little affected, and the basic structure of Chinese society remained the same as it had always been. Though Buddhism enriched Chinese life, it did not change it. The West, on the other hand, presented to the Chinese not only a new religion

LANTERN FESTIVAL   This tapestry panel of the eighteenth century depicts the scene of a lantern festival, traditionally celebrated on the fifteenth day of the first lunar month. There are the familiar dragon dance, the firecrackers, and the loud band, besides the lanterns. The Chinese characters on the flag behind the dragon read: "Peace on Earth" (literally, Peace within the Four Seas). The Chinese character *hsi* or "happiness" appears on the two lanterns on the right. Notice that all the people in this picture are male children or boys.

DRAGON BOAT FESTIVAL The dragon boat festival depicted in this tapestry panel (eighteenth century) is celebrated on the fifth day of the fifth lunar month. The most important event on this day is the dragon boat race, pitting sometimes one wealthy family against another. There are four dragon boats in this picture, each of which has a boy riding on the dragon's head. Notice also the Chinese type of houses on the lower right, the pagoda on top of a bridge on the upper left, and the dresses of the people on the lower part of the picture.

(Christianity), but also a new political institution (that of representative government), new economic theories (capitalism, socialism, etc.) and, in short, a new way of life. Rejecting Western culture at the beginning, eventually China had to modify its institutions and sense of values in order to survive in a fast-changing world. Whatever the future holds, certainly China will never be the same as it has been before. Presently many forces are at work, some traditional and others foreign in origin. Will traditional values survive in the long run? Or, will they become completely submerged under the pervasive Western influence? Or, will a synthesis of Eastern and Western cultures come into being eventually? China is in a period of transition, a period which goes back to the time when its doors were forced open for normal Western trade in 1842 (Treaty of Nanking). Beginning with the middle decades of the nineteenth century, all major events in China have been related to the Western impact, in one way or another. Before we proceed with the discussion of the Western impact, it is only proper that we should devote one chapter to an analysis of the traditional Chinese society, as a summary of the preceding chapters and as a prelude to the coming ones.

THE ECONOMIC SCENE

Economically, China is agricultural and has been agricultural for more than four thousand years. This simple fact conditioned to a great extent the nature of the traditional Chinese society. The agrarian civilization of China was one of the oldest in the world, and like an elderly man who had enjoyed a long life, it suffered inevitable weaknesses. The amazing thing is not that these weaknesses existed; it is amazing that the agrarian civilization of China continued to flourish without basic changes despite these weaknesses. Obviously there must have been intrinsic values within the civilization itself to remedy or correct these weaknesses, even though they could not be eliminated. The survival of the traditional Chinese society depended upon the continuous functioning of these corrective devices. Before we discuss the corrective devices, we have to know what the weaknesses were.

Of all the problems China had to face, perhaps none was more important than the perennial problem of land shortage and population pressure. It is difficult to say when this problem began; but in any event it became more serious with the passage of time. Such a problem did not exist during the Shang dynasty, because it is known that even in the most densely populated area (the North China Plain), there was still virgin land to be opened up, and forests could be found even in the suburb of Shang's capital Yin. In the twelfth century B.C. Chou conquered Shang. Chou, being more advanced agriculturally, quickly opened up the North China Plain, and tempted by the rich land in the south, extended its control southward to the Yangtze Valley. As new land was still available, there was no land shortage. The comparative abundance of arable land enabled the Chou regime to impose a feudal structure on all China, extending it to the lowest level, the peasants. Under Chou feudalism, each peasant family received one hundred *mou* (fifteen acres) for cultivation in return for feudal services which included the tilling of the lord's "common." Though a farm of fifteen acres is not large in the West, it was enviable in China. It may be said without exaggeration that Chinese peasants have never been so well off as they were under Chou feudalism. Subsequently, Confucian scholars (Confucius included) spoke constantly of the golden age of Chou.

Feudalism had to be destroyed eventually, because, among other reasons, there was simply not enough land to be distributed among the peasants as population continued to increase. While Confucians were still dreaming about the golden past, the Legalists were looking towards the future as they proposed the abolition of feudalism. When the Ch'in regime formally ended feudalism by declaring land to be private property subject to trade, it did what circumstances had clearly dictated. Since feudalism was abolished, it has never been successfully revived.

The two ancient conquerors, Ch'in Shih-huang and Han Wu-ti, enlarged China's "living space" through military conquests. Using South Manchuria (which had been settled by the Chinese previously) as the base of operation, they annexed Korea. Southward Chinese jurisdiction was extended to the shore of the South China Sea and included the modern Kwangtung province. Even the unproductive Yun-Kwei Plateau did not escape Han Wu-ti's attention. Beyond the southwestern frontier only the rugged terrain and the inhospitable jungle prevented the Han army from marching into the Salween and the Mekong valleys. In the north, land was intensively cultivated as long as there was enough rainfall, and this included the semi-arid, marginal land on the southern fringe of the Mongolian deserts. Of all the territories that constitute arable China today, only a small enclave on the Fukien coast and the island of Taiwan were not brought under Han control. (The former, hilly and unproductive, was spared for the time being, and the latter was protected by the 100-mile-wide Taiwan Strait.) Thus by the second century B.C. practically all land suitable for agriculture had been brought under Chinese control. The frontier of agriculture had virtually disappeared.

The importance of the disappearance of the agricultural frontier cannot be overemphasized. It means that subsequent increases in population had to be accommodated within the limited amount of arable land in China. Land shortage and population pressure was the main cause of the dynastic cycle, as has been stated in the preceding chapter. It is no coincidence that after the unification of China by Ch'in, major dynasties usually lasted two or three hundred years, enough time to reduce food production per capita to a dangerously low level. With the exception of Ch'in Shih-huang who in an enthusiastic mood predicted that his regime would last "thousands of emperors," no Chinese ruler ever believed that his dynasty would continue indefinitely. Sooner or later, there would be famine, rebellion, and war, and his dynasty, like so many before, would collapse in a mass social upheaval.

Since the amount of arable land was limited, the logical solution to the production problem seemed to be the increase of yield per unit area. Unfamiliar with the Chinese situation, many people blame the lack of technological advances for the Chinese inability to raise total production. While it is true that no major technological advance has occurred since the invention of the iron-shod plow in the sixth or fifth century B.C., the result would not have been materially different even if there had been such improvements. The fact is, the manual farming as conducted by the

Chinese has been and still is one of the most efficient in the world, as far as yield per acre is concerned. For instance, in the production of rice or wheat, a Chinese farm produces more per acre than a mechanized European or American farm. The introduction of machinery would have aggravated rather than alleviated the Chinese problem. The same farming method, highly efficient and suited particularly well to the Chinese situation, has not been changed for more than two thousand years. The prospect of reduced yield would have discouraged any prospective inventor of labor-saving devices. This might account for, partially at least, the lack of technological advances in Chinese agriculture. In short, the Chinese problem has been and still is the problem of land shortage.

All factors considered, it seems that there only could be two solutions to this problem: to reduce population pressure by practicing birth control and to make equally available to all what the land produced. Birth control was out of the question because, in addition to social and cultural considerations (such as the glorification of large families), the Chinese had no such knowledge and could not practice birth control even if they wished to. The second solution was not a true solution, but it was the best available to the Chinese. Because of the lack of a better term, we shall call it the principle of equalitarianism. The spirit of this principle was: no man should have too much at the expense of others.

The translation of this principle into practical policies met with varying degrees of success throughout Chinese history. Chou feudalism was perhaps the most successful in this respect because land was then comparatively plentiful, and the distribution of fifteen acres of land to each peasant family caused no practical difficulty. When Wang Mang attempted a similar arrangement, he failed miserably (Chapter III). His failure, however, did not discourage later rulers. Equal land distribution among peasant families was revived by subsequent regimes, notably Later (North) Wei and T'ang (Chapters IV and V). It could be carried out at the beginning of each of these regimes because dynastic change had substantially reduced population pressure and there was enough land available. The system deteriorated and eventually had to be abandoned as the central authority weakened and population continued to increase. None of these regimes practiced land distribution for any prolonged period, and beginning with the Sung dynasty it was abandoned altogether. Moreover, there were in each dynasty vested interests that were unaffected by the equalitarian principle, including the landholdings of members of the royal household and high-ranking government officials. Since land was subject to buying and selling, the tendency towards land concentration remained a serious, recurrent problem ever since the abolition of feudalism. However, the equalization of land ownership was one of the fondest dreams of all Chinese idealists who condemned land concentration whenever it occurred. In modern times it reappeared as one of Sun

Yat-sen's economic programs and in Mao Tse-tung's collective farms and communes.

Though it was difficult to translate the principle of equalitarianism into the equalization of land ownership, the principle was nevertheless built into Chinese customs. Contrary to many European countries where primogeniture was the rule, in China the property of the deceased was divided equally among his male children. However large the original size of a landholding, it would be eventually fragmented among a number of owners. Thus, land concentration never reached the same proportion as in historical Europe, and landholdings of plantation size were infrequent. The infrequent occurrence of large plantations might account for the absence of a large slave population such as could be found historically in many other countries. Landholdings being small, there was no need for slave workers. Those who have visited rural China must have noticed the crisscrossing footpaths that separate small, garden-like plots, most of which are a fraction of an acre in size. An old Chinese proverb says, "No family can be rich or poor consecutively for three generations." Though to become rich in three generations was more an expression of hope than a statement of fact, for a wealthy family eventually to become poor was in fact a commonplace.

Within a family the application of the equalitarian principle meant that all family members should have the same standard of living despite differences in earning power. A Chinese family was more like a clan in the Western sense, consisting of three or four generations and including brothers, cousins, and their wives and children. It was not merely a biological relationship; it was an economic unit, the members of which protected one another in financial matters. Men being unequal in natural endowment, their achievements in society (and in earning power) were bound to be different, and the Chinese believed that the strong had a moral obligation to help and protect the weak. Since the family came into being through a natural, biological relationship, it seemed to a Chinese that it was the most logical place to fulfill such moral obligations. In reality, of course, he did not rationalize in this matter; he was brought up to believe that a family was a closely knit unit and he acted on that premise. In theory and often in practice, all income of a family, including the earned income of its various members, would go into a common treasury, and each member would receive a certain amount for expenses regardless of the amount he had contributed to this common treasury. The actual amount he received usually varied in accordance with seniority (generation and age) rather than earning power. If the family prospered, all members benefited; if the family fortune declined, all suffered the same. Thus, a Chinese family served the same purpose as many of our social inventions put together—the insurance company, the Social Security Act, the unemployment compensation, and all other socialistic features of a modern society. The Chinese system was less costly, because it did not create so many middlemen.

The assumption of mutual obligations was extended beyond the immediate family members, to the clan, the neighborhood, and relatives and friends in general, though the extent of such assumption was steadily reduced as the relationship became less close. In other words, one's obligation towards his immediate family was higher than his obligation towards clan members, the obligation towards clan members prevailed over the obligation towards his neighbors, and so on. Nevertheless, all these obligations existed. A person was morally obligated to take care of his third or fourth cousin who became destitute, even though he had never met this cousin who was now seeking his help. One day opening the front door, one could also face a total stranger with a suitcase in his hand, who announced that their fathers had once been great friends and that he needed a place to stay for a few days (which often lasted a few weeks or months) until he could find employment. The prospective host did not have to invite the stranger in, but he would encounter social disapproval if he did not. Once coming in, the caller would be treated as a member of the family rather than as a guest, and he would undertake whatever tasks inside and outside the house he was capable of doing. He received no pay and did not expect any. When famine arrived in a village, the rich were morally bound to help the poor. When the rich men's last bit of grain was gone, they, rich and poor, all moved out to other towns and villages that, following an established custom, provided relief for the travelling refugees. The refugees came back early in the spring before the sowing season began.

One of the great institutions in China was the ever-ready granaries, another example of the equalitarian principle. The landowners were assessed to contribute a small portion of their harvests to the ever-ready granaries in good years, and the accumulated grain would be distributed among the poor as relief in time of famine or, in some cases, sold on the open market at below-the-market prices. The prosperity of the nation was often measured by the degree of fullness of its ever-ready granaries. If the grain they contained became rotten, prosperity must have lasted for a long time and historians duly recorded it with great jubilation. If the amount of grain continued to decline as a result of the lack of replenishment, there was a genuine cause for alarm.

Unable to escape the limitations imposed by nature, the Chinese incorporated into their custom and tradition many safeguards against economic hazards. Even social and moral values reflected the same concern. The Chinese, for instance, glorified thrift and condemned waste in unequivocal terms. Though thrift has been a virtue in practically every culture, the Chinese carried it to an almost unbelievable degree. Two stories might suffice to elaborate this point. A man described in *An Un-*

official History of the Literati (Chapter X) continued to raise his two fingers while lying on his deathbed speechless, and his relatives were at a loss to understand his last instruction in connection with the two fingers. Finally someone grasped what he meant and removed one of the two wicks in the oil lamp, and the man nodded his head and died in peace. The other story is in connection with the Ch'ing statesman Tseng Kuo-fan who turned down an applicant for a position despite high recommendations because in an interview over a dinner table the applicant had carefully picked up the unpolished rice in his rice bowl and set it aside on the table, instead of eating it indiscriminately with the good, polished rice. In Tseng's eyes a man so wasteful could not be trusted to rule the people. In this matter of thrift, the emperor and his officials were supposed to set the example. Historians praised Han Wen-ti, because, among other things, "the empress' skirt did not touch the ground" (it was cut short to save cloth); on the other hand, they condemned with vigor the luxurious habits of Ch'in Shih-huang and Sui Yang-ti who had built elaborate palaces for their personal comfort. Wang Mang won great admiration from the gentry-scholars partially because both he and his wife, despite great wealth at their command, were extremely thrifty people.

From the point of view of a modern society, the equalitarian principle had its obvious shortcomings. The implementation of such a principle necessitated an authoritarian organization, on the family as well as at the national level, because only an unchallenged authority could enforce it. Moreover, the principle discouraged individual incentive and enterprise, especially in connection with economic and financial matters. It took away a man's independence and made him a silent conformist to the status quo. These, of course, are all justifiable criticisms. However, it should be pointed out that individualism and independence are modern Western values and that they did not apply to historical China. In historical China conformity was a virtue and individualism was denounced in unequivocal terms. Criticism loses much of its validity if it does not take into consideration differences in social and economic environment. It is debatable whether the traditional Chinese society would have been better off if it had embraced modern Western values.

THE POLITICAL SCENE

The Chinese believed that a nation should be conceived as a huge family, and like a family, each member had his assigned privileges and responsibilities. At the head of this national family was the emperor who, like a father, should love and protect his subjects. He should see to it that flood control and irrigation works were in good order, famines would be relieved whenever they occurred, and justice would prevail within the empire. Moreover, he should by words and deeds set a moral example to the nation and possess the same virtues (such as filial piety) as he expected from his subjects. In performing his state functions he was assisted by a professional bureaucracy and, like him, all his officials should be "fathers and mothers" to the people whom they ruled. In return for his service, the emperor demanded unswerving loyalty and absolute obedience. Treason was punishable by death not only for the person directly involved but also for all his relatives. At least in one case, the death penalty was also extended to the accused's teachers who presumably had forgotten to teach their pupils to be loyal subjects. In addition, he demanded the payment of taxes to support his court, government, and army, and he could call his subjects to perform military service or corvée labor whenever the necessity arose. He would not interfere with their private lives as long as they complied with his basic demands. A subject could worship the way he wished, choose his own occupation, and move freely within the empire. Generally speaking, there was a great deal of personal freedom within the authoritarian state. Joyfully an ancient peasant sang:

> I begin to work when the sun rises;
> I rest when the sun sets.
> I dig a well for my drinking water;
> I plow the field to provide my food.
> Powerful as the emperors are,
> What has that power to do with me? [1]

The imperial power was hereditary, and the emperor was responsible to no one except the inscrutable Heaven. Accepting these two premises, the Chinese nevertheless built into their political system checks on imperial power expressed in theories and traditions. First, there was the ancient theory that people were more important than kings and that the government existed for the benefit of the governed only (Chapter II). If a king abused his power to the detriment of the people, the people were justified in revolting against him and in overthrowing his regime (Chapter III). Second, there were the unwritten customs and traditions which an emperor had to abide by if he wished to act legally. During the T'ang-Sung period, for instance, custom dictated that imperial decrees could take legal effect only after they had been approved by the prime minister. This custom caused a political crisis in 946 when the incumbent prime minister and his two deputies simultaneously resigned, and Emperor Chao K'uang-yin could not appoint a successor because there was no incumbent minister legally qualified to give approval to the appointment. There were numerous cases in which prime ministers returned imperial decrees back to the emperors on the ground that they were contrary in

[1] This anonymous folksong is one of the oldest on record and is dated at least 1,000 B.C.

letter and in spirit to the established custom or tradition. In one case the prime minister contemptuously burned an imperial decree, because in his opinion the woman whom the emperor had wished to promote to the lofty position of imperial concubine through this decree was clearly unqualified. Third, there were the dynastic rules formulated by the founding fathers of each dynasty and legally binding with regard to all their successors. During the Sung dynasty, for instance, one of the dynastic rules was that "under no circumstances should capital punishment be inflicted upon ministers and censors." This rule was dictated by Chao K'uang-yin and was faithfully observed by his successors. Lastly, the institution of censorate which empowered certain officials to criticize and remonstrate with the emperor also helped in preventing the abusive use of imperial power.

The basic weakness of these checks on imperial power was that they could be effective only as long as the emperors wished to observe them. A conscientious emperor like Chao K'uang-yin would abide by them voluntarily, but there was nothing anyone could do if a ruler chose to ignore them. A despotic ruler honored them when they suited his convenience, but ignored them when they failed to do so. That eunuchs could not participate in government was clearly a dynastic rule of the Ming. Yet, when Yung-lo came to the throne and felt that he had to reward his eunuch friends, he threw this rule overboard (Chapter IX). Generally speaking, emperors of the later periods in Chinese history were more despotic than earlier ones (Chapter IX), and they were more inclined to violate customs and traditions which restricted their power. In China theoretical and institutional guarantees were not effective means to check the abuse of power; the best guarantee was the inherent and acquired goodness of the rulers. Good rulers made good government, not vice versa (Chapters II and V).

In administering his empire, an emperor was assisted by a huge army of bureaucratic personnel. Before the abolition of feudalism in the third century B.C. little distinction was made between the government and the royal household, and all officials were regarded as the king's personal servants. The situation changed during the Ch'in-Han period when the territory to be administered was a large empire instead of small, independent kingdoms. The government was then separated from the royal household and made solely responsible for the administration of the empire. During the Han dynasty the head of the government was the prime minister (*tsai hsiang*) appointed by and responsible to the reigning emperor. Under him were thirteen ministries, including war, personnel, transportation, and postal offices. The thirteen ministries were merged into six ministries during the Sui dynasty, and the new arrangement remained unchanged throughout subsequent regimes. The Six Ministries, headed by a prime minister, were often referred to collectively as the cabinet (*nei-ko*). The institution of premiership, however, was abolished early in the Ming dynasty, and the Six Ministries were put under the direct jurisdiction of the emperor (Chapter IX). For the first time in Chinese history, the emperors became their own prime ministers.

As the affairs of the Six Ministries had to be coordinated, the Ming regime created a new post, the Grand Secretariat of the Cabinet (*Nei-ko ta-hsüeh-shih*). The official duty of the Grand Secretary was somewhat of a clerical nature; he could not make policy decisions which belonged exclusively to the emperor. However, with the passage of time he was delegated more authority; if he was able and if he enjoyed the emperor's confidence, he became prime minister *de facto*, if not *de jure*. The Ch'ing dynasty followed the same arrangement until 1729 when the emperor Yung-cheng superimposed on the Grand Secretariat a newly created office, the Privy Council or Office of Strategic Affairs (*Chün-chi ch'u*) over which he personally supervised. Originally created to plan and execute military campaigns, it soon became the policy-making organ of the nation, largely because the emperor personally supervised it. The Grand Secretariat, still in existence, handled the routine, administrative matters. This arrangement persisted until towards the end of the Ch'ing dynasty.

To a Westerner, perhaps the most interesting aspect of the traditional Chinese government was the institution of the censorate. It was an institution as old as the premiership, but it persisted even after the premiership had been abolished. Its official functions varied with different regimes, but its main duty remained the same: to criticize and impeach government officials. The censors were generally low-ranking officials but were empowered to speak candidly on their superiors, including the emperor. Their criticisms extended to an official's private life as well as his official competence because government officials were expected to set examples to the people they ruled.

The institution of the censorate was well developed as early as the Han dynasty. The highest official in charge was the Grand Censor (*Yü-shih ta-fu*), with the rank of deputy premier. Under him were two officials, one in charge of the censorship of government officials (*Yü-shih ch'eng*) and the other keeping a watchful eye on the conduct of the royal household (*Yü-shih chung-ch'eng*), including the emperor. On the local level each inspectional circuit was headed by a censor who visited all districts under his jurisdiction beginning with the eighth lunar month each year and reported his findings to the imperial government once every three years. He was a comparatively low-ranking official (annual salary: 600 piculs of grain); yet, upon his recommendation, the high-ranking governor (annual salary: 2,000 piculs of grain) could be rewarded or punished, promoted or demoted. His roving duties familiarized the imperial government with the lastest local conditions, and his independence of the provincial governor enabled him to speak freely on what he had observed. Sometimes he was given the power of promoting or dismissing local officials on the spot.

During the T'ang dynasty the institution of censorate was further strengthened by the establishment of the Board of Censors (*Yü-shih t'ai*). The duty of the censors was to scrutinize government policies and decisions and to criticize and impeach unfit or incompetent officials. Even the prime minister was not immune to their criticism. Independent of the Board of Censors were the imperial counsellors (*chien-kuan*) whose sole duty was to admonish or remonstrate with the emperor. They were chosen by the prime minister from men of highest integrity and broad knowledge, and theoretically at least, they should never be punished for their opinions. In reality, they often served as the mouthpieces of the prime minister and criticized the emperor as the prime minister himself would have criticized him. They acted as a cushion between the two most powerful offices in the nation, so that the emperor and the prime minister were able to maintain a harmonious relationship despite differences of opinion. An enraged emperor could summarily dismiss an imperial counsellor, but the prime minister's office was usually too lofty to suffer a similar indignity.

After the T'ang dynasty the influence and prestige of the censorate declined as monarchy became more absolute. By the Ming dynasty the office of imperial counsellors was abolished altogether, and replacing it was a low-ranking examiner (*chi-shih-chung*) whose sole duty was the examination of royal decrees before they were issued. He could send these decrees back to the emperor if, in his opinion, they were "improper" or "unconstitutional." His delaying action helped prevent unpopular measures from being enacted in haste and gave the emperor additional time to think them over. The regular Board of Censors was maintained, but their independence was greatly reduced. The censors could criticize and impeach their superiors, but they did so at their own peril. Those who wished to become martyrs could of course do whatever they pleased, including remonstrating with the emperor. As autocracy reached its historical apex under the Ch'ing regime, the influence of the censorate was also reduced to a minimum. The office of the examiner was incorporated as a part of the Board of Censors, and imperial decrees could no longer be delayed on "constitutional" grounds. One Ch'ing censor, in order to convince the then empress dowager (Tz'u Hsi) of the correctness of his point of view on a matter of imperial succession, presented his memorial and then ended his life by drinking poison. When a censor had to commit suicide to enable his opinion to be given adequate attention, the status of the censorate had become very sad indeed.

The local administration of different dynasties varied in details, but the basic structure and the spirit behind it remained substantially the same. Its relationship with the administration above and its duties with regard to the people below did not change. The local administration of the last dynasty, Ch'ing, will be discussed here as an example. China proper was then divided into eighteen provinces, each headed by a governor (*hsün-fu*). Two or three provinces were combined to form a viceroyalty, headed by a viceroy or governor-general (*tsung-tu*). To prevent a governor-general from having too much power over a large territory, the Ch'ing regime made the relationship of these two offices a parallel instead of a jurisdictional one. Both governors and governor-generals could petition and had direct access to the emperor. In case of conflict over business matters only the emperor (or whoever controlled the emperor, such as the empress-dowager) could render the final decision. Below the provincial level were the circuits (*tao*), each headed by an intendant or *tao-t'ai*. Each circuit was in turn divided into prefectures (*fu*) and districts (*chou*), prefectures generally being larger than districts. At the bottom of the administrative ladder were subprefectures (*hsien*), the grass-roots units of government. The head of a subprefecture, often translated as magistrate, was the people's immediate ruler; he collected taxes, administered justice, and was responsible for the maintenance of peace and order within his jurisdiction. Though his rank was one of the lowest, he was perhaps one of the most important officials in the nation. If he were wise and incorruptible, the people benefited; otherwise they would suffer. Below the subprefectural level, there was no organized government as such. Village affairs were taken care of by village elders or local gentry, in a rather informal manner. As a general rule, they settled disputes by negotiation and compromise. Only important issues, such as murder and armed robbery, were referred to the magistrate for decision.

All officials, high or low, received their positions through appointment. They were responsible to their superiors who appointed them rather than to the people whom they governed. In recruiting personnel to staff governmental positions, the Chinese invented a fairly objective, impartial procedure. The purpose was to find the most qualified men; birth, religion, and occupation were not supposed to be considerations. There were two major systems in recruiting government personnel, namely, selection (*hsüan-chü*) and examination (*k'o-chü*). The first system was more widely used during the earlier periods of Chinese history, and the latter system did not come into being until the seventh century. Many dynasties, however, used a combination of both.

The selection system was developed and perfected during the Han dynasty when the centralized government required a large army of civil servants to administer the affairs at the various levels of the empire. One aspect of this system was the selection by local officials of young men of sound character and good native intelligence to be educated at the central university in the capital. Upon graduation these young men would be appointed as the lowest-ranking officials with the local or central government. Moreover, local administrators could at anytime select those whom they regarded as the most talented (*mou-ts'ai*) or the most virtuous (*hsiao-lien*) to be interviewed by the imperial government for possible appointment to governmental positions. The neglect of selection duties on the part of local officials was punishable by law. During the Later Han dynasty the selection system was more institutionalized, and the number of persons to enter civil service each year was made proportional to the total population of each province, usually one for every 200,000 persons. To prevent influence peddling, all selectees were required to take a written examination, and only those who passed could enter the civil service.

The examination system per se was introduced during the Sui dynasty and was not fully developed until the T'ang dynasty. The candidates could be either graduates from public or private schools or those who had been selected by local officials (Chapter V). By the Sung dynasty the examination system had become so prestigious that in the eyes of the public it was the most honorable way of becoming a government official (Chapter VI). When the Mongols conquered China, even they had to conform partially to this tradition (Chapter VIII). It was in force throughout the Ming-Ch'ing period.

Like other systems, the examination system deteriorated with the passage of time, and the question frequently arose as to whether it was the best way of recruiting governmental personnel. Most of the controversies centered on the subject matter of the examinations. The T'ang and early Sung regimes emphasized the composition of poetry which, as has been pointed out in an earlier chapter, was no way of measuring a person's administrative ability. The emphasis on the interpretation of classics (*ching-yi*) during later periods did not improve the situation either. Chu Hsi, for instance, was so dissatisfied with the entire system that he once remarked that the nation would be better off if it stopped giving civil service examinations for thirty years. Ironically, it was his philosophy and the *Four Books* according to his interpretations that became the basic texts of all questions given in the examinations during the Ming-Ch'ing period. Candidates could no longer think and write freely and independently; if they did, their papers would be automatically rejected. Though unsatisfactory as a measurement of a man's true ability, the composition of poetry reflected to some extent his basic intelligence and literary training. Many people wondered whether the formalized expression of popularly accepted ideas could even serve that purpose.

The examination system further deteriorated when not only ideas but also the way to express them became highly conventionalized. The way officially approved was the so-called eight-legged form (*pa-ku*) which required parallel phrases or sentences (balanced like a person's legs) and the rigid observance of a well-defined structural style. First developed during the Ming dynasty, it remained the standard form throughout the

Ch'ing dynasty. That it could not serve the examination purpose was rather obvious, and as early as the seventeenth century, Ku Yen-wu denounced it as worse than Ch'ing Shih-huang's burning of books and burying scholars alive insofar as the promotion of new ideas was concerned. Despite severe criticisms like this, the eight-legged essays remained with the examination system, and the government was either unwilling or unable to find a better substitute. The examination system was finally abolished in 1906.

Serious as these shortcomings were, we should not let them deceive us when considering the basic merits of the examination system. Its shortcomings were those of a technical nature, and its advantages were fundamental and basic. Though much can be said about its unreliability, it cannot be denied that those who had passed the examinations were generally brighter and more intelligent than those who had failed. Whatever disadvantages education might have as a determining factor to judge a person's worth, it was still better than other personal attributes, whether they be birth or wealth. Before modern times China was the only country (except those countries that were under Chinese cultural influence such as Korea) in the world that had an objective, institutionalized method of recruiting governmental personnel. Within the examination system, power and wealth made no difference and only the level of education as measured by the examinations mattered. Attempts to evade the impartiality of the examination system by any sort of dishonest means were major crimes under Chinese law and were often punishable by death. Though much has been said about Chinese corruption, the examination system was one of the least corrupt of all Chinese institutions.

Moreover, the system provided a great deal of social mobility since even the humblest (except the "mean people" for some dynasties) could become a member of the ruling class by acquiring an education and passing the examinations. The absence of clear-cut class divisions might explain partially why parliamentary government never developed in China. As one recalls, parliamentary government developed in Western Europe as a result of the successful challenge by the middle class of the king's monopoly of government. Since in China the people had access to governmental positions through the examination system, there was less need to struggle against the king for the control of the government. With the exception of the throne itself, all offices were open to the public. The Western Europeans, unable to participate in the king's government, overthrew that government and replaced it with one of their own, known as parliamentary democracy. The Chinese, on the other hand, strengthened and prolonged absolute monarchy by joining it. By making all offices open to the people except their own, Chinese monarchs were much more clever than their European counterparts.

THE SOCIAL SCENE

Customarily the Chinese spoke of their society as composed of four classes: the scholars, the farmers, the artisans, and the merchants. The scholars were given the highest status because they performed what the Chinese regarded as the most important function: the transmission of an ancient heritage and the personification of Chinese virtues. The farmers' standing was second only to the scholars because they were the primary producers, feeding and clothing the nation. The artisans processed what the farmers had produced, and their function was not regarded as so essential as that of the farmers. At the bottom of the social scale were the merchants whom the Chinese regarded as outright exploiters, making profits from what others had produced or processed and contributing nothing themselves. Two other classes were often added to the four described above. One was the soldiers, whose expected role of burning and killing was very distasteful to the Chinese. Inasmuch as they took away the most valuable things from society, their standing in society was inferior to that of the merchants. Their image in the eyes of the public was not improved during modern times when the idle and adventurous swarmed to their ranks as mercenaries. The other class was the so-called "mean people" (*chien-min*), consisting of domestic slaves, prostitutes, entertainers, and members of lowly professions such as barbers. Though the contempt shown for this group could be explained historically, it was nevertheless a prejudice. It should be added, however, that the total number of this group was very small at any given time.

A more accurate classification of the Chinese people was perhaps the one advanced by Mencius some 2,300 years ago. He believed that in an ideal society there were two kinds of people: the educated who ruled and the uneducated who were the ruled. Though Mencius was only speculating on what an ideal society should be, the Chinese applied his theory almost to the letter until modern times. If we transcribe the customary division of classes (scholars, farmers, etc.) into his classification, all but the scholars would belong to the ruled category. Among the ruled it was difficult to say which group actually had a higher standing. Though traditionally the farmers were exalted and the merchants were condemned, such an evaluation of their comparative worth was done more in principle than in fact. It did not affect to any large extent the estimation of each class in the eyes of the general public. With the exception of the Former Han dynasty, discrimination against merchants was more theoretical than actual, though this discrimination, even on a theoretical plane, did discourage young men of talent from pursuing a commercial career. While it is true that a great landlord enjoyed more prestige than a rich merchant, it is not correct to say that a shopkeeper was regarded as inferior to a small, independent farmer. In the eyes of most people he was definitely superior to a tenant farmer. In China as in other societies, income crossed over the established social boundaries to become an important factor in determining social prestige. What made the traditional Chinese society seem unique was that income played only an auxiliary rather than a dominant role in the matter of social standing.

While the difference between farmers, artisans, and merchants was comparatively minor insofar as social standing was concerned, there was no question that scholars towered above them all in social prestige and general esteem. A number of reasons can be advanced to explain their exalted position. First, without an established religion (Confucianism was not a religion), China did not have a clerical hierarchy. On the other hand, some of the essential, useful functions traditionally carried on by the clergy in the West had likewise in China to be performed by someone. The teaching of morals, for instance, was such a function. Under the circumstances no one was in a better position to perform such functions than Confucian scholars. Second, the ultimate goal of practically all Confucian scholars (including Confucius) was to secure a position with the government, and in China as in many other agricultural societies, there was no higher prestige than that of becoming a king's minister. Since government officials were selected from scholars as a matter of principle, the prestige generally ascribed to government officials was also shared by scholars. Third, there was the difficulty of the Chinese written language. Though to learn colloquial Chinese (pai-hua) was perhaps no more difficult than to learn the English or Russian languages, it was definitely much more difficult to learn to read and write literary or classical Chinese. This required not only the mastering of more than 10,000 separate characters and their numerous combinations but also a fair knowledge of the great accumulation of Chinese literature. Unless the learner was a born genius, it would take a considerable part of his life just to learn to write in a presentable style. His style could always be improved no matter how good it was, and to improve it would be a life-long process. Most Chinese just could not afford the time. Thus, true mastery of a literary education was bound to be limited to a few. Knowledge, like commodities, commanded a high price when it was difficult to obtain.

The dividing line between the educated and the uneducated, the ruling and the ruled, was not a fathomless abyss unbridged. As education was an acquired attribute, class distinctions were earned, not hereditary. The nobility was noble partly because all noblemen were educated. The same thing can be said concerning the "old families" of the Wei-Tsin period. The only major exceptions were the Mongols during the Yüan dynasty who were noble despite the fact that they might be illiterate. But the Yüan regime was a non-Chinese regime, and its noblemen were never regarded as truly noble in the Chinese sense. Many of the Chinese eunuchs were also uneducated, but they were denounced as usurpers whenever they acquired power as a result of the emperor's abdication of authority. By and large the Chinese used education as a criterion to measure a man's worth. The emphasis on education made China one of the most mobile societies until modern times. Few pre-industrial societies had a faster turnover of the social and power elite, and such a fast turnover kept the Chinese society vital and dynamic. The constant absorption of new blood from the lower strata kept the elite in a state of continuous flux. The knowledge that one would be accepted as a member of the ruling group if he had clearly demonstrated his worth by passing the civil service examinations smoothed over the natural antagonism between the ruling and the ruled. There were no class struggles in the Marxist sense of that term because there were no definite, unchangeable classes.

The lack of class antagonism may have been partially responsible for the unchanged nature of the traditional Chinese society despite changes in political regimes. Dynastic changes meant little more than changes of royal households and should never be interpreted as the triumph of one class over another. With the establishment of a new regime, the same social structure remained intact and people moved between classes as freely as before. As social mobility was high, there was a general satisfaction with the social structure as it was, and no political regime ever wished to alter it. Such a state of contentment may partially explain the Chinese distrust for social innovations and their constant reference to history as the best guide and counsel. Confucius prided himself upon having faith in the ancient sages, and Wang Mang and Wang An-shih, two of the greatest reformers in Chinese history, quoted copiously from Confucian classics to justify their reforms. The reformers wanted to bring China back to its golden past, instead of building a new society for the future. As late as the nineteenth century scholars and statesmen, even when agreeing that reforms were essential, insisted that such reforms should be carried out only within China's historical framework. Since they kept on looking backward, there must have been many things in the past which, in their opinion, deserved to be preserved.

Recognizing that man's distinction in society depended upon earned and acquired attributes, the Chinese viewed with a broad mind religious and racial differences. Religion and race were not factors in class differentiations. Twice in history China was completely conquered by foreigners, and it was only then that race became a dominant factor in social divisions. In both cases, Yüan and Ch'ing, it was the ruling aliens who discriminated against the Chinese. As defined by Confucius, the difference between Chinese and barbarians was a cultural rather than a racial difference, and those who had accepted Chinese culture were regarded as Chinese regardless of their racial backgrounds. The Chinese pointed out with pride that the founders of some of their dynasties were alien in origin. The founder of the Chou dynasty, for instance, rose from a "barbarian" land, and the ancestors of T'ang's royal house could be traced back to a variety of "barbarian" blood. Yet Chou and T'ang were two of the greatest dynasties in Chinese history. The Manchu "barbarians" were accepted as Chinese rulers once they accepted and adopted Chinese culture. One of the diplomatic maneuvers frequently used by ancient emperors was to marry their princesses to "barbarian" chiefs, and no Chinese ever questioned the wisdom of such marriages on racial grounds. The absence of racial discrimination served the Chinese well: it enabled them to expand slowly and steadily until they occupied the geographical area we know today as China. At one time all peoples outside of the North China plain were regarded as barbarians. They became Chinese once they were culturally assimilated. The Roman Empire eventually split into many independent, quarrelling kingdoms; China, on the other hand, remained unified for the most part of her written history.

The absence of racial discrimination extended beyond the Mongoloids, people whose physical features were similar to those of the Chinese. During the historical past, Caucasoids (Persians, Arabs, Jews, and Europeans) were known to have taken permanent residence in China. It is even possible that at one time there was a sizable Negro population. Since historians failed to record exactly how they looked except the casual remark that they were dark, it is still debated whether they were Negroes. Whether they were Caucasoids or Negroids, there is no indication that they were discriminated against on account of race. When racial discrimination was introduced during the modern period, it was the Europeans in China who discriminated against the Chinese.

Unlike Europe where religious differences were a major factor in social cleavage, China did not attach much importance to religion as a determinant in social differentiation. There were Buddhist and Taoist priests, but they did not constitute a distinct class in the sense that they were higher or lower than the rest of the population. China had no established religion, and religion was left to families and individuals. Individual emperors might prefer one religion or another, but no Chinese emperor ever compelled the nation to follow his own example. There was nothing in Confucian ideology which prohibited the existence of other ideologies, and to be intolerant for the sake of intolerance was definitely anti-Confucian. Though from time to time there were individual zealots (Han Yü, for instance) who wrote inflammatory essays condemning Buddhism, the people as a whole were remarkably tolerant in religious matters. There were "Three Persecutions of Buddhism" in Chinese history, and the most severe persecution was conducted by T'ang Wu-tsung. Yet, the most severe persecution, which consisted of the reduction of the number of Buddhist monasteries and monks, was based upon economic rather than ideological reasons, and lasted only seven months (Chapter V). No Buddhist was put to the sword simply because he was a Buddhist. We should never read into these persecutions the same meaning as the Roman persecution of Christians and Christian persecution of heretics. In a typical Chinese household of modern times, the father was likely a Confucian and his wife was in most cases a devoted Buddhist; it was not unusual for them to decide to send their children to Christian missionary schools. In the minds of the Chinese, all religions taught people to be good: a religion defeated its basic purpose if it taught its followers to discriminate or hold hatred against other religions. Like farmers and artisans, the priests (Buddhist, Taoist, etc.) performed an essential, useful service, but they were not entitled to preferential treatment in the eyes of the Chinese. They did not possess the power of reward or punishment, either in this world or in the next. Their conduct and behavior would be judged on the same basis as the rest of the population.

Since education was the primary avenue to power and influence, it would seem that every Chinese family would have sent their children to schools. This, of course, was not the case. There were many considerations against what outwardly seemed to be the most logical decision to make. Most Chinese were small or tenant farmers, and they did not have the economic means to educate their children. A boy in school would not only mean the deprivation of one worker in the field; it would also mean that he would be taken away from farm production permanently once he was an educated man because an educated man was not supposed to do any manual work. Financially, education could be justified only when the educated man passed the civil service examinations and acquired a governmental position, and his chance of passing them, as we have said before, was very small indeed (Chapter VI). Failing to pass the examinations, his other alternative of making a living was to secure a position with small financial returns, such as school teaching or serving as a secretary-adviser (mo-liao) to some other official. In most cases he became an unemployed intellectual and had to be supported by his family for the rest of his life.

In view of the great risks involved, it was not surprising that educated men came mostly from the well-to-do families that had independent income from land or other sources. Though there were cases in which a peasant's son rose to become prime minister, most prime ministers came from the landlord class. In a more or less typical situation, a farmer would encourage the most promising of his children to acquire an education, and the whole family (including his other sons) would work to support him. If he succeeded in passing the civil service examination, the joy and the financial reward would belong to the entire family. If he failed, the family's prestige was nevertheless enhanced by the presence of an educated man, even though his intellectual capacity might not go much beyond the writing of a presentable letter and the composition of badly rhymed poems.

THE FAMILY SCENE

Like the Chinese nation, a traditional Chinese family was an autocratic organization. It was organized on two well-defined, unwritten rules: the superiority of the older over the younger generation and the superiority of males over females. In case of conflict, the first rule prevailed over the second. It could be compared to an army, each member receiving orders from his superiors and giving them to his inferiors. In a family of three generations the chain of command would look something like this:

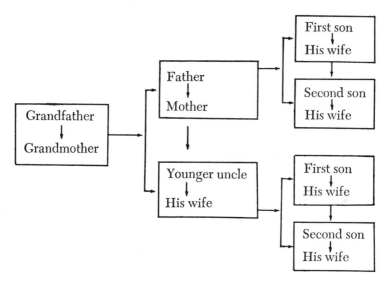

Within each generation the oldest son had authority over his younger brothers and sisters, though this authority was not so absolute as that of the parents. In case of disobedience on the part of a younger brother, the elder could appeal the case to the parents, who under normal circumstances were expected to support his stand. Since boys and girls were often segregated at an early age, the elder brother's commands—if he had any —to his unmarried sisters were first approved by his mother and then transmitted through her. All these, of course, were done in an informal manner.

These rules worked because they were based upon mutual responsibilities and obligations: love and protection on the part of the superiors and respect and obedience on the part of the inferiors. When the head of a family made a decision affecting each member, he took into consideration the family interest as a whole, and it was the absolute trust in his impartiality that made each member obey without complaint, no matter how adversely it would affect him personally. If a father decided that his second son was to be sent to school and the rest of his sons were to work at the family farm or shop, his decision had to be obeyed by all family members unless the father allowed himself to be persuaded to change his mind. Because of his broader knowledge, an educated son might be able to make more suggestions and command more attention with regard to family affairs, but education could not raise his status within the family circle. Theoretically, final decisions could only be made by the father, and in the absence of the father, the mother, even though both parents might be illiterate. Each member was held responsible for the behavior of his section of the family, his wife and children. To an outsider, the head of the family (father or grandfather as the case might be) was responsible for the actions of all members of the family, from his sons to his great grandsons.

Of course, there were individual variations from the pattern described above. A father might decide to abdicate his authority in favor of one of his sons (usually the oldest), and the mother, being out of touch with the outside world, might choose to stand on the sideline with regard to family decisions. But their authority was there, if they chose to exercise it. Generally speaking, the more "gentry" a family was, the stricter the chain of command. An emperor might be the Son of Heaven before his subjects. Yet within the family circle he was his mother's son; he should wait on her and obey her commands at all times and under any circumstances. Filial piety was the first virtue of the nation to which all must subscribe and from which even an emperor could not claim exemption. In the eyes of the public, a father was within his rights to put his daughter to death to save the family from disgrace if, for instance, she were found pregnant while unwed. But the son committed the greatest crime indeed if he took the law into his own hands against his father, no matter how much his father deserved the punishment. The Chinese believed that the father-son relationship was the most important of the five cardinal relationships among men (the other four relationships were between king and subjects, husband and wife, older and younger brothers, and friend and friend), and that the superiority of father over son had to be maintained at all costs.

Like other institutions, the traditional Chinese family had its advantages and disadvantages. It provided psychological and economic security; it created a sense of belonging. Its emphasis on mutual responsibility and family honor helped prevent wrongdoings among family members. Its disadvantages, on the other hand, were many and obvious. The Chinese glorified large families, and often three or four generations lived together. No matter how much each member was supposed to love the others, jealousies and resentments were bound to occur, especially among members of the same generation. Quarrels flared up from time to time, and harmony was often achieved only through the iron-handed suppression by the family elders. The inferiority of the female sex made the female role the least enviable, especially females of younger generations. The in-law difficulties, though universal, were greatly intensified in the Chinese situation. To avoid them was nearly impossible because a Chinese could not easily leave his parents and take away his wife to set up a new household. To do so would bring disgrace to the family, and the son would be universally condemned. To make the situation worse, he was expected to side with his mother against his wife in any disagreement between them, regardless of the merit of the case. The Chinese compared spouses to clothes which could be changed when necessity arose, but parenthood, being a biological relationship, could never be changed. Faced with a nonunderstanding mother-in-law, a young wife could have a miserable life.

Family tragedies often arose from difficulties between mothers and daughters-in-law, and almost without exception it was the latter who had to make the sacrifice. The sorrows of daughters-in-law were lamented by ancient poets and have been recorded in their poems and epics. The most famous epic in this regard is *The Peacock Flies Southeast* (*K'ung-ch'üeh tung-nan fei*), written by an anonymous writer of the third century. It is the story of a talented girl who learned to "weave at thirteen, tailor at fourteen, play the guitar at fifteen, and recite the *Odes* and the *History* at sixteen," and was married to a government clerk at seventeen. The couple were very devoted to each other, and this devotion apparently aroused the jealousy and resentment of the groom's mother. Maintaining that her daughter-in-law did not know how to please her, she insisted that her son should divorce his young wife. His mother's insistence left him no choice; however, he promised his wife that he would bring her back if somehow he could make his mother change her mind. After the girl went home to her parents, her mother and elder brother soon arranged to marry her to a son of a prefectural magistrate. Unwilling to break the promise she had made to her former husband and yet unable to disobey her mother and brother, she decided to drown herself. When the news arrived that she had committed suicide, her former husband joined her by hanging himself on a tree. According to the author, the event had actually occurred, and to those who are familiar with the traditional Chinese family, it is plausible. The Sung poet Lu Yu (1125–1210) had a similar experience, though it ended less tragically. He had to divorce his wife as ordered by his mother, but the couple maintained their affection for each other throughout the rest of their lives.

In the traditional Chinese family practically all marriages were arranged; only the lowest of the low would marry for love and romance. Today it is still fashionable to begin an engagement or wedding announcement by such an august remark as "By the order of our respective parents," even though the parents might have little or nothing to do with the happy occasion. In bygone days the sexes were segregated, and a maiden was not supposed to see a male stranger under any circumstances. The higher the family standing was, the stricter the segregation. Such being the case, marriages had to be arranged. In looking for a prospective wife or husband for their son or daughter, the parents had to consider a number of factors, and the most important factor was the other family's reputation and standing. The personal attributes of the prospective groom or bride came second: the boy should be talented and promising (for gentry families) or strong and hard-working (for peasant families), and the girl should be even-tempered, know her household work (such as sewing), and look wholesome, preferably on the plump side. The interested family revealed its intention to a go-between who approached the other family in the most casual manner; it had to be casual to avoid embarrassment. For a gentry family of high standing, the marriage procedure consisted of "six rituals" (liu-li), from the initial inquiry to the wedding itself. Most families, however, could not afford the expenses and passed over most of them. One ritual they could not pass over was the exchange of birth information: the hour, day, month, and year the prospective groom or bride was born. A fortune-teller was called in, and he would decide whether the proposed marriage was an auspicious one. A girl born in the Year of the Tiger would have a much more limited choice. She could not marry a man born in the Year of the Lamb because she would surely swallow him. But it would be all right for her to marry a man born in the Year of the Monkey because the monkey could always jump up to the back of the tiger. Needless to say, many prospects of happy marriages were ended right there.

In the Chinese thinking, a marriage was as much a marriage of two families as it was between the two persons directly involved. Its major purpose was the propagation of the male family line. Children bore their father's name, never their mother's. Individuals submitted themselves to their family's decisions, and rarely were they consulted about their prospective mates. Two great friends, learning that each other's wives were pregnant, might decide right then that their unborn babies were engaged if they turned out to be opposite in sex. Instead of seeing anything wrong with this kind of arrangement, the traditional Chinese society glorified it. Since marriage was arranged, the groom would be an ingenious man indeed if he had seen his wife before the wedding night. A woman performed her function well as a wife if she had borne her husband a son: it was then that her position with the family became absolutely secure. If she failed to perform such a function, her husband would be strongly pressed to take a concubine, mostly by his parents and sometimes by his wife as well. Socially and legally, a man could take as many concubines as he could afford. Since few could afford it, concubinage was confined to a small fraction of the population. Chinese emperors, who could best afford it, had scores or even hundreds of concubines.

Grim as Chinese marriage might seem, there is no indication that it was less happy than marriages arrived at any other way. Even though divorce was socially disapproved, it was legally permissible, and divorced persons could remarry if they chose to. Yet there were few cases of divorce. The concubine system may have saved many marriages, but it did not seem to be the main factor in the scarcity of divorce cases. Social disapproval was definitely a deterrent, and the families involved would normally exercise great pressure to prevent marriages from breaking up. Strange as it may seem, the fact that marriages were arranged might have been beneficial in some respects. A good family background as emphasized by the Chinese was perhaps a more important factor in happy marriages than a prospective mate's physical appearance. The customary subservience of wives to husbands and the Chinese attachment of great importance to children might be another contributing factor. It is not known, however, how many people remained married though unhappy. It will remain unknown, because the Chinese, as a matter of principle, did not believe that they should reveal to outsiders their feelings towards their spouses. Outward affection was taboo, even towards one's own wife. When a man and his wife had to appear together in public, the woman customarily walked ten paces behind.

How did sexual segregation come into being? Certainly there was no such thing at the beginning of recorded history. Then boys and girls enjoyed each other's companionship as much as they have under any other culture. Here is an example:

> You, shy, beautiful lass, my beloved,
>   Failed to meet me in a city corner you'd promised.
> Here I came; nowhere could you be found.
> Should I leave or should I have waited?
> For a long time I hesitated.

> You, shy, beautiful lass, my beloved,
>   Gave me a river reed flashing red;
> I love the river reed,
> I love more my beloved.

> I love the river reed, beautiful and enchanting;
> What beauty would it possess,
> Had it not caressed my beloved? [1]

[1] Translated from a poem in the *Book of Odes*.

In those ancient years a woman could be equally romantic:

> Are you thinking of me?
> Your love I cannot see.
> What prevents you from crossing the stream
> That separates you and me?

> If you stay your adoration for me,
> Others will not, certainly!
> Oh, how stupid you can be,
> How stupid you can be! [1]

As late as the second century B.C. it was still possible to conduct courtship. The Han poet Ssu-ma Hsiang-ju (179–117 B.C.) courted a rich widow with his lute and succeeded in persuading her to elope with him. Four centuries later the handsome P'an Yo (247–300) was reported to have been mobbed by women every time he went out. Such an occurrence would have been unthinkable in a later period. The indications are that sexual segregation became more and more rigid with the passage of time and was strictly enforced after the Sung dynasty. What caused the change? The acceptance of Confucian moralism was unquestionably one of the major reasons, especially the Sung School of philosophy. Chu Hsi, for instance, not only advocated strict sexual segregation but glorified widowhood as well; he thought he did society a great service by encouraging widows to join their dead husbands at the earliest possible moment. As his philosophy dominated the intellectual and ethical scene for the next seven hundred years, his bleak, puritanical ideas began to be accepted as the lofty goal which every gentry family strove to achieve. With the popularity of his ideas, the status of women declined.

Nothing can illustrate better the decline of women's status in society than the custom of foot-binding. It is not known exactly when or how this custom began. One reputable source maintains that it began in the court of Li Yü (Chapter VII) where a court dancer "bent her feet with silk so they were shaped like a crescent and whirled around as if she were dancing in the clouds." By the Sung dynasty foot-binding was widely practiced among the gentry families. The binding process began when a girl was four or five and continued until the desired result was achieved. The net result was a pair of crippled feet, only half the normal size. (Many mothers did such a thorough job that their daughters could barely walk.) Why did this inhumane custom ever get established and moreover persist for almost 1,000 years? Men, for unknown reasons, prefer small feet on women. A Western woman responds by squeezing her feet into shoes of smaller size, and Chinese women, perhaps more eager to please, bound their feet so they could walk forever as a modern

[1] Translated from a poem in the *Book of Odes*.

ballerina dances. Chinese gentlemen of older generations would not consider a woman attractive unless she had a pair of bound feet. However, it should be pointed out that this custom was by and large confined to a small portion of the population: the gentry families. The peasant women who had to work in the field neither desired nor could they afford such a painful luxury. The custom remained a major curse of the traditional Chinese society until the twentieth century.

THE INTELLECTUAL AND MORAL SCENE

The Chinese believed that the purpose of education was to make man a better man and that this moral purpose was inseparable from the learning process. In fact, moral indoctrination began as soon as the educational process began. A schoolboy of five or six might encounter the following assignment the first day he was in school:

> When a man is born (*Jen chih ch'u*),
> His nature is basically good (*hsing pen shan*).
> Human nature is similar (*hsing hsiang chin*);
> Only environment makes it diverse (*hsi hsiang yüan*).

These are the opening statements of the thirteenth century *Three-character Classic* (*San-tzu ching*), the chief primer for school children for almost seven hundred years. Needless to say, the schoolboy did not understand them, but he memorized and recited them like a song as his teacher had commanded. For the time being, the most important thing was to recognize and write the twelve characters that composed the two sentences. After he finished the *Three-character Classic*, his next book assignment might be the *Analects of Confucius*. The first paragraph of the *Analects* reads as follows:

Confucius says, Is it not a great pleasure to learn and to review constantly what you have learned? Will you not be pleased when a friend comes afar to see you? Is he not a gentleman indeed who shows no annoyance even though nobody knows his goodness?

By the time he was nine or ten the pupil should have covered the *Four Books*. If he was intelligent and his memory was good, he might have gone beyond the *Book of Odes* and the *Book of History*. Of course, he did not understand all that was said in these books, partly because of the nature of the subject matter and partly because they were written in a literary, classical style. However, he had acquired a large vocabulary, and it was then that he and his teacher would explore the hidden meanings of the ancient passages. When he reached the age of eleven or twelve, he was expected to write in an understandable manner. Once every ten or fifteen days he would be given a theme to write on: the theme was usually taken from one of the *Four Books* or *Five Classics* and consequently had a strong moral tone. One theme might be: "Confucius says, Do not travel afar while your parents are living. Elaborate." Another theme might be: "Mencius emphasizes the difference between righteousness (*yi*) and profit (*li*). Why?" Needless to say, all themes had to be written in a literary, classical style. Once he knew how to read independently the commentaries as well as the texts, the student's dependence on his teacher was lessened and he was practically on his own. How far he could advance depended upon his native ability, his ambition (or rather, the ambition of his family), and the economic status of his family. The decisive moment would arrive when he took the lowest level of the civil service examination.

It is easy to see that the traditional Chinese training was heavily one-sided, and little room was provided for other studies besides ancient classics and literature. Though Confucius himself believed that an educated man should master the "six arts" (rites, music, archery, chariot riding, calligraphy, and mathematics), academic learning was practically the only thing emphasized by all the later Confucian schools, especially those on the local level. After the civil service examination system was introduced, the students had little incentive to learn anything besides the classics and poetry because the examinations tested primarily these two fields. Thus the best product of the Chinese school system of old was a Confucian scholar, well-learned in Chinese philosophy, literature, and related subjects, but inadequately prepared in more practical fields. He knew nothing about technology and science, and his knowledge of what we today call social sciences was shallow and unsystematic. His sense of values was completely Chinese, as he had no way of knowing anything outside the cultural confine of China.

Of Confucius' "six arts" calligraphy was the only art form given great attention during the later periods. Calligraphy supposedly taught the virtue of patience and perseverance because long and constant practice was required before the writing would look even presentable. A child began to practice on his calligraphy as early as he learned to read, and usually he began by following the style of one of the great masters. The master could be, say, the ninth century Liu Kung-ch'üan (noted for his "bony" strokes), the thirteenth century Chao Meng-t'iao (famous for his graceful lines), or others; and the pupil's teacher would help him to select the style to follow in accordance with his natural inclinations. He practiced with brush and ink two or three hours a day; very likely he would continue to practice whenever he found time for the rest of his life. A man's calligraphic achievement, like a lady's face, was open for all to see, and too often it was regarded as a measurement of his cultural attainment. The incentive to improve it was enhanced during the Ch'ing dynasty when a paper written for the civil service examination would be automatically rejected if its author's calligraphy was judged as below standard. Well-executed pieces of calligraphy were hung in the most conspicuous places in a gentleman's house as if they were great paintings. Even in paintings there were accompanying poems (a practice developed during the later periods) which indicated unmistakably the painters' calligraphic achievements. A man whose calligraphy was poor would encounter a great deal of inconvenience. It was a severe handicap if he had to look for employment.

Since educational and moral purposes were considered inseparable, every branch of learning had to serve a moral purpose. Music refined a man's character; chariot riding and archery, two of the ancient subjects, taught the learner "the precedence of the seniors over the juniors" rather than physical fitness or military skill. The love poems in the *Book of Odes* were twisted to teach moral lessons, and history was written primarily to "punish the wicked and reward the virtuous." The writers of novels, short stories, and plays had in mind the same purpose. Even the author of *Flowering Plum in a Golden Vase* had to insist that the real purpose of his book was to teach a lesson against sexual indulgence (Chapter X). While the educated received their ethical teaching from works of old, the uneducated learned it from the examples set by the educated and from stories and plays they heard and saw in the tea houses and theatres. Since the basic standards of behavior were those recorded in the ancient classics, there was a moral code familiar to all and universally accepted. Its inviolability was strengthened through custom and usage.

The penalty for violating the moral code was severe and immediate. A thief would be lashed in public, and a murderer would have to pay with his own life regardless of the provocation. Chinese prisons were among the most inhuman places ever created for human beings; they vied with medieval dungeons as possible hells on earth. Though the educated were supposedly above corporal punishment, they received penalties perhaps even more severe if they ever committed crimes. The penalty was more severe because they had been expected to set examples for others. They were regarded as a disgrace to society and were perhaps ostracized forever. The sense of shame would be shared by their entire families and by their descendants for an indefinite time to come. They could no longer participate in the civil service examinations, and their chance for social recognition or any advancement would be gone forever. For practical purposes they would live as "living corpses" for the rest of their earthly terms. The severity of punishment was a strong deterrent to any wrongdoings.

The Chinese drew no subtle distinction between moral and legal codes. A moral offense was often dealt with as if it were a legal crime.

Filial disobedience was a moral offense; it was also punishable by law if the magistrate chose to enforce it. However, as long as an offense was of a minor nature and involved members of the same family, the law would refrain from intervening, trusting that the principle of equity could be better served without intervention. The law would intervene if different families were involved and if they could not settle their disputes through negotiation and compromise outside of the court. Society regarded a family, instead of an individual, as a moral unit. A family was held responsible for the conduct of its members, and the entire family was punishable if any of its members had committed a crime against society. Family members emulated one another in good behavior, and the restraining power of the entire family could usually prevent an individual from going morally astray. When Chang's child fought with Li's child, Chang was socially obligated to punish his child, and he could reasonably expect that his neighbor would do the same with his, because Chang was responsible for his child's behavior, not his neighbor's. It was ungentlemanly to blame others, and it was unthinkable for a father to give such "unfatherly" advice as "Hit him back." A child should be taught to criticize himself before he learned to criticize others, and he should never be allowed to shift the blame. He should be constantly reminded that people judged his family according to his behavior and conduct.

The families that supposedly set examples to other families were the gentry families. The definition of the word "gentry" was rather obscure, and it was more a product of public image than a combination of tangible factors. It varied from place to place: the same person whose status was too low to be considered a man of the gentry in a large city might be a leading member of the gentry class in his native village. However, there were things in common among the members of the gentry class: education, independent income, and a favorable public image. Education made one a member of the intelligentsia, a transmitter of the Chinese heritage; and an independent income freed him from the necessity of seeking undesirable employment. Since most Chinese derived their income from the land, an independent income usually meant the possession of a landholding. A favorable public image resulted from careful cultivation and came only with the passage of time, and a person was well situated indeed if his family had belonged to the gentry class for several generations. As there were numerous degrees within each of the three factors, there were numerous degrees of "gentility." Therefore, an ideal member of the gentry was a person whose intellectual capacity had been confirmed by his successful passing of the civil service examinations, whose income was large, and whose moral character was above reproach. The situation would be most ideal indeed, if he were a great landlord and a holder of the highest academic degree (*chin-shih* or "advanced scholarship"), and especially if his family had produced scholars and government officials for many generations. In such a case he belonged to *kao-men* (literally, high doors) or *shih-chia* (old families), the most enviable of all gentry families.

The gentry were the recognized local leaders. An appointed magistrate, who usually came from another province, had to secure their cooperation if he wished to govern successfully. Living in the same community for generations, if not centuries, the gentry had a deeper concern with local welfare than the temporarily appointed government officials. How a community thrived depended to a great extent upon their efforts and leadership. They financed and supported public works, schools, orphanages, and other useful projects. They were the guardians of public morals, and in moral matters they were expected to be more strict with themselves than with others. Within the Confucian confine, their private life could vary a great deal, depending upon not only individual inclinations but economic status as well. A gentry family of high standing might have a life such as that described in *The Dream of the Red Chamber,* while a less well-to-do person might encounter the same difficulties as the author of *The Six Chapters of a Floating Life* (Chapter X). However, as a personal embodiment of Chinese culture, they all loved poetry, calligraphy, and good paintings. They regarded themselves as superior, and their superiority was admitted by the general public.

SUMMARY

Those Chinese who came from rural areas where the Western influence was the least felt must remember the life described above, and perhaps remember it with a great deal of nostalgia. But for better or for worse, the traditional Chinese society is gone, and it does not seem that it can be revived. Its undermining began more than a century ago and has been virtually completed since the Communists took over the mainland in 1949. Perhaps its disappearance was inevitable. The traditional Chinese society was built on two major pillars: a sedentary, agricultural life and the ancient Confucian heritage. Industrialization would have undermined the former, and the pervasiveness of the Western culture would have broken down the latter. The presence of the Western culture may provide China with new answers to old problems and may direct it to a new path which it has never thought possible before. Of course, many ancient values will have to be sacrificed. It is still too early to tell into what kind of society China will eventually evolve.

℀ xii

The Western Impact (1)

Until the last century the Chinese had shown little interest in foreign countries. This lack of interest was due partly to the belief that China was culturally superior and had no need to learn anything from the outside world and partly to the fact that China looked down upon trade and was not interested in proselytizing, the two major motives that have brought foreigners to China in modern times. A man who went abroad and left his parents behind and the family cemetery unattended was universally condemned because he had violated a cardinal virtue of Confucianism, filial loyalty. To go abroad was often a legal as well as a moral crime and was punishable by death or long imprisonment. Thus, in the intercourse between China and the non-Chinese world, China had been largely passive. To be sure, there were times when an exuberant China sent out expeditions to learn about the outside world, such as Chang Ch'ien's "exploration of the West," the pilgrimages of Chinese Buddhists to India, and Cheng Ho's "seven voyages to the 'Western Ocean.'" These, however, were isolated cases, and each of them lasted for a comparatively short period. There were many Marco Polos who informed Europe about China, but there had been no Chinese Marco Polo in Europe until the nineteenth century. Western Europe emerged about 1500 and began to dominate the world; but of this fact, and of the profound changes brought about because of it, the Chinese knew nothing. For their ignorance they had to pay dearly, as we shall see later in this chapter.

In bringing China and the non-Chinese world together, foreigners played a much more active role. The Koreans, the Japanese, and the Indians had come to China at one time or another. Beginning with the Wei-Tsin period (220–420) there was also a steady inflow of Near Easterners who came to China as traders or missionaries. A Chinese book (*Loyang chia-lan chi,* or *A Story of Buddhist Temples in Loyang*) written in the sixth century records that there were more than ten thousand alien households in Loyang alone, and a sizable portion of them seems to have been Arabic and Persian. With the establishment of the Islamic empire in the seventh century, the inflow increased, and the newcomers, as one might expect, were mostly Arabs. With the passage of time the sea routes to China became more important, as ships were better built and became more seaworthy. Some of the foreigners came to trade, made a profit, and returned home; others settled permanently in the cities of the coastal areas, such as Canton, Ch'üanchou, and Yangchow. Within each of these cities, foreigners lived in segregated quarters (*fan-fang*), and from them the city government selected a respected or influential man as their chief. During the T'ang-Sung period (618–1279) Arabs constituted the largest number of foreigners in residence, and more often than not the chief was an Arab. If a foreigner committed a crime against his own countrymen, the customary law of his native land would apply; if the crime were committed against a man of a different nationality or a Chinese, the Chinese law would prevail. Foreigners often married Chinese women; they were not allowed, however, to take their Chinese wives back to their home countries.

After many years in China, many of these foreigners acquired Chinese names, learned the Chinese language, and even participated in the civil service examinations. In 848, for instance, an Arab named Li Yensheng passed the examination and became a holder of the highest academic degree ("advanced scholarship"). Foreigners like Li Yen-sheng would be eventually Sinicized; they would lose their Caucasoid physical features too, as they kept on intermarrying with the Chinese. However, some of them continued to hold their original religion despite assimilation in every other respect. A story was told during World War II that an

American soldier of Jewish faith went to visit a Chinese synagogue, only to be reminded of his "mistake" at the entrance. "Sir, this is a Jewish synagogue, not a Christian church," said the Chinese usher, bowing and smiling. As far as he was concerned, the fact that the American soldier was a white man automatically ruled him out as a Jew.

Besides the traders, other foreigners came to China to preach and proselytize. Among the most active were the Manichaeans, the Nestorians, and the Muslims. Manichaeanism was introduced to China by Persians towards the end of the seventh century and began to spread one century later. By the twelfth century it was strongly rooted in the Southeast where numerous Manichaean communities could be found. Several Chinese books which describe the Manichaeans have survived, and most of them treat their subject matter in a derogatory manner. The Manichaeans are described as "demon worshippers" and their activities as "incomprehensible." For one thing, they dressed differently. "Their leaders wear purple headwear and loose shirts, and their women cover themselves with black hats and white robes." "Their holy book deals with the two opposites, brightness and darkness, and it speaks of the three worlds, the past, the present, and the future." The Manichaeans would neither drink liquor or milk, nor eat meat or cheese. However, "men and women gathered at night to engage in licentious activities and would not disperse until daybreak." They helped one another whenever the need arose; "a new convert is supported by the entire congregation until he becomes established." "They call themselves members of one family and provide room and board for a travelling Manichaean even though they have never met him before." "They worship neither Buddha nor ancestors, and when a Manichaean dies, they bury him naked." Their deviation, in habits and beliefs, from the general cultural pattern, together with their clannishness, caused much misunderstanding and frequent friction between them and the rest of the Chinese population. Local governments occasionally persecuted them. After the twelfth century Manichaeanism declined steadily as a religious force, and many of its followers began to attach themselves to Buddhist or Taoist sects. It was not revived during the subsequent centuries.

The most important source on Chinese Nestorianism is a stone stele unearthed near Sian in 1623. The stele, bearing a cross in the middle of coiling dragons, was erected by a T'ang emperor in 781. The text on the stele, *The Spread of Syrian Nestorianism in China* (*Ta-ch'in ching-chiao liu-hsing Chung-kuo pei*), describes Nestorian activities in China in the seventh and eighth centuries. In 635, says the document, a Syrian priest named A-lo-pen brought to China the Nestorian Bible, and the emperor (T'ang T'ai-tsung) ordered one of his ministers to receive him in the western suburb. "The emperor had carefully examined its teachings and concluded that they were beneficial to men and the world and that they should be made known to all Chinese within the empire." In 638 the first Nestorian church in China, with twenty-one newly converted monks, was established at Ch'angan. During the reign of T'ang Kao-tsung (650–683), says the document, "Nestorian churches were established in all provinces . . . and its gospel was heard within the four corners of the empire." The Nestorian Bible had twenty-seven chapters, and the church was active in educational and philanthropical endeavors. "They fed the hungry, clothed the poor, medicated the sick, and buried the dead." The ability of Nestorian monks as medical doctors was verified by other sources. "The Nestorians are experts in eye diseases and diarrhea," says one source; "they can see illness before it occurs and they even undertake head surgery." In 683, says the Sung historian Ssu-ma Kuang, Emperor T'ang Kao-tsung complained of a severe headache and the loss of eyesight. A Syrian doctor was called in, and the emperor was saved from blindness. "Nestorian monks shaved their heads but grew long beards," says another historian. "They were not allowed to own slaves, nor could they have private property. They worshipped once every seven days and sang hymns seven times a day. They performed a ritual called baptism and they revered the cross."

It is doubtful whether the T'ang emperors who patronized the Nestorian church knew what it was about. A T'ang emperor (T'ang Te-tsung, 780–804) ordered a Nestorian monk to cooperate with Buddhists to translate Buddhist scriptures, even after the Buddhists had pointed out that there was a difference between these two religions. To the emperor, however, there was no reason why they should not cooperate, since both claimed that they knew so much about the next world. Emperor T'ang Hsüan-tsung ordered his four brothers to worship in the Ch'angan Nestorian church, and at the same time he decreed that his image and the images of his four predecessors be kept in the church, to be admired by all Nestorians. Nestorian monks were awarded governmental ranks and titles, and on Christmas Day, they received special incense for their church and a special dinner for themselves. There is no indication that the church ever resented the "pagan" behavior of Chinese emperors.

During T'ang Wu-tsung's persecution of Buddhists, Nestorian monks, together with Manichaeans and Zoroastrians, were ordered to return to civilian life. It is not known whether this persecution was the main cause of the decline of Nestorianism. In any case, this religion had only a small, scattered following even during its prime, and even its minor success seemed to have been due to government patronage. In the public mind, it was associated with the T'ang royal house. When Sung replaced T'ang, Nestorianism practically disappeared from the national scene.

Of the three minority religions described here, Islam proved to be the most enduring. The religion was founded by Mohammed in 622, and one generation later the first Muslim missionary had reportedly arrived in China. In the middle decades of the eighth century when T'ang's power began to decline, the Islamic Arabs gained control of Central Asia and extended their control eastward to include eventually the Tarim Basin. Islamic power continued to advance during the subsequent centuries; when it finally receded, it left behind millions of converts. Today the Muslims are one of the largest minorities in China, and most of them, as one would expect, live in the Northwest. During the T'ang-Sung period Muslims were found in the coastal cities as well as in the Northwest. These Muslims were either Arabic or Persian in origin and came via the sea routes as traders. Chinese historians described them as "abhorring pork and loving cleanliness"; few of them gave many details. One historian, however, was more explicit:

The "sea barbarians" (*hai-liao*) lived side by side with the Chinese in Canton and the most powerful of them was a man named P'u [believed to be the transliteration of the Arabic word Abu]. . . . The P'u family had been in the city for a long time, and being wealthy, lived a life of luxury far exceeding the level permitted under the law. However, since the local government was interested in encouraging more traders to come and since the family involved was not Chinese, it did not wish to concern itself with the violation. Thus, the P'u house became bigger and more luxurious as its wealth continued to grow at a fast rate. In 1192 when I was ten, I followed my father to Canton and had the opportunity of visiting the P'u house. The house was several stories high and covered a large area, though I can no longer remember the details. . . .

The barbarians worshipped spirits and loved cleanliness; it seemed that they had nothing to do all day long except to worship and to pray for better fortunes. The deity they worshipped sounded like Buddha but there was no image of him in the place where he was worshipped. Frankly, nobody knows what kind of deity he really was. In the place of worship there was a stone stele several *chang* high on which were carved strange, cursive words, and all worshippers prostrated themselves before it instead. . . . Behind the place of worship was a high, slender pagoda protruding skyward towards the clouds. It did not really look like a pagoda, and viewed from a distance, it looked more like a silver brush. It was made of earthen tiles and was painted with white powder. At the ground level was a door which led to a flight of circular stairs, and a person ascended the stairway to reach the top. The stairway, however, was invisible from the outside. Before ships arrived from the sea in the fourth or fifth lunar month, these barbarians went up and down the pagoda, making strange, unintelligible noises and praying for southern winds to come. Often the winds responded. At the pinnacle of the pagoda was a golden rooster which turned around with the change of wind. As I understand, one leg of the rooster has been missing.[1]

[1] A copy of the Chinese original appears in Fang Hao, *A History of Intercourse between China and the Non-Chinese World* (*Chung hsi chiao-t'ung shih*). (Taipei: The China Publishing Society, 1959), vol. 2, p. 236.

Throughout the T'ang-Sung period most of the foreigners who came to China were peoples of the Near East: the Persians, the Arabs, and the Jews. With the establishment of the Mongol empire in the thirteenth century also came the Europeans. For a long time Europeans had been fascinated by the possible existence of a "Prester John" in the Orient who, they believed, could be persuaded to attack the hated Saracens from the East if he could ever be reached. When the Mongols rose from the northern deserts and before they became a threat to Europe, many Europeans thought that their prayers had been answered. The Mongols, however, conquered people of all faiths indiscriminately, and Europe was consequently disenchanted. The sentiment of Europe, as expressed by the Bishop of Winchester in 1238, was: "Let us leave these dogs (Mongols and Saracens) to devour one another." Later when the fear of Mongol conquest had subsided, Europeans again entertained the hope of making an alliance with the Mongols. King Louis IX of France sent ambassadors to the Great Khan; so did the papacy. Though no military alliance was made, a Catholic outpost was established in Peking. The outpost was later elevated to an archbishopric, after several thousand converts had been made.

After the Mongols had conquered Central and Western Asia, the Arabs who had blocked the land and sea routes to China were no longer a barrier between Europe and China. With the arrival of the first Roman Catholic missionaries came also the first European merchants. Among them none exercised greater influence on later generations than Marco Polo, whose name has been mentioned in another connection (Chapter VIII). He came to China as a young man, and during his stay of seventeen years (1275–1292) in China, he served Kublai Khan in various capacities. After his return to his home city Venice, a war broke out between his city and Genoa, and he was captured as a prisoner-of-war. In a Genoese prison he dictated to a writer of romances named Rusticiano what he had observed in China and many other countries he had visited. The result was the *Description of the World* or *Travels of Marco Polo*. The information he provided on thirteenth century China was generally accurate, though here and there one notices some exaggerations, perhaps unintended. He described what he saw; there was no attempt to explain it in a more profound manner. His objectivity was sustained as long as the Saracens were not involved; he spoke highly, for instance, of the good customs of the Buddhists and Confucians (called "idolators" indiscriminately in his book). His book is of great value to Chinese historians, as it helps them understand better some of the most important events of the thirteenth century, such as the siege of Hsiangyang, the massacre of Ch'angchou, and the attempted conquests of Japan. The extant Chinese sources on these events are not comprehensive enough.

While Marco Polo could hardly be considered an important personality in China, the impact of his book on contemporary Europe was tremendous. That a more advanced society existed simultaneously with Europe was hard to believe, and most of the Europeans dismissed the book as mere fable. When the book finally won credence, it aroused great interest in China among the literate Europeans. Its readers included such men as Christopher Columbus. To the religiously devoted, there was a huge pagan world to conquer, and to the worldly merchants, there were enormous profits to be realized. The book was the most influential travelogue on China ever written in a European language, and it paved the way for the arrival of thousands of Europeans in the centuries to come.

As a result of the increasing contact between the East and the West, many of China's great inventions were brought to Europe. Among them were printing, paper making, the compass, and gunpowder. Even though Marco Polo might not personally have brought the art of printing to Europe, there were others who could have done it. It is inconceivable that this important invention could have eluded the attention of such an observant person as Marco Polo. There is also the possibility that Europeans learned the art of printing indirectly through the examination of Chinese paper currencies which were either obtained in Western Asia during the Yüan dynasty or had been brought back from China by travelling Europeans. Was there any relation between Gutenberg's movable type and the Chinese movable type which was invented some four centuries earlier? This question remains unanswered. There is no doubt, however, that the Chinese first invented the movable type as well as block printing.

When making books, the ancient Chinese wrote on bamboo or silk, and it was not until the first century B.C. that cloth rags were mixed with silk to strengthen it as a writing material. This rag-silk mixture, however, was not "paper" in the modern sense of that word. Chinese written records indicate that the first true paper, made of discarded fishing nets, appeared in 105 A.D. Recent findings seem to have pushed the date back a little further. Shortly afterwards paper was being made in all parts of China, and among its raw materials were tree barks, hemp dust, and cloth rags. By the eighth century the Arabs had learned the paper-making process from the Chinese, and the paper produced at Samarkand was acclaimed as the best outside of China. Towards the end of the century paper factories were also set up at Baghdad, and Chinese technicians were employed as supervisors. From the Near East the knowledge of paper making spread to Egypt, and then to France and Italy. Slowly this new paper replaced the traditional sheepskin as the writing material for most Europeans.

Though the invention of the compass was attributed to the legendary Yellow Emperor (Huang-ti), it did not appear in written records until the third century B.C. By the Han dynasty it was used by military commanders on the battlefield as well as by magicians (*ying-yang chia*) who depended upon it to locate the most propitious sites for burying the dead and erecting buildings. It does not seem that it was used as a navigational instrument then, because the earliest written record ever mentioning it in that capacity did not appear until 1119. The Arabs learned to use it as "a sailor's friend" towards the end of the twelfth century or early in the thirteenth century. The Europeans, in turn, learned its use from the Arabs, and soon it became standard equipment in every seagoing vessel.

Mention of sulphur and nitrates, two of the materials used to make gunpowder, appeared in written records as early as the Han dynasty. However, they were then used by alchemists to make elixirs, and it was not until the tenth century that they were mixed with carbon to make military explosives. The words "fire cannon," "rocket," "missile," and "fire ball" appear time and again in the official Sung history as well as two other books written during the same period. The first detailed description of using "fire cannon" in warfare was in connection with a battle fought in 1126 when the Sung army used it against the invading Nuchens. The so-called fire cannon was a tube made of bamboo filled with gunpowder which, when fired, threw a flaming missile towards the enemy. Since the barrel was made of bamboo, the flying missile could not cover a long distance. According to a description of a battle scene in 1132, it took two persons to carry a "fire cannon," and the cannons were fired from a moving platform after it had been moved close to the wall of the besieged city. Their effectiveness as a military weapon does not seem to have been great; Sung, which possessed this new weapon, was nevertheless unable to resist the invading army of the Nuchens. The Chinese invention of gunpowder never went much beyond its crudest form, and it was abandoned as a military weapon shortly afterwards. Since it could create a great deal of noise, the Chinese used it to make firecrackers for chasing out evil spirits and celebrating New Years. Today they still make the best firecrackers in the world market.

The Arabs improved gunpowder for military use, and by the thirteenth century Europeans like Roger Bacon had heard of its existence. One century later the Arabs used it to attack the Spanish city of Baza, and the very next year (1326) the city of Florence ordered the manufacturing of cannon and cannon balls. From Italy the making of gunpowder soon spread to other European countries, and by the 1350's it had become an effective weapon on the battlefield. In the seventeenth century both the Chinese and the Manchus had Portuguese cannons in the battle for the control of China.

In this cultural exchange the Chinese also learned a great deal from the non-Chinese world, such as the calendar, medical science, architecture, and music. Generally speaking, China contributed more to foreign cultures than it gained from them. Nevertheless, both sides benefited.

Beginning with the fourteenth century China remained static, whereas Europe surged ahead, not only technologically but in a variety of cultural activities. China was left behind, and in due time had to learn from Europe.

THE MISSIONARIES

Early in the modern period no group played a more important role in the cultural exchange between Europe and China than the Roman Catholic missionaries. We have noticed that the first Catholic missionaries came to China as early as the thirteenth century. Their impact, however, was not great then. The Latin community consisted of several thousand members (missionaries and converts), and the Church never made sustained efforts to enlarge it. When the Ming regime replaced the Yüan in 1368, the patronage hitherto extended to Christianity was withdrawn, and missionary activities all but ceased. They were renewed and intensified after the Reformation when the Church felt that it could more than compensate for its losses in Europe if it could conquer new territories for the faith in the non-European, pagan world. In the Society of Jesus the Church found one of its greatest proselytizing agents, and in training and in devotion to their assigned task, the Jesuits were superb. China, which had the largest population in the world and had more souls to be saved than any other country, was logically the greatest prize to win. If it were won, it would be the greatest victory for the Church since the conversion of the Roman Empire.

There were, however, numerous obstacles which seemed to be insurmountable at the beginning. In entering China the missionaries encountered one of the most advanced societies then known, and they had to establish for their religion some aspects of superiority before it could compete equally with other religions, some of which were older than Christianity and were deeply rooted in Chinese society. That the new faith recognized no other faith except its own was an added disadvantage because it aroused the resentment and anger of other religions. Its claim to the monopoly of truth in religious matters and its exclusiveness in its relationship towards other religions antagonized many Chinese who had long since learned the wisdom of compromise, even in religious matters. Regardless of the comparative merits of different religions which were highly partisan and perhaps impossible to determine, the religion that began its existence in a new territory by condemning all others would conceivably encounter more difficulties. Yet, in the matter of faith, the Roman Catholic Church could not and did not compromise. The uncompromising attitude taken by the Church concerning what it regarded as basic matters was the immediate cause of the banning of Christianity in 1724, as we shall see shortly.

In view of the difficulties involved, the fact that the early Jesuits could make a great impression upon the high officials in Peking attested to their devotion, tact, and ability. Among the Jesuit missionaries the Roman Catholic Church sent to China, Matteo Ricci was unquestionably one of the greatest. Ricci had studied mathematics and astronomy in Rome before he came to Macao in 1582, and with an understanding of the Chinese which had seldom been revealed among Europeans of his time, he plunged himself into the study of the Chinese language, literature, and philosophy. He first wore the garb of a Buddhist monk; but finding that Confucian scholars commanded more prestige, he changed to a mandarin robe. By such tact and by the knowledge he had acquired about Chinese culture, he won respect and esteem from Chinese scholars and officials. He wished to detach himself from European state power, the exercise of which, he believed, would do his mission more harm than good. In 1601 he arrived at Peking and was allowed to reside and preach. He concentrated his efforts on high governmental officials, with the hope that if they were converted to the new faith, the entire nation would follow. In less than five years, more than two hundred people had been baptized, including some high officials.

In retrospect, the contribution of Ricci and his fellow Jesuits lay more in their role as cultural ambassadors than in their mission as religious proselytizers. The total number of Chinese converts at the end of the seventeenth century, one hundred years after Ricci's arrival in China, was estimated between 100,000 and 250,000, a figure far from being impressive in a vast country like China. The lack of sensational success was not due to the lack of devotion and ability on the part of Christian missionaries; it resulted from the strong cultural resistance China could offer. As cultural ambassadors, however, these missionaries were unsurpassed. They enlightened Europe on China and informed China on Europe.

Arriving in Peking, Ricci presented to Emperor Ming Sheng-tsung (r. 1573–1619) an image of Christ, an image of the Virgin Mary, a Bible, a pearl-studded cross, two clocks, a world atlas, and a clavichord as "tribute." The emperor and his court officials were greatly impressed with the atlas and the clocks, but not much with any of the other presents. The atlas showed that there were five continents in the world and that "China is the greatest country in Asia and Italy is the greatest country in Europe." The clocks, as one Chinese official put it, showed the great ingenuity of "foreign devils." From the very beginning a tacit understanding seemed to have been reached. The missionaries would serve as advisers on science and technology in order to gain permission to preach and proselytize, and the Chinese tolerated or even encouraged their stay in

China so long as they could serve China in some useful yet worldly capacity. To the Chinese they were more scientists and technicians than missionaries.

The Jesuits had their first opportunity of showing their mathematical superiority in 1611 when the Ministry of Rites recommended the reform of the old calendar which had erred repeatedly in the prediction of the eclipse of the sun. Subsequently, at the urging of the Confucian scholar Hsü Kuang-ch'i who had been converted to the Catholic faith, the imperial government entrusted a group of Jesuits, headed by Joannes Adam Schall von Bell, to revise the calendar. The resultant calendar was regarded as superior to both the Chinese calendar and the frequently used Muslim calendar (*Hui-hui li*), and the Board of Astronomy in which many Jesuits served became the key position from which the missionaries extended their influence among the Chinese literati. When the Ming dynasty was overthrown in 1644, the new regime, Ch'ing, adopted the Jesuit calendar without much change. After the death of Schall in 1666, another Jesuit, Ferdinand Verbiest, served as an astronomical specialist with equal distinction. Despite occasional attacks by the defenders of the old calendars, the Shih-hsien calendar, as the Jesuit calendar was then called, was used throughout the Ch'ing dynasty. The Jesuits served the new regime as capably as they had served the old one.

Other Jesuit activities included map making, the translation of scientific works into Chinese, and the casting of cannon. Some Jesuits served as medical doctors, and others were called to become translators and consultants when China negotiated a treaty with the Russians (Treaty of Nerchinsk, 1689). Previously, the Chinese literati had been greatly impressed with Ricci's world atlas because this was the first time that the Chinese had ever heard of many foreign countries located on the atlas. As cartographers, the Jesuits' reputation continued to grow, and many Chinese were eager to learn from them. The Ch'ing government decided to take advantage of their talent, and from 1708 to 1715 they were sent by the emperor K'ang-hsi to all parts of China to make a geographical survey and record their findings on maps. The work was completed in 1717 and was entitled *The Complete Atlas of the Empire* (*Huang-yü ch'üan-lan t'u*). It was the first set of maps of China ever made by Western, scientific methods.

The books translated into Chinese were religious as well as technological, but it was the scientific and technological works that attracted the greatest attention among Chinese scholars. Some of these works were ancient classics such as Euclid's *Geometry*, translated jointly by Ricci and his Chinese friend Hsü Kuang-ch'i. The findings of Galileo were also rendered into Chinese. Other works were written by the missionaries themselves. One of the best-received books of this kind was *An Illustrated Explanation of Wonder Instruments* (*Ch'i-ch'i t'u-shuo*) by Joannes

Terrenz, the first systematic treatment of mechanical engineering ever to appear in China. The tremendous amount of knowledge these missionaries possessed amazed most Chinese and overwhelmed others. The following comment made by a Chinese scholar of the seventeenth century was perhaps typical of the reaction of the Chinese intelligentsia at that time:

The Westerners seem to be a hundred times more ingenious than the Chinese. Is it because they have been specially favored by Heaven? On the other hand, many of my friends know as much as they do; it does not seem that the Chinese are inferior to them in basic intelligence. The difference is that in China a man cannot achieve fame through technology and he spends all his time and energy in seeking wordly fortunes. He has no time for technical matters and is consequently inferior to a Westerner in this respect.[1]

Inspired by the Western missionaries, the Chinese then wrote a large number of scientific and technical books themselves. On mathematics alone there were seventy-six known works written during the seventeenth century. Had such inspiration continued, would the Chinese intellectual life have been markedly different from what it was in the eighteenth and nineteenth centuries? After the departure of the Jesuits, the Chinese intellectuals went back to their old routine of practicing calligraphy and writing eight-legged essays to prepare for the civil service examinations. The intellectual curiosity, temporarily stimulated by the Jesuits, soon disappeared.

In addition to map making, translation of books, and a variety of other secular activities, the Jesuits were often called upon to make military weapons. It may seem strange that the Church's representatives should even think of doing such a thing. However, if they had any scruple about their new duty, there was no indication of it. In fact, the close relationship between the acquirement of secular knowledge and warfare was very much in the mind of early Jesuits. Said Ricci in the introduction to Euclid's *Geometry*:

While the use of geometry in various fields is too large a subject to be treated here, it is clear that in warfare upon which a country's survival rests, the knowledge of geometry is absolutely essential. Therefore, a wise, brave general should first learn geometry, otherwise his wisdom and bravery would be exercised in vain. How can a general be considered good if he knows nothing about astronomy and other related sciences? A good general should be first familiar with the geography of the place where the battle is to be fought as well as his supply and logistic problems. Secondly, he should deploy his troops in accordance with the terrain of the battlefield. He could deploy them in a circular fashion if he wishes to deceive the enemy with regard to the size of his command, an angular shape if he wishes to impress his enemy with his own strength, and a formation shaped like a crescent if he intends to encircle his

[1] Fang Hao, *Chung hsi chiao-t'ung shih*, vol. 4, p. 84.

foe. If he proceeds to attack, he marches his soldiers like a sharp sword right through the enemy's ranks with the intention of routing them. Thirdly, he has to make sure that his offensive and defensive weapons are the newest available and that his soldiers are proficient in using them, as old weapons become obsolete with the arrival of new ones. I have read the history of various countries and all of them depend upon the perfection of new machinery [weapons] for offensive and defensive purposes. . . . The various kingdoms in the West had conquered and annexed one another before they were converted to Roman Catholicism some 1600 years ago. There were cases in which a small army could defend a besieged city successfully against an attacking force ten times as large, from land and sea. How did it manage to achieve the almost incredible? It was because its commanders were proficient in geometry.[1]

The use of geometry in warfare as described by Ricci seems to have been far fetched; nor was his interpretation of European history flawless. The motive behind this and similar writings was nevertheless clear: to gain the confidence of the Chinese literati in the practical application of the sciences in which the missionaries were experts and to use such influence as they would thus acquire for the eventual goal of converting China to Christianity. On the other hand, the Chinese government would use the missionaries' talents as well as it could, and it had no objection to their proselytizing activities. It had been tolerant of other religions before, and there was no reason why it should make Christianity an exception.

In 1623 the first group of Portuguese artillerymen arrived at Peking, accompanied by the Jesuit Joannes B. Rodrigues who served as a technical adviser as well as translator. The cannons they brought exploded during a demonstration and killed one of the party; the rest of the group was sent back to Macao. The second group arrived in North China with more and better cannons in 1629 and saw action against the Manchus in northern Hopeh near Peking. Meanwhile the Jesuits in Peking were busy designing and casting new and better weapons. Some of the Jesuits brought their creations to battlefields, and at least one Jesuit was injured in action. In 1640 Schall was ordered by the Ming emperor Ch'ung-chen to cast five hundred cannons, after he had successfully produced some twenty-nine. However, the Ming dynasty was overthrown before the project could be completed.

The Manchus, Ming's enemy, soon learned the use of cannon to good advantage. Some of the Jesuit cannons were brought to them by Ming generals who had surrendered, and others were captured on the battlefield. In 1631, improving upon the Jesuit model they had captured, the Manchus began to cast their own cannon. The new weapons, nicknamed "the red-barbarian generalissimos," were a major factor in the Manchus' successful campaign in South Manchuria. During the reign of K'ang-hsi

[1] A copy of the Chinese original appears in Chung hsi chiao-t'ung shih, vol. 4, pp. 87–88.

time and again Verbiest was called to supervise the casting of cannon. These cannons were reportedly better than any that had been in use before and were partially responsible for the success of the emperor's numerous campaigns. As a reward, Verbiest was promoted to the rank of deputy minister in the Ministry of Public Works in 1682.

The friendly relationship between the Chinese government and the missionaries did not last indefinitely. Ricci and his fellow Jesuits understood Chinese custom and tradition, and they knew that if Christianity were to make headway in China, it had to make some concessions to such ancient Chinese practices as the reverence for Confucius and ancestors. With great tact, Ricci emphasized the similarity between Christianity and Confucianism, and in a letter to a Buddhist layman who had challenged him in a debate, he said that one of his major purposes in coming to China was to teach filial loyalty. He found in ancient Chinese classics evidences to support Christianity, and he maintained that T'ien (Heaven) and Shang-ti were in fact the same as the Christian concept of God. The worship of Confucius and ancestors, said he, was not incompatible with the teaching of Christianity. While Chinese scholars were greatly pleased, his compromise with Confucianism antagonized his fellow Christians, including many in his own mission. Nicolaus Longobardi, Ricci's successor as head of the China mission, did not agree with many of his predecessor's beliefs, but he was too wise to press his point at the risk of losing China for the Church.

The success of the Jesuit mission in Peking encouraged the arrival of missionaries of other religious orders, notably the Dominicans and the Franciscans. With their arrival came also the sectarian rivalries so familiar in Europe. The disagreement between the Jesuits and other orders ranged from the purely academic, such as the meaning of the Chinese word T'ien, to a matter of vital concern, which was whether they should allow their Chinese converts to continue their worship of Confucius and ancestors. The so-called rites controversy split the Catholic missionaries in China into two rival camps. The Dominicans and Franciscans regarded such worship as pagan in nature and prohibited it, and the fight was on. While the Jesuits were spreading the Word among Chinese scholars in Peking and other large cities, the other two orders were active in proselytizing among the poor and the uneducated, especially in Fukien and Kwangtung provinces. Not only did they differ in the interpretation of Chinese customs and beliefs; their approach towards proselytizing was also different.

The controversy had to be resolved eventually by the papacy. Throughout the seventeenth century the papacy did not take a definite stand, and by implication each order was allowed to practice what it believed. However, the Dominicans continued to press their case, and in 1704 Pope Clement XI decided against the Jesuit stand and sent Cardinal

Tournon to China as papal legate to enforce the decision. So far the Chinese government had been content to stand on the sideline, and the emperor K'ang-hsi would have let the rivalry reach its own conclusion in good time if the decision had not been thrust upon him. The Jesuits appealed to him for help, and he, as expected, ruled in their favor. The legate was sent back to Macao where he died in 1710. The Pope, finding that his decree had not been obeyed, sent another legate to Peking in 1715 and issued the bull *Ex illa die* to reaffirm his decision with regard to the rites controversy. Now the issue was not merely a quarrel between two rival sectarian groups; it was a question of the supremacy of either the Church or the Chinese state. The Pope had spoken, and all missionaries must obey. On the other hand, it was unthinkable that K'ang-hsi, who prided himself on being a model Confucian monarch, would prohibit the worship of Confucius and ancestors among his subjects. After reading the papal bull, the emperor, who had been known for his even temperament, nevertheless made the following comment:

Reading this proclamation [papal bull], I have concluded that the Westerners are small indeed. It is impossible to reason with them because they do not understand larger issues as we understand in China. There is not a single Westerner who can read Chinese books, and their remarks are often incredible and ridiculous. Judging from this proclamation, it seems that their religion is no different from other small, bigoted sects of Buddhism or Taoism. I have never seen a document which contains so much nonsense. From now on Westerners should not be allowed to preach in China, so there will be no trouble.[1]

However, missionaries were allowed to preach in China as long as they did not attack the very foundation of the Chinese society, and many Jesuits continued to find ways to evade the decision of Rome and were thus allowed to stay. In 1742 Pope Benedict XIV issued the bull *Ex quo singulari* and cleared up whatever doubts the Jesuits might still have or pretended to have. The controversy came to an end, and one generation later the Society of Jesus itself was dissolved. Though its work in China was continued by other orders, it could not be replaced. The prohibition against the worship of Confucius and ancestors continued in force until 1939 when the papacy, after two hundred years, reversed its stand. However, there was no clear instruction insofar as the interpretation of *T'ien* and *Shang-ti* was concerned.

The rites controversy stunted the growth of Roman Catholicism in China for one hundred years. Chinese Catholics were allowed to worship the way they chose, but the size of their community (about 150,000) remained substantially the same throughout the eighteenth century. In the long run, perhaps the most unfortunate result was the dissociation of the Chinese intelligentsia from the Roman Catholic Church, and the

[1] *Chung hsi chiao-t'ung shih*, vol. 5, p. 140.

Church, without the intellectuals' cooperation, not only found its work difficult, but had to confine its activities to the uneducated. During the days of the early Jesuits, many Catholic scholars passed the civil service examinations and became respected and influential members in their communities. During the one hundred years after the rites controversy, there was not a single Catholic in China who could debate with Buddhist or Confucian scholars, as Ricci once did, on a convincing, intellectual basis. This was a serious setback for the Church in a country which honored scholarship and intellectual competence. To become a Catholic was now a mere matter of ritual rather than intellectual conviction, and the Church could appeal only to the less sophisticated section of the population. Often the Church was unjustifiably compared with the White Lotus Society and was characterized by such adjectives as ignorant, superstitious, and seditious. In a generally hostile atmosphere, the life of a Chinese convert was very difficult indeed. He was considered a disgrace to his family since he no longer honored his ancestors; his name would be taken away permanently from the family register; and he was not allowed to enter the family temple. Cut off from his family, he was ostracized by the entire society. Dissociated from the intellectuals, the Church was hard pressed even to find people who knew how to write. The Confucian scholars, looking at its poorly composed or crudely translated religious tracts, were doubly sure of their own superiority. This tendency was not corrected until the last few decades. Meanwhile, two hundred years of potential growth had been lost forever for the Roman Catholic faith.

THE TRADERS

Simultaneously with the missionaries came the traders, the other and worldly arm of the Western civilization. The Portuguese admiral Alfonso d'Albuquerque conquered Malacca in 1511 and was curious about the areas beyond. "Are the Chinese Christians?" he asked; "if not, what do they believe and what kind of deity do they worship?" Six years later (1517) a group of his countrymen arrived at Canton as traders. A Chinese official [1] who was then in charge of maritime affairs in Canton described them as follows:

One day there arrived suddenly two oceanic ships sailing straight towards the Huai-yüan harbor of Canton. Their owner was a man named Chia-pi-tan [*sic,* captain] who announced that he bore tribute to China from Fu-lang-chi [Portugal]. These men all had high noses and deep-set eyes. They wore white turbans and dressed up like Muslims. . . . As they knew nothing about proper

[1] The official was Ku Ying-hsiang who later rose to become the Minister of Justice of the imperial government. A copy of the Chinese original appears in *Chung hsi chiao-t'ung shih,* vol. 3, pp. 241–242.

manners, they were ordered to learn them at the Kuang-hsiao Temple for three days before they could be granted an audience. Since Fu-lang-chi was never a tribute-bearing country, the decision as to whether they should be received was referred to the imperial government. The imperial government consented to receive them, and these men were escorted on their way to Peking. When the present emperor [Ming Shih-tsung, r. 1522–1567] came to the throne, he was greatly annoyed at these men's lack of respect. He ordered that the Chinese interpreter be punished according to law and that these men be escorted back to Canton where they should be expelled from the country. Thus the matter came to a conclusion.

But the matter did not come to a conclusion. Other Portuguese traders continued to arrive, and their relation with the Chinese government continued to be unpleasant. They traded whenever it was convenient and robbed whenever there was nobody to stop them. The impression they made on the coastal Chinese contrasted sharply with the impression the Jesuits made on the Chinese intelligentsia a generation later. At the risk of their lives on the stormy seas, they came to China for one purpose only: to make the largest profits in the shortest time. They were professional adventurers, and they did not care whether they robbed or traded, as long as there were profits to be realized. Their conscience would not bother them since their victims were pagans. As one Portuguese trader (or pirate) put it, "Why should I be afraid of going to hell, as long as I have faith? The Almighty's mercy is unlimited." That the first Westerners the Chinese met happened to be people like these was extremely unfortunate. That they did not represent Europe or even Portugal is rather obvious. Nevertheless, the wrong impression had been created, and it persisted for more than two centuries afterwards. It remained a major handicap to normal relations between Europe and China long after the moral fiber of the traders had changed for the better. Moreover, it made the work of the missionaries all the more difficult. The Chinese reasoning was: if the missionaries were to teach morality and ethics, they were definitely more needed at home than in China.

The Chinese, on the other hand, were not completely without blame. Their contempt for trade as a profession and traders as a group made normal trade relations difficult, if not impossible. While the Chinese were not allowed to go to foreign countries to engage in trade, there was no national policy with regard to foreigners who came to China for such a purpose. Generally speaking, foreign trade was allowed as long as it was disguised as tribute missions. However, local officials were given the authority to determine whether the prospective traders were legitimate or only troublemakers, and these officials, like officials everywhere, were not immune from the pressure of vested interests, or even bribery. Moreover, they insisted that in a meeting with them, foreigners should behave in the same manner as the Chinese over whom the officials ruled. The Chinese demand, seemingly reasonable, was difficult to comply with. Imagine a rowdy sea captain performing Confucian rituals before a Chinese mandarin![1] Time and again this demand became a major point of controversy between China and European countries in the conduct of trade and diplomatic relations.

While the Portuguese went up and down the seacoast, trading or looting, the Chinese tried to confine their activities to as small an area as possible. In 1557 when a group of Portuguese merchants informed the Chinese that they needed a place to dry their goods before they could be respectably presented to China as "tribute," the local official in charge, heavily bribed, was happy to oblige. The place happened to be Macao, "lent" to Portugal on a permanent basis. The Chinese hoped that the Portuguese trade could be more easily controlled if it were confined to one port of entry and that the undesirable aliens could be isolated in a small area. Interestingly enough, Macao turned out to be the only territory that China ceded to a foreign country on a voluntary basis; it stands today as the last vestige in Asia of the once prosperous Portuguese empire.

As the Portuguese prospered, traders of other nationalities followed suit. The Dutch arrived early in the seventeenth century, and their presence was greatly resented by Portugal, which wished to preserve the lucrative trade for itself alone. Thinking that the Portuguese were already one group too many, the Chinese twice (in 1604 and again in 1607) refused the Dutch request for trade. The Dutch, unable to trade legitimately, resorted to smuggling, and operating from an island in the Pescadores, they carried on in a clandestine manner with the lawless elements of the coastal areas. Subsequently chased out by the Chinese authorities, they retired to Taiwan where, as we have noticed in a previous chapter, they ruled until 1662 when they were driven from the island by Cheng Ch'eng-kung. The Dutch fortunes took a definite turn towards the better in 1683 when the Ch'ing government rewarded them with four trading ports on account of their assistance in conquering Taiwan. Of the four ports only Canton turned out to be of great significance in a later period. Once the concession was made to the Dutch, the government decided that it might as well be made to all European countries that sought trade with China. By the beginning of the eighteenth century both England and France had sent ships to Canton. It should be added, however, that China regarded the opening to trade as a special favor granted to foreigners and that it was subject to revocation if "foreigners behaved in an uncontrollable, barbarian manner." The Ch'ing government did not believe that it had much to gain by trading with foreigners.

The trade as conducted at Canton reflected to a great extent the power flux of contemporary Europe. As the eighteenth century pro-

[1] One of these rituals was kowtow. For more details, see pp. 389–390.

FOREIGN FACTORIES AND TRADING STATIONS AT CANTON   The city wall of Canton
is in the background.

gressed, Great Britain slowly emerged as the greatest maritime power of
the world, and it also became the largest trading nation in Canton. The
East India Company maintained a regular staff at Canton and Macao, as
the size and value of the trade increased. As Canton continued to overshadow other trading ports in importance, the Chinese government decreed in 1757 that all foreign trade was to be confined to that city alone.
In 1784 when the first American ship, the *Empress of China,* sailed for
China, the British monopoly had been virtually established. Other countries continued to send ships to Canton, but it was to Britain that they
looked for leadership in their dealings with the Celestial Empire.

Though large profits were made, the British traders were not satisfied
with the semi-official status upon which the trade was conducted. Without an official treaty, the trade could be suspended unilaterally. Since
Britain had no diplomatic representation in Peking, whatever complaints
the merchants might have could not be presented directly to the imperial
government. Of complaints the merchants had plenty. They were confined to a secluded area outside of Canton during the time that a business transaction was made, and they had to retire to Macao after it had
been completed. Their movements were restricted, and they could not
bring to Canton their wives who had to reside at Macao. They could not
see any Chinese official in person, and any business they might have with

him had to be channelled through the Co-hongs. The Co-hongs were the twelve (and later thirteen) Chinese trade associations franchised by the Chinese government to deal exclusively with foreign traders. They bought all imports and sold all exports, and a foreign merchant could not deal with anyone else except them. They had a monopoly, and they did not hesitate to use it for their own advantage.

Whatever justifications the Chinese government might have had, the situation as described above was hardly satisfactory to the British. To find a remedy, England sent its first diplomatic mission to China in 1792. Lord George Macartney, the head of the mission, arrived in China in the summer of 1793. He sought, among other things, British representation at Peking, the opening of more ports for trade, and the reduction of tariff. To the Chinese, however, he was merely one of the many tribute bearers. "Since the English envoy has come far from the distant seas and for the first time visited a superior country," said the emperor Ch'ien-lung, "he should be treated with more consideration than the Burmese and Annamese who come here once every year." His Chinese escorts were instructed to teach him kowtow which, he was told, he must perform before the emperor. In Jehol where the emperor's summer palace was located, Lord Macartney was granted an audience (or audiences). Did he perform the kowtow? He said that he did not and that he had only bent one knee. On the other hand, Chinese sources, including those who were present during the audience, were equally sure that he did. Whether he did or did not, his request for diplomatic representation and others were rejected on the ground that they were inconsistent with Chinese custom. In 1816, the year after the battle of Waterloo, England sent another diplomatic mission to China. This mission, headed by Lord Amherst, was even less successful. His lordship was ordered to leave China immediately after he had made it clear that he would not perform the kowtow under any circumstances.

What was the kowtow? It consisted of kneeling and touching the forehead to the ground. It was a ritual performed by people of inferior status before their superiors, to show homage or deep respect. Ministers performed this ritual before kings, common people before government officials, and children before parents. The Chinese could not see any reason why the two English envoys would not perform it before their emperor as they did. The envoys were in Rome; therefore, they should do as the Romans did. When they refused to do so, the Chinese accused them of arrogance, bad manners, and bad faith. On the other hand, the two English gentlemen regarded this ritual as too humiliating. More than anything else, the controversy over the kowtow reflected the tremendous difficulties involved when two different cultures met head on for the first time. A Chinese had no objection to performing it before his parents or an emperor; many Westerners, on the other hand, preferred doing it before a beautiful woman.[1] What was humiliating to one side was glorified by the other. To a Westerner, trade was a right to be demanded; to a Chinese it was a privilege granted as a special favor. As a favor, it could be revoked. The Chinese looked down upon trade, whereas the Westerners attached great importance to it. Here was a cultural conflict which could not easily be resolved.

To compound the difficulties, the Chinese had no knowledge of the power and the civilization which England represented. The emperor K'ang-hsi often mentioned England and Burma and Annam in the same breath, and to him England was a remote, small, and uncivilized kingdom "impelled by humble desire to partake of our great civilization." The Chinese had no concept of international law as it was then known in Western Europe and would not have recognized it even if they had known it. The protocol and procedure that governed the normal conduct of trade and diplomatic relations were to them a new concept which they rejected. One century before, there had been the Jesuits in Peking who enlightened Chinese monarchs on Western countries, and their influence was partially responsible for the conclusion of a treaty with Russia in 1689. Now they were gone, and the Chinese had to grope in darkness.

As long as such ignorance persisted, the English traders in Canton had understandable grievances. At a time when mercantilism was the golden rule of Western Europe, the Chinese encouraged the import and discouraged the export trade. Ironically, this policy did not please foreign traders, because, having comparatively little to sell to China, their profits lay in buying as much as possible from China and reselling what they bought to Europe. There were also complaints against the tariff. Though the official rates as sanctioned by Peking were reasonable, local exactions were large. During each step of a business transaction, customs officials demanded payments for their services, and many such demands, in the eyes of the traders, were demands for bribes. As a result, the amount actually paid was several times larger than the statutory tariff. The monopoly of the Co-hongs was another source of irritation. The traders believed that if they were allowed to deal with whomever they pleased, their cost would have been smaller and their profits larger. Lastly, there was the problem of jurisdiction. The Chinese insisted that China had jurisdiction over all criminal cases in which a Chinese was involved. The foreign traders, considering Chinese law and court procedures "barbarous" and "uncivilized," were reluctant to agree to the Chinese demand, especially when they were the defendants.

In controversies of this nature, there are always two sides, perhaps equally persuasive. If the foreigners had to pay more duties than the

---

[1] Asked whether he would perform the kowtow before the Chinese emperor, John E. Ward, the American envoy to China in 1859, replied that he would only do so before God and women.

statutory tariff, the Chinese did not fare better if they were under similar circumstances. In other words, foreigners were not singled out for discrimination. There were times in Chinese history (such as the early Ming period) when government officials were honest and incorruptible. More often than not, bribery and corruption were a normal state of affairs. This argument, of course, did not excuse those Chinese officials who demanded bribes from foreign traders; it did, however, make their action understandable. As long as the "take" was reasonable, said one of the great Ch'ing emperors, it should be expected and should not cause undue alarm. Of course, there was the question whether the customs officials at Canton had been "reasonable." If the Co-hongs were monopolies (they were), so was the British East India Company. As to the jurisdictional problem, the Chinese had long maintained that whenever a Chinese was involved in a civil or criminal case in China, the Chinese government alone had jurisdiction and that a foreign government had jurisdiction only when both sides of a case were foreigners. In retrospect, the Chinese stand did not seem to be unreasonable in view of the fact that in accordance with the practice commonly recognized today, the territorial government alone has jurisdiction regardless of the nationalities of the parties involved unless the accused enjoys diplomatic immunity, which the foreign traders in Canton could not claim and did not have. Once a crime was committed, there was the difference in concept with regard to the ascertaining of responsibilities. The Chinese believed in joint responsibility; the Europeans, on the other hand, maintained that only the persons directly involved in a crime were subject to trial and punishment. From the Chinese point of view, a captain should be brought to account if one of his men had committed a crime and yet could not be found. To punish a captain because of a crime committed by one of his men was understandably "barbarous" to the Western world.

As each of the two sides insisted on the soundness of its own values and applied them accordingly, this problem of cultural conflict could only be solved if one side were strong enough to impose its will on the other. The Opium War (1839–1842), the first war between China and a European power, served exactly that purpose. When physical force was used, all alleged rights and wrongs became academic. It was the victor who dictated terms.

THE OPIUM WAR AND ITS AFTERMATH

Though mention of the opium-producing poppy can be found in ancient Chinese works, the use of opium as a habit-forming narcotic was of comparatively recent origin. Early in the seventeenth century the Spaniards introduced the smoking of tobacco in China, and shortly afterwards opium mixed with tobacco also appeared in China. Previously the Dutch had used this mixture in Java and in Taiwan which they then controlled, and from Taiwan it spread to nearby Fukien province. Once the mixture was in China, opium was separated from tobacco and was taken independently. Like every evil, opium possessed certain "charms" when it was first introduced to its victim: it reduced pain caused by headache, indigestion, and intestinal disorders, and midwives sometimes gave it to their charges during the time of childbirth. Even without any pain to reduce, a smoker nevertheless found it attractive. It cured depression, though only temporarily; it was even exhilarating while the effect lasted. However, once a person became an opium addict, he became a slave to his addiction. He was more concerned with the next puff than the next meal. If he had no money to buy it, he would sell whatever he had, including, sometimes, his own children. For opium, the black gold, was indeed expensive. Its denial to an addict meant unbearable pain, and its continuous denial would reduce him to a state of hysteria which could only be cured with the first inhalation. Even though a wealthy person might be able to afford such a habit, addiction would eventually ruin his health. He could no longer live a normal life, not only because he was physically weak but also because each working day had to be interrupted by smoking. In most cases he became a useless person. Moreover, once the habit was acquired, rarely could one get rid of it. For the opium merchant it meant that once he had a customer, he would continue to have that customer.

The first shipment of opium in quantity to China was made by the Portuguese from Goa. In 1729 when the emperor Yung-cheng issued a decree to prohibit opium traffic, the annual import was still small, amounting to 200 chests (each chest weighed approximately 133 lbs.) on the average. The prohibition was not strictly enforced, and the import of opium continued to increase. In 1790 the import from India alone reached 4,054 chests. With the opening of the nineteenth century the import increased by leaps and bounds, and shortly before the Opium War, it amounted to more than 30,000 chests per year. By then England had become by far the largest shipper, though France and the United States also participated. Before the opium trade, Europe had purchased more from China than it sold, and there had been a continuous flow of bullion from Europe to China. With opium, Europe more than paid for all the silk, tea, and porcelain it purchased, and the flow of bullion was consequently reversed. Before 1823 the yearly outflow of silver from China amounted to one million taels; it increased to twenty million taels from 1831 to 1834 and reached thirty million taels shortly before the war. By then opium addiction had spread from the members of the gentry class to "artisans, merchants, women, and even Buddhist monks and Taoist priests." "If the opium traffic is not stopped," said Lin Tse-hsü, later the Imperial Commissioner at Canton, "the country will become poorer and poorer and its people weaker and weaker. Eventually not only will there be inadequate funds to support an army, there will be no useful soldiers at all."

Repeatedly the Chinese government had imposed bans on the opium traffic, but each attempt failed to achieve its purpose. The avarice of foreign traders and the corruption of Chinese officials combined to defeat whatever measures the government took. Moreover, the long coastline made smuggling extremely difficult to stop, and local interests, fattening on the opium traffic, connived at, if not actually encouraged it. In 1838 when the opium traffic had reached alarming proportions, the emperor Tao-kuang (r. 1821-1851) sent one of his ablest servants, Lin Tse-hsü, to Canton, with the special charge to end it, "once and for all."

After Lin's arrival at Canton in the spring of 1839, he ordered that all foreign traders surrender the opium they possessed. They complied, and more than 20,000 chests of British-controlled opium were burned in public. However, the British refused to make a pledge that thereafter they would refrain from shipping more opium to China. Angered by their refusal, Lin threatened to ban all commercial traffic. In July, a Chinese was killed by a group of English sailors in Kowloon, and Lin demanded the surrender of the accused. As the British refused to surrender them, a fleet of Chinese war junks sailed towards the British naval force then staying at Hong Kong, with the ostensible purpose of seizing the accused seamen by force. The British fired, and the war began.

England could have gone to war before, but for reasons of its own it postponed the showdown until there was also the opium issue. To the Chinese, the issue was a moral one on which they believed that they could not make any compromise. Yet they did not want the war; nor were they prepared for it. It was unlikely that they had heard of Trafalgar or Waterloo; nor could their leaders foresee the grave consequences in having a war with a mighty power like England. In our modern concept of total war, the Opium War was no more than a skirmish. The British forces attacked and seized a few cities along the coast. When they threatened to attack Nanking, the Chinese sued for peace. There was no such concept then that a nation should fight to the last man and to the last inch of territory.

The Treaty of Nanking (1842), as the treaty which concluded the Opium War was called, contained thirteen articles. The major items were: (1) the opening of five ports (Canton, Amoy, Foochow, Ningpo, and Shanghai) for British trade, (2) the cession of the island of Hong Kong to Great Britain, (3) China's agreement to a uniform and moderate tariff on exports and imports which could not be changed save by mutual agreement, and (4) the payment by China of $21,000,000 as indemnity: $6,000,000 for the surrendered opium, $3,000,000 for the debts owed by Chinese to British merchants, and $12,000,000 for expenses occasioned by the war. A supplementary treaty, the Treaty of the Bogue, was signed one year later. With regard to this treaty, only two points need to be mentioned here. First, China agreed to grant Great Britain extraterritoriality in criminal cases, and second, Britain secured the most-favored-nation treatment. In accordance with this treatment, any additional privileges or immunities granted to any other power thereafter would automatically be enjoyed by British subjects. The most-favored-nation clause, though worded in different ways, was later included in every treaty concluded with a Western power, including Denmark and Mexico.

After Great Britain had obtained these concessions from China, other powers, through persuasion combined with the threat of physical force, demanded and received the same or even larger concessions. The American treaty (Treaty of Wang-hsia, July, 1844), for instance, extended the principle of extraterritoriality to include civil as well as criminal cases. France was given the right to build Roman Catholic missions at the treaty ports and the freedom to proselytize without interference from the Chinese government, though such concessions did not form a part of the official treaty (Franco-Chinese Treaty, October, 1844). Through the operation of the most-favored-nation clause, the new privileges were extended to all other countries which had, or were going to have, treaty relations with China. The concession given to France with regard to missionary activities, for instance, was granted to all countries which had Catholic or Protestant missionaries in China.

The Treaty of Nanking, hopefully hailed by many Westerners as the beginning of a new era in the relations between China and the Western world, created only a lull before another storm. The Chinese, who had behind them 4,000 years of ingrained ideas with regard to foreign relations, were slow to understand the new reality. Instead of boldly facing the future, they still dreamed about the golden past when the Son of Heaven chided barbarian chieftains for their unruly behavior and when there were no troublesome foreigners bent on making a profit at the expense of principle or morality. They were angered and frightened and were at a loss to know what to do. Their officials, caught between an antiforeign public and the demanding foreign powers, were a sorrowful lot; they evaded and stalled when the time arrived to implement the treaty provisions. In Canton, where the antiforeign feeling had been the strongest and was further intensified by the recent defeat, the mobs became violent and uncontrollable, and they refused to let foreigners enter their walled city. The foreigners were equally stubborn in their insistence, even though the treaty did not indicate explicitly that they had the right to enter the city. At this crucial moment when tension was building towards a climax, the viceroy of Kwangtung-Kwangsi, who was responsible for negotiating with the foreigners, was the inept, incredible Yeh Min-shen. He consulted a magician before he made any move, and the divine voice he heard always seemed to say: "Pay no attention to the trouble-some barbarians."[1] His superiors in Peking were equally unable to grasp the seriousness of the situation. "The object of the Manchu govern-ment," said a Western observer, "is to disgust Europeans, and break off all intercourse with them; it would gladly have nothing to do with them at any price." Yet, "China has now been brought too near to Europe for it to be permitted any longer to lead this isolated life in the midst of the world."

If the Chinese regarded the Treaty of Nanking as too harsh, the foreigners considered it too lenient. They wanted more ports opened for trade, especially in the interior, and they demanded diplomatic represen-tation at Peking. Since the Chinese government was reluctant even to honor existing obligations, it was clear to them that force had to be used if they wished to obtain additional concessions. The Opium War had revealed China's vulnerability, and there was reason to believe that an-other show of force would yield more rewarding results. "The time is fast approaching when we shall be obliged to strike another blow in China," said Palmerston, the Prime Minister of Great Britain. Now it was Eng-land's turn to play the role of the Son of Heaven, to punish, in the prime minister's own words, "these half-civilized governments such as those of China, Portugal, Spanish America," all of whom "require a dressing down every eight or ten years to keep them in order." Once minds were made up, the pretexts for starting another war were not slow in coming.

In the fall of 1856 a lorcha named *Arrow* was boarded by Chinese police and twelve of her Chinese crew of fourteen were arrested on the charge of piracy. The British consul at Canton protested on the ground that the ship had been registered in Hong Kong and was therefore legiti-mately British even though it was owned by a Chinese. The fact that the registry had expired before the arrest and consequently the ship was not legally entitled to British protection was apparently then unknown to both the Chinese and the British. The prisoners were eventually returned, but the British refused to accept the release as satisfactory because it was not accompanied by an apology. The British naval force at Canton at-tacked the city, and another war began.

Meanwhile, the French had decided to join the war. In February, 1856, a French Catholic missionary and some of his Chinese converts in Kwangsi were arrested and executed on the charge that they had insti-gated a rebellion. The missionaries' own admission that they had indoc-trinated their Chinese converts to look to "France as their support and liberation" against persecution seemed to have substantiated to some ex-tent the Chinese charge, though the exact circumstances of the so-called

---

[1] Yeh was later captured by the British during the ensuing hostilities and was taken to India as a prisoner. He wrote poems and calligraphy to be given to his captors as souvenirs before he died in 1859.

rebellion were not known. Moreover, no foreigners were allowed to step outside the treaty ports under the existing treaties, and the French missionary had been found deep in the interior. On the other hand, the Chinese, by arresting him and sentencing him to die, had obviously violated the extraterritorial right of France. Napoleon III had long dreamed of the spiritual conquest of China. When the news of the "judicial murder" arrived in Paris, he was eager to seize it as an opportunity to expand his spiritual empire.

The British and the French easily defeated the poorly trained, inadequately armed Chinese. When they threatened to attack Tientsin, the Manchu government sued for peace. The peace, called Treaties of Tientsin, granted new concessions and enlarged some old ones. Great Britain and France were to maintain resident ministers at Peking, and their nationals had the right of travelling in all parts of the interior of China. New ports were to be opened for trade, and foreign ships had the right of navigating the Yangtze River. Tariff rates would be adjusted downward from those that had been previously agreed, and China was to pay the two powers indemnities. There was also the article guaranteeing the protection of missionaries by Chinese authorities, since "the Christian religion, as professed by Protestants and Roman Catholics, inculcates the practice of virtue, and teaches man to do as he would be done by."

After the treaties had been signed, the Chinese refused to ratify them. This, of course, was the familiar Chinese delaying tactic, and the Western powers would have no part of it. Hostilities were renewed, and Tientsin and Peking were soon captured by the allies. In a vengeful mood, the British commander ordered the burning of the Yüan Ming Yüan, the Summer Palace ground which was the most beautiful place in the city and perhaps in all of China. The emperor Hsien-feng fled to Jehol, and China was again brought to its knees. Another treaty, the Peking Convention (1860) was signed. Kowloon was ceded to England, more ports were opened for trade, and more indemnities were paid. As other powers (including Russia and the United States) had the most-favored-nation clause in the treaties they had previously concluded with China, most of the privileges stipulated in the new treaties were also extended to them.

The treaties of 1858–1860, together with those of 1842–1844, provided the basis of the relationship between China and the Western powers until World War II. The Chinese called them "unequal treaties," because the benefits provided in these treaties went exclusively to the Western powers at the expense of China. They resented the special privileges foreigners enjoyed in China, privileges which they themselves did not have in their own country. The resentment against the special privileges was easily transformed into resentment against those who enjoyed them, and the Chinese, who had been tolerant towards peoples of different races and religions throughout their history, now became noticeably anti-foreign. For a century Chinese leaders blamed these unequal treaties for all real or imaginery ills that China suffered, and the call for abolishing them generated a patriotic fervor such as had never been seen in Chinese history. Though the Chinese case might often have been overstated, it is nevertheless true that we cannot understand the China of the last one hundred years unless we understand its grievances.

First, there was the right of extraterritoriality. Such a right denied the Chinese courts jurisdiction over foreign residents in China, and legally foreigners could do whatever they pleased without incurring the punishments provided by Chinese law. Only their consuls in the treaty ports had jurisdiction over them. In a case involving both Chinese and foreigners, the fairness of a consular trial was as much suspect by the Chinese as the fairness of a Chinese trial in a similar case had been suspect by foreigners before the treaty system. Moreover, when missionaries and other foreigners intervened on behalf of their Chinese protégés (converts and servants) who were involved in criminal or civil cases, local officials were expected to rule in their favor regardless of the merits of the case because these officials knew that their government was afraid that Western powers might seize any "mistrial" as an excuse to send troops to China to demand more concessions. If foreign powers intervened, they would be severely punished, as Lin Tse-hsü had painfully learned himself.[1] The fear of foreign intervention might or might not be justified, but such a fear did exist. As long as it existed, any court action involving a Chinese having foreign connections became a mockery of justice. Thus, with the passage of time, there developed in China a new privileged class, the foreigners and their protégés, above and beyond the reach of the law. Some of them learned to carry this exalted status with dignity, while others were eager to use it for their own advantage. All of them, of course, looked down upon the "natives" around them. This situation, as one would expect, caused great resentment on the part of the Chinese, and friction often occurred between Chinese and Chinese converts, especially in the interior regions. Since their government could not do anything to remedy the situation, eventually the people took this matter into their own hands. The result was the massacre of missionaries and Chinese converts, which will be discussed in the next chapter.

It was unfortunate that Christianity was reintroduced to China through the use of military force. It was elevated to a privileged position before it even had many followers. The way it was imposed on China and the privileged position it enjoyed made its failure almost a foregone conclusion. Ironically, its sponsors, insisting on a privileged position for their religion, did not give it a chance to compete fairly and equally with other religions in China. It could have succeeded, but it did not. To many

[1] Lin was stripped of his rank and title and was exiled to Ili after the Opium War.

Chinese the missionaries were an aggressive arm of Western imperialism, despite the many utilitarian things (such as schools and hospitals) they had brought to the Chinese people. To compound the difficulties, the early missionaries were not always well-trained. They were certainly not the best the West could have sent to China. Practically all of them were illiterate in the Chinese language, and some of them were barely literate in their own. Yet they were all determined to "lead the heathen Chinese out of the darkness." This attitude was of course not the best way of making friends and influencing people. While the Confucian scholars viewed their activities with a mixed emotion of bemusement and understanding, many lawless, unscrupulous elements swelled the Christian ranks because of the protection which the missionaries could provide in case they ran into difficulties with the law-enforcement officials. Thus, the Christian community, which had historically set an example in humility and virtue in many hostile lands, fell far short of being the ideal society in China which a good Christian would have wished. The Chinese attitude towards religion was similar to that of the ancient Romans. Christianity eventually conquered Rome, but it never made much headway in China. For this failure the unequal treaties were greatly responsible.

The low, conventional tariff (five percent *ad valorem*) as stipulated in the unequal treaties was declared by Chinese leaders to be an insurmountable barrier to China's industrial development. Tariff rates could not be raised save by mutual agreement, and it was virtually impossible to persuade foreign traders to agree to higher rates which increased the cost of their merchandise. No differentiation was made between luxuries and necessities, and the Chinese could not, for instance, impose higher duties on imported opium which had now become an open, legitimate item of trade. Deprived of tariff protection, native industries, still in an infant stage of development, could not compete with well-established foreign concerns. Only in certain industries, such as tea and silk, in which natural and geographical environment prohibited foreign competition, did the Chinese continue to prosper despite the unequal treaties. Moreover, as the Chinese government was not allowed to tax goods of foreign origins above the low, conventional tariff, it had to impose heavier taxation on the products of its own nationals in order to raise revenue for administrative expenses. Thus the unequal treaties forced the Chinese government to discriminate against its own nationals in favor of foreigners. It is difficult to say whether China could have developed a modern industry if the unequal treaties had never existed. As has been remarked in the Introduction, there were other factors in China unfavorable to industrial development. There is no denying the fact, however, that the regulated tariff was a great handicap to China's struggle to become a modern, industrialized society.

There were other provisions in the treaties which looked harmless at the beginning but which turned out to be detrimental from the Chinese point of view. The Treaty of Nanking stipulated the right of foreigners to reside in the treaty ports which, liberally interpreted, came to mean the right to reside in certain sections of the city over which the Chinese government had no jurisdiction. Originally intended for foreigners only, the "concessions," as foreign settlements in the treaty ports were called, eventually had more Chinese than foreigners who, with the passage of time, constituted only a small fraction of the total residents. The municipal government in each concession was controlled by the representatives of the foreign community and had sole jurisdiction over all its inhabitants, including the Chinese. Thus, within the boundaries of China there were numerous miniature "foreign countries" that were sovereign as far as China was concerned. They had their own tax systems, courts, and police. Deliberately or unintentionally, the foreigners in these concessions discriminated against the natives, and many Chinese have not forgotten the sign once hung on the entrance of one of Shanghai's parks: "Dogs and Chinese Not Allowed." What irritated local Chinese officials was the fact that a wanted criminal became immune from any penalty under Chinese law by simply stepping into a foreign concession unless the foreign government in the concession chose to repatriate him. If a foreigner decided to take into his protection a Chinese accused of having committed high treason, even the Son of Heaven could not bring him to justice. Most foreigners used their power with discretion; there were others who did not. Shanghai, said one Western observer, was an adventurer's paradise.

It should be pointed out, however, that when the treaties were concluded, neither China nor the Western powers had foreseen their implications. The Western powers were then interested in opening China for trade and, as if on second thought, also insisted on opening China for missionary activities. The extraterritorial rights, the regulated tariff, the foreign "concessions," and the freedom to navigate on China's internal rivers were not an end in themselves; they were aimed at enlarging profits and providing convenience for Western traders who, for business reasons, had to reside in China. If the treaty rights had been strictly interpreted, they would not have led to such abuses as later appeared. Their broad interpretations which caused such abuses clearly violated the intentions of the treaty makers. The Chinese, on the other hand, had no knowledge that these rights were a violation of their sovereignty when the treaties were concluded because few of them had any understanding of such a concept as national sovereignty, a concept which was Western in origin. As we have seen, China had long granted foreign residents (such as Persians and Arabs) a certain degree of extraterritoriality, and concessions of this sort did not seem to be incompatible with their dignity as a nation. Only when the treaty rights were abused was there a great deal of alarm. The agitation for the abolition of treaty rights provided the greatest driving force of Chinese nationalism. More than anything else, it united China as a modern nation.

THE TAIPING REBELLION

In the 1840's all evidence seemed to indicate that the Manchu dynasty had lost the mandate of Heaven. There were foreign invasions, domestic disturbances, natural disasters, famines, and a discredited, incompetent government which was unable to cope with them. The sequence was incomplete without a rebellion, and a rebellion there was. The Taiping Rebellion was the greatest social upheaval of nineteenth century China and the most serious challenge to the Manchu government before 1911. It was generated by indigenous forces, and it was suppressed by native resources. The professed Christianity of the rebels, however, was an indication of the Western influence.

From 1847 to 1849 natural disasters struck China repeatedly, and famines were reported in practically every province. The region most adversely affected was Kwangtung and Kwangsi where many peasants, driven by hunger, had appeared as organized bandits as early as 1847. Local officials were unable to maintain peace and order, and lawlessness spread over a large section of this region. The factors that had historically nourished a rebellion were present, and only a capable leader was required to organize it. In Hung Hsiu-ch'üan the dissatisfied peasants found their leader.

Hung Hsiu-ch'üan was born in 1812 near Canton to a small farmer. As the brightest member of the family, he was given the opportunity to study, while his two elder brothers continued to work on the family farm. He left school at the age of eighteen and, as was normally expected, went to take the lowest level of the civil service examination in Canton. He failed, and when he tried again in 1836, he did not fare any better. It was then that he was exposed to the teaching of Christianity for the first time, having read a pamphlet entitled *Good Advice to the World* (*Ch'üan-shih liang-yen*) handed to him by a street evangelist. He took the examination again the following year and failed for the third time. He then became seriously ill and was in a state of coma for forty days. When he woke up, he told an astonished audience that he had met God the Father and Jesus in his dream and that Jesus was God's elder son, whereas he, Hung, was His younger son. He was instructed by God the Father to kill the "demons," who later turned out to be the Manchus. It did not seem then that he had decided to lead a revolt, because as late as 1843 he took and failed the civil service examination for the fourth time. His bitterness could well be imagined, since he was an ambitious man. Of course, he had to bide his time until the opportune moment arrived. The moment did arrive when famine struck a wide area in his native province.

The base of his operation was a secret society called the Society of God Worshippers, efficiently organized under his command. It recruited its followers from poor peasants, and being looked down upon by Confucian scholars as another form of superstition, it was boycotted by the leaders of each community. Among the six "princes" whom Hung later appointed to assist him in establishing a Heavenly Kingdom of Great Peace, only three were educated, and the most powerful of the "princes," Yang Hsiu-ch'ing, had been a charcoal maker before he joined the rebellion. The society was very active in the southeastern section of Kwangsi, and as famine spread, it extended its influence towards other sections of the province. From time to time its members clashed with local militia men who were organized by the gentry leaders to combat the society as well as the widespread banditry. In the winter of 1850–1851, Hung raised the standard of revolt, calling for the overthrow of the Manchu dynasty.

The weakness of the Ch'ing regime had been shown in the Opium War. Now it could not even cope with the ill-trained, ill-equipped peasant rebels. The regular army collapsed before the rebels, and city after city fell into their hands. After each city was captured, the rebels singled out two groups for persecution: Ch'ing officials and Buddhist and Taoist priests. The persecution of the first group was to be expected; the persecution of the second group was unusual and was done on religious grounds, as the Buddhist and Taoist priests had allegedly worshipped "idols." A sizable number of these Buddhist and Taoist priests were killed, and their temples and monasteries were confiscated to provide homes for the homeless and the very poor. The discipline of the Taiping soldiers was generally good; a household only needed to paste the word "obedience" (*shun*) on its front door to assure that it would not be disturbed by the Taiping soldiers. In 1853 Nanking fell into the hands of the rebels. Hung proclaimed himself as *T'ien Wang*, or Prince of Heaven, and called his kingdom *T'ai-p'ing T'ien-kuo*, or Heavenly Kingdom of Great Peace. But there was to be no peace, not even an earthly one.

In retrospect, what made the Taiping regime unique was its attempted reforms. It decreed that all land belonged to the nation as a whole and that private property was forever abolished. Every household was to receive from the state a certain amount of land in proportion to its size. Since women were declared equals of men, they were entitled to an equal share. After a harvest, a household kept what it needed for its sustenance and handed over to the government the surplus. "Areas that suffer from famine shall receive help from areas that have had bumper harvests," said a Taiping decree, "so that everyone will enjoy the blessing of God, the Supreme Lord." "We shall till together and enjoy the fruits of

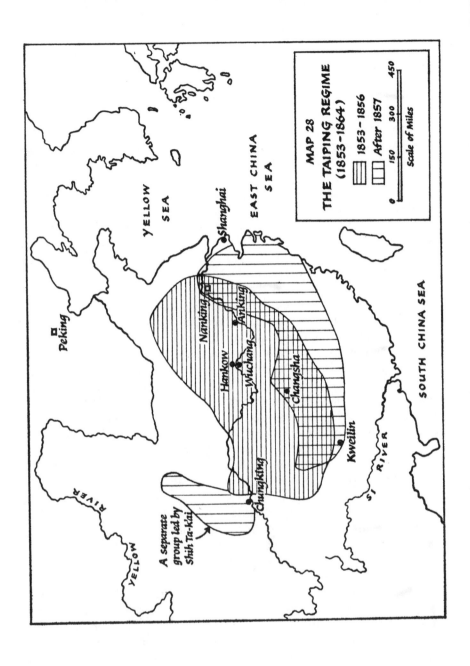

YELLOW SEA

EAST CHINA SEA

SOUTH CHINA SEA

Peking

Shanghai

Nanking

Hankow

Anking

Wuchang

Changsha

Kweilin

Chungking

YELLOW RIVER

SI RIVER

A separate group led by Shih Ta-kai

MAP 28
THE TAIPING REGIME
(1853-1864)

1853-1856

After 1857

0   150   300   450
Scale of Miles

our work in common. Food and clothing shall be shared; so shall money. No one shall have more than his neighbor has, and no one shall ever suffer from cold or hunger." Thus, four years after the *Communist Manifesto* (which nobody in China had then heard of) and one century before Mao Tse-tung's communes, a communistic society was established in China under the doctrine of Christian love.

The social reforms of the Taiping regime were equally drastic. Every twenty-five households were organized as a comradeship (*wu*), the basic administrative unit of the nation. Each comradeship was headed by a teacher-priest (*liang ssu-ma*), its secular as well as spiritual chief. In carrying out his administrative duties he was assisted by five comrade leaders (*wu chang*), one from each five households. The comrade leaders, under the supervision of the teacher-priest, were responsible for the training of the twenty-five soldiers (one from each household) in the comradeship and for the maintenance of peace and order. Every comradeship maintained a school which all children of school age must attend. In school the children were taught the *Old* and *New Testaments*, together with the decrees of the Prince of Heaven (Hung Hsiu-ch'üan). The *Three-character Classic* was completely revised to emphasize religious indoctrination. The opening statements of the revised version read as follows:

> The Great Supreme Lord (*Huang Shang-ti*)
> Created Heaven and Earth (*tsao t'ien ti*).
> He Created Mountains and Seas (*tsao shan hai*);
> He Made the World Complete (*wan-wu pei*).

On Sunday the comrade leaders led men and women to the comradeship church where they prayed and sang the glory of God. The aged, the orphans, the disabled, and all those who could not work were supported by the comradeship, and "none were to go hungry." All expenses occasioned by wedding, childbirth, and other festivities were drawn from the common treasury; during these festivities, "all heathen rituals should be dispensed with, and the participants had only to worship and pray to God the Father, the Supreme Lord."

The Taipings' communistic and collectivistic life may not appeal to us; some of their other reforms, however, were progressive and modern. They deplored the inferior role women had played in Chinese society and tried to elevate their position to the same level as that of men. Women were entitled to land distribution as has been said before, and were encouraged to attend school. In the Taiping government many talented women served as officials, and some of them even distinguished themselves on the battlefield. In the Taiping army women were a common sight. Civil service examinations were open to women as well as men, and candidates were asked to write an essay on such a topic as the refutation of Confucius' assertion that "Women and small people are the most difficult to deal with." Moreover, the Taiping law forbade concubinage, foot-binding, and prostitution. The transportation and smoking of opium were punishable by death.

Why did the Taipings fail? First, there was the lack of good leadership. Hung Hsiu-ch'üan was more a mystic than a statesman, and most of his top lieutenants were mediocre. His best friend and supporter, Feng Yün-shan, died in action early in the rebellion. After 1852 real leadership fell gradually into the hands of Yang Hsiu-ch'ing, while Hung withdrew more and more to a state of semiseclusion. As for Yang, the lack of a formal education was a great handicap; he had neither the foresight nor the statesmanship to steer the new regime through the first, most crucial years. He often went into a trance to speak in "the voice of God," forcing all, including Hung, to be obedient to him. He was a clever man, but not great. Once Nanking was captured, the Taiping leaders became complacent. After two attempts to conquer North China had failed in 1852–1853, they settled down in their new capital to enjoy the fruits of victory. This gave their enemy much needed time to prepare for a counter offensive. Even more damaging to their cause were the feuds that developed among the leaders themselves. Yang Hsiu-ch'ing, who often compelled Hung to kneel down before him to listen to "the voice of God," became arrogant and dictatorial, and Hung finally decided to get rid of him. When the massacre finally ended, Yang, his murderer, and the murderer of his murderer, together with hundreds of their lieutenants, were slaughtered in cold blood. Among Hung's top colleagues, only Shih Ta-k'ai, the only Taiping leader with a gentry background, was still alive. He left Nanking in disgust, went his separate way, and never returned. Being completely isolated, Hung could not trust anyone except his two half-brothers who, as has been noted before, had received no other training besides growing rice in the paddy fields. That the Taiping regime managed to last more than ten years in Nanking was largely due to the military genius of one man, Li Hsiu-ch'eng, who was not one of the original leaders of the rebellion. Eventually, however, even he was overpowered by the superior Manchu forces. The confession he made after his capture is one of the basic materials in studying the Taiping rebellion, especially its later stage.

Face to face with the Taiping regime and what it stood for were an ancient culture, the landed interests, some of the best brains of contemporary China, and finally, the Western interests in China. The odds against the Taipings were overwhelming. Their appeal to Chinese nationalism against "barbarian" Manchus fell on deaf ears because first, the Manchu regime had been Sinicized and had long been accepted by most, if not all Chinese; and second, whatever nationalist appeal the Taipings might have had was more than offset by the alien institutions and beliefs which they proposed for their new regime. Between the Sinicized Manchus and the "barbarized" Chinese, the Confucian scholars, supported by the majority of the Chinese population, did not hesitate to make a choice. The

Taipings were denounced as traitors to an ancient heritage, and the struggle against them was hailed as absolutely essential to the preservation of a great civilization. In the minds of these Confucian scholars, they were worse than the Western powers which had only recently defeated China, because the Western powers were only interested in making profits in China, whereas the Taipings deliberately undermined an established society and tried to destroy its ancient values. With the Taipings there could not be any compromise. Moreover, by proposing to nationalize all land, the Taipings infringed upon the vested interest of the most powerful class in China, the landed gentry. The same interests which had rallied to defeat Wang Mang eighteen centuries before now swarmed to the standard of the Manchus.

The man who symbolized and led the anti-Taiping forces to suppress the rebellion was Tseng Kuo-fan, one of the greatest Confucian statesmen of the nineteenth century. Tseng came from a gentry family in Hunan province and was well-schooled in Confucian learning during his boyhood. After passing the civil service examinations, he served successfully with the Ch'ing government and was eventually promoted to the vice-presidency of the Ministry of Rites. In 1852 he resigned his post to enter a period of mourning after the death of his mother, and it was then that he was ordered by the emperor Hsien-feng to organize a militia to defend his native province. He began his work earnestly in the following year, after the Taipings had swept across most areas south of the Yangtze River. The bannermen and the "green battalions" that had distinguished themselves on the battlefield early in the Ch'ing dynasty were now corrupt and useless, and the Ch'ing government had to depend upon provincial militias organized by local gentry to combat the rebels. While Tseng was busy in Hunan in organizing his army, a fellow gentry official named Li Hung-chang was doing the same in his native province, Anhwei. The Hsiang (Hunan) army led by Tseng and the Huai (Anhwei) army led by Li were the two major forces that eventually overthrew the rebel regime at Nanking.

In their war against the Taipings, Tseng and Li received help from an unexpected corner, the Western interests in China. Outwardly, it seems strange that the Western powers should assist the Manchu government against a Christian regime. At the beginning of the rebellion Christian missionaries showed considerable interest in the rebels who professed Christianity. A careful study of the Taiping beliefs soon disillusioned them because what Hung advocated could not be characterized in any way other than as outright heresy. The Taiping regime's prohibition of the opium traffic affected adversely the interests of Western traders who, together with their Chinese counterparts, had profited enormously by the spread of this vice. Moreover, the Western powers had only recently obtained many treaty concessions from the Ch'ing government, and there was no guarantee that the Taipings would honor these obligations if they replaced the Manchu regime. The feuds among the Taiping leaders and their inability to organize a real, respectable government dispelled whatever illusions some Westerners might once have had. When the showdown arrived, the Western interests sided with the Manchu government.

From 1860 to 1864 the bitterest fighting occurred in the Lower Yangtze. The Ch'ing forces were determined to take Nanking, and the Taipings, in order to defend their capital, were equally determined to occupy as large an area as possible. Shanghai, the most coveted prize in this region, was fought for by both sides. The Taiping commander Li Hsiu-ch'eng requested the Western powers to maintain neutrality, but his request was ignored. In Shanghai the Chinese as well as the Western commercial interests had grown enormously since the port had been opened for Western trade, and in view of the Taipings' communistic ideas, they understandably would do everything they could to prevent the Taipings from capturing the city. They sponsored and financed the organization of the so-called Ever Victorious Army, staffed by foreign officers and equipped with modern weapons. The army was first led by an American named Fred E. Ward, and after he was killed in action in 1862, the command was taken over by an Englishman, Charles G. Gordon. The Ever Victorious Army played an important role in the final campaign against the Taipings, as it captured many strategic cities for the Manchu regime in the Lower Yangtze.

In the summer of 1864, the Ch'ing forces, led by Tseng Kuo-ch'üan, a younger brother of Tseng Kuo-fan, made the final assault on Nanking. The city fell after a bloody battle which lasted fifteen days. Hung Hsiu-ch'üan, the Prince of Heaven, had committed suicide one month before, and his son and successor escaped from the city, only to be captured afterwards. "Not a single man of the 100,000 bandits in the city responded to the order of surrender," reported Tseng Kuo-fan to the imperial government, "and they burned themselves alive in groups as if they had no regret." Later he proceeded to Peking to report his victory in person. There he prostrated himself and kowtowed before the emperess dowager, Tz'u Hsi, who was then a co-regent for the boy emperor T'ung-chih.

ৠ xiii

The Western Impact (2)

THE IMITATION OF THE WEST

Hu Lin-yi, Tseng Kuo-fan's top lieutenant and governor of Hupeh, went to a hill overlooking the city of Anking (Anhwei province) where the attacking Ch'ing army was fighting a bloody battle against the besieged Taipings. Pleased with the progress of the battle, he remarked to his retainers that it was not difficult to defeat the "bandits" despite their "stubbornness." Coming down to the bank of the Yangtze he saw two foreign ships sailing upstream like "two galloping horses with wind-like speed." He was silent and his face became pale. On his way to the barracks, he vomited blood and almost fell from his mount. He had not been well before and now his illness took a serious turn for the worse. Several months later he died while still commanding troops in the army.

Like Hu, many Chinese leaders felt that the real danger to China was not domestic rebels like the Taipings but the seemingly invincible West. "I wish I knew what the future holds for us," remarked Hu, whenever foreigners were mentioned in the course of conversation. Now that China's door was wide open, it seemed that there was no way to resist the ever-increasing Western demands. The issue, however, had to be faced. "If we continue to buy Western ships and arms," said Tseng Kuo-fan, "eventually we shall have enough weapons to resist England and France." This may sound naive today, but it marked the beginning of China's imitation of the West. By then it had become apparent to a few articulate leaders that to become strong enough to resist Western demands, China had to learn the advanced technology of the Western countries. Only by possessing a strong military force, they believed, could China negotiate peace with the West on equal terms and fight a more effective war when the necessity arose. However, the basis of such a military force would not be solid and stable so long as it had to be equipped with vessels and weapons purchased abroad. Thus, in the opinion of many Chinese leaders, China had to have factories of its own, to produce equipment for its own needs. In 1865 the first modern shipyard was established at Shanghai, and the very next year another one was founded at Mawei, near Foochow. In 1870 the Tientsin Machine Factory was renovated to manufacture modern weapons, and in 1872 the China Merchants' Steam Navigation Company was organized at Shanghai. In 1878 coal was mined by using Western technology for the first time at Kaiping, and in 1880 initial steps were taken to build a railroad with Chinese capital. Psychologically, the most important innovation was perhaps the establishment of the Tsungli Yamen (Foreign Office) in 1861 which replaced the traditional Bureau of Barbarian Affairs in handling diplomatic relations with Western countries. By such an action China relinquished its age-old claim that it was the center of power as well as the fount of civilization. In fact, China was making an agonizing reappraisal of itself and its own position in a fast-changing world.

One might call this reappraisal a mental revolution of the first magnitude because it was the first time in Chinese history that a sizable portion of the intelligentsia openly admitted that there was a great deal to be learned from the "barbarians." To learn from the "barbarians," they, of course, had to read "barbarian" books. In 1862 the first foreign language school was established at Peking (T'ung-wen kuan). Western instructors were employed to teach Manchu and Chinese students of "great native intelligence" as measured by a competitive examination. Four foreign languages were taught: English, French, Russian, and German. One year later another foreign language school was organized at Shanghai. The main purpose of these schools was to train interpreters and translators, especially the latter. Translation, a seemingly easy task, became extremely difficult when a Western language was to be translated into the Chinese language of the literary style. It required great skill in the handling of Chinese words and proficiency in Chinese literature as well as a thorough knowledge of the subject matter. Two of the greatest translators of the modern period, Yen Fu and Lin Shu, were not products of the language schools, and the latter did not even know any foreign language. Yen Fu translated more serious books such as *Man's Place in Nature* by Thomas H. Huxley, *An Enquiry into the Wealth of Nations* by Adam Smith, *Logic* by John Stuart Mill, and *Spirit of Laws* by Montesquieu. Lin Shu, on the other hand, translated books of a lighter vein, such as *Camille* by Alexandre Dumas.

The logical place to learn what was then known as "Western affairs" (*yang-wu*) was obviously the Western countries themselves. In 1870 the government decided to send thirty boys each year to be educated in the United States. In Hartford, Connecticut, it bought a house as a dormitory for the students, and a Chinese official was appointed as supervisor. Students were also sent to England and France, though the largest number of them went to the United States. The study-abroad program, beneficial as it might be, soon encountered sharp criticisms. It was not only financially expensive, said the critics, but it denied the students a more basic education, namely, the study of Chinese classics and the appreciation of Confucian vitues. These critics advocated the establishment of Westernized schools in China where students could "learn Western skills without abandoning Chinese virtues." As one might expect, the first Westernized schools were vocational, technical institutions. The Foochow Marine Academy was founded in 1866, and in 1880 a naval academy came into existence in Tientsin. It was not until 1898 that a university with emphasis on liberal arts was established in Peking. The university, later known as the Peking University, has been one of the most famous universities in China.

Significant as these programs were, they were far from adequate to meet the demands for modernization. They were all small in scope, and the goal of each program was not steadily pursued. The lack of adequate funds and trained personnel was one reason, and the frequent change of policy with regard to these programs was another. Moreover, the primary sponsors of these programs such as Tseng Kuo-fan and Li Hung-chang had only a limited objective. What they wished to learn from the West was science and technology, and nothing else. They believed in the superiority of China's political and social structure, the Confucian ideology behind it, and the moral values that governed the relationship among men. All reforms, they maintained, should be conducted within China's own historical framework. "Chinese values should govern the basic matters," said one of them, "whereas Western learning is applicable only in the technical sphere." If such a principle were followed, China would then incorporate the best from both the East and the West. In short,

China was to remain Confucian and authoritarian, while acquiring the technological and military capacity to defend itself.

Even this limited objective of Westernization encountered strong opposition from the majority of the Chinese intelligentsia. The opposition resulted partly from a genuine concern over the possible consequence of exposing Chinese to such "strange" ideas as freedom and democracy, but mostly from habits and beliefs ingrained in an ancient civilization. The opposition was so strong that Li Hung-chang, the undisputed leader of the progressive group after Tseng Kuo-fan's death in 1872, often complained that he was fighting a lonely battle. "The intelligentsia always criticize me for honoring strange ideas," said he in a letter to a friend, "and it is difficult to understand the minds of some Chinese."

If it was difficult for Li Hung-chang to understand the Chinese mind, it was doubly so for a Westerner. In 1874, for instance, the British built a railroad between Shanghai and Sungkiang. The Chinese opposed the construction of this railroad on the ground that it violated the natural harmony of the landscape and that this violation would bring bad luck to them for generations to come. There was a storm of protest and under public pressure the government had to buy the railroad from the British in 1876, wreck it, and carry the wreckage all the way to Taiwan where it was dumped into a lake as an ill omen. During the subsequent decades the preservation of the natural harmony of the landscape (called *feng-shui* by the Chinese) was a great handicap not only to railroad construction but also to mining, the erection of telegraph lines, and other Western projects. In 1880 a Chinese official arrived in the United States as a superintendent of Chinese students and ordered all his charges to come to Washington, D.C., to listen to his lecture on "morality and good behavior." Upon seeing him the students refused to perform the kowtow. He was so angry that he sent a memorial to the imperial government in which he suggested that all Chinese students in the United States be ordered to return to China on the ground that even if they could acquire Western skills they, corrupted by Western ideas, could never be the same Chinese. The imperial government, acting on the superintendent's proposal, ordered these students to return home in the following year.

Between a small group of progressives and the ultraconservatives who constituted the overwhelming majority of the Chinese literati the ultimate arbitrator was the empress dowager, Tz'u Hsi. There are so many legends about this woman that sometimes it is difficult to differentiate facts from mere hearsay. One thing, however, remains certain. She was a ruthless woman endowed with great ability, and she used every talent she had to fight for the one thing she loved most: power. Principle and morality meant nothing to her if the observance of them was incompatible with the fulfillment of her personal ambition. In her struggle for power her closest allies were the eunuchs who until then had not been an important factor in Ch'ing politics. Such an alliance should be expected because, as a woman, she was under great handicaps in negotiating political alliances with men outside the palace. Her eunuchs served as go-betweens as well as spies and informers. She was able to inspire fear or even respect, but never love. Despite her ruthlessness and lack of principle, her strong personality commanded the loyalty and obedience of many eminent men in the second half of the nineteenth century such as Tseng Kuo-fan and Li Hung-chang.

The life of Tz'u Hsi sounds more like fiction than biography, and here only the briefest outline can be presented. Selected as a concubine by the emperor Hsien-feng while in her teens, she worked her way into becoming his confidante through her charm, talent, and skillful maneuvering. Her position in the royal household was greatly enhanced after she bore the emperor a son who was then made the heir apparent. When the emperor died in 1862, she and the empress Tz'u An were made co-regents on behalf of the child emperor T'ung-chih, and three royal princes, in observance of the dead emperor's will, were to assist them in the management of state affairs. Tz'u Hsi soon liquidated the three princes on trumped-up charges and became regent in fact as well as in name. Though Tz'u An, as the former empress, out-ranked her in seniority, she was too pliable a person to offer resistance to Tz'u Hsi's ambition. Tz'u Hsi's ruthlessness eventually alienated even her own son who, as he grew up, resented being a mere puppet. The rivalry between mother and son reached a climax in 1872 when the time had arrived for the imperial marriage. The young man favored a girl approved by Tz'u An and rejected the one recommended by his own mother. Tz'u Hsi, as the story goes, prohibited her son from visiting his newly married wife, thus hoping to force him to visit the girl whom she favored, the girl who had by then been made an imperial concubine. The boy refused to have anything to do with this scheme and visited street girls instead. He contracted a venereal disease and died two years later (1875) at the age of nineteen.

To a Westerner one of the most interesting parts of Tz'u Hsi's political career was her successful exploitation of the Confucian virtue, filial piety, to advance her own ambition. As has been said in a previous chapter, an emperor might be the Son of Heaven before his subjects, but he remained his mother's son in the royal household. As such, he was required by custom and tradition to be obedient to her and cater to her wishes, even when, as sometimes happened, state policies were involved. While most empress dowagers in history did not interfere with state affairs and were satisfied with ritualistic deference from their imperial sons, the ambitious ones, such as Tz'u Hsi, could transform this maternal dignity into real power, and by controlling their sons they controlled the nation. If a son or adopted son were a minor, the empress dowager could rule the nation openly without using the emperor as a puppet, because in such case she customarily became the regent.

After the death of T'ung-chih, Tz'u Hsi placed on the throne her three-year-old nephew (the son of her sister) who, after accession, was

TZ'U HSI ON HER PEACOCK THRONE

known as Kuang-hsü. She considered the boy her own son, and such a claim enabled her to continue to rule as a regent. The fact that she violated the dynastic rule by installing as the new emperor another member of the same generation did not bother her so long as the new emperor was a minor whom she could control. In 1881 Tz'u An died and Tz'u Hsi became the sole regent. As he grew up, Kuang-hsü, like his predecessor T'ung-chih, resented the empress dowager's domination. When the time had arrived for him to select a queen, the empress dowager imposed on him a girl he disliked, while the girl of his own choice was made a mere concubine (later known as the Pearl Concubine). The two personalities continued to clash despite their outward correctness: the empress dowager was always "loving and protective" and the emperor was always "pious and obedient." The clash reached a new height during the so-called Hundred Days' Reform (1898) which will be discussed later in this chapter. (See pp. 424–427.) After the failure of the Reform, the emperor was kept a prisoner in his own palace; and isolated from outside contact, his only comfort was his Pearl Concubine. Even this comfort was taken away in 1900 when the empress dowager, in a burst of anger, ordered her to commit suicide. The clash between the two personalities finally ended in 1908 when both died only one day apart. Thus, for almost a half century (1862–1908), one of the most crucial periods in Chinese history, the real power in China was the empress dowager, Tz'u Hsi.

Had the empress dowager, with great power at her command, backed up the progressives and thrown China's resources behind the modernization programs, the China of the late nineteenth century would have been remarkably different from what it was. This, of course, she did not do. First, there was the honest ignorance of what Westernization meant and what it promised, and second, she had to look at the reforms from her stand as a Manchu princess. Would the reforms help her position in the government or the Manchus' position in China? The answer was obviously "no." Practically all progressive leaders were Chinese, and the most reactionary among the conservatives were Manchus. What would have happened to the dynasty and to her personally if, as a result of the modernization programs, the Chinese became so powerful as to tip the traditional balance between these two ethnic groups? Moreover, how was it possible to import Western technology without importing Western ideas such as representative government and democracy? On the other hand, she knew that without being modernized technologically, China could not resist the increasing demands from foreign powers. Caught in a dilemma, she gave some encouragement to the modernization programs, but not enough to make them succeed. She was only too happy when a sizable fund originally appropriated for building a new navy was transferred to another account for the purpose of building a palace ground (known as Yi-ho Yüan) for her personal enjoyment. She could have been

China's Meiji Emperor (See p. 418.) but for her own reasons she did not choose to become one. If she were forced to make a choice between the salvation of China and the preservation of her own power and the power of the Manchus, there was no question about her decision. "I prefer to give China to the foreigners rather than to surrender it to my own slaves [Chinese]," she once remarked. As far as her personal objectives were concerned, she succeeded remarkably well. She was in power and so were the Manchus, as long as she lived. Three years after her death, the Manchu dynasty went with her.

To balance what has been said above, it should be pointed out that by taking a more conservative stand Tz'u Hsi had on her side the overwhelming majority of the Chinese intelligentsia. If she had done otherwise, she would have faced an uphill struggle as all of the progressives did. Since the conservative stand was more compatible with her personal interests, she did no more than what could be expected.

Despite the half-hearted support on the part of the government, the ingrained opposition arising from Chinese customs and traditions, and the inertia of the majority of the Chinese people, the advantages of Western technology were too obvious not to be recognized by certain sections of the population. Some of the new industries were financed jointly by foreign and Chinese capital; others were solely Chinese enterprises. Towards the end of the nineteenth century many railroads were built with the help of foreign capital, and several coal and iron-ore mines were operated by the use of Western technology. In the Wu-Han area the progressive governor-general Chang Chih-tung promoted Western-type industries with eagerness and energy, and financed them through local savings. In Shanghai small industries (such as textiles and flour mills) using machinery for production mushroomed overnight and attracted local capital which had been traditionally invested in landholdings. From 1864 to 1900 the total volume of China's foreign trade was more than trebled, though the excess of imports over exports also increased steadily. Economically, a new China was emerging, however slowly.

TERRITORIAL LOSSES

In the two decades after the Opium War, while England and France were battling China to enlarge their commercial interests, farther in the north another power was nibbling at Chinese territories. The emergence of Russia as an independent state after the overthrow of the Mongol overlordship was followed by a period of continuous expansion, and by the seventeenth century the Russian power had reached Siberia and clashed head-on with the rising power of the Manchu empire. Often there was friction between merchants and officials of both sides, and armed forces were sometimes called to resolve the differences. The situation was particularly serious in the Amur basin. As neither side could impose its will on the other in these remote areas, a compromise was reached in the Treaty of Nerchinsk in 1689. The Chinese granted Russian merchants the right to trade in the border areas in return for a generous boundary settlement. The boundary line ran along the Argun River, the Gorbitsa (a tributary of Shilka), and the watershed between the basins of the Lena and the Amur to the sea. This arrangement was supplemented by another treaty in 1727 (the Treaty of Kiakhta), which delimited the boundary line between the two countries west of the Gorbitsa, provided further details in the trade relations, and gave Russia a semirepresentation at Peking (a church, a priest, three curates, and five language students). This unofficial representation later provided Russia with valuable information on China and enabled it to have direct access to imperial officials at Peking, a privilege which England sought in vain throughout the eighteenth century.

The northern frontier was comparatively quiet until 1847 when China's weakness as revealed in the Opium War was seized upon by Russia as a golden opportunity for expanding territorially at China's expense. In that year the tsar appointed Count Nicholas Muraviev as governor-general of eastern Siberia with special instructions to investigate the Amur region. The Count, one of the ablest empire-builders, pursued his task in earnest, and by 1854 he and his agents had explored and then occupied the entire region north of the Amur River which under the Treaty of Nerchinsk was Chinese territory. In 1858 when England and France were invading China from the sea and the Taiping rebels were ravaging South China on land, Muraviev presented to the local Chinese officials a set of territorial demands. These officials, knowing that they could not count on the central government to send reinforcements to counteract any military action the Russians might take, consented to the demands. The Treaty of Aigun, signed between Muraviev and Yi-shan, the governor of Heilungkiang, contained three major items: (1) the cession to Russia of all territories north of the Amur River, (2) joint control of the land lying between the Ussuri River and the sea (the present Maritime Province), and (3) the right of both countries to navigate the Amur, the Ussuri, and the Sungari rivers.

Before Russia had had time to digest these territorial gains, another opportunity for demanding more territories presented itself in 1860 after England and France had defeated the Chinese and captured their capital Peking. The Russian minister to China, General Ignatief, promised the Chinese that he would use his good influence to persuade the allies not to engage in continuous destruction of that ancient city if the Chinese could see their way to cede to Russia the territory between the Ussuri and the sea. Looking at the victorious allies on a rampage, Prince Kung, the

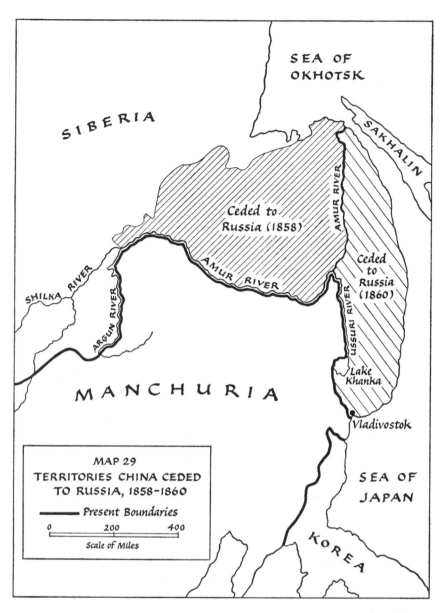

SEA OF
OKHOTSK

SIBERIA

SAKHALIN

AMUR RIVER

Ceded to
Russia (1858)

Ceded
to
Russia
(1860)

SHILKA RIVER

AMUR RIVER

USSURI RIVER

ARGUN RIVER

Lake
Khanka

M A N C H U R I A

Vladivostok

MAP 29
TERRITORIES CHINA CEDED
TO RUSSIA, 1858-1860

——— Present Boundaries

0   200   400

Scale of Miles

SEA OF
JAPAN

KOREA

highest Manchu official then in Peking after the emperor had fled, agreed and subsequently signed the Treaty of Peking (1860). By the two treaties (Aigun and Peking) Russia deprived China of 350,000 square miles of territory, a territory larger than Texas (267,339 sq. mi.), without ever firing a shot. At the southernmost tip of the newly acquired territory, the city of Vladivostok was founded, and the city remains today as Russia's largest naval base in East Asia.

Meanwhile in the south, England and France were engaged in conquering and annexing some of China's dependent states. These dependent states were sometimes called tributary states since their kings received investiture from China, adopted the Chinese calendar, and sent periodical tribute missions to the Chinese capital. China did not exercise actual control over these states and, as a rule, did not interfere in their domestic affairs. Generally speaking, the lord-vassal relationship was more a cultural than a political relationship. However, the dependent states did serve a political purpose in the sense that they formed a buffer zone between China proper and the less Sinicized and more hostile kingdoms and tribes beyond. The past showed that to protect China these dependent states had to be protected first, and that their loss to a foreign power would expose China itself to foreign invasions and might eventually even lead to the occupation of part or all of China. Throughout history China had striven to surround itself with a chain of friendly, dependent states, and the Ch'ing regime, like many Chinese dynasties before it, had a lord-vassal relationship with many of its border states such as Annam, Burma, Sikkim, and Korea.

Annam, which means "peace in the south" in Chinese, was known as Indo-China after the French conquest and comprises three independent Communist countries today, namely Vietnam, Laos, and Cambodia. France began to show interest in that country as early as 1843; however, it did not take military action until 1858. This military action and that which followed were taken on the ground that the Annamese government was hostile to Christians. In 1862 a treaty was concluded between the two countries which gave France the right to trade and proselytize in Annam and to navigate in the internal rivers. Besides, Annam ceded to France three provinces and paid indemnities to compensate French expenses occasioned during the military operation. To pave the way for annexation, France imposed another treaty on Annam in 1874 which recognized Annam as an independent country, thus cutting off its relationship with China. However, Annam continued to send tribute missions to China in 1876 and again in 1880. By 1884 the former Annam was quickly disappearing as a result of France's successful military operations, and French troops were pushing towards the Chinese border. China responded by sending troops to Annam, and amazingly, the Chinese, with native support, won victories against the French. Unable to make headway on land, France sent its fleet to ravage China's southeastern coast. Here the superiority of French naval power prevailed: it destroyed the Chinese naval base at Foochow and seized a naval port, Keelung, at Taiwan. Within the Ch'ing court, some officials favored continuing the war and others advocated a negotiated peace. The peace party, led by Li Hung-chang, eventually prevailed, after it had successfully convinced Tz'u Hsi that China was not prepared for a large-scale war and that continuing the conflict would subject the coastal cities to French bombardment or seizure. In 1885

China concluded a treaty with France in which China formally recognized Annam as a French protectorate.

Burma, an off-and-on Chinese tributary state since 1284, was conquered by Great Britain without provoking Chinese intervention. The conquest came about through three Burmese Wars (1824–1826, 1852–1853, and 1885), and, unlike the French conquest of Annam, this one did not involve missionaries. The Chinese formally recognized the conquest in 1886 when an Anglo-Chinese convention was signed. To save Chinese prestige, Great Britain promised to let the Burmese continue to send tribute missions to China once every ten years. However, only one such mission was sent, in 1895. Meanwhile, in 1890, Great Britain successfully "persuaded" the Chinese to recognize Sikkim as a British protectorate.

In retrospect, the country that proved to be more aggressive than either England or France was a neighboring Oriental country, Japan. During the initial stage of the Western impact, Japan reacted the same as China. However, it soon became convinced of the advantages of Westernization and began to apply Western technology to industry, commerce, and related fields. The modernization of Japan began with the Meiji Restoration (1867), and in one generation that country was transformed from a feudal, agricultural society to the most industrialized society in all Asia. The history of modern Japan is not our concern here; we can only relate those events that led to its conflicts with China. Japan's expansion began soon after its modernization began; in fact, a major purpose of the modernization programs was to provide Japan with the necessary economic and military capacity to play a more active role in East Asian affairs. Three years after Meiji became the emperor, a Japanese ambassador arrived in Peking asking for the same concessions that China had given to the Western powers. Li Hung-chang rejected the Japanese demand, saying that the unequal treaties had been forced upon China by the Western powers and that China had been duped into granting extraterritoriality to Westerners because it was unfamiliar with the European customs. "Now every time I see the dictatorial behavior of the Western consuls," he added, "I am grieved." However, a treaty of trade and commerce, minus the most-favored-nation clause, was signed between the two countries.

The first conflict between China and Japan involved Liu-ch'iu (Ryukyu) and Taiwan. Throughout the Ming-Ch'ing period Liu-ch'iu was China's vassal state and beginning in 1662 sent tribute missions to China once every two years. Japan, however, had claim on the islands too, as the king of Liu-ch'iu also sent tribute to the *Daimyo* of Satsuma from time to time. In 1871 some fifty-four Liu-ch'iu islanders, shipwrecked at Taiwan, were murdered by the aborigines. Japan proclaimed that Liu-ch'iu was its vassal state and asked China to punish the aborigines. Receiving no satisfaction from the Chinese, Japan sent a military expedition to Taiwan and occupied a strip of territory on the northern coast. When China responded by proposing to send a larger force to counteract the Japanese move, Japan requested England's good offices. The result was the treaty of 1874 which, by implication, recognized Japan's claim as protector of the Liu-ch'iu islands. Five years later, Japan deposed the Liu-ch'iu king and annexed the islands.

The conflict over Liu-ch'iu was the first of a long series of Japanese expansionist moves which were not to end until World War II. As Korea formed a natural bridge to mainland China, it was most logically Japan's next target. Since Han Wu-ti's conquest of Korea in the second century B.C., Korea had been sometimes a vassal state of China and sometimes independent. Military confrontations between China and Japan over Korea occurred in the seventh and again in the sixteenth century; in each case the greater manpower and economic resources China then possessed prevailed in the long run. Towards the end of the nineteenth century the power balance had shifted to Japan's favor, as that country had become militarily and technologically stronger. In 1876, as a result of a series of successful diplomatic maneuvers, a demonstration of force, and the outright occupation of some Korean islands, the Japanese secured a treaty with Korea which opened two Korean ports for Japanese trade and recognized that Korea as "an independent state, enjoys the same sovereign rights as does Japan." The detachment of Korea from its dependence on China, as the Japanese hoped, would enable them to have a free hand in that country. China, knowing its own military weakness, did not bother to protest. Instead, it persuaded Korea to open its ports to all Western countries, including England, France, the United States, and Russia, to counteract the increasing Japanese influence.

Meanwhile in Korea two political factions had developed, one progressive and the other conservative. The progressive group was led by returned students from Japan who wanted Korea to follow the Japanese example by initiating reforms. The conservative group, on the other hand, was headed by people close to the Korean king and leaned heavily on Chinese support. In 1884 the intrigues and strife between these two factions developed into open hostility, and both China and Japan, in the name of restoring peace and order, sent troops to Korea. The Chinese force, led by Yüan Shih-k'ai, dispersed the Japanese and placed the state power in the hands of the conservatives. In the following year a treaty was concluded between China and Japan in which each party pledged that in the case of future disturbances in Korea, it would notify the other party in advance before sending troops. By then it was clear that China was as determined to keep Korea as a dependent state as Japan was determined to detach it from China. If Korea were lost, the Ch'ing government reasoned, Manchuria, the home of China's royal house, would be exposed to Japan's attack. Between 1885 and 1894 China strengthened its control over Korea and made that country a protectorate, *de facto* as well as *de jure*. This was the first time that China had exercised such firm control since the beginning of the Ming dynasty.

In 1894 the Korean government had a rebellion to contend with. The rebellion was led by a semireligious group called the Eastern Learning Society which vowed to "expel and eliminate all Japanese invaders" and to "capture Seoul (Korean capital) to eliminate all aristocrats." The rebels occupied a large section of southern Korea and defeated the regular Korean army that was sent to suppress them. Korea requested China's help, and China responded by sending to Korea a military expedition, after notifying Japan of its intention. Japan moved quickly to counteract the Chinese move and succeeded in capturing Seoul. The Japanese deposed the Korean king and placed his natural father (known as Tai-wun-kun) on the throne. The new king concluded a treaty of alliance with Japan and requested his new ally to drive the Chinese troops out from Korea. Thus the war began.

After hostilities began, the Japanese won victories on both land and sea. From the Chinese point of view the most disastrous was the destruction of the Peiyang fleet, one of Li Hung-chang's most precious projects. After the Japanese troops had penetrated deep into South Manchuria and threatened Shanhaikuan, the Chinese sued for peace. Japan, enjoying the greatest victory it had ever won against China, refused to accept any man as China's minister plenipotentiary for negotiating peace except Li Hung-chang. Li, who had worked hard against great opposition to modernize China, was now compelled by circumstances to play a humiliating role: to go personally to Japan to ask the victors to moderate their demands. While in Japan he was shot by a Japanese citizen and was fortunate to escape serious injury. The incident, however, had no noticeable effect on the resultant treaty, one of the harshest China ever concluded with a foreign power. The Treaty of Shimonoseki (1895) called upon China (1) to recognize the independence of Korea, (2) to cede Taiwan, the Pescadores, and the Liaotung Peninsula to Japan, (3) to pay an indemnity of 200,000,000 taels, and (4) to open ports for trade and grant Japan the most-favored-nation treatment.

So harsh were the treaty terms that they sowed the seeds of hatred between the two countries for several decades to come. It was comparable to the Treaty of Paris of 1871 which helped to create a state of continuous hostility between Germany and France until the end of World War II. The Japanese were not merely interested in commercial expansion; their demand for large chunks of territories, the Chinese believed, revealed their ultimate ambition, the conquest of China. From 1895 on, Chinese nationalism was directed more at Japan than at any other foreign power, as Japan had shown herself to be the most aggressive of all foreign powers. From the Japanese point of view, however, the treaty was a masterpiece of diplomacy. The huge indemnity provided the much-needed capital for industrial expansion, and the most-favored-nation treatment enabled Japan to acquire the same tariff, extraterritoriality, and other concessions that Western powers enjoyed in China. Since Japan was geographically close to China, it was in a better position to exploit these concessions more effectively. Moreover, the treaty marked the beginning of the establishment of the Japanese empire. Korea, recognized as an independent state in 1895, became a Japanese protectorate in 1907, and was formally annexed by Japan in 1910. Taiwan was taken over by Japan outright and remained a Japanese possession until 1945.

In the case of the Liaotung Peninsula, however, the situation became more complicated. This peninsula, with its rich mineral resources, strategic location, and two excellent harbors (Dairen and Port Arthur), was as much coveted by Russia as it was by Japan. If it fell into the hands of a strong Japan, the Russian chance of securing it would become slim indeed. Shortly after the treaty was made public, Russia, supported by its ally France and also by Germany which had its own designs in this part of the world, demanded that Japan return the peninsula to China. Since Japan was in no position to fight a war against three major European powers, it reluctantly agreed to the Russian demand in return for a Chinese cash payment (30 million taels). The competition of the two countries for Manchuria eventually led to the Russo-Japanese War.

To Li Hung-chang the Treaty of Shimonoseki was as much a personal humiliation as a national disgrace. Moreover, he believed that Japan would not be content with what it had received and that sooner or later there would be another Sino-Japanese war. Knowing that China was unable to fight Japan alone, he was looking for a military alliance with a Western power. The memory of the recent wars with England and France was still fresh, and furthermore, it was unlikely that these two powers would fight a war against Japan to protect Manchuria for China. Russia, on the other hand, had a direct interest in seeing that Manchuria remain in Chinese hands because first, its occupation by Japan would threaten Russia's own security in Eastern Siberia, and second, Russia would like to reserve Manchuria as its own sphere for expansion. In 1896 Li Hung-chang went to St. Petersburg, outwardly to attend the coronation of Tsar Nicholas II but actually to negotiate a secret treaty of alliance with Russia. The treaty provided for mutual assistance against future Japanese aggression, for the use of Chinese ports by Russia in case of war, and for China's agreement to Russia's construction of a railroad (later known as the Chinese Eastern Railroad) across Manchuria to reach Vladivostok. Under no circumstances, said the treaty, should Russia use the construction of the railroad as an excuse to occupy Chinese territories.

Nevertheless, Russia was formally invited into Manchuria. The future of Manchuria was to be decided by the Russo-Japanese struggle, while the Chinese were forced to the sidelines.

CHINA'S STRUGGLE TO SURVIVE

The weakness of China as revealed during the Sino-Japanese War triggered a series of demands for Chinese territories on the part of Western powers. Germany, which was a newcomer among the imperialistic ranks and was anxious to secure a foothold in East Asia, made the first move. It notified the Chinese that it deserved a "reward" as a result of its intervention to force Japan to return to China the Liaotung Peninsula, and when the Chinese turned down its demand for the cession of the Kiaochow Bay (Shantung province), Germany decided to take military action. A gunboat was dispatched in July, 1897, but was destroyed by a typhoon while on its way to Kiaochow. Two months later two German Catholic missionaries were murdered by Chinese robbers in Shantung, and thereupon German troops landed in Kiaochow. Thus the Chinese government was forced to come to terms. The Kiaochow Bay was leased to Germany for ninety-nine years, and Germany was granted the right to build two railroads in Shantung and was also given the mining rights along the railroads. Moreover, "in all cases where foreign assistance, in persons, capital or material, may be needed for any purpose whatever within the Province of Shantung," the Chinese government bound itself to ask Germany for such assistance. In a term commonly used at the turn of the century, Shantung had become a German sphere of influence.

The German success was soon followed by Russian demands in the Liaotung Peninsula and French demands in southern China. Three weeks after Germany had acquired Kiaochow, China leased to Russia the southern tip of the Liaotung Peninsula (containing Dairen and Port Arthur) and gave Russia the right to build a railroad to connect Dairen with the main line of the Chinese Eastern Railroad in central Manchuria. Previously, France had acquired the right to exploit the mineral resources in Yunnan, Kwangsi, and Kwangtung as a "reward" for its intervention to force Japan to return the Liaotung Peninsula to China. Now, seeing that Germany and Russia had obtained new concessions from China, France demanded the same from the Chinese. In the spring of 1898 China agreed to give France (1) the right to build a railroad from Tonkin (Annam) to Kunming, (2) the lease of the Kwangchow Bay for ninety-nine years, and (3) the right to appoint Frenchmen as advisers to the newly proposed Chinese postal service. By virtue of this agreement, Yunnan, Kwangsi, and Kwangtung became the French sphere of influence.

England, whose interest in China had been so far more commercial

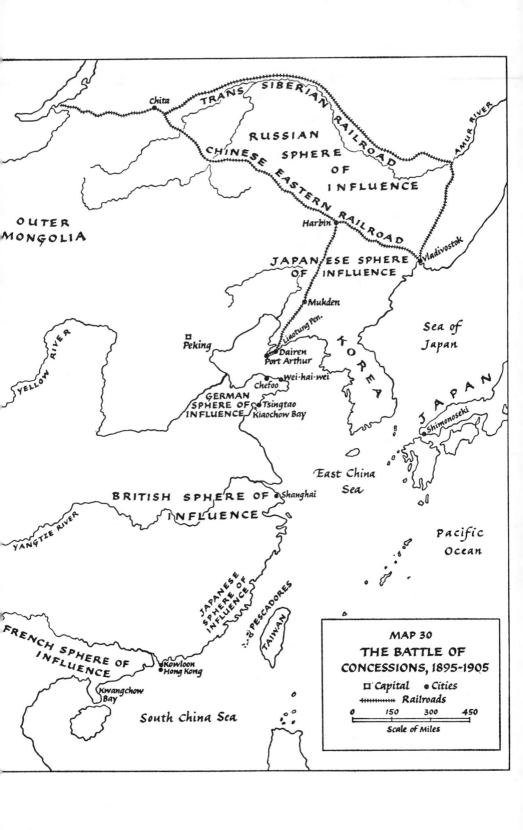

Chita

TRANS SIBERIAN RAILROAD

RUSSIAN SPHERE

OF

INFLUENCE

CHINESE EASTERN RAILROAD

AMUR RIVER

OUTER MONGOLIA

Harbin

JAPANESE SPHERE
OF INFLUENCE

Vladivostok

Sea of
Japan

Mukden

Liaotung Pen.

Peking

Dairen
Port Arthur

KOREA

YELLOW RIVER

Wei-hai-wei

Chefoo

GERMAN
SPHERE OF
INFLUENCE

Tsingtao
Kiaochow Bay

JAPAN

Shimonoseki

BRITISH SPHERE OF

INFLUENCE

Shanghai

East China
Sea

YANGTZE RIVER

Pacific
Ocean

JAPANESE
SPHERE OF
INFLUENCE

PESCADORES

TAIWAN

FRENCH SPHERE OF
INFLUENCE

Kowloon
Hong Kong

Kwangchow
Bay

South China Sea

MAP 30

**THE BATTLE OF
CONCESSIONS, 1895-1905**

□ Capital   ● Cities

╈╈╈╈╈╈ Railroads

0   150   300   450

Scale of Miles

than political, finally decided to join the other powers in the scramble for concessions. Three months after the French success England obtained from China the following concessions: (1) the promise by China that it would never alienate any territory in the Yangtze Valley, (2) British control of the Chinese Maritime Customs, (3) the lease of Weihaiwei to England as a naval station, and (4) the extension of the lease of Kowloon to ninety-nine years. Thus at the turn of the century, the economically most productive part of China had become divided into spheres of foreign influence. This was the procedure whereby Africa had been divided before, and the Chinese feared that the same fate would befall them. China, in the words of Sun Yat-sen, had become a subcolony with many masters. "Yet," said he, "none of the masters feels responsible for its welfare."

The defeat at the hands of Japan in the Sino-Japanese War and the territorial demands of the European powers stung China to a new realization that unless it was modernized quickly, it would not survive as a nation at all. Dismissing the cautious, gradual approach of Li Hung-chang as inadequate and ineffective, many Chinese believed that the nation must undergo speedy, drastic reforms before it was too late. The leader of the new sentiment was a Confucian scholar named K'ang Yu-wei. K'ang was born in 1858 to an aristocratic family in Kwangtung, a family which for generations had been prominent in scholastic and governmental circles. He was well educated in the traditional, Confucian scholarship and passed the provincial level of the civil service examination in 1894. On his way to Peking to participate in the metropolitan examination in the following year, he passed through Hong Kong and Shanghai where he was greatly impressed by the efficiency of the Western municipal administration. Previously he had petitioned the government for reforms, and now he was more than convinced that to survive, China had to imitate the West not only technologically but in a variety of other fields as well. In Peking he sent the emperor Kuang-hsü a petition on which he secured the signatures of hundreds of examination candidates. The petition, later known as the *Examination Candidates' Petition* (*Kung-che shang-shu*), strongly urged immediate reforms. "The need is urgent, and the time is short," said the petitioners. Though there was no immediate response from the emperor, the petition caused a great stir among the gentry-scholars. A political star had arisen on the horizon, and a new crusade was on its way.

To achieve his purpose of reform, K'ang had to win the support of the members of the scholar-gentry class. The only way to win their support, as he well knew, was to convince them that the reforms were not only compatible with Chinese tradition but would have been supported by Confucius himself. This was the same technique that had been used by Wang Mang in the first century and Wang An-shih in the eleventh century. In this respect K'ang's erudition in Confucian learning served him well, and he found in the *Spring and Autumn Annals* support for his proposed reforms. To strengthen his ideological stand, he wrote two books, *A Study of Confucius as a Reformer* (*K'ung-tzu kai-chih k'ao*) and *A Study of Forged Classics of the Hsin Dynasty* (*Hsin-hsüeh wei-ching k'ao*). A new organization, called the Society of Learning and Study (Ch'iang-hsüeh hui) was organized on a nation-wide basis to propagate his ideas. K'ang's most gifted disciple, Liang Ch'i-ch'ao, became the editor of a newly founded newspaper, *Current Affairs* (*Shih-wu pao*), and spoke eloquently to win many supporters. The ideological groundwork having been carefully prepared, the next most important thing was to convince the emperor of the necessity of reforms because the emperor alone could initiate action. It should be noted that K'ang and his colleagues were not rebels, and that they wanted to effect their reforms through the existing monarchic system.

Fortunately Emperor Kuang-hsü, who had taken over the reins of government from Tz'u Hsi in 1889 when he reached his majority, was in a receptive mood. He felt deeply the humiliation China had suffered at the foreigners' hands and he wished to become, to quote court sources, another George Washington or Peter the Great. He had read K'ang's books and he liked them. In the spring of 1898 K'ang and some of his colleagues were appointed as imperial officials, and they lost no time going into action. From June 11 to September 16, 1898, a series of imperial decrees were handed down, which, if carried out, would mean, among other things: (1) the abolition of the eight-legged essays and the introduction of tests on current affairs in all civil service examinations; (2) the elimination of superfluous, unnecessary government organs such as the Bureau of Royal Butlers (Kuang-lu ssu, in charge of the emperor's food) and the Bureau of Royal Stables (T'ai-p'u ssu); (3) the establishment of Westernized schools; (4) the organization and training of armed forces according to Western methods and the increased use of modern weapons; (5) the establishment of modern banks, the opening of mines, and the construction of railroads; and (6) the establishment of an economic bureau coordinating all industrial and commercial activities across the nation. During the one hundred days (hence the name: Hundred Days' Reform) the reformers reigned supreme since they had the emperor on their side.

Mild as these reforms were, they were too radical for the conservatives. They rallied behind the empress dowager Tz'u Hsi and urged her to take over the government and force the emperor to abdicate. The capital was full of rumors, including the rumor that the conflict between the emperor and the empress dowager had reached a climax and that the emperor's life was in danger. Some of the reformers attempted to stage a coup d'état to seize the empress dowager. The coup, if successful, would save the emperor and therefore their reforms—so they believed. Yüan Shih-k'ai, whose troops were stationed at nearby Tientsin, was approached by a reformer to carry out the coup, but Yüan, for his own reasons, reported the plot to the empress dowager instead. Thus the attempted coup failed before it could even get started. In the dawn of September 21, five days after the last decree of reform had been issued, the emperor was found kneeling and kowtowing before the empress dowager. He was trembling and speechless. "Stupid son," scolded the empress dowager; "I have been feeding you and taking care of you for more than twenty years and yet you listen to the words of those churls to plot against me." Then she issued a decree that the emperor was ill and that it was necessary for her to attend state affairs. The emperor was ordered to live in confinement and the reform was finished. K'ang and Liang managed to escape to foreign countries. However, other reform leaders were captured; they were subsequently sentenced to death or long imprisonment.

Why did the reforms fail? A superficial answer can be found in the sharp contrast between the two leading personalities: the empress dowager was strong and ruthless and the emperor was weak and undecisive, though always well-intentioned. The real reason, however, went beyond the difference in personalities. The failure of the reform movement should be viewed in the broad context of the confrontation between the East and the West and between imported progressivism and traditional conservatism. It failed because in 1898 the progressive force was still in a minority. Fifty years after the Opium War the country was not yet ready to accept Western ideas and to abandon even a small fraction of its traditional values. The reforms were opposed not only by Tz'u Hsi and her conservative supporters but by the majority of the intelligentsia as well. Despite his justification of reforms on the basis of Confucian ideology, K'ang Yu-wei was denounced as a cultural traitor and deviationist and was regarded as a dangerous man. "Even if Confucius really wanted reform, he desired only to restore the ancient Sage Kings of the Three Dynasties," said one scholar; "he had no intention of replacing Chinese institutions with barbarian [Western] systems." "K'ang Yu-wei imitates Confucius in external appearance, but follows the barbarians [Westerners] in his inner mind," echoed another. One government official even suggested to the emperor that K'ang should be beheaded. Moreover, some of the reforms affected adversely the vested interests of many of the intellectuals. These intellectuals had spent years in studying the classics and perfecting the eight-legged essays, and they depended on their skill in the ancient training to open doors to officialdom, power, and prestige. The abolition of the eight-legged essays in the civil service examinations, as they rightly feared, would block their avenue to advancement. Thus, by introducing one educational reform, K'ang made millions of enemies.

After K'ang Yu-wei's reforms had failed, those Chinese who wished to see a modern China rise from its deadening past eventually concluded that the Manchu regime must go. They joined the standard of another man who by temperament and choice was a rebel and revolutionary. His name was Sun Wen, better known as Sun Yat-sen. As to the career of this remarkable man, we shall have a great deal to say later in this chapter.

THE BOXER REBELLION, THE OPEN DOOR,
AND THE RUSSO-JAPANESE WAR

Tz'u Hsi, who in her advanced age was popularly referred to as the Old Buddha, remained outwardly placid and immobile after the storm over the reform movement had been blown away. Underneath the calm and almost kind appearance were anger, fear, and reinforced hatred. She wanted to depose the emperor, but she was not sure of the reaction of the foreign powers who, as generally understood, were in sympathy with the emperor and the progressive leaders. K'ang and Liang had escaped to foreign countries where they organized the Emperor Protection Society (Pao-huang hui) and openly criticized her and her reactionary policies. She wanted the foreigners to return the two "traitors" to China to be beheaded, but the foreigners refused to cooperate. Inside and outside the country there were numerous organizations working for her downfall and the downfall of her government. To her dismay even some of her own governors-general refused to consent to the deposition of the emperor. Who taught these Chinese to be "disloyal to their sovereign and impious towards their parents?" Of course, it was the foreigners. China would return to its virtuous path if all foreigners simply would leave China and take away with them all their gadgets such as railroads and telegraph poles. Yet she dared not say this to them because she was afraid of them, especially their fast ships and deadly weapons. If somehow these deadly weapons could be neutralized and could not do any harm to their intended victims! This would be a miracle, but miracles, as she was told, had happened before. Moreover, it was unthinkable that the great civilization of China would be trodden into pieces by these unscrupulous, contemptible barbarians. As she thought aloud, she increasingly surrounded herself with people of similar convictions. Around her were those who distrusted all books that were written in "illegible" horizontal lines and those who sincerely believed that sooner or later "Heaven will wipe out all barbarians who have recognized no ruler and no fathers for more than two thousand years." Their prayer seemed to have been answered when there appeared in North China the Society of the Righteous and Harmonious Fists (Yi-ho ch'üan). The society cried aloud: "Support the Manchus and eliminate the foreigners," and Tz'u Hsi and her reactionary advisers were greatly rejoiced. How could they eliminate the foreigners?

It was simple, said the Society's leaders. The foreigners had been able to defeat China because of their superiority in firearms, and "our members, when properly trained, are immune to bullets."

The Society of the Righteous and Harmonious Fists, better known in the English language as Boxers, was one of those numerous secret, semireligious organizations that have appeared time and again in Chinese history. Its religious beliefs were heavily dosed with superstition. It included among its dieties fictional as well as historical figures, including the monkey god invented by Wu Ch'eng-en in his romance, *Journey to the West* (Chapter X). Its followers were poverty-stricken peasants, the rural unemployed, disbanded soldiers, and all those who had nothing to lose except their lives. The nature and composition of this society would have implied that it was antilandlord and antigovernment, and for a considerable time it was. If it had been left alone to develop along its natural course, there would have been an open rebellion. However, by skillfully manipulating the Boxer leaders, local government officials were able to transform this antigovernment uprising into an antiforeign movement. As foreign pressure continued to increase towards the end of the nineteenth century, these officials had no difficulty in making the foreigners a scapegoat for China's miseries, especially the misery of the Boxers. The wrath of the Boxers, which at any other time would have been directed against the government, was now directed at the foreigners. Since the Boxers formed essentially a rural movement, they easily found their first target in the missionaries and their converts who lived in the rural areas.

That there had been friction between Chinese and missionaries has been said before; this friction was intensified as a result of Chinese misunderstanding of the nature of missionary activities. The Christians were accused of conducting immoral and illegal activities, such as "extracting eyes from infants to be compounded into direful drugs." Besides their extraterritorial status, their assumed superiority for having embraced the true faith and their alleged clannishness (in time of famine, for instance, the missionaries distributed rice only among their converts, derogatorily referred to by other Chinese as rice Christians) combined to make the situation worse. That most missionaries could not communicate in intelligible Chinese doubtless increased the confusion. During the nineteenth century there were isolated cases in which missionaries and converts were murdered, and in each case the foreign power from which these missionaries came quickly used the unfortunate occurrences as pretexts for demanding Chinese territories or other concessions. To the unsophisticated majority in China these missionaries were foreign agents and their Chinese converts were traitors to their own country and culture. Given the complexity of the situation, it was not surprising that the Boxers' first target was the missionaries and their Chinese converts.

The Boxer movement, like many other contentions between China and the Western powers, can best be understood in the context of an overall cultural confrontation during which friction and conflict were almost inevitable. Of all foreign groups in China, none was perhaps better motivated than the missionaries. One might argue about the desirability of sending missionaries to a country which had an advanced civilization of its own; there is no argument, however, about the sincerity of individual missionaries who believed that they were doing the most important thing that God willed. There was no question in their minds that the Chinese would eventually benefit from their work. They made great personal sacrifices by going to China, lived in uncomfortable, isolated places, and had to suffer and endure harassment, if not outright persecution, from the Chinese and their officials. If they did anything wrong, it was not intended. That their misfortunes had been often used by their home governments to advance their political and economic position in China was not their fault; as far as the missionaries were concerned, they preferred to see China converted to Christianity in a more peaceful way. "If the [Chinese] officials could be undeceived in regard to the real purposes of the missionaries, and if the missions in China could be conducted by really honest and sagacious men," said an American Minister to China in 1870, "I doubt if anything more than a passive resistance would be met with, which would soon be overcome by friendly intercourse and mutual forbearance." Unfortunately, not all missionaries were sagacious men; nor were Chinese officials always fair and wise. Thirty years after the above remark was made, a Chinese mob, called Boxers, fell mercilessly upon the missionaries and their Chinese converts. Their hatred was so bitter that they cared nothing for the consequences.

From the missionaries and their converts the Boxers broadened their targets to every Chinese who "smelt" foreign—people who advocated modernization and people who read books with horizontal lines. They burned churches, destroyed Westernized schools, dug out railroads, and cut telegraph lines. Had the local officials been wise, they would have suppressed this madness. They were not. The governor of Shantung, a bigoted Manchu named Yü-hsien, openly supported the Boxers' lawless activities. Only in South China did the governors take steps to suppress the Boxers despite the incitement from the empress dowager to do otherwise. One of the southern governors listened politely to a group of Boxer leaders who, appealing for his support, boasted about their magic powers, including their supposed immunity to Western bullets. The governor said that their claim had to be verified in front of impartial judges before he could give his support and ordered all of them to be shot in public, with, of course, Western bullets. Thanks to governors like him, the Boxer epidemic was confined to North China.

The question arises as to why such an intelligent person as the empress dowager believed this Boxer nonsense. It has often been said that her intense hatred of foreigners blinded her intellect and that in her advanced age she was no longer a rational person. This might be true, but still it does not explain adequately her obviously suicidal decision of declaring war on eight major powers all at once—any one of which could easily have defeated China. There is one lead to an otherwise puzzling situation. Shortly before the fatal decision was made, there had been a rumor that the foreigners had made new demands on China, one of which was that she should return the state power to the emperor. Knowing what she was, we can easily visualize how angry she would be. Without checking the validity of this rumor (which later turned out to be false), she plunged China into war because her position in China was always more important to her than China's position in the world.

Meanwhile in Peking the Boxers and their allies went on a rampage destroying everything foreign; among their victims was the German Minister to China, Von Ketteler. Their main target was the foreign legations which, against great odds, successfully defended themselves until reinforcements arrived. The rescue force consisted of 16,000 men sent by the allies: 8,000 Japanese, 4,500 Russians, 3,000 British, 2,500 Americans, and 800 French. Meanwhile, Russia was marching southward to seize Manchuria. The commander of the allied forces, Field Marshal Count Von Waldersee, was under the instruction from the Kaiser "to give no quarter and to take no prisoners," so that "no Chinese will ever again dare to look askance at a German." After the allied troops had arrived in Peking, there were large-scale massacre, rape, and looting, the like of which had not been seen since the days of the Mongols. The bulk of the German troops were held back to protect Kiaochow and the coast; otherwise the situation would conceivably have been worse. The empress dowager and the emperor fled to Sian, and China again lay helpless at the feet of the Western powers and Japan.

The existence of China could have ended then; it was saved by the disagreement among the powers as to how China should be divided among themselves. As they could not agree, they postponed their division of China by concluding a peace treaty with their vanquished foe. The main points of the treaty were: (1) the punishment of "war criminals"—some of them were later executed and others were exiled or demoted; (2) the destruction of all defenses ("now and forever") from Taku to Peking, (3) the right of foreign powers to station troops in legation sites; (4) the establishment by China of an effective 5 percent tariff; and (5) the payment of $333,000,000 in reparations of which Russia received the largest share. Against the background of a punitive vengeance the amount thus demanded was acknowledged to be far in excess of justifiable claims. A substantial portion of the American share, $25,000,000, was later voluntarily returned to China with the provision that the fund should be used to educate Chinese students in the United States. A similar arrangement was also made with England.

One of the products of the scramble for Chinese territories and the subsequent Boxer episode was the famed Open Door policy. It remained the basis of American foreign policy towards China until the Communists closed China's door in 1949. How did it come into being? It was a British idea at the beginning; only later was it revived by the United States. The British interests in China, as has been said before, were largely commercial. Such interests could be better served if China were to remain a free, open market. The scramble for spheres of influence in 1898 raised the unpleasant prospect that areas where another power had established a dominant position would be closed to British commerce and capital. Great Britain approached the United States for a joint pronouncement which would include the principle of equal commercial opportunity in all parts of China. When the Americans refused to cooperate, Great Britain went on to hunt for its own sphere of influence. After John Hay had become Secretary of State, he, unlike his predecessor John Sherman, was attracted to this Open Door idea. In September, 1899, he sent to Great Britain, Germany, and Russia his famous notes requesting that equal commercial opportunity for all powers be maintained within their spheres of influence. His notes did not attack the spheres of influence as such; nor did they explain how the incompatibility between two contrasting ideas, sphere of influence and equal opportunity of trade, could be resolved. The replies which Hay received from the three powers were noncommittal; even Great Britain conditioned its acceptance of the Open Door policy on the acceptance of it by other powers. However, the American Secretary of State announced in March, 1900 that the replies were "final and definitive."

The year 1900 was one of the least promising years to implement the Open Door. The Boxer uprising gave Russia the needed excuse to march into Manchuria, and it had intended to march further into North China until it was warned by Great Britain to keep out. Obviously, some of the powers, especially Russia and Germany, were bent on enlarging their spheres of influence and perhaps also gaining political control in them. If China were divided among them territorially, the Open Door idea would become meaningless, because naturally the power in control would introduce discriminatory measures against trade and capital from any other power within its territorial domain. In other words, the maintenance of China's territorial integrity was a prerequisite to the principle of equal commercial opportunity. In July, 1900, while Russian troops were pouring into Manchuria, Hay sent to the powers a circular note in which he stated that the United States aimed "to seek a solution which may bring about permanent safety and peace to China, preserve Chinese territorial and administrative entity, protect all rights guaranteed to friendly Powers by treaty and international law, and safeguard for the world the principle of equal and impartial trade with all parts of the Chinese empire." Except for Great Britain, none of the powers to which the note was addressed even bothered to answer.

The Open Door policy, like the Monroe Doctrine, was a unilateral declaration on the part of the United States. Its effectiveness relied on the willingness and capacity of the United States to enforce its observance. Since the United States did not attach such importance to the policy as to back it up with military force when the necessity arose, its effectiveness was rather limited. That the division of China was temporarily arrested in 1900 was due more to the rivalry among the powers than to the declaration of the American policy. However, to the Chinese who were in dire need of friends, this was a tremendous psychological lift. For the next fifty years China continued to seek help and support from the United States in its dealings with aggressors or potential aggressors, believing that the United States was the only major power that had no territorial ambition in China and could therefore be trusted.

The United States befriended China because, besides whatever sentimental reasons that can be cited, its interests in East Asia paralleled those of China. Though the American commercial interest was never large and accounted for only 2 percent of the total United States foreign trade at the turn of the century, there was always the hope that the volume could be considerably increased in view of the large Chinese population. Such a potential market could be best preserved for American goods if China remained independent and undivided. Politically, the American role in East Asia can best be understood in the context of the balance of power. From 1900 to 1949 China was the underdog in the power structure in East Asia, and during most of this period its potential or actual enemy was Japan. To be on the weaker side would have meant continuous support of China, and since this support was in line with America's commercial goal in China, the Open Door policy served both the political and economic interests of the United States. This, of course, only partially explains the American interest in China.

Among the different groups that influenced American policy towards China none was perhaps more important than the American missionaries. After 1900 the quality of all missionaries sent to China was greatly improved, and the approach to missionary work seems also to have changed. Now great emphasis was laid on educational and medical work, and the schools and hospitals thus established were among the best China ever had. These missionaries, like the early Jesuits, were scholars and teachers as well as evangelists. With tact and understanding they won respect and admiration from the Chinese among whom they lived. As the Chinese admired the missionaries, they also admired the country from which the missionaries came. For fifty years no foreign country was more popular in China than the United States. The missionaries, on their part, were equally enthusiastic about the Chinese and their culture, and their optimistic reports to their home churches unquestionably affected the attitude of Americans at home. Through the home churches the influence of the missionaries was eventually felt in the State Department and in Congress.

After the Boxer Protocol had been signed, the Russians stalled and delayed their evacuation from Manchuria. They were, in fact, exercising pressure on the Chinese government to legalize their occupation through the signing of a convention. The United States responded to the Russian threat with a reaffirmation of the Open Door, while England and Japan responded with a military alliance. England feared Russian penetration into North China, and Japan was uneasy about Russia's intention with regard to Korea. From England's point of view, the Anglo-Japanese Alliance (January, 1902) was merely a part of its global policy of containment against Russian expansion, "in Tibet, in Persia, in Turkey" as well as in Manchuria. To the Japanese, however, the Russian expansion had to be stopped if Korea were to be safeguarded and preserved as a stepping stone for the fulfillment of their own ambitions in Manchuria. The Anglo-Japanese Alliance pledged one party to neutrality if the other party was at war and to come to the other party's assistance if it had been attacked by more than one power.

In the summer of 1903 Japan proposed to Russia an arrangement whereby Russia would recognize Japan's special interests in Korea in return for Japan's acceptance of Russian rights in Manchuria "based on recognized treaties." If Russia agreed to this arrangement, it would mean, among other things, that its troops would have to withdraw from Manchuria. This the Russians would not do. The Japanese at home cried for war, and war came in the spring of the next year. Since the war had to be fought in Chinese territory, the Chinese government notified both belligerents that they should confine their fighting to the areas east of the Liao River so to minimize damage to Chinese life and property. This pleading, however, was ignored. During the hostilities Japan won victories on both land and sea. However, being a small country with limited resources, it could not continue the war indefinitely. Meanwhile, a revolution broke out within Russia; so both parties were ready for a negotiated peace. Through the good offices of the American President, Theodore Roosevelt, the Treaty of Portsmouth (September, 1905) was concluded. The major items of the treaty were: (1) the transfer to Japan by Russia of the Liaotung leased territory (including the two ports Dairen and Port Arthur), the southern section of the Chinese Eastern Railroad, and all the mining rights along the said section of the railroad; (2) Russia's acknowledgement of Japan's "paramount political, military, and economic interests in Korea"; and (3) the cession to Japan by Russia of the southern half of the island of Sakhalin.

By virtue of this treaty Japan not only safeguarded its interest in Korea (which it annexed later) but also acquired South Manchuria as its own preserve for economic activities. Meanwhile, Russia withdrew to North Manchuria which it regarded as its sphere of influence. Both parties, however, consented to withdraw their troops from Chinese territory and promised "not to obstruct any general measures common to all countries, which China may take for the development of the commerce and industry of Manchuria."

THE DOWNFALL OF THE MANCHU REGIME

After she returned from Sian where she had fled during the allied occupation of Peking, Tz'u Hsi was more than convinced of the Western superiority and was in a receptive mood for Westernized reforms. The measures that had been suppressed after the failure of the Hundred Days' Reform were reintroduced, and outwardly at least the empress dowager went along with enthusiasm. An imperial decree called for the organization of a national school system with a new curriculum which included not only the ancient classics but also "Western learning" such as European history, literature, and science. Students who possessed the financial means were encouraged to go abroad to study. Most of these students went to Japan because of its geographical proximity, while others went to Europe and the United States. In 1907 the American government made available the Boxer indemnity funds, and the number of Chinese students in the United States had increased to eight hundred on the eve of the revolution. Meanwhile in China the enrollment in Westernized schools continued to increase, reportedly reaching 1.6 millions by 1910. It was clear then that the old type of Confucian training would never come back again as the government had decided in 1905 to abolish the civil service examination once and for all.

Other reforms included the reorganization of the army and the navy and a newly found determination to stamp out the opium traffic. Though the Opium War was fought over the opium traffic, there was no mention of opium in the Treaty of Nanking. In 1858 the opium trade was legalized and importation of the drug continued to increase. As it increased, the Chinese began to grow opium poppy themselves. When the nation was again in a mood to carry out reforms, opium reappeared as a political issue. In 1906 the government adopted a policy of taxing domestic opium out of existence, and two years later Great Britain agreed to decrease annually its opium exports to China. In 1911 further agreement was reached with other powers besides Great Britain: all of them promised to cooperate with the Chinese government to stop the smuggling of the drug into China and to close opium shops and dens in the areas under their control. One year later the agreement came to naught, as the Manchu dynasty was overthrown and China entered the warlord period. Opium was to plague China for another forty years.

More interesting, if not more significant, was the attempted constitutional reform. To many Chinese it was the most basic of all reforms. The agitation for a written constitution began during the Russo-Japanese War, and many reformers optimistically predicted that "the outcome of this war depends on which nation has gained a constitutional government." When a small Japan with a constitution defeated a giant Russia without a constitution, it seemed to them that the merits of a constitution had been truly vindicated. Both the Chinese intellectuals and the Manchus wanted a constitutional government, though for different reasons. To the Chinese intellectuals it meant the opening of new opportunity to go into politics and secure government positions after the abolition of the civil service examinations. "In free political competition," said Liang Ch'i-ch'ao, "there will be no question as to whether the Manchus or the Chinese will have the predominant position under a constitutional government, since the political ability of the Chinese is far greater than that of the Manchus." The Manchus, for their part, wanted a constitution to legalize their control of the central government. There were also the Changs and Lis who honestly believed that a constitution was the first step to the modernization of China and would eventually make China as strong as Japan.[1] With all parties clamoring for a constitution, the empress dowager threw up her arms in despair and remarked majestically: "You say a constitutional monarchy can really make the nation strong; I will immediately send high officials to make a careful study of all constitutional monarchies."

It was unthinkable that Tz'u Hsi, who would not even share power with her nephew the emperor, would agree to share it with an elected parliament. Before the study group began to study "all constitutional monarchies," everybody knew what it would recommend: the Japanese model. In fact, under the draft constitution of 1908 the emperor enjoyed greater power even than the mikado. He was sacred and inviolable and he alone had the power to sanction or proclaim a law. The parliament whose deputies were chosen from a limited franchise could be opened or closed, prolonged or disbanded, at his choice. He was the commander-in-chief of the army and the navy, and he alone had the right of declaring war and concluding peace. The rights of speech, press, residence, and assembly could be exercised freely "within the boundary of law." Since the law could be changed by the government at any time, its boundary

[1] Chang and Li are two of the commonest surnames among the Chinese. They are like Brown and Smith among the English.

was extremely flexible, and the guarantee of civil rights existed mostly on paper.

Limited as these reforms were, if they had been introduced at the time when Tz'u Hsi became a co-regent in 1862 rather than at the year of her death (1908), the situation would have been vastly different. Now it was a matter of "too little and too late." The majority of the Chinese intellectuals who had until recently supported the Manchu regime became either apathetic or outright hostile. K'ang Yu-wei's Emperor Protection Society slowly but steadily lost its popularity; even his disciple Liang Ch'i-ch'ao had joined the revolutionary chorus: "The Manchus must go." Though the revolution drew its primary support from the intellectuals (especially those who lived abroad), it was supported by a large section of the people. China's numerous secret societies, which had a long tradition of rebelling against recognized authorities, could easily be transformed into a revolutionary potential. The overseas Chinese who had been discriminated against or even persecuted were anxious to see a modern, strong China that could extend to them a protective hand. Numerous young army officers saw the revolution as a new avenue for their own advancement, and many local gentry, if not openly sympathetic to the revolutionary cause, nevertheless wished to use it as a leverage to advance local autonomy. Finally there were the adventurers who joined the revolution for the sake of excitement, or for want of a better career to follow. Whatever motives each group of people might have, all agreed that China must be modernized and strong and that to build a modern China they must overthrow the Manchu regime.

The divergent elements of the revolution had to be organized before they could become a single striking force. They needed a leader, and they found him in Sun Yat-sen. Sun was born to a peasant family in a village near Canton in 1866, where for generations his family had had to work hard to wring a meagre subsistence from a small farm. He began his schooling at seven and at fourteen left his home to visit his elder brother in Hawaii, who by then had become a prosperous cattleman on a small island. He attended a missionary school in Honolulu and returned home in 1883. In 1886 he decided to enter the medical profession; he was enrolled at a medical school in Canton and one year later was transferred to the Alice Memorial Hospital at Hong Kong. It was then that he made valuable contacts with the anti-Manchu underground and won recognition as a potential leader. "I was using the school as headquarters for propaganda and using medicine as a medium for entering the world," said he many years later. Why did he forsake the profitable medical profession to enter the dangerous career of a revolutionary? Because the number of lives a doctor could save was rather limited, he replied, whereas a great statesman could save the lives of an entire nation.

To win supporters for his cause, Sun was at a disadvantage in competing with the reformer K'ang Yu-wei. K'ang came from an aristocratic family, had passed the civil service examinations, and was a brilliant Confucian scholar. Sun, on the other hand, came from a poor family, and his education was mostly Western. While K'ang appealed to the intellectual elite, Sun had to build his revolutionary base among the less respectable, many of whom were the members of the secret societies. "At first I despised Sun Yat-sen because I suspected that he was illiterate," said Wu Chih-hui who later became one of Sun's colleagues and friends. In 1894 when Sun organized his first revolutionary society (Hsing-Chung hui, or Society to Rejuvenate China) in Hawaii, his only followers were his brother and a dozen others. The headquarters of his organization was moved to Hong Kong the next year and there was some increase in membership. In that year he sent his close followers to Canton to stage a coup d'état. The plot, however, was discovered before it could be carried out, and the plotters were arrested and put to death. This was the first of a series of attempted coups that ended in failure. The Manchu government, which had been helpless in fighting against the foreigners, was nevertheless still capable of handling a small band of ill-organized and ill-equipped revolutionaries.

After the failure of his first attempted coup, Sun went to the United States and then to England. In London he was kidnapped by the Chinese legation personnel who planned to ship him back to China as a "bandit." During his captivity he managed to slip two notes out to his former teacher James Cantlie asking for help, and he was released after Cantlie notified Scotland Yard and the press. He stayed in London for the next two years where, according to a Scotland Yard report, "he went to the British Museum every day and spent most of his time there." It was then, he said later, that his basic ideas regarding the Three Principles of the People (Nationalism, Democracy, and People's Livelihood) first took shape. When the allies occupied Peking in 1900, he hastened back to organize another coup; but again he failed. From 1900 to 1905 he travelled between Japan, Southeast Asia, the United States, and Europe, concentrating his efforts on winning supporters and raising funds among the Chinese living abroad. By then many revolutionary societies had mushroomed both inside and outside China; some of them devoted themselves to the spread of revolutionary ideas through the clandestine publication of newspapers and magazines, and others took direct action by inciting open revolt and the assassination of "public enemies." In Japan there were several such "patriotic societies" among the 10,000 Chinese students. In the summer of 1905 Sun succeeded in persuading them to merge with his own and announced the formulation of the Alliance for Chinese Revolution (Chung-kuo ko-ming t'ung-meng hui), better known by its abbreviation, the Alliance, or T'ung-meng hui.

The organization of the Alliance was an important landmark in Sun's

revolutionary career. Until then his organization had been small and attracted only a scattered following. Into the new organization came not
only the young and idealistic students but also the veteran revolutionaries
such as Huang Hsing who until then had headed his own revolutionary
group. On November 17, 1905 the party organ, *The People* (*Min pao*),
first appeared in Tokyo. Its first editorial, written by Sun himself, emphasized the importance of the Three Principles of the People and the necessity of completing national, democratic, and social revolutions simultaneously:

> While it is clear that there should be no delay in beginning our national
> and democratic revolution in view of the present circumstances, such as thou-
> sands of years of autocratic rule, the oppression by an alien people [Manchus],
> and the intensified encroachment of China by foreign powers, it should also
> be kept in mind that the causes of social revolution which have accumulated
> themselves for a long time in Europe and the United States and which have
> not become serious in China should also be given adequate attention. As the
> disease is not serious, it is easy to cure. . . . People say that to strive for a
> strong China, we should imitate Europe and the United States. Strong as the
> Westerner powers are, their people remain poor. Labor strikes occur often,
> and the anarchists and the socialists have become increasingly active. In the
> near future a social revolution is bound to occur. . . . The seeds of evils in the
> Euro-American society were sown several decades ago, and such evils cannot
> be easily disposed of even after they have been discovered. If we can foresee
> these evils before they occur and prevent their occurrence by practicing the
> Principle of People's Livelihood, we can catch two birds with one stone: to
> complete political and social revolution at the same time. The day will arrive
> when we look over our shoulder and find Europe and America lagging far
> behind. . . .[1]

The above passage should be read against the background of 1905
when the labor movement in the West was still in its infant stage and
when organized labor had yet to win a strong voice in legislation and in
the formulation of governmental policy. Sun could not foresee what form
the social revolution would take; he did see, however, that such a revolution would occur, given the existing social and economic injustices. By then
his revolution had taken on a new dimension; it was social and economic as
well as political. The overthrow of the Manchu regime, whenever it occurred, was to be merely the beginning rather than the end of his revolution. It was clear to him even then that the establishment of economic
and social justice was much more difficult to achieve than the overthrow
of a discredited, corrupt regime. The Principle of People's Livelihood,

---

[1] Translated by the author from a photographed copy of the original that appears
in *The Pictorial Biography of Dr. Sun Yat-sen* (*Kuo-fu hua-chuan*) (Taipei, 1954)
by Lo Chia-lun, p. 43.

said he many years later, was the basis of the other two principles: Nationalism and Democracy.

Meanwhile, there was the Manchu dynasty to overthrow. From the establishment of the Alliance to the abdication of the last Manchu emperor in 1912, Sun was responsible for eight attempted coups and uprisings within China: six in Kwangtung, one in Kwangsi, and one in Yunnan. If an important city or a sizable area could successfully be brought under the control of the revolutionaries, Sun reasoned, a call for national uprisings would receive favorable response from various groups within China that wished to overthrow the existing regime but did not dare to take the first step. If the entire nation were in revolt, the Manchu regime would have to collapse. Sun's last coup was made in the spring of 1911 when Huang Hsing led his rebels to attack the governor-general's office at Canton. The promised military supplies did not arrive in time, and eighty-six revolutionaries died without seeing the establishment of the republic.

Ironically, what triggered the downfall of the Manchu regime was none of Sun's coups but an incident which was completely bourgeois in origin. In 1910 the Manchu government had concluded an agreement with an international banking agency (composed of banking interests of England, France, Germany, and the United States) to build a railroad linking Hankow and Canton. With the capital assured, it announced in May, 1911, the nationalization of railroads and revoked the construction rights which had been previously granted to private capital. Local interests in the provinces regarded the government's move not merely as an infringement on private enterprise but also as a deliberate attempt to break provincial autonomy which by then had become too precious to lose.

The increasing autonomy of provinces began in the 1860's when men of great influence and prestige such as Tseng Kuo-fan and Li Hung-chang were appointed as governors-general. Once begun, the process of decentralization accelerated. Towards the end of the nineteenth century even Tz'u Hsi made it a habit to consult the most important governors-general before she made an important move, though, being a strong ruler, she did not have to listen to their advice. The large measure of provincial autonomy was shown during the Sino-Japanese War when the North, under Li Hung-chang, was fighting a war against Japan and the South did not send one soldier to help. It was again shown during the Boxer Rebellion when the southern governors-general remained factually, if not legally, neutral, while the allies were marching towards Peking. In 1911, the empress dowager was gone, and there was not a single man in Peking, including the child emperor Hsüan-t'ung, who commanded the unswerving loyalty of the provincial authorities. Even without the revolution, the disintegration of the empire was already in sight.

More than anything else, the nationalization of railroads aligned the provincial interests against those of the central government and evoked a storm of protest such as none of Sun's coups had been able to do. Provincial leaders and local gentry, businessmen and bankers, intellectuals and students—all of them suddenly found that they had one aim in common: to preserve the railroads for their respective provinces. Organized by professional revolutionaries, radical students paraded in the streets, calling for the end of the Manchu regime. The situation was particularly serious in Szechuan where a general strike was called in all the railroads and related industries. In Chengtu many people were killed by police when they went to the governor's office to protest against the imprisonment of students. The news of Szechuan's defiance spread to other provinces, and the nation was in a mood for rebellion.

After the failure of Sun's last coup, his revolutionaries moved northward and concentrated their efforts in the Wu-Han area. They infiltrated the newly organized battalions of the Manchu regime where the young officers gave a sympathetic ear to the professional agitators. Their so-called secret meetings were nevertheless semiopen affairs, and it was reported that even the commander of the local garrison had sat in their meetings. However, the revolutionary leaders remained scrupulously in the background, and to avoid a repetition of past mistakes, they were carefully planning each step of a scheduled uprising. On October 9 the Manchu government discovered and seized the rebels' ammunition dump, and worse still, it got hold of a list of army officers who had secretly joined the revolutionary party. To forestall their arrest, the revolutionaries in Wuchang decided to take immediate action. On the night of October 10 they seized the government's ammunition dump and then attacked the governor-general's office. Instead of fighting the rebels, both the governor-general and the commander of the local garrison chose to flee, and the revolutionaries scored a victory far beyond their own expectations. After their successful coup, the most pressing need was to find a man of prestige to serve as their commander. Fortunately, in a routine search of the enemy's camps, they found a frightened colonel named Li Yüan-hung hiding underneath his bed. They dragged him out, put him under arrest, and then demanded that he become their commander. "I was surrounded by guns at the time, and I might have been killed instantly if I had not complied with their request," wrote Li a few days later to one of his friends.

The successful uprising at Wuchang prompted similar actions in other cities and provinces. In some cases the revolutionaries took control through the use of force, while in other cases the governors and governors-general declared their independence from the Manchu government and switched their loyalty to the revolution. By the end of the year practically all provinces south of the Yangtze had been freed from Manchu control.

Sun Yat-sen, who had been travelling in the United States during the Wuchang uprising, now returned to China to assume leadership. On January 1, 1912, he was sworn in as the first president of the Provincial Government of the Chinese Republic at Nanking, and the amiable Li Yüan-hung was named vice president. The new government pledged, among other things, to emancipate domestic slaves and to clean up, once and for all, the opium poison.

The Nanking government proved to be short-lived. In the north there was a strong, conservative force with which the revolutionaries had to reckon. This force was not led by the Manchu government but by the ambitious Yüan Shih-k'ai. The compromises which the revolutionaries had to make with this man paved the way for a new era of turbulence, popularly known as the period of warlords. The Manchu regime formally ended in 1912; China's woes, however, were far from being ended.

ʾ xiv

The Republic (1)

THE WARLORDS

The abdication of the last Manchu emperor, Hsüan-t'ung, on February 12, 1912, marked the formal end of the Manchu regime. Yet there was not a single force strong enough to replace it. In the south the revolutionaries were divided among themselves. Many governors who switched to the side of the revolution after the Wuchang uprising were more motivated by the preservation of their personal domains than the creation of a unified republic. Sun Yat-sen, the titular head of the revolution, had little or no influence over them. He was admired and respected, but he was not listened to. Equal confusion existed in North China where governors and military commanders fought among themselves and worked at cross purposes. The struggle for supremacy in China was a struggle among the political realists: the governors and military commanders who had the physical power to back up their demands. Meanwhile, China was plunged into the kind of chaos and war that prevailed at the end of any previous dynasty. If the past indicated anything, the country was looking for a strong man to emerge who could fight his way to supremacy and eventually unify all of China.

For a while the candidate most likely to succeed was Yüan Shih-k'ai whose name has been mentioned before in connection with the Sino-Japanese War. After that war he was given the important task of training a new army in the area near Tientsin, and it was then that he built a strong following among the young officers under his command. His role in the Hundred Days' Reform pleased Tz'u Hsi who later rewarded him with the governorship of Shantung. As the governor of Shantung, he suppressed the Boxers without in the meantime antagonizing the empress dowager, and by his successful maneuvers in a most difficult situation he won acclaim from both the Chinese and the foreigners as a clear-thinking, far-sighted statesman. In 1900, on the day before his death, Li Hung-chang recommended Yüan as his successor to govern Chihli (later known as Hopeh). "As I am looking around for men of ability all over the nation, I find no one better than Yüan," said Li in a memorial to the throne. As governor-general of Chihli and concurrently Superintendent of Trade in the Northern Ports (*Pei-yang ta-ch'en*), Yüan became one of the most powerful men in the nation. Once in a powerful position, he placed his followers in responsible and strategic positions in the imperial army as well as in the provinces. His army, called the Peiyang Army, was the most powerful fighting force in North China, and the Manchu government relied on it for the defense of the capital. Yüan's personal following constituted what was later known as the Peiyang clique, which produced many warlords in the years to come.

The Manchus in Peking were not unaware of the threat that Yüan's power posed for their own security. When Hsüan-t'ung was placed on the throne after the death of Kuang-hsü in 1908, the child emperor's father, Tsai-feng, dismissed Yüan from all the offices he held and ordered him home to "recuperate from the leg ailment which affected his gait." Rumor had it that he would have put Yüan to death had he not been afraid of violent reactions on the part of the officers of the Peiyang Army. In 1911 when most provinces had switched their loyalty to the revolution, the only thing that stood in the way of the revolutionaries' march towards Peking was the Peiyang Army, whose officers made it very clear that they would not fight "to the best of their ability" if Yüan were not made their commander-in-chief. The tables were now turned, and Yüan notified Tsai-feng that he would not resume his command until his conditions were satisfactorily met. He demanded the opening of parliament in the following year, the organization of a responsible cabinet, the legalization of political parties, and "full authority over, and the power to organize, all the armed forces." The Manchu government, under the dictate of circumstances, complied with all these demands. Shortly afterwards Yüan was made premier of the Manchu government. Thus, by one master stroke, Yüan became the ultimate arbitrator between the Manchu government in the north and the revolutionaries in the south.

The assumption of power by Yüan Shih-k'ai in the north was followed by negotiation with the revolutionaries in the south. Yüan's insistence on the legalization of political parties and other friendly gestures pleased the revolutionaries who promised him the presidency once the Manchu government was overthrown. On the day that he became president of the provisional government at Nanking, Sun Yat-sen telegraphed Yüan that he had accepted the office on a temporary basis, and that Yüan was to occupy it whenever he was ready. Why did the revolutionaries go so far as to make such extensive concessions? For one thing, Yüan was in command of the most powerful military force then in existence, and an open break with him would mean not only the continuance of the Manchu regime but also a prolonged civil war which the revolutionaries could not be sure of winning. The revolutionaries hoped that Yüan, as the president of the republic, could be made responsible to an elected parliament which they themselves would doubtless control. Obviously they underestimated their opponent's ambition, and because of their misjudgment, the new republic was destined for a turbulent beginning.

Under Yüan's pressure, the last Manchu emperor abdicated, and as previously agreed, Yüan was elected president of the new republic. Since he refused to come to Nanking to accept the presidency, the capital of the new republic was moved to Peking. No sooner did he take office than difficulties developed between the legislative branch of the government (the parliament) and the executive branch headed by the president. The provisional constitution which had been adopted in Nanking prior to the abdication of the Manchu emperor provided for a strong parliament which the new president would not tolerate. As the revolutionaries controlled the parliament, he proceeded to break their strength by all the means at his command. Early in 1913, Sung Chiao-jen, a key member of Sun Yat-sen's party, the Kuomintang, and a deputy in the parliament, was assassinated in Shanghai, and since Sung had been one of the most severe critics of Yüan's dictatorial behavior, all fingers pointed at the new president. Meanwhile, through persuasion, coercion, and outright bribery, Yüan strove to build a personal following among the parliamentary deputies. The outcome was the Progressive Party (*Chinputang*), composed of opportunist politicians as well as those who believed that Yüan alone possessed the power and the ability to unify China, and that they could honestly support him. Facing the opposition of the revolutionaries, in June of 1913, Yüan ordered the dismissal of three Kuomintang governors. The revolutionaries staged an armed revolt, only to be suppressed by

Yüan's powerful army. After the revolt, all Kuomintang members were disqualified as parliamentary deputies by the president's orders, and the provisional constitution was revised to give dictatorial power to the president.

Thus, less than two years after the establishment of the republic, Yüan achieved what he had set out to achieve: a personal dictatorship. The foreign powers strengthened his regime by advancing him a loan amounting to 25 million pounds, despite vigorous protests from Sun Yat-sen, who believed that Yüan would use the loan to strengthen his personal control. Had Yüan been satisfied with being a dictator, he would have been remembered differently in history, but instead, he chose to become emperor. By doing this he not only antagonized the Kuomintang but all those to whom monarchy had come to mean the most reactionary rule. Early in 1915 an organization called the Peace Planning Society was launched by Yüan's followers to prepare the way for transforming the republic into a monarchy with Yüan as the first emperor. In August an American professor, Frank J. Goodnow, who then served as Yüan's constitutional adviser, prepared a memorandum in which he pointed out the desirability "of establishing a constitutional monarchy if there was general demand for it." In view of the patronage the president possessed and the ceaseless activities of the Peace Planning Society, the "general demand" was not slow in coming. In each province Yüan's followers were busy creating "public opinion" and choosing the "right" people as provincial delegates to decide the basic structure of the government: constitutional monarchy or republicanism. When they finally cast their ballots, the count was 1,993 for monarchy and none for republicanism. Armed with this mandate, Yüan declared that a constitutional monarchy should be established in June, 1916.

What followed could not have been foreseen by the president, as he had been too much blinded by his own ambition. Led by Yunnan, several provinces successively declared independence, and Yüan, to save his presidency, belatedly relinquished his royal pretensions. By then it was already too late; the rebels insisted that he should resign from the presidency as well. Beset with worry and grief, he died on June 6, 1916.

Upon the death of Yüan Shih-k'ai, the man around whom China could have been unified was gone. The office of the presidency changed hands several times until Tuan Ch'i-jui, a member of the Peiyang clique and one of Yüan's early followers, managed to restore a semblance of order in the capital as the premier. The so-called national government controlled no more territory than Peking and its surrounding areas, though internationally it was recognized as representing China. The rest of China was divided among the so-called warlords, conquering and annexing the territory of one another with impunity. The disintegration of China which began as early as the 1860's was now complete. As the

central authority all but disappeared, there was nothing left except political anarchy. This situation was neither unique nor strange in Chinese
history; it had always been that way during the change of dynasties.
Those familiar with the course of history only blamed themselves for
being born in a wrong time, a wrong age. While the Westernized intellectuals were discussing the comparative merits of republicanism and constitutional monarchy, the peasants were waiting patiently for the next Son
of Heaven (or his modern equivalent, the Leader) to emerge who could
lead China back to peace and prosperity. Meanwhile, as the civil war
raged on, they had to endure the hardships inherent in a transitional
period. The lesson of history was not lost, either, in the minds of China's
ambitious leaders. They knew that to achieve supreme power one had to
fight his way with a superior military force. With such a force Yüan Shih-
k'ai almost succeeded in unifying China, and without it Sun Yat-sen had
had to relinquish his presidency almost as soon as he had acquired it.
Thus, despite the Western impact, the political game was played according to the ageless rule: might was right. Those who wished to succeed
had to build a strong military following around themselves, just as the
founders of the old dynasties used to do.

Before they succeeded in winning some respectability for their governments, the local strong men were called warlords. A warlord was a
man who fought for personal gains, territorial or otherwise, rather than
principles. His position might be that of a governor-general, a governor,
or simply a military commander with enough following to make his
weight felt. He was sovereign within the territory he controlled; he recruited his own bureaucratic and military personnel, levied taxes, and
administered justice. With no lofty principles to claim the loyalty of the
people he ruled, his major and perhaps only asset was his army. His army
was composed of mercenaries recruited from the rural unemployed who
would fight for anyone as long as they were regularly paid. Generous
warlords promised bonuses if their soldiers helped them win a victory. As
each battle involved no higher principle than the victory or defeat of two
equally selfish warlords, most of the soldiers went through the motions of
fighting and were not interested in heroism which would make them
unnecessary casualties. As they were the best assets a warlord had, he was
concerned for their safety, especially on the battlefield. The best victory
was won by an impressive show of force to scare the enemy away rather
than that won in a bloody battle which brought benefit to neither side
except a third warlord. Often the outcome of a prospective battle was
mutually agreed upon before it was actually fought after each side had
objectively compared its strength with that of its enemy; the weaker side
simply fled. Bloody battles did, however, occur from time to time when
both sides had grossly underestimated the strength of each other. One
battle fought in North China resulted in reported casualties of 20,000 for

the two sides, only to benefit a third warlord in the south. Generally speaking, battles like this were the exceptions rather than the rule, and all warlords agreed that war, as an instrument of policy, should be indulged in only as the last resort.

As the wars between the warlords involved no lofty principles, they were among the most polite ever recorded in history. A warlord did not hate his enemy; he only wished to acquire his opponent's territories. He held no grudge against the people living on the other side of the battle-line; he merely wanted to rule them so that they would pay taxes to him instead of his opponent. As far as the people were concerned, it did not make much difference which side won, because one warlord was as good or bad as the other. One warlord might promise lighter taxes than another; this consideration, however, was not important enough to cause one to commit himself fully to his side. In each battle the people were neutral, ready to welcome whoever happened to be the winner. Respecting the neutrality of the people, the warlords tried to disturb them as little as possible during each battle, for they all knew that killing taxpayers defeated the very purpose of warlordism. It was not unusual for two gentlemanly warlords to arrange a fight in a sparsely populated area to prevent unnecessary damage to life and property, while in the nearest city the people waited patiently for the outcome of the battle. When the news finally arrived, the city fathers opened the city gates; the victor, whoever he happened to be, rode in at the head of his army, to receive the city's tribute which was his due. Thus, despite what might be said about the evil of warlords, their war was much more civilized than other wars in which religious and other important issues were involved and when the principle of one side was the direct opposite of the principle of the other.

From 1916 to 1927 there were dozens, if not hundreds, of warlords. Small warlords attached themselves to big warlords as necessity arose but declared their independence as soon as they were strong enough to do so. Some of the big warlords had under their control two or three provinces, while in other cases two or three warlords might share one province. Under the nominal control of each of these warlords there were numerous small warlords feuding constantly among themselves. As wars were fought almost constantly, the territory within each warlord's control was in a continuous state of flux. As for the backgrounds of these warlords, they varied a great deal. Some were outright bandits, and others succeeded in maintaining a remarkable degree of respectability. At least one of them was a scholar of sorts who had passed the lowest level of the civil service examination during the Manchu regime.

Early in the 1920's power struggles revolved around three main personalities: Tuan Ch'i-jui in the capital and the surrounding areas, Wu P'ei-fu in the middle Yangtze, and Chang Tso-lin in Manchuria. Tuan Ch'i-jui, as premier of the republic, attempted to use force to unify China and bring all China under his control. He was challenged by Wu P'ei-fu, then a divisional commander in Hunan. Wu, with the help of his allies in the north including Chang Tso-lin, defeated Tuan in a battle fought near Peking (July, 1920). After Tuan was out of the way, Wu and Chang fought each other over the control of North China. In the spring of 1922 Chang marched southward and captured Peking, only to be driven back by Wu. Chang retreated to Manchuria where he continued to rule, and Wu became for the time being the overlord of North China. In South China the numerous warlords fought one another until Sun Ch'uan-fang succeeded in bringing under his control the Lower Yangtze and its surrounding areas in 1925. Outside the regions mentioned above there were numerous other warlords who remained beyond the control of the central government long after Chiang Kai-shek and his Nationalists had declared the establishment of a national government in 1927.

FOREIGN PRESSURE

The young republic, weak and divided, was an easy prey to foreign aggressors. After its advance in Manchuria had been stopped by the Russo-Japanese War, Russia shifted its expansion efforts to Outer Mongolia where resistance, if any, was not expected to be effective. In 1912, Outer Mongolia, supported by Russia, drove out the Chinese minister in residence and declared its independence. China protested to Russia in vain, and in an agreement concluded in the following year the Chinese consented to grant Outer Mongolia an autonomous status, in return for Russia's recognition of Outer Mongolia as a part of China. The political agreement was followed by a commerical treaty in 1914 whereby China agreed to give Russia the right to trade, to exploit the mineral, forest, and fishing resources, and to purchase land for farming and pastoral purposes in Outer Mongolia. Besides, all Russian goods exported from or imported into the Mongolian territory were to be duty-free. By virtue of this treaty Outer Mongolia became in fact a Russian sphere of influence, though nominally it was still a part of China.

In 1917 a revolution broke out in Russia; with the Russians engaged in civil war, China reasserted its control of Outer Mongolia in 1919. A Chinese general named Hsü Shu-tseng was named the Minister of Mongolian Affairs, with special instructions to "pacify and solace" the Mongolian people. Hsü, however, turned out to be a bad choice, and his ruthless, reckless behavior soon antagonized the powerful Mongol princes who, in cooperation with a group of White Russian mercenaries, drove Chinese officials out from the Mongolian capital. The establishment of a Mongolian empire was proclaimed, and the Living Buddha of Urga was declared emperor. In the summer of 1921 the Bolsheviks entered Outer

Mongolia, defeated the White Russians, and transformed the country into a Russian protectorate.

Previously, in the summer of 1919, the Soviet Union announced its willingness to give up all special rights and privileges which Tsarist Russia had acquired in China and to establish new relations with China based upon the principle of complete equality. Whatever motives prompted this announcement, it was greeted with great enthusiasm; many Chinese openly opined that the road to China's salvation was to follow the Soviet example, since the Soviet Union, they believed, was the only country that had no imperialistic ambitions in China. Two years after the Soviet announcement, the Chinese Communist Party was organized in Shanghai. In 1924 China concluded a treaty and supplementary agreements with the Bolshevik regime in which the latter agreed (1) to recognize Outer Mongolia as a part of China and to withdraw Russian troops; (2) to give up all special rights and privileges in China such as extraterritorial rights and concessions; and (3) to renounce the balance of the Boxer Indemnity which had not yet been paid. With regard to the Chinese Eastern Railroad, the treaty specified that it was a joint enterprise, "purely commercial," and that it might be redeemed by China in the future with "Chinese capital." Lenin might not have said that the road to world communism was through Peking; the fact that the Soviet Union was the first Western power to renounce the unequal treaties did, however, create a favorable impression. As such an impression spread, so did communism.

The early years of the republic saw not only Russian penetration into Outer Mongolia but also British penetration into Tibet. Previously, as Tibet was a center of contention between Russia and England, both powers had agreed to Chinese suzerain rights in that territory, thus making it a buffer zone between the two rival powers. In two conventions signed by Great Britain—the convention of 1906 with China and the convention of 1907 with Russia—Britain pledged itself not to annex Tibetan territory and not to enter negotiation with Tibet except through China, the suzerain power. In 1910 the ruler of Tibet, Dalai Lama XIII, revolted, and the Manchu government responded by sending troops to Lhasa. The Dalai Lama escaped to India where he stayed until the following year when revolution broke out within China. As the Chinese could no longer give adequate attention to Tibet, the Dalai Lama returned to Lhasa and, with British support, drove out the Chinese garrison. In 1912 the new Chinese republic ordered the re-entry of Chinese troops into Tibet, only to cancel its plans when Great Britain protested. In 1914 a conference between British, Chinese, and Tibetan delegates was held in the Indian city of Simla where a draft agreement was reached; the agreement was to become effective when it was ratified by the delegates' respective governments. The Chinese government refused to ratify it on the ground that the agreement, if carried out, would mean the loss of a considerable piece of Chinese territory. Meanwhile, World War I broke out in Europe and England was too busy at home to put pressure on the Chinese; so the matter was dropped for the time being. It reappeared after World War II when India and Communist China debated the legality of the Simla agreement. The disagreement eventually led to a border war, as we shall see in another chapter.

The Russian maneuvers in Outer Mongolia and the British penetration in Tibet were conducted under the pretence of supporting local autonomous movements against an inefficient, corrupt central authority; and as such, justifications could be advanced, however flimsy they were. Japan's intervention in China, on the other hand, was brazenly brutal and lacked any of the arguments one might advance to defend the Russian or British actions. For one thing, Japan's territorial ambition was directed against the heavily populated China proper rather than the outer territories sparsely inhabited by Mongolian and Tibetan minorities. Japan's ambition with regard to China was common knowledge to all parties concerned, but until World War I Japan had not been able to translate its ambition into reality, partly because of China's distrust of Japanese motives and designs after the Sino-Japanese War and partly because of the lack of adequate capital on the part of Japan to pursue an effective dollar diplomacy such as Western powers then pursued in China. Meanwhile Japan, to use the words of one of its statesmen, was waiting patiently for the arrival of a "psychological moment" when it could fulfill its ambitions.

Such a moment arrived with the outbreak of World War I. All major powers in Europe were engaged in a life-and-death struggle, and Japan finally was free to do whatever it pleased in East Asia. After the war broke out, it attacked Germany's Kiaochow leasehold at Shantung, "as a voluntary expression of friendship," said the Japanese foreign minister, "toward Great Britain under the Anglo-Japanese Alliance." The German garrison surrendered and Japanese troops not only took over the leasehold but also Chinese territories along the Kiaochow-Tsinan Railroad. Despite Chinese protests, it seemed that Japan intended to occupy Shantung indefinitely. Knowing Japan's ambition, China appealed to the United States for diplomatic support, the only country then in a position to give such support. The United States, however, did not wish to get involved because, to use the words of Acting Secretary of State Lansing, while the United States was prepared to promote China's welfare by peaceful methods, "it would be quixotic in the extreme to allow the question of China's territorial integrity to entangle the United States in international difficulties." China was now isolated, and Japan was in a position to press on towards its goal.

Early in 1915 Japan presented to China the world-shaking Twenty-One Demands, acceptance of which would have reduced China to a Japanese protectorate. The demands were divided into five groups, and the harshest was the fifth or last group. The implementation of Group I would mean the transformation of Shantung from a German into a Japanese sphere of influence. Group 2 would give Japan extensive industrial, commercial, and residential rights in South Manchuria and eastern Inner Mongolia, in addition to the extension of the lease of Port Arthur and Dairen from twenty-five to ninety-nine years. Group 3 concerned the Hanyeh-ping Company, the largest iron mining and smelting concern in Hupeh. The Japanese demand called for the transformation of the company into a Sino-Japanese joint enterprise, with actual control in the hands of the Japanese. Group 4 contained one article which called upon China "not to cede or lease to any other Power any harbor or bay or any island along the coast of China." By "any other Power" was meant, of course, any other power except Japan. Group 5 was the most drastic and was aimed at bringing all of China, rather than just a section of it, under Japanese control. Its major items were: (1) the employment of Japanese as political, financial, and military advisers in the Chinese central government; (2) the right of Japanese to own land for the construction of hospitals, temples, and schools; (3) the joint control of Chinese police force; (4) the purchase of Japanese arms by China and the establishment of ammunition factories jointly controlled by China and Japan; (5) the granting of railroad construction rights to Japan in the central lakes region; (6) China was to consult Japan if it wished to borrow foreign capital to finance railroad construction, mining, and other economic activities such as harbor improvement in Fukien province; and (7) China was to grant Japan the right of "preaching religion" in China. The last article was perhaps the most ironical; obviously the Japanese had in mind the Western missionaries who allegedly served the imperialist interests of their respective countries.

While the delegates of both countries were still negotiating on the demands, Japanese fleets sailed towards Chinese harbors and the Japanese army suddenly increased its strength in Shantung and South Manchuria. As great pressure was exercised, the Chinese president Yüan Shih-k'ai agreed to all the demands as listed in the first four groups and the one demand in relation to Fukien in the fifth group. China rejected, however, all the other demands in the fifth group, as their acceptance would have meant the end of China as a sovereign state. The Japanese could have pressed the matter further, but facing a violent reaction from Chinese in all walks of life, they decided to drop the most obnoxious demands for the time being. If the Sino-Japanese War of 1894–1895 marked the beginning of the Sino-Japanese hatred, the Twenty-One Demands solidified it. To the Chinese Japan's ultimate goal was the conquest of China, and to the Japanese China was a "power vacuum" which was a temptation not easily resisted.

In the summer of 1917 China joined the Allies and declared war on

Germany, partly because of the diplomatic pressure exercised by the Allies and partly because it wished to be represented in the peace conference after the war. It hoped, particularly, to regain the German leasehold in Shantung. It did not know then that early in the year England and France had agreed to support Japan's demand with regard to the said leasehold. During the Paris Peace Conference China demanded the return of the leasehold, but the Allies, bound by their secret agreements with Japan, sided with their stronger ally in the East in insisting that it be transferred to Japan. President Wilson of the United States, though sympathetic to the Chinese cause, could not do anything to help, as the Japanese delegation threatened to leave the conference if its demand were not met. The angry Chinese delegation left Paris without signing the Versailles Peace Treaty.

The Shantung question reappeared in the Washington Conference in 1921–1922. This conference was called for two purposes: naval disarmament and the consideration of the "Far Eastern question" that threatened international peace. The rapid expansion of the Japanese navy had caused considerable apprehension in Washington as it posed a threat to the security of such American possessions as the Philippines. As the relations between the United States and Japan continued to worsen after World War I, the American government was anxious to seek a multilateral agreement to maintain the *status quo* in the Western Pacific so that Japan would not change the existing power structure and thus disrupt a delicate balance to its own advantage. To complicate the matter, Japan had a military alliance with England, so that in case of a shooting war between the two governments across the Pacific the United States might conceivably be at war with England too, and possibly even Canada which was then a British Dominion. When the Anglo-Japanese Alliance was formed in 1902, the allies had in mind Russia and possibly Germany as potential enemies. Now that Germany had been defeated and Russia after the Bolshevik revolution was no longer a threat to British interests in East Asia, England was anxious to leave the alliance without in the meantime making Japan "lose face." Like the United States, it was also seeking a multilateral agreement to replace the Alliance. In November, 1921, at the invitation of President Harding of the United States the delegates of nine countries (England, France, the United States, Italy, Japan, China, the Netherlands, Belgium, and Portugal) gathered in Washington, D.C. for the scheduled conference.

Three important treaties emerged from their consultations. The Four Power Pacific Treaty (between the United States, Great Britain, Japan, and France), which replaced the Anglo-Japanese Alliance, called upon the contracting parties to respect one another's rights in the regions of the Pacific in respect to their "insular possessions and insular dominions" and to settle any controversy "arising out of any Pacific question" by peaceful means. The Five Power Naval Treaty called for a ten-year holiday in capital ship construction and the limitation of the tonnage of capital ships and aircraft carriers in a ratio of 5:5:3:1.75:1.75 for England, the United States, Japan, France, and Italy, respectively. Moreover, the *status quo* in the Western Pacific with regard to each other's territorial possessions and "fortifications and naval bases" was to be maintained. As far as China was concerned, the most important document was the Nine Power Open Door Treaty signed by all powers represented in the conference. The treaty called upon all signatories, other than China, "to respect the sovereignty, the independence, and the territorial integrity of China" and "to use their influence for the purpose of effectually establishing and maintaining the principle of equal opportunity for the commerce and industry of all nations throughout the territory of China." On paper the treaty was a great victory for China and the United States, as it incorporated the two basic principles of the Open Door. For the first time the Open Door became an international committment as well as a statement of American policy. However, the treaty did not provide sanctions, economic or military, in case its terms were violated by one or more of the contracting parties. As it was worded in the most general and abstract terms, the treaty was subject to different interpretations. Naturally each signatory would interpret it to advance its own interests in China.

Unsatisfactory as the treaty might be, the Chinese delegation did not go home empty-handed. The concessions they won from the powers were noteworthy in view of the fact that China had no bargaining power whatsoever in the conference and that it relied solely on the good will of the powers concerned and the "righteousness" of its case. Shantung was to be returned to China, though Japan would retain control of the Kiaochow-Tsinan Railroad. France agreed to return to China the Kwangchow Bay, Japan the Kiaochow Bay, and England the Bay of Weihaiwei. Japan, however, refused to discuss the return of Port Arthur and Dairen, and England was equally determined to keep Kowloon. As to the main objectives of China such as the restoration of tariff autonomy, the abolition of extraterritoriality, and the withdrawal of foreign troops and police from foreign concessions in China, the Chinese delegation was woefully unsuccessful. The powers, however, agreed to discuss these matters at a future date. In the case of extraterritoriality, a commission composed of the treaty powers was to be organized to study Chinese law and the judicial system before each treaty power would consider "gradual" steps to be adopted for the eventual abolition of the extraterritorial system. As to the foreign spheres of influence in China, they were a subject so touchy that none of the major powers wished to discuss it.

However unsatisfactory from the Chinese point of view, the various treaties and agreements concluded during the Washington Conference enabled the existing power structure to be maintained and initiated a ten-year period of international peace and stability in the Pacific region. In the 1920's a moderate group was in power in Japan which preferred economic and commercial expansion to outright military aggression. To be sure, there were occasional armed clashes between China and Japan, none of which, fortunately, developed into full-scale war. It was not until 1931 when militarism re-emerged in Japan that armed aggression was again undertaken to extend Japanese control over mainland China.

CHINA REAWAKENED

During the past one hundred years each major military or diplomatic defeat was followed by a reappraisal of Chinese values and an increasing interest in Western culture. The Opium and *Arrow* Wars were followed by Li Hung-chang's advocacy of a Westernized armed force; the Sino-Japanese War and the creation of foreign spheres of influence precipitated the Hundred Days' Reform; and the Manchu government's incompetence in handling the Boxer Rebellion gave rise to intensified activities among the revolutionaries who eventually overthrew the Manchu regime. In each case the process of Westernization was not pursued on a sustained basis, and the conservative force representing the indigenous culture prevailed in the end. After the passing of each crisis China returned to its long slumber, unchanged and seemingly unchangeable. It should be added, however, that while the conservatives continued to win each round, their strength also steadily declined; and with each round the progressive forces began to gain ground, however slowly. For instance, the concept of a Chinese republic sounded fantastic in the 1890's, but it became a reality in 1912, imperfect though it was.

In the long run the winds of progress blew ever stronger. Each new generation was more receptive to new ideas than the preceding one, and Confucianism, the ideological stronghold of the conservative forces, became less sacred and more vulnerable with the passage of time. Confucian ideology, as has been said before, was the product of a sedentary, agricultural society, and the changed conditions resulting from the Western impact necessitated a more liberal interpretation of the ancient doctrine. Moreover, with the abolition of the civil service examination system in 1906 the mastering of Confucian classics, which had been traditionally the key to officialdom, power, and influence, was no longer emphasized as it had been. As the sanctity of Confucianism was subject to question, the traditional Chinese society built on Confucian virtues was slowly undermined. The process was speeded up by an annual inflow of the so-called returned students who had received part or most of their education abroad. Though not all returned students advocated "complete Westernization," they favored the change of the traditional Chinese society in one way or another. As they became leaders of the new China, their beliefs inevitably affected the thinking of the Chinese people as a whole.

As foreign pressure continued to mount in the early years of the republic, it was not surprising that the reawakening of China should initially take the form of strong nationalism. Though Chinese nationalism in its modern sense could be traced back to the years immediately following the Opium War, it had been confined to a small group of sensitive intellectuals who felt that the Chinese nation as well as its culture had been threatened by "barbarian" invasions. Most Chinese knew nothing about it and perhaps did not even care. However, the basis of nationalism continued to broaden with successive defeats at the hands of the Western powers and Japan, and as the loss of territories and the significance of the unequal treaties became better known, more Chinese became nationalistic. In 1915 when the supposedly secret Twenty-One Demands were intentionally leaked to the press and became public knowledge, there was such a violent reaction among the Chinese that even the Japanese were surprised. A modern press, introduced to China in the latter part of the nineteenth century, played an important role in the spread of nationalistic ideas. The Confucian gentry who had been concerned mostly with local affairs were aroused by the possible consequence of a China completely dominated by Japan. Wherever newspapers were found, the seeds of nationalism were sown.

In 1919, when news arrived in China that the Chinese delegation had failed to secure the return of Shantung in the Paris Peace Conference, thousands of students demonstrated in the streets of Peking; they beat one Chinese diplomat and burned the house of another, both of whom were accused of having sold China out when they negotiated with Japan on the Twenty-One Demands. Similar demonstrations occurred in all parts of China, and the students demanded "the preservation of Chinese sovereignty and the abolition of the unequal treaties." In large cities like Shanghai and Hankow, workers supported the students' demands by calling strikes, and merchants responded by closing their shops. Chinese were warned not to purchase goods of Japanese origin, and when the Japanese government protested, the students changed their slogan from "Boycott Japanese goods" to "Purchase Chinese goods only." This patriotic movement was later known as the May Fourth Movement because the first student demonstration occurred in Peking on May 4, 1919.

The May Fourth Movement was of course more than an antiforeign movement. It reflected the dissatisfaction of the new generation of intellectuals with China's domestic as well as international status. The Manchu regime had been overthrown, but China's difficulties were far from over. The country was divided among numerous warlords, fighting ceaselessly to advance their personal gains. The foreign powers, especially Japan, took advantage of this sad state of affairs and exploited it to their own advantage. This domestic disunity, as many Chinese readily conceded, was the cause, rather than the result, of foreign encroachments. Therefore, China should first "put its own house in order" before its voice could command any respect in international conferences. The yearning for a unified China was shared by people of all walks of life who had everything to lose in the long war conducted by the warlords. The merchants, for instance, resented the repeated taxation whenever their merchandise passed through a warlord's domain with the resultant increase in cost. Farmers were sometimes forced to pay land taxes twenty or thirty years in advance, only to see another warlord come to power who demanded the same preferential treatment. This legalized robbery was accompanied by an illegal variety conducted by the soldiers in the countryside. These soldiers, unpaid or underpaid, lived on the peasants like parasites. They stole their food, besides tampering with the chastity of their daughters. How long would this miserable state of affairs continue? Who could deliver the people from their sufferings? When Chiang Kai-shek finally arrived with a strong force of well-disciplined soldiers, the nation sighed with relief. Perhaps he could achieve what others had failed to do: the unification of China under a strong, centralized government.

While the intellectuals could do nothing to change the political situation, they attempted to create a new atmosphere in which a modern China could emerge. These intellectuals were not the Confucian scholars of the old type; they were the products of Western schools abroad or Westernized schools in China. Each year many students who had been educated in Europe, America, and Japan returned home, and many of them found employment in the newly established universities and colleges. They preached in their classrooms what they had learned abroad, and their students who subsequently became secondary and primary school teachers transmitted their ideas to an even larger audience. None of their ideas were original, and more often than not they mimicked their more illustrious professors in Europe or America. But for the Chinese who had lived for more than two thousand years in a staid Confucian atmosphere, these new ideas were more than welcome. From France came vitalism; from England, utilitarianism; and from the United States, pragmatism—plus a number of other "isms" too numerous to mention. It is difficult to assess the net impact of these ideas on China's intellectual life; superficially understood, as philosophies, they perhaps served no better purpose than arousing curiosity and stimulating inquisitiveness. Their advocates needed battering-rams to tear down the ancient stronghold of Confucianism which they blamed for China's "backwardness," and to use ideology to combat ideology, they wielded whatever weapon they had recently learned to use, be it pragmatism or utilitarianism. A nihilistic attitude characterized many of the new intellectuals who were determined to destroy the old values but were at a loss to find new ones to replace them. Some of them called for "complete Westernization," and others cried aloud for "science and democracy." Few of them, however, wished to be bothered with details and went beyond the stage of shouting slogans.

The intellectual aspect of the May Fourth Movement has often been referred to as the Chinese renaissance. The most concrete outcome of this intellectual revival was the colloquial (*pai-hua*) movement. As has been said in a previous chapter, all writing in China, to be presentable and respectable, had to be composed in a literary or classical style. To be able to write in a literary fashion required a tremendous amount of preparation in traditional literature on the part of the learner. The question often arose as to whether the colloquial language, the language as it was actually spoken, could be used as a means of literary expression. The traditionalists said "No," and for more than two thousand years no writer, except occasionally novelists, ever attempted to use it for serious writing. As democracy, in whatever form, was the goal of the new intellectuals, it naturally occurred to them that an informed public, upon which a workable democratic government ultimately depended, could not come about unless the written language was made easier to learn. The old question was again raised, and this time a small group of intellectuals answered "Yes."

What ensued was perhaps one of the most important though bloodless revolutions in Chinese history. The leader of this colloquial movement was the American-educated Hu Shih who demonstrated through his own writings that the spoken language could be literary and that in a piece of literature it was the content rather than the form that really counted. *The Marsh Heroes* and *The Dream of the Red Chamber*, which most people had read and yet pretended to look down upon, acquired new halos as great masterpieces of literature, even though they were written in colloquial Chinese. Following Hu's example, other writers began to experiment with colloquial Chinese, and it was proved beyond doubt that works written in the new medium could also be literary. All of a sudden the colloquial style acquired a respectability that it had never enjoyed before; it soon replaced the classical style as the standard form in newspapers, magazines, and all other means of communication aimed at large audiences. School textbooks were rewritten in the easily understood style, and students wrote letters home in the spoken language, much to the chagrin of their more conservative parents. Their parents perhaps became angry when they found in the letters punctuation marks which, according to the ancient custom, should never be used unless they were meant as a deliberate insult to the literary ability of the prospective reader. As the popularity of the colloquial style increased, writers also introduced the punctuation marks like those used in English.

The continuous inflow of Western ideas not only caused the intellectuals to reappraise their ancient beliefs; it slowly undermined the traditional Chinese society which we described in Chapter XI. Old and new values met head-on, and nowhere was the conflict so evident as it was within the family. The conflict was most acute in families whose children had received education abroad or in Westernized schools in China. Filial loyalty, a cardinal Confucian virtue and the strongest tie which held the Chinese family together, suddenly became a form of "parental oppression," and many parents could not understand how all of a sudden they had become "intolerable tyrants" in the eyes of their children. Boys revolted when their parents proposed to arrange their marriages; some of them ran away from home when wedding dates had already been set. They had read many books which emphasized love and romance as the correct basis of marriage, and they could not see why they should marry women whom they had never met. Their parents, on the other hand, were equally adamant in proclaiming the soundness of their own values and condemned in unequivocal terms this "love-and-romance nonsense" which to them was not only indecent but outright immoral. "No decent girl would let a man talk to her while she remains a maiden," said the parents; "if she does, we certainly do not wish to have her as our daughter-in-law." The battle between the older and the younger generations went on, sometimes with heartbreaking results. The parents might decide to disown children who had been openly rebellious, and their children, unable to change the "old-fashioned" ideas of their parents, might prefer to cut off the family relations anyway.

Thus during the transitional period when old values were slowly losing their grip and when new ideas had not been fully accepted, difficulties were bound to occur. Arranged marriages were denounced as "outdated" and "unscientific"; yet the dating system had not been approved by even the "most broad-minded" people. Under the circumstances, how could a young person ever find a husband or wife? In many instances a happy compromise was worked out: the parents would consult their son before they decided on his future bride and might even arrange meetings when the prospective life partners could see each other at a safe distance. Once the engagement was announced, it was a golden contract almost sacred. If it were violated, the family whose daughter had been "scorned" would suffer a disgrace which neither the society nor itself could ever forget.

A much publicized incident which occurred in the 1920's may help to illustrate the intensified conflict between the old and the new. A group of bandits raided a train and carried away many passengers to hold for ransom. Among the people seized was the daughter of a distinguished gentry family. After the girl had been released following the payment of a handsome ransom, the question arose as to whether her fiancé should honor the engagement by marrying her, since, presumably, she had been compromised by the bandit chieftain. The debate went on in many news-papers and magazines, with progressives and conservatives lining up on the opposite sides of the argument. The progressives, led by returned students from Europe and America, urged the young man to honor the engagement on the ground that his fiancée was not responsible for the unfortunate happening and that the bond of marriage was love, not chastity. The conservatives, on the other hand, maintained that chastity was one of the great virtues of maidenhood and that even though the unfortunate circumstance was not of her own making, she should be willing to make a personal sacrifice by refusing to marry the young man in order to maintain the good custom of China. In fact, this kind of argument could have occurred only in China!

It should be added that such a cultural conflict as this was confined to families which had been more or less influenced by the Western culture. For the overwhelming majority of the Chinese people, especially those on the peasant level, the old values still reigned supreme. Generally speaking, cultural conflict was more evident in the cities than in the rural areas, more wide-spread along the coast than in the interior regions, and more pronounced among the educated than the uneducated. In large sections of China two criteria were often used to measure the degree of Western influence: whether the parents had stopped binding their daughters' feet and whether the women, married or unmarried, had cut their hair short to resemble the hairdo popular in the West. Prior to the Western impact, a maiden braided her hair into a long pigtail hanging on her back, and a married woman coiled it into a bun on the back of her neck. It took great courage for the first woman in a community to cut her hair short, and once it was done, other women, finding the new hairdo more easily managed, began to follow suit. The short hairdo became a symbol of "Westernization" (*yang-hua*) or "emancipation," but more often than not the so-called emancipation was more apparent than real. Most girls were still taught to obey their fathers at home and their husbands after they were married.

The lessening of family ties was made inevitable by the increase of geographical mobility resulting from the introduction of modern means of transportation (first railroads and then automobiles) and the establishment of new industries. This situation was particularly noticeable in large cities and their immediate environs. The new industries needed workers, and this need was met by the influx of the unemployed or semi-employed from the rural areas. Once people lived in the cities, they acquired many urban characteristics such as independence and individualism as far as their families were concerned. This did not mean that their families had completely lost control; it did mean that as individuals they were more self-reliant in regulating their personal lives. In the 1920's the Nationalist and Communist agents were active in organizing them into unions and often urged them to go on strikes for political as well as economic purposes. If they could challenge the authority of their employers, why could they not challenge that of their parents? This newly acquired independence was not only discernible among the workers but also among other groups who had to live and make a living in the cities.

The establishment of new industries also changed the old concepts regarding industrialists and merchants—a group of people who had been traditionally looked down upon. As Western influence spread, the old concepts began to change until Western values eventually became the norm. Profit was no longer an unsavory word as long as the profit was legitimately realized. Nor was wealth something to be modestly hidden or to be ashamed of; it was to be proudly displayed. The traditional image of an ideal young man, poor but studying diligently for the civil service examinations, gave way to a new brand of young men who, shrewd and aggressive, knew how to turn a fast profit. This trend was particularly noticeable in large cities, a trend which made China look more and more like an industrial society in Europe or America. It should be remembered, however, that by and large the old values still existed in most parts of China and that there was a vast difference between a few Westernized cities and the large rural areas.

Though large industries such as railroads and maritime shipping were mostly controlled by foreigners, there was enough room left for native entrepreneurs. Rural savings, which had been traditionally invested in land, were channeled into industrial development, and new factories mushroomed in many large or medium-sized cities. The new industries were for the most part light industries catering to the needs of consumers and were not impressive by European or American standards. For one thing, capital outlay could not be large because the Chinese, true to their ancient tradition, preferred to raise capital on a family rather than a corporate basis. Most of these new industrialists were former landlords who found investment in modern industry more profitable than landholdings. As more landlords invested their money in industrial and commercial enterprises, the traditional distinction between the gentry-scholars and merchants was no longer so clear as it once had been. Needless to say, the stigma traditionally attached to the merchant class had all but disappeared.

SUN YAT-SEN AND HIS PHILOSOPHY

While the various warlords were fighting among themselves and annexing each other's territories, Sun Yat-sen, the founder of the Chinese republic, was a disappointed man. He was respected as an honorable man but, not having a military following of his own, his words carried little weight with the realistic warlords. His old revolutionary comrades were scattered all over the country—some gave him polite attention and others joined the warlords. In 1917, together with a few of his followers, he set up an independent government in Canton; but he left this government after only one year because the southern warlords had skillfully taken it over. In 1920 he returned to Canton; and the following year with the help of a warlord named Ch'en Chiung-ming, he proclaimed the establishment of a new national government with himself as the president. Thus two governments existed simultaneously in China, one in Peking and another in Canton, each claiming that it represented all of China. It was then that Sun asked the Western powers, especially the United States, for financial and diplomatic support, and the Western powers, recognizing the Peking government, turned down his request. Undaunted, he organized an expedition to "crush the northern warlords." His army, poorly organized and poorly led, was defeated, and one of his key supporters, Ch'en Chiung-ming, deserted him. He was forced to resign from his presidency and left for Shanghai in May, 1922.

It was during Sun's stay in Shanghai that a very important event occurred, with enormous consequences for decades to come. In January, 1923, Sun met the Soviet emissary Adolph Joffe, and they issued a joint statement after their conferences. In this statement the Soviet Union pledged its assistance to Sun for the realization of China's political unity and independence and, to allay Sun's fear of Communist domination over China, it declared that Communism and the Soviet system were unsuited to China's present needs. Late in that year the Soviet agent Michael Borodin arrived in Canton where he helped to reorganize the Kuomintang (National People's Party) after the Bolshevik model. Members of the Chinese Communist Party joined the Kuomintang as "individuals" and pledged to support Sun as their revolutionary leader. Meanwhile, their own party was not dissolved and existed side by side with the Kuomintang. In the reorganized Kuomintang emphasis was laid on party loyalty and discipline, indoctrination and propaganda among the masses, and the creation of a revolutionary army under the command of the party. The new programs were formally approved by the party's first national congress convened in January, 1924. To train officers for the revolutionary army, the Whampoa Military Academy was established. Chiang Kai-shek, who had been sent by Sun to study the organization and training of the Red Army in the Soviet Union in the summer of 1923, then returned home as the president of the new school.

Early in 1924 Sun Yat-sen gave a series of lectures to his followers in Canton. These lectures, later compiled into one volume, were known as San Min Chu-yi, or Three Principles of the People. This volume, together with Sun's other works such as Plans for National Reconstruction (Chien-kuo fang-lüeh), the Fundamentals of National Reconstruction (Chien-kuo *ta-kang*), the *Political Philosophy of Sun Yat-sen* (*Sun Wen hsüeh-shuo*), and the *First Step to Democracy* (*Min-ch'üan ch'u-pu*), provided the ideological basis for the Nationalist revolution. To the members of the Kuomintang or Nationalists, Sun's philosophy was the ultimate in truth and wisdom. In areas within the Nationalist control it was a standard course taught in every school, from grade to college level and is still taught in Taiwan today.

Sun believed that his political philosophy was a combination of the very best from "the East and the West." While borrowing extensively from the prevailing Western ideologies, he hoped to preserve for his new China what he regarded as the best in China's ancient heritage. He was not an originator of any philosophical system in a metaphysical sense; the merits of his works lay more in their practical wisdom. He strove to solve the problems China then faced and hoped eventually to build a new society in which economic prosperity and social justice would exist simultaneously with political independence. He was a great patriot, and all his works should be read in that context. The basic ideas in the *Three Principles of the People* had been conceived as early as the turn of the century and matured with the passage of time. It was not until 1924, however, that they were put down in a more systematic form. Sun became seriously ill and then died before he had time to complete his lectures on his third and last principle, the *Principle of People's Livelihood*. The lectures, hastily composed, present many imperfections in organization and style. Had he lived a few years longer, he would doubtless have corrected them. The lectures have been published as they were originally delivered, because no one in the Nationalist government has had the audacity to suggest correction and improvement. To the Nationalists it is the bible.

In the *Principle of Nationalism*, Sun appealed to the national pride of the Chinese, with their ancient culture and great heritage. This great nation was in danger, said he, unless all Chinese transformed their traditional loyalties to families and clans into a new loyalty as embodied by the nation. The problem of the Chinese was not that they had too little individual freedom as had been the case with many European countries before the modern period, but that they had too much. They were like sands on the beach, said Sun, which, being too individualistic, produced no strength. They should be cemented together to from a solid rock, and in that case they would be able to resist foreign aggression and abolish the unequal treaties. The abolition of the unequal treaties should be China's first concern because, as long as these treaties existed, China could never be the master in its own house. China's status in the international family, Sun maintained, was worse than that of India, because India, being a colony of Great Britain, served only one master, whereas China, having unequal treaties with so many powers, was a subcolony of many masters all of whom exploited China without rendering anything in return. It was suicidal to practice internationalism while one's own country was in danger of being submerged, and only when China became a free, independent country in the truest sense could it become a member of the international community as an equal partner. Before that day arrived, nationalism, instead of internationalism, had to be its goal. To achieve national independence, "China should ally itself with all countries that treat us as equals." The countries that treated China as an equal presumably included the Soviet Union which was then helping Sun to unify China.

The achievement of international equality for China should be accompanied by a similar achievement among the various peoples within China, according to Sun. The traditional chauvinistic attitude of the Han (Chinese) people towards the minority groups should be condemned and dispensed with, and all peoples in China, regardless of their ethnic backgrounds, should enjoy the same social, economic, and legal rights. They should choose their own representatives to sit in the National Assembly when a constitutional government was established, and all policies with regard to the minorities should be aimed solely at the betterment of their welfare. Eventually, Sun continued, a new nation would be created in which all people in China would identify themselves as Chinese, regardless of their original ethnic backgrounds. This could be done, said Sun, and he cited the United States as an example. "The United States was composed of a variety of peoples originated from Europe; yet, today these are only one people, the American people, one of the most glorious peoples in the entire world."

In advancing his *Principle of Democracy*, Sun pointed out that men, contrary to the general belief, were not born equal. Men were endowed differently by nature, and within any group of people, some were wise and others were stupid, while most of them were somewhere between the two extremes. Equality, therefore, was created rather than inherited, and equality should mean equality in opportunity rather than achievement, because no two persons could achieve the same. In the political sense, everyone should have the same political rights (which were "created" for him) such as the right to vote, but the actual operation of the government should be in the hands of the able and the wise. The people were like bus riders and the government officials were like bus drivers, said Sun. The people should hire the best bus driver they could find; but once they hired him, they should not keep on telling him how to drive. How could one know that he was a good driver? He should take a road test, of course. Therefore, before any man was allowed to run for political office, he should pass a written examination in political science and related fields, impartially administered like the old civil service examinations. A man's popularity with the voters was a poor measurement of his ability; an uneducated or inadequately educated man should not be entrusted with public office, however popular he was. The right to vote, on the other hand, should be enjoyed by all above the legal age, without property, sex, education, and other limitations.

To make the government responsible to the people and yet to conduct an efficient administration without their constant meddling, the powers of the government and the rights of the people should be separated and well balanced, according to Sun. The government should have five powers (*neng*): executive, legislative, judiciary, examination, and censorship. The examination branch of the government was not only responsible for administering examinations to government employees but would keep an objective record of their services for promotion or demotion purposes. The censorship (sometimes translated as control) branch of the government was a revival of the censorate of the imperial days; it was empowered to criticize or impeach all government officials who had failed in their assigned duties or who for personal reasons were unfit for public office. To balance the five powers which the government possessed, the people should have four rights (*ch'üan*): the right to elect and recall public officials, the right to initiate legislation when their representatives had failed to introduce it, and the right of referendum with regard to all important legislation. The government, said Sun, should be like the board of directors of a corporation, and the people like the stockholders. The directors were experts and their way of conducting business should not be interfered with unnecessarily. On the other hand, they were hired employees and should be held responsible for the welfare of the stockholders.

Having lived under autocratic government for thousands of years, the Chinese, said Sun, were not yet prepared to exercise the political rights described above. The democratic or constitutional government could not be achieved overnight, he warned. Instead, there should be three stages in the revolutionary process, and the main tasks during each of the stages should be successfully completed before the arrival of the next stage. The first of these would be the military period during which the revolutionaries would use military force to unify the country and subject it to military rule. Once the country had been unified, the second stage, that of political tutelage, would arrive. During this period, the actual control of the government would be vested in the revolutionary party, the Kuomintang, whose main task was to educate the people in the use of the four rights. Self-government should begin with the lowest administrative unit, the subprefecture, and then be extended to the provincial level. Only after each province had functioned under a provincial constitution would come the third and last period, the establishment of a national, constitutional government. Then the historical rule of the Kuomintang would be completed and it should hand over the control of the government, happily and willingly, to the representatives of the people. What could the people do if the Kuomintang, long entrenched in power, refused to surrender its power or even order elections? This question was not answered.

Sun's economic theory, as described in the *Principle of People's Livelihood*, can best be described as a moderate socialism. Seeing the increasing conflicts between capital and labor during his lifetime, he rejected capitalism as an economic system. On the other hand, he was equally unwilling to accept socialism of the Marxist version. For one thing, he believed that the motivation of social progress was not class struggle as expounded by Karl Marx; it was cooperation, he said. The problem China faced was not how to distribute wealth of which it had little but how to create it. To create it, people must be given an incentive. While large industries that "affect the welfare of the people as a whole" should be government owned and controlled, there should be enough room left for private enterprise and individual initiative. Transportation and communication systems, for instance, should be made government monopolies because competition in this field was costly and uneconomical. On the other hand, there was no reason that industries that "are not monopolistic in nature and do not affect the life of the people as a whole" should not be left in private hands where free competition would be most beneficial. In the development of China's industrial potential, foreign capital was to be welcomed as long as foreign investment did not affect China adversely as a sovereign nation. Communism was at best a distant goal; for the time being the most important task was to create wealth, by private as well as public resources. "In China there is no such difference as that between the rich and the poor," Sun declared; "there is only the difference between the extremely poor and the moderately poor." "We shall strive to eliminate poverty before we can talk about the distribution of wealth."

Sun's land policy can be summarized in the often repeated statement: "Land belongs to the tillers." This purpose, however, should be achieved by peaceful, gradual means rather than radical methods such as nationalization of all land and its redistribution among peasants. In a speech made in 1921 Sun suggested some initial steps for the eventual realization of this important goal. Under his plan a landlord was allowed to assess the cash value of his land estates and report his assessment to the government. If the government believed that the assessment was above the true worth of his landholdings, it would tax him in accordance with his own assessment. If, on the other hand, the assessment was below that measured in terms of market price, the government would purchase the reported land by paying a price according to the landlord's own assessment. Presumably, land thus obtained would be resold to tillers on easy terms. Any appreciation of land values resulting from circumstances other than the landlord's own improvement should be credited to the society as a whole and be expropriated by the government. Sun believed that his plan would not only prevent land concentration in the hands of a few but would also lead to the acquiring of land ownership by tillers. Moreover, as land was no longer a profitable field for investment, the nation's savings could be channeled to industrial development which was badly in need of capital investment.

To millions of Chinese, Sun's works summarized the wishes and aspirations of a new China. To them Sun was not merely a politician or even a statesman; he was a Messiah. Personally, he was honest and selfless; even his enemies had never doubted the sincerity of his motives. In December, 1924, he was invited by the northern warlords (Tuan Ch'i-jui, Chang Tso-lin, and "Christian General" Feng Yü-hsiang) to Peking to negotiate a peaceful unification of all China. Already seriously ill, he was moved to Peking on his sickbed. As it happened, this became his final attempt to unify his beloved country; his health deteriorated further after his arrival in the capital. He died on March 12, 1925. After the establishment of the Nationalist regime his body was moved to Nanking where it was housed in a magnificently built mausoleum.

CHIANG KAI-SHEK

After Sun's death a power struggle developed among his followers. Chiang Kai-shek, a long time disciple, eventually emerged triumphant. Chiang was born in 1887 in Ch'ik'ou, a village on the coast of Chekiang province. The family had been farmers for generations and were well-to-do according to local standards. His father died when Chiang was only nine and it was his mother, said he many years later, who gave him love and protection so essential to the healthy growth of a fatherless child. She was somewhat disappointed when Chiang, after his graduation from high school, decided to pursue a military instead of a scholarly career. However, she gave her consent after the young man had definitely made up his mind. He applied and was accepted by the Paoting Military Academy (Hopeh province), then the leading school for training army officers in accordance with Western standards. After his graduation he was sent by the Manchu government to Japan for additional training where he was greatly impressed with the discipline and hardship which accompanied the training of a Japanese soldier. In 1910 he enlisted in a Japanese artillery battalion as a trainee with the rank of private, second class, but was soon promoted to a higher rank. His battalion commander, when interviewed many years later, said that he knew that Chiang would accomplish a great deal; yet, he could not even dream that the young soldier would become a "great, historical figure." In Japan Chiang joined the Alliance [1] and was introduced to Sun Yat-sen shortly afterwards. "He is

[1] The Alliance was a revolutionary organization headed by Sun Yat-sen. For more details, see pp. 437–438.

an unusual man," commented Sun. He was said to be serious, sincere, and full of enthusiasm about the revolution. In 1911 he returned to China to participate actively in the overthrow of the Manchu regime. He led a group of revolutionaries to attack the Manchu governor's office at Hang-chow and returned that city to the newly established republic at Nanking. However, when Yüan Shih-k'ai banned the Kuomintang, Chiang, like other revolutionaries, went underground.

We know little about Chiang's activities during the early years of the republic. When he reappeared on the political scene early in 1922, he joined Sun Yat-sen's government at Canton. Two years later he was ap-pointed president of the Whampoa Military Academy, the first major break in his political career. When Sun died in 1925, Chiang had built a strong following among his student-officers. They formed what was later known as the Whampoa clique, one of the bases of Chiang's political strength. They, in turn, trained other officers who all pledged loyalty to Chiang as their leader. Later when the Whampoa Military Academy was renamed the Central Military Academy and was moved to Nanking, Chiang remained its president. Several hundred cadets graduated each year and they, when they joined the army as second lieutenants, not only carried their loyalty to Chiang with them but also indoctrinated their soldiers with their own beliefs. In a country where political victory was ultimately decided on the battlefield, it is not difficult to see what a political asset this strong following was. With such an asset, Chiang was able to achieve what Sun had failed to bring about: the defeat of most of the warlords and a symbolic unification of all China. Early in the 1930's he was officially proclaimed the Leader (*ling-hsiu*), demanding and re-ceiving absolute loyalty from all government officials, civilian or military, in the Nationalist government. He was the ultimate power, regardless of the official positions he happened to hold at any given moment. One might find ample grounds to criticize a personal power so vast; it should be remembered, however, that throughout Chinese history political power had always been built around men instead of institutions or ideologies.

In the summer of 1926 Chiang Kai-shek was appointed by the revolu-tionary regime in Canton commander-in-chief of all armed forces, with special instructions to eliminate the warlords and unify China. The mili-tary campaign, known as the Northern Expedition, was accompanied by speedy and overwhelming success. The Wu-Han metropolis was captured in October and Nanking was occupied in March, 1927. Why did the warlords collapse so quickly? For one thing, their soldiers had neither the training nor the fighting spirit possessed by the revolutionaries who had been indoctrinated to fight for a cause: a unified, strong China as outlined in Sun Yat-sen's *Three Principles of the People*. Moreover, because the Northern Expedition became as much antiforeign as it was antiwarlord, the belief that the warlords were supported by foreign interests damaged their position in the eyes of their countrymen. Chang Tso-lin and Wu P'ei-fu, for instance, were regarded as Japanese and British puppets, respectively.

The antiforeign sentiment was intensified immediately before and during the Northern Expedition as a result of a number of incidents. Early in 1925 a group of Chinese workers called a strike for higher wages against a Japanese textile mill in Shanghai, and the management dismissed the leader of the strikers, shot to death another worker, and wounded many others. Supporting the workers' stand, the angered students demonstrated in Shanghai's International Settlement and made speeches condemning "the imperialists and their brutalities." During one of the demonstrations (May 30th) the students were fired upon by British police and many of them were killed and injured. A general strike of protest was called: workers left factories, merchants closed their shops, and students vacated classrooms. The antiforeign movement soon spread to other large cities, and England resorted to the use of force to suppress it. In Hankow, British troops machine-gunned demonstrators on June 10, while in Canton several hundred were killed and injured on June 23 when British men-of-war opened fire from the nearby harbor. The entire nation was aroused, and the partriots urged all Chinese to boycott English and Japanese products. Chiang Kai-shek's Northern Expedition, which had been launched primarily for the defeat of the warlords, now became increasingly nationalistic. To millions of Chinese the success of the Northern Expedition would not only mean the unification of China but also the abolition of the unequal treaties.

After the revolutionaries reached the Yangtze Valley, the Kuomintang split into two rival factions. The revolutionary regime, which had been moved to Wu-Han after the capture of that metropolis, was then controlled by the Kuomintang leftists and their Communist allies. It had forcibly taken over the British concession at Hankow and was violently anti-foreign. Chiang Kai-shek, then fighting in the Lower Yangtze, was greatly concerned over the possible consequence of the official policy which to him had unnecessarily invited so many foreign enemies. Moreover, the Communists and the Kuomintang leftists were converting the Northern Expedition from an antiwarlord campaign into a social and economic revolution. They had successfully organized peasants and workers, expropriating land from landlords and calling strikes for political purposes. Within areas under the Kuomintang control, production stood at a standstill and no property owners were safe against mob violence. It was then that Chiang Kai-shek decided to change the course of the revolution and took a step so drastic that it affected Chinese history for decades to come.

In April, 1927, Chiang sent his troops to seize Shanghai and ordered the liquidation of all Communists who had been active in organizing strikes and demonstrations to prepare in advance the taking over of that city by the revolutionaries. With the help of Shanghai's conservative businessmen and secret societies he scored a quick victory. Not only was Shanghai captured, but countless Communists and leftists were captured and shot. Chou En-lai who was then a primary organizer of the Communist activities in Shanghai barely escaped. This marked the beginning of the intense hatred between Chiang and the Communists which has been intensified with the passage of time. As Chiang's coup was not authorized by the Central Committee of the Kuomintang, the Wu-Han govern-

MEMORIAL PAGODA   This pagoda is located outside of Nanking where soldiers killed during the Northern Expedition are buried.

ment dismissed him from his post as the commander-in-chief. Chiang retaliated by setting up a separate government at Nanking. As the intra-party struggle continued, the war against the warlords was temporarily suspended. Under strong party pressure, Chiang finally resigned from his post and went into exile in Japan.

Meanwhile, even the leftist Kuomintang members began to suspect Communist motives and came closer to Chiang's point of view: that the Communists were Moscow agents and that their ultimate purpose was to eliminate the Kuomintang and subject China to Soviet rule. A supposedly secret telegram from Joseph Stalin to the Chinese Communists became known to Wang Ching-wei, a leader of the Kuomintang, in which the Soviet leader outlined the steps to be taken by his Chinese comrades for the control of the Kuomintang and the liquidation of the "recalcitrant" ele-ments who refused to cooperate with the Communists. Wang and his colleagues were alarmed and proceeded to do the same thing for which they had criticized Chiang before, which was the purging of Communists from the Kuomintang ranks. The Communists, being a minority, offered only ineffectual resistance. The Communist purge paved the way for a reconciliation between the left and right factions of the Kuomintang. In August, 1927, the separate Nanking government was abolished, and the Wu-Han government moved to Nanking. Chiang returned to China early in 1928. The Northern Expedition was resumed, and despite Japanese obstruction Peking was eventually captured. Chang Tso-lin, the last of the strong warlords, was murdered (presumably by the Japanese) while re-treating to Manchuria. His son and successor Chang Hsüeh-liang (the "Young Marshal") declared his allegiance to the revolutionary regime in December, 1928. In name at least, China was unified.

As the radical elements had been either purged or had voluntarily left the party, the new government at Nanking (officially, the National Government of China) was conservative in tone. In the fall of 1927 Chiang was converted to Christianity as a Methodist and late in that year he was married to Soong Meiling, a beautiful, talented young woman who came from a businessman's family and had been educated in the United States. These two happy occurrences well foretold the national and international policies the Nationalist government was going to follow. The *Three Principles of the People* was still the ideological basis of the new regime, but it was not to be interpreted literally. The equalization of land ownership, for instance, had come to mean the reduction of rent charged by landlords, and the pro-Soviet policy originated by Sun Yat-sen was abandoned. Sun's widow, Soong Ch'ing-ling, accused Chiang of hav-ing betrayed her husband's trust and left China for Moscow. The new regime was supported wholeheartedly by the landowners and the bour-geoisie, as it was more consistent with their concept of a revolutionary regime. In foreign policy, China was to be more Western orientated, and the goal of abolishing the unequal treaties, while not abandoned, should be achieved through peaceful means and by negotiation. By and large, the conservative policy of Chiang and his colleagues was supported by the nation as a whole, and the Communists, through their constant agitation for violence, had antagonized not only property owners but all those who wanted nothing better than peace after so many years of civil war. Upon the new leader, Chiang Kai-shek, China placed much of its hope, as he was young, energetic, and self-assured.

THE NATIONALIST REGIME

After Peking had been captured by the Nationalists and when China was again nominally unified, the Nationalist government in Nanking formally declared that the military period had come to an end and that the second period of the revolution, that of political tutelage, had begun. During the period of political tutelage, the state power was vested in the Kuomintang which formulated policies and appointed government personnel. No other political party was allowed to function because the Kuomintang alone, according to Sun Yat-sen, had the right and obligation to prepare the country for the eventual realization of a democratic, constitutional government. The highest organization of the party was the National Party Congress, composed of delegates from all provinces and overseas Chinese communities. When the congress was not in session, party power was vested in a Central Executive Committee and a Supervisory Committee; the members of both committees were elected by the congress. The standing committee of the Central Executive Committee was in fact the most powerful organ of the party. As the government was responsible to the party, the man in control of the party was also the strongest man in the government. He might not occupy the position of president of the republic, but whatever position he held, he made the final decisions with regard to government as well as party policies. During most of the period under discussion, 1927–1949, Chiang commanded the majority vote in the standing committee as well as the Central Executive Committee.

Even during the prime of the Nationalist regime, the unification was more apparent than real. Recognized by all foreign powers as China's legal government, it had no more than one-third of the nation under its direct jurisdiction in the 1930's—the central lakes region, the Lower Yangtze, part of North China, and later, Fukien and Kwangtung provinces. The other two-thirds were controlled by local strong men who were given such titles as governor as long as they were not in open rebellion. Time and again they revolted, and the central government had to use force to suppress them. Once they were defeated, they were either al-

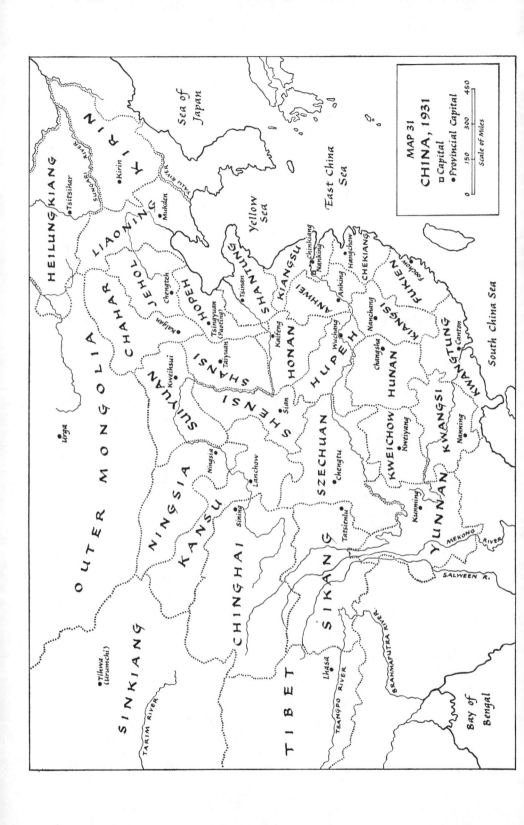

MAP 31
CHINA, 1931
□ Capital
● Provincial Capital

0 150 300 450
Scale of Miles

lowed to retain their territories or were brought back to Nanking to occupy some high but powerless positions. In some cases they were "advised" to go abroad for a prolonged vacation. Why did Chiang not pursue the goal of unification to its logical conclusion by conquering all warlords? To him these warlords were merely selfish, unprincipled men who could be easily pushed aside once he successfully defeated the real enemy, the Communists. Having an ideology, a program, and strong and able leadership, the Communists were the greatest challenge to everything he stood for, and he did not mind making alliances with the warlords to help bring about the defeat of the Communists. With communism there could not be any real compromise. From time to time he was called upon to deal with other problems such as warlords' rebellions and Japanese aggression, but he never let those problems distract him from his main political goal: the destruction of communism in China. As far as he was concerned, the die was cast as early as 1927.

Despite recurrent warfare against warlords, continuous conflict with the Communists, and Japanese aggression after 1931, the Nationalist regime was not without significant achievements during its short stay in Nanking (1927–1937). For the first time since the overthrow of the Manchu regime, there was a fairly honest government which most Chinese could support with good conscience. Though much has been said about Nationalist corruption, it was perhaps no worse than what could be found in many other countries. It was not until the end of World War II when a runaway inflation had eaten up the income of most wage earners that corruption became a major disease. Chiang was personally incorruptible, though we cannot say the same thing about all of his followers. He practiced and glorified a Spartan type of life, and he invited others to do the same. Despite criticism of his foreign and domestic policies, his popularity continued to grow. His popularity was never so high as when he decided to make a stand against Japan in 1937.

Before the war with Japan began, the Nationalist government made conscientious efforts to improve the nation's economy. Thanks to the fact that China was largely agricultural, the world-wide depression of the 1930's did not affect China as it did more industrialized countries. However, the devaluation of currencies in foreign countries affected adversely the Chinese monetary system. Silver, which had been the standard medium of exchange for many centuries, began to flow abroad, following the raising of silver price in the United States. In 1935 the government decreed the nationalization of silver and imposed severe penalties for using it in business transactions. All silver was to be handed over to the government in exchange for the "legal tender" (*fa pi*) issued by government-controlled banks. All bullion thus collected was the bank reserve backing the soundness of the paper currency. The currency reform was more successful than had been expected; for one thing, it enabled the government to finance the war against Japan which began in 1937. However, towards the end of World War II the continuous printing of unredeemable paper money resulted in an inflation unprecedented in modern history which eventually destroyed the financial structure.

Other economic achievements of the 1930's included the construction of railroads and highways. The Che-Kan (from Hangchow to Nanchang) Railroad and the Yüeh-Han (from Canton to Hankow) Railroad were both completed in 1936. The construction of highways was also emphasized, reaching 68,000 miles by 1937. A Sino-American enterprise, the China Aviation Company, was founded in 1930 with regular flights between major cities in China. Meanwhile, efforts were made to convert the middle and lower Yangtze—areas under the direct control of the Nationalist government—into a highly industrialized region. Heavy and light industries were equally emphasized, and the government took initial steps towards the exploitation of China's mineral resources. Unfortunately, most of the industrial programs were still in the blueprint stage when war began in 1937.

On the rural level, a land law passed in 1930 was intended to reduce some of the worst evils in tenancy. Rents were not to exceed 37.5 percent of the main crop, and tenants could not be evicted unless they had failed to pay rent consecutively for two years or had not worked the land for a year without good reason. Unfortunately, the law was not strictly enforced, and ingenious landlords had schemes for obtaining the same rent without violating the letter of the law. For one thing, tenancy was difficult to obtain and tenants did not have the bargaining power possessed by landlords. As credit was rare and not easily available, usurious interest was a rule rather than an exception. When the government made available low-interest loans in rural areas, more often than not such loans wound up in the hands of landlords whose credit rating was certainly higher than that of the peasants. Moreover, flood and drought were a recurrent problem. In 1931 an unprecedented flood along the Yangtze caused the death of more than 100,000 and affected an area of more than 70,000 square miles. Following the disaster, the government built a long dyke along the middle and the lower valley of the river, extending more than 2,600 miles. This extraordinary work reduced damages in the subsequent floods, though it could not eliminate them. Despite the government's efforts, the majority of the peasants were no better off than they had been before. The government's inability to solve the rural problems gave the Communists a great opportunity to exploit them. As to this, we shall have more to say in the next chapter.

To prepare the nation for the eventual realization of a constitutional government, the Nationalist government launched an extensive educational program. However, due to the lack of adequate funds and trained personnel, the result was anything but impressive. All children were supposed to have at least six years of schooling, but this goal proved to be impossible to reach. In the rural areas children began to work in the fields at a tender age, and even if the tuition were free, their parents simply could not afford to take them away from the field to send them to school. Whenever schools were established in rural areas, only the comparatively well-to-do could take advantage of the opportunity. Unable to promote education on a mass scale, the government concentrated its attention on institutions of higher learning. Many universities, colleges, and teacher-training schools were established. They were of uneven quality, of course; but the best among them could be compared favorably with the leading institutions in other countries. For one thing, high school graduates had to pass rigid entrance examinations before they were admitted; in many cases, only one in twenty candidates could be accepted. Academic learning was universally emphasized; sports and other forms of recreation had been looked down upon and still were. However, as institutions of learning were few and expensive, only a few could ever enter their doors. The waste of the nation's talent was simply enormous.

In the field of foreign relations the Nationalist government directed its major attention to the abolition of the unequal treaties. German, Austrian, and Hungarian rights in China were liquidated in World War I, and Russia renounced its special privileges following the Bolshevik revolution. Now China under the Nationalist regime wished other Western powers and Japan to do the same. During the two year period (1928–1929) a series of treaties were concluded with these powers which conceded to China the principle of tariff autonomy. Thus after eighty-seven years (1842–1929) the system of regulated tariff finally came to an end. The government was only partially successful, however, in securing the return of the concessions. Some were regained, but others, including the International Settlement at Shanghai, remained in the hands of foreigners. As to extraterritoriality, the Western powers and Japan refused to give ground. They criticized China's judicial system and would agree to the gradual abolition of the extraterritorial system only after China had revised its legal codes, modernized its prisons, and conducted a variety of other reforms. As negotiations were stalemated, the Nationalist government announced that extraterritoriality would come to an end on January 1, 1932. When the powers refused to budge, the Chinese government capitulated in December, 1931. By the beginning of World War II China was one of the few "sovereign" countries where foreigners still enjoyed extraterritorial rights. Both Turkey and Siam had successfully eliminated them.

☃ XV

The Republic (2)

THE COMMUNISTS

The forerunner of the Chinese Communist Party was the Marxist Study
Association organized by a group of intellectuals in Shanghai in the spring
of 1920. Until this time the leader of this group, Ch'en Tu-hsiu, had been
an ardent advocate of American republicanism; but then, impressed with
the Soviet Union's anti-imperialist stand and its willingness to relinquish
its special rights in China, he saw communism as the cure-all of China's
foreign and domestic ills. In the summer of that year he and his colleagues organized the Communist Youth Corps as a prelude to the organization of a Communist Party. The party formally came into being in
July, 1921. The total number of registered Communists was no more than
fifty, and when the First Party Congress was called into session that year
there were only thirteen delegates from "all parts of China" to attend the

476

meeting. The party had little strength then, and it needed a popular hero to bolster its prestige. G. Maring, the Comintern agent who had been sent to China to help organize the Chinese Communist Party, contacted Sun Yat-sen for a possible alliance, and Sun, believing that the New Economic Policy as then pursued in Russia under Lenin was similar to his own idea of economic development, agreed to the alliance. The alliance with the Soviet Union was formally announced after Sun's meeting with another Soviet agent Joffe. When the Kuomintang held its First Party Congress in January, 1924, all Communists pledged their loyalty to Sun as their leader, and some of them were elected as alternate members of the Central Executive Committee of the Kuomintang—including an obscure young man named Mao Tse-tung.

During the Northern Expedition (1926–1927) the Communists were very active in propaganda work and in the organization of peasants and workers. They took a strong antifeudal and anti-imperialist stand by which they meant the elimination of landlordism as an economic institution and the liquidation of the special privileges and rights which the treaty powers then enjoyed in China. To achieve their purpose, they did not hesitate to use the most dubious methods. When Nanking was captured in the spring of 1927, the Communist-inspired mobs, waving anti-imperialist flags, invaded British and American consulates and churches, killed foreigners indiscriminately, and did much damage to property. The British and American ships in the nearby Yangtze opened fire and bombarded the city, and for a while it seemed that a severe punishment of the Boxer type was in order. It was against this background that Chiang Kai-shek struck back against the Communists, and his success in Shanghai was followed by a mass purge. The Nationalists and the Communists went their separate ways, and ever since then the Communists have accused him of betraying the revolution.

The victory of Stalin over Trotsky in Russia in 1927 was followed by a similar change of leadership among the Communists in China. Ch'en Tu-hsiu and his colleagues were replaced by the Stalinists, headed by a Moscow-trained Chinese named Li Li-san. Goaded by Stalin, the Communists staged a series of uprisings in southern and central China in the latter part of 1927. All of them failed, including the "autumn harvest" uprising in Hunan led by Mao Tse-tung. After the failure, the Communists were a dispirited and disorganized force; each group was more concerned with its survival than with the proletarian revolution. One group, led by Mao Tse-tung, arrived at Chingkangshan, a mountainous area in southern Kiangsi. Soon it was joined by a Communist militarist named Chu Teh and his group. The Chu-Mao coalition became the nucleus around which a strong Communist force was eventually built up. Meanwhile, other Communist groups were scattered in many isolated areas in South China, each fighting for its own existence. To coordinate the efforts of the various groups and to plan a unified strategy, a party congress was called in Shanghai in May, 1930. The congress passed a resolution reaffirming the "correctness of the leadership of the proletariat" and condemning those comrades (such as Mao Tse-tung) who elevated the peasants above the workers as the basis of the revolution. The party leadership remained in the hands of the doctrinaires who believed that to succeed the Communists had to capture large cities where the proletarians lived, while the peasants, traditionally conservative and politically inert, could only be considered auxiliaries to the revolution. In July, 1930, the Communists felt strong enough to carry out the resolution. They attacked Changsha and the Wu-Han cities with the purpose of building an urban, revolutionary base. They succeeded in capturing Changsha, only to be driven out by the reinforced Nationalists a few days later. Though the action had been planned and urged by the Comintern, the Kremlin dropped Li Li-san after his failure, and party leadership passed into the hands of a group of students who had recently returned from Moscow.

Meanwhile Mao and Chu, who had been the reluctant partners in Li's *putschism*, went their separate ways and practiced their own brand of communism. The failure of Li and his Moscow-dictated strategy had convinced them of the correctness of their own theory: that in an industrially backward, agricultural China where industrial workers were few, the basis of the revolution could not be any other group except the peasants who constituted the majority of the population. Of the two, Mao was the leader who formulated policies and planned strategy. More versed in Chinese history than in Communist ideology, he was in closer touch with reality than those doctrinaire Communists trained by Moscow.

Mao Tse-tung was born in 1893 to a peasant family in Hunan. His father, a shrewd farmer who also speculated in the rice market, brought prosperity to the family much to the envy of the neighborhood. He was a strict disciplinarian, however, and ruled the family with an iron hand. Many years later his son still remembered vividly how he had hated the "dictator." Being intelligent and promising, young Mao was sent to school where, we are told, he hated his teacher with equal intensity because the teacher forced him to study Confucian classics which he disliked. Defiant of authorities and established conventions, he imagined himself as a Chinese Robin Hood, striking against the rich and helping the poor. Had there been no Karl Marx and Lenin, he would have been a rebel in the traditional sense, perhaps like those in *The Marsh Heroes*, a book which he enjoyed reading and greatly admired.

To say that Mao was a born rebel is of course not enough. Like any other Chinese who knew how to read, he was greatly disturbed by China's international status. The thought that China might be conquered by Japan or divided among foreign powers aroused in him a strong sense of nationalism. "It was the duty of all people to help save China," he declared. How could China be saved? His early solution was a simple one: China had to possess Western inventions—railroads, telegraphs, steamships, and "machines of all kinds." After he grew older, he realized that this would not be enough. The real solution, he declared, lay in the conversion of China to a Communist society because "the emancipation of China depends upon the successful liberation of all colonial and semicolonial countries from capitalist, imperialist rule." By reaching such a conclusion he made China's struggle for freedom and independence a part of the world Communist movement. Thus three facets appeared in Mao's personality: the rebel, the nationalist, and finally, the Communist.

After finishing his education in the village school, Mao went to Changsha, capital of Hunan, where he was enrolled as a student in a normal school. A prospective teaching career, however, was not to his liking, and he left the school one year later so that he could devote his entire time to "patriotic work." He read avidly the newspapers and pamphlets put out by the various revolutionary groups. Among the revolutionaries, he admired Sun Yat-sen and hoped to join his organization. In 1918 he went to Peking where he found a job as an assistant librarian with the Peking University. This position gave him an opportunity to read books of different ideologies and also to audit the lectures of many prominent professors, including Hu Shih. The head of the library and his immediate superior was Li Ta-chao, an avowed Marxist, and under Li's guidance, he became Marxist orientated. In 1921 when the Communist Party was organized, he was one of its charter members. During the first Kuomintang-Communist cooperation (1924–1927) Mao strongly urged his own party to rely upon the peasants as "the most dynamic, most revolutionary force" because "they have been despised and trodden down by the gentry for centuries." "The leadership by the poor peasants is very essential," he continued; "without them there will be no revolution." His proposal was rejected by the party leaders who regarded his idea as unorthodox and heretical.

After the failure of Li Li-san's *putsch* in 1930, Mao's prestige within the party increased. Many Communists, while still giving lip service to the dictatorship of the proletariat, began to accept Mao's strategy as the most feasible. In 1931 the establishment of a Soviet Republic was proclaimed in southern Kiangsi with Mao as its chairman. Within the area under their control, the Communists liquidated the landlords, expropriated their land, and distributed it among the peasants. This gave the peasants a stake in defending the republic. Quickly the Communists applied their organizational ability and mobilized all men and women on a permanent, military basis. Even small children were mobilized to spy on their "enemy," the Nationalists. A program of intensified indoctrination was conducted, and the peasants were taught to hate "the imperialists, the landlords, and their lackey, Chiang Kai-shek." By the early 1930's the Communists had extended their control over a great part of Kiangsi and large areas of Fukien and Hunan provinces.

Meanwhile the Nationalists, under the leadership of Chiang Kai-shek, had not been idle. From December, 1930, to June, 1932, they launched four military campaigns against the Red republic; all of them, however, ended in failure. The failure was partly due to the strength of the thoroughly indoctrinated peasant Communist army and partly due to other circumstances beyond the Nationalists' control. For instance, the third campaign was called off after Japan had invaded Manchuria in September, 1931, and the fourth campaign came to nought when the Nationalists had to move troops to North China to face another Japanese invasion early in 1933. Ironically, the Japanese militarists had been the Communists' inadvertent allies throughout the civil war. They put pressure on China whenever the Nationalist government was busy fighting its domestic enemy; by doing so they reduced the pressure that the Nationalists had been exercising on the Communists. In 1933 the Nationalist government obtained a truce from Japan by signing away part of North China, and in the following year it launched the fifth and the best planned campaign against the Soviet Republic in Kiangsi. The military offensive was accompanied by an economic blockade so thorough that soon the Communists began to feel the pinch. For one thing, the lack of an adequate supply of salt had become so serious that the peasant soldiers were simply too weak physically to continue the fight. Rather than risk total annihilation the Communists left Kiangsi and began the so-called Long March. Breaking through the encirclement with 80,000 men, they walked 6,000 miles until they reached Yenan in northern Shensi in the fall of 1935. When they arrived at their destination, only 20,000 men remained. Meanwhile the Nationalist troops were pressing northward for the final campaign of liquidating the Communist remnants.

It seemed that the Communists, as an organized group, would have ended then, but they were saved by a totally unexpected event, the Sian Incident. When Japan invaded Manchuria in 1931, the Manchurian army, under the leadership of the "Young Marshal" Chang Hsüeh-liang, was ordered by the Nationalist government to withdraw southward to China proper. After the Communists had arrived in northern Shensi, this army was deployed face to face with the Communists in the north. The Communist agents immediately began to work among the officers and soldiers of the Manchurian army, and their line of argument, from the point of view of people who had recently lost their homes in Manchuria, was very convincing indeed. The civil war should cease at once, said the Communists; and all Chinese, regardless of geographical and ideological differences, should form a united front against the Japanese invaders. The deployment of the Manchurian army along the front, the Communists continued, was Chiang's standard way of using one enemy to eliminate another, since the Manchurian army was not trained and commanded by Chiang's personal followers. The Communist strategy worked well; even the "Young Marshal," after a meeting with Chou En-lai, became convinced of the Communists' sincerity. Not only did the two opposing armies cease to fight; they fraternized. Angered by this development, Chiang flew to Sian, the "bandit-extermination headquarters," on December 12, 1936, for a personal inspection. He was seized by the Manchurian army under the "Young Marshal's" order, and his bodyguards were either killed or captured. The mutineers demanded the termination of the civil war and the formation of a united front against Japan. Chiang, however, refused to negotiate with them and ordered them to release him immediately and to accept the consequences of their mutiny. On December 25 not only was he released; he brought his captor, the "Young Marshal," as his prisoner back to Nanking.

What had happened between December 12 and 25? The official explanation was that the "Young Marshal," after conferring with Chiang, was greatly moved by the latter's uprightness and selfless devotion to the state and agreed to release him. On the other hand, there was no question that the Communists had played a decisive role in the final outcome. Why did the Communists want their bitter enemy to be released? Paradoxical as it might seem, the answer is not difficult to find. By insisting on Chiang's release, the Communists acted according to their own best interests. Soon after the news arrived in Nanking that Chiang had been kidnapped, the Nationalist air force began to drop bombs on Sian, and Chiang's best army, then stationed in the Lower Yangtze, began to move northward. If Chiang were killed, there would have been a bloodbath which the Communists would not wish to face as their force, even with the help of the Manchurian army, was much inferior. By insisting on Chiang's release, they hoped to strike a bargain with him which would prolong their own existence. Moreover, despite their personal feelings, it was clear to them that there was no man except Chiang Kai-shek behind whom the nation could rally for a prolonged effort against the Japanese aggression. In the spring of 1937 Chou En-lai held a series of discussions with Chiang and his representatives, as a result of which the second period of cooperation between the Kuomintang and the Communists began. Before the agreement was even completed, Japan struck again. The war with Japan was not to be ended until August, 1945.

JAPANESE INVASIONS

For two decades after the establishment of the Nationalist regime in Nanking, there were three major forces in China's political arena: Japanese militarists, Chinese Nationalists, and Chinese Communists. The triangular conflict between the three groups overshadowed all other events during this period. If Japan were to conquer China, nothing would be more to her advantage than for that country to remain continually weakened and divided. A unified China, better utilizing its vast manpower and natural resources, would be an insurmountable obstacle to the fulfillment of Japan's ambition. In April, 1928, when the Nationalists were marching northward to capture Peking, Japan sent its troops to Shantung and interposed them between the northern militarists and the Nanking forces, ostensibly for the purpose of protecting Japanese residents in that province. A clash ensued which ended with the withdrawal of the Nationalist forces from Tsinan and its occupation by the Japanese. It was not until March, 1929, after a long period of painful negotiation, that Japan agreed to withdraw from Shantung. Meanwhile the almost perennial conflict between the two countries also took a turn for the worse in Manchuria. The "Young Marshal" who succeeded his father as the overlord of Manchuria proved to be more nationalistic than his father had ever been. After he had pledged his allegiance to the Nanking regime in December, 1928, a large number of Kuomintang agents came to Manchuria with his blessing, and these agents, preaching an anti-imperialist gospel, found an attentive audience among the local Chinese who resented the privileged position enjoyed by the Japanese. Japan's privileged position in Manchuria was secured through a series of treaties and agreements between these two countries dating from 1905 to 1915. China, weak as it was, never resigned itself to the *status quo*, as it believed that the existence of Japan's privileges in Manchuria was a violation of its sovereign rights. On the other hand, Japan was anxious to enlarge the existing concessions whenever the opportunity presented itself. After Russia had agreed to relinquish its special privileges in Manchuria (with the exception of the Chinese Eastern Railroad) following the Bolshevik revolution, the primary target of Chinese nationalism in Manchuria was Japan. Neither side would retreat from its established position, and this eventually led to an armed conflict, with Japan, the stronger power, playing a more aggressive role.

One of the many difficulties between the two countries concerned the South Manchuria Railroad (from Changchun to Dairen), the primary agent of Japan's economic interests in Manchuria. It was more than a railroad; it was a vast industrial complex organized to exploit the economic resources of South Manchuria. To safeguard the monopolistic interest of the railroad, Japan obtained from China a promise in 1905 that the Chinese government would not "construct any main line in the neighborhood of and parallel to that railway, or any branch line which might be prejudicial to the interests" of the South Manchuria Railroad. When the "Young Marshal" came to power, he proceeded to carry out an economic development of his own, including the building of railroads in South Manchuria with Chinese capital. This infuriated the Japanese who viewed the Chinese program as a challenge to their dominant position.

The Chinese contended that since Manchuria was their territory, they had every right to develop it the way they thought fit.

Another difficulty between China and Japan had to do with Korean residents in Manchuria. On the Manchurian side of the Yalu River a large number of Korean farmers had settled. As the number of Koreans increased, the Chinese took various measures to restrict Korean immigration, as they feared that the continuous acquisition of land by Koreans would eventually lead to the alienation of that part of the country to Japan, of which Korea was then a part. This fear was intensified when Japan made it clear that under no circumstances would it recognize the naturalization of Koreans as Chinese. Invoking its extraterritorial rights, it declared that it alone had jurisdiction over Koreans in China. Whenever clashes occurred between Chinese and Korean farmers, China and Japan each proceeded to use force to protect its own group. It was one of these clashes that became the immediate cause of what has been known as the Manchurian Incident.

At Wanpaoshan, a small village near Changchun, a dispute occurred in 1931 over the right of some Korean farmers to construct an irrigation ditch across the lands of some Chinese farmers. Both Chinese and Japanese police appeared on the scene, and their appearance resulted in bitter feelings between the Chinese and Korean farmers. The sensational accounts of this seemingly minor incident in the Japanese and Korean press led to anti-Chinese riots in Seoul and Tokyo; the aroused mobs killed and injured several hundred Chinese. The Chinese responded with a vigorous boycott of Japanese goods. While the feelings of both sides ran high, a Japanese military officer named Nakamura was killed by Chinese soldiers in northwestern Manchuria. It was then that the Japanese militarists decided to make a drastic move: to occupy all of Manchuria. Japan could not have chosen a more propitious moment. The world had just entered the worst depression in modern history, and it was unlikely that the major powers would interfere with the implementation of Japan's "grand scheme."

On the night of September 18, 1931, Japanese forces seized Mukden. This was followed by an almost unopposed occupation of all large cities in Manchuria. Towards the end of that year the victorious Japanese army pushed its operation towards the Great Wall and occupied the province of Jehol. The Nationalist government, then busy fighting a domestic war against the Communists, decided not to oppose the Japanese invaders. Such a policy aroused public anger, and students demonstrated in the streets and demanded Chiang Kai-shek's resignation. Chiang resigned in December, 1931, only to regain power shortly afterwards.

Why did the Nationalist government let China's richest territory go without offering military resistance? First, the China of 1931 was certainly in no position to fight against a strong, industrialized Japan. The Chinese hoped that if Japan met with no opposition, it would be satisfied with Manchuria. If China decided to resist, went the argument, large parts of China, especially the coastal areas, would be under Japanese attack or even occupation. Moreover, as far as Chiang was concerned, the Communists (whom he termed a "disease of the heart") were a much worse and more deadly enemy than Japan (which he termed a "disease of the skin"), and he would yield to Japanese demands in order to gain time to eliminate the Communists. However the Japanese militarists, for obvious reasons, would not give him time. Flushed with their easy victory in Manchuria, they attacked Shanghai early in 1932. A warlord's army (the Nineteenth Route Army), which was then stationed at Shanghai and over which Chiang had no direct control, decided to take up the battle against the Japanese. Fighting against great odds, it held the invaders at bay for more than two months. Overnight the soldiers of the Nineteenth Route Army, composed mostly of Cantonese, became national heroes. As the Japanese invasion of Shanghai threatened the commercial interest of foreign powers in that city, they exercised pressure on both sides to negotiate for a truce. They succeeded and the Battle of Shanghai was over. Subsequently, the Nineteenth Route Army withdrew to Fukien where its commanders proclaimed the establishment of an independent republic. Striking with flashing speed, Chiang liquidated their republic before it could get off the ground.

Unable to resist Japanese aggression single handed, China appealed to the League of Nations and the United States for help. The Western powers were sympathetic but decided to do nothing aside from giving verbal and moral support. They were opposed to sanctions of any kind "other than the sanctions of adverse public opinion and official nonrecognition of conquests or settlements achieved by other than peaceful means." The nonrecognition of conquests was later known as the Stimson Doctrine, as it was first enunciated by the American Secretary of State Henry L. Stimson. Later the League incorporated the doctrine in a resolution proposed by Great Britain. It appointed a commission of inquiry to study the dispute between China and Japan with regard to Manchuria. In its report (known as the *Lytton Report,* named after the chairman of the commission, the Earl of Lytton), the commission criticized Japan's military action as unwarranted and proposed ten conditions as indispensable to any satisfactory solution. The last condition was perhaps the most interesting and significant. It said in effect that as long as China was without a strong central government and remained politically unstable, the difficulties with Japan would continue. To put it more bluntly, Japanese aggression would continue as long as China was weak and divided and did not possess the physical strength to resist such aggression. The commission urged "temporary international cooperation in the internal reconstruction of China, as suggested by the late Dr. Sun Yat-sen."

Meanwhile, Japan was consolidating and expanding its military gains. It created a puppet regime called Manchukuo early in 1932, consisting of Manchuria and the Jehol province. The last Manchu emperor Hsüan-t'ung, who had then acquired the unbelievable name of Henry P'u-yi, was "kidnapped" by Japanese agents from Tientsin to serve as the figurehead of the new regime.[1] One year after the establishment of Manchukuo, Japan renewed its military operations. By the spring of 1933 it drove out all Nationalist forces in eastern Hopeh where it succeeded in establishing another puppet regime. In May, 1933, the Nationalists signed the so-called Tangku truce whereby they agreed to withdraw from the Peking-Tientsin area where, under the Boxer Protocol, Japan was entitled to, and did, station troops. By then it was clear that Japan intended to bring all of North China under its control. In 1935 it proceeded to create a North China autonomous region, embracing five provinces: Chahar, Suiyuan, Shansi, Hopeh, and Shantung. It was on the verge of succeeding when China decided not to retreat any more. In Lukouchiao (Marco Polo Bridge), south of Peking, fighting broke out between Chinese and Japanese troops on the night of July 7, 1937. In August, Japan attacked Shanghai, and a full-scale war began.

Why did China finally decide to fight? The answer has to be found in the domestic situation. When Japan invaded and then occupied Manchuria, Chinese patriotism was aroused, and as Japan continued to advance in North China, the nationalistic fervor steadily built to a climax. That China could not militarily cope with Japan was brushed aside as unpatriotic thinking, and in a wishful mood, swords were glorified as more effective weapons than tanks. Students went repeatedly to the streets, calling for resistance against Japan, and they caused such an uproar that at one time they even forced Chiang Kai-shek to resign. The boycott of Japanese goods was vigorously pursued; sad to say, it had no noticeable effect on either the policy or the military strength of the Japanese government. Newspapers and magazines that were not controlled by the Nationalist government continued to agitate for a war of resistance regardless of consequences. "If China as a nation has to be terminated, let it be terminated by a war rather than continuous retreat." The fires of patriotism were fanned by the Communists who called for the cessation of the civil war and the formation of a united front against the Japanese. As Japan

[1] P'u-yi was captured by the Russians towards the end of World War II and was subsequently repatriated to Communist China. "What is he doing now?" asked a Western correspondent in 1962. "He is having a happy life in the People's Republic," replied a high-ranking Communist Chinese official. "What does he do for recreation?" "He loves gardening." P'u-yi died in 1967 at the age of sixty-one.

continued to advance in North China, their appeal became more convincing to a large section of the Chinese.

While the nation was clamoring for a war of resistance, Chiang Kai-shek was immobile. Yet, in view of the position he held, he was the only man who could lead the nation in war. There was no question that he resented Japanese aggression as other Chinese did, but he hated the Communists more. He had to liquidate the Communists first before he could think seriously about an all-out war against Japan. "Until all hopes are exhausted, we shall not forsake peace," he announced; "until the last moment arrives we shall not talk casually about sacrifices." Meanwhile, some of the leaders who had talked too loudly about sacrifices were sent to jail. How long could he withstand public pressure? This question was answered for the nation by the Sian Incident. When a rapprochement was reached between the Kuomintang and the Communists, the Nationalist government agreed to go to war if Japan pushed further for territorial gains. Ten days after the Lukouchiao Incident, Chiang announced that the "last moment" had arrived. "Once we go to war to save the nation," he continued, "there is no alternative to victory." "We will fight to the bitter end, whatever the sacrifices. If we compromise with our enemy in the course of the war, we compromise our very existence. What Japan has done to us cannot be tolerated by any nation with self-respect." Throughout the war, time and again Japan proposed peace negotiations. True to his words, Chiang turned them down without the slightest hesitation.

THE UNDECLARED WAR

The undeclared war that began in the summer of 1937 was referred to by Japan as the "China Incident"; but to the Chinese it was a life-and-death struggle. It was, to use an ancient Chinese metaphor, like an egg trying to make a stand against a rolling rock; and the Japanese rock, rolling on and on, captured the two major cities in North China, Tientsin (Map 5) and Peking, shortly after the hostilities began. When Japan attacked Shanghai in August, Chiang Kai-shek threw his best troops into the battle. Overnight there was such national unity as had never been seen before in modern history. Even the warlords sent their representatives to Nanking, offering their services in the hour of common peril. They were requested to dispatch troops to the front and they responded without hesitation. Their response was selfless indeed, in view of the fact that once a warlord lost his army he ended his career as a warlord. Most of the warlords' soldiers left their home provinces for the first time, determined to exchange their lives for those of the invaders. Some gave a good account of themselves; most of them, however, served no better purpose than to consume Japanese bullets, as they were equipped with nothing better then knives, swords, and a variety of odd weapons. These soldiers and their commanders who had never done anything more bellicose than bullying peasants and fighting the most polite of battles panicked when they saw Japanese tanks rolling towards them. Ironically, as they were destroyed *en masse*, the warlordism which had plagued China since the beginning of the republic thereby faded out of the Chinese scene. What the central government had not been able to achieve was accomplished by the warlords' own selfless patriotism.

In Shanghai where the Nationalist government's crack troops were committed, the Chinese performance surprised even the foreigners who watched the battle from the French and the International Settlements whose neutrality the belligerents respected. The day after hostilities began in that city carrier-based Japanese aeroplanes were sent out to destroy the nascent Chinese air force, and some of the aeroplanes, painted with Chinese emblems, destroyed many Chinese aircraft that failed to take off in time.[1] During the initial stage of the war, the Chinese air force did well in the air as long as planes and pilots lasted. Eventually the overwhelming numerical superiority of the Japanese prevailed, and Japan obtained complete control of the air. On the ground it was the same story. Chinese forces fought well for almost three months in Shanghai until they were flanked by the invaders who had landed near Hangchow. They retreated hastily to Nanking which was quickly surrounded by the Japanese. The fall of that city was followed by what has been called the rape of Nanking. For a whole week's period, the victorious Japanese plagued the city with plunder, rape, and mass murder. Thousands of civilians were slaughtered in cold blood, in addition to countless numbers of surrendered soldiers.[2]

After the capture of Nanking Japan waited for China to sue for

[1] In the afternoon of August 14, 1937, the author was playing with other boys in the family backyard when he saw two single-engined planes fly over the house roof. The planes flew so low that the Chinese emblems on the planes were clearly visible. The boys jumped and waved. A few minutes later bombs were dropped on the nearby airport, and the city was in a panic. The magistrate ordered the evacuation of all residents to the countryside, as he was afraid that the Japanese planes would come back to bombard the city. The Japanese planes, however, did not come back that evening. They waited until the Japanese had captured Shanghai. Then they destroyed the city (Kwangteh, Anhwei Province) with incendiary bombs.

[2] How far man can degenerate during the time of war may well be illustrated by the following incident. After the capture of Nanking two Japanese soldiers entered a murder contest, each claiming that he could kill more in a given day than the other. In the morning they went for a killing spree and met again in the evening to compare statistics, each claiming more than a hundred murdered men, women, and children to his credit. As their "heroic deeds" were also described in detail in the Japanese press, the Chinese government, after the end of the war, insisted on the return of the two "heroes" to be tried as war criminals. The two Japanese said that they had done this only to impress their girl friends at home. On their way to the execution ground they shouted repeatedly: "Long live the friendship between China and Japan!"

peace, but Chiang Kai-shek refused to oblige. The China of 1937 was completely different from that of the nineteenth century when the capture of a few key cities by a foreign power would usually bring about China's surrender. More than three decades of nationalistic indoctrination had thoroughly changed the mental outlook of every Chinese, and no political leader within the Nationalist government dared to speak openly for a negotiated peace, whatever his private opinion. Instead, he spoke bravely of the scorching of every inch of earth before the advancing invaders and of China's ultimate victory, however remote it might be. Facing a stubborn Chiang, Japan announced early in 1938 that it would no longer deal with him. In the fall of that year Japan renewed its offensive. Canton fell on October 21, and Hankow, the provisional capital after the fall of Nanking, was captured by the invaders on October 25. Still refusing to surrender, Chiang moved his capital to Chungking. The frustrated Japanese, who had wished to put a quick end to the "China Incident" so that they could concentrate their efforts on their prospective, more formidable enemies such as the Soviet Union and the United States, decided to create their own Chinese leaders to deal with. They created two puppet regimes, one for North China with its capital at Peking and one for the Yangtze region with its capital at Nanking. Yet they were unable to persuade any prominent Chinese, not even the old warlord Wu P'ei-fu, to head the two puppet governments. Their fortunes in this respect took a turn for the better in December, 1938, when Wang Ching-wei, a high-ranking Nationalist official, deserted his own government at Chungking to collaborate with the enemy. Wang, a long time disciple of Sun Yat-sen, made the important move on the ground that continuous resistance against Japan was hopeless and suicidal and that by cooperating with Japan he might be able to mitigate the harsh Japanese rule in the occupied areas. He did not know then that World War II would break out in Europe in a few months. Nor had he any idea that he would be treated as merely another puppet once he was installed as "President of China." Within the occupied territories the Japanese organized development companies to explore and exploit China's natural resources. The Chinese refused to cooperate in this endeavor and used such negative methods as work stoppage and sabotage to defeat practically every Japanese move. Thus, despite great efforts, the utilization of Chinese resources to meet Japan's military and financial needs was largely unsuccessful.

By the end of 1939, two years after the outbreak of hostilities, Japan had conquered the northeastern one-third of the country, the most populous and productive region in China. By then Japan had overextended itself and its forces were spread too thin. The battle line remained substantially the same until towards the end of the war when Japan made the final attempt to force China to surrender by penetrating deep into Kwangsi and Kweichow. After the outbreak of World War II in Septem-

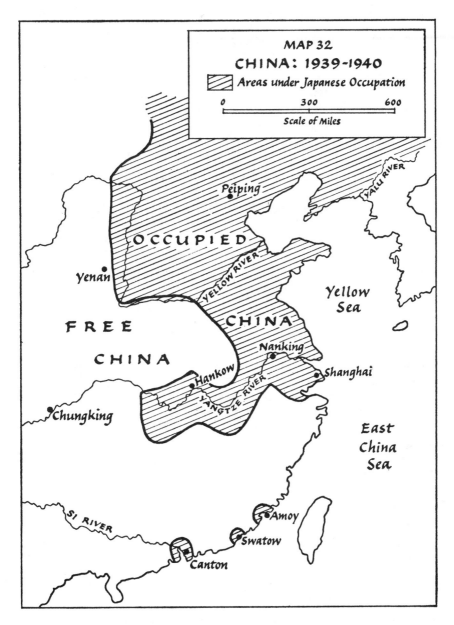

MAP 32
CHINA: 1939-1940

Areas under Japanese Occupation

| 0 | 300 | 600 |

Scale of Miles

ber, 1939, Japan had other enemies to think about, and the "China Incident" became more and more a liability. As for China, it was nearly exhausted. It could not launch a massive offensive on its own, though by its very existence it was able to tie down a large number of Japanese troops on Chinese soil. A stalemate was thus reached, without the prospect of a decisive victory for either side. Meanwhile Japan, with complete control of the air, continued to send planes to bomb Chungking, a terror technique designed to force Chiang out of the war. Chungking, China's wartime capital, is a mountainous city on the upper Yangtze. During the war the Chinese dug into the mountains and constructed numerous connecting tunnels as air shelters. When the sun rose, the air raid alarm sounded and everyone entered the tunnels, only to emerge after the sunset when the Japanese planes had gone. One summer day, while enemy aeroplanes were still overhead, people were pushing one another towards the tunnel gates which were locked and guarded by soldiers. The soldiers, under the orders of their commander, refused to open the gates until the air was clear of enemy planes. When they finally opened the gates, they saw nothing except dead or half-dead bodies in the tunnels. Anywhere between 5,000 and 10,000 persons were reported to have suffocated to death on this occasion.

As the best troops of the Szechuan warlords had been sent to the front at the beginning of the war and were destroyed by the Japanese, the Nationalist government was able to move to that province without encountering much opposition. Szechuan, in fact, was the economic as well as the political center of unoccupied China. Before the fall of such industrial cities as Shanghai and Hankow, the Chinese had managed to move some of their industrial plants to the interior where they were reassembled for renewed production. They were carried by river boats and by animal and human strength, since there was not a single operative railroad within the unoccupied areas. These plants enabled the Chinese to continue the manufacturing of small arms and daily necessities such as soap and matches. The greatest difficulty was of course the supply of trucks and gasoline because the Chinese did not produce the former and had only a limited supply of the latter. Transportation was a serious problem, and every old motor vehicle was patched up again and again to keep it moving. Many trucks were converted into alcohol and charcoal powered vehicles; they did not move as fast as they should, but they moved.

As the Nationalist government moved to the interior, so did China's better universities. The Peking University was merged with two sister universities of North China and, renamed the Southwestern University, found its new home at Kunming. The National Central University was moved from Nanking to Chungking, and the National Chekiang University, after a long and eventful journey, finally settled down at Tsungyi in Kweichow, hundreds of miles away from its original home in Hangchow. Two students from these three universities, then operating under the most difficult circumstances, eventually became China's first Nobel Prize winners. Thanks to the richness of the Szechuan soil, there was no starvation on a mass scale, as had often been the case in North China. However, there was a great shortage of industrial products.

For interior China, the war was not without its compensating factors. The arrival of new industries from the coastal areas gave this region a new orientation in economic life; it was hoped that a more balanced economy could be achieved even after the coastal Chinese returned home at the end of the war. Culturally, the interior region had been less advanced than the coastal areas. The arrival of eastern universities such as those mentioned above slowly raised the educational standard of the area, and parents did not have to send their children afar to receive the best kind of education then available. As the institutions of higher learning improved, they eventually benefited secondary and primary schools, since better teachers became available. Socially, the impact was even greater. The war had increased geographical mobility and brought together people of different regions. Provincialism which had always been strong in China was now greatly reduced, and people were more inclined to think of themselves as Chinese rather than as Cantonese or Szechuanese. Though friction did occasionally occur between the interior and coastal Chinese, it never reached serious proportions. In fact there was a harmony far beyond any previous expectations. Warlordism was by and large eliminated, and the Nationalist regime was perhaps the most enlightened the interior Chinese had seen for a long time. For example, opium addiction which had been common before the war was now vigorously suppressed. New hospitals, public or private, were established to attend to the needs of the addicts, though the supply of drugs and medicine was a serious problem. Opium traders, once they were caught, could expect long imprisonment or capital punishment.

Before December, 1941, the Chinese hope for an ultimate victory was not more than an unshakable faith; it bore no relation to a realistic appraisal of the existing domestic and international situation. China had been pushed towards the poor, interior regions; economically and militarily, it had a difficult time maintaining itself, let alone launch an offensive to recover the lost territories. To be sure, China received some outside help, first from the Soviet Union and then from the United States. The American help consisted of lend-lease aid, technical advisers, and the famed Flying Tigers, an American volunteer air force formed by Claire Chennault to challenge the Japanese domination of the air. This help prevented a bad situation from deteriorating faster; it deteriorated nevertheless. When the United States entered the war against Japan after Pearl Harbor and officially became China's ally, the international situation, if not the domestic one, completely changed. For one thing, China then no longer fought alone. Though there was no immediate relief, there was a real hope for the future for the first time since the war began. Despite the initial setbacks which the United States and Great Britain suffered in the Western Pacific, there was no question in the Chinese mind that the allies would win because, for one thing, the alternative was simply unthinkable.

Whatever doubt they might have had before about ultimate victory, they did not have it any more.

After Pearl Harbor American aid, in the form of military and financial assistance, became much more substantial. Believing that Chinese soldiers, properly trained and equipped, could make a great contribution to the defeat of Japan, President Franklin D. Roosevelt ordered the delivery of military equipment to China and a training program for Chinese soldiers. A financial grant of $500,000,000 was a great help in stabilizing the Chinese currency at a time when a runaway inflation, rather than any Japanese offensive, had become the major concern. The man sent by the President to implement American policy was General Joseph Stilwell who arrived in China early in 1942. His major objective was to hold Burma so as to keep open the Burma Road over which, it was hoped, American supplies would be transported to Chungking. Burma fell to Japan despite his efforts, and American supplies then had to be flown over "the Hump" (the Himalayas) from India. The amount of military equipment thus supplied could not be large, and to make the situation worse, the overall strategy as decided in Washington and London was "Europe first, the Pacific Ocean area second, and the China-Burma-India theatre last in terms of priorities."

The Sino-American cooperation was not without its difficulties. Soon after Stilwell's arrival, disagreement developed between him and Chiang Kai-shek. This disagreement involved not only a conflict in personalities but also a basic difference in policy. Stilwell, a soldier who placed victory against Japan above anything else, insisted on the arming of all anti-Japanese elements in China, including the Communists. Chiang, more a statesman than a soldier, saw easily the serious consequence to his Nationalist government if the Chinese Communists were armed with American weapons. Though the Kuomintang and the Communists were officially allies, tensions between them had been slowly building up by 1942. Eventually Chiang insisted on Stilwell's dismissal, and in October, 1944, Roosevelt agreed and appointed a more diplomatic general, Albert Wedemeyer, as his successor. Chiang and the new American general got along beautifully. The Ledo Road (later renamed as Stilwell Road) was then constructed, linking Assam (India) and the upper Burma Road in Yunnan. A large quantity of American equipment came in; as a result China was able to create new armed divisions with modern weapons. Before they could be committed to the battlefield against the Japanese, the atomic bombs were dropped, and the war was over. Later, these divisions were used against the Chinese Communists when the civil war broke out again.

Chinese victories were much more impressive on the diplomatic front than they were on the battlefield. In January, 1943, the United States and Great Britain concluded treaties with China providing for the immediate relinquishment of extraterritorial rights and the settlement of related matters. This meant that the Chinese courts, for the first time in one hundred years, had jurisdiction over British and American citizens in China; it also meant that the powers concerned could no longer maintain troops on Chinese soil without Chinese consent and that the remaining concessions would be returned to China. The last remnants of the unequal treaties were thus eliminated. Later in the same year, urged by President Roosevelt, Congress passed a law which permitted a small number of Chinese—105, to be exact—to migrate to the United States as immigrants each year. For the first time since 1882 (Chinese Exclusion Law) a Chinese could be naturalized as an American citizen. China's greatest diplomatic victory, however, was scored at Cairo, where Roosevelt, Winston Churchill, and Chiang Kai-shek met in November, 1943, to discuss policy matters concerning Japan. The policy statement, known as the Cairo Declaration, pledged the allies to continue the war until Japan accepted "unconditional surrender." Manchuria, Taiwan, and the Pescadores would be returned to China, and Korea would become free and independent "in due course." When the news of the agreement reached Chungking, never had there been a foreigner so popular as Franklin D. Roosevelt. And as far as Chiang Kai-shek was concerned, his popularity and prestige reached a new height.

The enthusiasm, however, proved to be somewhat premature. In February, 1945, Roosevelt, Churchill, and Stalin met at Yalta to discuss the final phase of the war with regard to Germany and Japan. In exchange for the Soviet Union's promise to enter the war against Japan "two or three months after Germany had surrendered," the two Western statesmen promised Stalin the following concessions: (1) Outer Mongolia over which China claimed jurisdiction would become independent; (2) Dairen would be internationalized and Port Arthur would be leased to the U.S.S.R. as a naval base; and (3) the Chinese Eastern Railroad and the South Manchuria Railroad would be jointly operated by China and the Soviet Union and "the preeminent interests of the Soviet Union shall be safeguarded." In other words, Manchuria was to become a Soviet sphere of influence, though "China shall retain full sovereignty" in that area. The special privileges which Lenin had condemned and renounced in 1919 were returned to his successor Stalin with extra bonus. Since the Yalta Agreement was reached without Chinese knowledge, "the President [Roosevelt] will take measures in order to obtain this concurrence [from Chiang Kai-shek] on advice from Marshal Stalin." Chiang was not informed of the contents of this agreement until months later; when the Chinese people learned of them after the war, there was strong resentment. However, as long as China depended upon the United States for military and diplomatic support, there was nothing it could do with regard to the agreement made by the Big Three. In July, 1945, Chiang sent his brother-in-law T. V. Soong to Moscow to negotiate a treaty with the Soviet Union. The treaty called for China's recognition of the independence of Outer Mongolia "if a plebiscite indicates that result" and the implementation of other Yalta terms. In return the Russians promised assistance and support for the Nationalist government as headed by Chiang Kai-shek.

Following the dropping of the first atomic bomb on Hiroshima on August 6, the Soviet army marched into Manchuria. The Japanese army offered little resistance, and the invaders soon took over Manchuria. After Japan surrendered on August 12, the Russians were in a good position to help their comrades, the Chinese Communists.

COMMUNIST ASCENDENCY

After the war broke out in July, 1937, the Communist army was renamed the Eighth Route Army and fought side by side with the Nationalists against the Japanese invaders. Since they had no heavy equipment, their contribution to the war efforts was confined largely to guerrilla activities. The aggressiveness of a common enemy had temporarily forced the two old rivals (Nationalists and Communists) to cooperate; but, as the war reached a stalemate towards the end of 1939, the old enmity returned and tensions began to develop. From hindsight it seems that their cooperation had never been intended to be more than a temporary arrangement; distrust and hatred of long standing could not be wiped out simply by a joint declaration of good will. Early in 1941 the tensions which had been slowly building up flashed into the first open conflict as Nationalist troops attacked and partly wiped out the Communist New Fourth Army, a guerrilla force then operating in the Lower Yangtze. This turned out to be only the beginning of a long struggle to come. When the United States entered the war after Pearl Harbor, both sides acted as if the war against Japan had already been won, and they began to think in terms of a postwar struggle between themselves. From the Nationalist point of view the areas controlled by the Communists should be contained and if possible reduced. The Communists, on the other hand, were anxious to bring as many areas under their domination as possible, so that they would be in a better position to challenge the Nationalist authority when Japan was out of the picture. Both sides were more concerned with their struggle against each other than their common war against Japan, and they deployed their forces accordingly. When General Stilwell suggested the arming of the Communists with American weapons, the reaction of Chiang Kai-shek was predictable.

Knowing what lay ahead, Mao Tse-tung planned his strategy accordingly. He was reported to have ordered his comrades to devote 70 percent of their energy to Communist expansion and 20 percent to "coping with" the Kuomintang, leaving 10 percent to be used against Japan. He might not have used exactly the same words, but the policy he followed during the war coincided well with what he had allegedly said. The Japanese invaders could at best control large cities, strategic points, and main lines of communication and transportation after they had driven out the Nationalists. For one thing, they simply did not have enough forces to cover every town and village. The puppet Chinese force they created was anything but reliable; the presence of the Japanese and their Chinese collaborators in the countryside was bitterly resented by the villagers. This situation offered the Communists a unique opportunity. They infiltrated the Japanese lines in small groups and went to the villages to organize. They called for a united effort against Japan and brought under their banner people from all walks of life, including former Kuomintang officials. Since they had abandoned their extreme methods such as land confiscation, even conservative landlords chose to cooperate with them. Their basic support came of course from the peasants who constituted the overwhelming majority of the people in the rural areas. To win their support, the Communists lowered rent and interest rates and encouraged the organization of cooperatives and the establishment of schools. They even allowed peasants to choose their own administrative officials on the village level, while reserving for themselves the power of control. Their efforts did not go unrewarded; to the villagers, including many landlords, the Communists were patriotic Chinese who desired nothing for themselves except the nation's survival. As they continued their efforts, large areas within the occupied territory were brought under their control. The Japanese held the big cities, but the Communists dominated the countryside. However, when the Communists attempted to extend their organizational work to areas nominally within the Nationalist control, the Nationalists struck back, as they had done in the case of the New Fourth Army early in 1941.

The physical struggle between the two parties on the wide expanse of China was accompanied by an ideological battle of sorts. Mao Tse-tung and Chiang Kai-shek spoke out from their respective capitals, Yenan and Chungking, about the kind of society they wished to create for the Chinese people. Mao, in a major speech made early in 1940, outlined the New Democracy which he said was an integration of the truths of Marxism and China's nationalist characteristics. There was no place for doctrinaire Marxists in China, he declared. In economic matters he pledged his support to Sun Yat-sen's principle of people's livelihood. Big banks and big industrial and commercial enterprises should be owned by the government. However, the government should not take over other capitalist production that "cannot dominate the livelihood of the people." It would "adopt certain necessary measures to confiscate the land of landlords and distribute it to those peasants having no land or only a little land, abolish the feudal relations in the rural areas, and turn the land into the private property of the peasants." In other words, there would be no compromise with the landlords.

Who, then, should wield political power in the New Democracy? Mao divided the existing governments in the world into three groups: (1) "republics under bourgeoisie dictatorship" such as most of the Western countries, (2) "republics under the dictatorship of the proletariat" such as the Soviet Union, and (3) "republics under the joint dictatorship of several revolutionary classes." China, said he, belonged to the third category, where the power of the government should be vested in the proletariat, the peasantry, the intelligentsia, and other sections of the petty bourgeoisie. Lest anyone forget that he was a Communist, he added that the "several revolutionary classes" should be led by the proletariat, even though from the vantage point on top of his Yenan cave there was not a single proletarian in sight. The kind of government described in the third category, he continued, was not only correct for China; it was "the transitional form of state to be adopted by revolutionaries in colonial and semicolonial countries." "So long as there are revolutions in colonies or semicolonies, the state and political form will of necessity be basically the same in nature, i.e., a new democratic state under the joint dictatorship of several anti-imperialist classes." The New Democracy, however, was the party's present or minimum program. The ultimate objective was the creation of a socialist or Communist state. Mao did not say when it would be the most propitious time to implement socialism or communism. For the time being, he was most interested in making his program moderate enough to attract the support of the largest possible number of people.

In 1943 Chiang Kai-shek published two books in succession, *China's Destiny* and *Chinese Economic Ideology*. Like Mao, he blamed imperialism and the unequal treaties for China's past ills and pledged the implementation of Sun Yat-sen's three principles of the people. Whereas Mao regarded such implementation as appropriate only during what he called the transitional period, Chiang considered it the final fulfillment of China's political and economic goals. The theoretical basis of the new society was not such alien ideologies as Marxism or *laissez-faire;* it was such ancient virtues as loyalty and filial piety. Marxism with its theory of class struggle had no place in China which had always been a society of cooperation and mutual help, and to preach class struggle was to artificially create class hatred which had never existed. On the other hand, Chiang had no use for such Western virtues as individualism, because in his opinion, they were motivated by man's selfishness and could not be properly called virtues. Private enterprises were allowed, but they should be carefully controlled so as to protect the people from the evil of economic exploitation. Politically, the new society should practice democratic centralism. Power was to be created by a democratic process, but once created, it should command the obedience and respect of the people as a whole. Only when the government was "able," said Chiang, could it successfully carry out Sun Yat-sen's three principles of the people.

Ideologies notwithstanding, the outcome of the struggle between the Nationalists and the Communists was to be decided in a contest of physical strength. At the end of World War II, the Communists controlled large areas inside the former Japanese-occupied territory and within marching distance of some of the large eastern cities, whereas the main strength of the Nationalist army was far away in the interior. The Allied Command ordered Japanese troops not to surrender to any Chinese groups except those authorized by Chiang Kai-shek. When the Communists attempted to seize some of the major cities, the Japanese repulsed them. Thanks to American help, the American equipped Nationalist Chinese divisions were airlifted to these cities, disarmed the Japanese, and took over control. The Communists protested, but there was not much they could do.

In Manchuria, however, the situation was somewhat different. The Russians, who had been scheduled to withdraw from Manchuria "three months after the defeat of Japan," decided to stay longer. They used this valuable time to strip Manchuria of industrial equipment to be shipped to Russia as "war booty" and also to provide a protective wing for the activities of their Chinese comrades. They turned over the surrendered Japanese arms to the Chinese Communists who thereby for the first time were equipped with modern weapons, including tanks and heavy artillery pieces. By doing this the Russians violated the Sino-Soviet treaty of 1945 as well as the Yalta Agreement which specified that they should not assist any Chinese group other than the Nationalist government. With such assistance the Chinese Communists were eventually able to drive the Nationalists from Manchuria.

China's internal development during and immediately after World War II was a great disappointment to the United States which had been hoping for the emergence of a "friendly, unified China as a stabilizing influence in the Far East." Largely through Roosevelt's insistence and efforts China was elevated to be one of the "Big Five" and later became a permanent member of the Security Council of the United Nations. As the prospect of civil war loomed larger, the United States government instructed its Ambassador to China, Patrick J. Hurley, to play an active role in bringing the Nationalists and the Communists together. As a result of his efforts Mao Tse-tung arrived at Chungking on August 28, 1945, to confer with Chiang Kai-shek for a peaceful settlement of their differences. Mao's six-week stay in Chungking did not bring about any constructive results, as the two sides were far apart in their views about the methods to

MAO TSE-TUNG (LEFT) AND CHIANG KAI-SHEK DRINKING A TOAST   This picture was taken in the fall of 1945 after Mao Tse-tung had arrived in Chungking to talk with Chiang Kai-shek on the terms to organize a coalition government. During his stay in the Nationalist wartime capital Mao's personal safety was said to have been guaranteed by the American government. The negotiations between the two Chinese leaders came to nought. Four years later, the Communists overran mainland China and drove Chiang Kai-shek to his island stronghold, Taiwan.

be used in unifying China. For one thing, the Nationalists insisted on the complete integration of the Communist army with the Nationalist force, a condition which the Communists would not accept. Later, when they agreed to the existence of a separate Communist army, there was no agreement as to how large such an army should be. The Nationalists would not agree to more than twenty divisions, and the Communists would not be satisfied with less than forty-three. As a result, they were hopelessly deadlocked. The nature of their disagreement would mean that even if a coalition government had been formed, it would not have been a national government in the true sense of that term, because no government could function "nationally" as long as there was a separate military force operating within its territory over which it had no control.

In December, 1945, the United States proposed the convocation of a national conference to end the civil war, while pledging continuous assistance to the Nationalist government as the only legal government of China. Early in 1946 President Harry S. Truman sent General of the Army George C. Marshall as his special ambassador to China with special instruction to effect a compromise between the Nationalists and the Communists which, it was hoped, would eventually lead to the establishment of a democratic coalition government. Marshall's efforts came to nought and he returned to the United States early in the following year. Before his departure, he blamed the recalcitrance of both parties for the failure and regarded the assumption of leadership by the liberals as the only hope for the future. The liberals, consisting mostly of intellectuals who had received their education in Europe and America, had their own organization, called the Democratic League. They had good intentions and constructive ideas, but they lacked one thing most essential in Chinese politics: an independent army. Nevertheless, they played an important part in the political consultative conference which came into session early in 1946. The conference, called to "broaden the democratic basis of the Nationalist government," eventually broke down as the Nationalists and the Communists could not agree to the composition of the state council, the policy-making organ in the proposed coalition government. When the political consultative conference was finally dissolved, the members of the Democratic League were forced to choose sides. As one might expect, the leftists switched their loyalty to the Communists, and the rightists to the Nationalists. With the departure of Marshall and the dissolution of the political consultative conference the civil war was renewed in earnest.

What followed is a familiar story. At the beginning of the renewed civil war, Mao Tse-tung warned his followers that there was a long struggle ahead. He predicted that it would take five years before they could match the Nationalists in military strength and that they would triumph at the end of ten years. In all likelihood, his quick victories on the battlefield amazed even himself. Manchuria fell to the Communists in the fall of 1948, and this was followed by the conquest of North China. Sometimes entire divisions switched to the Communist side and carried with them their American weapons. One of the best Kuomintang armies of some 300,000 strong which had been pampered for more than ten years just for this occasion evaporated with hardly a fight. As the Communists marched southward and threatened Nanking, the Nationalists decided to make a strong stand at Hsuchow (northern Kiangsu) where one of the most decisive battles was fought. There was heroism on both sides, but the Nationalist troops went to defeat when the flanking Communists cut off their logistical support. After this battle Chiang resigned from the presidency and his successor Li Tsung-jen proceeded to negotiate peace with the Communists. The Communists demanded virtually unconditional sur-

A GATE STRUCTURE LEADING TO THE INNER CITY OF PEKING   The Chinese characters in the background read: "Eliminate anarchy to reconstruct the country; exterminate bandits (Communists) to save the people." The city was then under the Nationalists' control. In the foreground is the ornate *p'ai-lou,* or arch.

render and the punishment of "war criminals" headed by Chiang Kai-shek. As there was no common basis for a negotiated peace, the Communist offensive was resumed in April, 1949. The capture of Nanking was followed by the surrender of Shanghai one month later. By the end of that year all of China proper was brought under Communist control. Meanwhile, Mao Tse-tung and his colleagues proclaimed the establishment of a People's Republic on October 1, 1949.

THE DEFEAT OF THE NATIONALISTS

The causes of the Nationalists' defeat were many-fold, and we can easily overemphasize one at the expense of others which were perhaps equally valid. Just as in many other wars, the weaknesses of the vanquished combined with the strength of the victor to bring about the final outcome. Moreover, there were factors working to the advantage or disadvantage of one side or the other that were beyond the control of either. The Japanese invasions, for instance, helped the Communist cause immensely, even though they were never meant that way by the Japanese. In the final analysis, however, the blame has to be placed upon the Nationalists themselves. At the end of World War II they were far superior to the Communists militarily. It is clear that the subsequent change of political fortunes was due to factors other than the military, and that these factors were advantageous to the Communists.

Politically, prior to 1948 when a constitution went into effect, the Nationalist regime operated under the theory of political tutelage. The power of governing was vested in the Kuomintang, and all important government officials were appointed by and responsible to the party. In view of the Chinese circumstances (the lack of a democratic tradition, for instance) a great deal could be said for this theory, and it could have worked had the Kuomintang remained the dynamic, revolutionary party conceived by Sun Yat-sen. No political party is better than its members, and the members, being human, are subject to human frailties. Once power was secured, the Kuomintang leaders were more interested in the power itself and what it could bring to them than in the social and economic programs which they had pledged themselves to carry out. Had there been popular elections threatening to oust them or an opposition party to serve as a watchdog, this abuse could have been reduced if not prevented, but the theory of political tutelage under which the Nationalist government operated ruled out either of these two possibilities. Party leaders became the power elite, and not subject to popular control, gradually they lost touch with the masses and became isolated from them. As the party leaders were essentially the same people from 1927 to 1949, so, by and large, were the government officials who formulated and carried out policies. A change of cabinet meant no more than a reshuffling of a few "infallible" men, and public offices were granted as a reward for loyalty to party leadership rather than party programs. Among the best qualifications that many of these high-ranking officials possessed was that they were once members of the Alliance and had heard an excellent speech made by Sun Yat-sen. To be sure, not all of them were bad men. Yet by occupying these high positions without either the inclination or the ability to accomplish something worthwhile, they frustrated the ambitions of younger aspirants to leadership, and in that sense they were harmful to their own party.

A political organization such as this inevitably encouraged the maintenance of the *status quo* and discouraged social and economic reforms. A man in power would naturally abstain from doing anything that might jeopardize his own position. To assure his security in power, he measured the worth of his subordinates not in accordance with their ability or performance but upon the evidence of their loyalty to him. It was not an ordinary kind of loyalty: it was the sort of blind, absolute obedience such as that once given to the ancient emperors. By insisting on such a condition for employment or promotion, the Kuomintang leaders isolated themselves from the country's most talented people who naturally had independent opinions of their own. Moreover, a man of strong moral fibre would not humiliate himself by being so slavish. As personal loyalty was generally emphasized, there was a proliferation of political cliques within the Kuomintang; each clique was built around one or two party leaders who evaluated and rewarded men in accordance with their loyalty towards them. Above these cliques was Chiang Kai-shek who was "the greatest, the wisest, and the most virtuous." Personal loyalty was of course not a bad thing in itself as long as the followers had other qualifications as well. Only when it became the only virtue overshadowing all others was it an abuse. A man could be corrupt and incompetent, but he could still hold his office as long as his loyalty to his superior was not in doubt.

Thus overemphasized, the expression of loyalty often degenerated into a shameless contest of adulation and flattery. Many clever but unscrupulous men literally flattered their way to some of the highest positions in the land. In this respect we cannot give a better example than by citing the career of a man named Chang Chih-chung. An ex-policeman who used to direct traffic at Hankow, Chang had no great talent or ability as far as we know. Yet in a short time he rose to become a general of the army, a governor, and a member of the Central Executive Committee of the Kuomintang. During the Japanese war he was given a military command to defend Changsha. He set fire to the city and fled as fast as he could even though there was not a ghost of the enemy nearby. Despite vigorous protests from the Hunanese who had seen their beloved capital reduced to ashes, he was not brought to trial; instead, he rose to even higher and more responsible positions. Why was he not punished? Because, said his apologists, his loyalty to the Leader was invaluable. In 1949 when he was sent by the Nationalist government to negotiate a truce with the Communists, he quickly switched sides and proclaimed that Mao Tse-tung, after all, was the true savior of China. Chang, unfortunately, was not an isolated case; there were thousands of his type within the Nationalist government.

In rural areas the Kuomintang members were inevitably the "recognized leaders of each community," namely, the gentry. The party did not attempt to attract membership from among the peasants and it did not have peasant members. To the peasants the local Kuomintang headquarters was just another government they had to support, if they noticed its existence at all. The new gentry in the countryside was different from the scholar-gentry of the old type whose members, because of their Confucian training, had a strong sense of obligation towards the less fortunate peasants. Since Confucian virtues had become "old-fashioned," the members of the new gentry enjoyed power and used that power for their own advantage without feeling an "old-fashioned" obligation. They could then exploit the hapless peasants with a clear conscience since they may also have gone to Western schools and heard of such ideas as *laissez-faire*. Whatever laws the central government might have enacted to improve the lot of peasants (such as the land law of 1930), those laws could not be carried out without the cooperation of the gentry class. Since their implementation worked to the disadvantage of this class, it is not difficult to understand the hostile attitude of this class towards these laws. The gentry obstructed, stalled, and used every means available to see to it that these laws were not strictly enforced. Usually the gentry members succeeded.

The accumulated evil of a bureaucratic rule became all too evident at the end of the Japanese war. Thousands of Kuomintang officials took the first aeroplanes to the formerly occupied areas to perform the function of *chieh-shou* (literally, take and receive) which in numerous cases was a legalized robbery of the people in the occupied areas. The situation was most serious in Taiwan where it eventually provoked an open revolt. These carpetbaggers who had been regarded as liberators from Japanese oppression behaved like conquerors and damaged the reputation of the Nationalist regime beyond repair.

In the countryside the landlords who had been driven out by the Japanese came home to reclaim their land which was now tilled by those left behind. By accusing those who had been left behind as collaborators, these landlords not only regained their lost land but often enlarged it too, as they could easily force the "collaborators" to sell out at a nominal price. The once tranquil countryside became a battleground of land grabbing, setting relatives against relatives and friends against friends. Whoever won, the peasants could not see any difference. Much land had been laid waste during the war, and without proper care land productivity had been greatly reduced. Yet the landlords, old or new, demanded the payment of the same amount of rent. In many cases they demanded the payment of all rents that were due but were not collected during the war years. By spring when the sowing season began, most of the peasants had exhausted their food supply, and to borrow from the landlords they had to pay an annual interest of something like 200 percent. In a more or less typical case a peasant who borrowed one bushel of rice in May would have to pay the lender two bushels in September when harvests were collected. Once he paid his debt, he was on a starvation diet. Whether there had been Communists or not, the situation had become too serious to continue.

What was happening in the countryside was either unknown or brushed aside as insignificant by the Nationalist hierarchy. At this crucial moment the formulation of policy was in the hands of a group of professional soldiers who looked at everything in military terms and resolved to solve every problem by military methods. It never occurred to them that communism was more a socio-economic than a military problem and that to eliminate communism one had to eliminate the social and economic ills upon which communism thrived. Those who were not military-minded enough were accused of being soft on communism and were dealt with accordingly. The militarists did not succeed in eliminating communism, but they did succeed in silencing those who believed that there were better, more effective ways of combatting communism.

The social and economic ills were reflected most poignantly in the runaway inflation. The war against Japan had been financed largely through inflation, especially during the latter stage of the war when the most productive areas in China had been lost to the Japanese. The ratio of exchange between Chinese and American dollars was 3 to 1 before the war began in 1937. In August, 1945, when the war ended, the official rate was 20 to 1, though the black market price, which reflected more correctly the true worth of the Chinese dollar, was many times larger. Early in 1946 the official rate was raised to 2,020 to 1 and was again raised to 73,000 to 1 at the end of that year. By the summer of 1948 to print a paper bill cost more than the face value it bore, and the government lost money every time a piece of paper money came off the printing press. Early in 1949 shortly before the government made a last attempt to reform the currency, one American dollar was worth 1.2 million Chinese dollars. According to independent newspapers, the maintenance of an official exchange rate which bore no relation to reality enabled a few high government officials and their relatives to enrich themselves. They purchased American dollars according to the official rate and then resold them in the black market where the exchange rate was many times larger. By repeating the same process they made themselves fabulously wealthy. It was widely rumoured that a sizable portion of the American financial aid designed to stabilize the Chinese currency reappeared in America and other foreign countries under private accounts and was invested in such profitable businesses as oil wells in Texas.

The runaway inflation prevented capital from being invested in industrial enterprises which produced goods and created jobs. As it continued, a businessman found it more profitable to hoard than to produce. When every businessman thought along the same line and acted accordingly, hoarding itself became a cause of inflation, as prices were forced to go up when businessmen refused to part with their merchandise. By 1949, shortly before the Communists took over, a decent meal cost a million dollars, and a pair of shoes several millions. In the countryside, people resorted to barter trade, since they no longer trusted the government's "ghost money." In the Lower Yangtze, for instance, every salable product, from chairs to chickens, was priced in terms of rice. Thanks to the thoroughness of the government's currency reform in the 1930's, rarely could one find a Mexican dollar which had been in circulation before the currency reform.[1] Rice, bulky and perishable, was not the best kind of medium of exchange, but the peasants had to do what they could under the existing circumstances. After four thousand years of civilization, they went back to the prehistoric ways.

Despite what has been said above, the Nationalist regime was perhaps no better or worse than most Chinese regimes in history. What made its shortcomings so striking was that in the twentieth century the requirements for a good government were a great deal higher and more substantial. The numerous problems a modern government had to face were also more complicated. The broadening of education made people more politically conscious and consequently less fatalistic. For every problem they demanded a solution, and solutions were difficult to find. The Western impact brought with it the force of nationalism which, in its modern form, had never been in existence before. After a century of humiliation at the hands of the Western powers and Japan, people demanded the abolition of the unequal treaties, the recovery of lost territories, and the restoration of China as an independent, sovereign state. In view of China's political and military weaknesses these were difficult goals to reach. The Western impact also brought the concept of democracy, and authoritarian rule was no longer taken for granted. People became more articulate in demanding that government existed for the governed only and that their voice be heard in the council of government. Right or wrong, many believed that the Nationalist government was too slow in achieving either the nationalistic or the democratic goal.

While the question as to whether the Nationalists or the Communists were more nationalistic or democratic was a subject of great controversy, what tipped the balance in favor of the Communists was their success in convincing the peasants that they could do better for them in the field of social justice and economic welfare. In the countryside the most serious had been and still was the land problem. All attempts to resolve it had failed, the last of these attempts having been made by the Taipings.[2] The Communists resolved it by liquidating landlords and dividing the expropriated land among the peasants. This was not a true solution because the Chinese problem was essentially a problem of shortage rather than of distribution. For the time being, however, their program appealed to the peasants who fought their wars and fought so well that they conquered mainland China for the Communists. Why did the same peasants not fight for the Nationalists? Here we return to one of the basic weaknesses of the Nationalist government: its inability to think in social and economic

[1] The Mexican dollars may have been brought to China by the English (who had taken them from the Spanish) in the seventeenth and eighteenth centuries.
[2] See Chapter XII, pp. 400–406.

terms in its anti-Communist crusade. It regarded communism as a military issue which, unfortunately, it was not. If it were, it would have been eliminated a long time ago.

THE NATIONALIST REGIME ON TAIWAN

In the spring of 1949 when it became increasingly clear that mainland China could no longer be defended against the seemingly invincible Communists, Chiang Kai-shek began to move part of the Nationalist troops to Taiwan. Previously he had ordered the transfer of China's gold reserve to the island, and now with the men and the money it was hoped that Taiwan could make a successful last stand against the Communists and perhaps serve as a base of operation for the eventual reconquest of the mainland as well. The hope for the future, however, contrasted sharply with the grimness of the present. The Communists were pushing relentlessly towards the Southwest, and the remaining Nationalist troops were either defeated or chose to surrender without a fight. Li Tsung-jen, then the Acting President, wanted Chiang to send back his troops to hold the Southwest, and Chiang wisely refused, as it was unlikely that any Nationalist forces could stop the Communist advances on the mainland. Taiwan, on the other hand, could be better defended. The Communists had no amphibious forces, and the Nationalists, by virtue of possessing a few naval ships, could give a good account of themselves. The Taiwan Strait, one hundred miles wide, thus saved the Nationalist regime from total extinction.

Gloomy as the domestic situation was, the international situation was even worse. In the summer of 1949 the United States issued the famous *White Paper* in which it placed the blame for the Nationalists' downfall on their own "corruption and incompetence" and adopted the policy of "waiting for the dust to settle." In January, 1950, President Truman said that the United States did not have "any intention of utilizing its armed forces to interfere in the present situation" and would "not provide military aid or advice to the Chinese forces on Formosa." The Nationalist fortunes had never looked worse. There was confusion, uncertainty, and despair. In view of what the Communists had done to the so-called counter-revolutionaries on the mainland, the Nationalists had no illusion about what lay ahead for them if the Communists captured the island. At least two high-ranking Nationalist officials—two of the most decent ones—had committed suicide, and others were prepared for the worst to come. On March 1, 1950, Chiang resumed the presidency after Acting President Li Tsung-jen, who was then staying in the United States to "seek American aid," failed to return. Whatever shortcomings Chiang might have, he was not a quitter. His assumption of leadership inspired confidence and hope among the otherwise dispirited Nationalists. They were all in one ship which had to be kept afloat at all costs. Across the Taiwan Strait on the mainland the Communists amassed a large invasion force. Further north in Peking, Chu Teh (1886–1976), commander-in-chief of the People's Liberation Army, announced that the urgent task of the nation was to "liberate" Taiwan from the "Chiang Kai-shek clique."

From hindsight it seems that what saved Taiwan from Communist conquest was neither Taipei nor Washington but a miscalculation on the part of Moscow. In June, 1950, North Korea, at the instigation of Moscow, invaded South Korea, and the United States, which had been anything but enthusiastic about the Nationalist regime on Taiwan, was then forced to reverse its policy. It declared that "in these circumstances [North Korean invasion] the occupation of Formosa by Communist forces would be a direct threat to the security of the Pacific area" and ordered the Seventh Fleet to prevent any attack on Taiwan. The intervention by the Chinese Communists in the Korean War and their subsequent animosity towards the United States drew Washington and Taipei closer each day, culminating in the conclusion of a mutual defense treaty in December, 1954. As long as the People's Republic maintained her hostility towards the United States, the United States would of course reciprocate by staunchly supporting the Nationalist regime on Taiwan. Prior to President Richard M. Nixon's trip to Peking in February, 1972, the unequivocal support of the Nationalist regime had been in fact America's established policy. Now that the Chinese Communists are actively seeking a rapprochement with the Americans as a counterbalance to the Soviet threat, the United States, facing the same threat on a global scale, suddenly finds herself in a dilemma that no one knows how to resolve. On the one hand, she, since the Cairo Declaration of 1943, has always recognized Taiwan as an integral part of China, and such recognition was reaffirmed in the *Shanghai Communiqué* of 1972 (p. 585). Following a legalistic point of view, she cannot intervene on behalf of Taiwan if the Chinese Communists decide to take the island by whatever means they deem necessary, including force. On the other hand, she has a treaty of alliance with Taiwan that calls upon her to defend that island if it is attacked by hostile forces. In other words, she has made two commitments that are contradictory to each other. It will take a great deal of skill and patience to work out a formula that satisfies both the Nationalists and the Communists.

Whatever the future of Taiwan may be, the Nationalist regime, since relocated on the island, has been most energetic and dynamic, noticeably different from what it was on the mainland. Its defeat at the hands of the Communists was not without its blessings. The opportunists who had used their party label to get rich quick or to exercise power for whatever it could bring to themselves were cleaned out under the impact of disaster. Some retired to enjoy their ill-gotten wealth, and others were either liquidated by the Communists or became turncoats and joined them. Those on Taiwan knew that they had to make their government a respectable going concern or suffer final defeat. To be sure, the regime is not a democracy in the truest sense since it is still a one-party government that tolerates no opposition. Nominally, the highest organ of the government is the National Assembly, consisting mostly of those delegates who had been elected on the mainland and then fled to Taiwan at the end of the civil war. Though they have not seen their constituents since then, they supposedly represent their interests. Somehow the legal fiction has to be maintained because the government claims that it represents all of China, while the Communists on the mainland are merely "bandits." Since Chiang Kai-shek's death in 1975, his son Chiang Ching-kuo (1910–　) has been the chairman of the Kuomintang and, beginning in 1978, president of the Nationalist government. Western sources describe the younger Chiang as a dynamic, popular leader, dedicated to building the island as a showcase of progress and prosperity. In many ways he has succeeded remarkably well.

Politically Chiang Ching-kuo's most popular measure has been the recruitment of more and more native Taiwanese to join his government. Today (1978) the vice president of Taiwan is an islander, and five of the twenty-two members in the Kuomintang's standing committee are also native-born. Many Taiwanese doubtless wish the process to be sped up, but in the long run the problem will perhaps be solved by itself. In the first place, the Taiwanese are culturally and racially Chinese, and the difference between them and the mainlanders is that their ancestors happened to arrive on the island earlier. As the children of both groups go to the same schools, are taught the same subjects with the same language, and invariably intermarry, whatever artificial differences there are between the two groups will eventually disappear. Besides, the mainlanders have been in Taiwan for thirty years; as they die of old age, one after another, all the people born in Taiwan will indeed be Taiwanese as well as Chinese. Then the question of differences between the two groups, let alone antagonism, simply will not arise.

Political stability on Taiwan is accompanied by an economic progress that can only be described as phenomenal. As has been pointed out in a previous chapter, Taiwan is richly endowed with agricultural resources. During the Japanese occupation, the island was intensively developed, industrially as well as agriculturally. Today under the Nationalist rule both industrial and agricultural outputs have far outdistanced peak performances during the Japanese occupation, thanks to Chinese diligence, generous provision of American aid, and steady inflow of foreign investments. The American economic aid stopped in 1965, but Taiwan has continued to score impressively in economic growth. For instance, the gross national product increased by 11.5 percent from 1975 to 1976, and the total volume of foreign trade increased by 37 percent over the same period. Per capita income increased from U.S. $292 in 1970 to U.S. $861 in 1977; it will increase to U.S. $970 in 1978, according to a governmental source. By 1981 when the present Six-Year Plan is completed, per capita income is supposed to be as high as U.S. $1,400, which will elevate Taiwan to one of the most developed countries in the world. The increase of per capita income means improvement of the standard of living for the overwhelming majority of the population. In 1975, we are told, there were thirty-six telephones, eighty-two television sets, sixty-three refrigerators, thirty-one washing machines, and fifty newspaper subscriptions in every one hundred households. It is interesting to note that despite the subtropical climate that spoils food easily, people in Taiwan would buy a television set before they would think of purchasing a refrigerator.

All this achievement may not look impressive from an American point of view, but it is an enormous improvement upon what the Chinese, either on Taiwan or on the mainland, have experienced or known. Most importantly, the economic prosperity also encompasses the peasants, traditionally the hardest working but most deprived people in China. As early as 1949 the Nationalist government embarked upon a program of land reform that began with the reduction of rent to 37.5 percent of the main crops and ended with the realization of Sun Yat-sen's teaching that "all land belongs to the tillers." Today practically all farmers own the land they till, and the success of the land reform has been credited with the building of a solid base on which industry can grow. As a result, the Taiwanese farmer enjoys an economic prosperity undreamed of twenty years ago. He sends his children to school and may even own such things as a television set, a refrigerator, and a motorcycle. Nevertheless, his income is smaller than that of an industrial worker, largely because of the small size of his landholdings. How to increase his income without in the meantime allowing landlordism to reemerge has been a most difficult problem for both the government and the farmers themselves.

While the economic prospect continues to be good at this moment, there are two shadows on the horizon that seem to grow bigger and bigger each day. One is the continuous increase of population that may cancel any economic gain that can be made. The island of 13,884 square miles is only half the size of South Carolina, but is currently (1978) supporting a population of 17 million, a population almost as large as that of California. Taiwan, with a population density of 1,224 people per square mile, is in fact one of the most populated countries in the world. In recent years, however, the annual rate of population growth has declined from 2.5 to 2.0 percent, thanks to a nationwide family planning program. This is no small achievement in view of China's traditional emphasis on large families. Even with this small rate of increase, population will double in one generation, which means 0.015 cultivated acres per capita. Then, in addition to many other considerations, the island simply will not be able to grow enough food to feed its own people.

The other shadow that darkens Taiwan's future is its international status. Today most countries have recognized Peking as the legitimate government of China; Taiwan, as a result, has become more and more isolated in the international community. What will happen to Taiwan if the United States also recognizes the People's Republic as the government representing all Chinese, including those in Taiwan? If she does, the result could be catastrophic to the islanders in view of the enormous differences in manpower and industrial and military strength between Taiwan and the mainland. The past clearly shows that the Chinese Communists have not been charitable or lenient towards their opponents or vanquished foes. It is true that the Nationalists also talk about the recovery of the mainland, but such talk stems more from an ideological commitment or simple faith than from an objective assessment of the situation involved. Barring a major civil war on the mainland which the Nationalists might be able to take advantage of, most people in Taiwan are only too happy with the maintenance of the status quo, namely, two separate political identities *de facto*. Fortunately for them, the Chinese Communists are now too occupied with the Soviet threat from the north to disturb the status quo in the south, and Taiwan is safe as long as this threat persists. Since the Chinese Communists, without America's moral or material support, can no more resist the Soviet Union than Taiwan, without American support, can resist mainland China, the United States enjoys a leverage over both the Nationalists and the Communists. In the final analysis, the United States will have to decide whether the status quo should or should not be allowed to continue. The people in Taiwan know this well, and they watch every American move with great expectation and anxiety.

ༀ xvi

The People's Republic (1)

On the morning of October 1, 1949, hundreds of thousands of people gathered at the T'ienanmen Square in Peking. Thousands of red flags fluttered against the autumn wind, and a two-hundred-piece band played one martial song after another. The crowd was joyful and anxious. Finally it heard the band play a familiar tune:

> The East is Red;
> The Sun is Rising.
> On the Horizon of China
> Appears the Great Hero Mao Tse-tung.

High on the T'ienanmen Tower a tall, plump man in grey uniform, flanked by many dignitaries, slowly ascended the marble stair toward the

STUDENTS PARADE ON THE TIEN-AN-MEN SQUARE Mao Tse-tung's picture appears on the upper left. The Chinese slogans on the wall read: "Long Live the People's Republic of China" and "Long Live the Grand Unity of All People in the World."

central platform decorated with huge red lanterns. Having at last reached the front of the platform, he turned and waved to the crowd below with a faint smile. The crowd went wild with applause which, being so noisy, drowned out even the band. By then the band had come to the last line of the music:

> He is the Great Savior of the People.

Immediately after the last music note subsided, a clear, masculine voice roared from the loudspeaker: "Ladies and Gentlemen, our national anthem." The band struck up again.

> Arise, you brave men
> > Who do not wish to become slaves;
> Let us use our blood and flesh
> > To build a new Great Wall of national defense.

The colorful but solemn ceremony marked the official beginning of the People's Republic of China, sometimes called Communist China in the Western world. The central figure of the show was Mao Tse-tung who only one year before had predicted that it would take four years for his Communist legions to win the civil war. Now, as he stood on the top of the T'ienanmen Tower where many ancient emperors may have stood before, he must have thought with great satisfaction of his own career, a rise from an insignificant librarian making 17 Chinese dollars (U.S. $5.67) a month to the dictator of all China, commanding the absolute obedience of 600 million people. How many people in the world had achieved so much in such a short time? Every place where he had been—the farm where he had once tended his father's pigs, the normal school at which he had once been a student, and the little room where he had once worked as an assistant librarian—was subsequently declared a national shrine. Since the last days of the emperors many people had fought for the position he now held; yet only he had succeeded. Why? For one thing, he knew how to make the finest promises. "We will work bravely and industriously to create our own civilization and happiness and will at the same time promote world peace and freedom. Our nation will never again be insulted. We have stood up." To hundreds of thousands of people who stood on the T'ienanmen Square on that memorial day, the sweetest word was perhaps "peace." The war had lasted too long; the sufferings had been too great to endure. Was it chance that T'ienanmen Square was chosen as the place to announce the establishment of the People's Republic because T'ienanmen, literally, means the Gate of Heavenly Peace? Could Chairman Mao lead the Chinese people successfully through that gate?

Since the disintegration of the Manchu empire no Chinese regime had a more propitious beginning. For the first time since 1911 the country was unified and the power of the central government was effectively exercised over all parts of China. The Kuomintang enemy had been decisively defeated, and people of all walks of life, regardless of their personal feelings, had no choice but to accept the new regime. Would the new regime be one of the greatest in Chinese history like Han, T'ang, and Ming, or would it last only a short time like Ch'in and Hsin? Whatever future historians might record, Mao Tse-tung had no doubt about his own position in history. Without a blush, he thought that he was the greatest conqueror China had ever produced. Witness his poem:

Snow (To the Melody *Shen Yüan Ch'un*)

This is the scene in the northern land;
A hundred leagues are sealed with ice,
A thousand leagues of whirling snow.
On either side of the Great Wall
One vastness is all you see.
From end to end of the great river
The rushing torrent is frozen and lost.

The mountains dance like silver snakes,
The highlands roll like waxen elephants,
As if they sought to vie with heaven in their height;
    And on a sunny day
You will see a red dress thrown over the white,
    Enchantingly lovely!
Such great beauty like this in all our landscape
Has caused unnumbered heroes to bow in homage.
But alas, these heroes—Ch'in Shih Huang and Han Wu Ti
Were rather lacking in culture;
Rather lacking literary talent
Were the emperors T'ang T'ai Tsung and Sung T'ai Tsu;
    And Genghis Khan,
Beloved Son of Heaven for a day,
Only knew how to bend his bow at the golden eagle.
    Now they are all past and gone:
To find men truly great and noble-hearted
We must look here in the present.[1]

Minus the modern, Marxist trimmings, the position of Mao Tse-tung was the same as that of the strongest emperors in China's past. While the emperors of imperial China spoke of the mandate of Heaven to justify their rule, Mao and his colleagues repeated endlessly the mandate of the people—which really amounted to the same thing because in both cases the mandate was secured on the battlefield. They said that they would exercise power through a process called democratic centralism, but the theory of democratic centralism was, to use a popular Chinese metaphor, merely a new bottle for the same old wine: a true dictatorship disguised under an attractive modern phraseology. In name, state power was created through popular elections; however, since every level of popular election was controlled by the Communist Party, the so-called people's democracy was to all intents and purposes a Communist dictatorship. Under the concept of democratic centralism that required absolute obedience to power once power had been created, this Communist dictatorship was in fact a dictatorship by the CCP leadership. It was meant to be not only peremptory but also permanent.

Nevertheless, when the People's Republic was established in 1949, Mao Tse-tung still called his government a New Democracy, or a "joint dictatorship of all the revolutionary classes." The revolutionary classes, according to Mao, were the proletariat, the peasants, the national capitalists, and finally, the petty bourgeois which meant the intellectuals

---

[1] This poem was written by Mao Tse-tung in August, 1945. The great heroes mentioned in this poem can be found elsewhere in this book. T'ang T'ai Tsung and Sung T'ai Tsu were the imperial or "temple" titles for Li Shih-min and Chao K'uang-yin respectively. Source of this poem: Mao Tse-tung, *Nineteen Poems* (Peking: Foreign Languages Press, 1958), p. 22.

and their allies who, while of a gentry or bourgeois background, had chosen to cooperate with the Communists. Opposite the revolutionary classes were the "reactionaries" such as the landlords, the capitalists who had cooperated with foreign interests in China (as opposed to the national capitalists), and the Kuomintang officials under Chiang Kai-shek's leadership. The New Democracy, said Mao, was a "democracy for the people and dictatorship for the reactionaries." "We certainly have no benevolent policies toward the reactionaries," he declared. Minority parties, such as the reconstructed Democratic League, were still allowed to function, as they supposedly represented the interest of the national capitalists and the petty bourgeois. Each of them, "recognizing its transient nature during the transitional period when classes still exist," had to write into its constitution the statement that it accepted the Communist Party's leadership. Thus, even during the period of a "joint dictatorship of all the revolutionary classes," the minority parties were never meant to be anything but a democratic window dressing for the one-party dictatorship.

The transition from a "joint dictatorship of all the revolutionary classes" to the "dictatorship of the proletariat" when all the minority parties cease to exist can be best demonstrated by comparing the Constitution of 1954 with the Constitution of 1975 which was in force until 1978. The Constitution of 1954 consists of a preamble and 106 articles in four chapters; its successor is a much shorter document, having only 30 articles. The former is described as the fundamental document during the period of transition when "all democratic classes, democratic parties and groups, and popular organizations," led by the CCP, "will continue to play their part in mobilizing the whole people in common struggle to fulfill the fundamental task of the state." The latter document, says the CCP, marks "the beginning of the new historical period of socialist revolution and the dictatorship of the proletariat" when the CCP is the "core of leadership of the whole Chinese people" and "Marxism–Leninism–Mao Tse-tung Thought is the theoretical basis guiding the thinking of our nation" (Article 2). "The National People's Congress is the highest organ of state power under the leadership of the Communist Party of China," states Article 16, and this statement effectively transforms the state power, including the armed forces the state commands, into an instrument to carry out the CCP's dictates. The party commands the state, and the state in turn commands the people whose fundamental rights and duties, says Article 26, are "to support the leadership of the Communist Party of China." There is no mention in the constitution of what the people can or should do if they are dissatisfied with the CCP leadership; such dissatisfaction is simply not allowed, constitutionally speaking.

Under both constitutions the Chinese are supposed to have "freedom of speech, freedom of the press, freedom of assembly, freedom of association, freedom of procession, and freedom of demonstration," but these freedoms, under the 1975 Constitution, are conditioned by the fact that all citizens must support the CCP leadership at all times and without reservation. In other words, a Chinese can exercise these freedoms to praise or support the CCP leaders or the policies and programs they have adopted, but not to criticize or oppose them. He can, if he so chooses, shout "Long live Chairman Mao" as loudly and as many times as he wishes, but he will be declared a counterrevolutionary and punished accordingly if he ever whispers that "Chairman Mao sometimes makes mistakes." Even in a Communist utopia, says Chang Ch'un-ch'iao, the man primarily responsible for the drafting of the 1975 Constitution, there are the "capitalist roaders" and the class enemies to whom freedom of speech must be denied and against whom all the good Communists must maintain a permanent vigilance. The utopia is called a dictatorship of the proletariat; actually it is a dictatorship by the CCP leadership. The proletariat have no more say about their government than any other group of the Chinese people. The CCP leaders, as personal embodiments of true Marxism-Leninism and Mao Tse-tung's thought, are supposed to know what is good or bad for every Chinese.

A non-Communist would have to characterize this Communist utopia as retrogressive or totalitarian, but the CCP, from the very beginning of its existence, has made it clear that this is indeed its final goal. All the things it has advocated in the past, such as a national and democratic revolution, a united front, the New Democracy and the joint dictatorship of all the revolutionary classes, are merely strategies to meet objective conditions at a given time, either to assure its own survival when confronted with overwhelming and hostile forces or to reduce resistance to the attainment of its goal. Now that the final goal, namely the dictatorship by the CCP leadership (which is euphemized as the dictatorship of the proletariat), has been realized, the chairman of the CCP, whoever he happens to be, is by definition the dictator of all China. Extraordinary though this development may seem, it in fact has its roots in Chinese history. As has been mentioned earlier in this book, monarchal power has steadily increased since the monarchal system began in China several thousand years ago; logically it has to be at its historical height at this Communist stage. To justify or rationalize the position he holds, the chairman of the CCP has to be built up as a man larger than life itself. Before his death in 1976, Mao Tse-tung was hailed everywhere in China as the greatest leader, teacher, and helmsman, embodying all the possible virtues. His remarks, however contradictory they might appear to a less adulatory mind, were regarded as the ultimate in wisdom, more binding than any law or the constitution itself. Ideologically and politically he was considered infallible. No Chinese emperor in the past, not even Ch'in Shih-huang whom Mao Tse-tung admired, had been built up to such superhuman proportions. A similar buildup is currently in progress for his successor Hua Kuo-feng, even though, historically, a successor to the founding father of a dynasty was not supposed to have possessed the same amount of virtue as the founder himself.

The 1978 constitution, enacted by the Fifth National Congress (parliament) in March, 1978 and containing 60 articles, does not differ materially from the 1975 constitution, though some concessions are made to the spirit of the 1954 constitution. The document reaffirms Marxism-Leninism-Maoism as the state's commanding ideology, the necessity of all citizens to support the CCP leadership, and the importance of organization and discipline to carry out the principle of "democratic centralism." It makes concessions to the 1954 constitution by restoring "people's procuratorates" which the 1975 constitution has abolished. Nevertheless, the existence of "people's procuratorates" under the 1954 constitution did not in any way prevent arbitrary arrests and massive punishments that reached horrendous proportions during the Cultural Revolution of the 1960's. Only the future can tell whether human rights will fare better under the new constitution. The document also calls for the competition of ideas among "a hundred schools of thought," but no one, having heard or read about the 1957 debacle (pp. 521–522), will take this offer seriously. In the end it is the CCP and its leaders that determine the course of events, constitution and statutes notwithstanding. As if to underscore this point, Hua Kuo-feng was confirmed by the Fifth National Congress as head of both the Party and the government, a combination of posts that even Mao Tse-tung did not enjoy prior to his death in 1976.

Though power is concentrated and comes from above, the CCP leaders ultimately have to depend upon individual members to carry out party directives and to influence other Chinese to do the same. They carefully screen each candidate for membership, hoping to recruit to the party ranks thoroughly indoctrinated and highly motivated individuals. The most important qualification for party membership, according to the CCP, is "proletarian consciousness" which, in plain language, means absolute loyalty to the party leadership and total dedication to implementing the party line. Since the leaders can be in or out of power, depending upon the outcome of infighting among themselves, and since the party line can vary from one time to another, depending upon the ideological orientation of the party faction that happens to be in power at a given time, this loyalty or dedication can, theoretically, create a serious problem for party members. But it does not. As a rule, the party members have been thoroughly conditioned to swing with ease from one end to another in accordance with the prevailing political wind, and they have no difficulty in condemning one party leader or one party line that they enthusiastically endorsed only the previous day. "Loyalty" and "dedication" are virtues absolute in themselves; it is not important to whom one pledges one's loyalty or to what line one dedicates one's effort, as long as the leader is a Communist or the line has been officially sanctioned. For those who may have acted independently or committed themselves too deeply to one party leader or one party line to make a complete about-face when occasion calls for it, the consequence could be very serious. They could be condemned and humiliated, often in public gatherings, ending with a punishment that ranges from "reform through physical labor" to expulsion from the party membership. During the antirightist campaign of 1957–1958, for instance, approximately one million Communists were either expelled from the party or put on probation, and the number of Communists suffering the same fate during the Cultural Revolution of 1966–1976 was doubtless larger. To be expelled from the party is considered the ultimate in disgrace, as disgraceful to a Communist as excommunication was to a Christian during medieval times. One can never resign from the party, but one may be expelled from it.

As long as a person remains a party member in good standing, he is supposed to personify all the virtues of a model citizen and set an example for other Chinese to follow. He is a leader or "active member" in his family, his school, his factory or farm or whatever other group to which he happens to belong. He and his fellow Communists receive directives from the party headquarters, and it is their duty to carry them out, with as much enthusiasm as possible. Three or more party members are organized as a cell, and many cells form a party branch covering a mine, a factory, or an army unit. Above the branches are party organizations that operate in a city, county, or commune. Further above are headquarters with jurisdiction over entire provinces, special municipalities, and autonomous regions. The party branch, however, is the basic operational unit responsible for the implementation of the party's directives. Though the party was founded by intellectuals, its present membership consists almost exclusively of workers and peasants, since the early members of a bourgeois or landlord background have mostly died. Party membership commands enormous prestige, competition for acceptance is intense, and there are always more applicants than the party is willing to accept. Total membership at this moment (1978) approximates 35 million, or 4.1 percent of the population. These party members, says the CCP, are the vanguards of the proletarians, willing to "climb the highest mountain or swim into the deepest ocean" to carry out the party's directives. Throughout Chinese history there has never been an organization so authoritarian and effective as the Chinese Communist Party.

To influence the non-party Chinese to follow the party's directives, the Communists involve themselves actively with the various "people's organizations" such as the peasant association, the trade union, the youth league, and women's organizations, that operate in practically all Chinese communities. Their duty is to generate enthusiasm for, and then carry out, whatever programs the party organization has decided upon. In this regard the most effective of the "people's organizations" are the street committees in the urban areas and the production teams in the rural regions. Since nearly all adult Chinese belong to either of these two organizations, the CCP, by controlling these organizations through its active members, controls the entire country. Working among the non-party Chinese, the Communists are urged by their leaders to use persuasion rather than coercion to make the party will prevail, though in practical terms the non-party Chinese do not have any choice except to be persuaded. Besides, all media of mass communication, such as newspapers, magazines, radio, and television, are controlled by the CCP and never express any opinion or idea contrary to the party line. To be sure, some of the propaganda is apolitical in nature when, for instance, the CCP urges the people to work harder for a good harvest, send their children to school, or practice hygiene to improve public health. By combining ideological indoctrination with social service, the CCP not only makes the indoctrination tolerable but also successfully creates the impression that the party, indeed, cares for the people.

LEFTISTS, RIGHTISTS, AND THE PURGES

"Left" and "right" are relative terms, since one's right is bound to be someone else's left. In the ideological spectrum, however, the relative position of "left" and "right" is shaped more like a circle than a straight line; one need only look in the other direction to realize that what has been customarily regarded as one's right becomes suddenly one's left. In fact, the shape of political ideology can be plausibly compared to that of the spherical earth. China is a Far Eastern country only because most Americans habitually look eastward toward the Europe of their ancestors; she is actually a Far Western country in terms of geographical distance from the center of America. The ideological relationship between the leftists and the rightists may be drawn as follows:

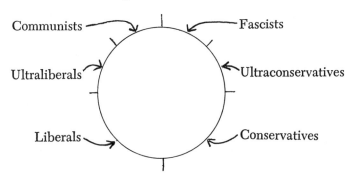

Most people, not being ideologically committed, float constantly in front of the circle. They can be either liberal or conservative, depending mostly upon how each issue affects their personal interest, and rarely do they wander far from the middle. As one moves toward the back of the circle, either left or right, and becomes more and more ideologically committed, one suddenly realizes, at a certain point, that one's distant antagonists are actually one's closest neighbors. The Fascists and the Communists have a great deal in common in the sense that both favor a personal dictatorship, a totalitarian form of government, a regimented citizenry, and the sacrifice of individual welfare for the alleged common good. There is a major difference between them, however. While the Fascists want to exterminate certain so-called inferior racial or religious groups in order to make room for "superior" people like themselves, the Communists, on the other hand, want to liquidate what they call class enemies—landlords, capitalists, etc., in order to create the kind of utopia that has been described earlier. Since it is much easier to change one's socioeconomic status than to camouflage one's race or religion, the Communists have an appeal unmatched by the Fascists. They hate each other with the greatest intensity not because they are vastly different in ideology but because, surprisingly enough, they both want to occupy the same rear section of the ideological circle.

The Fascist movement is not our concern here; we shall confine our discussion to the Communist movement in China. From the ideological circle drawn above, it is obvious that to gain power the Chinese Communists had to move rightward in order to win as many sympathizers and supporters as possible. But the early leaders of the CCP did not do that. Carried away by their newly acquired ideology that called upon them to wage permanent warfare against all the feudal and imperialist enemies, they kept on moving toward the left and thus continued to narrow their small base of support, culminating in the "Long March" which was really a prolonged, tortuous retreat in defeat. At the time of total disaster (January, 1935) Mao Tse-tung took over the CCP leadership and slowly guided the party toward the right. Completely reversing its old stand, the CCP began to advocate a national democracy instead of a proletarian dictatorship, a united front of all patriotic forces against Japanese aggression instead of a world revolution, rent and interest reductions instead of land confiscation and redistribution. "How can we succeed in our revolution if we do not allow the landlords to make a decent profit?" Mao Tse-tung once asked rhetorically. He did not object when the Western press characterized him as a land reformer, but few realized that to him land reform was merely an "unavoidable phenomenon at a certain stage of historical development"—a means to an end but not an end in itself. As the CCP moved rightward, it pushed the Kuomintang further to the right until all of its normal support evaporated. The success of Mao Tse-tung's strategy was crowned with the establishment of the People's Republic in 1949.

With the attainment of absolute power in 1949 when it no longer needed to make compromises, the CCP, under the leadership of Mao Tse-tung, reversed the trend that had its beginning in 1935. As it journeyed leftward to its natural home, namely the dictatorship of the proletariat, the first group of people to be eliminated from the power structure had to be those bourgeois elements that supposedly represented the national capitalists and the petty bourgeois, the same people who had at one time been regarded as two of Mao Tse-tung's "four revolutionary classes." Less than three years after the promulgation of the 1954 Constitution which specifically stipulated that all non-Communist but democratic forces had a constructive role to play in the new society, Mao Tse-tung launched an ideological campaign that ended with their total collapse. In February, 1957, Mao, in his famous speech "On the Correct Handling of Contradictions among the People," called upon the Chinese people to speak frankly on what they felt about communism and the Communist society. "Let a hundred flowers bloom and let a hundred schools of thought contend," he declared; "we Marxists are not afraid of criticism." Cautious at first, the intellectuals, led by those who had been educated in Europe and America, took his offer seriously and began to criticize. They deplored the disintegration of the traditional Chinese family under communism, the ruthlessness with which party cadres had carried out the program of land confiscation and redistribution, the disadvantages that China had suffered in her military and economic alliance with the Soviet Union, and many other matters. They even attacked the CCP leadership for its lack of foresight and wisdom.

As criticisms mushroomed out of control, Mao Tse-tung suddenly concluded that these criticisms were of a destructive instead of a constructive nature and that the critics were "poisonous weeds" instead of "flowers." He ordered a general crackdown. All criticisms, he said, must tend to strengthen rather than weaken or cast doubt on the CCP leadership; the "poisonous weeds" must be rooted out before they could spread further and cause more harm. The CCP called for counterattacks; before the summer was over, all the "bourgeois and democratic forces" had disappeared from the national scene. "The purpose of conducting the Hundred Flowers Campaign," said Liu Shao-ch'i, then Mao Tse-tung's designated successor, "was to set a trap to let 'poisonous weeds' grow, so that, by growing taller and taller, they would become more visible and easily mowed down."

The antirightist campaign of 1957–1958 proved to be only the first step toward the radicalization of China. Other steps had to follow if China was to become a truly Maoist society. Since by then none but a Communist could hold a position of power or influence, the target of purges had to be the Communists themselves. As one purge followed another, yesterday's purgers became today's purged, and each purge pushed the CCP further leftward, culminating in the Great Proletarian Cultural Revolution that was supposed to have brought about the real-ization of a Communist utopia. The radicalization of China continued during the Cultural Revolution and did not come to an end until Mao Tse-tung himself died in 1976. The arrest of his radical followers, includ-ing his wife Chiang Ch'ing, was in fact an anticlimax since they could not go on with their radicalization without the master's guiding hand. Robespierre was dead, and China, for the first time in twenty-seven years (1949–1976), moved cautiously rightward.

In a speech delivered to the party's faithful in 1971, Mao Tse-tung stated that there had been "ten major struggles over the party line" after the founding of the CCP in 1921.[1] The ten major "struggles," a euphemism for purges, were as follows:

	Date	Leaders Purged	Reasons Given for the Purge
1	1927	Ch'en Tu-hsiu (1896–1943) Liu Jen-ching (1899–) P'eng Shu-chih (1896–)	Trotskyism
2	1929 and 1931	Ch'ü Ch'iu-pai (1899–1933)	Leftist adventurism
3	1930–31	Li Li-san (1899–)	Leftist adventurism
4	1931	Lo Chang-lung (1901–1949)	Antiparty separatism
5	1932–33 and 1935	Wang Ming (also known as Ch'en Shao-yü, (1904–)	Leftist radicalism
6	1938	Chang Kuo-t'ao (1897–)	Rightist deviationism
7	1954	Kao Kang (1902–1954) Jao Shu-shih (1901–)	Antiparty separatism
8	1959	P'eng Teh-huai (1898–) Huang K'o-ch'ang (1902–) Chang Wen-t'ien (1898–) Chou Hsiao-chou (1912–)	Rightist deviationism

[1] For a complete text of this speech, see Dun J. Li, *Modern China: From Mandarin to Commissar* (New York: Scribners, 1978), pp. 324–329.

| 9 | 1966 | Liu Shao-ch'i (1898–) Teng Hsiao-p'ing (1904–) | Attempt to revive capitalism |
| 10 | 1971 | Lin Piao (1907–1971) | Attempt to revive capitalism |

To make the list complete, we have to add the following:

| 11 | April, 1976 | Teng Hsiao-p'ing | Rightist deviationism |
| 12 | October, 1976 | The "Gang of Four": Chiang Ch'ing (1915–) Chang Ch'un-ch'iao (1915–) Wang Hung-jen Yao Wen-yüan (1927–) | Leftist radicalism |

Ideological difference and power struggle were so interwoven with each other that it is difficult to say which of the two was the more dominant factor in each purge. We are further handicapped by the fact that only the side of the victors has been made known, never that of the purged or defeated. The major purges before 1949 have been mentioned earlier in this book; here we shall discuss only those that occurred after that date. In the case of Kao Kang, it seems that he, as the overlord of Manchuria, had maintained a secret liaison with Moscow without Peking's knowledge, doubtless hoping that Stalin would support him in an eventual bid for supreme power in China. After Stalin's death in 1953, his prospective successors, in their effort to ingratiate themselves with Mao Tsetung and gain his support, informed him of Kao Kang's secret dealings with Stalin. Betrayed and disgraced, Kao Kang committed suicide. In the case of P'eng Teh-huai, it seems that he, as the defense minister, had argued strongly for the modernization of the Chinese armed forces in the party's high council, thus defying Mao's dictum that "in war it is men, not weapons, that determine victory or defeat." He may also have argued for an enlarged role of the military men in the formulation of the nation's policies, thus contradicting the CCP's established policy that "the party commands the guns, not the other way around." Whatever chance of success he might have in his challenge to Mao's authority, Mao quickly undercut him by lining up other military men on his side, notably Lin Piao who, after the purge, was appointed the defense minister to replace the purged victim. From then on Lin Piao's star kept on rising until he himself was purged in 1971.

Fortunately, both the Kao Kang and the P'eng Teh-huai purges involved only the party's hierarchy; the rank and file, together with the rest of the nation, were not seriously affected. With the Great Proletarian Cultural Revolution, launched by Mao Tse-tung in May, 1966, a totally new situation began to emerge. Practically every Chinese was affected, and its impact varied in direct proportion to the position a person held in the party, the government, or the armed forces. Why should Mao Tse-tung start a revolution against his own party, of which he was then the chairman? Basically two reasons have been advanced, and China experts have debated among themselves as to which of the two, naked power struggle or genuine ideological differences, was more important. In 1958 Mao Tse-tung, at the towering height of his own career, started an economic campaign known as the Great Leap Forward. The details of this campaign will be discussed later in this chapter; suffice it to say that the Great Leap Forward, aimed at the speedy industrialization of China, quickly deteriorated into a gigantic step backward. Before long millions of Chinese were actually suffering from hunger and cold. In April, 1959, Mao Tse-tung was replaced by Liu Shao-ch'i as head of the state so that, according to an official explanation, he could from then on concentrate on "ideological work." Most likely he had been eased out from the position of absolute power, a position he had held after 1935. "I was worshipped like a Buddha, but nobody paid any attention to what I had to say," said he a few years later. While Mao's power was in an eclipse, such moderates as Liu Shao-ch'i and Teng Hsiao-p'ing proceeded to consolidate their own gains in the party, the government, and the armed forces. Mao Tse-tung had never been satisfied with a lofty position with little real power; so to regain his lost power, he had to launch the Cultural Revolution to get rid of the moderates.

Nevertheless, genuine differences in ideology did exist between the moderates and the radicals. The moderates, once in power, slowly moved away from the kind of pure communism exemplified in the Great Leap Forward and started to adopt a Chinese version of Lenin's NEP in which material incentive, as well as ideological indoctrination, was relied on as the motivating force for social and economic advancement. By the early 1960's the moderates had succeeded so well in their pragmatic policies that the economy not only recovered from the Great Leap disaster but also resumed its normal progress. To the Maoist radicals, however, this retreat from pure communism was a step backward from the CCP's effort to build a higher civilization. If unchecked, this pragmatic trend would lead China to revisionism, a branch of communism that was supposed to have prevailed in the Soviet Union. Capitalism would once again raise its ugly head, classes would reemerge, and communism itself might come to an end in China. The radicals called upon the Chinese people to oust the "capitalist roaders," a term that they used to characterize the moderates, so that China and communism could be returned to their rightful path. Since the call was issued in the name of Mao Tse-tung, then worshipped like a god despite his loss of control over the CCP apparatus, the impact was immediate. Overnight millions of students emerged in the streets to challenge the established authorities and, shouting such slogans as "Dare to rebel" and "Dare to be violent," they roamed up and down the country in the name of "exchanging revolutionary experience." To encourage them in their lawless activities, Mao Tse-tung even composed a song for them to sing. The song read in part:

> Revolution is not like giving a party,
> Composing a piece of literature, or
> Making fine embroidery.
> It is not refined, leisurely, or polite;
> It is not gentle, modest, or respectful.
> Revolution is violence;
> It is the overthrow of one class by another—
> By violent action!

These young zealots, known as the Red Guards, stormed into CCP headquarters across the nation, dragged out the party secretaries, put dunce caps on their heads, and paraded them in the streets as class enemies, while encouraging onlookers to spit on them. No less a dignitary than Teng Hsiao-p'ing had suffered this kind of humiliation. Different groups of Red Guards tried to outdo one another in exhibiting their "revolutionary spirit." In the process they desecrated the burying ground of Confucius on the ground that he was an arch-counterrevolutionary, intimidated and harassed Sun Yat-sen's widow whom they denounced as a decadent bourgeoise, besieged Premier Chou En-lai and threatened to oust him, and kidnapped Mrs. Liu Shao-ch'i, wife of the president of the People's Republic who, according to the Red Guards, also happened to be "China's number one capitalist roader." The country was turned upside down, all in the name of upholding Chairman Mao's teachings. For years the moderates had instructed others to obey the Chairman's directives without reservation; they felt totally helpless when the Red Guards, waving the Chairman's edict, ordered them to bow low to receive punishment as "capitalist roaders."

After the moderates had been purged from their position of power and when the party and the government could once again be reconstructed in the Chairman's image, Mao Tse-tung called upon the army to restore order. He sent most of the Red Guards to the countryside where, according to the CCP, they could "continue to honor Chairman Mao" by engaging in manual labor. Many were ordered to go as far as the frozen wilderness of Tibet, the barren desert of Sinkiang, and the forests and swamps of northern Manchuria. The young zealots were now pushed aside, after having served a Maoist purpose successfully. To reward Lin

Piao, then the defense minister, for the army's role in restoring order, Mao Tse-tung designated him as his political heir during the CCP's Ninth Congress in 1969.

Having been designated as Mao Tse-tung's successor, Lin Piao wanted to make sure that upon Mao's death no potential rivals would wish to challenge his right of inheritance. He took a series of steps to strengthen his own position, notably by placing his followers, most of whom were military men, in the key positions of the party and the government. He prepared so well for the succession that eventually Mao Tse-tung himself was alarmed. Did his political heir intend to succeed him long before he was ready to make his planned trip to see Marx? During the Second Plenary Session of the CCP's Ninth Congress, held in August, 1970, Lin Piao attempted to get himself elected president of the People's Republic, a post that had been left vacant after the downfall of Liu Shao-ch'i. Mao Tse-tung blocked this move by stating that he did not want anyone, including himself, to occupy that post. He had in mind, of course, that Liu Shao-ch'i, when occupying that post, had deprived him of the kind of authority that he once enjoyed. Frustrated, angered, and fearful of his own future, Lin Piao initiated a plot to assassinate the B52, a code name used by the plotters to denote their intended victim, Mao Tse-tung. The plot failed, and Lin Piao, together with his wife and son, was killed in a plane crash while fleeing from China to the Soviet Union in September, 1971. During the subsequent campaign to root out his supporters, Lin Piao was denounced as "a greedy power-grabber of the capitalist class, an evil schemer, a counterrevolutionary, a double-crosser, a rebel, and a traitor, all compounded in one person," even though only two years earlier he had been hailed as a true Marxist-Leninist and "Chairman Mao's closest comrade-in-arms."

During the Cultural Revolution a new political force was created. It became more powerful during the anti–Lin Piao campaign of the early 1970's and then came to a sudden end in October, 1976, less than one month after Mao Tse-tung's death. This force was known to the Chinese as *Wen-keh p'ai,* or Cultural Revolution Clique, but it was generally referred to as the CCP's leftist or radical faction in the Western press. It was led by none other than Chiang Ch'ing, Mao Tse-tung's wife. Prior to the Cultural Revolution the standard policy of the CCP had been total separation of a leader's public life from his private one, designed as a sharp contrast to the allegedly widespread nepotism in what the CCP called feudal, bourgeois, and decadent societies. Shortly before and during the early stage of the Cultural Revolution, when he did not have total control over the CCP administration, Mao Tse-tung, by necessity perhaps, regularly sent the person whom he trusted most, namely his wife, to various parts of China to organize the opposition. In due course Chiang Ch'ing became a power in her own right; she and her protégés

(Chang Ch'un-ch'iao, Wang Hung-jen, Yao Wen-yüan, and others) quickly formed a new, powerful group. This group, stressing the importance of ideological purity and the conduct of class struggle to perpetuate the revolution, constituted the CCP's leftist or radical wing. On the other side of the ideological and political spectrum were the "Long March heroes" who occupied key positions in the armed forces and the government. This group, emphasizing the necessity of peace and order and the economic construction of China, formed the CCP's rightist or moderate wing. The moderate wing was led by Chou En-lai, a superb, experienced politician who proved to be more than Chiang Ch'ing's match.

Chou En-lai was born in 1898 to a wealthy aristocratic family in Huaian, Kiangsu province. He attracted public attention for the first time in 1919 when, as a student leader in Tientsin, he was arrested and thrown into jail for his participation in the May Fourth Movement. Released from jail in 1920, he went to France as a work-study student. But neither work nor study was his primary interest. He became an activist in radical politics and, in due course, helped found a branch of the Chinese Communist Party in France. After the reorganization of the Kuomintang in 1924 and the acceptance of Communists as Kuomintang members, he served as Chiang Kai-shek's deputy and political commissar in the Whampoa Military Academy. He was organizing workers in Shanghai when Chiang Kai-shek suddenly launched a bloody purge of the Communists in the spring of 1927. According to one report, Chou En-lai barely eluded the dragnet and thus saved his own life by camouflaging himself as a woman. For several years after 1927 he headed the party's military affairs department, often clashing with other party leaders, including Mao Tse-tung. In January, 1935, Mao assumed the undisputed party leadership by ousting a group of Moscow puppets known as the CCP's international faction. From then on Chou En-lai was satisfied with playing a secondary role to whoever happened to be the top leader.

From hindsight it seems that his decision not to aspire to the number one position in the party was in fact his secret formula for political survival. Whoever happened to be the top leader, he needed a good administrator and an able diplomat, which Chou En-lai was. Time and again Chou was called upon to represent the CCP in negotiations with all and sundry, including the Russians, the Americans, and, of course, the Chinese Nationalists. He impressed everyone he met, including Chiang Kai-shek. "He is the only decent Communist I have ever met," Chiang Kai-shek was reported to have remarked, "if there is such a thing as a decent Communist." Seemingly reasonable and agreeable, he, nevertheless, made each move in accordance with what he regarded as the CCP's best interest. "Do not forget that I am a Communist," he reminded his bourgeois visitors whenever they were carried away by his personal charm. During the Sian Incident, when all other Communist leaders, including

Mao Tse-tung and Chu Teh, wanted to kill "that s.o.b.," Chou En-lai alone insisted that Chiang Kai-shek's life must be spared. Chou En-lai was right; it seems clear, then and now, that the CCP's interest would be better served if Chiang Kai-shek remained alive (p. 481).

With the establishment of the People's Republic in 1949, Chou En-lai became its premier and remained in that post until he died in January, 1976. There were purges and counterpurges, and many veteran Communist leaders, including the "Long March heroes," fell by the wayside. Yet Chou En-lai survived. He bent with the prevailing political wind and successively condemned P'eng Teh-huai, Liu Shao-ch'i, and Lin Piao as Mao Tse-tung had instructed. Certainly it was no small feat to have survived the Cultural Revolution. With the rise of Chiang Ch'ing and her radical followers in the wake of the Cultural Revolution, Chou En-lai, despite his subservience to Mao Tse-tung, became the natural leader behind whom the moderates sought protection. In view of his lifelong service to the CCP and the enormous popularity he enjoyed among the party's rank and file, conceivably he could be pushed up to the number one position once Mao Tse-tung died. Chiang Ch'ing could not tolerate a prospect of this kind since she wanted to succeed Mao Tse-tung herself. Her resentment must have increased tenfold when Chou En-lai, after learning that he had cancer and would not survive long, not only resursected Teng Hsiao-p'ing from political oblivion but also appointed him the first deputy premier who, upon Chou's death, would doubtless succeed as the premier. This was the same Teng Hsiao-p'ing whom Chiang Ch'ing and her radical supporters had publicly humiliated and condemned as a "capitalist roader" during the Cultural Revolution. The future was ominous. Conceivably Teng Hsiao-p'ing would succeed not only Chou En-lai but Mao Tse-tung as well.

As long as Chou En-lai lived, the moderates were united; they were more than able to hold their own. Then he died. Shortly after his death, the radicals launched an antirightist campaign that successfully stripped Teng Hsiao-p'ing of all positions of power. Hopeless at the moment, the moderates were nevertheless strong enough to block the radical candidate Chang Ch'un-ch'iao for the premiership. A deadlock ensued; yet the government must go on. Finally both sides agreed to a compromise candidate named Hua Kuo-feng who, without a nationwide following and a power base of his own, could easily be pushed aside when the right moment arrived; at least that was what the radicals thought. Had Mao Tse-tung lived two or more years, chances were that this would indeed happen, since the radicals were gaining strength fast, especially in the people's militias that had been built up as a counterbalance to the regular army, home of the moderates. Unfortunately, Mao Tse-tung died too early for them to realize their dream.

With Mao Tse-tung's death on September 9, 1976, the radicals were suddenly confronted with a now-or-never situation. They moved quickly to seize power and, according to an official source, went so far as to forge the dead man's will to achieve their purpose. The moderates had no choice but to rally behind Hua Kuo-feng, and leaders of the regular army did their part in "keeping the people's militias in their proper place." On October 6, 1976, Chiang Ch'ing, Chang Ch'un-ch'iao, Wang Hung-jen, and Yao Wen-yüan, jointly referred to as the "Gang of Four," were arrested. Subsequently a nationwide campaign was conducted to root out their supporters, who could offer only feeble resistance. "A major civil war would have occurred had the Gang of Four succeeded in their evil scheme," said Hua Kuo-feng.

In August, 1977, the CCP convened its Eleventh Congress to sanctify the new power structure of the moderates. A new Central Committee was formed, and its 26-member Political Bureau consisted mostly of those noted for their pragmatism and their devotion to China's modernization. The standing committee of the Political Bureau, which constituted the power center of the Party and the nation, had five members, namely Hua Kuo-feng, Yeh Chien-ying, Teng Hsiao-p'ing, Li Hsien-nien, and Wang Tung-hsing. Hua Kuo-feng served as the premier as well as chairman of the CCP; theoretically, he was the most powerful man in the nation. Nevertheless, many believed that the real power of the state lay with the third-ranking Teng Hsiao-p'ing who had strong support in the army, in the government, as well as among the CCP's rank and file. This was the same Teng Hsiao-p'ing who, once denounced as a "capitalist roader," a "rightist deviationist," a "demon," and a "freak," had been twice purged by Mao Tse-tung, Chiang Ch'ing, and their radical colleagues. The power reversal could not have been more dramatic and complete.

With people like Teng Hsiao-p'ing in full control of the power of the state, the Cultural Revolution was declared to have officially ended. Many CCP leaders, who had been purged during the Cultural Revolution, returned to their former positions of power and influence. Though Mao Tse-tung had occupied too lofty a position to be downgraded right away, a process of "de-Maoization" began almost as soon as he died. The new leaders stressed the importance of peace, order, discipline, and economic progress, just as empatically as the radicals had spoken of the necessity of class struggle and a perpetual revolution. A new chapter of the CCP had begun, and the People's Republic, for the first time after its establishment, moved cautiously rightward.

INDUSTRIAL DEVELOPMENT

To an outside observer it is doubtless depressing to see millions of Chinese, at the push of a button, emerge in the streets to demonstrate against a leader who, only a year or a month before, had been hailed as a true defender of the proletarian revolution. They shout at the top of their lungs "Long live X" and "Down with Y," completely oblivious to the fact that with the same enthusiasm they have, not a long time before, shouted "Long live Y" and "Down with X." It is easy, of course, to dismiss the Chinese as "robots" or "blue ants"; the fact is that no human beings, certainly not in such large numbers, can be degraded for so long unless they feel that the degradation is more than offset by certain compensations. In other words, the dictatorship of the CCP leadership, deplorable though it is from an objective point of view, must at this time serve a useful Chinese purpose. It may even be argued that a dictatorship of this kind, with its emphasis on self-sacrifice and self-discipline, is the only way that China can pull herself out from the abyss into which she has fallen in modern times.

It is difficult for an outsider who does not have a similar background to understand the nature and depth of this abyss and China's frustration over her inability to do anything about it. Shortly before the Communist assumption of power, China had experienced the ultimate insult that one nation could inflict upon another, namely, Japan's attempt to conquer China on the ground that the Chinese could not really govern themselves. Domestically, miseries abounded, especially among the peasants who constituted the overwhelming majority of the Chinese population. The miseries originated in one basic source, namely, poverty on such an extensive and intensive scale that no one but a witness could really believe it. One example might be more than sufficient to demonstrate this point. In 1944, at the height of the Sino-Japanese War, 1.5 million people died in the province of Honan alone, not from Japanese guns but from starvation brought on by a prolonged drought. It was this kind of misery that the Communists confronted when they assumed power in 1949. When a man is hungry, human rights are not high on his list of priorities, and he will support any regime that assures him three regular meals a day in return for his hard labor. A Chinese peasant does not compare his life with that of a European or American about whom he knows little; he compares himself with his father or grandfather whose sufferings he knows intimately. Today he has enough to eat and wear, and he even sends his children to school. He is grateful to the CCP and does whatever its leaders tell him to do. His support and the support from people like him are in fact the CCP's real strength.

To lift all Chinese, especially the peasants, from the kind of deprivation that had been so much a part of their experience, the CCP, as soon as it attained supreme power, set out to implement an ambitious plan of economic development. The model of development was that of the Soviet Union. Like the Russians, the Chinese believed that heavy industry formed the basis of both agriculture and light industry and must therefore be developed first. This meant, of course, that there would not be substantial improvement in living standards for the moment, but the CCP assured the Chinese people that great sacrifices had to be made in the present in order to build a great future. As we shall see later on, the overemphasis on industry at the expense of agriculture proved to be a serious mistake. But the Chinese, blinded by their desire to follow the Soviet model, did not know it then.

While dreaming about the future, the Chinese Communists faced a stupendous task in 1949. Wars had been an almost normal state of affairs since the fall of the Manchu regime in 1912, and whatever economic accomplishments had been made before 1937 were more than cancelled during the Sino-Japanese War and the civil war that followed. The Communists themselves did an effective job of wrecking railroads and destroying mines then under the Nationalist control. In Manchuria, which had been built up as an industrial showcase during the Japanese occupation, industrial equipment and sometimes entire plants were dismantled by the Russians and then shipped to Russia as "war booty." Much of what was left suffered heavy damage during the civil war that followed. In 1949 the output of producer goods dropped by 70 percent from its previous peak, and the decline in the production of consumer goods was 30 percent. The shortage of technical and managerial personnel, the inadequate supply of raw materials, the diffusion of labor forces, the disruption of rail and water transportation all combined to make reconstruction work extremely difficult. The Nationalists did not help the situation by staging a naval blockade shortly after they had been driven out from the mainland. Shanghai, once a booming city of industry and commerce, was virtually dead.

Slowly and gradually the Communists succeeded in overcoming their initial difficulties. They took possession of the enterprises formerly belonging to the Nationalist government or officials. They took over foreign assets either by outright confiscation as in the case of American firms upon the outbreak of the Korean War or by a more devious method in which foreign firms, having encountered numerous Communist-inspired labor disputes, were forced to sell their assets to the Communist government at a nominal price. As for those capitalists who could not be classified as either reactionaries or counterrevolutionaries, the government decided to let them run their firms as usual and keep production going at a time when there was a serious shortage of manufactured goods. This lenient attitude towards the so-called national capitalists contrasted sharply with the harsh policy the new regime then pursued towards the landlords in the countryside, who lost not only their land but also, in numerous cases, their lives as well.

In due course this lenient attitude towards the so-called national capitalists was to be changed. Upon its entry into the Korean War, the

Communist government launched a series of economic campaigns to finance it, and the properties of many businessmen were confiscated on a variety of trumped-up charges. Those businessmen who were spared during these campaigns were "persuaded" to take the government as their partner in forming joint state-private enterprises. Compared with their state counterparts, these joint state-private enterprises were generally small in terms of output as well as the number of employees. In spite of their being called state-private enterprises, they were without an exception run by state employees responsible to the government. Nevertheless, former managers were more often than not asked to stay on their jobs and former owners, unless classified as "reactionaries" or "counterrevolutionaries," were allowed to receive part of the profit as a dividend, computed roughly at 5 percent of their original investment. In 1956 the government reported that 98.7 percent of the value of industrial output had been produced by enterprises either controlled or owned outright by the state.

Through strenuous efforts, the new regime was able to restore industrial production to the pre-1949 peak by the end of 1952. Confident and ambitious, it launched its First Five Year Plan in 1953. The plan called for speedy development of heavy industry and creation of new industrial centers in the Northwest and the Southwest, away from the coastal areas. Of the 42.74 billion *yuan* (c. U.S. $17 billion) earmarked for capital expenditure, more than 77 percent was to be spent on heavy industry, while the rest was divided among agriculture, forestry, water conservation, and cultural, educational, and health activities. By 1957 when the First Five Year Plan was completed, the government reported fulfillment and overfulfillment of all production quotas. The output of capital goods was increased by more than 204 percent with an average growth rate of 24.9 percent per year, and the production of consumer goods was increased by 85.1 percent with an average growth rate of 13.2 percent per year. The production of steel, for instance, was increased from 1.8 million metric tons in 1953 to 5.4 million metric tons in 1957.

Having scored a great success in the production of capital goods, a more cautious planner would have called for the concentration of energy on other sections of the economy to achieve a more balanced growth. Unfortunately, the Chinese Communists did not see the rationale of this approach. Carried away by their recent success, they pushed relentlessly toward even higher goals along the same line. When the Second Five Year Plan began in 1958, the prospect for continuous economic growth had never looked better. Yet by the end of the year the whole economy began to fall apart. Discarding all precautions, the government called for the Great Leap Forward: the increase of production by 100 percent in key industries. The Chinese were urged to work even harder, "concentrating twenty years' progress in a single day" and surpassing Great Britain in fifteen years. Thousands of small blast furnaces appeared in the countryside, producing tons of iron and steel that looked good in statistics but were mostly useless, even to make farm implements. The government claimed an increase of 131 percent in pig iron production to 13.7 million metric tons, and an increase of 107 percent in crude steel production to 11.1 million metric tons, all in a single year. The increase in the production of other industrial items was less spectacular but nevertheless substantial. All these production figures, however, proved to be more illusory than real since local Communists, to impress their superiors in Peking, sent fantastic reports about their economic achievements, achievements that could not be substantiated by on-the-spot inspections. The Peking government quickly had to revise its claim downward, much to its own embarrassment.

After 1958 economic production on all fronts dropped sharply, until it reached disastrous proportions by 1961. Factories lay idle because of the shortage of raw materials, and thousands of workers had to be sent to the countryside to increase agricultural production. Transportation broke down; demand could not find supply and vice versa. The most adversely affected area, unfortunately, happened to be the most important, namely, the production of consumer goods. As food and cloth were rationed and rerationed to make what was available go as far as possible, many people actually suffered from hunger and cold. The once bright picture had suddenly become dismal and bleak.

What had happened? First, there were serious errors in both planning and implementation of various industrial projects. The plans were too ambitious, exceeding the capacity of both natural and human resources then at the government's disposal. Coordination was poor among the various economic agencies, each of which pursued its own goals with little or no regard for supplementary and complementary work done by the others. Second, the failure to expand agricultural production to keep pace with industrial development resulted in the inadequate supply of industrial raw materials as well as food. When cotton crops failed, for instance, textile plants had to be closed or operated on a part-time basis. Third, serious floods and droughts occurred successively after 1958. The government had either to abandon its ambitious industrial projects or face mass starvation and possibly revolt. Naturally it took the former course. Millions of city dwellers were sent to the countryside to help agricultural production, and, temporarily at least, industrial production was relegated to a position of secondary importance. Finally, the increasing economic difficulties came at a time when the Soviet Union and the People's Republic became more and more antagonistic towards each other. Not satisfied with the role of a smug bystander, the Soviet Union actually called off the assistance it had formerly pledged. Many industrial plants could not be completed when the Soviet Union not only refused to send additional equipment but also withdrew all of its technicians.

Underlying the various causes of this economic disaster was the basic question involving the very nature of a planned economy. While a planned economy admittedly possesses many advantages, it is also true that no planners, however capable, can anticipate the operation of numerous economic forces, many of which are clearly beyond human control. This difficulty was compounded by the inflexibility of Communist dogmas and the eagerness to accomplish what physically could not be accomplished in a short time. Under the capitalist system, with each corporation planning its own expansion and production, the failure of one company to anticipate market demand will not affect the economy as a whole, since it is inconceivable that all corporations would make the same mistakes at the same time. Moreover, as the scope of planning is restricted and affects only a small section of the economy, misjudgments can have only a limited impact as compared with planning that involves the economy of the entire country and affects hundreds of millions of people. In the latter case, a minor error on the planning board will be magnified a million times on the implementation level and may result in irreparable damage to the economy as a whole. To complicate the matter, the Communist planners, under the dictate of political considerations, were often inclined to disregard economic realities.

The Great Leap Forward stunted economic growth for a brief period, and its failure was partly responsible for Mao Tse-tung's temporary loss of control within the Communist power structure, as noted earlier. In 1961 when the economy reached its nadir, even the most sanguine Communists began to have second thoughts about the Great Leap, and more pragmatic administrators, under the leadership of Liu Shao-ch'i, began the arduous task of putting the broken pieces together. Material incentive was emphasized for the workers; industrial plants were ordered to operate on a profit-or-loss basis; the overall management of industry was decentralized; and for the first time, great attention was given to the production of consumer goods. By 1964 the recovery had been so encouraging that the production of all goods actually returned to the 1958 level. In some industries, such as coal and petroleum, the production even outdistanced any on record. At a time when a strong sense of well-being permeated the nation, Mao Tse-tung, suddenly and without warning, launched the so-called Cultural Revolution. Fearful that if the prevailing trend continued, the socialism that he had carefully built would eventually disappear in China, Mao Tse-tung, through his ardent supporters, accused Liu Shao-ch'i and his associates of having followed a "revisionist" policy and the capitalist road and demanded their ouster from positions of power. Rampaging the countryside, the

Red Guards attacked any "revisionist" (who was "socialist in appearance but capitalist in reality") they could find. In many cases, they encountered strong resistance from the workers who, understandably, did not relish the thought of losing part of their pay in order to conform to someone else's ideology.

The Cultural Revolution affected practically every aspect of Chinese life, including industrial development. The Maoist radicals, by emphasizing the importance of ideological purity and the necessity of maintaining an incorruptible, Spartan form of life, tended to downgrade economic progress per se. To them "politics should be always in command," and work was as much a political or spiritual exercise as it was a means to achieve a materialistic end. A good worker was one with the correct outlook toward man and his society, as outlined in Marxism-Leninism-Maoism, not necessarily one who knew how to produce more. Wages, though a necessary means to sustain life, must be kept at a minimum so that the worker, living on bare necessities, would not be corrupted by creature comfort and would not degenerate into a bourgeois. Workers who had distinguished themselves, as either ideological purists or high achievers (and preferably both), should of course be recognized. They were hailed as labor heroes and given more responsibilities; they might even be considered for membership in the CCP, the exclusive club for the political and social elite. Material incentive had no place in a Communist utopia, and a true proletarian, completely selfless and constantly working for the benefit of all mankind via class struggle, had a much higher goal to attain than the improvement of living standards.

This idealistic, romantic approach to life and work was laudable, replied the moderates, if it could be translated to reality without the greatest hardship and difficulties. But this could not be done. To make it work an individual's life and thought would have to be controlled from cradle to grave: was this not too high a price to pay? As the possibility of backsliding was always present even among a group of the most regimented individuals, eternal vigilance had to be maintained, in the form of not only daily or weekly criticism and self-criticism meetings but also repeated ideological campaigns on a massive scale. During the ideological campaigns too often one group of people was set against another, and the country was turned upside down. "Class struggle" and "perpetual revolution" might be the necessary means to preserve the purity of a proletarian society, but the cost was also enormous, especially in terms of lost production. Was not the goal of life happiness, including happiness in a material sense? What was wrong with creature comfort, the moderates argued, even in a Communist society, if it could be universally shared? Why should material incentive be unequivocally condemned if it was the most effective means to induce a worker to work harder and produce more? How could China be a good example for the rest of the world to follow if her people continued to live in poverty? How could she even survive as a nation, let alone promote world revolution, if she remained industrially backward, however ideologically pure she really was? To industrialize and modernize, said the moderates, China should not mind borrowing ideas from any source, including capitalist countries. No country had a monopoly of all that was good; if a capitalist country happened to be superior to China in a certain area, such as technology, by all means China should borrow from her. "It does not matter whether a cat is black or white," said Teng Hsiao-p'ing, "as long as it catches mice."

From 1966 to 1976 the moderates and the radicals waged a tug of war between them, and each claimed credit for what had been accomplished and blamed the other for what had failed. Wherever the credit or blame really belonged, there is no question that substantial progress was made during this period. Steel production, for instance, rose from 11 million to 25 million metric tons from 1966 to 1975, but it dropped to approximately 21 million metric tons in 1976. The drop was caused not only by the increasing tempo of political infighting between the radicals and the moderates but also by natural disasters such as the T'angshan earthquake that damaged factories and mines and interrupted rail and water transportation. The production of industries other than steel also declined proportionally.

On all accounts, the most important industrial development during the period from 1966 to 1976 was in the petroleum industry. Prior to the discovery of large oil reserves in the early 1960's, China had no petroleum industry to speak of. Before 1949 she depended mostly upon the United States for the satisfaction of her oil needs. When that supply was cut off upon the establishment of the People's Republic, she began to purchase oil from the socialist camp, primarily the Soviet Union and Rumania. In the wake of the Sino-Soviet split that began in 1959, the Soviet Union cancelled all the oil exports to China in order, said the Soviet leaders, to "impress our Chinese comrades on the importance of socialist solidarity." Mao Tse-tung called the Soviet move blackmail and immediately sent Chinese geologists to search for domestic sources of supply. Soon these geologists found oil reserves so large and extensive that no one had dreamed of their existence before. The estimate of these reserves ranges anywhere from 22 billion to 220 billion barrels, concentrated primarily in two areas: the Tach'ing oil fields in northern Manchuria and the Takang and Shengli oil fields around the Gulf of Pohai. Production of crude oil has been increased at an annual rate of 20 percent since 1960 and will reach 3 to 4 million barrels a day by 1980. In 1970, for the first time in her history, China produced enough oil for her own consumption; in 1973 she began to export oil, primarily to Japan. According to Peking, oil exports may reach 1 million barrels a day by 1980.

Impressive though it was, the production of oil would have been even greater had China sought the assistance of foreign technology. Why did she not seek foreign assistance in industrial development? The question was in fact a major issue between the moderates and the radicals during the ten-year period between 1966 and 1976. Saddened by their experience with the Soviet Union which cut off all forms of aid in 1959 and helped send the Chinese economy into a downward spin, the radicals, led by Mao Tse-tung and Chiang Ch'ing, insisted that China must rely on her own effort for economic development, so that she would not be subject to foreign blackmail again. They contended that it was preferable to develop China's economy slowly without foreign assistance than to develop it faster with it. The principle of self-reliance should in fact underlie all of China's economic endeavors, including foreign trade. China would buy with what it could sell, and export and import should be balanced as much as possible on an annual basis. Foreign credit from either corporate or governmental sources should be avoided so that China's industrial establishments would not be mortgaged to "the greedy, capricious imperialists" who had in the past reduced China to a semi-colonial status. In the long run, having the oil buried in the ground was a much wiser decision than having it pumped out faster with foreign assistance; so said the radicals.

While agreeing with the radicals on the importance of self-reliance, the moderates believed that China could not develop her industry, especially her defense industry, fast enough to meet modern demands without learning from abroad and adopting foreign technology. They contended that the kind of ruthless exploitation of China by foreign powers, prevalent before 1949, could not possibly reemerge and that China's experience with the Soviets should be regarded as more an exception than a rule. It was possible to invite foreign assistance without foreign domination, and China could not keep pace with the developed countries as long as she insisted on isolating herself from foreign contact. Science and technology did not have an ideological content and certainly did not recognize national boundaries. It was China that had to suffer for not recognizing this fact.

Generally speaking, the principle of self-reliance prevailed during the period between 1966 and 1976. While providing foreign aid in moderate amounts for the developing countries in Southeast Asia and Africa, China herself shunned major borrowings, in capital as well as in technology, from the more industrialized countries. With the downfall of the "Gang of Four" in October, 1976 there has been a noticeable but slow and gradual change. The Chinese Communists, under the leadership of Hua Kuo-feng and Teng Hsiao-p'ing, have expressed increasing interest in the exchange of scientific and technological information with developed countries like the United States and Japan, in the purchase of sophisticated equipment such as computers and jet engines, and in the enlargement of foreign trade in general. Early in 1977 the *People's Daily,* a Communist organ, published for the first time a 1956 speech of Mao Tse-tung's in which the Communist leader stressed the importance of "learning from abroad" and the adoption of Western technology. While its editor, for obvious reasons, did not choose to emphasize the fact that the speech was made before the Sino-Soviet split and long before the Cultural Revolution, the fanfare that accompanied publication of the speech indicates clearly that the old policy of total self-reliance has been greatly modified, if not completely abandoned. At the moment the major block to the enlargement of foreign trade has less to do with the principle of self-reliance than it has with China's inability to sell enough abroad in order to finance the imports she needs. For instance, how many tons of hog bristles (which remains a major item of export) must she sell in order to purchase one computer or one jet engine? The situation may change drastically if the newly developed petroleum industry lives up to its expectation. If oil exports continue to increase, China will be able to purchase more industrial equipment and sometimes entire plants to facilitate her industrial growth, the rate of which may speed up considerably from then on.

Early in 1978 the People's Republic signed a $20 billion trade pact with Japan that called for the exchange of Chinese coal and petroleum for Japanese steel, machinery, and technology for a period of eight years. This is the largest trade agreement she has concluded with a foreign power in more than two decades. Meanwhile she has repeatedly expressed her desire to sell oil directly to the United States, in exchange for American petroleum technology which is the most advanced in the world. To show their determination to guide China in a different direction, the moderates in power have written into the 1978 constitution the so-called four modernizations—the modernization of agriculture, industry, national defense, and science and technology. By the year 2000, the moderates say, China will be fully and completely modernized.

AGRICULTURE

Agriculture has been the most important section of the Chinese economy, and the problems it poses are also the most difficult to resolve. The Communists rose to power on their promise to solve the land problem; the success or failure of their regime has ultimately to be judged by their ability to keep that promise.

The role of China's traditional agriculture was a simple one: to provide enough food to meet the basic needs and to produce enough cotton, hemp, and silk for clothing. This goal, however, was no longer sufficient for the Communist regime that came into existence in 1949. Besides producing necessities for domestic consumption, Chinese agriculture, according to the Communists, had to produce a large surplus to be shipped to the Soviet Union and other socialist countries in exchange for industrial equipment and materials necessary to implement China's industrialization programs. The demand on agriculture was greater than it had ever been. If historically China had not been able to produce enough to meet domestic needs, how could the new regime hope that she could produce huge surpluses to meet the new demand? The Communists said that she could. They asserted that if "feudal" relationships in the countryside were abolished, if landownership were socialist rather than private, and if modern science and technology were applied to farming, then the historic problem of land shortage and population pressure would be solved. Thus convinced, they began, as soon as they took power, to apply their brand of Marxism-Leninism to the Chinese land problem.

Knowing that they would encounter great resistance if they attempted to carry out their socialist reconstruction in one giant step, the Chinese Communists decided to advance toward their eventual goal by stages. The first stage was the reduction of both rent paid to the landlords and interest charged by rural moneylenders. This was the policy the Communists followed in areas under their control during the Sino-Japanese War, and its moderation won them great admiration as agrarian reformers, especially in the Western world. Before the summer of 1950 the same policy was also followed in Central and South China.

The second stage was that of land confiscation and redistribution, which came about only after the Communists had completely eliminated the Kuomintang influence and had brought an area under their unchallenged control. Land redistribution did not come to the Yangtze region until the fall of 1950, though it had been carried out in Manchuria and North China before this time. In each village where land was to be redistributed, Communist cadres went to work to stir up hatred. They divided all the villagers into five classes: landlord, rich peasant, middle peasant, poor peasant, and farm laborer. Their strategy, in observance of an order from Peking, was to ally with poor peasants and farm laborers, neutralize rich and middle peasants, and strike against landlords. At so-called struggle meetings convened by the Communists, each landlord was brought before the villagers to confess his sins, real or imaginary. The trial and conviction of the "notorious" landlords, many of whom were executed on the spot, was followed by land redistribution, whereby each peasant received anywhere from 0.15 to 0.45 acre of land, depending upon the localities. By the spring of 1953 land redistribution was said to have been completed for more than 80 percent of the Chinese villages.

The small amount of land each peasant received after land redistribution indicates clearly the tragic nature of the problem: too little land

and too many people. Moreover, as land was further fragmented, its productivity became smaller still. What would the government's next step be? It could not proceed immediately with collectivization, which would deprive the poor peasants of their recently acquired land and antagonize them; yet, it was obviously uneconomical for anyone to cultivate a garden-sized farm. In short, there had to be intermediary steps between land redistribution and collectivization. Consequently in the spring of 1953, the government called for the implementation of the third stage of its socialist reconstruction program, namely, the organization of mutual-aid teams. Within each mutual-aid team peasants shared manpower, draft animals, and agricultural tools, mostly on a seasonal or temporary basis. This form of cooperation was readily accepted because, first, it had existed before, and second, it clearly benefited all parties concerned.

Mutual-aid teams existed for only one year, however, before the government moved to implement the next or fourth stage of its socialist reconstruction program, namely, the merge of mutual-aid teams into agricultural cooperatives. All members in a cooperative pooled their land, draft animals, farm implements, and labor. When harvests were collected, they were remunerated in accordance with their contributions, especially labor which carried more weight than any other factor. The cooperatives, however, did not enjoy the same kind of enthusiastic support as the mutual-aid teams for the simple reason that psychologically it was easier for a peasant to identify himself with a small plot of land he owned himself than with a large tract of land which, he was told, he jointly owned with others. Whenever resistance was encountered, the government would use every means at its command, including the denying of credit, to bring the recalcitrant peasants into line. By the summer of 1956 more than 90 percent of the peasant households had been organized into cooperatives.

Whatever misgivings the peasants might have had about the cooperatives were mollified considerably by two consecutive good harvests in 1956 and 1957. Believing that the pooling of farming land had indeed increased production, Mao Tse-tung decided, in the spring of 1958, to merge cooperatives into even larger units. These large units were called people's communes which, according to Mao's ardent supporters, were communism *par excellence,* the final stage of the government's socialist reconstruction program. Peasants were ordered to hand over to the communes all that they possessed with the temporary exception of houses, courtyards, and trees. Private ownership completely disappeared overnight, and all peasants became the rural proletariat, working for the communes and paid in wages. The first commune, named Sputnik after the Soviet Union's first orbiting satellite, came into existence in Honan in April, 1958, and by the end of the year more than 24,000 communes, comprising 99 percent of the rural population, had been organized. The

CCP predicted greater production and higher standard of living for all the participating peasants.

Optimism died quickly, however. The organizational dislocation caused by the launching of the communes and the excesses generated by the Great Leap Forward, plus repeated flood and drought after 1958, sent agricultural production into a tailspin, and by 1961 millions of people were actually hungry. Under the impact of disaster, the doctrinaire Communists slowly, though reluctantly, handed over the administration of the economy to their more pragmatic colleagues; and beginning in 1962, agriculture, as well as industry, started to move upward. The Communist leaders finally realized that no man, however highly motivated, could endure indefinitely a working schedule of fifteen or sixteen hours a day, plus one or two hours of political indoctrination, without eventually suffering a mental or physical breakdown. They issued a new order that directed all commune members to have at least twelve hours for meals, sleep, and recreation during each working day. As a concession to petty capitalism, each peasant was allowed to have a private plot of his own, the produce of which could be either retained for his own consumption or sold in a free market. But the combined size of the private plots, said the new instruction, should not exceed 5 percent of the total area in each commune. Ironically, it was the produce of these private plots, rather than the commune farm, that helped the nation survive its worst depression on record.

The communes that were established in 1958 have undergone many changes and modifications. To provide more efficient management, the original 24,000 communes have been broken up to form the existing 74,000 smaller ones. Moreover, the harsh regimentation of life that accounted for the early abuse has since been considerably allayed. The commune system, consequently, has become less draconic and more workable. Aside from its political and social implications, which may not be all good, the system definitely possesses certain advantages, given China's special circumstances. First, the enlargement of farms enchances the prospect of using machines that may eventually replace most if not all the manual labor; it facilitates the use of fertilizers and the application of insecticides; and it makes easier the work of irrigation, flood control, and field drainage. Moreover, it enables individual peasants to be specialized in different aspects of farming labor. Second, as each commune is encouraged to build its own industries to produce goods to meet local needs, not only will the rural unemployed and semiemployed find a new opportunity for employment, but the demand made on the state-owned enterprises will also be eased. The state enterprises, from then on, could concentrate on the production of those goods that require advanced technology and large capital outlays. Third, the well-disciplined, organized life in the commune enables the government to mobilize large labor forces to undertake giant tasks of common concern on short notice, especially in wintertime when commune members are not busy in the field. The meaning of this point becomes self-evident when it is pointed out that despite the Communist regime's effort to industrialize, China's main asset in production is still manpower. In 1969, for instance, as a result of employing 1,750,000 workers, three major water-conservation projects were completed, including a waterway of 340 miles that brought irrigation benefits to five provinces. Last, since each commune is designed to be culturally as well as economically self-sufficient, it has established its own schools, job training centers, and recreation facilities. The commune, for instance, has played an important role in adult education and in the elimination of illiteracy in China.

Since manual labor, instead of machines, is the key factor in the operation of a Chinese farm, the commune, even in its reduced size, is still too large to serve as an operational unit. A commune is normally divided into production brigades, each of which corresponds to a village. A brigade is in turn divided into production teams, and generally speaking, the members of each team come from the same neighborhood. People from the same neighborhood, headed by a team captain, work and rest together; jointly they are responsible to the production brigade, the basic operational unit in a commune. The head of the production brigade, usually a Communist cadre, is the most important man in a village; he, in consultation with others, not only supervises all activities in the brigade but also serves as a conduit between the state and the peasants. It is his duty to persuade the peasants that the state's decisions are wise and should be carried out, whatever they happen to be. Usually he succeeds in his efforts, but sometimes with great difficulties. A recurrent disagreement between the state and the peasants has to do with the way in which the fruits of labor are divided. The peasants, naturally, want to keep as much as possible for themselves, while the state is bent on enlarging its own take. Caught between the two contradictory demands, the CCP cadre has to be extremely skillful not to antagonize either one.

Generally speaking, each year's harvests are divided three ways. One portion will be sold to the state's purchasing agencies at a price fixed by the state. To all intents and purposes this sale amounts to a taxation on income, since the state, at its own discretion, can raise or lower not only the percentage of its share but also the prices, thus increasing or decreasing its own take. In a year of good harvests the state will take more; it will take little or nothing if a drought or flood has reduced the output substantially. After the state has taken its share, the rest of the crops will be divided between "collective reserve" and "distributed income." The former, corresponding to the retained or undivided profit in a Western corporation's balance sheet, can be used either for capital expansion, such as the purchase of a new tractor, or for education and social welfare, such as the improvement of school or medical facilities and the establishment of a new "happy home for the aged." The distributed income is more like disposable income than wages since, unlike wages, it is not subject to taxation. The amount of disposable or distributed income a peasant actually receives depends upon not only the total amount of crops assigned for distributed income but also the number of working units he has accumulated throughout the year. A working day constitutes a working unit; since all the peasants in a production brigade or team work approximately the same number of days each year, their income, theoretically at least, is also about the same.

Since the establishment of the commune system in 1958, the assortment of collective revenue among state purchase, collective reserve, and distributed income has been a major issue not only between the CCP and the peasants but also among the Communist leaders themselves. As a group, the CCP moderates have argued for a larger percentage assigned for distributed income, the increase of which means, in a most tangible way, the enhancement of the peasants' standard of living. The CCP radicals, on the other hand, want to keep distributed income within a bare minimum not only for the purpose of generating more capital for state and local enterprises but also as a means of maintaining a more puritanic and, to them, more socialist form of life. They look with disfavor on the development of a private economy within a socialist framework and condemn such practices as cultivating family-owned vegetable gardens and raising and selling pigs for the enhancement of personal income. These practices, they say, are a Trojan horse that would undermine the very foundation of a socialist society. They want to reduce the private section of the peasants' economic activities until it ceases to exist, and they brand anyone advocating otherwise as a "capitalist roader" who must be knocked down immediately before he can "raise his ugly head." Nevertheless, despite their strong opposition to it, petty capitalism continued to flourish in the countryside even during the height of their power (1966–1976). For instance, a typical peasant might raise two pigs, one for his production team and one for himself and his family. Theoretically, the team pig was the more important of the two, but no one, not even the local Communist leader, wished to press him too strongly on this point. Now that the "Gang of Four" has been ousted from the position of power, petty capitalism most likely will do even better.

Before his death in 1976, Mao Tse-tung time and again called upon the Chinese peasants to learn from Tachai which, for more than ten years, has been hailed as a rural community *par excellence*. Tachai is a small hamlet in Shansi province, located in one of the less productive areas in North China. Frequently ravaged by drought or flood, its fields seem to have always contained more rocks than earth. People in this hamlet had periodically lingered between starvation and death prior to the Communist triumph in 1949; they, like peasants elsewhere in China, attributed their misfortune to fate. Fortunately, the situation has improved enormously since then. According to the 1975 statistics, the hamlet had a total of 83 households and 450 persons. Total land under cultivation was 128 acres, or 0.28 acre per person—a seemingly hopeless situation. Yet the hamlet produced not only enough to satisfy its own needs but also a surplus to subsidize the state, year after year. How did it accomplish the nearly impossible? The answer is good planning, backbreaking labor, and determination. As an example, the hamlet reported that for four years from 1971 to 1975 its members devoted all the winter time to "the leveling of thirty-three hills, large and small, and the filling of fifteen valleys with rocks and earth" for the creation of new land for cultivation. "In 1972 when there was a serious drought," the report continued, "we decided to bring water, pail by pail, to the fields and only water those spots where the seeds were actually planted. Though this meant harder work for everyone, we believed that this was the right thing to do because first, not a single drop of water would be wasted and second, all of our neighbors would be left with enough water to do their own spring planting." There may have been some exaggeration in this report, but the spirit behind it is undeniable. As a result of this dauntless spirit and superhuman effort, the grain production in Tachai has increased year after year. Per capita income for 1974 was U.S. $216, or ten times as much as that for 1955.

A per capita income of U.S. $216 would mean abject poverty to a West European or North American, but it is a handsome sum to a peasant in Tachai or anywhere else in China. It means freedom from hunger and cold—the most basic of all the freedoms. One may not like communism as an ideology or political system, but it is under the Communist leadership that the Chinese peasants, with determination and hard work and with no help from anyone, have been able to pull themselves up from the abyss of total helplessness and deprivation. One has to be familiar with the peasant life in old China in order to appreciate fully this point. This does not mean that the Communists have not made any mistakes; they have. In 1959–1961, for instance, millions of peasants were starving because a bad policy was implemented at the most inopportune time; even then few, if any, were actually starved to death. There is a world of difference between "being starved," which is common, and "being starved to death," which is rare. The sad thing is that prior to the establishment of the People's Republic, no Chinese regime during the past century and a half could make the claim that none of its citizens had actually been starved to death in a period of twenty-nine years. Today (1978) the per capita income for peasants is about U.S. $250 per year, less than one third of that in Taiwan and a fraction of that in the United States. Yet it is the highest ever recorded in the modern period.

The rise of per capita income for peasants results directly from the increase of total grain production on a nationwide basis. Total grain production rose from 113 million to 164 million metric tons between 1949 and 1952 and reached a historical height in 1958 when a total of 250 million metric tons was reported. The quixotic drive during the Great Leap Forward changed the picture drastically; by 1961, the "year of disaster," total grain production dropped to 162 million metric tons. The recovery began in 1962, and by 1964, total grain production once again reached the level of 200 million metric tons. The increase has continued since, though the rate of increase varied from year to year, depending on weather conditions. The 1975 harvest is estimated at 283 million to 289 million metric tons, and the 1976 harvest, according to Peking, was another record high. If Peking's claim proves to be valid, total grain production may have passed the landmark of 300 million metric tons for the first time in Chinese history.

Total grain production does not, of course, tell the whole story; equally important is the increase of population which must be smaller than the increase of grain production in order to show an increase in per capita consumption. Unfortunately, the People's Republic took only one census since its establishment in 1949; that was in 1953 when total population in China was reported to be 590 million. The figure of 750 million was often used in the 1960's, and the population for 1977 is estimated at 850 million to 890 million. Roughly speaking, while total grain produc- has increased by 50 percent (from 200 million to 300 million metric tons) from the 1960's to the 1970's, population increased by only 13 percent (from 750 million to 850 million) during the same period. Simple mathematics indicates that the standard of living for the peasants has risen substantially, though it is still low by Western standards. In the long run, however, a solution to the ageless problem of population pressure and land shortage has to be found in the population side of the equation since food production cannot be increased indefinitely, while the increase of population, theoretically at least, has no end. In recent years, the Chinese population has increased at an annual rate of 1.5–2 percent, so the country needs an annual increase of at least 5 million metric tons in grain production in order to maintain the same per capita consumption. Realizing the necessity of controlling population growth, the People's Republic has encouraged such practices as birth control and late marriages. The eventual goal is a population of zero growth, and a married couple in China is not supposed to have more than two children. But, for reasons that will be discussed later the Chinese have great difficulties in attaining this goal.

☙ xvii

The People's Republic (2)

CLASS AND CLASS STRUGGLE

An ideologically committed man creates for himself a prison that is his ideology. The more committed he is, the stronger the prison is and the less likely he will regain his freedom. A Communist is a person committed to the Marxist ideology, an ideology originating in a man whose training and experience were confined to those of Western Europe and whose knowledge of China was fragmentary at best and nonexistent at worst. Prior to the May Fourth Movement (1919) few of China's intellectuals had heard of Karl Marx and such men as Ch'en Tu-hsiu and Li Ta-chao, who later founded the Chinese Communist Party, had committed themselves to creating for China a Western-oriented society, with emphasis on science and democracy. They began to study Marxism only

546

after they had learned to admire Lenin's "new state," or, more precisely, that part of Lenin's policy that called upon the "new state" to relinquish the special rights and privileges that Czarist Russia had gained in China during the nineteenth century. In other words, it was the Marxist prescription for the destruction of imperialism, which meant freedom and independence for China, that attracted these Chinese intellectuals to Marxism. Overnight they transformed themselves from admirers of John Locke and Thomas Jefferson to disciples of Marx and Lenin.

These intellectuals quickly learned that one could not accept Marxism eclectically and that once a Marxist, one had to embrace the entire gamut that ran from dialectic materialism to the theory of class struggle. "History is a history of class struggle," said Karl Marx, and his latter-day Chinese followers had to look at Chinese history from a point of view totally different from that of traditional historians in China. More modest and less pretentious, the latter never believed that there was one system or theme that could explain all the intricacies of human events, other than the common-sense notion that somehow historical forces seemed to have always moved in a circular fashion ("a country divided will be united and a country united will be divided," etc.). This open-minded, pragmatic approach to history persisted until the twentieth century when a variety of theories arrived from the West. Among them the best thought-out but most dogmatic was the Marxist interpretation of history which, claiming to be scientific, was supposed to have universal applications. Presumably Chinese history could also be interpreted in a Marxist manner.

Since the founding of the Chinese Communist Party in 1921, Communist and leftist intellectuals have studied the development of Chinese society from a Marxist point of view; namely, Chinese history, like history elsewhere, has to be a history of class struggle. The Marxist shoes are supposed to fit feet of all sizes; if they do not, the feet have to be operated on in order to accommodate the shoes. In other words, historical facts have to be added or subtracted, emphasized or deemphasized, molded or distorted, in order to confirm the "universal truth of Marxism." Nevertheless, the Marxist interpretation of Chinese history was no more than an academic exercise prior to 1949, with little impact on Chinese political, social, and economic life, and non-Marxist historians could either accept part or reject all of it. The situation changed with the establishment of the People's Republic, a state that proclaimed Marxism-Leninism its commanding ideology. Historians could not teach or write without embracing the Marxist or "scientific" viewpoint of history, and all other interpretations were totally suppressed. Still historians were allowed to disagree among themselves as long as they disagreed within the Marxist framework. This comparatively moderate policy ended suddenly in 1966 when Mao Tse-tung launched the Cultural Revolution. Everything had to be radicalized, including the teaching and writing of history. According to the radicalized version, the entire span of Chinese history is divided into the following periods:

Primitive society: *c.* 600,000 B.C.–*c.* 2,000 B.C.
Slave society: *c.* 2,000 B.C.–481 B.C.
Feudal society: 481 B.C.–1840 A.D.
Semifeudal and semicolonial society: 1840–1949
Socialist society: 1949–

The key element in the periodization of Chinese history, as listed above, is the "means of production." During the period of "primitive society," say the Marxist historians in China, the means of production, namely the stone instruments, was so simple and primitive that it could be easily made, and its ownership, being universal, did not make the owner a member of the exploiting or oppressive class. No division between exploiting and exploited classes existed, and the primitive society was in fact the first commune, where the concept of private property had not yet arrived. The history of class struggle, therefore, really began with the historical period after a written language had been invented. In China's case, it began in approximately 2,000 B.C. when China entered the stage of "slave society." Then the means of production was slaves, and the ownership of slaves made one a member of the ruling or exploiting class. Since there is no indication that slaves were either numerous or widespread during the period between 2,000 B.C. and 481 B.C., the Marxist historians, to rationalize this period into the Marxist mold, have to claim that the word "people" (*min*), that appears frequently in the ancient records, is really synonymous with the word "slaves" (*nu*). If this were indeed the case, why, then, did the ancients say that "people (*min*) are more important than kings (chün)" and that "Heaven (*t'ien*) sees as people (*min*) see and Heaven hears as people hear"? Quoting statements like these, Confucian scholars have for centuries claimed that an ideal society had actually existed during this period when an individual's position in society was determined by his education and moral worth rather than the class to which he belonged. The truth seems to lie somewhere in the middle, pleasing neither the Confucian nor the Marxist historians.

Marxist or Maoist historians are much more at home with the period of "feudal society" when the major means of production was indeed land and when landowners enjoyed obvious advantages over the landless. It is not true, however, that the landowners and the landless constituted two distinct classes with an unbridgeable gap between them and that their relationship was that of an uncompromising, relentless class struggle. Oversimplification always contains an element of falsehood. The relationship between the landowners and the landless was neither a relationship of class struggle nor that of "harmony and accommodation" as many traditional historians have claimed. The actual relationship depended upon the time and the circumstances and the kind of persons directly involved. Most of the peasant uprisings, characterized by the Maoists as "class struggle in the highest form," were actually led by landlords, and Hung Hsiu-ch'üan, one of the most celebrated leaders of peasant uprisings with whom the Chinese Communists identify themselves, came from a landowning background. It is reasonable to believe that during the twenty-three hundred years (481 B.C.–1840 A.D.) that the Maoists refer to as "feudal period," most Chinese leaders in all fields of activities actually originated in the same background as that of Hung Hsiu-ch'üan, Sun Yat-sen, and Mao Tse-tung, namely small landowners and independent farmers. Had landownership constituted the sole means to the attainment of ruling class status, the great landlords would have had complete control of Chinese society throughout the entire period, They, of course, did not.

The semifeudal and semicolonial society came about, according to the Maoist historians, when the capitalists from the West and later Japan joined ranks with the Chinese landowners as the exploiters of the Chinese masses. It was semifeudal because the power of the landlords, no longer absolute, depended upon the imperialists for its continuance; it was semicolonial because China was economically exploited by the treaty powers, though politically she was not conquered by any of them. The period began in 1840 when China was defeated in the Opium War and when the economic exploitation of China by the imperialists began. Class struggle during this period acquired a "national characteristic" because it was waged against foreign imperialists as well as domestic landlords. Under the dual oppression of imperialists and landlords, Chinese capitalism could not develop, and the Marxist stage of a bourgeois society was consequently bypassed in China. To free China, the Maoists say, meant an anti-feudal (anti-landlord) and anti-imperialist struggle that reached a successful conclusion in 1949 when the People's Republic was established.

In short, the written history of China, covering a period of four thousand years, is divided into basically two periods, the slave period before 481 B.C. and the feudal period after that date. Class struggle was conducted between slave owners and slaves during the first period and between landlords and peasants during the second period. The imperialists, in fact, did not come to the scene until the last one hundred years of the second period. Aside from other considerations, the obvious shortcoming of this periodization is that it contains too few periods. Before a better system can be devised, most historians, including this author, prefer the traditional periodization by dynasties.

As Mao Tse-tung used to say, all fields of learning have to serve a political purpose, and the periodization of Chinese history is not an exception. Though the Communist movement in China was described as an anti-feudal and anti-imperialist struggle, there could be different emphasis at different times, depending upon which of the two, landlords or imperialists, were more profitably regarded as a class enemy at a given time. From 1931 when Japan invaded and conquered Manchuria to 1945 when she was defeated, the CCP regarded the Japanese imperialists as a worse enemy than the domestic landlords and called upon all Chinese, including the landlords, to form a united front to resist the Japanese aggression. After Japan's defeat, the CCP, most naturally, concentrated on the Kuomintang as the class enemy and urged "all the revolutionary classes" to conduct a "relentless struggle" against the political party that supposedly represented only the landlords' interest. The strategy worked beautifully, and the People's Republic, called a "dictatorship of four revolutionary classes," came into existence in 1949. Nine years later, the national capitalists and the petty bourgeois, once regarded as "revolutionary," were eliminated from the political scene, and the People's Republic came to be known as a "proletarian dictatorship based upon the alliance of workers and peasants." By 1975 the so-called proletarian dictatorship had become a dictatorship by the CCP leadership, as has been discussed in the preceding chapter. Since then the Communist rank and file have no more say about their government than other Chinese; they are merely the agents who carry out the directives of the CCP leadership. In reality, only the top Communist leaders constitute the ruling class; all the other Chinese, including the Communist rank and file, are subjects, whose "fundamental rights and duties," according to the 1975 Constitution, "are to support the leadership of the Chinese Communist Party." Thus the Chinese government, after so much change in modern times, ends where it began. To all intents and purposes, today's chairman of the CCP is yesterday's Son of Heaven.

There is a difference, however. In traditional China all of the emperor's subjects were customarily divided into four classes (scholars, farmers, artisans, and merchants) but the real factors in class differentiation were education and wealth (pp. 354–359). Social mobility was large because of the operation of the civil service examination system (pp. 179–181). With the establishment of the People's Republic, a classless society was supposed to have arrived, but contradictions existed even in a classless society, said Mao Tse-tung in 1957, notably the contradiction between the government and the people and between the leaders and the led. These contradictions, Mao Tse-tung continued, were "among the people" and were "nonantagonistic"; they could and must be resolved by peaceful means, such as persuasion and education. This assessment seemed to have been correct in 1957 since the "class enemies" (landlords, "monopolistic" capitalists, etc.) had been effectively liquidated by then. Nine years later, Mao Tse-tung made a complete about-face when he asserted that China had gone "revisionist" and that the government was controlled by a group of "capitalist roaders" against whom the Chinese people must wage a relentless class struggle. After the CCP moderates had been successfully purged and when, once again, Mao Tse-tung emerged as the dictator of all China, the CCP began to present a totally new view of Chinese society. Classes in the People's Republic not only existed, said the CCP, but eternal class struggle must also be waged against class enemies. Though moderated somewhat since Mao's death in 1976, this view has remained one of the party lines.

How can there be classes, let alone class struggle, in a society completely dominated by the CCP, the "party of the people"? First, the conventional concept of factors that differentiate classes, such as power, wealth, and social prestige, is not applicable in the People's Republic, and the so-called class enemies are the former landlords and capitalists and their descendants who, as a group, are actually the most deprived people in the country. In other words, class struggle is conducted on behalf of the privileged against the underprivileged, the powerful against the powerless, and the majority against the minority, in direct contrast to what the term "class struggle" normally means. The rationalization behind this novel concept of class struggle is that once born to a reactionary class, one can never completely eliminate one's reactionary sentiment— nor can one's descendants. Though no Communist theoretician has speculated on the number of generations during which the reactionary characteristics are supposed to persist, the Communists have done thorough work in tracing each person's genealogy in order to determine whether he is a friend or an enemy. Would the Communist leaders apply the same principle to themselves? Of course not. If they did, most if not all of them would have been declared reactionaries and therefore class enemies. It seems that the makers of a rule have always made themselves an exception to the rule.

Second, there is genuine concern among the Communist purists that if nature were allowed to take its own course and if permanent vigilance were not maintained against capitalism, some people would be bound to become richer and more privileged and would acquire a higher class status than others. Since men are not endowed with the same intelligence, organizational skill, or propensity to work, the end result will be different even though they all start at the same point. In that case classes will emerge and China, like the Soviet Union, will become "revisionist"—socialist in appearance but capitalist in reality. Therefore, class struggle must be maintained even before classes emerge, and those who think or behave like capitalists, namely those who place personal welfare above social well-being, must be regarded as "capitalist roaders" and class enemies. They must be knocked down before they can become full-fledged capitalists. Class struggle, therefore, is a never-ending process, and revolution is permanent and continuous. How, then, can a classless society be preserved when the natural development of events is bound to create classes? In order to preserve a classless society, what is the limit to the price China is willing to pay, not only in terms of social disturbances and the chaos that class struggle invariably creates but also in terms of the loss of individual freedoms and incentive to produce more goods and services that will certainly benefit all members of the society? There is no easy way to answer these questions, as long as China is committed to the creation of a classless society.

Committed to the creation of a classless society, even the moderates, presently in power, do not know how to resolve this dilemma. The 1978 constitution, for instance, calls upon the government not only to deprive landlords, rich peasants, and reactionary capitalists of their political rights, but also to punish the newly emerged capitalist class. Since landlords, etc. have ceased to exist in China for more than 29 years, these terms could only mean either their former varieties or, most likely, descendants of these varieties. Likewise, since there is no emerged capitalist class in China today, the term cannot but mean those who "think" or "behave" like capitalists, rather than capitalists per se. "Class struggle," therefore, has acquired a new definition totally unexpected by Marx and Engels. As true believers in the Maoist theory of contradictions, all good Communists, moderate or radical, have to invent class enemies when, all across China, there is not a single one of them in sight.

Too often, however, the terms "class" and "class struggle" have been used in a most facetious manner. After a person has been successfully purged, whether he was Liu Shao-ch'i, Lin Piao, or Teng Hsiao-p'ing, he would be invariably described as "having a big landlord background," "a capitalist roader who loves creature comfort," "an antisocialist who became a Communist by deception," and therefore a class enemy. During the Cultural Revolution Chiang Ch'ing and her protégés used this tactic successfully in ousting the moderate leaders from positions of power, only to be branded themselves as "capitalist roaders" and "class enemies" after they failed to seize absolute power in the wake of Mao Tse-tung's death. In the heat of a power struggle, words become weapons; they lose their normal meanings. Today's "true Marxists-Leninists" may be tomorrow's "capitalist roaders," and vice versa.

EDUCATION

In education as in practically everything else, the history of the People's Republic can be divided into three periods: the transitional period of accommodation and consolidation from 1949 to 1966, the period of radicalization from 1966 to 1976, and the period since 1976. During the first period, the CCP, while maintaining what it regarded as the best of China's cultural heritage, also introduced and carried out much-needed reforms. The second period was marked by the CCP's total rejection of the Confucian tradition and its enforcement of a new educational policy that resulted in the demoralization of educational personnel and the lowering of academic standards. Though the third period is too short to warrant any definitive assessment, a slow process of de-radicalization or de-Maoization seems to have already begun and may, if continued, return China to the first period.

The first period was by far the most constructive as the government attempted to increase enrollment at all levels of schools, raise academic standards among the institutions of higher learning, and eliminate illiteracy. Ten years after the establishment of the People's Republic, it was reported that nine out of ten children of school age were attending schools and that more than twelve million students were enrolled in the middle schools. Enrollment continued to increase throughout the early 1960's; by 1966 when the Cultural Revolution began, practically all children old enough to attend were in school. The Chinese law then required every child to have at least six years of schooling, and the provisions of this law were enforced in all but the most remote or isolated areas. Secondary education was more selective, however, due to the lack of adequate funds and trained personnel, as well as the general poverty of the nation. Nevertheless, the number of secondary schools and the kind of education they offered continued to improve throughout the first period.

As one would expect, colleges were even more selective than secondary schools. For a middle school graduate to be accepted in a university or college was considered an unusual privilege, reserved for those who were not only highly intelligent but also politically most reliable. Nevertheless, even the institutions of higher learning made great progress during this period. The total number of colleges and universities rose from 227 in 1950 to 1,000 in 1958, and total enrollment increased from 110,000 to approximately 650,000 during the same period. In 1966 more than 1,000,000 students were attending colleges and universities. The quality of these schools was uneven, of course, but the best among them could be compared favorably with the best in many Western countries. As one would expect, the government favored colleges of science and engineering. While Peking University remained a college of general studies, its sister institution, Tsinghua, was reorganized as a vast polytechnic university. It coordinated its research with governmental projects, whether the project was the construction of a dam or the designing of a new jet engine. In 1958 the famed Chinese University of Sciences and Technology was established in Peking; it admitted students of exceptional academic ability and high political reliability. The faculty was drawn from the research members of the Academy of Sciences, the leading center of research in the People's Republic. In 1957 the Academy had 68 research institutes with a total personnel of more than 17,000. It purchased books and subscribed to scholarly journals from all the scientifically advanced countries, including the Soviet Union and the United States. It had many of China's renowned scientists as its research fellows.

Equally impressive was the new regime's successful effort in eliminating illiteracy. Throughout Chinese history education had always been the right of a privileged few. An ordinary peasant viewed the written word with reverence and awe; it was something obviously useful but incomprehensible to him. Since the People's Republic was supposed to be a democratic state based upon the alliance between workers and peasants, one of the first priorities for the new regime was to teach workers and peasants how to read, if for no other reason than the fact that the government wanted them to be informed about its policies and programs, so it could continue to enjoy their support. Adult or part-time schools were established in every corner of the country so that workers and peasants could learn in the evenings or in wintertime when peasants were not busy in the fields. One of the government's most ingenious devices was to encourage educated children to teach illiterate parents, and both parents and children were hailed as heroes if they succeeded in their effort. The campaign to eliminate illiteracy went so well that by the middle 1950's all Chinese, with the exception of those too old to learn, knew enough Chinese characters to read a local newspaper or write a personal note. This may not mean very much on the surface, but it was an achievement never before attained in China.

In short, education on all levels—elementary, secondary, and college —made steady progress throughout the 1950's and the early 1960's, and the progress would have continued had there not been a so-called Great Proletarian Cultural Revolution. Responding to Mao Tse-tung's call to smash into pieces the established authorities, including educational authorities, millions of students deserted their classrooms and poured into the streets, shouting such slogans as "Down with revisionism!" and "Down with bourgeois education!" They roamed across the length and breadth of China in the name of "exchanging revolutionary experience" and "upholding Chairman Mao's teachings." All schools, with the exception of those on the elementary level, were closed; administrators and teachers either had to join their charges in shouting revolutionary slogans and attending endless indoctrination meetings or run the risk of being condemned as counterrevolutionaries and punished as such. Four years later when schools were finally reopened, the old educational system had been destroyed for good.

Why did Mao Tse-tung deliberately and purposely destroy an educational system that had functioned so well and effectively? Aside from being part of a power struggle, the reason may also be found on a personal and ideological level. Mao Tse-tung did not have much formal education; earlier in his career when he worked as a clerk in the Peking University library, he doubtless resented those pseudo-sophisticated students who, coming from a wealthy or well-to-do background, looked down upon him as a "country bumpkin." Among the charter members of the CCP he was perhaps the only one without an academic degree, and it is not difficult to imagine his attitude towards those who could read *Das Kapital* in the German original and their attitude towards him. He educated himself in Chinese history and literature, especially folk literature, such as *The Marsh Heroes* and *The Romance of the Three Kingdoms* (pp. 329–331), and in due course he learned to write exceedingly well, especially in classical poetry. Isolated from intellectuals who, he suspected, had always looked down upon him, he increasingly identified himself with the peasants from whom he came and about whom he knew intimately. His triumph over the Moscow-trained intellectuals in 1935 was in many ways a triumph of *The Marsh Heroes* over *Das Kapital;* it was on the shoulders of the peasants, he said, that the future of the Chinese revolution would rest. During the war years, he accepted intellectuals as part of the united front out of necessity, but he never trusted them. A self-educated man and an enormously successful one, he always had a low opinion of formal education.

A peasant's lot improved considerably after 1949, but the establishment of the People's Republic did not in any way advance his position vis-à-vis that of the intellectuals. Under the educational system prior to the Cultural Revolution students in colleges and universities were still those from an intellectual background, and the children of workers and peasants, while enjoying an elementary or perhaps even a secondary education, were proportionally underrepresented in the institutions of higher learning. The reason was simple. To be accepted by a college or university, one must pass the highly competitive entrance examination where children of an intellectual background invariably did better than those of the culturally deprived. If this trend persisted, not only would the gap between the intellectual elite and the masses continue to widen but the very nature of China as a socialist society would also be undermined. How could China remain a "proletarian dictatorship based upon the alliance of workers and peasants" if the children of workers and peasants could not compete with other children in obtaining a college education—the first step toward leadership in the new society?

If educational standards were too high for a worker or a peasant to reach, they obviously had to come down to meet him. This may not be justified from an academic point of view; it was justifiable, according to the Maoist educators, from a social point of view. The new educational system, devised during the Cultural Revolution, had at least the following characteristics:

First, under the new system academic learning was supposed to be combined with ideological training, but the former was discriminated against in favor of the latter. The ideology to be studied was Marxism-Leninism-Maoism, with emphasis on Maoism. For students on the elementary school level, the ideological emphasis did not create too great a problem since a child could learn Chinese characters from a sentence like "I love Chairman Mao; Chairman Mao loves me" as well as he could learn from a sentence such as "I love my dog; my dog loves me"; and there was no special disadvantage to substituting "imperialist running dogs" and "proletarian heroes" for "oranges" and "apples" when teaching addition and subtraction. But, as a child grew older and became more mature, the constant repetition of Chairman Mao's sayings inevitably became a bore, especially to brighter students. Why should a student read the Chairman's works ten or one hundred times when two or three times seemed to be more than enough? Would the time not be better spent reading a scholarly journal or some other material equally useful? If these questions were raised, they would have to be raised in silence.

Second, the Maoist educators emphasized technical training at the expense of intellectual pursuit for its own sake. As a result, practically all the traditional courses of general education were deleted, and the required length of time for all levels of education was greatly shortened. Time for elementary school was reduced from six to four years, middle school also from six to four years, and college from four to three or two years. Most children did not have the opportunity to go beyond the eighth grade, at the end of which they were supposed to have learned a useful and employable skill. The few lucky ones continued their education in the so-called workers' universities operated by industrial plants. Called universities, they were actually job training centers, teaching technical skills in specialized fields.

Third, the new educational system called for the combination of academic learning with manual labor. The CCP rose from the peasants, and the romanticization of the soil has been a long-established tradition. Callouses and sweat were supposed to have a cleansing effect on one's body and soul, in addition to their obvious contribution to production. All students, even those in the elementary school, were supposed to devote part of their time to physical labor, and most schools, as a result of students' participation in production, were able to raise crops, vegetables, and livestock for part of their own support. Though often justified on ideological grounds, this half-study and half-work program entailed practical benefits nevertheless, since most schools, operating on a low budget, could not have survived without additional income from the physical labor of students and teachers. Because physical labor was regarded as a character-building medium, entire schools were sometimes closed so students and teachers could journey to the countryside to help the peasants.

Fourth, in the new educational system children of workers and peasants were given more opportunities than children of an intellectual background. This was especially true for the few institutions of higher learning that had always had more applicants than they could accept. An applicant must first be recommended by a factory or commune where he had worked for at least two years, and the recommendees were normally those who came from a peasant or worker background, who were ideologically pure and politically reliable, and who had worked doubly hard as manual workers and thus won admiration from their colleagues. High intelligence and academic preparations were the factors least emphasized, and a bright student's chance of having a college education was not very great if in the meantime he did not possess the qualifications mentioned above. Examinations or tests were taboo for the simple reason that had they been held, they would quickly reveal that the best Maoist students might not be the best academic performers. Such a result would be extremely embarrassing to both teachers and students.

Certain results were inevitable as a result of implementing the Maoist educational system. One was the general and sharp decline of academic standards, and the other was the increasing radicalization of every college campus, until colleges looked more like hotbeds of political intrigue than centers of learning. By 1973, after the quality of higher education had so deteriorated that mathematics majors could not do simple algebra and physics majors had never heard of Archimedes, even the Maoist educators had to agree that some academic screening was necessary. In addition, since all the nominees for college entrance were "outstanding Maoist warriors from a worker and peasant background" and since colleges, being limited in space, could accept only a small percentage of them, it seemed that a competitive examination of an academic nature was the only proper answer. However, hardly had a written examination been introduced before it became a major controversy involving not only the educators but also the CCP's top leaders.

The controversy can best be demonstrated by relating an incident involving a young man identified in the Chinese newspapers only as "author of an examination answer" (ta chuan che) or "author of the blank examination book" (ta pai-chuan che). Knowing in advance that he would not be accepted by the Liaoning University (Manchuria) because of inadequate academic preparation, he composed a letter addressed to "comrade leaders" before he entered the examination hall. Even though the examination was open-booked, he scored only 38 points in the Chinese language, 61 points in mathematics, and 6 points in physics and chemistry, out of a maximum of 100 points for each subject. In each examination he copied the letter he had prepared in advance, in which he attacked the whole concept of a written examination as unfair to people like him and asserted that he, as captain of a production team with an impeccable proletarian background, should be preferred over the "academics" for entrance to college. The incident could have ended here had the CCP's radical leaders not taken over his cause. His letter, with an editor's supporting comment, appeared in the *Liaoning Daily* (a regional newspaper), and the same letter and comment were later reprinted in the *People's Daily* (a national newspaper). A *cause célèbre* was created overnight, with the CCP's top leaders, radical and moderate, lining up on both sides of the ideological struggle. "This kind of method [written examination] in selecting college students," said Chang Ch'un-ch'iao, "will inevitably close the door to even the most promising among our proletarian youth. It is not proletarianism; it merely raises hope for revisionism." The moderates contended, correctly of course, that the radicals had heated up the issue in order to undermine the authority of Chou En-lai who had authorized the written examination.

Against the background of an educational policy that stressed the importance of "baptizing by sweat," a unique but most controversial innovation during the Cultural Revolution was the so-called May Seventh School, named after a directive issued by Mao Tse-tung on May 7, 1966. The directive called upon all the intellectuals to combine bookish learning with manual labor and urged them to go to the countryside to learn from "poor and middle peasants." Two things happened shortly afterward. One was the massive exodus of city youth to the countryside to live and work among the peasants, after millions of them, as Red Guards, had performed their "revolutionary duties" by restoring Mao Tse-tung to his unchallengeable position as the dictator of all China. Later, as colleges could not accommodate the massive yearly output of graduates from a lower level, the exodus to the countryside, known in Chinese as *hsia fang,* was institutionalized, and most students were expected to work on the farms for two or more years regardless of their personal feelings or the feelings of their parents. Many city youths were sent as far away as Manchuria and Sinkiang "to be tempered with hardship so they can become better men and women," while their parents shed tears in silence. The presence of city youths in the countryside was not a welcome sight to the peasants either, since the peasants had a problem of surplus labor themselves and would have wanted to employ their own people first. Nevertheless, the exodus helped the cities where school facilities were inadequate and where a large concentration of unemployed and unemployable youths would have created enormous problems. This is a good example of how the solution to practical problems was rationalized in ideology, albeit great human sufferings resulted from the solution.

The other aftermath of the May Seventh Directive was of course the May Seventh School that mushroomed across the country beginning in 1968. Called a school, it was actually a labor camp where participants labored in the fields from dawn to dusk, with evenings devoted to criticism and self-criticism meetings and to the study of Marxism-Leninism-Maoism. Most of the participants seemed to come from the following groups: (1) intellectuals of a landlord or bourgeois background such as artists, writers, and teachers, including college and university professors; (2) white-collar workers, including bank presidents, who had never had manual labor experience; (3) CCP workers, including high-ranking officials, who had backslid in their ideological purity and who had degenerated into "old-time bureaucrats"; (4) criminal or moral offenders among the better educated who, having been punished legally, with a jail sentence, for example, might be reformed by physical labor; and (5) CCP leftists or rightists who had been purged by their political enemies and who might be won over to the ideological or political side of the men then in power. As a normal procedure, each participant was assigned to a peasant from whom he was supposed to learn not only such things as how to use a shovel or a hoe but also the philosophy of life. A professor of nuclear physics, for instance, might have a semiliterate peasant assigned to him as a tutor. The peasant would relate to him, among other things, how much underprivileged people like peasants had suffered under the reactionary rule of the Kuomintang and how important it was for privileged people like the professors to serve the masses. The length of a participant's stay in the labor camp could vary from a few months to a few years, depending upon how sincerely he had been converted to Marxism-Leninism-Maoism. In theory the decision on his "graduation" was made jointly by all the participants in the May Seventh School; actually it was made by the CCP leader in charge.

It would be wrong to say that all the educational innovations introduced during the period of Cultural Revolution were bad or disastrous. In medical science, for instance, two innovations proved to be extremely valuable. One was the renewed interest in traditional Chinese medicine, and the other was a new institution known as the "barefoot doctors." Chinese medicine was as old as Chinese history, and certain Chinese practices, such as the use of acupuncture and herbs for the prevention and cure of diseases, dated from at least 1,000 B.C. Medical works have been written and compiled since the days of Pien Ch'üeh (fifth century B.C.), perhaps the most renowned physician in Chinese history, and open-heart surgery was performed by a physician named Hua T'o as early as the third century A.D. In short, prior to modern times when China fell behind the West in medicine as well as in practically everything else, the Chinese had had a medical tradition unmatched in richness by any other country in the world. Yet, even the best of China's medical practices were empirical rather than scientific, since none of them had ever been studied and recorded under controlled conditions. Chinese doctors knew what they had to do when an illness occurred, but they did not know the reason behind their prescription. When pressed for an explanation, they expressed it in philosophical rather than scientific terms. To a modern man, determining the nature of an illness by feeling the pulse was a myth, if not an outright fraud, and Chinese medicine quickly fell into disrepute. A physician trained in Western medicine had nothing but contempt for the traditional practitioners.

Mao Tse-tung grew up in the countryside where Western medicine was not available, and he must have observed Chinese medicine at work and found it effective. To his credit he called upon the medical profession to take a good look at traditional practice and bring it up to date. Realistically speaking, China had no choice but to continue to rely on traditional medicine, since the population was large and Western-trained physicians were too few. When the medical profession responded to Mao Tse-tung's call, it quickly learned that traditional Chinese practices, tested under laboratory conditions, not only worked but also, in some cases, worked better than their Western counterparts. The most celebrated example was of course acupuncture which, since then, has won acceptance even among the Western physicians outside of China. How, then, can one explain that during open-heart surgery the patient remains conscious and maintains a running conversation with the operating physician—even though the only "anesthetic" he has is a couple of twisting needles on his toes—and that he walks away from the operating table without assistance almost as soon as the operation is over? No scientist, Chinese or Western, can provide a rational answer. The fact is that, despite advances in modern science, there is a broad area about which we know practically nothing.

The "barefoot doctors" program was introduced on the premise that it was better to have some medical care than to have none at all. Indeed, the medical needs of China's 850 million people would not be met for a long, long time to come if everyone who practices medicine has to have an M.D. degree. The length of medical training is usually long as compared to other professions, and the funds required for such training are enormous. Besides, most medical practices, such as handing out aspirin tablets to cure a headache and giving a penicillin shot to ease inflammation, do not require advanced training. Under the "barefoot doctors" program middle school graduates from the countryside are given two years' training in medicine, with more emphasis on practical skills than on theories. Upon graduation they are returned to the community they came from and serve the people there. They "climb high mountains and ford deep gorges" in their regular tours among the peasants, giving advice on medical care and personal hygiene and providing treatment that does not require advanced knowledge or sophisticated equipment. If a patient is seriously ill, they can call upon a regular physician for assistance or make arrangements to have the patient sent to a hospital. They are invaluable to the government's birth control program because, without their advice and counsel, most peasant women would not know how to proceed. To identify them with the people they serve, they are paid as peasants rather than as doctors and have to do manual labor in the fields when they are not on medical tour—the word "barefoot" indicates that they are no different from other peasants. According to an official source, they numbered 1.5 million in 1976.

One may, legitimately, either approve or disapprove Communist China's educational policy of emphasizing technical skills at the expense of academic learning, but the study of Marxism-Leninism-Maoism to the exclusion of all other ideas in the field of humanities and social sciences has to be regarded by anyone other than a Maoist as an unmitigated disaster. How Chinese history is distorted through a Maoist kaleidoscope has been discussed earlier; here we shall relate the CCP's policy towards Confucius, regarded by most Chinese as the greatest educator China has ever produced. After the establishment of People's Republic in 1949, the entire Chinese heritage was reappraised and reevaluated, and the name of Confucius was inevitably mentioned in every discussion. How should he be characterized—as a reactionary, a progressive, or a man somewhere in between? Without an answer to this question, the educational foundation could not be formulated, and the entire educational process would be thrown into chaos. For instance, should students be encouraged or discouraged to read the *Four Books* and the *Five Classics?* Should Confucian philosophy and ethics be taught in schools? If not, how could one proceed with the teaching of Chinese history where the name of Confucius seemed to appear on every other page? To answer these questions, educators and learned scholars held three major meetings in 1957, 1961, and 1962, respectively, so as to reappraise Confucian thought from a "proletarian viewpoint" and subject it to the "dynamics of dialectic materialism." Vigorous debates were conducted at a time when free expression was still allowed within the Marxist framework. The radical faction, represented by Professors Kuan Feng and Tu Yü-shih, summarized its reason for opposing Confucius as follows:

> Basically speaking, the political philosophy of Confucius should be viewed as an attempt, on the part of the slave owners, to harmonize or smooth out the contradictions between different classes. Confucius was hoping that by reforms the old institution of the West Chou dynasty could be restored. In terms of political action, he was more than a conservative or reactionary. He always stood on the side of the slave owning nobility.

The radicals constituted only a small minority of the participants in these meetings. The majority opinion, as expressed by Professor Feng Yu-lan, was as follows:

The philosophical view of Confucius marks the liberation of man's thought from the yoke of supernatural power. It teaches us the adoption of a positive attitude toward the reality of life. The love advocated by Confucius is expressed in universal terms, transcending class differences.

A similar opinion was also expressed by Professor Fan Wen-lan, perhaps the best known Marxist historian in China:

What is the attitude we should adopt toward Confucian teachings, rich as they certainly are? The most beneficial attitude, as has been pointed out by Mao Tse-tung, is to differentiate the dregs from the essence, and we should reject the dregs in order to preserve the essence. Confucius has left behind a beautiful heritage which all of us Chinese must value highly.

During the early 1960's when the CCP's moderates were in power, the government honored Confucius by restoring his birthplace, and the visitors to Confucius's tomb, we are told, numbered thousands each day. Suddenly Mao Tse-tung launched the Cultural Revolution: thousands of Red Guards visited Confucius's tomb every day, not to pay respect but to urinate on it. Overnight the great sage was transformed into cultural enemy number one. He was described as an out-and-out reactionary, and there was absolutely nothing to recommend in his teachings. Beginning in August, 1973, when the CCP's Tenth Congress was held, a nationwide anti-Confucius campaign spread across the country, requiring all people in schools, factories, and communes to denounce Confucius. Since Confucianism formed the main trend of thought in all the humanities courses taught in China, the CCP, of necessity, had to delete these courses from curriculum requirements. There were more Chinese history courses offered at Harvard, said an American reporter who visited China in 1972, than there were at the Peking University. This was in fact an understatement, and the situation deteriorated further after 1972.

Yet no one, not even Mao Tse-tung, could wipe out the entire Chinese heritage by one stroke of a pen. If there was nothing in Confucianism that recommended it, there must be some other philosophy in the past that could be safely taught in schools. The CCP chose Legalism, the philosophy that stresses law, as opposed to moral persuasion, as the best means to maintain a peaceful, orderly society. The Legalist philosophers also advocate the creation of an absolutist state headed by an omnipotent prince to whom all citizens must pledge their loyalty and support, the sacrifice of individual well-being for the common good, and, most importantly, the teaching of Legalism to the exclusion of all other ideologies. Maoism is not Legalism, of course. Nevertheless, there is enough similarity between them that comparison helps clarify each of them. Both, for instance, elevate power as a primary motivating force for man and society. The Maoists say, "Politics should be always in command," but the expression of every human relationship in terms of power has created many bizzare and tragic events. Han Fei, the brilliant and most eloquent Legalist philosopher, was murdered by his "best friend" and ideological ally Li Ssu (p. 91); Mao Tse-tung, founder of Maoism, was the target of an assassination plot engineered by his "closest comrade-in-arms" and political heir Lin Piao. Ch'in Shih-huang, the best Legalist practitioner in Chinese history, burned books and buried scholars alive (p. 101); Mao Tse-tung, who was compared to Ch'in Shih-huang by his admirers and detractors alike, banned non-Maoist teachings from the classroom and sent dissenting scholars to the May Seventh School to be reformed by manual labor.

This does not mean that Ch'in Shih-huang and Mao Tse-tung did not make any contributions to China and the Chinese; their contributions were in fact enormous. It merely suggests that the price the Chinese had to pay was also enormous. To a person believing in independent thinking and free expression, the most repulsive aspect of Maoist society has been its intolerance, and total suppression, of competing ideas. According to an official source, the *Selected Works of Mao Tse-tung* sold 260 million copies between 1966 and 1976, and a condensed version, *Quotations from Chairman Mao Tse-tung*, sold even more. In the spring of 1977 the fifth volume of the *Selected Works* was published, and its publication was hailed as a major political and cultural event. While the presses, all owned by the government, were working overtime to print the Maoist works, they had neither the inclination nor the time to print anything else. Culturally the People's Republic has not been a great success.

Since Mao Tse-tung's death in September, 1976, not only has the anti-Confucius campaign been halted altogether, but there has also been a new emphasis on academic learning. Renowned scholars and scientists who were purged during the Cultural Revolution for no other reason than their education and training in the capitalist West have been restored to their former positions, and the Academy of Sciences, a center for basic research, once again functions. Written examination has been reintroduced as a normal procedure to measure a student's performance; no longer can a student graduate from college without learning something academic, no matter how "proletarian" his background is or how "pure" he is as a Maoist revolutionary. After passing a competitive entrance examination, a high school graduate can indeed go straight to college, without having first to work in a commune or factory for two or more years. Every child is now required to have at least eight years of schooling, and in some schools, we are told, children have to learn a foreign language, usually English, beginning in the third grade. Science and technology are emphasized on all levels of the educational ladder, though the new educators in charge have not yet come out with a formula whereby the "universal truth of Marxism" can be successfully combined with the humanities tradition of China. Most interestingly, Beethoven and Mozart are once again performed, apparently with the CCP's approval. Early in 1978 when Shakespeare, in translation, was made available for the first time in more than a decade, people braved bitter cold and lined up for blocks to purchase it, and it was sold out before most of the prospective purchasers even reached the door of the bookstore. Having been undernourished for so long, how hungry the Chinese must be!

NEW MAN; NEW SOCIETY

In the wee hours of a February morning, 1972, American newsmen were awakened by strange noises outside their hotels in Peking. Walking to the windows, they rubbed their eyes and could hardly believe what they saw. Down below thousands of Chinese—men and women, old and young—were clearing the streets of the fresh snow that had fallen during the evening. They worked silently in teams, with shovels, brooms, and hand wagons, hardly exchanging a word among themselves, as if each person knew exactly what he or she should do under the circumstances. They piled and packed the snow neatly around the trees that lined up on both sides of the streets, so the trees would receive the moisture they needed. An hour later, the streets were cleared of the snow and deserted; presumably every snow remover had gone home to resume sleep. These American newsmen had come to China to cover President Richard M. Nixon's historical trip to China after that country had been closed to the American media for more than twenty years. They were more than anxious to see for themselves how things had worked out in the new society. Nevertheless, even the most knowledgeable among them had not expected to witness a scene like that described above. The cultural shock was so great that they talked about it for days afterward.

The snow removers the Americans saw on that cold, February morning in Peking were the Maoist men and women in action—the new citizens in a new society who, in this case, were sacrificing personal comfort for the common good. More than two thousand years before the establishment of the People's Republic, the Ch'in dynasty had attempted to create the same kind of people—the Legalist men and women who were as "industrious in peace" as they were "brave in war" and who, at the government's command, would "march into raging fire and boiling water" to glorify the state. Unfortunately the Ch'in dynasty did not last long enough to see its indoctrination effort yield concrete results. The

People's Republic, on the other hand, has been much more successful. During the T'angshan earthquake (1976), for instance, a man had a choice of rescuing either his two children or the local CCP leader; without hesitation, he preferred the life of the Party leader over those of his own children. The *People's Daily*, a Maoist organ, praised him highly and urged other Chinese to follow his "selfless example." This does not mean, however, that the CCP has succeeded in converting every Chinese into a totally dedicated, completely selfless Maoist. In fact, during the fall of 1976 when power changed hands in the wake of Mao Tse-tung's death and when discipline deteriorated amid the general chaos, bank robberies were reported, and stealing, we are told, also became quite common. News of this nature was shocking, to say the least, in a society where no one, supposedly, needs to lock his door at night. Nevertheless, since the effort to create a Maoist society involves 850 million people and since the demand on a Maoist man is so stringent as to be almost superhuman, success is obvious despite infrequent failings and occasional backslidings. Even moderate success would have required mental conditioning ("brainwashing") from cradle to grave.

The conditioning begins with babyhood when nursery rhymes are supposed to contain "revolutionary messages." The buttons of jackets for kindergarten children are located in the back and a playing block is deliberately made too heavy for one child to carry—the purpose of all this is to encourage children to help one another and cultivate the spirit of cooperation at as early an age as possible. In their songs the children sing the praise of Chairman Mao and the CCP; when playing games, they aim their toy guns at the "imperialists, the revisionists, and their running dogs." After a child has learned enough Chinese characters to read independently, among his first assignments would be the *Diary of Lei Feng* and the "Three Old Stories." Lei Feng was a truck driver in the army: he maintained his truck in top condition, found the most effective way to save gas and oil while driving, and had never had an accident until he was killed in one. He devoted his off-duty hours to the study of Chairman Mao and to helping other people in need. The "Three Old Stories," written by Mao Tse-tung himself, deal with a "Long March" soldier who died of an accident while making charcoal, a Canadian physician named Norman Bethune (d. 1939) who attended the Communist wounded during the war, and the "Old Foolish Man" who wanted to remove a mountain that blocked sunlight to his house. "If I cannot finish removing it, my children will," said the "Old Foolish Man." "If my children cannot finish removing it, my grandchildren will, and so on until it is removed." The "Old Foolish Man" is a fable as old as China itself; it would have remained on the shelf collecting dust had Mao Tse-tung not chosen to retell it in his own words. Nevertheless, the message is clear. As Rome was not built in a single day, it would take hard work, determination, and patience to build a Maoist China and, eventually and hopefully, a Maoist world.

It would be wrong to say, of course, that the People's Republic has no juvenile delinquency or serious crimes. Proportionally speaking, nevertheless, she has perhaps the smallest number of crimes in terms of a large population. During 1966–1967 when the Red Guards ran wild across the country, taking lives and destroying property, the justification was that they had to "smash the capitalist roaders into pieces" before they could create a true Maoist society. In other words, their crimes should be viewed as an act of war rather than crimes *per se.* Aside from mental conditioning, which is doubtless the most important factor, other reasons can be cited for the low crime rate. First, the Chinese family ties, while loosened under the Communist regime, are still stronger than their Western counterparts, and such ties impose restraint on all, including members of the younger generation. Second, as the media, including television and movies, are not dominated by sex and violence, Chinese are not subject to the temptation of antisocial behavior as people in the West are. Besides, they must regularly attend criticism and self-criticism meetings during which they are expected to confess not only their "dirty deeds," if any, but also their "dirty thought." Third, for any infraction of the law, written or unwritten, justice is swift and punishment extremely severe. Murder, armed robbery, and rape are punishable by death, and one cannot convince a Maoist that capital punishment does not deter crimes. For crimes of a less serious nature, such as stealing and embezzlement, the sentence to be imposed depends as much upon how the conviction is obtained as upon the nature of the crime. If the conviction results from the offender's voluntary and full confession and if, in the meantime, the court is convinced of his sincere desire to reform, the sentence may be very light. If, on the other hand, the evidence has been independently obtained without his cooperation or despite his denial, the sentence could be very harsh. Once brought before a court of justice, a person is on his own, since the People's Republic has no such professions as lawyers, psychoanalysts, and social workers who might intervene on his behalf. Nor is there a jury system. The power of the judge—usually a CCP member—is enormous.

The mental conditioning of a citizen continues even after he has left school, and it reaches as far as such personal matters as love, romance, and marriage. According to the law, a man and a woman can marry at the age of 20 and 18, respectively. However, since the beginning of the Cultural Revolution when nationwide family planning was introduced, a man and woman would rarely marry before twenty-eight and twenty-four, respectively. The real purpose of encouraging later marriages is to slow down population growth, even though, officially, it is to preserve a woman's health so that it would not deteriorate quickly as a result of too much childbirth. Without marriage, what does a young person do in the meantime? Nowhere can the power of mental conditioning be better shown than in this matter called sex. Chinese and Westerners are conditioned differently in their respective attitudes toward sex; the result, consequently, is also different. In the West the drive toward sexual satisfaction is considered an indication of manhood (or womanhood), and those not interested in the opposite sex are regarded as abnormal at best and psychopathic at worst. In fact, there is a specialized field of learning that explains all human behavior in terms of sex. The Chinese, on the other hand, have for centuries downgraded sex as a beastly desire that must be suppressed in order to advance "heavenly reason"; the ability to abstain from sex is praised as an indication of strong character and moral intrepidity. This does not mean, however, that all Chinese have succeeded in attaining the Neo-Confucian goal, as concubinage and prostitution were widespread in traditional China. Nevertheless, it has remained a noble goal for a Chinese gentleman to achieve.

The Chinese Communists inherit this ascetic tradition and make it a Communist virtue as well. In the *Diary of Lei Feng*, a book mentioned earlier, there is no mention of any romantic feeling for a woman at all, let alone lust for her. Yet this is a hero that the CCP wants all Chinese to emulate. To the CCP love, romance, and marriage, whenever they occur, must be more social than personal in nature, and the success of a sexual relationship depends upon how the parties concerned can serve society politically rather than how they are attracted to each other emotionally and physically. If the political base of a marriage is solid, attractions of a personal nature will, given time, come by themselves. For a woman to attract a man by physical appearance or, worse still, by such artificial devices as makeup and fancy clothing, is an insult to womanhood, and women can never reach the same status as men as long as they spend more time worrying about how they look than how, as equals of men, they can accomplish and perform. Not surprisingly, all women in the People's Republic dress themselves in the same manner as men (baggy jackets and trousers, usually in black or blue), and the fashion industry is unheard of.

Thus Victorian puritanism, which the Victorians idealized but seldom practiced, has emerged in full blossom in Maoist China. This Maoist puritanism outdistances even the Confucian version of traditional China when chastity was always one-sided in favor of the stronger sex. Now that prostitution and concubinage have been totally eliminated, men have to abide by the same puritanic rules as women. How do the newly liberated women fare in the People's Republic? Not only have they become more numerous as manual workers, in factories as well as in the field, they are also doing well professionally as teachers, physicians, nurses, scientists, technicians, artists, and writers. They receive the same pay as men when engaged in the same kind of work, and they continue to draw the same pay during maternity leave which, under normal circumstances, is limited to two months. Even in politics where men traditionally dominated, Chinese women are also very active. In the lowest organizations of political life, such as street committees in the urban areas and village governments in the countryside, the heads and deputy heads are mostly women, though the percentage of women's participation becomes smaller and smaller as the political organizations become more and more powerful and authoritative. For instance, before her ouster from the position of power, Chiang Ch'ing was the only female whose voice commanded attention in the CCP's Political Bureau. Sadly, most women who achieved power status also happened to be the wives of those in power, such as Wang Kuang-mei (Mrs. Liu Shao-ch'i) before 1966, Yeh Ch'ün (Mrs. Lin Piao) before 1971, and Chiang Ch'ing (Mrs. Mao Tse-tung) before 1976. Today (1978) two of the most prominent women in China are Soong Ch'ing-ling (Mrs. Sun Yat-sen) and Teng Ying-ch'ao (Mrs. Chou En-lai) who occupy prestigious but basically powerless positions, more as a tribute to their dead husbands than as an indication of their own political strength. Of the 26 members of the CCP's Political Bureau, only one is a woman, and no woman serves in its all-powerful standing committee. Even in the People's Republic women have a long way to go in attaining equal status.

Thus, marriage and family remain the normal course for most Chinese women to follow, despite their enhanced status, and an unmarried woman pursuing an independent career is extremely rare. Since women are more home-oriented than men, the CCP depends upon them rather than their husbands to mold the family in Maoist fashion. Husband and wife are supposed to place the welfare of the community—a factory or a commune—above that of the family, and indoctrinate their children on the same point. Any violation of this general principle must be reported to the community to which the family belongs, and the violator is required to confess his sins in public and promise to reform. Parents cannot hide wrongdoings by their children, and vice versa. Often one member of a family is designated as an ideological coordinator who presides over the reading of Chairman Mao's works as well as criticism and self-criticism meetings among the family members. Since the ideological coordinator, usually the politically active member of the family, may not necessarily be the father and since children can criticize their fathers in the criticism and self-criticism meetings, the traditional authority associated with the father is no longer the same. The Confucian family system is virtually dead.

There are other changes as well, mostly for the better. Traditionally a man could divorce his wife on a variety of grounds, such as adultery, failure to bear him a son, and inability to please his parents. But a woman could not divorce her husband under any circumstances. Now divorce, as well as marriage, is not only sexually nondiscriminatory but also much more rational. The law says that divorce will be granted when husband and wife both desire it, without either having to resort to accusations that are purported to make the other party look guilty. Nevertheless, divorce rate is small compared to that in the West. The Communists attribute this fact to the very nature of a socialist society where the bond of marriage is only a means to a higher social end, whereas the bourgeois foundation of marriage, being a purely personal relationship, is extremely fragile. The Communist explanation is at best an oversimplification since in traditional China, where all marriages were arranged, the divorce rate was small too.

The relationship between parents and children, like that between husband and wife, is reciprocal and mutually obligatory. Children have the duty to support and assist their parents, says the Chinese law, just as parents have the duty to rear and educate their children. Upon retirement at an advanced age, parents normally live with their married children. Only when they have no children of their own would they go to the "happy home for the aged"—an impersonal and unhappy place even under the best conditions. Thus, even in modern times there is a great need to have children, and for this reason family planning has not been an unqualified success, especially in the rural areas. Since one normally lives with the family of a son rather than a daughter, having a male child is as much an economic necessity as it is a cultural bias. A peasant would stop having more children if he has already had one boy and one girl or two boys, but he would keep on trying to have a boy if all of his children happened to be girls. Multiply this situation millions of times, and the result is an imbalanced growth of population between males and females. The imbalance will become a serious social problem if continued, especially in a society where all men and women are supposed to get married.

Sometimes even the CCP is forced by tradition to make compromises. Take religion as an example. Freedom of religion is allowed as long as it does not lead to the establishment of an independent church that challenges the CCP authority. In practical terms this freedom exists only in name because there is also a freedom of antireligion which the government favors. Besides, the CCP feels that time is on its side since the young, growing up in an atheist state, have less and less to do with religion, which they equate with superstition. Ancestor worship has by and large been replaced by Mao worship, and Mao Tse-tung's image, instead of the ancestral tablets, is now occupying the most honored place inside a house. Still, during the *Ch'ing-ming* ("Clear and Bright") festival of honoring the dead, the custom of visiting ancestral cemeteries continues, though it is not encouraged. The cemeteries occupy valuable tracts of land that could have been used for forestry or agriculture, in a country where usable land is small and population large; and the CCP would have preferred cremation had there been no strong opposition to it. But there is strong opposition. Asking the Chinese not to stage elaborate funerals is one thing; asking them to burn their honored ancestors to ashes is an entirely different matter. (Thousands of Chinese blocked Chou En-lai's funeral procession when they learned that their beloved premier was to be cremated, being convinced that the cremation had been ordered by Chou's political enemies as a posthumous degradation. The procession was allowed to continue only after Chou's widow had convinced them that the cremation was indeed Chou's own wish.) As a concession to tradition, burial is allowed, but it has to be six feet underneath the ground, so the land above can still be used for production purposes.

Inside his house a man can, of course, indulge in a moment of free thinking or a little fantasy, provided that he does not communicate his thought to others, including his closest relatives and friends. Outside the house the mental conditioning is relentless. Wherever he turns, he sees Mao and Maoist sayings, printed in large characters—nor is there any way for him to escape the ubiquitous loudspeaker that constantly urges him to obey Chairman Mao's teachings. As a means of enforcing ideological conformity, the government controls all the media, not only newspapers, magazines, radio, and television but also works of art and literature. Before the Cultural Revolution, when free expression was still allowed within the Marxist framework, one could still read or write a story of love and romance involving a proletarian hero and his heroine or paint a picture, such as a landscape, that had no political meaning in it. With Chiang Ch'ing serving as the cultural czar during the Cultural Revolution, all the "feudal," "bourgeois," or "nonrevolutionary" works of art and literature were banned from circulation, including not only Shakespeare, Tolstoi, and Ts'ao Hsüeh-ch'in but also veteran Communist writers whose revolutionary zeal was judged below the standard. Under the Maoist slogan, "Politics must be always in command," an artist could literally not paint anything except propaganda posters and a writer could not write anything except the eulogies of Chairman Mao and the CCP. As Chiang Ch'ing moved steadily leftward in her pursuance of absolute power, more and more works were removed from the shelf until, eventually, Marx, Lenin, and Mao Tse-tung were the only safe authors to read. For instance, Liu Shao-ch'i's *How to Be a Good Communist* was once regarded as a classic and required reading for everyone. After 1966 anyone caught reading this book would run the risk of being condemned as a "capitalist roader" and suffer the consequences. Since the political winds shifted constantly, one was never sure whether, at a given time, a particular book was or was not on the prohibited index. The safest course to follow was not to read any book at all, with the exception, of course, of *Quotations from Chairman Mao* and *Selected Works of Mao Tse-tung*.

Reading, at best, is for those more or less intellectually inclined, and most people would not have missed it had they not read a serious book all their lives. Popular entertainment, on the other hand, has a universal appeal. The CCP, as early as the Yenan days, recognized the value of popular entertainment as an effective means of political propaganda, and its cultural department organized and supervised singing, dancing, and theater troupes to tour regularly among the areas under its control, ostensibly to entertain but actually to indoctrinate. *Yang-ko* ("planting song"), a dance form that consists of two big steps forward and two small steps backward, was most popular among the peasants and soldiers. When the CCP came to power in 1949, suddenly it found in its hands not only such simple forms of entertainment as *yang-ko* but also the most advanced types, including films, opera, ballet, radio, and later television, all of which could be used effectively for political purposes.

For a seventeen-year period before 1966 when the Cultural Revolution began, traditional themes in movies and the theater were allowed to exist side by side with the newly developed revolutionary ("propaganda") stories, and a person could spend an evening in an opera house watching either a historical drama involving Liu Pang and Hsiang Yü (pp. 103–104) or a contemporary story that condemned the wicked landlord and praised the oppressed peasant. With the arrival of the Cultural Revolution, everything had to be revolutionized, including movies and the theater. All the traditional themes were banned, and a person had a choice of either staying home or being propagandized. The Peking opera, for instance, was so "revolutionized" that its old admirers had difficulties getting used to the new form—a hybrid that infuriated the old-timers without in the meantime making many new converts. The Peking opera was an art form dating back to Emperor T'ang Hsüan-tsung of the eighth century (pp. 189–190), beloved by and most endearing to all Chinese for centuries. Now it was butchered beyond recognition.

Perhaps Communists like Chiang Ch'ing have no choice in this matter. If they allow traditional themes to compete freely with the newly developed ones, even the most ardent Maoists would not patronize the latter. In that case, the power of mental conditioning through a most powerful medium would end, and the Chinese, constantly exposed to "feudal," "bourgeois," and "reactionary" thought, might indeed backslide to "capitalist roaders" or worse. While Chiang Ch'ing was in power, love and romance, traditional but most popular themes that made people laugh and cry, were totally eliminated from the theater, and a hero or heroine was invariably a person who would die, if necessary, for Chairman Mao and the CCP. Each story developed along familiar lines, and one knew the ending even before the story began. It was none other than Teng Hsiao-p'ing who once remarked that Chinese theater was so bad that none would attend it of his own accord. Only in sports and sports-related performances did genuine enthusiasm continue since, obviously, not much political propaganda could be instilled into them. For instance, the Shenyang (Manchuria) Acrobatic Troupe, that toured Europe and America in the early 1970's and thrilled thousands, was as popular in China as it was abroad. Even in sports, political propaganda emerged whenever an opportunity presented itself. When interviewed, rarely would a Chinese sportsman not attribute his success to Chairman Mao and the CCP.

The absurdity with which political ideology was projected into the performing arts can best be demonstrated in the controversy over a film entitled "A Gardener's Song" (*Yüan-ting chih ko*). It is a Chinese version of "Good-bye, Mr. Chips" that depicts a dedicated teacher who devotes her whole life to the education of the young. The script was approved in advance by Hua Kuo-feng, then First Secretary of the CCP, Hunan province, and the film proved to be a moderate success when it was shown. Apparently the making of this film had not been cleared with Chiang Ch'ing, who subsequently instigated a concerted attack by all the media under her control, including the *People's Daily*. The film was condemned as "revisionist" and "antiproletarian" because, first, it "overemphasized" the importance of academic learning (three Rs in this case) at the expense of proletarian ideology, and, second, it "unjustifiably" elevated the position of intellectuals, such as teachers, as if intellectuals, instead of the CCP leaders, were the pillars of a socialist society. In 1974 the film was banned from showing in all the theaters, only to reemerge in November, 1976, after Chiang Ch'ing had been arrested and Hua Kuo-feng himself had succeeded Mao Tse-tung as the most powerful man in China.

Since their ascension to power in October, 1976, the CCP moderates have made repeated promises that freedom of expression in works of art and literature will be encouraged and that writers and artists should no longer fear the kind of retaliation that blackens the Chiang Ch'ing period. Would these promises, if kept, undermine the very nature of a socialist society? Would China not then become as "revisionist" as the Soviet Union? Who would go to see a movie entitled "Eternal Glory to Our Great Leader and Teacher Chairman Mao Tse-tung (released in December, 1976) if a Chinese version of "The Love Story" is available? Give people freedom, and there is a good chance that they would become "bourgeois" and "decadent." Worse still, they may not even support the CCP leadership as required by the Constitution. This is a dilemma the CCP leaders cannot and will not solve.

FOREIGN RELATIONS

Externally as well as internally, the China after 1949 was different from the China before that date. No longer was it a geographical expression, a pawn in international politics. It was united, strong, and confident, asserting vigorously what it regarded as its national rights. Fifty years earlier the various powers had debated among themselves on how to solve their "China problem" by partitioning her among themselves; as late as the 1930's the Japanese imperialists had tried to convince everyone who wished to listen that the only way to solve the "China problem" was to let them do whatever they pleased in China, since the Chinese could not really govern themselves. After the establishment of the People's Republic, the "China problem" remained, though of a diametrically different nature. The problem was how to contain China and Chinese influence within its national border, so the interest of other powers in areas outside of China would not be adversely affected. In either case, China looms large and has always been a "problem."

The foreign relations of the People's Republic conveniently fall into three groupings: one, with the Soviet Union and other Communist countries; two, with the developing countries known as the Third World; and three, with the Western countries headed by the United States.

Since the Communist success in China was achieved without substantial assistance from the Soviet Union, it had been hoped in Western circles that the new regime would pursue a foreign policy independent of Moscow. Such a hope was dashed in the summer of 1949 when Mao Tsetung announced that China would "lean to one side," the side of the socialist camp headed by the Soviet Union. On October 2, 1949, the day after the new regime was formally inaugurated, the Soviet Union extended its recognition, and Soviet leadership was soon followed by other Communist countries. In December Mao journeyed to Moscow to confer with Stalin—his first trip outside China; in February he brought home a treaty of friendship and alliance designed to last thirty years. The conclusion of this treaty was followed by negotiation of trade and loan agreements in which the Soviet Union pledged financial and technical support for China's reconstruction programs.

The test of this new alliance came in the summer of 1950 when North Korea, egged on by Moscow, invaded South Korea. The United States, with some assistance from other members of the United Nations, came to the aid of the South Koreans. By October, 1950, the United Nations forces had not only recovered all the territories the South Koreans had lost, but were also pushing northward to the Yalu River, the boundary between China and Korea. For a while, it seemed that Korea would be unified under United Nations sponsorship. Much to the surprise of the outside world, the People's Republic, then barely one year old, intervened and fought the United Nations forces to a stalemate. The final settlement restored Korea to its prewar status, divided as it had been before the conflict. Despite staggering losses in men and materials, the People's Republic emerged from the Korean War with accrued prestige because it had successfully prevented the United Nations from unifying Korea under a pro-Western regime. The significance of its military "success" was not lost to the Kremlin; as long as the Soviet Union had China as its ally in East Asia, its eastern flank would be safe against the attack of the so-called imperialist warmongers.

The years 1950–1958 marked the heyday of Sino-Soviet cooperation. A series of agreements, generally favorable to China, were reached between the two Communist countries. The Soviet Union agreed to provide China with industrial equipment and technical advice, and such assistance was uninterrupted by Stalin's death in 1953. Though China had to pay for everything it received, the Soviet Union agreed to take whatever products China could deliver, mostly food and industrial raw materials. The Soviet aid helped China's industrialization program enormously, and it was partially responsible for the economic progress China made during the period 1950–1958.

Economically stronger and more self-assured, the People's Republic began to call upon the Soviet Union to relinquish the economic privileges that the latter had acquired before 1949. We may recall that the Yalta Agreement of February, 1945, gave Russia vital concessions in Manchuria, such as joint control of the Chinese Eastern (Changchun) Railroad and lease of the naval base of Port Arthur. These concessions were finalized in a treaty between Nationalist China and the Soviet Union later in the same year. After the establishment of the People's Republic, further concessions were made to the Russians in the form of four Sino-Soviet joint companies organized to exploit China's natural resources. In the fall of 1952 the Soviet Union agreed to transfer to China, with full title and without compensation, all Russian rights in the management of the Chinese Eastern Railroad and all properties belonging to it. Three years later, China took full control of the four joint stock companies. This was followed by the transfer of Port Arthur to China in May, 1955. Thus, for the first time since 1842 (Treaty of Nanking), the last vestige of the much-denounced unequal treaties was finally wiped out.

Within the Communist bloc the influence of China continued to grow vis-à-vis the Soviet Union and other Communist countries. In 1956 when the Soviet Union faced mass revolt in Eastern Europe after its de-Stalinization campaign, the Chinese premier Chou En-lai journeyed to Poland and Hungary as a peacemaker. Chou's successful mission marked the apex of China's prestige and influence within the Communist bloc.

After this, the relationship between the two Communist giants soon began to deteriorate; the deterioration became all the more evident after Nikita Khrushchev had successfully purged his opponents and consolidated his own power in the Soviet Union.

Outwardly, the disputes involved such questions as the feasibility of peaceful coexistence with the capitalist countries and the best method —war or peaceful competition—to communize the world, but the real issue was much more complicated. Emerging from World War II as the strongest country on the Eurasian continent and surrounded by allies and satellites, the Soviet Union was, for the time being, satisfied with the power structure of the world as it was, whereas the People's Republic was not. The People's Republic wanted to wrest Taiwan from the Nationalist control, neutralize Japan, secure Southeast Asia for less hostile governments, and, in short, create a buffer zone between herself and the American power in the Western Pacific, in the same manner as the Soviet Union had successfully done in Eastern Europe. To achieve any or all of these goals would mean a joint confrontation of the People's Republic and the Soviet Union with the United States, which the Soviet Union refused to contemplate. First, the ultimate consequence of such a confrontation was unthinkable in a nuclear age and second, the Soviet Union herself had nothing to gain if China realized any or all of the aforesaid goals. When in 1959 Khrushchev journeyed to the United States to confer with President Dwight D. Eisenhower on ways to ease world tension, the People's Republic accused the Soviet Union of having replaced "international proletarianism" with "capitalist collaboration" and of having sold out China in order to appease the "unappeasable American aggressors." As this kind of attack continued and was returned in kind by the Soviet Union, normal relations between these two countries all but ceased. The most damaging from the Chinese point of view, as noted earlier, was the stoppage of Russian economic aid and the recall of Russian technicians from China.

It took two sides to create a dispute, and the Soviet Union was equally responsible, if not more so, for the Sino-Soviet split. Stalin, one of the shrewdest politicians of the twentieth century, knew the limit beyond which he could not impose his will, especially on a country that, having recently freed itself from a semicolonial status, was extremely sensitive in terms of national pride. During the period 1953–1958 when the prospective successors to Stalin competed for absolute power, each of them made an effort to ingratiate himself with Mao Tse-tung whose support they sought, and Sino-Soviet cooperation continued. It was during this period that China enhanced her position within the Communist bloc, as mentioned earlier. In 1958, after Nikita Khrushchev had succeeded in making himself the sole successor to Stalin, he proceeded immediately to treat China like one of his many vassals. He neither understood the humiliations China had suffered at the hands of the Western powers and Japan during the modern period nor exhibited the kind of suavity that his position demanded. Among other things, he demanded the granting of military bases for Soviet uses within the territory of China, ostensibly for the purpose of "fighting American aggression" but actually as the first step to converting China into a full-fledged Russian satellite. He thought he had made an offer the Chinese could not refuse because, after all, China was then totally isolated and needed Soviet support to cope with the Americans. Much to his surprise, an irritated and angry Mao Tse-tung refused, saying that China did not fight for one hundred years to get rid of the British and other foreigners in order to invite in the Russians. From then on, the Sino-Soviet relations went from bad to worse.

Between 1961 and 1963 repeated attempts were made to repair the rift in the international Communist movement, but the rift was too deep to be repaired. In the fall of 1964 Khrushchev was ousted from his position of power by Leonid Brezhnev who, the Chinese hoped, would reverse the "revisionist" policy of his predecessor and thus revive the solidarity of "international proletarianism." Chou En-lai went to Moscow to see what he could do, only to return home disappointed. "Brezhnev is just another Khrushchev," he concluded. As both sides could not agree, the conflict escalated, involving not only the question of Soviet dominance in the international Communist movement but also disputes over borders and territories.

As noted earlier in this book (pp. 414–417), Russia, through the use of force or the threat of it, had acquired large territories from a weak China during the nineteenth century. The People's Republic now called upon the Soviet Union to acknowledge the seizure of these territories as unjust and unfair and the treaties that sanctioned it as unequal treaties. The Soviet Union refused to make such an acknowledgment and quickly changed all the names in the disputed territories from Chinese to Russian. As tension heightened, both sides rushed reinforcements toward their four-thousand-mile frontier, and clashes occurred from time to time. In the spring of 1969 the Chinese and the Russians twice fought over the possession of a disputed island in the Ussuri River; in the summer of the same year another battle was fought over a border pass in Sinkiang. Fortunately, cooler heads prevailed shortly afterward, and both sides agreed to hold border talks that began in Peking in October, 1969. These talks have been conducted, off and on, for the past nine years (1969–1978), and so far no agreements have been reached.

Why is it so difficult for both sides to reach an agreement, especially since the Chinese have stated explicitly that they do not demand the return of the disputed territories? While outsiders can only speculate, the key issue seems to be Mongolia. Though Mongolia, under Soviet sponsorship, declared its independence from China as early as 1921, the independence was not acknowledged by China (Nationalist) until 1945 when she yielded to American pressure and agreed to implement the Yalta Agreement (p. 493). Beginning in 1949 when the People's Republic was established, the Chinese reentered Mongolia to compete with the Russians in influence, but they lost out in the wake of the Sino-Soviet split in 1959. Independent in name only, Mongolia has been a Soviet-occupied satellite since 1921, an intolerable situation from the Chinese point of view. A reading of the map will show why: Russian troops, stationed in Mongolia, are within easy reach of all of North China, including Peking. Once Peking is captured, Manchuria will be completely encircled and will fall into the Soviet hands like a ripe apple. Today the Soviet Union has in Mongolia not only crack divisions but also missiles with nuclear warheads pointed at Peking and many other Chinese cities. Each time the two countries meet to discuss their differences, the Chinese demand that the first item on the agenda should be withdrawal of all troops and military equipment to territories within their respective boundaries. Since the Russians have no intention of ending their occupation of Mongolia, the stalemate continues. The Soviet Union could, if it so chose, annex Mongolia *de jure*, as well as *de facto*, but such a step would make the Sino-Soviet enmity irreversible. Obviously, her interest is not served by having a permanent enemy on her eastern frontier.

As far as China's relations with Communist countries other than the Soviet Union are concerned, they vary in accordance with her Soviet relations. As long as communism remained a monolithic movement, the People's Republic condemned such deviators as Yugoslavia, which was characterized as a "capitalist lackey." With the Sino-Soviet split, she not only made an all-out effort to befriend an anti-Soviet country like Albania but also encouraged such countries as Yugoslavia and Rumania to be more independent of Moscow. When Czechoslovakia, under Alexander Dubcek, defied Moscow's wishes by liberalizing its regime, the People's Republic encouraged her and provided her with moral support. She condemned the Soviet Union in the strongest terms when the latter invaded Czechoslovakia in the summer of 1968 and succeeded in overthrowing the Dubcek regime. The Soviet Union justified the invasion by invoking the theory of limited sovereignty: that the Soviet Union has the right to intervene in a socialist country's internal affairs if the social and economic structure of that country is being undermined by undesirable capitalist influence which, in this case, was West German and American in origin. Conceivably the Soviet Union could apply the same theory, known as the Brezhnev Doctrine, to the People's Republic. It was then that Mao Tse-tung raised the slogan: "Dig the tunnels deep, store grain everywhere, and be prepared for war." He was anticipating a Soviet attack at any time.

If the United States cannot do much about "freeing the captive nations" (Poland, Hungary, etc.) in Eastern Europe, obviously the People's Republic, much weaker than the United States, can do even less. She, in fact, attaches much more importance to the developing countries around the globe, known as the Third World. There are at least two reasons for this attachment. Sentimentally, she and the other developing countries share a similar colonial past and economic backwardness, and her model of development, centered on self-reliance and labor-intensive programs, is, from her point of view, more appropriate than either the Soviet or the American model. Politically, the People's Republic believes that the Third World, including herself, holds the key to the future, as well as the balance of power between the United States and the Soviet Union. Whoever leads the Third World, which has the largest population, territory, and natural resources, will have the greatest influence in the long run. It is no secret that the People's Republic would like to be that leader herself.

China's attempt to gain influence in the Third World has met with some success but mostly failures. The failures result largely from two factors. First, being economically underdeveloped herself, she cannot offer the kind of industrial and military assistance that the two superpowers are capable of. Second, the fact that she is Communist and prefers every other country to be Communist raises doubt about her motive. Besides, the dictate of national interest often overshadows all other considerations, including the common identity as members of the Third World. The best example in this regard is China's relations with India. After the establishment of the People's Republic, no country outside the Soviet bloc was more friendly towards the new regime than India which, among other things, continued to propose Communist China for membership in the United Nations. This friendship was demonstrated to the world during the Bandung Conference of 1955 when twenty-nine Asian and African states gathered in Indonesia to express identity of interest in "struggling against imperialism and colonialism." It was then that Chou En-lai and Jawaharlal Nehru, the Indian premier, formulated the so-called five principles of peaceful coexistence (*i.e.*, mutual respect for territorial integrity and sovereignty; mutual non-aggression; non-interference in each other's internal affairs; equality and mutual benefit; and peaceful coexistence) as a basis for relations not only between China and India but also among "all the peace-loving nations in the world." Yet in October, 1962, open warfare erupted between these two countries.

The conflict involved two pieces of territory, one in eastern Ladakh (Kashmir) and the other in the eastern end of the Himalayas between Bhutan and Burma. The basic cause of this conflict can be traced back to the first decade of this century when Great Britain, then ruling India, played the "great game" (as Lord Curzon called it) by penetrating deep into Tibet (pp. 449–450), which the then weak, divided China could not

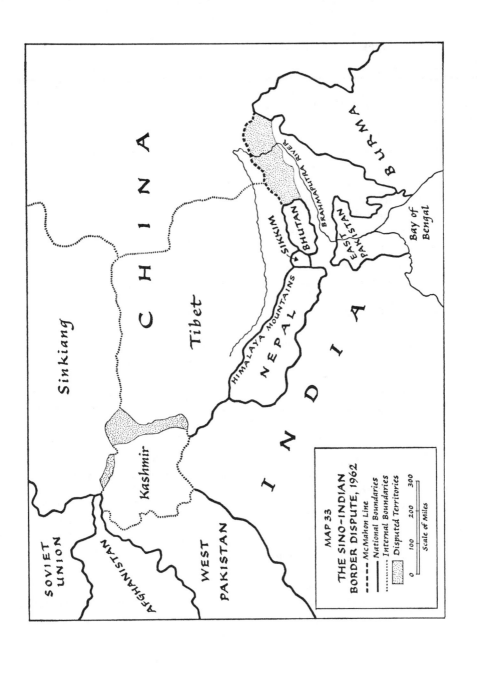

MAP 33

THE SINO-INDIAN
BORDER DISPUTE, 1962

- - - McMahon Line
——— National Boundaries
· · · · · Internal Boundaries
▚▚▚ Disputed Territories

0   100   200   300
Scale of Miles

protect. During the Simla meeting of 1914, Britain's representative, Sir Arthur McMahon, determined the eastern portion of the border by drawing a line on a map along the Himalaya peaks from Bhutan to Burma, later known as the McMahon line. The Chinese government repudiated the McMahon line by refusing to ratify the Simla Agreement, on the grounds that the traditional demarcation line, based on ethnic factors, was the one located further in the south. Subsequent Chinese governments, both Nationalist and Communist, have taken a similar stand. When India, after independence, made the same claim on these territories as the British, the People's Republic accused India of being imperialist and expansion-minded; India, of course, said the same thing about the People's Republic. When nationalist fervor was aroused, all principles were thrown overboard, including the five principles previously mentioned. Fortunately, the hot war of 1962 ended almost as quickly as it began. Today China holds the disputed territory in eastern Ladakh, while India remains in possession of the disputed territory south of the McMahon line (see Map 33).

During the brief war both the United States and the Soviet Union provided India with moral and material support, with the former providing the major portion of it. But, for reasons never clearly defined, India slowly turned her back on the United States and leaned further and further toward the Soviet Union, culminating in the Soviet-Indian treaty of friendship in 1971. In the India-Pakistani war that erupted later in that year, China supported Pakistan while the Soviet Union backed India, but her support, being more moral than material, did not prevent Pakistan's defeat and the creation of a new state called Bangladesh. According to Richard M. Nixon, then the American president, all of Pakistan would have been conquered by India had the United States not threatened to intervene on Pakistan's behalf. In short, it was the United States, instead of the People's Republic, that prevented Pakistan from being exterminated as a nation.

China's inability to influence events because of her economic and military weakness can be best shown in her relations with Indonesia. At one time Indonesia had not only the largest but also the most Peking-oriented Communist party outside of the Communist-controlled countries. Feeling strong and assured, the Indonesian Communists staged a coup in September, 1965. The coup failed almost as soon as it began, and its failure was quickly followed by a countercoup launched by the Indonesian army and its supporters. In the process of gaining control of the state, they slaughtered more than 400,000 Communists or alleged Communists, including thousands of resident Chinese who, out of necessity if not conviction, had shown some pro-Peking sympathy during a time when Indonesia considered the People's Republic "the best of her friends." Peking protested, but decided to take no action other than agreeing to take into China all the Chinese whom the Indonesian government regarded as undesirable and wished to repatriate. Since most of the Chinese whom the Indonesians had either slaughtered or repatriated were either born or had lived in Indonesia for generations, the lesson of this tragic incident was simply unforgettable. The ethnic Chinese in Southeast Asia, who numbered more than nineteen million, have rightly concluded that whatever protection Peking has promised them is illusory and that a better means to achieve survival as a minority group in a foreign country is to have nothing to do with Peking whatsoever.

Judging from subsequent events, it seems that the Indonesian lesson was not lost on Communist China either. Not only did she finally realize that she was still a second-rate power, unable to influence events as a great maritime power could, but it was also apparent to her that the developing countries were not interested in ideology or revolution and that they regarded as friends only those countries that could assist them economically. When she finally emerged from the domestic chaos created by the Cultural Revolution and became more active in international affairs, she directed her attention more toward economic and technical aid. Being less affluent than either the United States or the Soviet Union, understandably she had to be very selective when choosing recipients. Two of the recipients were Tanzania and Zambia. To them the Chinese extended an interest-free loan of U.S. $423 million to build a 1,860-kilometer railroad that would link Kapiri M'Poshi in the heart of Zambia to Dar es Salaam, the Tanzanian capital on the eastern coast of Africa. Since the railroad traversed a most difficult terrain and involved engineering work of the most advanced type, the Chinese took upon themselves the full responsibility to construct it. It took two years to survey the route, and actual construction did not begin until October, 1970. In July, 1976, the entire line was officially open to traffic, and the Chinese won praise for successful completion of a most difficult task. The construction of the Tanzania-Zambia Railroad remains the most important project that the People's Republic undertook abroad.

"We have lost some white friends," said Chiang Ch'ing in 1975, obviously referring to the Soviet satellites in Eastern Europe who had joined the Soviet Union in condemning China as a "splitter" and "spoiler"; "but we have more than made up for the loss by gaining many, many black friends." The Chinese courtship of the Third World paid off handsomely in October, 1971, when the United Nations Assembly, by a majority vote, admitted the People's Republic as a U.N. member. When the final vote was announced, most delegates burst into a tumultuous, prolonged applause, and many black delegates from Africa were actually dancing in the aisle—a sight that could not have been more pleasing to Mao Tse-tung and his colleagues. Communist China's quest for a U.N. seat began as soon as the regime itself began, but it had been futile until

1971, largely because of American opposition. Nevertheless, by 1971 the United States had softened its opposition to such an extent that it would agree to Communist China's U.N. membership if the Nationalists in Taiwan were allowed to remain a member. The majority in the United Nations did not agree, and the American proposal went down in defeat. By the vote referred to above, the Nationalist regime in Taiwan was ousted from the United Nations, and the People's Republic replaced it as a permanent member in the Security Council as well as a member of the General Assembly and other U.N. organs. Six months later, President Richard M. Nixon himself appeared in Peking to confer with Mao Tse-tung and Chou En-lai. Sino-American relations have not been the same since.

When the People's Republic was formally established in 1949, it was generally assumed that the rest of the world, including the United States, would have to recognize her, however unpleasant this political reality might seem. The assumption proved to be incorrect, however, especially after Communist China had concluded a treaty of mutual defense with the Soviet Union in February, 1950, and then, later in the same year, participated in the Korean War. The United Nations passed a resolution condemning Communist China as an aggressor, and to most people in the Western world, especially the Americans, the newly created Communist regime was merely another tool with which the Soviet Union attempted to communize and then dominate the world. The United States took the lead in urging all the "peace-loving peoples" to boycott Communist China through a trade embargo as well as diplomatic nonrecognition, especially trade in strategic materials. Many influential Americans believed that the Communist regime in China was only a "passing phase" and that the denial of diplomatic and economic support would weaken that regime to such an extent that it would eventually have to topple. Though Communist China did not topple, the American effort in isolating her was, nevertheless, remarkably successful. With the exception of Great Britain, which recognized the People's Republic before the diplomatic boycott was officially launched by the United States, all the major Western countries followed the American lead by recognizing the Nationalist government in Taiwan rather than the Communist government on the mainland as the legal representative of the Chinese people. A vicious circle thus ensued: the West's belief in the existence of an unbreakable, monolithic Communist movement dominated by Moscow gave Communist China no choice except to rely heavily on the Soviet support that in turn provided substance for this belief. As this circle continued, few people in the Western world doubted the existence of an international Communist conspiracy that, directed and masterminded by the Kremlin, had as its ultimate objective the domination of the world.

The Sino-Soviet split that began in 1959 slowly undermined this long-held belief. Understandably, each Western country responded to the split in accordance with the degree of her own emotional or national involvement with this belief. Having a large Communist party operating legally in her own country and with no more territory to lose in Asia after 1954, France recognized the People's Republic in 1964. The United States, on the other hand, found the recognition of Communist China much more difficult, not only because she had been most emotionally involved in the anti-Communist crusade, but also because she had made firm commitment to the support and defense of her anti-Communist allies in East and Southeast Asia, especially the Nationalist government in Taiwan. Nevertheless, the American attitude toward Communist China has undergone a slow and gradual change throughout the years. Underlying this changed attitude is the belief that continued hostility towards the People's Republic will not serve a useful purpose and may in the end force that country into the arms of the Soviet Union, a prospect that no one except a Communist would relish. Moreover, the very concept of the balance of power dictates that one should always ally oneself with the weak against the strong, and there has never been any question as to which of the two Communist giants, the Soviet Union or the People's Republic, can cause more harm to the Western world in general and the United States in particular. The question has never been whether there should or should not be a Sino-American rapprochement; the question has always been why it came so late as 1972. Had it occurred in 1959 when the Sino-Soviet split began or as late as 1961 when the split became clearly irreversible, the tragic involvement of America in the Vietnam War would have been avoided; Laos and Cambodia would have been preserved as pro-American, non-Communist countries; and both Lyndon B. Johnson and Richard M. Nixon would have gone down in history as much greater presidents than they are commonly regarded today. Most importantly, the enormous expansion of Soviet influence around the globe would have been greatly curtailed, if not stopped altogether.

Hindsight is, of course, always better than foresight, and the miscalculation of the twentieth century will doubtless be examined and reexamined for many years to come. Whatever the reasons were, Sino-American rapprochement was regarded by both sides as impossible as long as the United States sank deeper and deeper into the Vietnam quagmire. From the American point of view, the intervention in Vietnam was necessary in order to prevent Chinese communism from spreading southward; without this intervention, according to an official explanation, all of the Southeast Asian countries would fall into Communist hands like so many dominoes. From China's point of view, the domino theory was merely a façade behind which America could carry out its "aggressive and sinister scheme" to encircle her with China-hating American satellites. America, with so many China experts in the government and in its great universities, must know that China had no intention of engaging in such self-defeating adventure as expanding southward toward Southeast Asia—to do so would certainly have aroused nationalist sentiment against the Chinese and would indeed defeat the very purpose China wanted to achieve, namely, the establishment around China of a buffer zone of friendly states that separated her from hostile forces further beyond. Thus, while the United States viewed its Vietnamese intervention as purely defensive, the People's Republic regarded it as a first step for possible invasion of China itself. As mutual distrust deepened, the Vietnam War dragged on endlessly from one year to another.

While the United States was occupied with Vietnam and later Laos and Cambodia, the Soviet Union was unwittingly given the golden opportunity to expand on a global scale. Not only was she able to bring enormous pressure upon China in the hope of converting her into an outright satellite à la Poland and Hungary, but she also penetrated into the Eastern Mediterranean, the Middle East, North Africa, and, by her pseudo-alliance with India, the Indian Ocean as well. She even established a client state (Cuba) only ninety miles off the coast of Florida. In short, she had succeeded in achieving what her Czarist predecessor could only dream about. In 1954 when the American involvement with Vietnam officially began, the Soviet Union was a secondary power compared to the United States; in 1975 when the United States finally ended her involvement, the Soviet Union was on a par with the United States in terms of global influence as well as industrial and military strength. While single-mindedly chasing an elusive rabbit in Vietnam, the United States, sadly, ignored the giant bear that stalked in its rear, growing bigger and bigger with each advancing step. In competing with a dynamic country like the Soviet Union, one cannot waste twenty years without suffering the consequences.

Early in the 1960's, while the United States was exercising pressure on China via Vietnam, the Russians were doing the same thing in the north. Both were supporting India in her territorial claims across the Himalayas. Even North Korea, which had been saved by "Chinese volunteers" from extinction one decade earlier, jumped onto the bandwagon by allying herself with the Soviet Union, doubtless believing that the Soviet Union, rather than China, could help her to unify all of Korea. The People's Republic was surrounded and isolated: in the whole world she had no ally except tiny Albania, which most Chinese doubtless had difficulties locating on the map. "Attacked by both the imperialists [United States] and the revisionists [Soviet Union], we would have no place to go except the Himalaya mountains," said Ch'en Yi, then the foreign minister. What Ch'en Yi failed to mention was that had the Chinese withdrawn to the Himalayas, the Indians would be there waiting for them.

To break through the encirclement, Ch'en Yi suggested, and Mao Tse-tung agreed, China must seek an understanding with the United States, by conceding South Vietnam if necessary, so that China could concentrate on coping with the Russians. Shortly afterward, the United States escalated the war in South Vietnam and started massive bombing of North Vietnam; some of the American planes penetrated deep into China's territorial space. The Chinese leaders concluded that they could not approach the United States under these circumstances.

The possibility of a Sino-American rapprochement reemerged in 1969 when the United States responded to the Soviet proposal of an attack on China's nuclear installations with a giant nuclear explosion in the Aleutian Islands, next to Russia's Siberian border. The message to the Russians was loud and clear; Mao Tse-tung and Chou En-lai concluded that President Nixon, a Machiavellian politician like themselves, was a man with whom they could do business. Imagine their puzzlement when news arrived from the south that Prince Sihanouk had been ousted by an America-backed coup and, worse still, American ground troops had invaded Cambodia (spring, 1970). The Cambodian invasion delayed but did not end the possibility of a Sino-American rapprochement. One year later, Henry A. Kissinger, then President Nixon's foreign policy adviser, made the first of his "secret trips" to Peking. In February, 1972, President Nixon was in Peking himself.

In the *Shanghai Communiqué* that concluded the Nixon trip, the United States and the People's Republic endorsed the principle of peaceful coexistence, cultural exchange, and mutual effort to normalize state relations. On the crucial issue of Taiwan, the United States "acknowledges that all Chinese on either side of the Taiwan Strait maintain there is but one China and that Taiwan is part of China. The United States government does not challenge that position. It reaffirms its interest in a peaceful settlement of the Taiwan question by the Chinese themselves." Though too much can be read into this document, it is safe to say that the Soviet Union looms large behind it, even though her name is not mentioned. By establishing an American connection through this document, the Chinese government hopes that the Soviet Union will think twice before launching an attack on the People's Republic. There is benefit for America too. With American backing, the People's Republic could serve as a bulwark against the Soviet expansion toward the Western Pacific, and the United States could then concentrate on Western Europe and the Middle East where the Soviet threat is equally great. Had any of the three key areas—China, Western Europe, and the Middle East—been converted into a Soviet sphere of influence, the balance of power would be strongly tilted in favor of the Soviet Union and perhaps irreversibly. In short, the United States and China need each other.

The Chinese Communists, time and again, refer to the Soviet Union as the worst, most predatory imperialist country in the world. Other imperialist countries in the past, such as England and France, were primarily motivated by greed for profit. Even their colonies were merely a means to an end rather than an end in themselves. When profit ceased to exist, they were only glad to be relieved of the colonial burden and readily granted their former colonies independence. The Czarist and Soviet empire, on the other hand, is primarily territorial, and her territorial ambition poses a direct threat to all the countries geographically contiguous to her, including China. Moreover, once annexed by the Soviet Union, a country or territory can rarely free itself. For instance, the United States eventually returned the Ryukyu Islands, including Okinawa, to Japan, but the Japanese have tried in vain to recover the Kuril Islands from the Soviet Union. Beginning as a small principality in the fourteenth century, Russia has grown to become the largest empire in the world. Other empires have come and gone, but the Russian empire is still expanding.

To combat Russian expansion, the People's Republic calls upon all the people in the world, leftist, rightist, and centrist, to form a united front, in the same manner as all the progressive forces had been united in resisting Germany and Japan before and during World War II. The correct policy to follow is not appeasement, disguised as "detente," but a policy of tit for tat, whenever and wherever the "new Czars" make their move. Most interestingly, the People's Republic, by comparing the United States to Great Britain at the time of Munich, is hoping that an American Winston Churchill will eventually emerge, to face the "new Hitlerites" in the Kremlin with courage and without fear. From their experience, say the Chinese Communists, strength rather than reason is the only thing the Soviets understand.

An outsider may question the necessity of China's obsessive fear of the Soviets. But, as long as that fear persists, all other issues, including Taiwan, become minor in importance. Relying on an American understanding to ward off Russian threats, the People's Republic cannot afford to antagonize the Americans and certainly will not attempt to "liberate" Taiwan without America's open or implied consent. Taiwan is safe from "liberation" as long as the Sino-Soviet animosity continues. Likewise, North Korea will not invade South Korea without the joint support of both the Soviet Union and the People's Republic, and this joint support is extremely unlikely as long as the two Communist giants are at odds with each other. Not surprisingly, the United States, after twenty-seven years, has begun to withdraw its troops from South Korea, confident that there will not be a renewal of the Korean War. Thus the Sino-Soviet split has worked in many ways totally unexpected when the split began in 1959.

THE PAST AND THE PRESENT

There are three elements in the Chinese Communist movement: socioeconomic, nationalist, and Communist; and the Communists attained their Communist goal in 1949 by successfully exploiting the socioeconomic and nationalist forces that had been in existence long before the organization of the Chinese Communist Party. The grinding poverty of the nation and the uneven distribution of income set the socioeconomic forces in motion, and the Communist exploitation of these forces took the forms that ranged from the most extreme to the generally moderate. Prior to 1937 it was the extreme form that prevailed. Wherever in control, the Communists advocated and carried out a program of land confiscation and redistribution. Though this program won for them many converts among the poor peasants, it generated stiff resistance from people outside the Communist-controlled areas. In short, this extreme form of communism did not work. Beginning in the summer of 1937 when the Sino-Japanese War began, the Communists, in order to win the support of as many Chinese as possible in their war effort against Japan, made a complete about-face, suspended land confiscation, and advocated a new program of rent and interest reductions. The new program worked like magic, since even many landlords did not object.

Moreover, the war of resistance against Japan released a nationalist fervor of unprecedented scale, which worked further to the Communists' advantage. Many Chinese went to the Communist side, for no reason other than the fact that the Communists were then the most uncompromising in the anti-Japanese struggle; among them were intellectuals of a gentry or bourgeois background who certainly had more to lose than to gain if communism triumphed in China. With this kind of support, the Communists, who began the anti-Japanese war as a ragtag army of thirty thousand, emerged as a well-disciplined striking force of two million at the end of the war, ready to contend for the highest prize in the nation. A strong argument can be made that had the Japanese militarists not invaded China for the ostensible purpose of saving that ancient country from the evil of communism, communism would not have succeeded in China, and the Nationalist regime, despite its many shortcomings, would have reigned supreme on the mainland today.

Thus communism succeeded despite the Communists' basic beliefs, since the means they used to achieve this success, such as rent and interest reductions and the sponsorship of Chinese nationalism, were not especially communistic, and non-Communists could have conscientiously advocated the same thing. Not until the Communists had firmly established themselves in power did the Communist programs reappear. Land was confiscated and redistributed, and industrial properties were appropriated either outright or in a disguised form (*e.g.*, joint state-private enterprises). The Communists may use non-Communist methods to achieve power, but in the end they are, of course, Communists.

Radical and extraordinary though the Communist movement may seem, similar movements have occurred in China's historical past. An example is the Taiping Rebellion of the nineteenth century (pp. 400–406) that, had it succeeded, would have made the Communist movement of our time comparatively mild. An ironical difference is that while the Taipings called their movement godly and Christian, based upon the teachings of the Holy Bible, even the most egoistic Communists do not claim that their movement is divinely inspired. The failure of the Taiping Rebellion left China's basic problems unattended and unresolved, and from then on a series of reforms was attempted, climaxed in our own time by the Kuomintang movement led by Chiang Kai-shek and the Communist movement led by Mao Tse-tung. Thus the Communist movement, viewed from a historical perspective, is merely the latest stage of a long development, dramatic though it may seem on the surface.

As noted earlier, the Communists rode to power on the peasants' discontent as well as the intellectuals' dissatisfaction with China's international status. Though neither of these two phenomena was new, the Communists were the most effective group in converting them into political strength. The sad fact is that the Chinese did not have a tradition of changing their government by ballot or other peaceful methods; to stage a rebellion against an unpopular government was not only done in practice but also justified in the loftiest of the Confucian principles. The civil war that followed was often regarded by traditional historians as a democratic process couched in violence, in the sense that among all the contenders for the throne, the one with the largest popular support would eventually win. In short, the method may not have been democratic, but the result was. If a foreign power chose to intervene, she by definition had to intervene on the side of the minority and thus thwart the "democratic process," since she did not have to intervene if she wished the will of the majority to prevail. More often than not the real motive of her intervention was the advancement of her own interest at the expense of the majority. This was the case with the Manchus in the seventeenth century; this was also the case with the Japanese in our own time. Japan's attempt, prior to and during the Sino-Japanese War, to ally herself with Nationalist China in an anti-Communist crusade was such a farce that even the most anti-Communist Chinese could not swallow it—indeed, it may have, from hindsight, irreparably tipped the balance in the Communists' favor. With an enemy like Japanese militarism, the Chinese Communists did not need any friends.

Peasant revolt, without intellectual leadership, was no more than organized violence and certainly could not succeed. The Yellow Turbans' Rebellion of the second century (pp. 130–131) and Chang Hsien–chung's Rebellion of the seventeenth century (pp. 299–301) belong to this category. Prior to the modern period, the motive that prompted intellectuals to lead or join a rebellion was mostly personal ambition; the altruistic compassion for the economically deprived, which figured so prominently in their public statements, was at best secondary in importance. The situation changed, however, with the impact of the West in the nineteenth century. From then on, practically all the Chinese intellectuals were concerned with China's weakness as a nation and the possibility that she might be conquered or partitioned by the Western powers and Japan. When an intellectual decided to join a revolution or rebellion, nationalism was more often than not his primary motivation. Sun Yat-sen, for instance, decided to overthrow the Manchu regime in 1885 when China was defeated by France. Likewise, when the two university professors, Ch'en Tu-hsiu and Li Ta-chao, decided to join the rebels' ranks by founding the Chinese Communist Party, they honestly believed that communism was the only effective means whereby China could regain her freedom and independence. Ironically, their heavy reliance on the Comintern guidance and support in promoting revolution in China made them appear no less slavish to foreign interests than their opponents and thus rendered them ineffective as national leaders. Not until Mao Tse-tung had *de facto* dissociated the Chinese Communist movement from the Comintern control and made it truly "nationalistic" did it gather momentum and eventually succeed.

Now that the Communist regime has been in power for twenty-nine years (1949–1978), what is a historian's verdict of it, tentative though this verdict must be? The answer, as one might expect, is not clear-cut. On the positive side, not only has the Communist regime eliminated the last vestige of the unequal treaties and thus made China truly sovereign and independent for the first time in the modern period, but it has also elevated her to the status of a major power, an important factor in international affairs. In short, it has successfully achieved the nationalist goal. Economically, it has raised the standard of living, especially for the peasants, though the standard of living in the People's Republic is still low compared to that in the United States, Japan, or even Taiwan. Socially, it has enhanced the position of peasants and workers, the traditionally downtrodden classes, and also the position of women who, for the first time in Chinese history, are men's coequals. It has, by and large, achieved the socioeconomic goal.

It must be quickly added, however, that for these achievements the Chinese have paid an enormous price. The Communist regime is perhaps the most dictatorial in all of China's history: it tolerates no opposition and brooks no differences. Every Chinese must support the CCP or suffer the consequences. He is denied not only the freedom of speech but also, most regrettably, the freedom of silence—a freedom precious to all of those who, being apolitical, want to be left alone. It is true that prior to the Communist assumption of power the Chinese did not have political freedom either, namely, the freedom of choosing their own government and leaders. Nevertheless, they did have civil liberties, such as the liberty of choosing one's own occupation and residence. Today a Chinese cannot move from one occupation to another, or one place to another, without Communist approval. Nor can he read whatever he wishes and paint or compose whatever he pleases. There is no individual creativity unless it can be channelled to serve a social or socialist purpose, and the cultural atmosphere of contemporary China has been anything but exuberant.

One may argue that the denial of human rights and civil liberties is necessary to the attainment of the nationalist and socioeconomic goals referred to above and that, as these goals are attained, human rights and civil liberties will gradually be restored. In other words, the Communist dictatorship is merely a means to an end, a necessity during a transitional period when drastic measures must be adopted to pull China from the abyss into which she has sunk in modern times. If this argument is valid, obviously there must be a new society beyond the Communist dictatorship, a society in which individual freedom exists side by side with social justice and economic affluence. In short, a formula of historical development for an economically backward society like China could be either "feudal—Communist—bourgeois" or "feudal—Fascist—bourgeois," instead of "feudal—bourgeois—Communist," which Karl Marx once prescribed for highly industrialized societies. If this formula for underdeveloped countries makes sense, we should not be surprised if in some future time the "capitalist roaders" indeed emerge triumphant in China.

Selected Bibliography

Note: These books are selected for their readability, broad intellectual appeal, and availability in paperbacks.

Chai, Ch'u and Winberg, *The Changing Society of China*. New York: New American Library, 1962.

Chang Chung-li, *The Chinese Gentry*. Seattle: University of Washington Press, 1955.

Ch'en, Jerome, *Mao and the Chinese Revolution*. New York: Oxford University Press, 1967.

Chiang Yee, *Chinese Calligraphy: An Introduction to Its Aesthetic and Technique*. Cambridge, Mass.: Harvard University Press, 1973.

————, *Chinese Eye: An Interpretation of Chinese Painting*. Bloomington, Ind.: Indiana University Press, 1964.

Chow Tse-tsung, *May Fourth Movement: Intellectual Revolution in Modern China*. Stanford, Ca.: Stanford University Press, 1967.

Clubb, O. Edmund, *Twentieth Century China*. New York: Columbia University Press, 1972.

Creel, Herrlee G., *Chinese Thought from Confucius to Mao Tse-tung*. Chicago: University of Chicago Press, 1971.

————, *Confucius and the Chinese Way*. New York: Harper, 1960.

Fairbank, John K., *The United States and China*, 3rd ed. Cambridge, Mass.: Harvard University Press, 1971.

Fung Yu-lan, *A History of Chinese Philosophy*, translated by Derk Bodde. New York: Free Press, 1966.

————, *The Spirit of Chinese Philosophy*, translated by E. R. Hughes. Boston: Beacon Press, 1962.

Houn, Franklin W., *A Short History of Chinese Communism*. Englewood Cliffs, N.J.: Prentice-Hall, 1973.

Hsu, Francis L. K., *Americans and Chinese*. Garden City, N.Y.: Natural History Press, 1972.

————, *Under the Ancestors' Shadow*. Stanford, Ca.: Stanford University Press, 1967.

Hsu Kai-yu, *Chou En-lai: China's Gray Eminence*. Garden City, N.Y.: Doubleday, 1969.

Hudson, G. F., *Europe and China*. Boston: Beacon Press, 1961.

Li, Dun J., *China in Transition: 1517–1911*. New York: Van Nostrand, 1969.

————, *The Civilization of China*. New York: Scribners, 1975.

————, *The Essence of Chinese Civilization*. New York: Van Nostrand, 1967.

————, *Modern China: From Mandarin to Commissar*. New York: Scribners, 1978.

————, *The Road to Communism: China Since 1912*. New York: Van Nostrand, 1969.

Lin Yutang, *The Importance of Living*. New York: Putnam, 1974.

Liu Wu-chi, *An Introduction to Chinese Literature*. Bloomington: Indiana University Press, 1966.

Mao Tse-tung, *Selected Works*, 5 vols. San Francisco: China Books, 1977.

————, *Quotations from Chairman Mao Tse-tung*. San Francisco: China Books, 1967.

Meisner, Maurice, *Li Ta-chao and the Origins of Chinese Marxism*. New York: Atheneum, 1970.

Mu Fu-sheng, *The Wilting of the Hundred Flowers*. New York: Praeger, 1962.

Polo, Marco, *The Travels of Marco Polo*, translated by R. E. Latham. London: Penguin, 1958.

Schram, Stuart, *Mao Tse-tung*. Baltimore: Penguin, 1967.

Snow, Edgar, *The Long Revolution*. New York: Random House, 1973.

————, *Red China Today*. New York: Random House, 1971.

————, *Red Star Over China*. New York: Grove Press, 1968.

Spence, Jonathan D., *Emperor of China: Self-Portrait of K'ang Hsi*. New York: Random House, 1975.

Van Slyke, Lyman P. (ed.), *The Chinese Communist Movement: A Report of the United States War Department, July 1945*. Stanford, Ca.: Stanford University Press, 1968.

Waley, Arthur, *The Book of Songs*. New York: Grove Press, 1960.

————, *Three Ways of Thought in Ancient China.* Garden City, N.Y.: Doubleday, 1956.

————, *The Way and Its Power.* New York: Grove Press, 1958.

Wright, Arthur F., *Buddhism in Chinese History.* New York: Atheneum, 1965.

————, *Confucianism and Chinese Civilization.* New York: Atheneum, 1964.

Wright, Mary C., *The Last Stand of Chinese Conservatism: The T'ung-chih Restoration, 1862–1874.* Stanford, Ca.: Stanford University Press, 1957.

Romanization
of Chinese Names

There is no unanimity among scholars as to how Chinese names should be romanized. The easiest way out of this difficulty is to follow the Wade-Giles system throughout regardless of other considerations. In that case, Confucius becomes *Kung ch'iu* or *Kung Fu-tzu;* Chiang Kai-shek becomes *Chiang Chieh-shih* or *Chiang Chung-cheng.* This, certainly, will not do. In general, the following rules are followed in this book:

1. All historical names of persons and places, with the exception of those which have long been standardized (such as Confucius and Mencius), are romanized according to the Wade-Giles system: *Chao K'uang-yin, Li Shih-min, Ch'üanchou,* etc.

2. The names of people in modern China are the same names they themselves prefer to be called or the names which have long been used in con-

temporary literature: *Sun Yat-sen, Chiang Kai-shek,* etc. With the exception of these two cases, personal names are romanized according to the Wade-Giles system.

3. Postal names are used for all major Chinese cities: *Peking, Nanking,* etc. For cities little known in Western literature or cities whose postal names cannot be easily located, the Wade-Giles system is used: *Ch'ench'iao,* for instance.

4. Whenever historical cities bear the same names and are on the same sites as their modern counterparts, postal names are used: *Kaifeng, Yangchow,* etc.

5. Whenever a name is romanized identically as another name according to the Wade-Giles system even though they are indicated by two entirely different Chinese characters or two different sets of Chinese characters, they are romanized differently in order to avoid confusion. A Chinese kingdom during the Spring and Autumn period bears the same Chinese character as a Chinese regime flourishing between the third and the fifth century, and both are romanized as *Tsin,* even though they could have been romanized as *Chin* according to the Wade-Giles system. On the other hand, the Nuchen regime established in the twelfth century is romanized as *Chin* because it bears a different Chinese character which means *gold.*

6. A personal name which consists of two Chinese characters is linked with a hyphen: *Hung-chang, Tse-tung,* etc. A hyphen is used even when the name is not really a name but a title: *Wen-ti* (Emperor Wen), *Wu-ti* (Emperor Wu), etc. As a general rule, only a person's real name (*ming*) is given, rarely his courtesy name (*tzu* or *hao*). This is done in order to reduce the number of names that have to appear in this book.

7. Geographical names, whether they are the names of cities, mountains, or seas, have no hyphens even though they contain two or more Chinese characters: *Pohai, Ch'angan,* etc. Hyphens appear only when the names are Sinicized foreign names: *Hsiung-nu, Wu-sun,* etc. An exception is made in cases when there have been standardized English equivalents long in usage: *Genghiz Khan* instead of *Ch'eng-chi-ssu Han,* for instance.

In summary, the Wade-Giles system is followed unless there are compelling reasons for not doing so. However, the system provides only approximate pronunciation for Chinese words; the pronunciation of most Chinese words simply does not have its equivalent in English. A useful purpose will be served if students observe the following simple guide:

a as in f*a*r	*e* as in *e*rror
i as the first *e* in *e*vade	
o as in *o*ver	*u* as in r*u*le
ai as the *i* in t*i*me	*ou* as the *o* in *o*bey
ao as the *ow* in n*ow*	ü as ü in German
ch' as in *ch*urch	*k'* as in *k*ite
p' as in *p*ay	*t'* as in *t*ie
ts' as in boa*ts*	*tz'* as in quar*tz*
ch as the *j* in *j*est	*k* as the *g* in *g*o

p as the *b* in *b*oy

ts and *tz* as *dz*

j has no English equivalent but is pronounced more like *r* than like *j*.

ss is pronounced as *s*

t as the *d* in *d*ay

hs as *sh* in *sh*arp

Chronological Chart

Dynasties	Government and Politics
Hsia (c.2205–c.1766 B.C.)	Yü, founder of the Hsia dynasty The Great Flood (legend?) Chieh, last Hsia ruler
Shang (c.1766–c.1122 B.C.)	T'ang, founder of the Shang dynasty Frequent shift of capital until it was settled at Yin (modern Honan province) in 1401 B.C.
Chou (c.1122–249 B.C.) West Chou (c.1122–771 B.C.) East Chou (770–249 B.C.) Spring and Autumn period (722–481 B.C.) Warring States period (403–221 B.C.)	King Wen, King Wu, and Duke Chou Feudalism established, c. 1122 B.C. Feudal states: Lu, Ch'i, Tsin, etc. Interstate warfare after 771 B.C.; interstate conferences; decline of feudalism Duke Huan of Ch'i and Duke Wen of Tsin Rise of Ch'u Warring States: Ch'in, Ch'i, Ch'u, Chao, Han, Wei, and Yen
Ch'in (221–207 B.C.)	Shih Huang-ti; Li Ssu China unified, 221 B.C. Legalism adopted as the state philosophy: the burning of books Central control and bureaucratic administration over all parts of China
Han (202 B.C.–220 A.D.) Former Han (202 B.C.–9 A.D.) Hsin dynasty (9–23 A.D.) Later Han (25–220 A.D.)	Liu Pang (Han Kao-tsu) Han Wu-ti Defeat of Hsiung-nu and conquest of Korea Usurpation of the Han throne by Wang Mang Liu Hsiu Usurpation of power by eunuchs Massacre of eunuchs, 189 A.D. Ts'ao Ts'ao

Socio-economic Developments	Culture
Domestication of animals Cultivation of wheat and millet Sericulture	Black pottery Animism
Trade; cowrie shells being used as medium of exchange	White incised pottery Bronze vessels and weapons Carved ivory and jade Written language (*chia-ku wen*) Ancestor worship Oracle bones
The "well-field" system (*ching-t'ien chih*) The rise of the merchant class and the growth of cities after the eighth century B.C. Sinicization of South China Iron Age Introduction of metallic coins Shang Yang's social and economic reforms Roaming scholars	*Book of Odes* Confucius Mo Ti *Book of Taoist Virtue* Chuang Chou Mencius Ch'ü Yüan and Sung Yü Han Fei *Chou-pi Mathematics*
Standardization of weights and measures *The Ch'in Code* Irrigation projects and public works	*Small Script* declared as standard for all writing
Persecution of merchants Wang Mang's reforms Resurgence of the landed class under the Later Han regime Personal loyalty	Tung Chung-shu Confucianism declared as the state philosophy Ssu-ma Ch'ien Ssu-ma Hsiang-yü Alchemy Compass Pan Ku; Pan Chao Invention of paper Introduction of Buddhism Wang Ch'ung *The Peacock Flies Southeast*

Dynasties	Government and Politics
Three Kingdoms	Ts'ao P'i; Liu Pei; Sun Ch'üan
Wei (220–265) Shu (221–265) Wu (222–280)	
Tsin (265–420)	Tsin Wu-ti Barbarian invasions
West Tsin (265–317) East Tsin (317–420)	Sack of Loyang, 311 and 316 Tsin Yüan-ti
Southern and Northern Dynasties	China divided Liu Yü
South: Liu Sung, 420–479; Ch'i, 479–502; Liang, 502–557; Ch'en, 557–589 North: Later (North) Wei, 386–535; East Wei, 534–550; West Wei, 535–556; North Ch'i, 550–577; North Chou, 557–581	Wei Hsiao-wen-ti Liang Wu-ti
Sui (590–618)	Sui Wen-ti Sui Yang-ti Civil service examination introduced
T'ang (618–906)	Li Shih-min (T'ang T'ai-tsung) T'ang Kao-tsung: conquest of Central Asia and Korea Empress Wu The Three Secretariat system; six ministries Fu-ping chih T'ang Hsüan-tsung An Lu-shan's revolt Hui-heh; T'u-fan
Five Dynasties (907–960)	Warlordism Loss of the Sixteen Yen-Yün Districts Chou Shih-tsu
Later Liang, 907–923 Later T'ang, 923–936 Later Tsin, 936–947 Later Han, 947–950 Later Chou, 951–960	

Socio-economic Developments	*Culture*
The nine rank system	Decline of Confucianism Taoism; Buddhism
Mass migration to the Yangtze region, fourth century Clans Moral decline of the gentry class	Pilgrimage to India: Fa-hsien Calligraphy: Wang Hsi-chih T'ao Ch'ien Seven Sages of the Bamboo Grove
Invaders Sinicized Hsiao-wen-ti's land reform Elite families	"Parallel form" Golden age of Buddhism
Ever-ready granaries Grand Canal	Block-printing
Land distribution *Liang-shui fa* Arab and Persian traders	Hsüan-tsang Ch'an Buddhism Zoroastrianism; Manicheanism; Nestorianism, Islam Cultural expansion Essayists: Han Yü; Liu Tsung-ch'üan Poets: Li Po; Tu Fu; Po Chü-yi Painters: Li Ssu-hsün; Wu Tao-tzu; Wang Wei Dance and music
Foot-binding	Printing of Confucian classics Li Yü

Dynasties	Government and Politics
Sung (960–1279) North Sung, 960–1126 South Sung, 1127–1279 Liao, 907–1125 West Hsia, 990–1227 Chin, 1115–1234	Chao K'uang-yin (Sung T'ai-tsu) "Disarmament beside the wine cups" Agreement of River Shan The Tangut war Sung Shen-tsung Fang La rebellion Fall of Kaifeng, 1126 Sung Kao-tsung Yo Fei Rise of the Mongols
Yüan (1260–1368)	Genghiz Khan Kublai Khan Corruption of Mongol princes
Ming (1368–1644)	Chu Yüan-chang (Ming T'ai-tsu) Yung-lo (Ming Ch'eng-tsu) Seven Voyages to the "Western" Ocean The tribute system Japanese pirates Eunuchs Chang Hsien-chung; Li Tzu-ch'eng
Ch'ing (1644–1912)	K'ang-hsi Ch'ien-lung Opium War Taiping Rebellion Sino-Japanese War Boxer Rebellion K'ang Yu-wei: Hundred Days' Reform Tz'u-Hsi
Republic (1912–)	Yüan Shih-k'ai Warlordism Sun Yat-sen Chiang Kai-shek Nationalist Government at Nanking Manchurian Incident, 1931 Sino-Japanese War Communist ascendency Nationalist Government in Taiwan

Socio-economic Developments	Culture

Wang An-shih's reforms
Decline of women's status
Paper currency
	Four Colleges
	Movable type
	Philosophers: Chou Tun-yi; Chu Hsi;
	    Lu Chiu-yüan
	Tz'u poets: Liu Yung; Li Ch'ing-
	    chao; Hsin Ch'i-chi
	Essayist: Su Shih
	Historians: Ou-yang Hsiu; Ssu-ma
	    Kuang
	Painting: Mi Fei
	Vernacular tales

Caste system	Road construction; Grand Canal Music drama: *The Romance of the* *West Chamber* *The Marsh Heroes* *The Romance of the Three Kingdoms*
Plantations Commercial expansion Gentry Deterioration of peasantry	*Yung-lo Encyclopedia* Wang Shou-jen T'ang Yin and Tung Ch'i-ch'ang School system "Eight-legged" essays Ku Yen-wu Jesuits *Flowering Plum in a Golden Vase*
Population increase Opium addiction Taiping's social and economic reforms Introduction of modern industries	The Han Learning *Four Treasuries* Introduction of Western culture Christianity *The Dream of the Red Chamber* *An Unofficial History of the Literati*
The May Fourth Movement Three Principles of the People Emancipation of women Traditional society undermined	The *pai-hua* (colloquial) movement Modern schools Science and democracy Hu Shih

Dynasties	Government and Politics
People's Republic (1949–)	The Chinese Communist Party and its congresses Mao Tse-tung: New Democracy; dictatorship of the proletariat; dictatorship of the CCP leadership The Soviet-Chinese alliance (1950) and split (1959) Korean War and Indochina War The Constitutions of 1954, 1975, and 1978 Political purges: Kao Kang, P'eng Teh-huai, Liu Shao-ch'i, Teng Hsiao-p'ing, Lin Piao, and "Gang of Four" Rise and fall of CCP radicals (1966–1976) Sino-Soviet border clashes (1969): intensification of Sino-Soviet enmity Shanghai Communiqué: Sino-American rapprochement (1972) Reemergence of CCP moderates (1976–)

Socio-economic Developments	Culture
Rural revolution: land confiscation and redistribution (1950); mutual-aid teams (1953); cooperatives (1954–1958); people's communes (1958–) Industrial progress (1949–1958); Great Leap Forward and economic decline (1959–1961); restoration of economic progress (1962–) Self-reliance in economic development Discovery and exploitation of new oil reserves Decline of the Confucian family system: the marriage law of 1950 Class struggle and continuous revolution The creation of a Maoist man and a Maoist society: regimented life; Maoist puritanism; criticism and self-criticism meetings; reform by physical labor Reemphasis on "four modernizations": modernization of agriculture, industry, national defense, and science and technology (1976–)	Marxism-Leninism-Maoism Mao worship Educational progress (1949–1966); educational decline (1966–1976); progress restored (1976–) Chiang Ch'ing the cultural czar (r. (1966–1976): banning of traditional literature and art forms and their replacement by revolutionary varieties; anti-Confucius campaign; elevation of Legalism; Maoist interpretation of history Culture as a means to facilitate proletarian dictatorship or dictatorship by the CCP leadership Retreat from rigidity in all fields of cultural activities (1976–)

Index

Note: In order to facilitate the location of an entry, the index is compiled in such a way as to ignore the presence or absence of apostrophe, hyphen, or umlaut.